Economics

22 Years 2025-2004

ISC

CHAPTERWISE QUESTION BANK

Economics

Class 12

Author
Pratima Jain Roy

arihant
SUCCESS AND NOTHING LESS

arihant
SUCCESS AND NOTHING LESS

ARIHANT PRAKASHAN
(School Division Series)

ADMINISTRATIVE & PRODUCTION OFFICES

Regd. Office
'Ramchhaya' 4577/15, Agarwal Road, Darya Ganj, New Delhi -110002
Tele: 011- 47630600, 43518550

Head Office
Kalindi, TP Nagar, Meerut (UP) - 250002, Tel: 0121-7156203, 7156204

SALES & SUPPORT OFFICES

Agra, Ahmedabad, Bengaluru, Bareilly, Chennai, Delhi, Guwahati, Hyderabad, Jaipur, Jhansi, Kolkata, Lucknow, Nagpur & Pune.

PO No : TXT-XX-XXXXXXX-X-XX

Published By Arihant Publications (India) Ltd.

For further information about the books published by Arihant, log on to www.arihantbooks.com or e-mail at info@arihantbooks.com

PRICE ₹280.00

Follow us on

Achieving 99+
Marks in Board Exams

Achieving 99+ marks in board exams is definitely an ambitious goal, but with the right approach and these 7 tips from toppers, you can definitely increase your chances of success!

Here are the 7 Topper Tips to ace your board exams:

1. Master the art of consistency

Consistency builds understanding and confidence, both crucial for excelling in exams.

2. Build a winning study strategy

Create a personalised timetable that prioritises subjects based on your strengths and weaknesses.

3. Befriend the syllabus

Focus on high-weightage topics and prioritise mastering core concepts before moving on to advanced ones.

4. Embrace active learning

Explain concepts to yourself or in study groups to solidify understanding.

5. Conquer the past

Solve Past Years' Papers and Sample Papers under timed conditions to practice time management and understand paper pattern.

6. Seek help, when needed!

Don't hesitate to clarify doubts with teachers, tutors, or study groups. Asking questions strengthens your understanding and prevents confusion.

7. Prioritise well-being

Eat nutritious meals, get enough sleep, regular exercise and practice stress management techniques like meditation to stay calm and focused during exams.

These tips are just a starting point, and you can personalise them to fit your learning style and preferences.

Description of

Newly Added Features

01

Theory of Consumer Behaviour and Demand

TREND ANALYSIS

01 Utility and Laws of Utility Analysis

Average No. of Questions Across all Sets

Types of Questions	2023	2020	2019	2018	2017
1 Mark	1	—	—	—	—
2 Marks	—	1	—	1	—
3/4 Marks	—	—	—	—	1
6 Marks	1	1	—	1	—

Trend Analysis

At the start of each chapter, Trend Analysis is given to indicate the types of Questions asked from different topics of the chapter. This feature helps students to know the importance of different topics of the given chapter from exam point of view and helps them to prepare accordingly.

6 Marks Questions

1. Explain the consumer's equilibrium through indifference curve approach with help of diagram.

Ans Consumer's equilibrium is that situation in which a consumer buys such a combination of goods from which, he gets maximum satisfaction, given the prices of the commodity and the money income of the consumer. Consumer's equilibrium under ordinal

Common Mistake Students generally don't mention about the convert IC at the point of equilibrium. It is the sufficient condition of equlibrium.

Common Mistakes

It focuses on some of the general but critical mistakes that students commit while solving the questions. This feature helps students to develop the habit of avoiding mistakes while solving questions

2. Explain four properties of indifference curve. **Specimen 2023**

Or Discuss any two properties of indifference curve. **2015**

Or Explain the properties of indifference curve. **2008**

Ans The properties of an Indifference Curve (IC) are explained below

(i) **An IC slopes downward from left to the right**
This shows that an IC has a negative slope. This property is based on the assumption that if a

Value Points

For getting maximum marks, following value points can be included in the answer

- Use diagram to prove the properties of IC.
- Explain the properties with reference to the digram only.

Value Points

'Value Points' are given with selected questions with the purpose to help students to know the key points to be covered in the answer to get full marks.

4. Define marginal utility. When can it be negative? **2015**

Or When does marginal utility becomes negative? **2009**

Ans The utility derived from the consumption of an additional unit of a commodity is termed as 'marginal utility'. It is defined as change in total utility due to consumption of an additional unit i.e. marginal utility can be negative when total utility falls. In other words, when total utility is highest, marginal utility becomes zero. If consumer continues to consume more even after this, then total utility falls and marginal utility becomes negative.

Concept Enhancer Students generally draw MU from y-axis. Marginal utility curve does not start from y-axis as utility not defined at that point.

Concept Enhancer

Concept Enhancer gives the brief description of the concept, which has been used to solve the question. This feature provides revision of important concept along with practice of question solving.

Most Important Topics

from each Chapter

On the basis of analysis of last 5 Years' Board Examination Papers, we have identified Important Topics from each chapter.

Chapter Name	Important Topics	Weightage in Last 5 Years' Boards				
		2025	2024	2023	2020	2019
Theory of Consumer Behaviour and Demand	Utility and Laws of Utility Analysis	1M, 4M, 2M		1M,6M	2M,6M	
	Consumer's Equilibrium	1M	6M		4M	2M,6M
	Concept of Demand and its Determinants	1M, 1M	4M	1M	3M	
	Law of Demand and its Exception				2M	4M
	Movement and Shift in Demand Curve					3M
Elasticity of Demand	Meaning and Types of Elasticity of Demand	2M	1M,2M	1M,2M, 2M,2M	3M	4M
	Degree and Factors Affecting Elasticity of Demand			6M		
Supply and Elasticity of Supply	Concept of Supply and its Determinants		2M			
	Law of Supply and Change in Supply	2M	1M	1M,3M	3M	3M
	Elasticity of Supply	2M		2M	6M	2M
Concept of Production	Production Function			1M,3M	2M	3M
	Law of Variable Proportion	1M,2M	1M,4M		6M	2M
Cost and Revenue	Concept of Cost	1M, 1M, 2M	1M,2M	1M,1M, 2M	3M	3M
	Concept of Revenue	2M	2M		4M	4M
	Producer's Equilibrium	1M				6M
Forms of Market and Application Tools of Demand and Supply	Main Market Forms	2M,2M, 2M, 2M,2M, 2M, 2M	1M,1M, 4M	2M,6M	6M	2M,6M
	Market Equilibrium under Perfect Competition	2M	1M,6M	2M,2M, 6M	6M	4M
	Price Determination and Changes in Equilibrium	2M	1M,2M	1M,3M	2M,6M	6M

Chapter Name	Important Topics	Weightage in Last 5 Years' Boards				
		2025	2024	2023	2020	2019
Theory of Income Determination	Aggregate Demand and Aggregate Supply		1M,1M, 1M,2M	1M,1M, 1M	6M	3M
	Short-run Equilibrium and Multiplier	2M	2M	4M	2M,4M	2M,6M
	Deficient and Excess Demand	2M, 4M	1M	1M	6M	3M
Money and Banking	Money, its Functions and Supply of Money	1M		1M,3M	3M,3M	2M,3M
	Banks : Commercial Banks and Central Bank	1M, 1M, 1M, 4M	8M	1M,2M	3M,6M	3M,6M
Balance of Payments and Exchange Rate	BoP and its Components	2M, 2M	1M,4M		2M	6M
	Disequilibrium in BoP	1M, 2M, 2M			6M	
	Foreign Exchange Rate	1M	1M,4M	6M		2M
Public Finance	Fiscal Policy and Public Revenue	1M, 2M, 2M	2M	1M	2M	2M
	Public Expenditure, Public Debt and Debt Financing			1M,2M	3M	3M
	Government Budget and Budget Deficit	1M	1M,1M, 2M	2M	3M	3M
National Income	Circular Flow of Income		4M	4M	3M	4M
	Basis Concepts of National Income Accounting	2M, 2M, 4M		3M,3M	3M	3M
	Measurement of National Income	4M, 4M, 4M	8M	2M,6M, 6M	2M,6M	2M,6M

Dream, Believe, Achieve Insights from ISC Toppers

Follow all the 5P's

• Persistence • Passion • Perseverance • Purpose • Practice

MANYA GUPTA
ISC Topper (99.75%)

Aim for high marks, that's what I was doing. I convinced myself that if I aim for 100 I will at least get a 95. That was my logic, but I ended up getting a 100.

I studied with the help of my school and tuition classes. I didn't study daily much, but before the exams, I used to pull all-nighters and study.

ARYAAN
ISC Topper (99.75%)

Studying for 3-4 hours every day along with six hours of school helped me secure 399 out of 400 marks, scoring 99.75%.

I'm very active on all social media platforms but it has never hindered my studies. I strike a balance between hard work and fun.

The degree of toughness of any subject is merely a subjective outlook. I made sure that I incentivised myself at times when I didn't feel like sitting at my study table, especially for theoretical subjects.

I simply believe in revising the concepts which were taught at school or tuitions that very day and minimise backlogs as much as I could.

POOJA KEJRIWAL
ISC Topper (97.5%)

I believe there is no substitute to hard work. There was no fixed hours of preparation. I read a topic till the time I completely understood it. I had to be satisfied with the topic covered.

See it is important to take breaks and everyone has their own way of entertainment. I do chat with friends on social media. I think it is fine until it becomes an addiction.

There is no secret formula as such, but one should not panic and have faith in his/her preparation.

DEVANG KUMAR
ISC Topper

DIMPLE KOTHARI
ISC Topper (97.5%)

- Don't run behind marks, crave for knowledge, experience because ultimately that's gonna help you.
- Don't let peer pressure dominate you.
- If you want to obtain good marks, leave all social media-This is a myth. I was active on Instagram & WhatsApp before my examinations, and even during my examinations. It's just that you need to remember that everyone has the same 24 hours, it's how you utilize it as well as enjoy it better than others.
- Both early morning and late night studies are best ~ you need to choose what's better for you.
- Don't hesitate to ask questions. If you have any doubts, please clarify. Everyone has different learning styles and speed, so it's nothing to be ashamed of.
- Never give up.

Please Note that all the information is collected from different websites.

Contents

ISC Chapterwise Question Bank 2025-2004

1.	Theory of Consumer Behaviour and Demand	1-29
2.	Elasticity of Demand	30-43
3.	Supply and Elasticity of Supply	44-60
4.	Concept of Production	61-74
5.	Cost and Revenue	75-97
6.	Forms of Market and Application Tools of Demand and Supply	98-123
7.	Theory of Income Determination	124-140
8.	Money and Banking	141-153
9.	Balance of Payments and Exchange Rate	154-166
10.	Public Finance	167-185
11.	National Income	186-212

- Assertion/Reasoning Based MCQs 213-219
- ISC Examination Paper 2024 221-230
- ISC Examination Paper 2025 231-240
- ISC Sample Papers (1-3) 241-251
- Latest ISC Specimen Paper 252-260

Latest Syllabus

Class XII (2025-26)

There will be two papers in the subject.

Paper I Theory : 3 Hours — 80 Marks

Paper II Project Work — 20 Marks

Note: *The syllabus is intended to reflect a study of the theory of Economics with specific reference to the Indian Economy. Therefore, examples and specific references to the Indian Economy must be made wherever relevant.*

PAPER I THEORY — 80 Marks

S. No.	UNIT	TOTAL WEIGHTAGE
1.	**MICROECONOMIC THEORY (40 Marks)**	
	(i) Demand	16 Marks
	(ii) Elasticity of Demand	
	(iii) Supply	
	(iv) Market Mechanism	
	(v) Concepts of Production	12 Marks
	(vi) Cost and Revenue	
	(vii) Main Market Forms and Equilibrium of a Firm	12 Marks
	MACROECONOMICS (40 Marks)	
2.	**Theory of Income and Employment**	8 Marks
3.	**Money and Banking**	8 Marks
4.	**Balance of Payments and Exchange Rate**	6 Marks
5.	**Public Finance**	6 Marks
6.	**National Income**	12 Marks
	TOTAL	**80 Marks**

1. Micro Economic Theory

(i) Demand: meaning, factors affecting demand; Demand function; Law of Demand; derivation of demand curve; movement and shift of the demand curve; exceptions to the Law of Demand.

Law of Diminishing Marginal Utility, Law of Equimarginal Utility, consumer's equilibrium through utility approach (Cardinal) and indifference curve analysis (Ordinal).

The concept of demand: meaning, types of demand. A demand function to be specified incorporating the determinants of demand. Diagrams should be used in explaining the Law of Demand, reasons for downward slope of demand curve, its derivation using demand schedule. Derivation of market demand curve from individual demand curve.

(a) Cardinal Utility Analysis: meaning of utility, total utility, marginal utility, relationship of TU and MU, Law of Diminishing Marginal Utility (schedule and diagram, Only assumptions to be taught, criticisms not required), Consumer's equilibrium – one commodity (schedule and diagram), Law of Equimarginal Utility (statement, schedule) and conditions of consumer's equilibrium using marginal utility;

(b) Ordinal Utility Analysis: Indifference Curve – its meaning and properties (including MRS and DMRS), indifference map, consumer's budget line, Consumer's equilibrium – condition (to be explained with the help of a diagram).

(ii) Elasticity of demand: meaning, types of elasticity of demand, measurement of elasticity of demand; factors affecting elasticity of demand.

Various methods of measurement of the elasticity of demand: point method - percentage method, expenditure method and geometric method. (Numericals required on percentage method only). The cross and income elasticity of demand must be explained. Degrees of elasticity of demand to be explained. Use diagrams wherever necessary.

(iii) Supply: meaning; difference between stock and supply; determinants of supply; Law of Supply; movement and shift of the supply curve; elasticity of supply

Difference between stock (intended supply) and supply (actual supply) with the help of relevant examples. A supply function should be specified and explained. Law of Supply: Meaning, supply schedule and supply curve. Derivation of market supply curve from individual supply curve. Movement and shift of the supply curve, exceptions to the Law of Supply. Elasticity of Supply: Meaning, degrees of elasticity of supply and measurement of elasticity of supply by percentage method and geometric method.

(iv) Market Mechanism: Equilibrium and disequilibrium; Equilibrium price and effect of changes in demand and supply on the equilibrium price. Simple applications of tools of demand and supply.

A basic understanding of the concept of equilibrium. The effects of changes in demand and supply - both along the curves and shift of the curves to be explained. Basic understanding of Price control, rationing, Price ceiling and Floor price with the help of demand and supply curves.

(v) Concept of production and production function: (short run and long run production function), returns to a factor, returns to scale (meaning only) total, average and marginal physical products; Law of Variable Proportions and its three stages.

A production function (concept only). Law of Variable Proportions: statement, assumptions, schedule (for the purpose of understanding and not for testing), diagram and explanation to the three stages.

(vi) Cost and revenue: Basic concepts of cost; fixed cost, variable cost, total cost, marginal cost and average cost – their relationships; opportunity cost; short run and long run cost curves. Revenue: meaning; average revenue, marginal revenue and total revenue and their relationships under perfect competition and imperfect competition, Producer's equilibrium.

Basic concepts – private cost, economic cost, social cost, money cost, real cost, explicit cost, implicit cost.

Cost concepts – Fixed cost, variable cost, total cost, marginal cost, average cost with schedule and diagram; relationship between average cost, marginal cost, total cost (only concepts of long run and short run cost curves, derivations not required). Opportunity cost – meaning only. Difference between accounting cost and opportunity cost.

Revenue – Average revenue, marginal revenue, total revenue – concepts and relationships under perfect competition and imperfect competition. Producer's equilibrium (Profit maximization goal) – meaning; conditions: (a) TR and TC approach along with diagram (b) MR and MC approach along with diagram.

(vii) Main market forms: perfect competition, monopolistic competition, oligopoly, monopoly, monopsony; characteristics of the various market forms; equilibrium of a firm in perfect competition under short run and long run.

Features of perfect competition, monopolistic competition, oligopoly, monopoly and monopsony (meaning only). Equilibrium of a firm in perfect competition under short run (explanation and diagram, shut down point and break-even point) and long run (diagram not required).

2. Theory of Income and Employment

Basic concepts and determination of Income and Employment

The concept of demand (exante) and effective (expost) demand. Aggregate demand and its components, propensity to consume and propensity to save (average and marginal), equilibrium output, investment multiplier (its meaning and mechanism with the help of a diagram). Simple numerical based on the above. Meaning of full employment. Problems of excess demand and deficient demand; measures to correct them.

3. Money and Banking

(i) Money: meaning, functions of money, supply of money.

Meaning, kinds of money, functions of money (primary, secondary and contingent) to be explained; supply of money (only meaning of M_0, M_1, M_2, M_3 & M_4). Inflation: meaning, demand pull and cost push (diagrams not required)

(ii) Banks: functions of commercial bank; high powered money, credit creation by commercial banks; Central Bank: functions.

Basic understanding of the functions of commercial banks, credit creation process with limitation. The regulatory role of the Central Bank, its functions and the way it controls the flow of credit needs to be explained. A brief mention may be made of quantitative CRR, SLR, Bank Rate policy (repo rate and reverse repo rate) and Open Market Operations and qualitative methods.

4. Balance of Payment and Exchange Rate

Balance of Payment – meaning, components; foreign exchange – meaning, determination of exchange rate (Flexible).

Balance of Payment - Meaning and components; Causes of disequilibrium and how the disequilibrium can be corrected; Foreign Exchange Rate – meaning, meaning of fixed and flexible exchange rate, determination of exchange rate in a free market. Concepts of depreciation, appreciation, devaluation and revaluation (meaning only).

5. Public Finance

(i) Fiscal Policy: meaning and instruments of fiscal policy.

Meaning and instruments of fiscal policy – Public Revenue: Meaning, taxes (Meaning and types), difference between direct and indirect taxes; Public Expenditure: Meaning and importance; Public Debt: Meaning and redemption; Deficit Financing: meaning.

(ii) Government Budget: meaning, types and components.

Meaning and types of Government budget – union, state; components – revenue and capital. Concept of deficit budget: revenue deficit, fiscal deficit, primary deficit – their meaning and implications.

6. National Income

(i) Circular flow of Income.

A simple model explaining the circular flow of income with two, three and four sector models with leakages and injections.

(ii) Concepts and definition of NY, GNP, GDP, NNP, private income, personal income, personal disposable income, National Disposable Income and per capita income; relationship between the income concepts.

A brief understanding of the mentioned national income aggregates is needed. The concepts of GNP and NNP should be explained both at factor cost and market prices, real GDP and nominal GDP, National Disposable Income (Gross and Net), GDP and Welfare, GDP as an indicator of Economic welfare.

(iii) Methods of measuring National Income: product or value-added method; income method and expenditure method with simple numericals based on them.

Simple numericals based on all the methods to be covered for better understanding of the concept. Precautions and difficulties of measuring National Income for each method.

PAPER II PROJECT WORK 20 Marks

Candidates will be expected to have completed two projects from any topic covered in Theory.

The project work will be assessed by the teacher and a Visiting Examiner appointed locally and approved by the Council.

Mark allocation for each Project [10 marks]

Overall format	1 Mark
Content	4 Marks
Findings	2 Marks
Viva-voce based on the Project	3 Marks

Analysis of Pupil's Performance: ISC Economics

Topics found difficult / confusing by candidates

TOPICS FOUND DIFFICULT BY CANDIDATES

- Question 1 (iv): AR and market demand curves.
- Question 1 (x): Shift of market and individual supply curve.
- Question 1 (xvi): Ex-ante demand in Keynesian model and in micro sense.
- Question 3: The floor price.
- Question 5 (i): Freedom of entry and exit leading to normal profit in the long run; selling cost under Oligopoly.
- Question 7 (i): Fiscal deficit proves to be counter productive.
- Question 8 (i): Current account and capital account of BoP.
  (ii): Fixed foreign rate determination.
- Question 10 (ii) : Short run equilibrium of a perfectly competitive firm.
- Question 11: Indifference curve analysis.
- Question 12: Numerical on national income.

CONCEPTS IN WHICH CANDIDATES GOT CONFUSED

- Market supply curve and individual supply curve.
- AP and TP relationship
- The floor price.
- Fiscal deficit being counter productive
- The words- combat this situation, implication, etc

SUGGESTIONS FOR CANDIDATES

- Study all the topics given in the syllabus; candidates should not resort to selective studying.
- Practice all the numerical problems covered in the syllabus.
- Understand the meaning of the concepts thoroughly and read through the complete content or chapters.
- Understand the diagrams and practice them correctly.
- Practice higher-order MCQs, assertion and reasoning statements from different topics, and analytical and application-based questions.
- Clearly understand the cause-and-effect relationships for every economic concept.
- Read the question paper thoroughly during the stipulated 15 minutes allotted for reading.
- During the reading time, students should prepare a basic outline of their answers in their minds for different questions.
- Understand all three methods of calculating national income, along with the steps and the items that need to be included and excluded. Practice a variety of problems on national income.
- Solve the previous years' ISC Question papers, Specimen Papers, CFQs and inculcate time management.
- Stay connected with real-life situations and different policies adopted by the government and try to analyze these in relation to knowledge gained from studying various topics in the syllabus.

01

Theory of Consumer Behaviour and Demand

TREND ANALYSIS 5 YEARS

Average No. of Questions Across all Sets

	Types of Questions	2023	2020	2019	2018	2017
01 Utility and Laws of Utility Analysis	1 Mark	1	—	—	—	—
	2 Marks	—	1	—	1	—
	3/4 Marks	—	—	—	—	1
	6 Marks	1	1	—	1	—
02 Consumer's Equilibrium	1 Mark	—	—	—	—	—
	2 Marks	—	—	1	—	—
	3/4 Marks	—	1	—	—	1
	6 Marks	—	—	1	—	—
03 Concept of Demand and its Determinants	1 Mark	1	—	—	—	—
	2 Marks	—	—	—	—	1
	3/4 Marks	—	1	—	1	—
	6 Marks	—	—	—	—	—
04 Law of Demand and its Exception	1 Marks	—	—	—	—	—
	2 Marks	—	1	—	—	—
	3/4 Marks	—	—	1	—	—
	6 Marks	—	—	—	—	1
05 Movement and Shift in Demand Curve	1 Mark	—	—	—	—	—
	2 Marks	—	—	—	—	1
	3/4 Marks	—	—	1	1	—
	6 Marks	—	—	—	—	—

TOPIC 1

Utility and Laws of Utility Analysis

Consumer

A consumer is one who takes decisions about what to buy for the satisfaction of wants. This decision can be taken as an individual or as a member of household, as a producer and even government is a consumer of various goods and services. Consumer seeks to maximise utility by spending his income on various goods and services.

Utility

It is the want satisfying power of any good/commodity or services.

There are two approaches to measure utility as given below

(i) **Cardinal utility approach** It was given by Professor Alfred Marshall. It refers to the measurement of utility in terms of cardinal

numbers (i.e. numerical values) 1, 2, 3, etc.
e.g. A basket of oranges offers 10 utils of utility to a consumer. Utility is measured in terms of 'utils'.

(ii) **Ordinal utility approach** It was given by Professor Hicks and Allen. It refers to the measurement of utility in terms of psychological satisfaction on consuming one good in comparison to the other (i.e. utility is ranked based on preferences). e.g. A pizza offers greater satisfaction to a consumer than a chapati.

Concept of Cardinal Utility

The two main concepts of cardinal utility are as follows

(i) **Total Utility** (TU) Total satisfaction obtained by a consumer by consuming given amount of a particular commodity is called 'total utility'. It is the sum total of utility derived from consumption of all units of a good/commodity.

Total Utility (TU)
$$= MU_1 + MU_2 + MU_3 + \ldots + MU_n \text{ or } \sum_{i=1}^{n} MU_i$$

(ii) **Marginal Utility** (MU) The utility derived from the consumption of an additional unit of a commodity is termed as 'marginal utility'. It may also be called as the utility obtained from the consumption of an additional unit.

Mathematically, it is calculated as

$$MU_{nth} = TU_n - TU_{n-1} \text{ or } MU = \frac{\Delta TU}{\Delta Q}$$

Here, MU = Marginal Utility
TU_n = Total Utility of n units
TU_{n-1} = Total Utility of '$n-1$' units
ΔTU = Change in Total Utility
ΔQ = Change in Quantity

Relationship between Total Utility (TU) and Marginal Utility (MU)

Main points of this relationship are as follows

(i) MU is derived from TU.
(ii) MU always diminishes, as the satisfaction that we derive from an additional unit is less than that of the previous one.
(iii) When MU falls but remains positive, TU rises, though at a diminishing rate.
(iv) When MU becomes zero, TU reaches its maximum and becomes constant (known as 'saturation point').
(v) When MU becomes negative, TU starts falling.

Note MU can be zero or negative but TU cannot be zero.

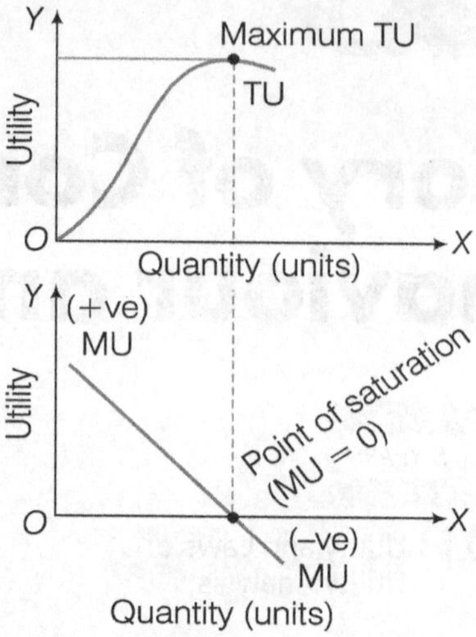

Laws of Utility Analysis

Utility analysis has two main laws

1. Law of Diminishing Marginal Utility (DMU)/ Gossen's First Law of Consumption

According to this law, as the consumer consumes more and more units of a good, then marginal utility derived from each successive unit, falls continuously and eventually becomes negative. In other words, when a consumer consumes successive units of a good, total utility initially increases, reaches its maximum and eventually falls.

This law can be explained with the help of following schedule and diagram

Units of apple consumed	MU from apple (utils)	TU from apple (utils)
1	20	20
2	15	35
3	10	45
4	05	50
5	0	50
6	–5	45

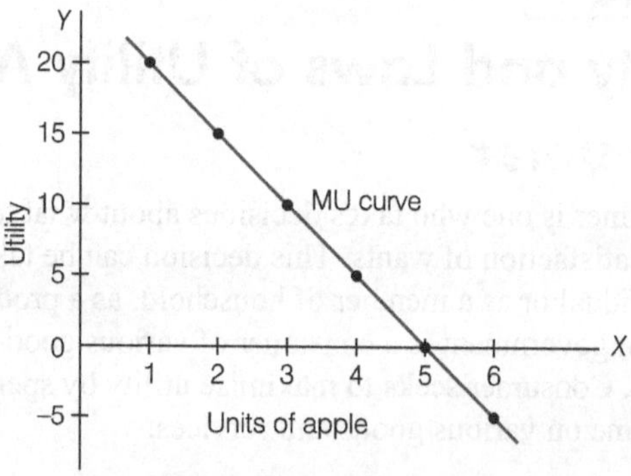

Law of DMU is based on certain assumptions, which are as follows

(i) Cardinal measurement of utility.
(ii) Marginal utility of money is constant.
(iii) Consumer is a rational consumer.
(iv) Income of the consumer and prices of goods are constant.
(v) Consumption should be of identical units.
(vi) Consumption should be continuous.
(viii) Consumption should be of standard units.

2. Law of Equi-marginal Utility/ Gossen's Second Law of Consumption

According to this law, the consumer maximising his total utility will allocate his income among various commodities in1 such a way that the marginal utility of the last unit of money (rupee) spent on each commodity is equal.

This law was propounded by H.H. Gossen.

According to **Prof. Marshall,** "If a person has a thing which he can put to several uses, he will distribute it among these uses in such a way, that he has the same marginal utility in all."

Equation for '*n*' number of commodities

$$\frac{MU_1}{P_1} = \frac{MU_2}{P_2} = \frac{MU_3}{P_3} = \dots = \frac{MU_{nth}}{P_{nth}} = MU_M$$

We can explain it with the help of following schedule.

Assume, $P_X = ₹10$, $P_Y = ₹2$ and $MU_M = ₹1$.

Units of 'X'	MU_X	P_X	MU_X in terms of $₹\left(\frac{MU_X}{P_X}\right)$	Units of 'Y'	MU_Y	P_Y	MU_Y in terms of ₹ (MU_Y/P_Y)
1	100	10	10	1	24	2	12
2	80	10	8	2	22	2	11
3	60	10	6	3	20	2	10
4	40	10	4	4	18	2	9
5	20	10	2	5	16	2	8

In the above schedule, $\frac{MU_X}{P_X} = \frac{MU_Y}{P_Y}$, when consumer is consuming 1 unit of good X and 3 units of good Y and also, when he is consuming 2 units of good X and 5 units of good Y. Now, let us assume that his money income is ₹ 30. So, for first combination, he pays $1 \times 10 + 3 \times 2 = ₹16$, which is less than his money income, therefore he is not in equilibrium.

For the second combination, he pays $2 \times 10 + 5 \times 2 = ₹30$, which is equal to his money income. Also, at this level, total utility is maximum.

Therefore, equilibrium is struck when he consumes 2 units of X and 5 units of Y.

Consumer's Equilibrium

It refers to the condition/situation in which a consumer gets maximum satisfaction from the consumption of the commodity with his given income.

Conditions for Consumer's Equilibrium

Following are the two conditions of consumer's equilibrium

(i) **One commodity case** Condition for consumer's equilibrium when he is assumed to consume only good, say X, is given as

$$\frac{MU_X}{P_X} = MU_M$$

Where, MU_X = Marginal Utility of Commodity X; P_X = Price of X; MU_M = Marginal Utility of Money

It implies that in state of equilibrium marginal utility derived in terms of money is equal to price of commodity.

In the above equation, if we assume $MU_M = 1$ (for the sake of simplicity).

Then, $$\frac{MU_X}{MU_M} = P_X$$

or $$MU_X = P_X \qquad [\because MU_M = 1]$$

The following schedule will help in a better understanding of the above concept

Units consumed	MU_X (utils)	MU_X in terms of ₹ $\left(\frac{MU_x}{2}\right)$	Price	Gain/ Loss
1	10	5	3	2
2	8	4	3	1
3	6	3	3	0
4	4	2	3	–1
5	2	1	3	–2
6	0	0	3	–3

In the above table, it is assumed that MU of a rupee is 2 utils.

From the above table, it is clear that consumer is at equilibrium when he is consuming 3 units, because

$$\frac{MU_X}{MU_M} = P_X$$

or $$\frac{6}{2} = 3 \text{ or } 3 = 3$$

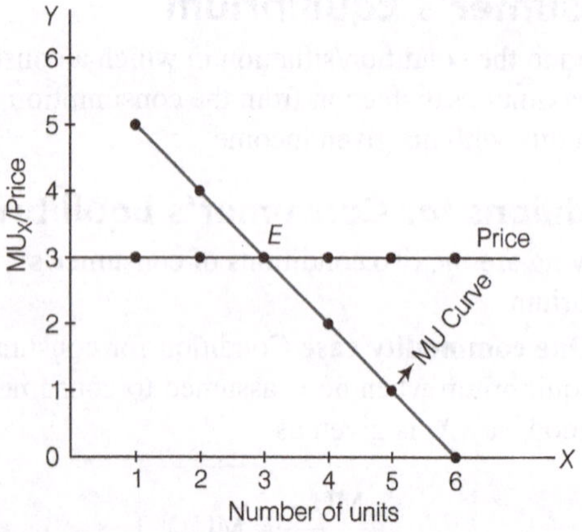

Where, E = Point of Equilibrium; $P_X = MU_X$

(ii) **Two commodity case or Equimarginal utility**

When a consumer consumes two commodities say X and Y, condition for consumer's equilibrium will be

$$\boxed{\frac{MU_X}{P_X} = \frac{MU_Y}{P_Y} = MU_M}$$

Where, MU_X = Marginal Utility of Commodity X

MU_Y = Marginal Utility of Commodity Y

P_X = Price of X

P_Y = Price of Y

MU_M = Marginal Utility of Money

It implies that in state of equilibrium, utility per rupee obtained by the consumer from good X or good Y, should be equal to Marginal Utility of Money (MU_M).

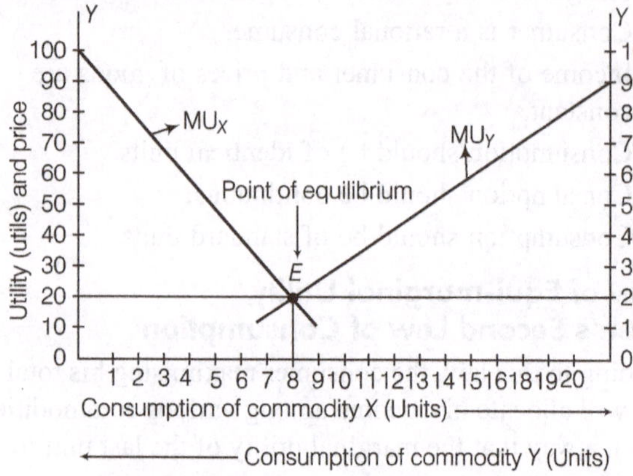

Following diagram will help in better understanding of the above concept

If, $MU_M = 1$

then $\frac{MU_X}{P_X} = \frac{MU_Y}{P_Y}$ *or* $\frac{MU_X}{MU_Y} = \frac{P_X}{P_Y}$

If $P_X = P_Y$

then, $MU_X = MU_Y$

Conditions of Consumer's Equilibrium using Marginal Utility Approach

(i) Marginal utility of per rupee must be same across all goods purchased by the consumer.

(ii) Marginal utility of money remains constant.

(iii) Law of diminishing utility remains valid.

PYQs Previous Years' Questions

1 Mark Questions

1. The aggregate utility obtained from the consumption of a specific unit of a commodity is called ***ISC 2023***

(a) marginal utility (b) total utility
(c) maximum utility (d) additional utility

Ans (b) total utility

2. Additional utility derived from the consumption of an additional unit of a commodity is called ***ISC Sem I 2021***

(a) average utility
(b) marginal utility
(c) total utility (d) additional utility

Ans (b) marginal utility

3. What is the formula for calculating MU? ***ISC Sem I Specimen 2021***

(a) $TU_n + TU_{n+1}$ (b) $TU_n - TU_{n+1}$
(c) $TU_n - TU_{n+1}$ (d) $TU_n - TU_{n-1}$

Ans (d) $TU_n - TU_{n-1}$

4. When a consumer consumes two goods then he will be in equilibrium at ***ISC Sem I Specimen 2021***

(a) $MU_X = P_X$ (b) $\frac{MU_X}{P_X} = \frac{P_Y}{MU_Y}$

(c) $\frac{MU_X}{P_x} = \frac{MU_X}{P_Y}$ (d) None of the above

Ans (c) $\frac{MU_X}{P_X} = \frac{MU_X}{P_Y}$

5. Total utility refers to the total satisfaction derived by the consumer from the consumption of *ISC Sem I Specimen 2021*
(a) an additional quantity of a commodity
(b) a minimum quantity of a commodity
(c) a maximum quantity of a commodity
(d) a specific quantity of a commodity

Ans (a) an additional quantity of a commodity

2 Marks Questions

1. Differentiate between total utility and marginal utility. *ISC Specimen 2023*

Ans

Basis	TU	MU
Meaning	It is sum total of utility derived from consumption of different units of a good.	It is an additional utility derived from consumption of additional unit of a good.
Formula	TU = ΣMU	$MU = TU_n - TU_{n-1}$

2. State the Law of Diminishing Marginal Utility. Mention any two assumptions of the law. *ISC 2020*

Ans According to Law of Diminishing Marginal Utility, as the consumer consumes more and more units of a good, then marginal utility derived from each successive unit, falls continuously and eventually becomes negative.

Two assumptions of this law are
(i) Marginal utility of money is constant.
(ii) Consumer is a rational consumer.

3. Define total utility. How is marginal utility derived from total utility? *ISC 2018*

Ans Total satisfaction obtained by a consumer by consuming given amount of a particular commodity is called 'total utility'. It is the sum total of utility derived from consumption of all units of a commodity. The utility derived from the consumption of an additional unit of a commodity is termed as 'marginal utility'.

Total Utility (TU)

$$= MU_1 + MU_2 + MU_3 + \ldots\ldots + MU_n$$

or ΣMU_n

Marginal Utility (MU) can be derived from total utility.

$$MU_{nth} = TU_n - TU_{n-1} \quad or \quad MU = \frac{\Delta TU}{\Delta Q}$$

Here, MU = Marginal Utility
TU_n = Total Utility of n units
TU_{n-1} = Total Utility of $n-1$ units
ΔTU = Change in Total Utility
ΔQ = Change in Quantity

4. Define marginal utility. When can it be negative? *ISC 2015*

Or When does marginal utility becomes negative? *ISC 2009*

Ans The utility derived from the consumption of an additional unit of a commodity is termed as 'marginal utility'. It is defined as change in total utility due to consumption of an additional unit i.e. marginal utility can be negative when total utility falls. In other words, when total utility is highest, marginal utility becomes zero. If consumer continues to consume more even after this, then total utility falls and marginal utility becomes negative.

Concept Enhancer Students generally draw MU from y-axis. Marginal utility curve does not start from y-axis as utility not defined at that point.

5. State the Law of Equi-marginal Utility. *ISC 2012*

Ans According to this law, the consumer maximising his total utility will allocate his income among various commodities in such a way that the marginal utility of the last unit of money (rupee) spent on each commodity is equal. Mathematically,

$$\frac{MU_1}{P_1} = \frac{MU_2}{P_2} = \frac{MU_3}{P_3} = \ldots\ldots = \frac{MU_n}{P_n} = MU_M$$

6. State any two assumptions of Law of Diminishing Marginal Utility (DMU). *ISC 2011*

Ans Refer to Q. No 2 (2 Marks) on page 5.

7. State the Law of Diminishing Marginal Utility (DMU). *ISC 2007*

Ans Refer to Q. No 2 (2 Marks) on page 5.

3/4 Marks Questions

1. Explain with the help of a diagram the relationship between total utility and marginal utility. *ISC 2017*

Ans The relationship between Total Utility (TU) and Marginal Utility (MU) can be summarised as follows
(i) MU is derived from TU.
(ii) When MU falls but remains positive, TU rises, though at a diminishing rate.
(iii) When MU becomes zero, TU reaches its maximum and becomes constant.
(iv) When MU becomes negative, TU starts falling.

The adjacent diagram shows the relationship between TU and MU.

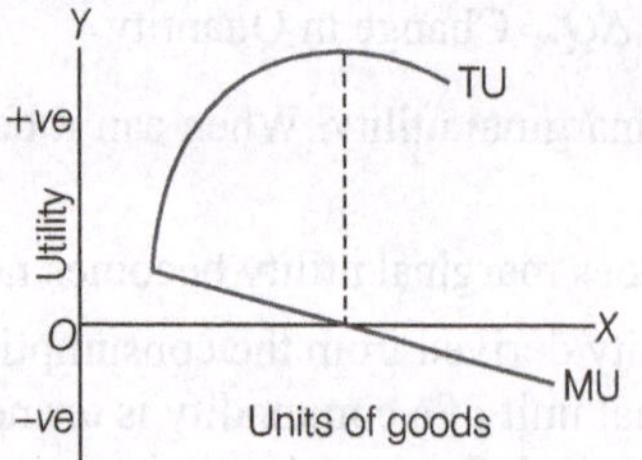

Total Utility and Marginal Utility Curves

Common Mistake Students usually mention TU as maximum when MU is zero. However, TU is both maximum and constant and not just maximum.

2. Discuss two differences between cardinal utility and ordinal utility. **ISC 2016**

Ans Difference between cardinal utility and ordinal utility

Basis	Cardinal utility	Ordinal utility
Meaning	This approach to utility assumes that utility is measurable in terms of numbers such as 1, 2, 3, etc. The unit of measurement under this approach is 'utils'.	This approach to utility refers to the measurement of utility in terms of psychological satisfaction on consuming one good in comparison to other.
Example	A basket of oranges offers 10 utils of utility to a consumer.	A pizza offers greater satisfaction to a consumer than a chapati.

3. The following table shows the marginal utility derived from the purchase of books. The price of the book is ₹ 500. Draw a diagram to explain consumer's equilibrium where MU = P. **ISC 2012**

Number of books	MU
1	700
2	600
3	500
4	400
5	300

KEY IDEA
For equilibrium, assume constant value of marginal utility of money.

Ans Consumer's equilibrium is attained at the point where the following condition gets satisfied

$MU_X = P_X$ ($MU_M = 1$) (assumed)

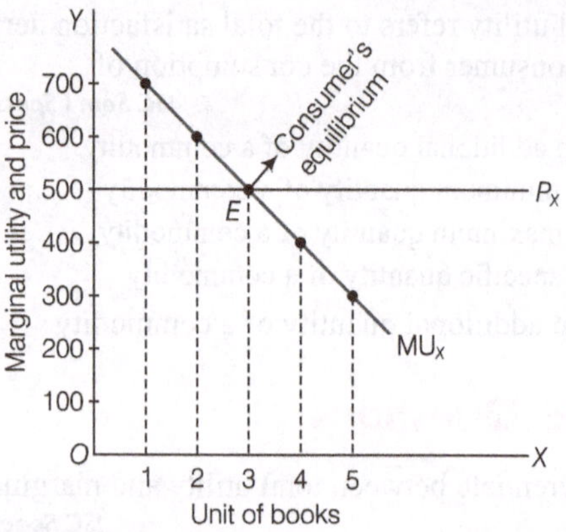

In the diagram, number of books purchased are taken on OX axis and MU and price of the book are plotted on OY axis. As the table shows, with every additional unit of book purchased, MU derived is falling. According to the consumer's equilibrium condition, the consumer can maximise his satisfaction by consuming the units of a given commodity where $MU_X = P_X$ i.e. Marginal utility derived from consumption of a commodity is equal to the price of that commodity.

In the diagram, equilibrium situation is shown at point E, where prices (₹ 500) equal to the marginal utility derived (500) when the consumer purchases 3 units of book. So, he is at equilibrium when he purchases 3 books.

6 Marks Questions

1. With the help of a diagram, explain how the consumer will attain equilibrium on consumption of a single commodity at a given price. **ISC 2023**

Or Explain with the help of a diagram the consumer's equilibrium through utility approach. **ISC 2015**

Or Using the utility approach, discuss how a consumer attains equilibrium. **ISC 2010**

Ans Consumer's equilibrium is that state/condition where he attains his maximum satisfaction given his resources. This is a situation of rest or stability.

Under utility approach, there are two situations or cases of consumer's equilibrium which are as follows

(i) **One commodity case** When a consumer buys only one commodity, his behaviour is guided by the law of DMU. In this case, consumer will attain equilibrium when following condition gets satisfied

$$\frac{MU_X}{P_X} = MU_M$$

Here, MU_X = Marginal Utility of Commodity X,
P_X = Price of X,
MU_M = Marginal Utility of Money

Here, consumer is assumed to consumes good X at a price of P_X. In the above equation, if we further assume $MU_M = 1$, then the condition will be $MU_X = P_X$.

Assumptions of consumer's equilibrium are as follows

(a) It is assumed that the consumer is rational. He aims at maximising the utility from his purchases.

(b) Utility is measured in terms of money.

(c) The law of diminishing marginal utility operates.

(d) Consumer's income and price of the goods is given and remains unchanged.

Schedule of Marginal Utility

Units of shirts	Marginal utility
1	700
2	650
3	600
4	500
5	350

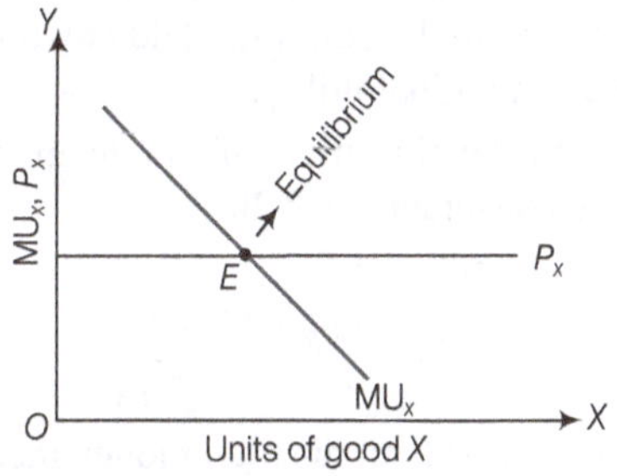

The above diagram shows that the consumer is at equilibrium at point 'E'.

At this point $MU_X = P_X$.

(ii) **Two commodity case** When a consumer wants to buy two commodities/goods, his equilibrium will be determined in accordance with the law of equi-marginal utility.

In this case, consumer is assumed to consume good X and good Y at price P_X and P_Y, respectively, condition for equilibrium will be

$$\frac{MU_X}{P_X} = \frac{MU_Y}{P_Y} = MU_M$$

If, $MU_M = 1$, then $\frac{MU_X}{P_X} = \frac{MU_Y}{P_Y}$

or $\frac{MU_X}{MU_Y} = \frac{P_X}{P_Y}$

Further if, $P_X = P_Y$

$\Rightarrow \quad MU_X = MU_Y$

Following diagram will help in better understanding of the above concept

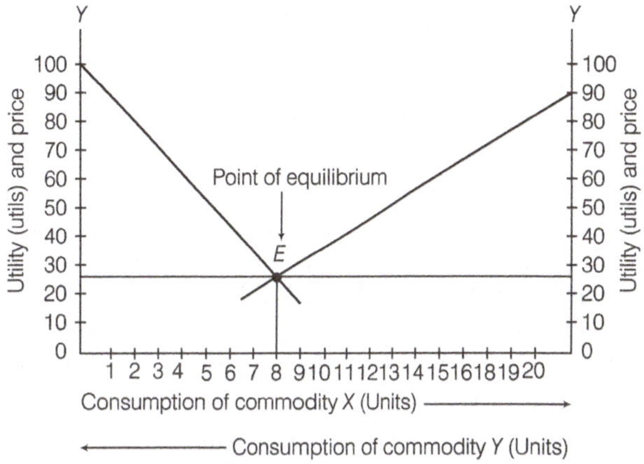

Value Points

For getting maximum marks, following value points can be included in the answer

- When nothing is mentioned regarding commodity, then explain both situation, i.e. one commodity and two commodity case.
- Assumptions of consumer's equilibrium should be added.

2. The marginal utility schedule of a rational consumer is given below. If the price of a commodity is ₹ 35, explain with the help of a diagram, how the consumer attains equilibrium. **ISC 2020**

Number of the commodity bought	1	2	3	4	5
MU	50	45	40	35	30

Ans Consumer's equilibrium is attained at the point, where following condition gets satisfied

$MU_x = P_x$

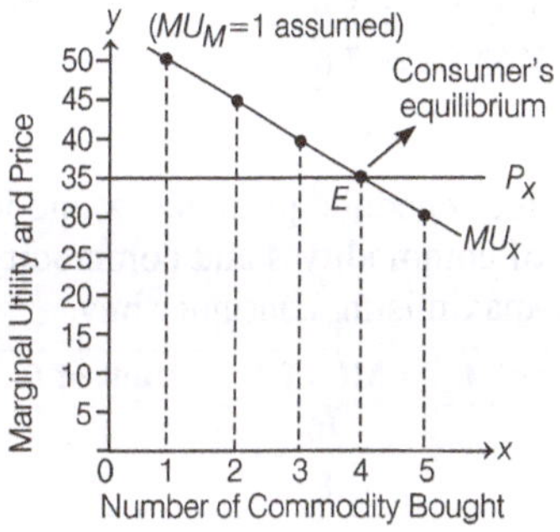

In the diagram, number of commodity bought is taken on *OX* axis and Marginal utility and price are taken on *OY* axis.

According to consumer's equilibrium condition, the consumer can maximise his satisfaction by consuming the units of a given commodity where $MU_x = P_x$, i.e. Marginal utility derived from consumption of a commodity is equal to the price of that commodity.

In the diagram, equilibrium situation is shown at point *E*, where price (35) is equal to the marginal utility derived (35) when the consumer purchases 4 units of commodity. So, he is at equilibrium when he purchases 4 units of commodity.

3. A consumer consumes goods *X* and *Y*. Given below is his marginal utility schedule for goods *X* and *Y*. Suppose, the price of *X* is ₹ 2, *Y* ₹ 1 and income ₹ 12. State the law of equi-marginal utility and explain how the consumer will attain equilibrium. **ISC 2018**

Units	1	2	3	4	5	6
MU_x	16	14	12	10	8	6
MU_y	11	10	9	8	7	6

Ans According to given schedule, price of a good *X* is ₹ 2 and that of good *Y* is ₹ 1.

Units	MU_x (Utils)	MU_x (₹) (MU_x/P_x)	MU_y (Utils)	MU_y (₹) (MU_y/P_y)
1	16	08	11	11
2	14	07	10	10
3	12	**06**	09	09
4	10	05	08	08
5	8	04	07	07
6	6	03	06	**06**

The consumer will buy 3 units of good *X* and 6 units of good *Y*. The marginal utility derived from good *X* and good *Y* are equal, at these particular level according to the condition laid down in the law of equi-marginal utility $MU_{x(₹)} = MU_{y(₹)}$

Also, this level is attainable in the given income of the consumer, i.e. ₹ 12

3 units of *X* @ ₹ 2 = ₹ 6
6 units of *Y* @ ₹ 1 = ₹ 6
₹ 12

4. (i) Study the schedule given below and identify how much of commodity *A* and commodity *B* will a utility maximising consumer buy.

Units of *A*	MU of *A*	Units of *B*	MU of *B*
1	10	1	30
2	8	2	24
3	6	3	20
4	4	4	16
5	2	5	14
6	1	6	8

Note Price *A* = ₹ 2, Price *B* = ₹ 4, Income = ₹ 20

(ii) Explain the law of equi-marginal utility using the above schedule. **ISC 2014**

Ans (i) According to the given schedule, price of commodity *A* is ₹ 2 and that of commodity *B* is ₹ 4.

Units of *A*	MU_A (utils)	MU_A (₹) (MU_A/P_A)	Units of *B*	MU_B (utils)	MU_B (₹) (MU_B/P_B)
1	**10**	**5**	1	30	7.5
2	8	4	2	24	6
3	6	3	**3**	**20**	**5**
4	4	2	4	16	4
5	2	1	5	14	3.5
6	1	0.5	6	8	2

The consumer will buy 1 unit of good *A* and 3 units of good *B*.

The marginal utility derived from good *A* and good *B* are equal, at these particular level according to the condition laid down in the law of equi-marginal utility.

Also this level is attainable in the given income of the consumer, i.e. ₹ 20.

1 unit of *A* @ ₹ 2 = ₹ 2
3 units of *B* @ ₹ 4 = ₹ 12
₹ 14

which is less than his total money income and hence attainable.

(ii) **Law of equi-marginal utility** This law states that the consumer maximising his total utility will allocate his income among various commodities in such a way that his marginal utility of the last rupee spent on each commodity is equal.

From the above schedule, it can be said that when prices of the commodities are unequal, then marginal utility must be converted in terms of rupee to compare and hence, law is satisfied where 1 unit of good *A* and 3 units of good *B* has been consumed by the consumer.

5. A marginal utility schedule of a person is given below. Discuss the law underlying the given schedule.
ISC 2013

Pen (units)	1	2	3	4	5
MU (utils)	25	20	15	10	5

Ans The law underlying the given schedule is the Law of Diminishing Marginal Utility (DMU).

As per the Law of DMU, the level of satisfaction obtained from the consumption of each additional unit of a commodity consumed, keeps on declining as more and more unit of a commodity are consumed.

This law was formulated by the famous economist, H.H. Gossen and propagated by Alfred Marshall.

It is based on the following assumptions
(i) Cardinal measurement of utility.
(ii) Consumption should be continuous.
(iii) Marginal utility of money is constant.
(iv) Income and prices are constant.
(v) Goods are same in all aspects. i.e. colour, shape, size, quality, etc.
(vi) Goods consumed are of standard unit.

As the schedule illustrates that when first unit of pen is purchased, the marginal utility derived is maximum. But with every successive unit of pen used, the marginal utility goes on decreasing from 25 utils to 5 utils when 5th unit of pen is used. This is in accordance with the law of diminishing marginal utility.

Concept Enhancer Marginal utility can be zero or negative as these are just avaliable options and consumer may not actually choose these levels.

TOPIC 2

Consumer's Equilibrium : Indifference Curve Approach (Ordinal Theory)

Indifference Curve and Indifference Map

Indifference Curve (IC) is the locus of all possible bundles/combinations of two goods that gives consumer equal satisfaction. The group or set of indifference curves showing different combination of two goods is called indifference map.

Properties of Indifference Curves

There are four main properties of Indifference Curves (IC) which are as follows

(i) It is downward sloping from left to the right. If the consumer decides to have more of good X, then he must have less of good Y.
(ii) Due to decreasing marginal rate of substitution, it is convex to the origin.
(iii) Two IC cannot give equal satisfaction to consumer, so they can not intersect each other.
(iv) Higher IC represents higher income and higher satisfaction to consumer.

Slope of Indifference Curve

An indifference curve is negatively sloped. It is a downward sloping curve from left to right because to increase the consumption of one unit, the consumer has to decrease the consumption of the other, because his income is given and fixed.

Law of Diminishing Marginal Rate of Substitution (DMRS)

Marginal rate of substitution is the rate at which one commodity is gained at the sacrifice of the other. In other words, it is the rate at which the consumer is willing to exchange one good for the other good.

According to this law, Marginal Rate of Substitution (MRS) falls continuously. As consumer consumes more and more units of good 1, he would like to sacrifice lesser and lesser units of good 2. Hence, MRS diminishes and indifference curve becomes convex to the origin.

$$\text{MRS} = \frac{\Delta Y}{\Delta X}$$

Here, MRS = Marginal Rate of Substitution
ΔY = Quantity of Good Y sacrificed
ΔX = Quantity of Good X obtained

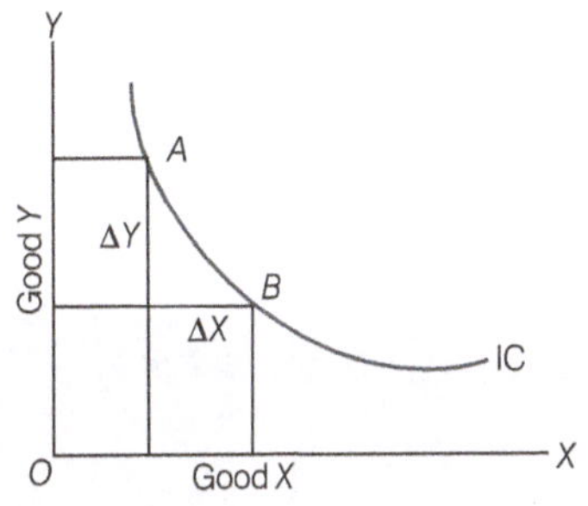

Consumer's Budget

It is the real purchasing power of consumer from which he can purchase certain quantitative bundles of two goods at a given price.

Budget Set

It represents all those combination of two goods which a consumer can afford to buy. The budget set is thus, the collection of all bundles that the consumer can buy with his/her income at the prevailing market prices.

Budget Line

It indicates exactly that combination of two selected goods that a consumer can afford at a specified price for the goods given his particular money income.

$$P_X Q_X + P_Y Q_Y = M$$

Here,

M = Given Money Income

P_X and P_Y = Per unit Price of Good X and Y, respectively

Q_X = Quantity of X

Q_Y = Quantity of Y

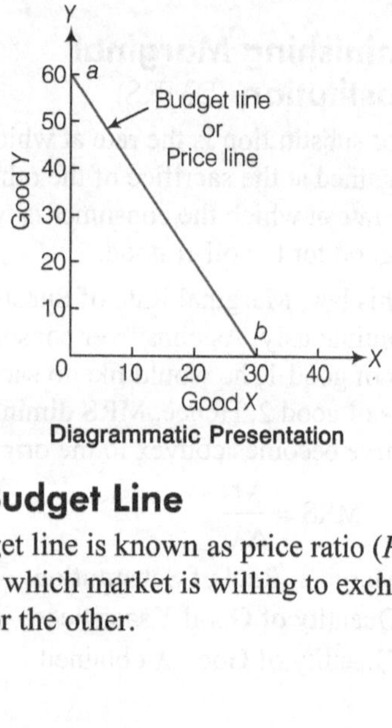

Diagrammatic Presentation

Slope of Budget Line

Slope of budget line is known as price ratio (P_X/P_Y), i.e. the rate at which market is willing to exchange one commodity for the other.

The main properties of a budget line are

(i) Negatively sloped line.

(ii) Slope of the budget line is equal to the price ratio of two commodities.

(iii) It is straight line, as we assume given prices of the two commodities to be constant.

Condition for Consumer's Equilibrium Under Ordinal Approach

The condition for consumer's equilibrium under ordinal approach is as follows

(i) $MRS_{XY} = P_X/P_Y$

i.e. Slope of Indifference Curve = Slope of Budget Line

Here, MRS_{XY} = Marginal Rate of Substitution between Goods X and Y

P_X/P_Y = Price Ratio between Goods X and Y

(ii) MRS continuously falls – The indifference curve must be convex to the origin at the point of equilibrium. Consumer is equilibrium at point 'E' where the IC is tangent to the budget line.

The consumer is attaining maximum satisfaction at this point within his given income.

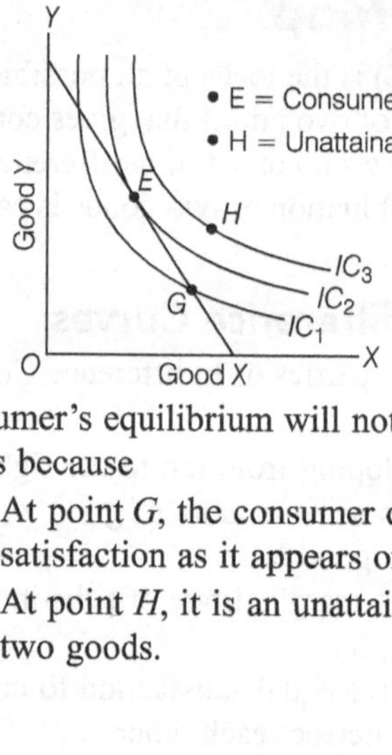

Consumer's equilibrium will not fall at the following points because

(a) At point G, the consumer derives lesser satisfaction as it appears on a lower IC.

(b) At point H, it is an unattainable combination of two goods.

PYQs Previous Years' Questions

1 Mark Questions

1. Indifference curve is convex to the origin due to *ISC Specimen 2023, 21*

(a) Axiom of transtivity
(b) Law of DMU
(c) Law of DMRS
(d) Axiom of non-satiety

Ans (c) Law of DMRS

Or Convexity of indifference curve implies ...... marginal rate of substitution. *ISC Sem I 2021*

(a) increasing (b) decreasing
(c) constant (d) zero

Ans (b) decreasing

2. The indifference curve means *ISC Sem I 2021*

(a) equal consumption of two goods
(b) equal utility from the consumption of combination of two goods
(c) equal income of the consumer
(d) equal prices of goods consumed

Ans (b) equal utility from the consumption of combination of two goods

3. The slope of the indifference curve is equal to *ISC Sem I Specimen 2021*

(a) one
(b) marginal utility
(c) marginal rate of substitution
(d) None of the above

Ans (c) marginal rate of substitution

2 Marks Questions

1. Explain an indifference map, with the help of a diagram. *ISC 2019*

Ans The set of indifference curves showing different combination of two goods is called indifference map.

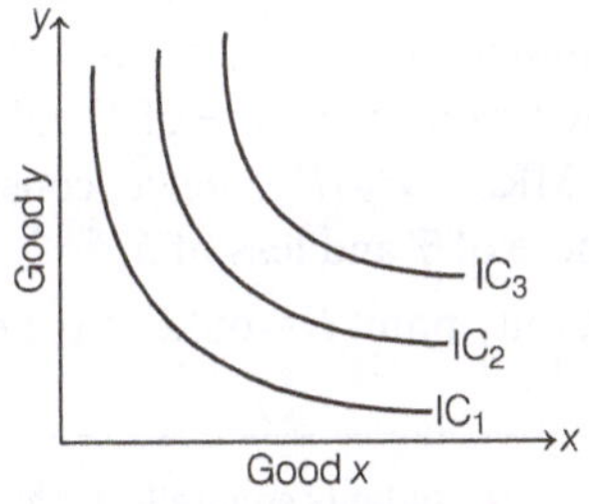

Indifference Map

2. What is meant by budget line? *ISC 2016*

Ans Budget line indicates exactly that combination of two selected goods that a consumer can afford at a specified price for the goods, given his particular money income.

$$P_X Q_X + P_Y Q_Y = M$$

Here,
M = Given Money Income
P_X and P_Y = Per unit Price of Goods X and Y, respectively
Q_X = Quantity of X Q_Y = Quantity of Y

Concept Enhancer Budget line is only a part of budget set or constraint.

3. Define the term 'Marginal Rate of Substitution' (MRS). *ISC 2006*

Ans Marginal Rate of Substitution (MRS) is the rate at which consumer is willing to sacrifice one good (say good Y) in order to gain one additional unit of the other good (say good X).

The formula to calculate MRS is

$$\text{MRS} = \frac{\Delta Y}{\Delta X} = \frac{\text{Loss in } Y}{\text{Gain in } X}$$

4. Explain one property of indifference curve with the help of diagram. *ISC 2005*

Ans Indifference curve is downward sloping from left to right, as consumer has to sacrifice some units of good Y, in order to gain every additional unit of good X, to be on the same indifference curve. In other words, on a single indifference curve, consumption of both the goods cannot be increased simultaneously, because income of the consumer does not change.

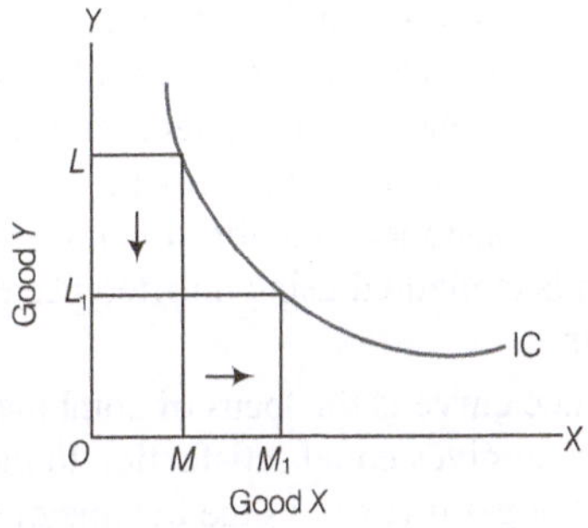

5. State two differences between utility analysis and IC analysis. **ISC 2005**

Ans Two differences between utility and IC analysis are

(i) While studying consumer's equilibrium, utility analysis can be used for a single or double commodities. Whereas, IC analysis can be used only for two commodities.

(ii) Utility analysis assumes that utility is measurable. Whereas, IC analysis assumes that utility from two goods can only be compared.

3/4 Marks Questions

1. Explain the concpet of Diminishing Marginal Rate of Substitution and show how it affects the indifference curve. **ISC 2020**

Ans Refer to text 'Law of Diminishing Marginal Rate of Substitution' on page 9.

2. Explain any two characteristics of an indifference curve. **ISC 2017**

Ans Two characteristics of an indifference curve are

(i) Indifference curves slope downward to the right or are negatively sloped, as consumption of both the goods cannot be increased at once.

(ii) Indifference curve is convex to the point origin, due to diminishing marginal rate of substitution.

6 Marks Questions

1. Explain the consumer's equilibrium through indifference curve approach with help of diagram. **ISC Specimen 2023**

Or Explain how a consumer attains equilibrium using Indifference curve analysis. **ISC 2019**

Or Explain the concept of consumer's equilibrium with the help of indifference curve analysis. **ISC 2016**

Or Explain how a consumer attain equilibrium using the indifference curve analysis. **ISC 2014**

Ans Consumer's equilibrium is that situation in which a consumer buys such a combination of goods from which, he gets maximum satisfaction, given the prices of the commodity and the money income of the consumer. Consumer's equilibrium under ordinal approach is explained using indifference curve and budget line.

Indifference curve is the locus of combination of two goods which gives equal satisfaction to the consumer, whereas budget line shows the income of the consumer (i.e. the bundle of two goods that the consumer can afford to buy with his income).

The conditions for consumer's equilibrium are

(i) Indifference curve must be tangent to the budget line (i.e. slope of indifference curve must be equal to the slope of budget line).

(ii) Indifference curve must be convex to the origin.

The assumptions for consumer's equilibrium are

(i) **Rationality** The consumer is rational. He wants to obtain maximum satisfaction from his given income and prices.

(ii) **Utility is ordinal** It is assumed that consumer can rank his preference according to the satisfaction that each combination of goods offer him.

(iii) **Consistency of choice** It is also assumed that the consumer is consistent in the choice of goods.

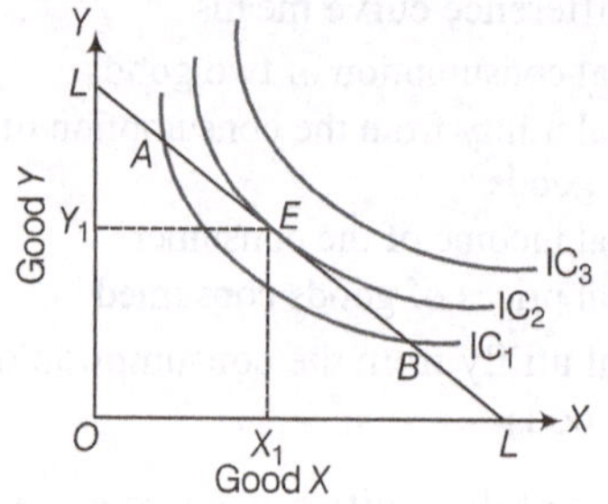

In the given diagram, consumer will be in equilibrium at point *E* where, MRS $= P_X/P_Y$.

i.e. Slope of Indifference Curve = Slope of Budget Line

Here, MRS = Marginal Rate of Substitution between Goods *X* and *Y*

P_X/P_Y = Price Ratio between Goods *X* and *Y*.

At equilibrium, consumer will try to achieve highest possible indifference curve with his given income. Though, IC_1 is affordable but consumer can reach at IC_2 which is a higher indifference curve, while IC_3 in not affordable to the consumer.

Also except *E*, point *A* or point *B* cannot be the point of equilibrium as at point *A*, MRS $> P_X/P_Y$. So, consumer will consume more of *X* and less of *Y* while at point *B*, MRS $< P_X/P_Y$, hence, consumer will consume more of *Y* and less of *X*.

As a result, only point *E* would be the equilibrium point.

Common Mistake Students generally don't mention about the convex IC at the point of equilibrium. It is the sufficient condition of equlibrium.

2. Explain four properties of indifference curve. *ISC Specimen 2023*

Or Discuss any two properties of indifference curve. *ISC 2015*

Or Explain the properties of indifference curve. *ISC 2008*

Ans The properties of an Indifference Curve (IC) are explained below

(i) **An IC slopes downward from left to the right** This shows that an IC has a negative slope. This property is based on the assumption that if a consumer consumes more of one commodity (food), he must consume less quantity of the other (clothing) because of his limited resources or income. He will have the same level of satisfaction from different combinations of two commodities.

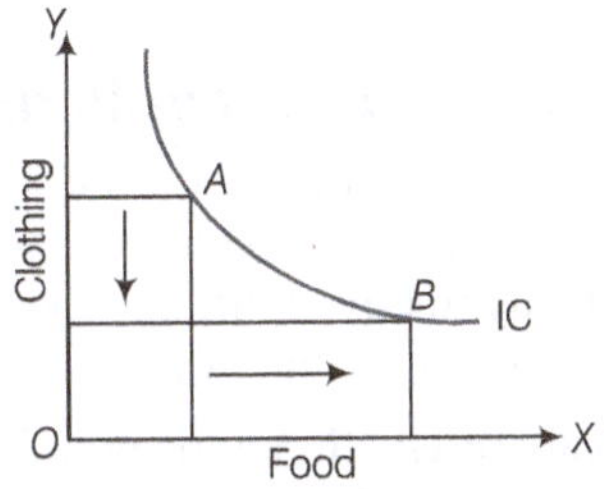

(ii) **An IC is convex to the origin** Convexity of IC implies that it bows inwards to the origin. In other words, the slope of IC decreases as we move down the IC due to the assumption of diminishing marginal rate of substitution.

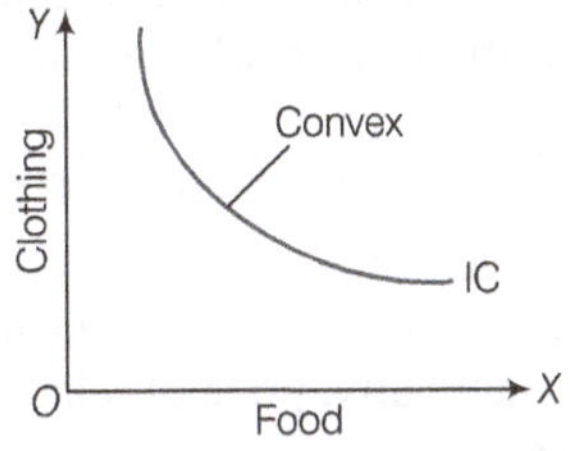

It indicates that the rate at which the consumer is willing to substitute cloth for food diminishes with every additional unit of food.

The consumer is willing to sacrifice less of '*Y*', in order to get more of '*X*'.

$$MRS = \frac{\Delta Y}{\Delta X}$$

(iii) **Higher IC yields higher satisfaction** Higher IC represents those combinations which yield more satisfaction than the combinations on lower IC, since the former will be giving us more amount of both the commodities. Combination *B* on IC_2 will give more commodities than combination *A* on IC_1. Same holds true for combination *C* with respect to *B* and *A*.

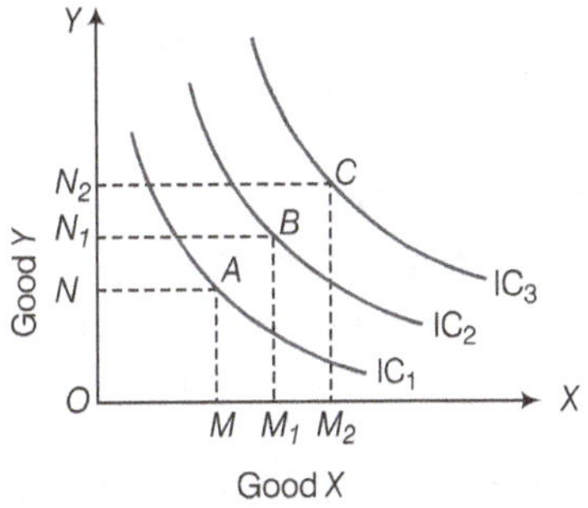

(iv) **Indifference curves never intersect each other** Indifference Curves (IC) are parallel to each other.

Between two indifference curves, there is no common set of points as both represent bundles of goods achievable at different income levels. i.e. two indifference curves cannot give same level of satisfaction

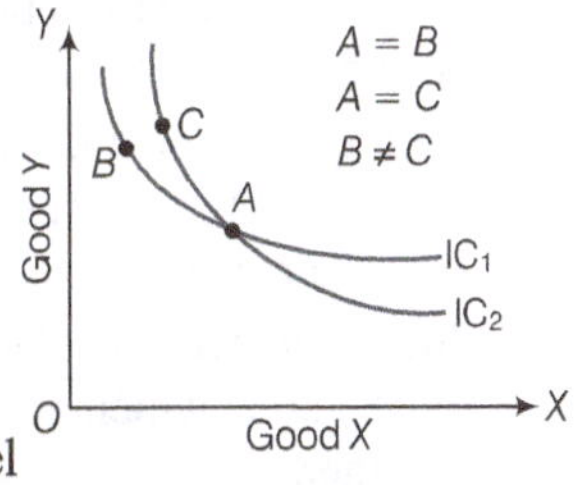

Value Points

For getting maximum marks, following value points can be included in the answer

- Use diagram to prove the properties of IC.
- Explain the properties with reference to the digram only.

TOPIC 3

Concept of Demand and Its Determinants

Demand

It refers to various amounts of commodities that a consumer is willing and able to purchase in the market in a given period of time and at various prices. A specific quantity of a good/commodity that a consumer is willing and able to purchase at a particular price during a particular time period is called as 'quantity demanded'.

Types of Demand

Various types of demand are as follows

(i) **Individual demand and market demand** The demand by an individual consumer for a commodity is termed as 'individual demand'.

Whereas, market demand is the sum of all individual demand that prevail in the market at different prices of the same commodity.

(ii) **Ex-ante demand and ex-post demand** Ex-ante demand refers to the amount of goods that consumers want to buy during a particular time period.

Whereas, ex-post demand refers to the amount of the goods that the consumer actually purchase during a specific period.

(iii) **Joint demand** It refers to the demand for two or more goods which are used jointly or demanded together.

e.g. Car and petrol, milk and sugar, bread and butter, etc. They are also known as 'complementary goods'.

(iv) **Derived demand** The demand for a commodity that arises because of the demand for some other commodity is called 'derived demand'. e.g. Cement, brick, etc, whose demand arises due to demand for house. Demand for labour is also derived demand.

(v) **Composite demand** Demand for goods that have multiple uses is called 'composite demand'. e.g. Steel, wood, milk, etc.

Demand Schedule and Demand Curve

Demand schedule is a tabular representation of quantity demanded at different possible prices. While, demand curve is graphical representation of demand schedule.

Under the concept of demand schedule, we will consider two types of schedules; one is individual demand schedule and the other is market demand schedule.

Individual Demand Schedule and Curve

Individual demand curve is the table which shows various quantities of a commodity which an individual buyer is ready to buy at different possible prices of the commodity at a given point of time. The graphical presentation of individual demand schedule is known as 'individual demand curve'.

Market Demand Schedule and Curve

Market demand schedule is the table which shows various quantities of a commodity which all the buyers in the market are ready to buy at different possible prices of the commodity at a given point of time.

The graphical presentation of market demand schedule, which is the horizontal summation of individual demands, is known as market demand curve.

Demand Function

It shows the relationship between demand for a commodity and its various determinants like own price of the commodity, price of related good, income of the consumer, etc.

$$D_X = f(P_X, P_r, Y, T, E, C, P, D, G)$$

Determinants of Individual Demand

(i) **Own price of commodity** (P_x) There is inverse relationship between price of commodity and quantity demanded.

(ii) **Price of related goods** (P_r) There are two types of related goods

(a) **Substitute goods** They are those goods which can be used in place of one another. e.g. Tea and coffee. Increase in the price of the commodity will increase demand for its substitute goods and *vice-versa*.

(b) **Complementary goods** Complementary goods are goods that people tend to use together. e.g. car and petrol. Increase in price of commodity will decrease the demand for its complementary goods.

(iii) **Income of consumer** (Y) There are types of goods

(a) **Normal goods** Normal goods are those goods whose demand increases with increase in income of consumer and *vice-versa*.

(b) **Inferior goods** For inferior goods, with a rise in income, the demand for good falls and *vice-versa*.

(iv) **Taste and preferences** (T) Demand for the goods is affected by consumer habits, fashions, likes and dislikes.

(v) **Consumer expectation** (E) Current demand of consumer is affected by expectations of future prices, incomes, price of related goods.

Determinants of Market Demand

(i) **Number of consumer in the market population** (D_X) There is direct relationship between number of consumer and market demand.

(ii) **Own price of the commodity** (P_X) There is inverse relationship between price of commodity and quantity demanded.

(iii) **Price of related goods** (P_r) There are two types of related goods

(a) **Substitute goods** They are those goods which can be used in place of one another. e.g. tea and coffee. Increase in the price of the commodity will increase demand for its substitute goods and *vice-versa*.

(b) **Complementary goods** Complementary goods are goods that people tend to use together. e.g. car and petrol. Increase in price of commodity will decrease the demand for its complementary goods.

(iv) **Income of the consumer** (Y) There are two types of goods

(a) **Normal goods** Normal goods are those goods whose demand increases with increase in income of consumer and *vice-versa*.

(b) **Inferior goods** For inferior goods, with a rise in income, the demand for goods falls and *vice-versa*.

(v) **Taste and preferences** (T) Demand for the goods is affected by consumer habits, fashions, likes and dislikes.

(vi) **Market expectations** (E) Current demand of market is affected by expectations of future prices, consumer income and price of related goods.

(vii) **Government's policy** (G) Favourable economic policies of government (i.e. reduction in GST) increase the market demand and *vice-versa*.

(viii) **Climate and season** (C) Market demand depends on climate and season (i.e. Demand for T-shirts, cotton clothes, ice-creams and cold drinks, etc increases in summer.)

(ix) **Distribution of income** (D) Market demand is influenced by income distribution pattern in economy.

PYQs Previous Years' Questions

1 Mark Questions

1. The figure given below shows the relation between the quantity demand for the good X and the price of the good Z. What type of goods are X and Z? **ISC 2023**

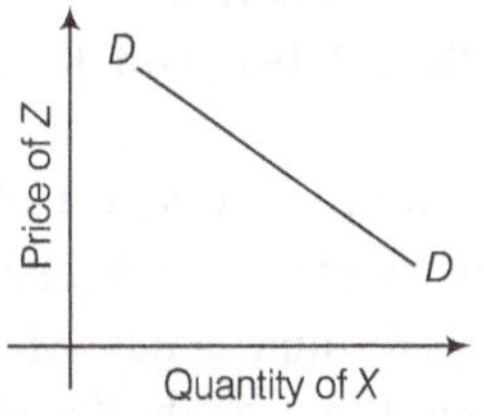

(a) Unrelated goods
(b) Substitute goods
(c) Complementary goods
(d) Giffen goods

Ans (c) Complementary goods

2. When price is ₹ 5 per unit of a commodity, A's demand is 11 units, B's demand is 14 units and C's demand is 8 units, then market demand will be **ISC Sem I 2021**

(a) 11 units
(b) 14 units
(c) 17 units
(d) 33 units

Ans (d) 33 units

3. An increase in income leads to decrease in demand for instant noodles, then instant noodles is **ISC Sem I 2021**

(a) normal good
(b) inferior good
(c) substitute good
(d) complementary good

Ans (b) inferior good

4. Which factor causes the demand for a commodity to decrease? **ISC Sem I 2021**
(a) Increase in income
(b) Fall in price of substitute goods
(c) Expectation that prices will increase
(d) Increase in market size

Ans (b) Fall in price of substitute goods

5. If the price of petrol increases, the demand for cars will **ISC Sem I Specimen 2021**
(a) increase (b) decrease
(c) expand (d) vary

Ans (b) decrease

6. What is ex-ante demand also known as? **ISC Sem I Specimen 2021**
(a) Intended demand (b) Actual demand
(c) Effective demand (d) Unplanned demand

Ans (a) Intended demand

7. The demand for a commodity refers to **ISC Sem I Specimen 2021**
(a) desire for a commodity
(b) need for a commodity
(c) quantity demanded at the lowest prices during a particular period of time
(d) quantity demanded at various possible prices during a particular period of time

Ans (d) quantity demanded at various possible prices during a particular period of time

2 Marks Questions

1. What is meant by ex-ante demand and ex-post demand? **ISC 2017**

Or How is ex-ante demand different from ex-post demand? **ISC 2010**

Ans **Ex-ante demand** It refers to the amount of goods that consumers want to or are willing to buy during a particular time period.

Ex-post demand It refers to the amount of goods that the consumers actually purchase during a specific period.

2. What is the shape of the demand curve? **ISC 2014**

Or How does an increase in the price of a commodity affect its quantity demanded? Show it with the help of a diagram. **ISC 2013**

Ans Keeping all other factors constant, there is an inverse relationship between price of a commodity and its quantity demanded, i.e. with the rise in price, quantity demanded for the commodity falls and *vice-versa*. Demand curve is negatively sloped.

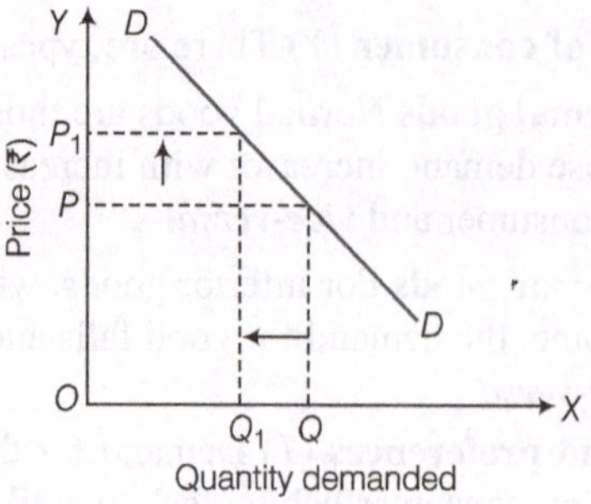

Concept Enhancer A demand curve can be non-linear as well. In that case, its shape is known as rectangular hyperbola.

3. What is composite demand? **ISC 2005**

Ans Demand for goods that have multiple uses is called 'composite demand'. e.g. Steel, wood, milk, etc, because, while demanding that product, one will first access the uses that it can be put to and then determine their demand.

Common Mistake Students generally get confused between composite demand and complementary demand. Demand is said to be complementary when two goods are demanded together.

3/4 Marks Questions

1. Explain any two factors affecting the demand of a commodity, other than its price. **ISC 2020**

Ans Various factors affecting demand are

(i) **Income of the consumer** Income level of the consumer has a positive or direct effect on the demand for a good (if the good is a normal good) i.e. with the rise in income of the consumer, demand for normal goods also increases and *vice-versa*.

In case of inferior goods, there is an inverse relationship between income of the consumer and demand of the commodity.

(ii) **Price of the related good** Related goods are of two types

(a) Substitute goods (like tea and coffee)

(b) Complementary goods (like car and petrol)

In case of substitute goods, with the rise in the price of substitute goods, demand for the commodity concerned increases and *vice-versa*. On the other hand, if the goods are complementary, with the rise in the price of complementary goods, demand for the commodity concerned falls and *vice-versa*.

2. Discuss how prices of related goods affect the demand for a commodity. **ISC 2018**

Ans **Price of the related goods** Related goods are of two types

(i) Substitute goods (like tea and coffee)

(ii) Complementary goods (like car and petrol)

In case of substitute goods, with the rise in the price of substitute goods, demand for the commodity concerned increases and *vice-versa*. On the other hand, if the goods are complementary, with the rise in the price of complementary goods, demand for the commodity concerned falls and *vice-versa*.

3. Complete the demand schedule for commodity X.

Price (₹/unit)	Quantity demanded by individual A (dozens)	Quantity demanded by individual B (dozens)	Market demand (C)(dozens)
15	50	85	?
20	45	?	105
25	?	45	85
30	35	35	?

Draw the market demand curve from the above schedule. **ISC 2011**

Ans

Price (₹/unit)	Quantity demanded by individual A (dozens)	Quantity demanded by individual B (dozens)	Market demand (C) (dozens)
15	50	85	**135**
20	45	**60**	105
25	**40**	45	85
30	35	35	**70**

As, $C = A + B = 50 + 85 = 135,$

$B = C - A = 105 - 45 = 60$

$A = C - B = 85 - 45 = 40$

$C = A + B = 35 + 35 = 70$

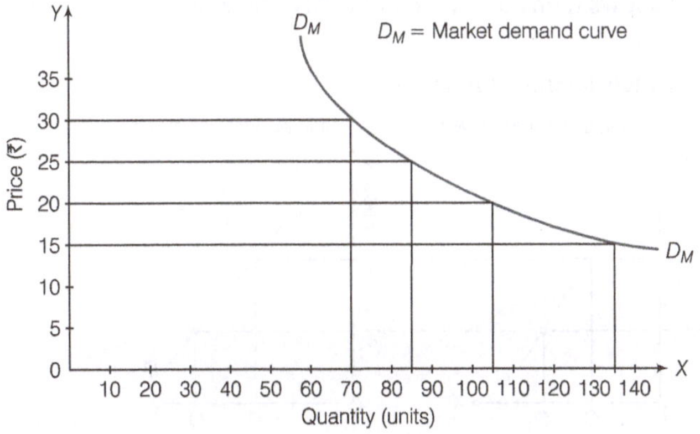

6 Marks Question

1. Discuss four factors other than price, that affect demand of a commodity. **ISC 2012**

Or

Explain any four factors affecting demand for a commodity. **ISC 2007**

Ans Various factors affecting demand are

(i) **Income of the consumer** Income level of the consumer has a positive or direct effect on the demand for a good (if the good is a normal good) i.e. with the rise in income of the consumer, demand for normal goods also increases and *vice-versa*.

In case of inferior goods, there is an inverse relationship between income of the consumer and demand of the commodity.

(ii) **Price of the related good** Related goods are of two types

(a) Substitute goods (like tea and coffee)

(b) Complementary goods (like car and petrol)

In case of substitute goods, with the rise in the price of substitute goods, demand for the commodity concerned increases and *vice-versa*. On the other hand, if the goods are complementary, with the rise in the price of complementary goods, demand for the commodity concerned falls and *vice-versa*.

(iii) **Consumers' tastes and preferences** Tastes and preferences depend on social customs, fashion, habits of people climate, etc which keep on changing leading to change in customers' taste and preferences. As a result, the demand for different goods changes. e.g. consumers may switch over from cheaper old fashioned goods to costlier new goods.

(iv) **Consumers' expectation** Expectation plays a major role in shaping the demand for a particular commodity.

If a consumer expects that the supply of a particular commodity may fall in future hence, he will increase his demand now and *vice-versa*.

Factors Affecting Demand
- Income of the consumer
- Price of the related good
- Consumers' tastes and preferences
- Consumers' expectation

TOPIC 4

Law of Demand, Derivation of Demand Curve and Exception to the Law of Demand

Law of Demand

According to the law of demand, keeping other factors constant, there exists an inverse relationship between price of the commodity and its quantity demanded.

According to **Professor Alfred Marshall**, "The quantity demanded increases with a fall in price and diminishes with a rise in price".

Law of demand is based on certain assumptions, which are as follows

(i) Price of related goods are constant.
(ii) Income of the consumers do not change.
(iii) Taste and preferences do not vary.
(iv) Expectations remain constant.
(v) Commodity should be a normal goods.

We can explain it with the help of following schedule and curve

Demand Schedule

Price (₹)	Quantity demanded (units)
1	8
2	6
3	4
4	2

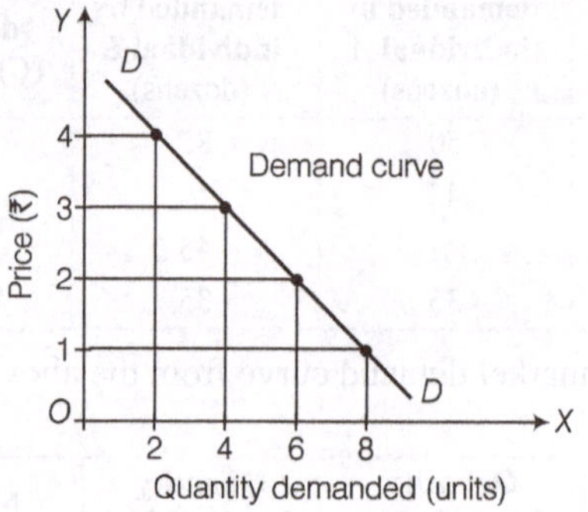

Derivation of Demand Curve

Demand curve is a graphical presentation of the law of demand or in other words, demand curve is derived from law of demand. It is a downward sloping curve. It is the graphical representation of individual demand schedule.

Individual Demand Schedule

Price	Quantity demanded	Inverse relationship between price and quantity
1	20	P↑Q↓
2	15	or
3	10	P↓Q↑
4	5	

Derivation of Market Demand Curve

It is the horizontal summation of the individual demand curves. It shows demand for a commodity made by all the persons in the market at different possible prices at a point of time.

Market demand curves derived from individual demand curves by their lateral summation.

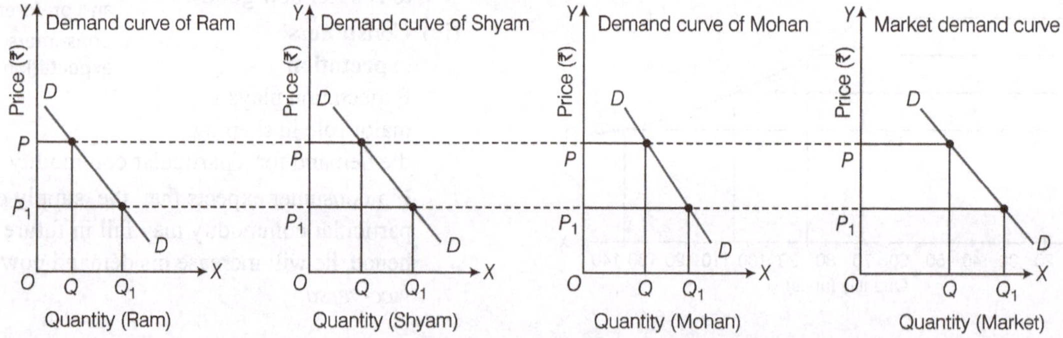

Demand and Income of the Consumer

Normal Goods and Inferior Goods

(i) **Normal goods** These are those goods which have a negative price effect (i.e. demand falls as price rises) and positive income effect (i.e. demand rises with increase in income).

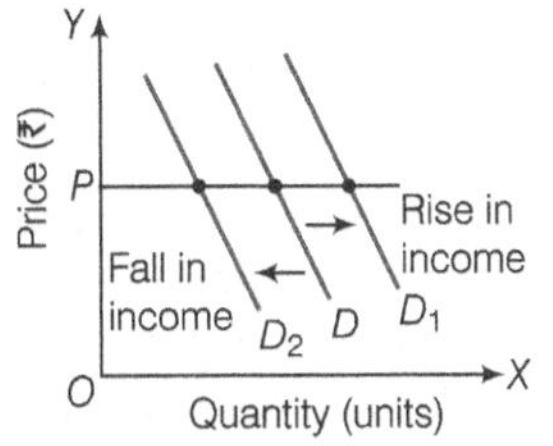

Normal Goods

(ii) **Inferior goods** These are those goods which have a negative income effect i.e. demand for inferior goods falls as consumer's income rises and *vice-versa*.

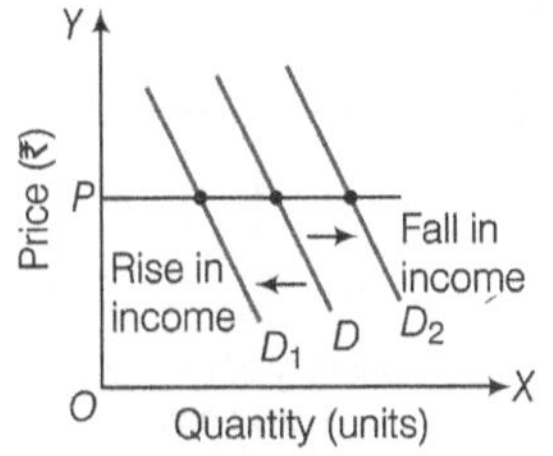

Inferior Goods

Reasons for Downward Slope of Demand Curve

The causes for downward slope of demand curve are as follows

(i) **Law of diminishing marginal utility** According to this law, as the consumption of a commodity increases, the utility from each successive unit goes on diminishing. Accordingly, for every additional unit to be purchased, the consumer is willing to pay less price.

(ii) **Income effect** Change in own price of a commodity causes a change in real income (purchasing power) of the consumer. With a fall in price, real income increases. Accordingly, demand for the commodity expands and *vice-versa*.

(iii) **Substitution effect** It refers to substitution of one commodity for the other when it becomes relatively cheaper due to change in relative prices. Hence, consumer switch to the cheaper good when there is change in price. e.g. CNG and petrol.

(iv) **Size of consumer group** When price of a commodity falls, it attracts new buyers who can afford to buy it, hence quantity demanded rises.

(v) **Different uses** Many goods have alternative uses. e.g. milk is used for making curd, cheese and butter. If price of milk reduces, it will be put into different uses. Accordingly, demand for milk expands, when its price falls.

Exceptions to the Law of Demand

It means those goods which have a direct relation with price, i.e. fall in price does not lead to increase in demand and *vice-versa*.

The exceptions to the law of demand are

(i) **Giffen goods** These are those goods which have a direct relation with price i.e. with the rise in price demand rises and *vice-versa*.

(ii) **Conspicuous consumption** The law of demand will not apply in case of costly items such as diamonds. These commodities will be demanded, even if the prices have gone up very high.

(iii) **Conspicuous necessities** Certain things become the necessity of modern life, so we have to purchase those inspite of their high price.
The demand of television sets and automobiles has not gone down, inspite of the increase in their price.

(iv) **Ignorance** If the consumer is not aware of the competitive price of the commodity, he may purchase more of the commodity even at higher price. Such ignorance of the buyers makes the law of demand ineffective.

(v) **Expectation regarding change in price** When buyers expect a further rise in prices in future, they purchase increased quantity of that good even at high prices and *vice-versa*.

(vi) **Emergencies** During emergencies like war, famines, etc, people may predict shortage of goods in future. In that case, they may buy large quantities even at high prices.

PYQs Previous Years' Questions

1 Mark Questions

1. Which of the following is not an exception to the law of demand? **ISC Sem I 2021**

(a) Articles of snob value
(b) Veblen effect
(c) Substitution effect
(d) Giffen good

Ans (c) Substitution effect

2. The reason for downward sloping demand curve is **ISC Sem I Specimen 2021**

(a) inverse relation between price and demand
(b) inverse relation between income and demand
(c) direct relation between price and demand
(d) Both (a) and (b)

Ans (a) inverse relation between price and demand

3. Price effect is **ISC Sem I Specimen 2021**

(a) Income effect – Substitution effect
(b) Substitution effect – Income effect
(c) Income effect + Substitution effect
(d) Income effect + Substitution effect – Negative effect

Ans (c) Income effect + Substitution effect

4. Giffen goods are **ISC Sem I Specimen 2021**

(a) normal goods, whose demand falls with a rise in their price
(b) inferior goods, whose demand falls with a rise in their real income
(c) Inferior goods, whose demand falls with a fall in their price
(d) Superior goods, whose demand falls with a rise in their real income

Ans (c) inferior goods, whose demand falls with a fall in their price

2 Marks Questions

1. Explain the meaning of income effect. **ISC 2020**

Or Define income effect. **ISC 2008**

Ans It occurs when the price change affects the consumer purchasing power and thus, lead to a change in quantity demanded. When the price of a commodity falls, the real income of the consumer increases.

A part of this increased real income may be used to buy more of the commodity. Thus, a fall in the price of a commodity, increases the demand for it.

Concept Enhancer Income effect is negative in case of inferior good and positive in case of normal good.

2. Explain the demand curve for a necessity commodity. **ISC 2014, 2004**

Ans The demand for necessities of life are not affected by change in their price. They are maintained at an constant level, because they are necessary to survive. Therefore, their demand curve is a horizontal straight line parallel to the *x*-axis. Necessities of life are an exception to the law of demand.

D is the demand curve for necessities of life.

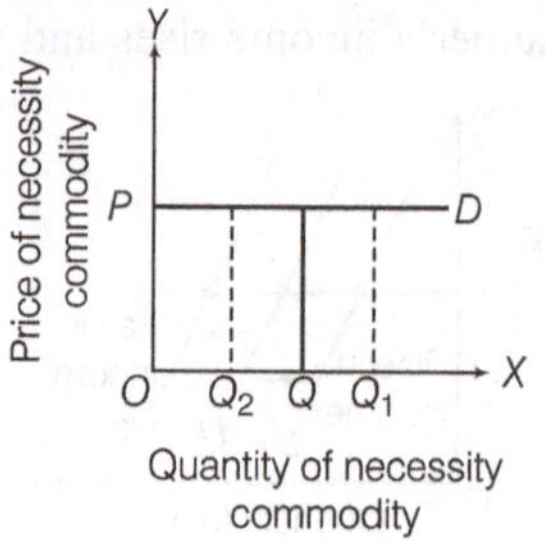

3. Explain with an example, what kind of a commodity will have an inverse relationship between income and demand? **ISC 2012**

Or What are inferior goods. **ISC 2007**

Ans Goods having inverse relationship between income and demand are known as inferior goods.

e.g. At lower levels of income, consumers generally consume bajra, toned milk, etc, but with the rise in income of the consumers, demand for such goods falls.

Common Mistake In most cases, students draws upward sloping demand curve (positive relation) for inferior good. Demand curve for inferior good is also downward sloping (inverse relation).

4. How does an increase in income affect the quantity demanded of an inferior commodity? **ISC 2009**

Ans Inferior goods has a negative income effect, hence when there is increase in income, demand for inferior goods will fall and *vice-versa*.

5. Give two exceptions of law of demand. *ISC 2007*

Ans Two exceptions of law of demand are as follows

(i) **Giffen goods** These are those goods which have a positive price effect, i.e. with the rise in price, demand for giffen goods rises and *vice-versa*.

(ii) **Conspicuous consumption** The law of demand will not apply in case of costly items such as diamonds. These commodities will be demanded, even if the prices have gone up very high.

4 Marks Questions

1. Discuss any two exceptions to the law of demand. *ISC 2019*

Or Explain how the following phenomena are exception to the law of demand.

(i) Expectation regarding future prices

(ii) Conspicuous consumption by a consumer. *ISC 2012*

Ans (i) **Expectation regarding future prices** In the presence of expectations, law of demand does not hold true. If the price of a commodity is increasing, then consumer may expect price to increase further in near future, hence he would demand more at present to avoid future hike in prices, as a result of which, demand will rise despite of rise in prices. In the same way, if consumers expect prices to fall in future, then they will postpone their demand for future despite of current fall in prices.

(ii) **Conspicuous consumption by a consumer** The law of demand does not apply to status symbol commodities which are termed as veblen goods. These goods are demanded more at higher prices by (rich) consumers to increase their social prestige or as a source of display of wealth or richness. e.g. diamond, expensive watch, expensive furniture, etc.

2. Discuss the relationship between income of the consumer and demand for a commodity with respect to normal goods, inferior goods and necessities. *ISC 2015*

Ans Relationship between income of the consumer and demand for a commodity

(i) **Normal goods** These goods have a positive income effect, i.e. with rise in income, their demand also rises and *vice-versa*.

(ii) **Inferior goods** These goods have a negative income effect, i.e. with rise in income, their demand falls and *vice-versa*.

(iii) **Necessities** The demand for necessities is not dependent on the income of the consumer. It is constant at all levels.

6 Marks Questions

1. Explain any four reasons for the demand curve to be downward sloping. *ISC 2017*

Or Explain how the income effect and substitution effect are the reasons for the downward slope of the demand curve. *ISC 2013*

Or Discuss two reasons for the downward slope of demand curve. *ISC 2011*

Ans Four reasons for a downward sloping demand curve are explained below

(i) **Law of diminishing marginal utility** According to this law, as the consumption of a commodity increases, the utility from each successive unit goes on diminishing. Accordingly, for every additional unit to be purchased, the consumer is willing to pay less price.

(ii) **Income effect** Change in own price of a commodity causes a change in real income (purchasing power) of the consumer. With a fall in price, real income increases. Accordingly, demand for the commodity expands and *vice-versa*.

Reasons for Downward Sloping DD Curve
- Law of diminishing marginal utility
- Income effect
- Substitution effect
- Size of consumer group

(iii) **Substitution effect** It refers to substitution of one commodity for the other when it becomes relatively cheaper due to change in relative prices. Hence, consumers switch to the cheaper good when there is change in price. e.g. CNG and petrol.

(iv) **Size of consumer group** When price of a commodity falls, it attracts new buyers who can afford to buy it, hence quantity demanded rises.

2. Discuss four causes for the inverse relationship between price and quantity demanded for a commodity. How are giffen goods an exception? *ISC 2011, 2009*

Ans Reasons for downward sloping demand curve

(i) **Law of diminishing marginal utility** According to the law, as the consumer consumes more and more units of a good, marginal utility derived from consumption of each additional unit will diminish.

A consumer pays for a commodity because it possesses utility and he would like to pay lesser and lesser price for each additional unit, as he is getting lesser and lesser utility. Hence, a consumer will buy greater quantity only at a lower price.

(ii) **Income effect** It refers to change in quantity demanded of a commodity when real income of the consumer changes owing to change in own price of the commodity.

Suppose at the price of ₹ 3 per kg, the demand for sugar was 50 kg, here consumers are spending ₹ 150 on sugar. If price falls to ₹ 2.5 per kg, the consumer will purchase 60 kg with the same amount of income (money). Thus, the demand for sugar rises with the fall in prices and falls with the rise in prices.

(iii) **Substitution effect** It refers to change in quantity demanded of commodity *X* when relative price of the commodity (*Y*) changes owing to change in P_X or P_Y. Hence, consumer will start to substitute the commodity which is relatively less expensive.

Suppose, the price of rice and wheat were ₹ 4 and ₹ 3 per kg, respectively. If the price of rice falls to ₹ 2.50 per kg, it means rice has became cheaper in comparison to wheat, as a result, consumers would start to substitute rice for wheat. Reverse will happen when the price of rice rises.

(iv) **Additional consumer** When price of a commodity falls, some additional consumers come to the market, as they can now afford the given commodity which leads to increase in demand in the market, so reduced price attracts additional consumers and *vice-versa*.

Giffen goods an exception Giffen goods are those goods which have a positive price effect i.e. with the rise in price, demand for giffen goods rises and *vice-versa*. In other words, giffen goods are those inferior goods on which the consumer spends a large part of his income and whose demand falls with fall in their prices. These commodities have a peculiarity, that with a fall in the price, the consumers tend to migrate from giffen goods to superior goods. e.g. it was observed in a country that the workers usually consume bread and meat.

When the price of bread had gone up, they started to consume more of bread as bread was the part of their main diet. They cannot afford to purchase superior food because of their limited income. Thus, there was increase in demand for bread at the cost of meat.

3. State the law of demand with two assumptions. Briefly discuss two exceptions of the law of demand. *ISC 2010*

Ans **Law of demand** According to the law of demand, keeping all other factors constant, there is an inverse relationship between price of a commodity and its quantity demanded.

Two assumptions of law of demand are

(i) No change in the price of related goods.

(ii) No change in the income of the consumer.

Exceptions of law of demand Exceptions of law of demand are as follows

(i) **Giffen goods** These are those goods which have a positive price effect, i.e. with the rise in price, demand for giffen goods rises and *vice-versa*.

(ii) **Conspicuous consumption** The law of demand will not apply in case of costly items such as diamonds. These commodities will be demanded, even if the prices have gone up very high.

4. Explain the law of demand with the help of a diagram and schedule. Give two reasons, why it slopes downwards to the right? *ISC 2006*

Ans Law of demand states that keeping all other factors constant, there is an inverse relationship between price and quantity demand of a commodity.

Assumptions of law of demand are

(i) Income of the consumer remains constant.

(ii) Price of the related goods do not change.

(iii) Taste and preference do not change.

(iv) Expectation remains stable.

We can explain this with the help of schedule and diagram as given below

Schedule and Diagram showing Law of Demand

Price of sugar (per kg)	Quantity demanded
1	50
2	40
3	30
4	20
5	10

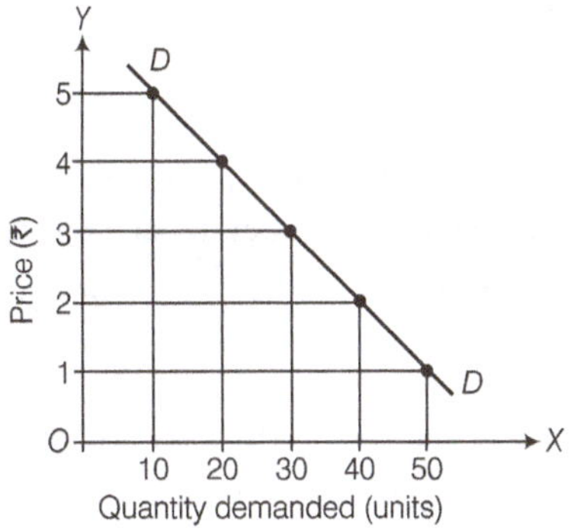

Two reasons for downward slope of demand curve are

(i) **Law of diminishing marginal utility** According to this law, as the consumption of a commodity increases, the utility from each successive unit goes on diminishing. Accordingly, for every additional unit to be purchased, the consumer is willing to pay less price.

(ii) **Income effect** Change in own price of a commodity causes a change in real income (purchasing power) of the consumer. With a fall in price, real income increases. Accordingly, demand for the commodity expands and *vice-versa*.

TOPIC 5

Movement Along the Demand Curve and Shift in the Demand Curve

Movement Along the Demand Curve

It means, when quantity demanded changes due to change in own price of the commodity, keeping other factors constant. It is also known as change in quantity demanded.

There are two types of movement along demand curve

(i) Expansion of quantity demanded (rightward/ downward movement).

(ii) Contraction of quantity demanded (leftward/ upward movement).

Reasons for Movement Along the Demand Curve

Movement occurs due to change in price of the commodity, keeping all other factors constant.

(i) Increase in price leads to contraction in quantity demanded.

(ii) Decrease in price leads to expansion in quantity demanded.

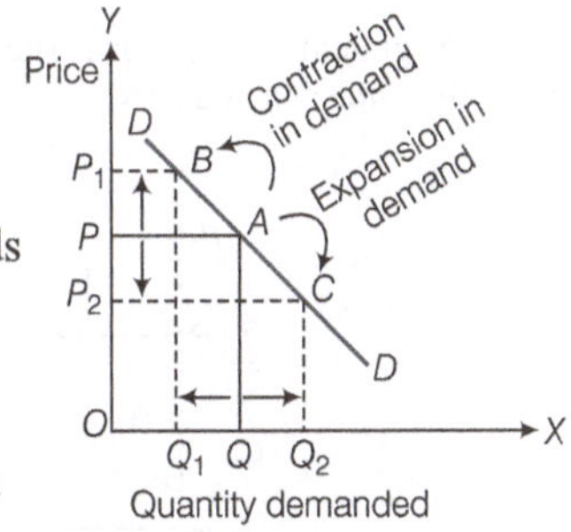

Movement along the Demand Curve

Shift in Demand Curve

It means, when demand for a commodity changes due to change in other factors keeping own price of the commodity constant. It is also known as change in demand.

A shift of the demand curve can be due to

1. Increase in Demand

When demand for a commodity increases inspite of no change in the price of the commodity, it is called increase in demand. The reasons may be as follows

(i) Increase in income of the consumer.

(ii) Decrease in price of complementary goods.

(iii) Increase in price of substitute goods.

(iv) Change in taste and preference in favour of the commodity.

2. Decrease in Demand

When demand for a commodity falls inspite of no change in the price of the commodity, it is called decrease in demand.

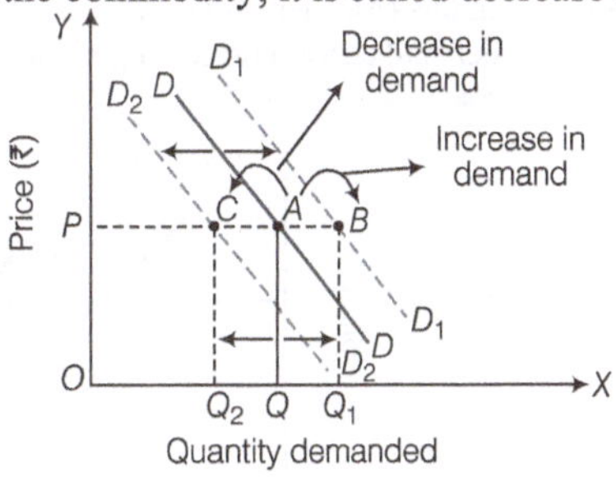

Shift in Demand

The reasons may be as follows

(i) Decrease in income of the consumer.

(ii) Increase in price of the complementary goods.

(iii) Decrease in the price of the substitute goods.

(iv) Change in taste and preferences against the commodity

PYQs Previous Years' Questions

1 Marks Questions

1.

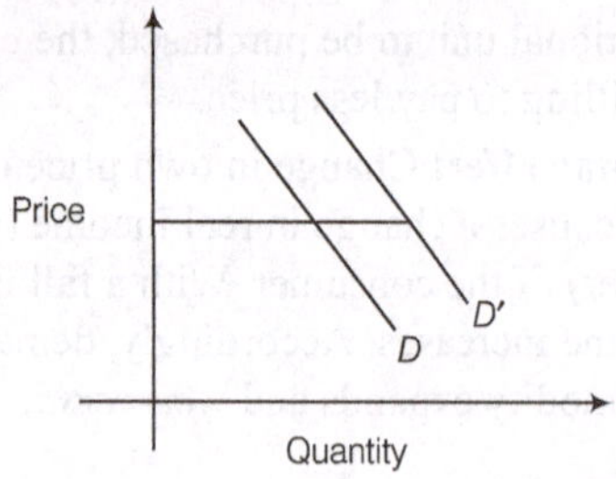

In the figure given above, D is demand curve for normal good. It shifts to D′ which is a case of *ISC Specimen 2023*

(a) extension of demand due to increase in income
(b) increase in demand due to rise in expected future price
(c) contraction in demand due to increase in price of substitutes
(d) increase in demand due to rise in price of a complementary good

Ans (b) increase in demand due to rise in expected future price

2. What relation do you notice between price and demand in the table given below? *ISC Sem I Specimen 2021*

Price	Demand (Units)
10	20
8	25

(a) Increase in demand (b) Decrease in demand
(c) Extension in demand (d) Contraction in demand

Ans (c) Extension in demand

3. Which of the given options is a reason of change in demand? *ISC Sem I Speciemen 2021*

(a) Change in consumer's income
(b) Change in prices of related goods
(c) Population increase (d) All of the above

Ans (d) All of the above

4. The reason for decrease in demand is *ISC Sem I Specimen 2021*

(a) rise in price
(b) increase in the price of substitute goods
(c) increase in the price of complementary goods
(d) decrease in income in case of inferior goods

Ans (c) increase in the price of complementary goods

2 Marks Questions

1. Differentiate between increase in demand and contraction in demand with the help of diagrams. *ISC Specimen 2023*

Ans

Meaning	Increase in demand	Contraction of demand
Meaning	It takes place when demand for a good increases due to factor other than price.	It takes place when quantity of a good falls due to rise in price.
Diagrammatic presentation	In this case, demand curve shifts to the right with new demand curve representing higher quantity at the same price. 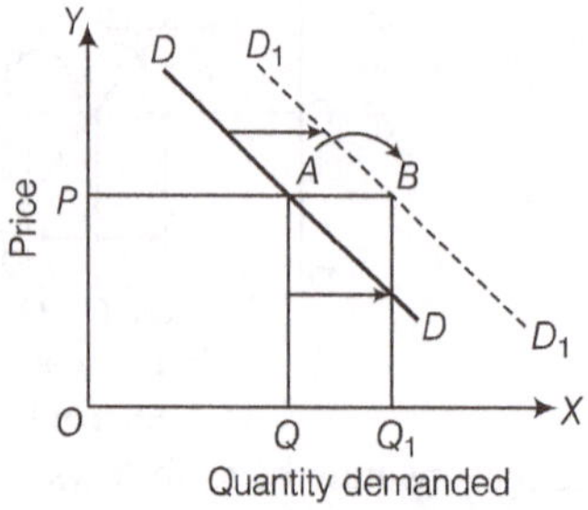	Diagrammatically, this is shown as an upward movement on the same demand curve. 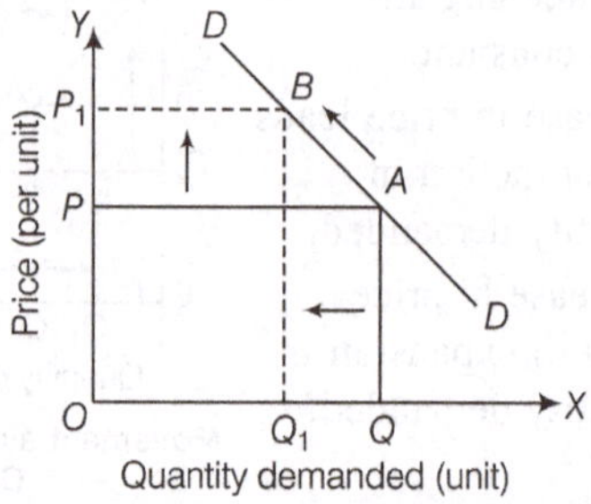

2. Give a reason for each of the following **ISC 2017**

(i) The demand for a good increases when the income of the consumer increases.

(ii) X and Y are substitute goods. A rise in the price of X results in a rightward shift of the demand curve of Y.

Ans (i) Income of a consumer represents his purchasing power. With increase in income, the consumer's purchasing power also increases and this leads to increase in demand for a normal good.

(ii) Substitute goods are those which can be used one in place of other. So, if price of good 'X' rises, then consumers will substitute good 'X' with good 'Y' and because of this demand of good 'Y' will increase at the same price. This will cause a rightward shift in the demand curve of good 'Y'.

3/4 Marks Questions

1. How does an increase in income affect the demand for the following **ISC 2019**

(i) A normal good (ii) An inferior good

Ans (i) Increase in income causes the demand for a normal good to increase. More is demanded at the same price causing rightward shift in demand curve.

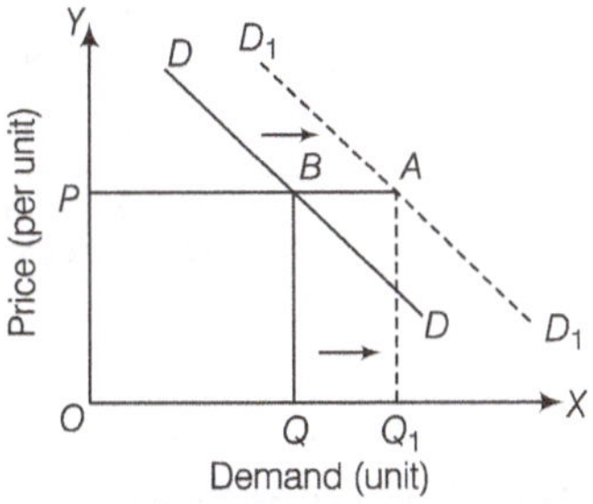

For Normal Good

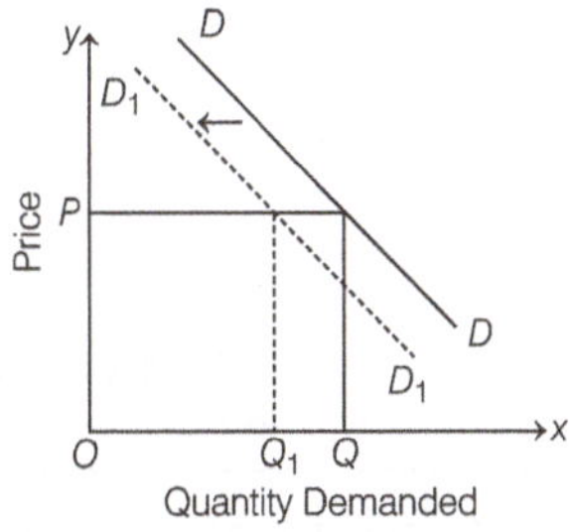

For Inferior Good

(ii) Increase in income causes the demand for an inferior good to decrease. Less is demanded at the same price causing leftward shift in demand curve.

2. Differentiate between contraction of demand and decrease in demand, using diagrams. **ISC 2018**

Ans Difference between decrease in demand and contraction of demand are

Basis	Decrease in demand	Contraction of demand
Reason	This is caused by change in determinants, other than own price of the commodity.	This is caused only by change in own price of the commodity.
Impact	This happens when at the same price, less is being demanded.	This happens when at a higher price, less is being demanded.
Diagrammatic presentation	Diagrammatically, this is shown as a backward shift in demand curve.	Diagrammatically, this is shown as an upward movement on the same demand curve.

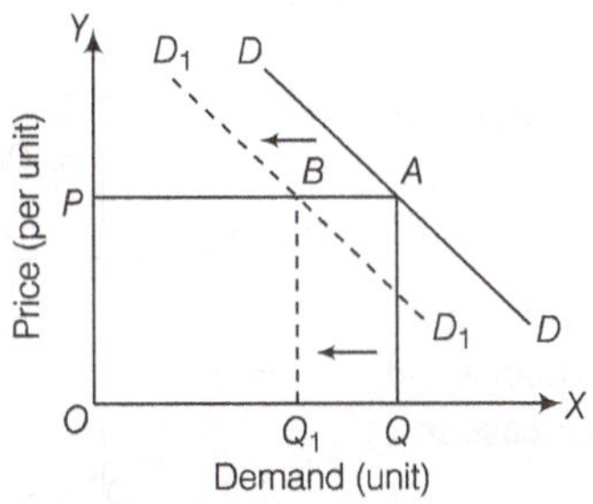

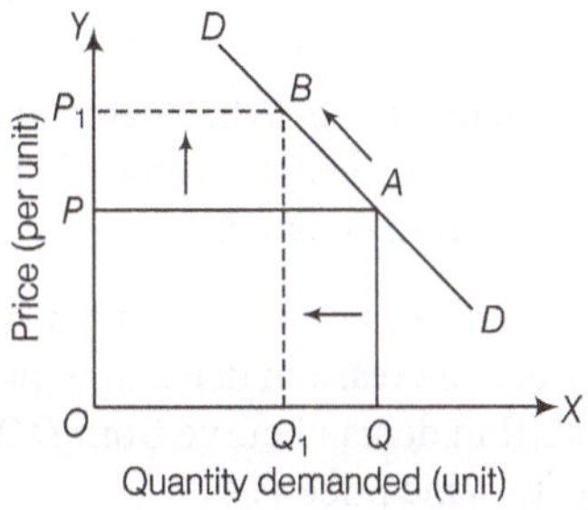

3. Differentiate between extension of demand and increase in demand, using diagrams. ***ISC 2015***

Ans Difference between extension of demand and increase in demand

Basis	Extension of demand	Increase in demand
Meaning	When quantity demanded for a commodity rises due to fall in the price of the commodity, keeping other factors constant, it is known as 'extension in demand'.	When demand for a commodity increases due to favourable changes in other factors, keeping own price of the commodity constant, it is known as 'increase in demand'.
Causes	The only cause here is fall in the price of the commodity.	The reasons may be increase in consumers' income, increase in price of substitute goods or decrease in price of complementary goods.
Effect on demand curve	In this case, demand curve does not shift, rather there will be a downward movement along the demand curve, indicating decrease in price and increase in quantity demanded. 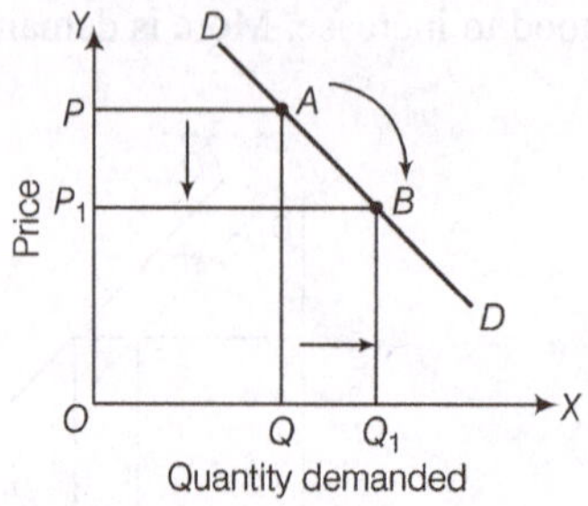	In this case, demand curve shifts to the right with new demand curve representing higher quantity at the same price. 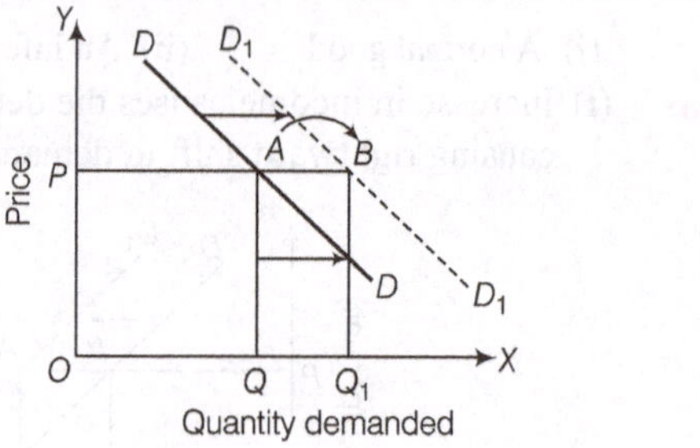

Common Mistake Students get confused between the causes of increase in demand and extention of demand. Extension of demand is caused by fall in the price of the commodity.

4. With the help of diagrams, show the shift and movement on the demand curve. ***ISC 2010***

Ans **Movement along the demand curve** It means when quantity demanded of a commodity changes due to change in own price of the commodity, keeping other factors (like income, taste and price of related goods) constant.

There are two types of movement which are known as

(i) Expansion in quantity demanded

(ii) Contraction in quantity demanded

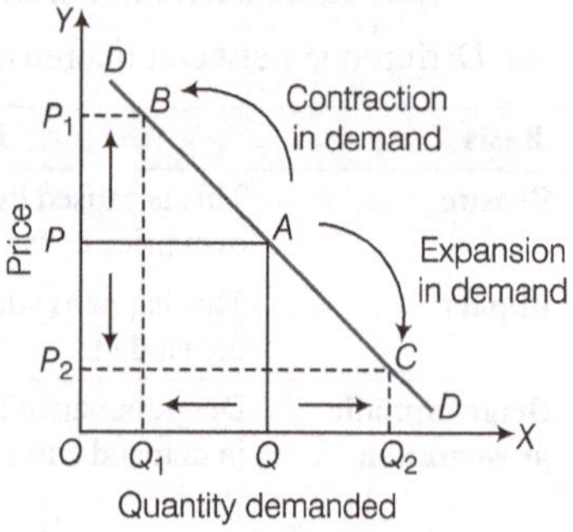

In figure, say market price is *P*. If price falls to P_2 quantity demanded rises to Q_2, this movement from *A* to *C* is known as expansion in quantity demanded. Similarly, movement from *A* to *B* is known as contraction in quantity demanded (i.e. due to rise in price from *P* to P_1).

Shift in demand curve When demand for a commodity either increases or decreases due to change in other factors, keeping own price constant, it is known as shift in demand.

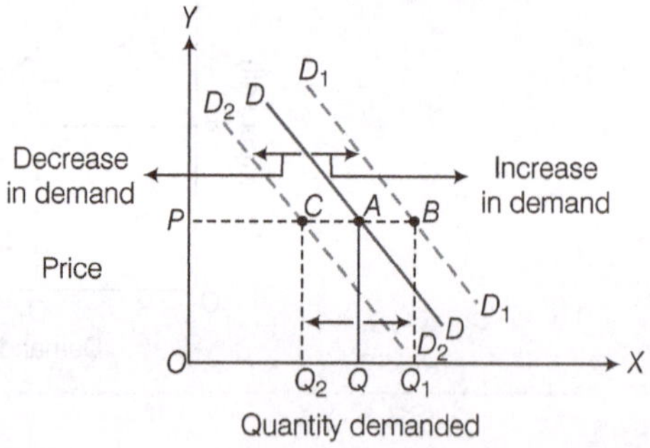

In the given figure, shift in demand curve from *DD* to D_1D_1 (rightward shift) indicates increase in demand with same price *P*. On the other hand, leftward shift in demand curve from *DD* to D_2D_2 indicates decrease in demand with same price *P*.

6 Marks Question

1. Discuss with the help of diagram, the concepts of increase of demand and extension of demand. *ISC 2006*

Ans **Increase in demand** When demand for a commodity increases due to favourable changes in other factors, keeping own price of the commodity constant, it is known as increase in demand. The reasons may be increase in consumer's incomes, increase in price of substitute goods or decrease in price of complementary goods. In this case, demand curve shifts to the right with new demand curve representing higher quantity at same price.

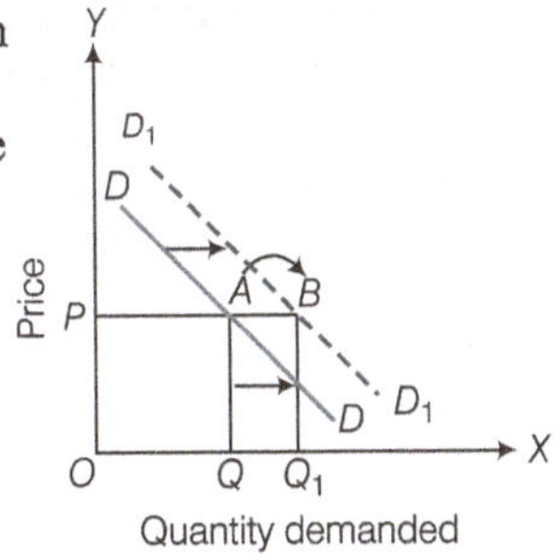

Extension in demand When quantity demanded for a commodity rises due to fall in the price of the commodity, keeping other factors constant, it is known as extension in demand.

In this case, demand curve does not shift, rather there will be a downward movement along the demand curve, indicating decrease in price and increase in quantity demanded.

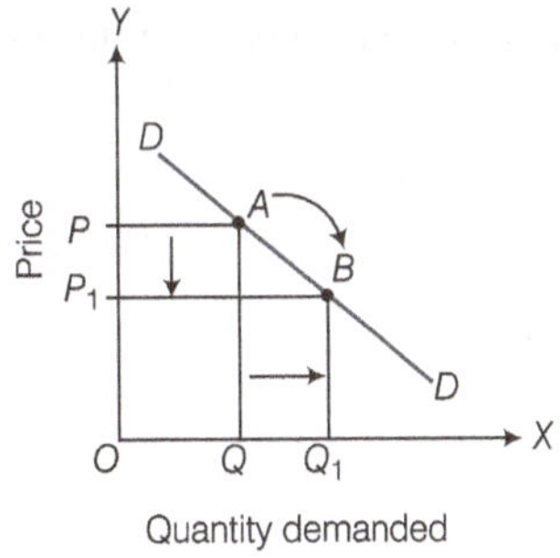

Value Points

For getting maximum marks, following value points can be included in the answer

- Specific causes of increase and extension of demand
- The effect taking place, i.e. shift or movement in demand curve.

Case Based Questions

Case 1

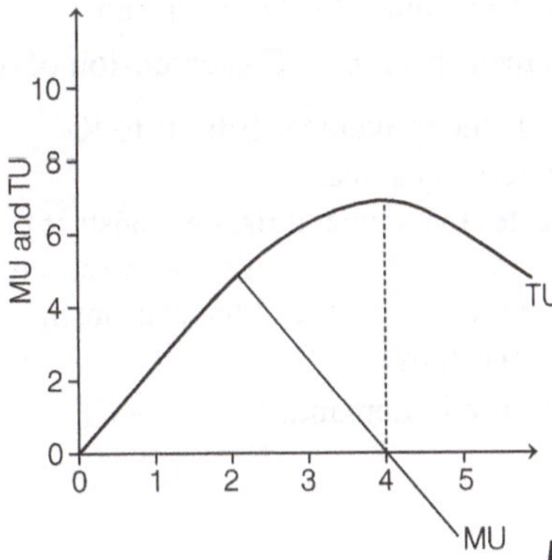

ISC Sem I 2021

(i) When TU is maximum, then MU is

(a) zero (b) maximum
(c) positive (d) negative

Ans (a) zero

(ii) When TU decreases MU is ....

(a) increasing (b) decreasing
(c) negative (d) zero

Ans (c) negative

(iii) When TU is increasing at a diminishing rate then MU ....

(a) decreases but is positive
(b) increases
(c) negative (d) becomes S shaped

Ans (a) decreases but is positive

Case 2

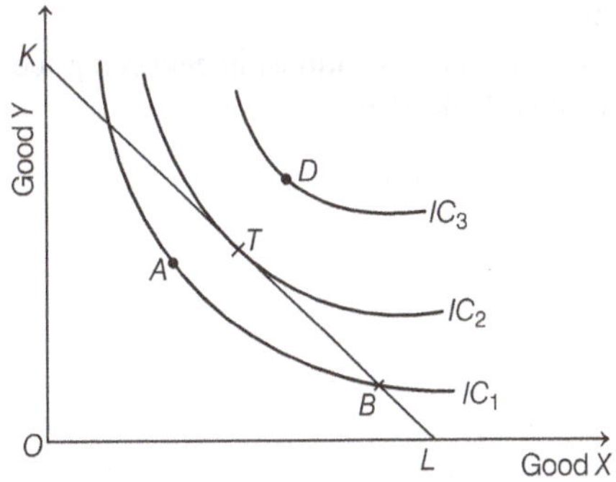

ISC Sem I 2021

(i) In the diagram above, the point of consumer equilibrium is

(a) D (b) T (c) A (d) B

Ans (b) T

(ii) The point which is unattainable is

(a) A (b) T

(c) B (d) D

Ans (d) D

(iii) The condition for consumer's equilibrium is

(a) $MU_x = P_x$ (b) $\frac{MU_x}{P} = \frac{MU_y}{P}$

(c) $MC = MR$ (d) $MRS_{xy} = \frac{P_x}{P_y}$

Ans (d) $MRS_{xy} = \frac{P_x}{P_y}$

Case 3

Due to the pandemic the prices of vegetables and fruits have increased but the demand for quantity has not fallen.

ISC Sem I Specimen 2021

(i) What is the reason for the demand remaining the same?

(a) Demand for food is inelastic since food is a necessity.

(b) Demand for food is elastic

(c) Demand is for the inferior goods.

(d) Demand is for the luxury goods.

Ans (a) Demand for food is inelastic since food is a necessity.

(ii) What are the exceptions to the law of demand?

(a) Emergences (b) Quality-price relationship

(c) Veblen goods (d) All of these

Ans (d) All of these

(iii) Which of the following statements pertains to law of demand?

(a) There is a direct relationship between price and quantity demanded.

(b) There is an inverse relationship between price and quantity demanded.

(c) There is a direct relationship between price and quantity demanded, other things remain the same.

(d) There is an inverse relationship between price and quantity demanded, other things remain the same.

Ans (b) There is an inverse relationship between price and quantity demanded.

Case 4

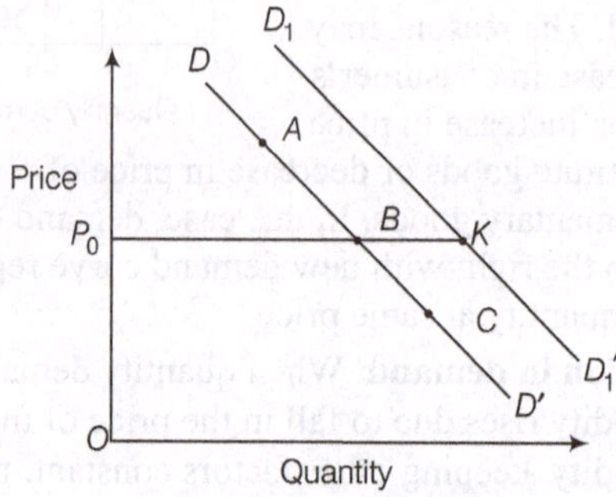

Figure I

ISC Sem I Specimen 2021

(i) In figure 1, the

(a) movement from A to B is contraction of demand.

(b) movement from B to C is extension of demand.

(c) movement from A to C is contraction of demand.

(d) movement from C to B is extension of demand.

Ans (b) movement from B to C is extension of demand.

(ii) In figure 1, the movement from B to K

(a) is increase in demand.

(b) indicates that demand rises at constant price.

(c) takes place due to rise in demand caused by rise in money income of the consumer.

(d) All of the above.

Ans (a) is increase in demand.

CHAPTER TEST

01 Mark Questions

1. Total utility is maximum when
(a) marginal utility is zero
(b) marginal utility is at its highest point
(c) marginal utility is equal to average utility
(d) average utility is maximum

2. Which one of the following is not an assumption of the theory of demand based on analysis of indifference curve?
(a) Given scale of preferences as between different combinations of two goods
(b) Diminishing marginal rate of substitution
(c) Constant marginal utility of money
(d) Consumers would always prefer more of a particular piece of goods to less of it, other things remaining the same

3. The consumer is in equilibrium at a point where the budget line
(a) is above an indifference curve
(b) is below an indifference curve
(c) is tangent to an indifference curve
(d) cuts an indifference curve

4. An indifference curve slopes down towards right since more of one commodity and less of another result in
(a) same satisfaction
(b) greater satisfaction
(c) maximum satisfaction
(d) decreasing expenditure

5. Same good may give different level of satisfaction to different consumers. State true or false.

6. Cardinal approach of utility assumes utility to be qualitative in nature. State true or false.

7. When only one unit of a commodity is consumed, marginal utility will be equal to ………….

8. The first psychological law of consumption is also known as ………… .

9. What is marginal utility of money?

10. Rationality is an important feature for an economic agent. What do you understand by the rationality of a consumer?

02 Marks Questions

11. What do you mean by utility?

12. State the equilibrium equation in case of single commodity.

13. Define individual demand.

14. Justify the statement 'higher indifference curve represents higher level of satisfaction'.

15. Why is an indifference curve convex to the origin?

04 Marks Questions

16. Differentiate between demand and quantity demanded.

17. Explain the derivation of market demand curve from the individual demand curves.

06 Marks Questions

18. Explain the law of diminishing marginal utility using schedule and diagram.

19. Briefly explain the following
(i) Normal goods (ii) Inferior goods
(iii) Giffen goods

20. Explain the following
(i) Derived demand (ii) Joint demand
(iii) Composite demand (iv) Market demand

Answers

1. (a) marginal utility is zero
2. (c) Constant marginal utility of money
3. (c) is tangent to an indifference curve
4. (a) same satisfaction
5. True
6. False
7. total utility
8. law of diminishing marginal utility

02

Elasticity of Demand

TREND ANALYSIS 5 YEARS

Average No. of Questions Across all Sets

	Types of Questions	2023	2020	2019	2018	2017
01 Meaning and Types of Elasticity of Demand	1 Mark	1	—	—	—	—
	2 Marks	3	—	—	—	—
	3/4 Marks	—	1	1	—	1
	6 Marks	—	—	—	—	—
02 Degree and Factors Affecting Elasticity of Demand	1 Mark	—	—	—	—	—
	2 Marks	—	—	—	—	—
	3/4 Marks	—	—	—	—	—
	6 Marks	1	—	—	1	—

TOPIC 1

Meaning and Types of Elasticity of Demand and Measurement of Elasticity

Elasticity of Demand

It explains the degree of responsiveness of demand when there is a change in either price, income of the consumer or price of related goods.

Types of elasticity of demand are as follows

1. Price elasticity of demand (Due to change in price of the commodity)
2. Income elasticity of demand (Due to change in income of the consumer)
3. Cross price elasticity of demand (Due to change in price of related goods)

These types of elasticity of demand are briefly discussed below

1. Price Elasticity of Demand

It measures the degree of responsiveness of quantity demanded of a commodity, to change in its price.

Price elasticity of demand for a commodity is defined as the percentage change in quantity demand for the commodity divided by the percentage change in its price.

Price elasticity of demand of a commodity can be measured as

$$e_p = (-)\frac{\text{Percentage Change in Quantity Demanded for the Commodity}}{\text{Percentage Change in the Price of the Commodity}}$$

Three methods of measuring price elasticity of demand are as follows

(i) **Percentage or proportionate method** In this method, price elasticity of demand is measured by the ratio of the percentage change in quantity demanded to the percentage change in price.

$$e_p = (-)\frac{\text{Percentage Change in Quantity Demanded}}{\text{Percentage Change in Price}}$$

...(Percentage method)

$$= (-)\frac{\dfrac{\text{Change in Quantity Demanded}}{\text{Initial Quantity}}}{\dfrac{\text{Change in Price}}{\text{Initial Price}}\times 100}\times 100$$

$$= \frac{(-)\dfrac{\Delta Q}{Q}\times 100}{\dfrac{\Delta P}{P}\times 100}$$

$$or \quad = (-)\frac{\Delta Q}{Q}\div\frac{\Delta P}{P} = (-)\frac{\Delta Q}{Q}\times\frac{P}{\Delta P} = \frac{\Delta Q}{\Delta P}\times\frac{P}{Q}$$

Thus, $e_p = (-)\dfrac{\Delta Q}{\Delta P}\times\dfrac{P}{Q}$ ...(Proportionate method)

Where, e_p = Price Elasticity of Demand
Q = Initial Quantity
ΔQ = Change in Quantity
ΔP = Change in Price
P = Initial Price

Note Price elasticity of demand is a negative number because price and quantity demanded are inversely related. For simplicity, we generally ignore the negative sign.

(ii) **Total expenditure or total outlay method** In this method, price elasticity of demand can be measured in terms of change in total expenditure due to change in the price of commodity.
According to total expenditure method,

(a) If price and total expenditure change in the same direction, then elasticity of demand will be less than unity (one) ($e_p < 1$) or inelastic.

(b) If price and total expenditure change in the opposite direction, then price elasticity of demand will be greater than unity ($e_p > 1$) or elastic.

(c) If price changes but total expenditure remains constant, then price elasticity of demand will be equal to unity ($e_p = 1$) or unitary elastic.

Total Expenditure (TE)
= Price (P) × Quantity Demanded (Q)

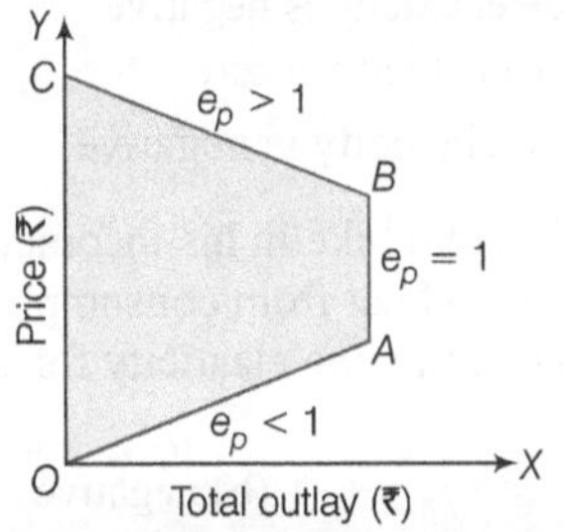

(iii) **Geometric or point method** This method measures the price elasticity of demand at different points on the straight line linear demand curve. It is also called as point method.

$$e_p = \frac{\text{Lower Segment of the Demand Curve}}{\text{Upper Segment of the Demand Curve}}$$

When there are infinitely small changes take place in price and demand, then it is used.
In the diagram, point E divides the demand curve into two equal portions
(a) Lower portion EN (b) Upper portion EM

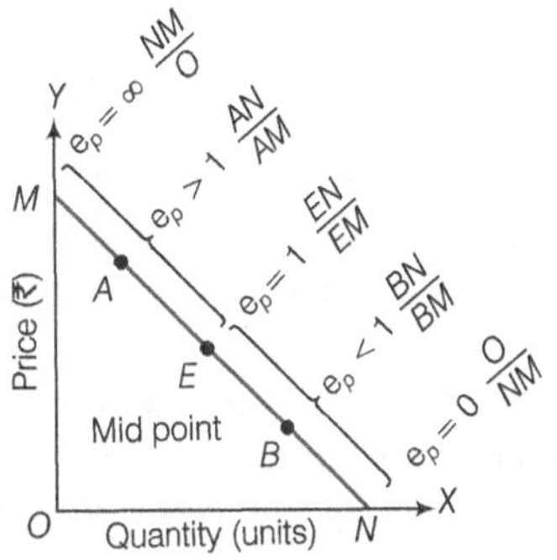

Point B is located in the lower portion and point A in the upper portion.

- e_p at point $M = \dfrac{MN}{O} = \infty$
- e_p at point $A = \dfrac{NA}{AM} = e_p > 1$ (because AN is greater than AM)
- e_p at point $E = \dfrac{NE}{EM} = e_p = 1$ (because E is the mid-point)
- e_p at point $B = \dfrac{NB}{BM} = e_p < 1$ (because BN is smaller than BM)
- e_p at point $N = \dfrac{O}{MN} = 0$

2. Income Elasticity of Demand

It measures the responsiveness of quantity demanded of a commodity, due to change in consumer's income. Thus, income elasticity of demand can be measured as the percentage change in quantity demanded divided by the percentage change in consumer's income.

$$e_y = \frac{\text{Percentage Change in Quantity Demanded}}{\text{Percentage Change in Income}}$$

$$or \quad e_y = \frac{\dfrac{\Delta Q}{Q}\times 100}{\dfrac{\Delta Y}{Y}\times 100} = \frac{\Delta Q}{Q}\div\frac{\Delta Y}{Y} = \frac{\Delta Q}{Q}\times\frac{Y}{\Delta Y}$$

or $e_y = \frac{\Delta Q}{\Delta Y} \times \frac{Y}{Q}$

Where, e_y = Income Elasticity of Demand
ΔY = Change in Income
Y = Initial Income
ΔQ = Change in Quantity
Q = Initial Quantity

Three types of income elasticity of demand are

(i) **Positive income elasticity of demand** Demand of commodity increases with increase in consumer's income and *vice-versa*. e.g. Normal goods.

(ii) **Negative income elasticity of demand** Demand for goods decreases with increase in income. e.g. Inferior goods.

(iii) **Zero income elasticity of demand** There is no effect of increase in consumer's income on the demand of commodity. e.g. Necessaries goods.

3. Cross Price Elasticity of Demand

It measures the responsiveness of demand of one commodity, due to change in price of related commodities. Three types of cross elasticity of demand are

(i) Positive cross elasticity of demand
(ii) Negative cross elasticity of demand
(iii) Zero cross elasticity of demand

Cross elasticity of demand can be measured with the help of following formula by percentage or proportionate method

$$e_{xy} = \frac{\text{Percentage Change in Demand of Good X}}{\text{Percentage Change in Price of Good Y}}$$

or $$e_{xy} = \frac{\frac{\Delta Q_X}{Q_X} \times 100}{\frac{\Delta P_Y}{P_Y} \times 100} = \frac{\Delta Q_X}{Q_X} \div \frac{\Delta P_Y}{P_Y}$$

$$= \frac{\Delta Q_X}{Q_X} \times \frac{P_Y}{\Delta P_Y}$$

or $$e_{xy} = \frac{\Delta Q_X}{\Delta P_Y} \times \frac{P_Y}{Q_X}$$

Where, e_{xy} = Cross Elasticity of Demand of X for Y
Q_X = Initial Quantity Demanded of Commodity X
ΔQ_X = Change in Quantity Demanded of Commodity X
ΔP_Y = Change in Price of Commodity Y
P_Y = Initial Price of Commodity Y

Relationship between Cross Elasticity of Demand and Goods

(i) If the cross elasticity of demand between the goods is positive, then the goods are substitute of each other.

(ii) If the cross elasticity of demand between the goods is negative, then the goods are complementary of each other.

(iii) If the cross elasticity of demand is zero, then the goods are not related with each other.

PYQs Previous Years' Questions

1 Mark Questions

1. If the price of a commodity and total expenditure on that commodity change in the same direction, the price elasticity of demand will be **ISC 2023**

(a) greater than one
(b) less than one
(c) equal to zero
(d) equal to infinity

Ans (b) less than one

Concept Enhancer Using total expenditure method, we cannot predict elasticity equal to zero and elasticity equal to infinity.

2. If two goods are complementary, then their **ISC Sem I 2021**

(a) income elasticity arc negative
(b) cross price elasticity is positive
(c) cross price elasticity is negative
(d) cross price elasticity is zero

Ans (c) cross price elasticity is negative

3. When Zubair had a hike in his income, he switched over to rice and wheat from consumption of maize and jowar. Then income elasticity for the latter goods is **ISC Sem I 2021**

(a) positive (b) negative
(c) zero (d) constant

Ans (a) positive

4. At the midpoint of a downward sloping straight demand curve touching two axes **ISC Sem I 2021**

(a) $e_d = 2$ (b) $e_d = 0.5$

(c) $e_d = 1$ (d) $e_d = 4$

Ans (c) $e_d = 1$

5. What is the nature of relationship between price and demand in case of elasticity of demand? **ISC Sem I Specimen 2021**

(a) Qualitative

(b) Quantiative

(c) Competitive

(d) None of the above

Ans (b) Quantitative

6.

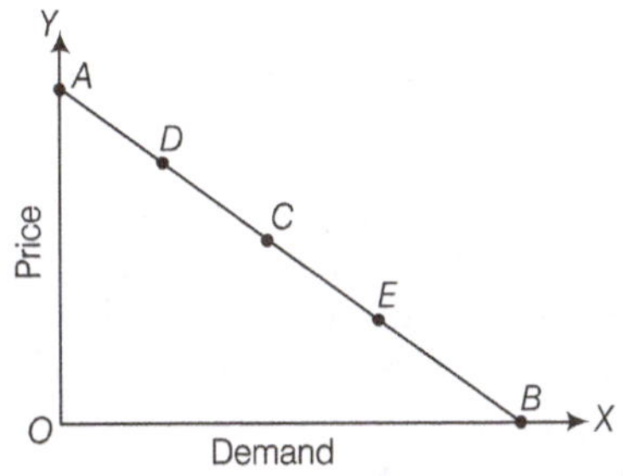

In figure, the demand is **ISC Sem I Specimen 2021**

(a) perfectly elastic at A, unit elastic at B and relatively inelastic at E

(b) relatively elastic at D, perfectly elastic at C and unit elastic at E

(c) unit elastic at C, relatively inelastic at E and perfectly inelastic at B

(d) relatively inelastic at D, unit elastic at C and perfectly elastic at B

Ans (c) unit elastic at C, relatively inelastic at E and perfectly inelastic at B

7. Cross elasticity of demand is .... for substitute goods. An increase in the price of one commodity leads to .... in the demand for another commodity. **ISC Sem I Specimen 2021**

(a) positive, increase

(b) negative, increase

(c) positive, decrease

(d) negative, increase

Ans (a) positive, increase

8. When a fall in the price of the commodity results in increase in total expenditure, the elasticity of demand will be .... **ISC Sem I Specimen 2021**

(a) $e_p = 1$ (b) $e_p = 0$

(c) $e_p < 1$ (d) $e_p > 1$

Ans (d) $e_p > 1$

9. When the price of a good falls by 7%, its quantity demanded rises from 40 units to 50 units. What will be the price elasticity of demand for this good? **ISC Sem I Specimen 2021**

(a) 2.84 (b) 2.85

(c) 2.86 (d) 3.57

Ans (d) $E_d = -\left(\frac{40-50}{40} \times 100\right) / 7 = \frac{25}{7} = 3.57$

10. When the price of a commodity falls by ₹ 2 per unit, its quantity demanded increases by 10 units. Its price elasticity of demand is (–) 1. Initial quantity demanded at previous price, ₹ 10, was **ISC Sem I Specimen 2021**

(a) 49 units (b) 50 units

(c) 51 units (d) 52 units

Ans (b) $E_d = \left(\frac{\Delta Q}{\Delta P}\right) \times \frac{P}{Q}$

$E_d = -1;\ \Delta P = ₹ -2;\ \Delta Q = 10;\ P = ₹\ 10$

$$-1 = \left(\frac{10}{-2}\right)\left(\frac{10}{Q}\right)$$

$\therefore \quad Q = 50$

11. The price elasticity of demand for a commodity is (–) 1.5. When its price falls by ₹ 1, its quantity demanded rises from 30 units to 33 units. What was its previous price? **ISC Sem I Specimen 2021**

(a) ₹ 15.25 (b) ₹ 15.50

(c) ₹ 15.75 (d) None of these

Ans (d) $E_d = \left(\frac{\Delta Q}{\Delta P}\right) \times \frac{P}{Q}$

$E_d = -1.5;\ \Delta P = ₹ -1;\ Q = 30;\ Q_1 = 33;\ \Delta Q = 3$

$$-1.5 = \left(\frac{3}{-1}\right)\left(\frac{P}{30}\right)$$

$\therefore \quad P = ₹\ 15$

12. A consumer buys 200 units of a good at a price of ₹ 5 per unit. When the price changes, he buys only 100 units. If price elasticity of demand is 2, the changed price will be **ISC Sem I Specimen 2021**

(a) ₹ 5.75 (b) ₹ 6.25

(c) ₹ 6.75 (d) ₹ 7.25

Ans (b) $E_d = \left(\frac{\Delta Q}{\Delta P}\right) \times \frac{P}{Q}$

$Q = 200;\ P = ₹\ 5;\ Q_1 = 100;\ E_d = 2$

$$2 = \left(\frac{-100}{\Delta P}\right)\left(\frac{5}{200}\right)$$

$\Delta P = 1.25$

$\therefore \quad P_1 = 5 + 1.25 = 6.25$

13. A consumer buys 80 units of a good at a price of ₹ 8 per unit. Price falls to ₹ 6 per unit. How much quantity will the consumer buy at a new price if $e_p = (-)2$? **ISC Sem I Specimen 2021**

(a) 100 units
(b) 110 units
(c) 120 units
(d) 130 units

Ans (c) $E_d = \left(\frac{\Delta Q}{\Delta P}\right) \times \frac{P}{Q}$

$Q = 80;\ P = ₹\,8;\ P_1 = ₹\,6;\ \Delta P = -2;\ E_d = -2$

$$-2 = \left(\frac{\Delta Q}{-2}\right)\left(\frac{8}{80}\right)$$

$$\Delta Q = 40$$

$$\therefore \quad Q_1 = 80 + 40 = 120 \text{ units}$$

2 Marks Questions

1. The price of a good decreases from ₹ 100 to ₹ 80 per unit. If the price elasticity of demand for the good is 2 and the original quantity demanded is 30 units, calculate the new quantity demanded. **ISC 2023**

Ans According to the question,

$$P = 100 \text{ and } P_1 = 80$$

So, $\Delta P = P_1 - P = 80 - 100 = -20$

$$e_d = 2 \text{ and } Q = 30, Q_1 = ?$$

$$e_d = (-)\frac{\Delta Q}{\Delta P} \times \frac{P}{Q}$$

$$2 = (-)\frac{\Delta Q}{-20} \times \frac{100}{30}$$

$$\therefore \quad \Delta Q = 2 \times 6 = 12$$

$$Q_1 = Q + \Delta Q = 30 + 12 = 42$$

2. The initial demand for a commodity was 100 units. With a rise in price by ₹ 5, the demand for the quantity decreases by 5 units. The elasticity of demand is 1.2. Calculate price before change in demand. **ISC 2023**

Ans According to the question,

$Q = 100, \Delta P = 5, \Delta Q = 5, e_d = 1.2$

$$e_d = (-)\frac{\Delta Q}{\Delta P} \times \frac{P}{Q}$$

$$1.2 = (-)\frac{-5}{5} \times \frac{P}{100}$$

$$P = 1.2 \times 100 = 120$$

3. Define income elasticity of demand. When can it be negative? **ISC 2023**

Or What is meant by income elasticity of demand? **ISC 2016**

Ans Income elasticity of demand measures the responsiveness of quantity demanded of a commodity, due to change in consumer's income. Thus, income elasticity of demand can be measured as the percentage change in quantity demanded divided by the percentage change in consumer's income. Symbolically,

$$e_y = \frac{\text{Percentage Change in Quantity Demanded}}{\text{Percentage Change in Income}}$$

Income elasticity is negative in case of inferior goods.

Concept Enhancer When income elasticity is zero, demand curve will be vertical line.

4. The demand for a commodity at ₹ 4 per unit is 100 units. The price of the commodity rises and as a result, its demand falls to 75 units. Find the new price, if the price elasticity of demand of that commodity is 1. **ISC 2014**

Ans Original Price $(P) = ₹\,4$
Original Quantity Demand $(Q) = 100$ units
New Quantity Demand $(Q_1) = 75$ units
New Price $(P_1) = ?$
Price Elasticity of Demand $(e_P) = 1$

$$e_P = (-)\frac{\Delta Q}{\Delta P} \times \frac{P}{Q};\ e_P = (-)\frac{Q_1 - Q}{P_1 - P} \times \frac{P}{Q}$$

$$1 = (-)\frac{75 - 100}{P_1 - 4} \times \frac{4}{100};\ 1 = (-)\frac{(-)25}{P_1 - 4} \times \frac{4}{100}$$

$$P_1 = 4 + 1 = 5$$

$\therefore$ The new price of the commodity will be ₹ 5.

Common Mistake Generally, students forget to use minus (–) sign while calculation of price elasticity of demand. While calculating price elasticity of demand minus (–) sign should be used in the formula.

5. What does zero cross elasticity of demand between two goods imply? Give an example to explain. **ISC 2013**

Ans Zero cross elasticity of demand means goods are not related to each other, i.e. percentage change in price of one good does not impact quantity demanded of the other good. e.g. A change in the price of sugar is not likely to influence the demand for fan, so their cross elasticity of demand will be zero.

6. What will be the price elasticity of demand of the points A, B, L and K in the diagram given below?

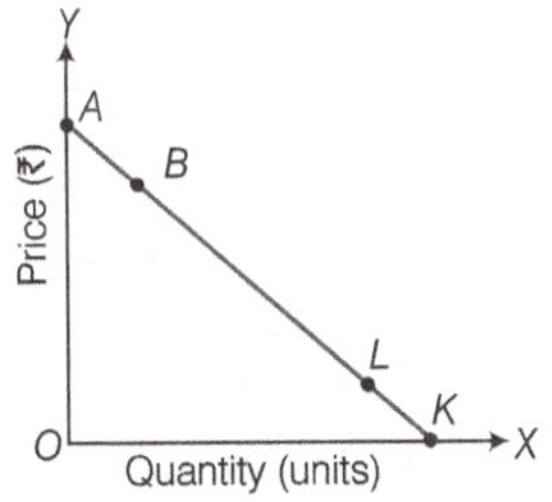

ISC 2012

Ans According to geometric method,

Price Elasticity of Demand

$$(e_p) = \frac{\text{Lower Segment of the Demand Curve}}{\text{Upper Segment of the Demand Curve}}$$

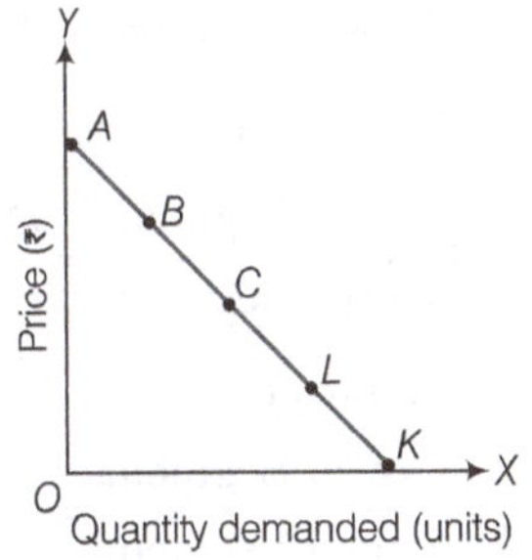

At point A, $e_p = \frac{AK}{0} = \infty$ (Perfectly elastic demand)

At point B, $e_p = \frac{BK}{BA}$ [where, $BK > BA$]

$e_p > 1$ (Highly elastic demand)

At point L, $e_p = \frac{LK}{LA}$ [where, $LK < LA$]

$e_p < 1$ (Less elastic demand)

At point K, $e_p = \frac{0}{KA}$

$e_p = 0$ (Perfectly inelastic demand)

7. If demand increases by 50% due to an increase in income by 75%, calculate the income elasticity of demand. **ISC 2011**

Ans Income Elasticity of Demand (e_y)

$$= \frac{\text{Percentage Change in Demand}}{\text{Percentage Change in Income}} = \frac{50}{75} = 0.67$$

Concept Enhancer In this case, positive coefficient of elasticity indicates that the given good is a normal good.

8. What would be the elasticity of demand of a commodity when

(i) Price and total expenditure move in the opposite direction?

(ii) Price and total expenditure move in the same direction? **ISC 2011**

Or What is the price elasticity of demand when

(i) The change in price and total expenditure move in the opposite direction?

(ii) The change in price and total expenditure move in the same direction? **ISC 2008**

Ans (i) When change in price and total expenditure move in the opposite direction, the price elasticity of demand will be greater than unity ($e_d > 1$).

(ii) When price and total expenditure change in the same direction, then elasticity of demand is less than unity ($e_d < 1$).

9. What is cross elasticity of demand? **ISC 2006**

Ans Cross elasticity of demand measures the responsiveness of quantity demanded of one good (say good X) due to change in price of other good (say good Y).

Mathematically,

$$e_{xy} = \frac{\text{Percentage Change in Demand of Good } X}{\text{Percentage Change in Price of Good } Y}$$

or $$e_{xy} = \frac{\Delta Q_X}{\Delta P_Y} \times \frac{P_Y}{Q_X}$$

10. What is meant by price elasticity of demand? **ISC 2005**

Ans Price elasticity of demand measures the responsiveness of quantity demanded due to change in price of the commodity.

According to percentage method,

$$e_p = (-)\frac{\text{Percentage Change in Quantity Demanded}}{\text{Percentage Change in Price}}$$

$$= (-)\frac{\frac{\text{Change in Quantity Demanded}}{\text{Initial Quantity}} \times 100}{\frac{\text{Change in Price}}{\text{Initial Price}} \times 100}$$

$$= (-)\frac{\frac{\Delta Q}{Q} \times 100}{\frac{\Delta P}{P} \times 100} = (-)\frac{\Delta Q}{Q} \div \frac{\Delta P}{P}$$

$$= (-)\frac{\Delta Q}{Q} \times \frac{P}{\Delta P} = (-)\frac{\Delta Q}{\Delta P} \times \frac{P}{Q}$$

Thus, $e_p = (-)\frac{\Delta Q}{\Delta P} \times \frac{P}{Q}$

Where, e_p = Price Elasticity of Demand
Q = Initial Quantity
ΔQ = Change in Quantity
ΔP = Change in Price, P = Initial Price

Note Price elasticity of demand is a negative number because price and quantity demanded are inversely related.

3/4 Marks Questions

1. When price of commodity X changes from ₹ 40 per unit to ₹ 20 per unit, its demand increases by 20 units. If price elasticity of demand is 0.5, calculate the initial and the final quantity demand of commodity X. ***ISC 2020***

Ans Initial Price (P) = ₹ 40 ; New Price (P_1) = ₹ 20
Initial Quantity $(Q) = x$; New Quantity $(Q_1) = x + 20$
Change in Price $(\Delta P) = P_1 - P = 20 - 40 = -20$
Change in Quantity $(\Delta Q) = 20$ (Given)
Price Elasticity of Demand $(e_P) = 0.5$

$$e_p = (-)\frac{\Delta Q}{\Delta P} \times \frac{P}{Q}$$

$$0.5 = (-)\frac{20}{-20} \times \frac{40}{x}$$

$\Rightarrow \quad 0.5x = 40$

$\Rightarrow \quad x = 80$

$\therefore$ Initial Quantity (Q) = 80 units and
New/Final Quantity $(Q_1) = x + 20$
$\Rightarrow \quad 80 + 20 = 100$ units

2. Explain the various degrees of price elasticity of demand at different points on a straight line demand curve. ***ISC 2019***

Or In a straight line demand curve touching the two axis, show the different degrees of elasticity of demand. ***ISC 2010***

Ans Geometric method measures elasticity at a point on the straight line linear demand curve.
According to this method,

$$e_p = \frac{\text{Lower Segment of the Demand Curve}}{\text{Upper Segment of the Demand Curve}}$$

Using geometric method, we can measure elasticity at any point on the above demand curve (AF) with C as the mid-point.

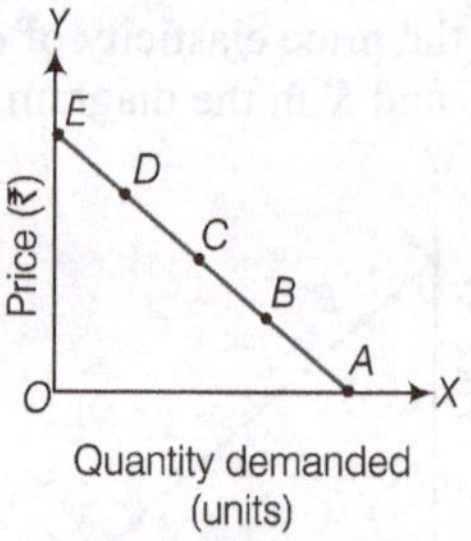

At point A, elasticity will be

$$e_p = \frac{\text{Lower Segment}}{\text{Upper Segment}} = \frac{0}{AE} = 0 \text{ (Perfectly inelastic)}$$

Similarly, at different points, elasticity will be

At point B, $e_p = \frac{\text{Lower Segment}}{\text{Upper Segment}} = \frac{BA}{BE}$

$e_p < 1$ (Less than unity) [as $BA < BE$]

At point C, $e_p = \frac{\text{Lower Segment}}{\text{Upper Segment}} = \frac{CA}{CE}$

$e_p = 1$ (Unity) [as $CA = CE$]

At point D, $e_p = \frac{\text{Lower Segment}}{\text{Upper Segment}} = \frac{DA}{DE}$

$e_p > 1$ (Greater than unity) [as $DA > DE$]

At point E, $e_p = \frac{\text{Lower Segment}}{\text{Upper Segment}} = \frac{EA}{0}$

$e_p = \infty$ (Infinity)

3. Find the elasticity of demand of x and y on the basis of the demand schedule given below and specify which one is more elastic. ***ISC 2017***

Good x		Good y	
P_x (₹)	D_x (units)	P_y (₹)	D_y (units)
8	10	8	10
4	12	6	25

Ans Elasticity of Demand of Good $x = (-)\frac{P}{Q} \times \frac{\Delta Q}{\Delta P}$

$$= (-)\frac{8}{10} \times \frac{(12-10)}{4-8} = (-)\frac{8}{10} \times \frac{2}{-4} = 0.4$$

Elasticity of Demand of Good $y = (-)\frac{P}{Q} \times \frac{\Delta Q}{\Delta P}$

$$= (-)\frac{8}{10} \times \frac{(25-10)}{6-8} = (-)\frac{8}{10} \times \frac{15}{-2} = 6$$

Demand for Good y is more elastic.

4. The quantity demanded of a commodity at a price of ₹ 10 per unit is 40 units. Its price elasticity of demand is (–2). The price fall by ₹ 2 per unit. Calculate the quantity demanded at the new price. **ISC 2016**

Ans Original Price (P) = ₹ 10 per unit

Original Quantity (Q) = 40 units

Change in Price (ΔP) = – (₹ 2 per unit)

Price Elasticity of Demand (e_d) = –2

We know that, Price Elasticity of Demand

$$(e_d) = \frac{\Delta Q}{\Delta P} \times \frac{P}{Q}$$

So, $$-2 = \frac{\Delta Q}{-2} \times \frac{10}{40} \quad \text{or} \quad -2 = \frac{\Delta Q}{-8}$$

or Change in Quantity (ΔQ) $= -2 \times -8 = 16$ units

So, quantity demanded at new price

$= 40 + 16 = 56$ units

Note As price falls, quantity demanded will increase.

5. Price elasticity of demand of a product is unity. A household buys 50 units of this product when its price is ₹ 10 per unit. If its price rises to ₹ 12 per unit, how much quantity of the product will be bought by the household? **ISC 2013**

Ans Given, $e_p = 1$, Let new quantity be 'x'.

According to percentage method,

$$e_p = (-)\frac{\Delta Q}{\Delta P} \times \frac{P}{Q} \Rightarrow 1 = (-)\frac{x-50}{12-10} \times \frac{10}{50} (\because e_p = 1)$$

$$10 = -x + 50 \quad \Rightarrow \quad x = 50 - 10 = 40$$

∴ 40 units will be bought by household at ₹ 12 per unit.

Where, e_p = Price Elasticity of Demand

ΔQ = Change in Quantity

ΔP = Change in Price, Q = Initial Quantity

P = Initial Price

6. Calculate the quantity demanded of a commodity when its price increases from ₹ 4 to ₹ 6. The original quantity demanded was 40 units and the price elasticity of demand is 0.5. **ISC 2012**

Ans Given, $e_p = 0.5$

P	4	6
Q	40	?

Let new quantity be 'x'

$$e_p = (-)\frac{\Delta Q}{\Delta P} \times \frac{P}{Q}$$

$$0.5 = (-)\frac{x-40}{6-4} \times \frac{4}{40} \Rightarrow 0.5 = (-)\frac{x-40}{20}$$

$\Rightarrow 10 = -x + 40$

$x = 30$ i.e. new quantity

Where, e_p = Price Elasticity of Demand

ΔQ = Change in Quantity, ΔP = Change in Price

Q = Initial Quantity, P = Initial Price

7. The price of a commodity falls from ₹ 50 to ₹ 30, resulting in an increase in the purchase of the commodity from 200 units to 220 units. Calculate the price elasticity of demand. **ISC 2010**

Ans $P = ₹\,50, P_1 = ₹\,30$

$Q = 200, Q_1 = 220$

$\Delta P = P_1 - P = 30 - 50 = -20$

$\Delta Q = Q_1 - Q = 220 - 200 = 20$

$$e_p = (-)\frac{\Delta Q}{\Delta P} \times \frac{P}{Q} = (-)\frac{20}{-20} \times \frac{50}{200} = \frac{1}{4}$$

$e_p = 0.25$ (Less elastic)

Where, e_p = Price Elasticity of Demand

P = Initial Price

P_1 = New Price

Q = Initial Quantity

Q_1 = New Quantity

ΔP = Change in Price

ΔQ = Change in Quantity

6 Marks Question

1. Describe any two methods of measurement of elasticity of demand. **ISC 2007**

Ans Elasticity of demand can be measured by using following three different methods

(i) Percentage or proportionate method

(ii) Geometric or point method

(iii) Total expenditure or total outlay method

Percentage Method Refer to Q. No. 10 (2 Marks).

Geometric Method Refer to Q. No. 2 (3/4 Marks).

Value Points

For getting maximum marks, following value points can be included in the answer

- Use linear demand curve under geometric method.
- For total outlay method, all coefficients of elasticity of demand should be mentioned.

TOPIC 2

Degrees and Factors Affecting Elasticity of Demand

Degrees of Elasticity of Demand

There are five degrees of elasticity of demand

1. Perfectly Inelastic Demand ($e_d = 0$)
2. Less Elastic or Inelastic Demand ($e_d < 1$)
3. Unitary Elastic Demand ($e_d = 1$)
4. More Elastic or Elastic Demand ($e_d > 1$)
5. Perfectly Elastic Demand ($e_d = \infty$)

1. Perfectly Inelastic Demand ($e_d = 0$)

It means despite of change in price, quantity demanded does not change.

This is generally happens in the case of necessity goods, where price may change but demand does not change. In this case, demand curve will be vertical straight line parallel to *Y*-axis. e.g. Life saving drugs.

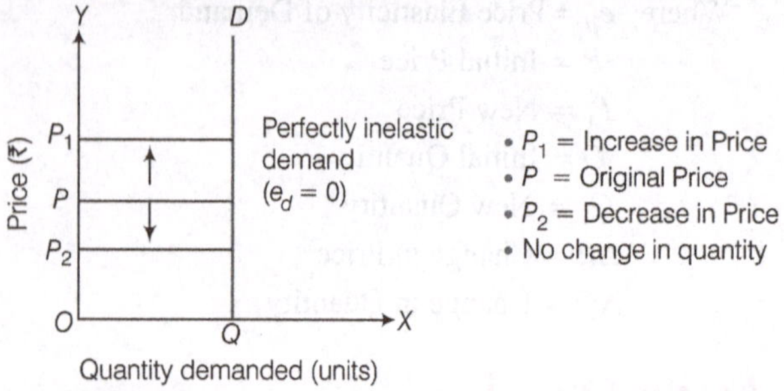

2. Inelastic Demand ($e_d < 1$)

It means percentage change in quantity demanded is less than percentage change in price. In this case, demand curve will be downward sloping but steeper than unitary elastic. e.g. Food, fuel, etc.

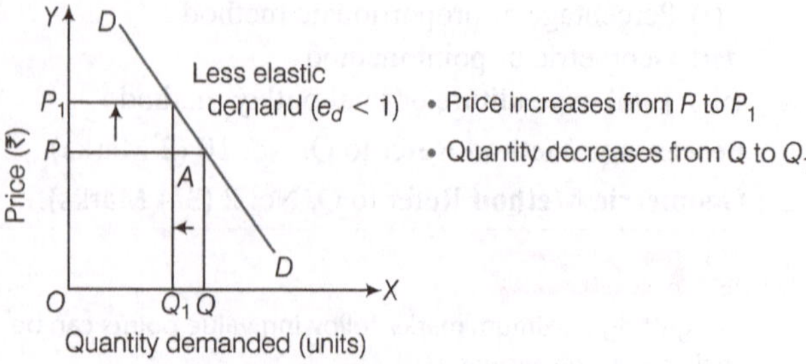

3. Unitary Elastic Demand ($e_d = 1$)

It refers to the situation when percentage change in quantity demanded will be equal to percentage change in price.

Demand curve will be proper downward sloping. e.g. Normal goods.

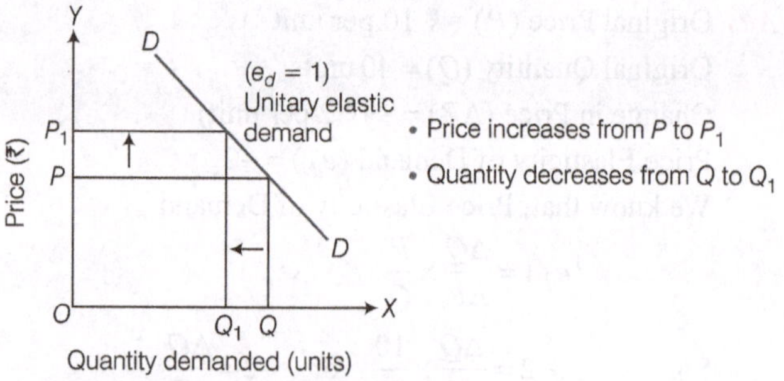

4. More Elastic Demand ($e_d > 1$)

It refers to the situation in which percentage change in quantity demanded is greater than percentage change in price. In this case, demand curve will be downward sloping but flatter than unitary elastic. e.g. Luxuries.

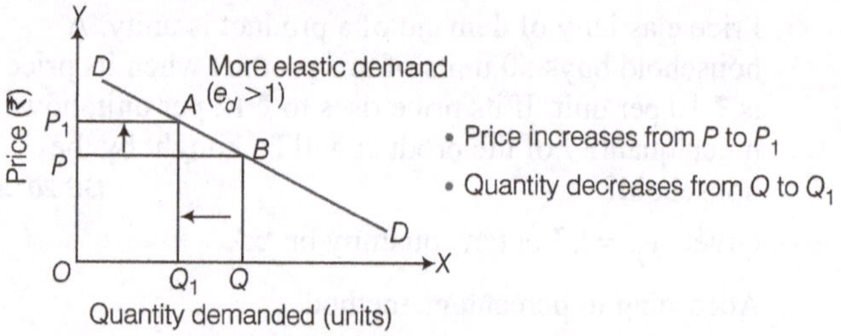

5. Perfectly Elastic Demand ($e_d = \infty$)

Under this situation, it is assumed that infinite units are demanded at a given price, but even if there is a slight increase in price, demand falls to 0. It is an imaginary condition. In this case, demand curve will be horizontal straight line parellel to the *X*-axis.

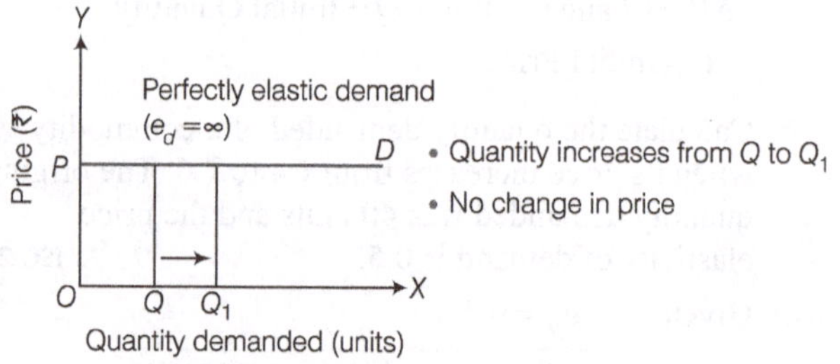

Factors Affecting Price Elasticity of Demand

Following factors affect of price elasticity of demand

(i) **Existence of substitutes of commodity** A good having more close substitutes will have an elastic demand and a good having few close substitutes will have an inelastic demand.

(ii) **Nature of the commodity** The price elasticity of demand is likely to be low for necessities (i.e. food items) and high for luxuries (i.e. jewellery).

(iii) **Proportion of income spent** The products that take up a high percentage of income (i.e. cloth) will have a more elastic demand and *vice-versa*.

(iv) **The number of uses of a commodity** The more number of uses a commodity can be put to, more elastic is the demand.

(v) **Time period** More time period, more price elasticity of demand and *vice-versa*.

(vi) **Postponement of consumption** The demand for commodities is elastic, whose consumption can be postponed for sometime (i.e. TV).

(vii) **Price range** Costly goods have highly elastic demand while demand for inexpensive goods is inelastic demand.

(viii) **Habit of the consumers** The demand for good is inelastic if its consumption becomes a habit for the consumers (i.e. tobacco, alcohol, etc).

PYQs Previous Years' Questions

1 Mark Questions

1. A demand curve parallel to X- axis signifies *ISC Specimen 2023*

(a) perfectly elastic (b) perfectly inelastic
(c) elastic (d) inelastic

Ans (a) perfectly elastic

2. 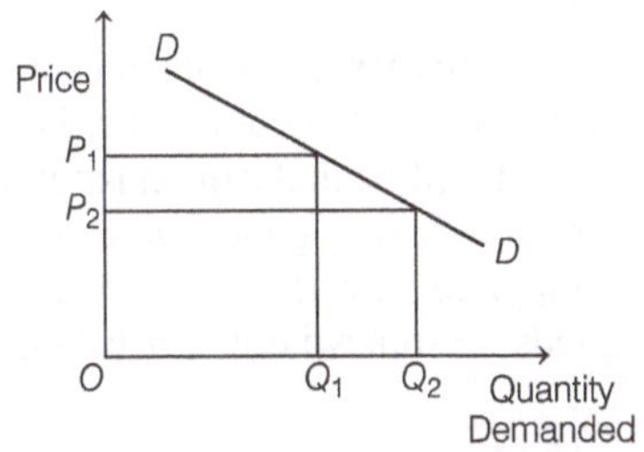

In the diagram above, demand curve represents *ISC Sem I 2021*

(a) unit elastic (b) perfect inelastic
(c) highly elastic (d) highly inelastic

Ans (c) highly elastic

3. When demand curve is parallel to X-axis, what would be it elasticity of demand? *ISC Sem I Specimen 2021*

(a) $e = \infty$ (b) $e = 1$
(c) $e > 1$ (d) $e < 1$

Ans (a) $e = \infty$

4. Which of the given options shows the effect of elasticity of demand? *ISC Sem I Specimen 2021*

(a) Nature of good (b) Level of income
(c) Availability of substitutes (d) All of these

And (d) All of these

5. The demand for a certain brand of fruit juice is elastic because *ISC Sem I Specimen 2021*

(a) it falls under luxuries
(b) its consumption can be postponed
(c) its substitutes are available in the market
(d) it is a multiple use product

Ans (a) it falls under luxuries

2 Marks Question

1. Draw demand curves showing $e_d = 0, e_d = \infty$ *ISC 2009*

Or

Draw a perfectly elastic demand curve. *ISC 2006*

Ans Demand curve for $e_d = 0$

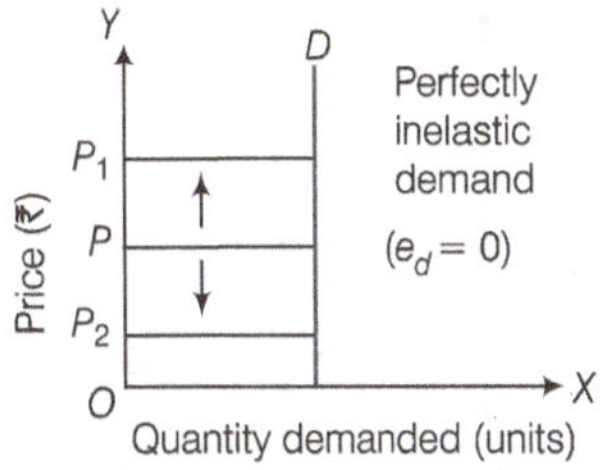

Demand curve for $e_d = \infty$

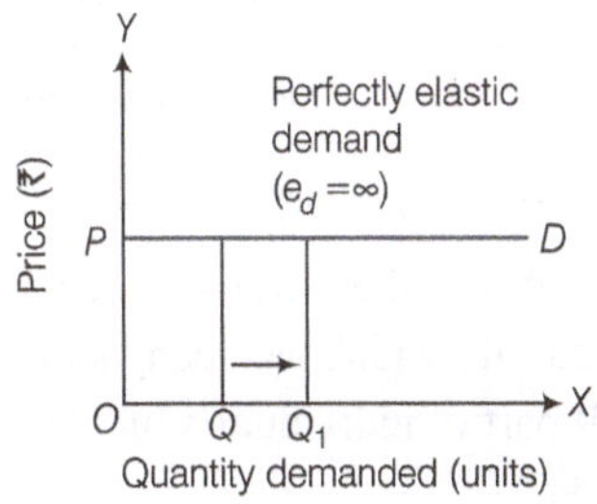

3/4 Marks Questions

1. Draw the diagrams to show elasticity of demand when it is
(i) Greater than one (ii) Less than one
(iii) Unity **ISC 2015**

Ans The demand curves exhibiting the necessary elasticities are

(i) **Greater than one** Percentage change in quantity demanded is more than percentage change in price.

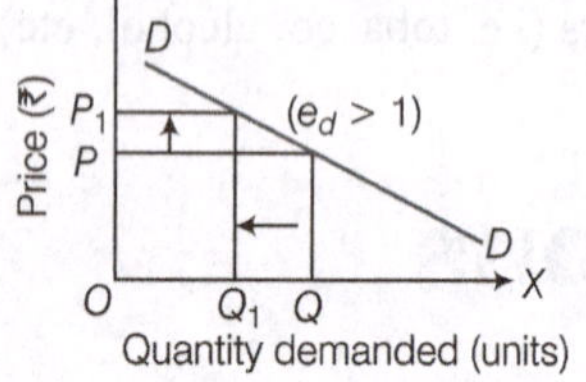

(ii) **Less than one** Percentage change in price is more than percentage change in quantity.

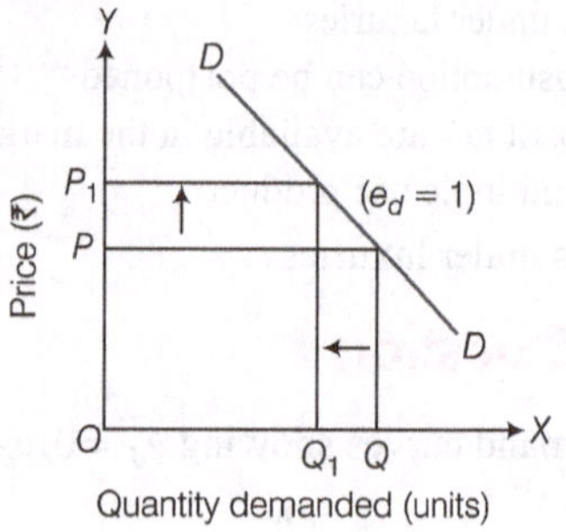

(iii) **Unity** Percentage change in price and percentage change in quantity demanded are equal.

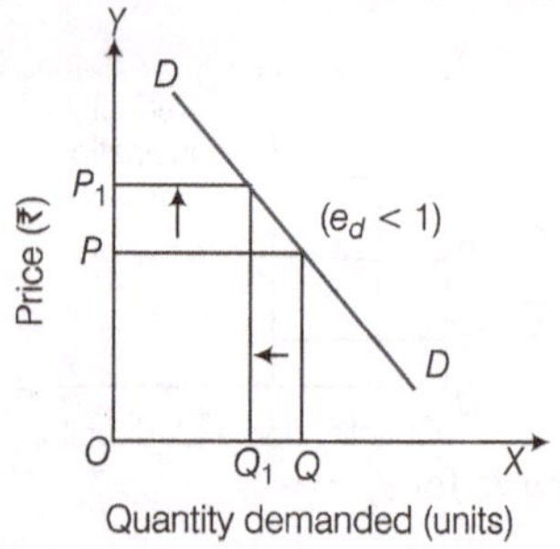

Common Mistake Students don't indicate the change in demand due to price in the diagram. There should be proper arrows marked for the same.

2. Discuss the effects of elasticity of demand on
(i) A commodity which has many substitutes.
(ii) A small part of individual's income spent on a commodity. **ISC 2014**

Ans (i) A commodity having many substitutes will be elastic in nature, as if the price of a particular commodity rises, consumers can easily switch over to its substitutes which are relatively cheaper. e.g. Tea and coffee.

(ii) The commodities on which consumer spent a very small fraction of his income will have inelastic demand, because the price of such commodities is so less that consumer can afford to buy such commodities easily. e.g. Match box, needle, etc.

3. How is the elasticity of demand of a commodity affected by the following factors
(i) Existence of substitutes of a commodity,
(ii) Nature of a commodity. **ISC 2012**

Ans (i) **Existence of substitutes of commodity** Demand for goods which have close substitutes (like tea and coffee) is relatively more elastic. Because, when price of such a good rises, then consumers have the option of shifting to its substitutes. Goods without close substitutes like salt, etc are generally found to be less elastic in demand.

(ii) **Nature of a commodity** It has its impact on elasticity of demand. If the commodity is a necessity, then it will be inelastic in nature. On the other hand, luxury goods which have generally high price, have elastic demand. Comfort goods lie somewhere in between.

6 Marks Questions

1. Explain any four factors affecting price elasticity of demand. **ISC 2023**

Or Explain any two factors affecting the price elasticity of demand. **ISC 2018**

Or Explain any four determinants of price elasticity of demand. **ISC 2011, 2006**

Ans Factors affecting price elasticity of demand are

(i) **Existence of substitutes of commodity** Demand for goods which have close substitutes (like tea and coffee) is relatively more elastic. Because, when price of such a good rises, then consumers have the option of shifting to its substitutes. Goods without close substitutes like salt, etc are generally found to be less elastic in demand.

(ii) **Proportion of income spent** Commodities on which consumer spend a small proportion of their income (like needle, match box, etc) will have an inelastic demand. On the other hand, goods on which the consumers spends a large proportion of their income (like television, furniture, etc) tends to have elastic demand.

(iii) **Postponement of consumption** Demand for a commodity will be elastic, if its consumption can be postponed for future, e.g. Television. However the consumption of food items like fruits, vegetables, etc cannot be postponed, hence they are inelastic in nature.

Factors affecting Price Elasticity of Demand
- Existence of substitutes of commodity
- Proportion of income spent
- Postponement of consumption
- Habits of the consumers

(iv) **Habits of the consumers** Habits or preferences of the consumers also affects the elasticity of demand. If consumers are habitual of consuming a particular commodity, they will continue to consume such commodities, even if their price changes, demand for such commodities are inelastic. e.g. Smokers do not quit smoking, even if price of cigarette increases.

2. Discuss any four degrees or magnitudes of elasticity of demand. ***2008***

Ans Different commodities have different price elasticities. Some commodities have more elastic demand, while others have relatively less elastic demand. Basically, the price elasticity of demand ranges from zero to infinity. It can be equal to zero, less than one, greater than one, equal to unity or equal to infinity.

According to **Doctor Marshall**, "The elasticity or responsiveness of demand in a market is great or small accordingly as the amount demanded increases much or little for a given fall in price and diminishes much or little for a given rise in price."

Different degrees of elasticity of demand are

(i) **Perfectly inelastic demand** ($e_d = 0$) It means despite of change in price, quantity demanded does not change. This generally happens in the case of necessity goods, where price may change but demand does not change. In this case, demand curve will be vertical straight line paralled to Y-axis.

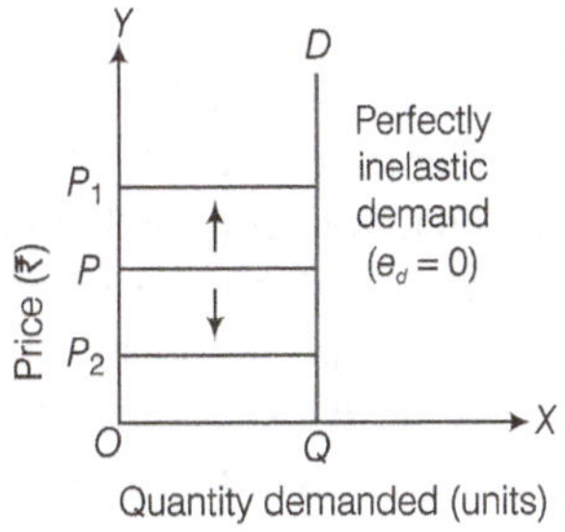

In the given figure, D shows the perfectly inelastic demand. At price OP, the quantity demanded was OQ. Now the price increases to OP_1 from OP, the demand remains the same and *vice-versa*.

(ii) **Inelastic demand** ($e_d < 1$) It means percentage change in quantity demanded is less than percentage change in price. In this case, demand curve will be downward sloping but steeper than unitary elastic.

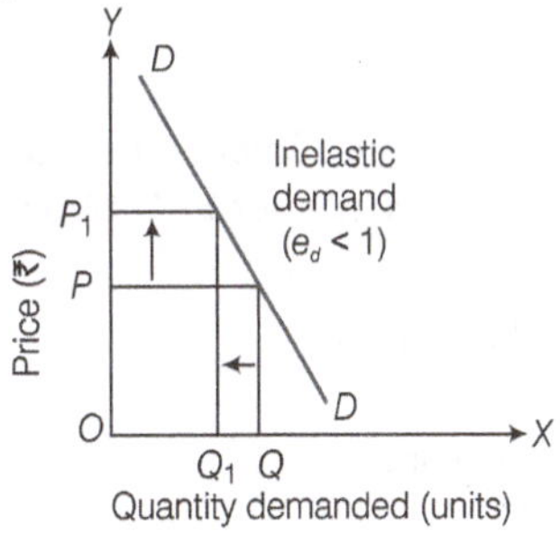

In the given figure, DD demand curve represents relatively elastic demand. When price was OP, quantity demanded was OQ. Now if price rises to OP_1, then the quantity demanded reduces by less than proportionate change in price, i.e. OQ_1.

Degrees of E_d
- Perfectly inelastic demand
- Inelastic demand
- Unitary elastic demand
- More elastic demand

(iii) **Unitary elastic demand** ($e_d = 1$) It refers to the situation when percentage change in quantity demanded will be equal to percentage change in price. Demand curve will be proper downward sloping.

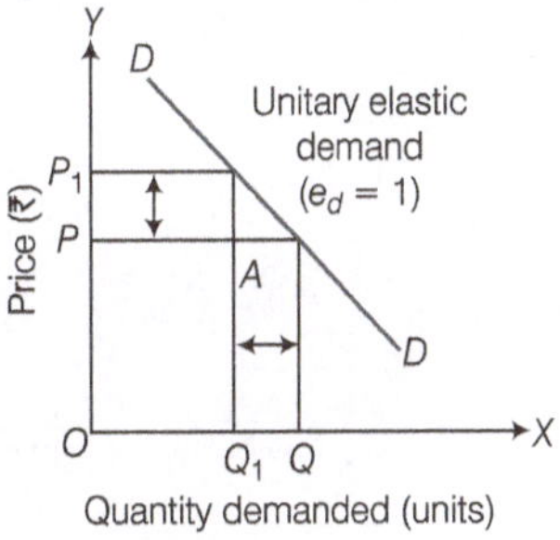

In the given figure, DD demand curve represents unitary elastic demand. When price was OP, the quantity demanded was OQ. Now price rises to OP_1, the quantity demanded falls to OQ_1. PP_1 and Q_1Q are equal in terms of price and quantity demanded. The proportionate change in both the variables remain the same. Thus, $e_d = 1$.

(iv) **More elastic demand** ($e_d > 1$) It refers to the situation in which percentage change in quantity demanded is greater than percentage change in price.
In this case, demand curve will be downward sloping but flatter than unitary elastic.
In the given figure, DD demand curve represents elastic demand. When price was OP, quantity demanded was OQ, as price rises to OP_1 quantity demanded falls to OQ_1. In this case, PP_1 is less than Q_1Q.

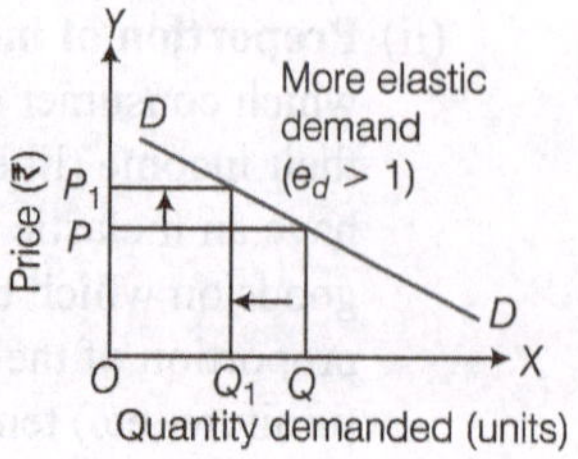

Value Points

For getting maximum marks, following value points can be included in the answer
- Change in price and demand should be shown while explaining the degrees of E_d.
- Meaning of each degree of E_d should be mentioned.

Case Based Question

Case 1

When price of a good is ₹ 12 per unit, 24 units are demanded. When the price rises to ₹ 14 per unit, 20 units are demanded. *ISC Sem I 2021*

(i) The price elasticity is
(a) one
(b) greater than one
(c) zero
(d) between zero and one

Ans (a) Price elasticity

$$= -\frac{\Delta Q}{\Delta P} \times \frac{P}{Q} = -\frac{-4}{2} \times \frac{12}{24} = 1$$

(ii) The shape of the above demand curve will be
(a) positively sloped (b) negatively sloped
(c) parallel to X- axis (d) parallel to Y- axis

Ans (b) negatively sloped

(iii) The price elasticity of demand measures
(a) slope of budget line
(b) percentage change in the price of the good
(c) responsiveness of quantity demanded to the change in price
(d) sensitiveness of price to change in quantity demanded

Ans (c) responsiveness of quantity demanded to the change in price

CHAPTER TEST

01 Mark Questions

1. The elasticity of demand for a commodity will be higher when
(a) the more of that commodity is considered a necessity
(b) the more is buyer's demand loyalty
(c) there is more availability of substitutes
(d) All of the above

2. Elasticity of demand indicates
(a) changes in quantity demanded
(b) rate of change in quantity demanded
(c) change in prices
(d) change in income

3. From the following commodities, which has the lowest elasticity of demand?
(a) Car (b) Salt
(c) Tea (d) House

4. When the percentage change in quantity demanded is less than percentage change in price, then price elasticity of demand is
(a) less than unity (b) more than unity
(c) equal to unity (d) None of these

5. If a consumer spends higher proportion of income on a good, its demand will be inelastic. State true or false.

6. Flatter demand curve has lower elasticity of demand. State true or false.

7. The elasticity of demand at the mid-point of a linear demand curve will be ....

8. Slope of demand curve and elasticity of demand are .... proportional.

9. What will be the income elasticity of demand for giffen goods?

10. Why luxury goods are highly elastic in nature?

02 Marks Questions

11. What is the difference between price elasticity of demand and income elasticity of demand?

12. Why is demand inelastic in short-term or short-run?

13. Draw a demand schedule for salt with relatively inelastic demand.

14. Price elasticity of demand of good X is (–) 2 and of good Y is (–) 3. Which of the two goods are more price elastic and why?

15. Draw demand curve for the following cases
(i) Elastic demand
(ii) Inelastic demand

03/04 Marks Questions

16. In a situation when price of a commodity falls and price elasticity of demand is greater than unity, should total expenditure on the commodity be increasing, decreasing or constant? Give reason.

17. 'If a product's price increases, a family's spending on the product has to increase'. Defend or refute the statement.

18. The quantity demanded of a commodity at a price of ₹ 8 per unit is 600 units. Its price falls by 25% and quantity demanded rises by 120 units. Calculate its price elasticity of demand. Is it demand elastic? Give reason in support of your answer.

19. A 3% fall in the price of good X leads to 9% rise in its demand. A 5% rise in the price of good Y leads to 5% fall in its demand. Calculate the price elasticity of demand for good X and good Y. Which is more elastic and why?

06 Marks Question

20. The elasticity of demand of good X is half the price elasticity of demand of good Y. A 25% rise in the price of good Y reduces its demand by 100 units from 400 units. Calculate percentage rise in demand of good X when its price falls from ₹ 10 to ₹ 8 per unit.

Answers

1. (c) there is more availability of substitutes
2. (b) rate of change in quantity demanded
3. (d) House *4.* (a) less than unity
5. True *6.* False
7. unity *8.* inversely

03

Supply and Elasticity of Supply

TREND ANALYSIS 5 YEARS

Average No. of Questions Across all Sets

Topic	Types of Questions	2023	2020	2019	2018	2017
01 Concept of Supply and its Determinants	1 Mark	—	—	—	—	—
	2 Marks	—	—	—	—	—
	3/4 Marks	—	—	—	1	—
	6 Marks	—	—	—	—	1
02 Law of Supply and Change in Supply	1 Mark	1	—	—	—	—
	2 Marks	—	—	—	—	—
	3/4 Marks	1	1	1	1	—
	6 Marks	—	—	—	—	—
03 Elasticity of Supply	1 Mark	—	—	—	—	—
	2 Marks	1	—	1	—	1
	3/4 Marks	—	—	—	—	—
	6 Marks	—	1	—	—	—

TOPIC 1

Concept of Supply and Determinants of Supply

Supply

It refers to the quantity of a commodity that a seller is willing to sell at a given price in a given period of time. In other words, supply refers to quantity of goods offered for sale at different possible prices.

Quantity supplied refers to a specific quantity of a good that a producer is willing to sell at a particular price during a particular time period is called as quantity supplied.

Supply can be classified as

(i) **Individual supply** Supply of a particular commodity by an individual firm at a given price in the market is termed as 'individual supply.'

(ii) **Market supply** It is the aggregate of individual supplies, which prevails in the market at a particular price.

Supply Schedule

It is a table showing various quantities of a commodity offered for sale corresponding to different possible prices of that commodity or it is a table showing a relationship between price and quantity supplied of a commodity at a given period of time. Supply schedule has two aspects

1. Individual Supply Schedule

It is a table showing different quantities of a commodity that an individual firm is ready to sell at different prices during a given period of time.

2. Market Supply Schedule

It is a table showing different quantities of a commodity that all the firms in a market are willing to sell at different prices of that commodity at a given time period.

Supply Curve

It is a graphical presentation of supply schedule showing various quantities of a commodity offered for sale at different possible prices of that commodity. It shows the positive relationship between price of commodity and its quantity supplied. It is upward sloping curve. Supply curve has two aspects

1. Individual Supply Curve

It is a graphical representation of individual supply schedule, showing positive relationship between price and quantity supplied of a commodity.

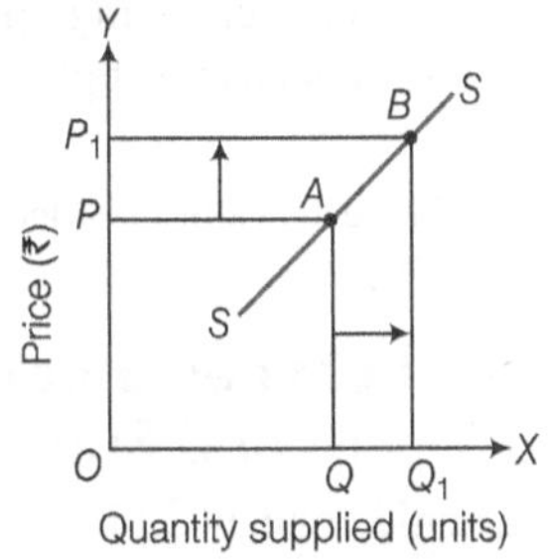

Individual Supply Curve

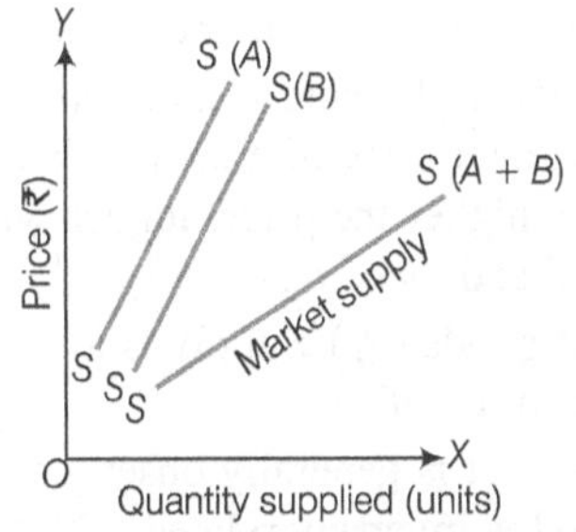

Market Supply Curve

2. Market Supply Curve

It is a graphical representation of market supply schedule or in other words, market supply curve is the horizontal summation of the individual supply curves.

Derivation of Market Supply Curve from Individual Supply Curve

Market supply is the horizontal summation of individual supply curve at different prices.

Supply Schedule

Price (₹)	Qty Supplied by A	Qty Supplied by B	Qty Supplied by C	*(A+ B+C)* Market Supply
5	10	30	20	60
10	20	40	30	90
15	30	50	40	120

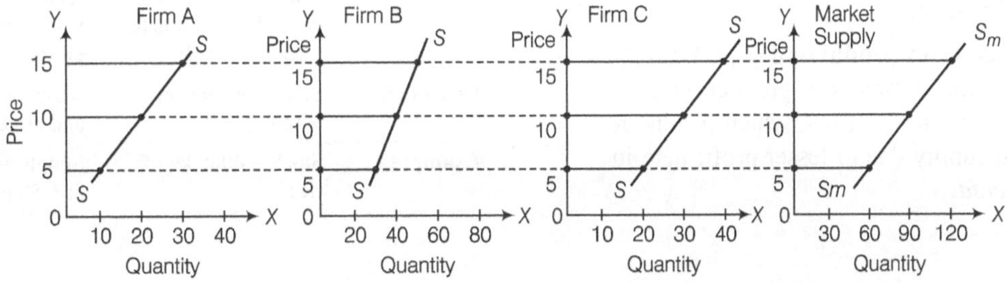

Supply Function

Supply function studies the functional relationship between supply of a commodity and its various determinants. It is expressed in the following equation

$$S_x = f(P_x, P_r, N_f, G, P_f, T, E_x, G_p)$$

Here, S_x = Supply of Commodity
f = Functional Relationship
P_x = Own Price of Commodity X
P_r = Price of the Related Goods
N_f = Number of Firms in the Industry
G = Goal of the Firm
P_f = Price of Factors of Production
T = State of Technology
E_x = Business Confidence/Expectation
G_p = Government's Policy

Factors Affecting Supply/ Determinants of Supply

The various factors affecting supply of commodity are

(i) **Price of a commodity** (P_x) There is a direct relationship between own price of a commodity and its quantity supplied, higher the price, higher will be the quantity supplied and *vice-versa*.

(ii) **Price of the related goods** (P_r) Supply is affected by the change in the price of
  (a) **Substitute goods** It is generally observed that supply of a good is inversely related with the price of substitute goods. So, rise in the price of tea will lead to a fall in the supply of coffee.
  (b) **Complementary goods** It is observed that supply of a good is directly related with the price of its complementary good. So, rise in the price of car will lead to an increase in the supply of petrol.

(iii) **Goal of the firm** (G) If goal of the firm is to maximise profits, more quantity of the commodity will be offered only at a higher price. On the other hand, if goal of the firm is to maximise sales, more will be supplied even at the same price. Sales-maximiser firm supplies greater quantity than a profit-maximiser firm.

(iv) **Price of factors of production** (P_f) With the rise in the price of factors of production, the cost of production also rises, which results in decrease in supply due to lesser profit margin and *vice-versa*.

(v) **State of technology** (T) New discoveries bring reduction in costs of production and increase in production hence profits. This will increase the level of supply also. A cost saving technology shifts the supply curve to the right.

(vi) **Number of firms in the industry** (N_f) Increase in the number of firms implies increase in market supply and decrease in the number of firms implies decrease in market supply of a commodity.
An increase in the number of firms, shifts market supply curve to the right i.e. supply increases and *vice-versa*.

(vii) **Business confidence/expectation** (E_x) In the situation of high business confidence, investment tends to rise and supply starts rising and *vice-versa*.

(viii) **Government policy** (G_p) The production of the commodity is discouraged, if high rate of GST is imposed on goods, then supply will decrease, so supply curve will shift to the left. In the same way, tax concessions encourage producers to increase supply. In this case, supply curve will shift to the right.

Note The first five factors affect individual supply. All the factors affect market supply.

Difference between Stock (Intended Supply) and Supply (Actual Supply)

'Stock' is a static concept and 'supply' is a flow concept.

The difference between supply and stock mainly depends upon the nature of commodity. For perishable commodities like fish and fruits, supply and stock will be same. The commodities, which are non-perishable like TV, AC can be held back if prices are not favourable. In short, stock is potential supply.

In other words, stock refers to the quantity of goods that are available with the seller to offer for sale. On the other hand, supply refers to the quantity of good that a seller is actually able to sell at varied prices.

Basis	Stock	Supply
Meaning	It is the total amount of commodity which is in the custody of the seller. So, it is the intended supply.	Supply is that part of stock which a seller is ready to sell at a certain price during a certain period of time.
Dependence	Stock depends on output.	Supply depends on stock and price in market.
Example	Stock = 4000 kg of rice.	Supply = 900 kg for sale at ₹ 50 per kg.

PYQs Previous Years' Questions

1 Mark Questions

1. Stock of a commodity is also called *ISC Sem I 2021*
   (a) intended supply
   (b) actual supply
   (c) market supply
   (d) individual supply

Ans (a) intended supply

2. Adoption of cost saving technological progress will *ISC Sem I 2021*
   (a) increase the supply
   (b) reduce cost of production
   (c) reduce cost and increase supply
   (d) supply will not change

Ans (a) increase the supply

2 Marks Questions

1. Distinguish between intended supply and actual supply. *ISC 2014*

Ans Difference between intended supply (stock) and actual supply (supply)

Basis	Intended supply	Actual supply
Meaning	It refers to total amount of the commodity that can be supplied in market.	It refers to the quantity that are actually supplied in the market for sale.
Dependence	It depends on output.	It depends on stock and price in market.

2. Mention two factors, other than price, which influence the supply of a commodity. *ISC 2006*

Ans Two factors affecting supply are
   (i) **Input prices** Change in the prices of input causes opposite change in the supply of commodity.
   (ii) **Government's policy** Taxes and subsidies also influence the supply of a commodity.

3/4 Marks Questions

1. Derive a market supply curve from two hypothetical individual supply schedules. *ISC 2018*

Ans Derivation of market supply curve from two individual supply schedules

Price (₹)	Quantity Supplied by A	Quantity Supplied by B	Market Supply $(A + B)$ (units)
2	10	15	25
4	15	25	40
6	20	35	55
8	25	45	70
10	30	55	85

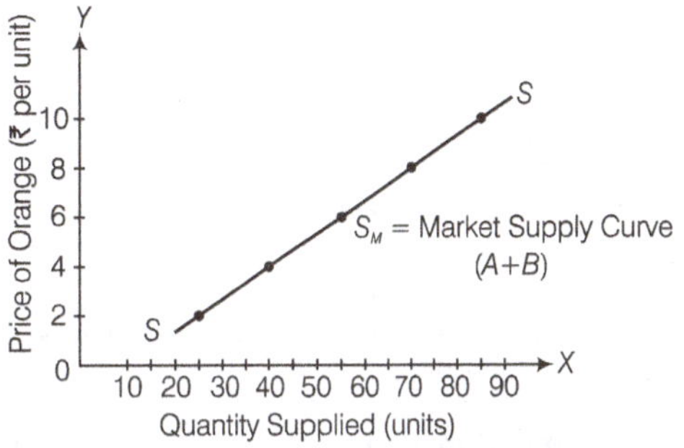

Market Supply Curve

The market supply is derived simply by adding the quantities supplied at each price by the two firms. Market supply curve is the graphical representation of market supply schedule which is shown by S_M to S_M curve. Market supply curve shows the total quantity supplied $(A + B)$ at various prices.

Concept Enhancer Market supply curve is the horizontal sum of individual supply curves, as it adds quantity at each price.

2. Complete the following table and draw a supply curve for the firm A *ISC 2013*

Price (per unit)	Supply of A	Supply of B	Market Supply
2	5	5	?
3	?	10	17
4	9	?	24
5	11	20	?

Ans

Price (Q) (per unit)	Supply of A $(C - B)$	Supply of B $(C - A)$	Market Supply $C\,(A + B)$
2	5	5	**10**
3	**7**	10	17
4	9	**15**	24
5	11	20	**31**

For, $A = C - B$ $\quad B = C - A$

$A = 17 - 10$ $\quad B = 24 - 9$

$A = 7$ $\quad B = 15$

(i) $C = A + B = 5 + 5$, $\quad C = 10$

(ii) $C = A + B = 11 + 20$, $\quad C = 31$

Supply curve for the firm 'A' is given below

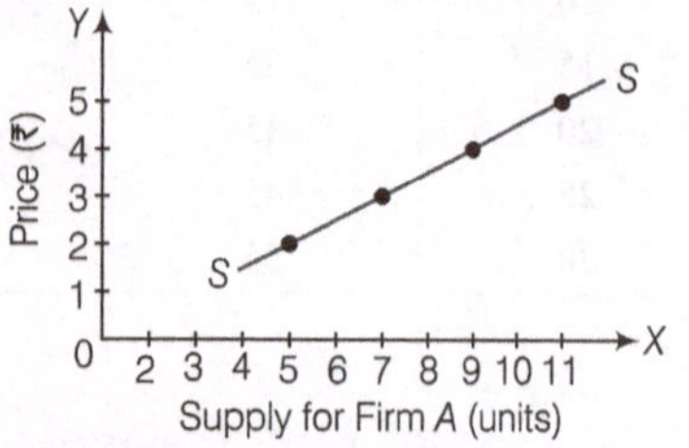

Value Points

For getting maximum marks, following value points can be included in the answer

- Show the formulae in the numerical answer.
- In diagram, only firm A's supply curve should be shown as asked in question.

3. Explain supply function. ***ISC 2011***

Ans Supply function studies the functional relationship between supply of a commodity and its various determinants. It is expressed in the following equation

$$S_x = f(P_x, P_r, N_f, G, P_f, T, E_x, G_p)$$

Here, S_x = Supply of Commodity

f = Functional Relationship

P_x = Own Price of Commodity X

P_r = Price of the Related Goods

N_f = Number of Firms in the Industry

G = Goal of the Firm

P_f = Price of Factors of Production

T = State of Technology

E_x = Business Confidence/Expectation

G_p = Government's Policy

6 Marks Questions

1. Discuss four determinants of supply of a commodity. ***ISC 2017, 2013***

Or Define supply. Explain four factors affecting supply. ***ISC 2009***

Ans Supply refers to the quantity of a commodity that a seller is willing to sell at various prices in a given period of time. In other words, supply refers to whole quantity of goods offered for sale at different possible prices.

Determinants of supply Four determinants of supply of a commodity are

(i) **Price of the commodity** (P_x) Price of the commodity and supply have a positive relation i.e. when the price of a commodity rises, it becomes more profitable for the producers, hence, he will supply more at the increased price.

On the other hand, if the price of the commodity falls, supply will also fall.

(ii) **Number of firms in the industry** (N_f) Increase in the number of firms in the industry leads to increase in supply, whereas decrease in the number of firms in the industry lead to decrease in supply.

Determinants of Supply
- Price of the commodity
- Number of firms in the industry
- Price of factor
- Technique of production

(iii) **Price of factor** (P_f) It is an important determinant of supply for a commodity. If the input price of a commodity rises, then the commodity becomes less profitable or expensive to produce, hence producers will supply less units of such commodities. On the other hand, if input prices fall, then profitability rises and supply will also rise.

(iv) **Technique of production** (T) If the technique of production is such that it reduces the cost of production and hence, raises profit, then supply will also increase. On the other hand, if technique of production raises cost, then supply will fall.

2. Differentiate between stock and supply. With the help of diagrams, explain the relationship between time period and supply. ***ISC 2006***

Ans **Difference between stock and supply** Supply (actual supply) of a commodity refers to that quantity which producers are willing to offer for sale at a particular price during a particular period of time.

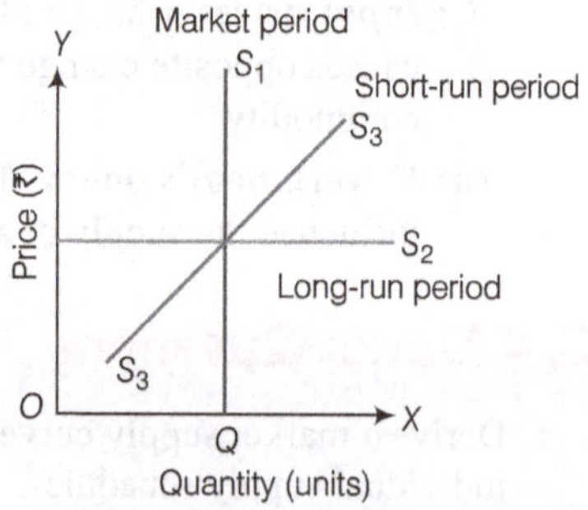

Stock (intended supply) of a commodity is the total amount of the commodity available with the producers at any given time.

Time period is generally divided into three different phases, which are as follows

(i) **Market period** (Very short period) It is very short period of time in which supply of a good cannot be changed. In this period of time, supply (actual supply) and stock (intended supply) are equal to each other.

In case of agricultural products like fruits and vegetables, supply cannot be changed instantly even if their price changes. As a result, supply curve for market period will be vertical line parallel to Y-axis (S_1) indicating that supply is not a function of price.

(ii) **Short-run** (Short period) It is the period in which supply can be adjusted to some extent. Producers can increase the production (hence the supply) by running the same plant for longer hours like two shifts instead of one. Short period is not enough for the firm to set-up new plants or new machines. Therefore, in the short-run, supply curve is upward sloping like S_3S_3 in the given figure.

(iii) **Long-run** (Long period) It is the period which brings stability in the market. The firms are now earning only normal profit and have reached their equilibrium. They will not like to disturb their equilibrium. Therefore, they are willing to supply indefinite quantities at the prevailing price. Supply curve becomes parallel to X- axis as S_2 as shown in the figure.

TOPIC 2

Law of Supply, Movement along Supply Curve and Shift in Supply Curve

Law of Supply

Law of supply states that keeping other factors constant, their is a direct/positive relationship between price of a commodity and its quantity supplied.

Assumptions of Law of Supply

Assumptions of law of supply are

(i) Input prices are constant.
(ii) Price of related goods are constant.
(iii) Goal of producer does not change.
(iv) Technique of production remains constant.
(v) Government's policy does not change.
(vi) Market expectation does not change.

Exceptions of the Law of Supply

Following are the exceptions of law of supply

(i) **Agricultural produce** (products) Due to natural and seasonal factors, law of supply does not applied.

(ii) **Rare articles** (like old manuscripts, postage stamps, etc) Certain goods are such that in spite of changes in price, there is no change in their supply e.g. Old coins.

(iii) **Supply of labour force** High wages rate decrease the supply of labour and *vice-versa*. After reaching a certain labour supply, it can be further increased. After this situation, labour supply falls. This makes backward bending labour supply curve.

(iv) **Clearance sale** When the seller wish the clear existing stock of goods, he supplies more at lower price.

(v) **Expectations of further changes in price** If sellers anticipate that price will fall further in future, then they will supply more on less current price and *vice-versa*.

Movement along the Supply Curve

A movement along the supply curve is caused by changes in the price of the goods, other factors remaining constant. It is also called change in quantity supplied of the commodity.

Here, we move on the same supply curve either upwards or downwards.

Movements along a supply curve can take the form of

1. Extension or Expansion of Supply

When the quantity supplied increases with the rise in price, it is called expansion of supply. In this case, we move upward on the same supply curve. It is explained in the given diagram, as with an increase in the price from OP to OP_2, quantity supplied also increases from OQ to OQ_2.

2. Contraction of Supply

When the quantity supplied decreases with the fall in price, it is called contraction of supply. In this case, we move downward on the same supply curve.

It is explained in the given diagram, as with a fall in price from OP to OP_1, quantity supplied falls from OQ to OQ_1.

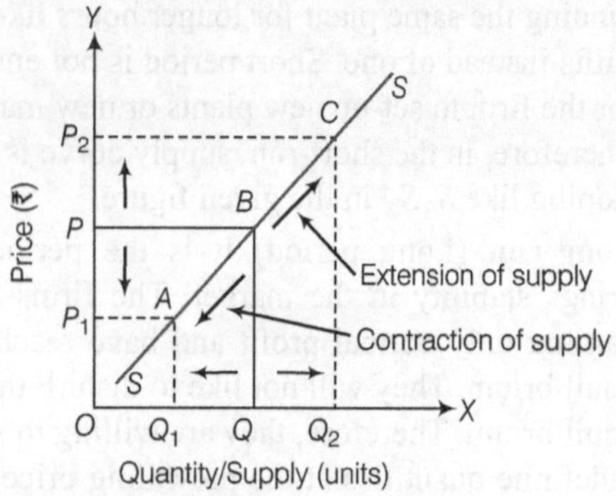

Shift in the Supply Curve or Change in Supply

Shift in supply curve or change in supply shows the situation of increase or decrease in supply, even when, own price of the commodity remains constant. These are caused by other factors, which are

(i) Price of related commodities
(ii) State of technology
(iii) Cost of production
(iv) Government's policy
(v) Change in the goal of the firm.

In a shift, a new supply curve is drawn.

There are two possible conditions

1. Increase in Supply

When supply of a commodity increases due to favourable changes in factors other than price, it is called increase in supply. It is explained in the given diagram, as supply curve SS shifts to S_1S_1 (rightward shift) signifying increase in supply, keeping price constant.

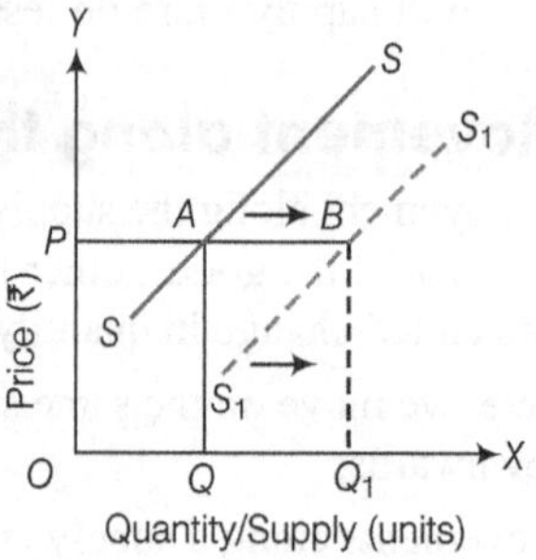

Causes for the Increase in Supply

Increase in supply may occur on account of the following factors

(i) Fall in the price of substitute goods.
(ii) Rise in the price of complementary goods.
(iii) Changes in the goals of producers to being sales-maximiser.
(iv) Fall in the price of factors of production.
(v) Improvements in technology.
(vi) Increase in the number of firms in the market.

2. Decrease in Supply

When supply of a commodity decreases due to unfavourable changes in factors other than price, it is called decrease in supply. It is explained in the given diagram, as supply curve SS shifts to S_1S_1 (leftward shift) signifying decrease in supply, keeping price constant.

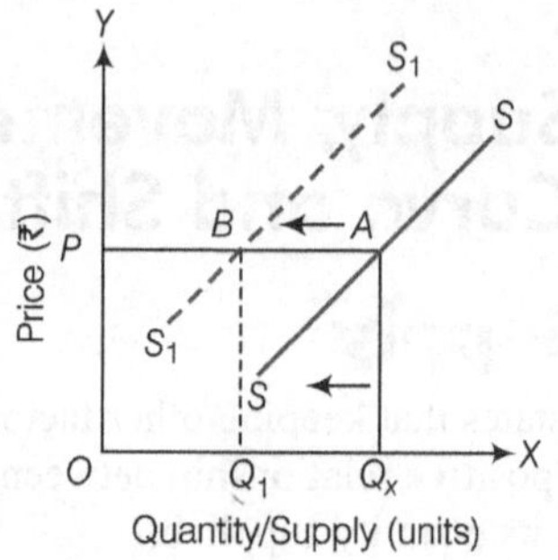

Causes for the Decrease in Supply

Decrease in supply may occur on account of the following factors

(i) Rise in the price of substitute goods.
(ii) Fall in the price of complementary goods.
(iii) Changes in the goals of producers to being profit-maximiser.
(iv) Rise in the price of factors of production.
(v) Outdated technology.
(vi) Decrease in the number of firms in the market.

PYQs Previous Years' Questions

1 Mark Questions

1. Which one of the following is not a *ceteris paribus* assumption of the law of supply? **ISC 2023**
   (a) Indirect taxes and subsidies on the firm's products remain constant
   (b) Technology used by the firm in production remain constant
   (c) Prices of the factors of production paid by the firm remain constant
   (d) Price of the commodity produced by the firm remains constant

Ans (d) Price of the commodity produced by the firm remain constant

2. Which of the following does not cause a shift of supply curve of a good? **ISC Sem I 2021**
   (a) Price of inputs (b) Price of good
   (c) Goods and Service Tax (d) Subsidy

KEY IDEA
Change in price of the commodity leads to movement along the same supply curve.

Ans (b) Price of good

3. Movement along the supply curve occurs due to **ISC Sem I 2021**
   (a) increase in own price of the commodity
   (b) decrease in own price of the commodity
   (c) change in factors other than own price of the commodity
   (d) increase and decrease in own price of the commodity

Ans (c) change in factors other than own price of the commodity

4. If the Government provides tax concessions and subsidies, the supply curve will **ISC Sem I 2021**
   (a) shift leftwards (b) shift rightwards
   (c) remain constant (d) demand curve will shift

Ans (b) shift rightwards

5. The shape of supply curve of perishable commodity will be **ISC Sem I 2021**
   (a) vertical (b) horizontal
   (c) upward sloping (d) downward sloping

Ans (d) downward sloping

Concept Enhancer Perishable goods are those goods which has very short shelf life, they are generally used for immediate consumption.

6. The supply of labour decreases with increase in wage rate because **ISC Sem I 2021**
   (a) labour starts substituting leisure for wages
   (b) labour starts substituting wages for leisure
   (c) demand for labour changes
   (d) supply of labour is dependent on demand

Ans (a) labour starts substituting leisure for wages

7. An increase in wages for labour will lend to **ISC Sem I 2021**
   (a) upward movement along the supply curve
   (b) downward movement along the supply curve
   (c) supply curve will shift towards left
   (d) supply curve will shift towards right

Ans (a) upward movement along the supply curve

8. When supply increases due to improvement in technology, it is known as **ISC Sem I Specimen 2021**
   (a) extension in supply
   (b) increase in supply
   (c) contraction in supply
   (d) decrease in supply

Ans (b) increase in supply

9. Which of the given options is the correct reason for a backward bending supply curve? **ISC Sem I Specimen 2021**
   (a) Labour first prefers work over leisure and then leisure over work
   (b) Labour first prefers leisure over work and then work over leisure
   (c) Both (a) and (b)
   (d) Neither (a) nor (b)

Ans (a) Labour first prefers work over leisure and then leisure over work

10. What is the reason for the upward sloping supply curve? **ISC Sem I Specimen 2021**
   (a) Direct relation between price and quantity
   (b) Number of producers
   (c) Profit maximisation (d) All of the above

Ans (d) All of the above

2 Marks Questions

1. The following headline appeared in the newspaper "Crop damage in Himachal Pradesh sent tomato prices soaring in Delhi." Analyse the statement with reference to the relationship between price and supply. ***ISC Specimen 2023***

Ans The above case indicates shortage of supply due to crop damage. This will lead to increase in price of tomatoes in Delhi, but supply cannot be increased beyond a certain limit owing to the shortage. This situation can be considered as an exception of law of supply.

2. Technical advancement leads to cost saving. With the help of a diagram, explain the effect of technical advancement on the supply curve. ***ISC 2016***

Ans Technological progress tends to lower the marginal cost and average cost of production, because better technology facilitates higher output with the same inputs.

Accordingly, producers are willing to supply more at the existing price. As a result, supply of producer increases and the supply curve shifts rightwards.

With technical advancement, supply curve SS shifts to S_1S_1.

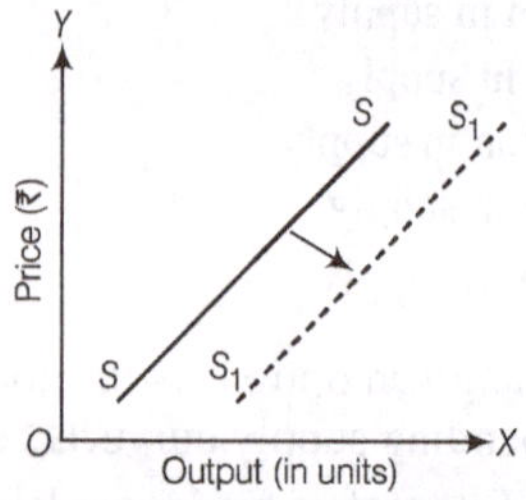

Common Mistake Students generally don't use diagrams while explaining the impact. A diagram is must in such cases.

3. State what causes a movement along the supply curve and show it diagrammatically? ***ISC 2012***

Ans Change in quantity supplied due to change in its own price, keeping other factors constant is known as movement along the supply curve. When price of the commodity rises, quantity supplied expands.

It is known as extension in quantity supplied, this is shown as an upward movement along supply curve.

On the other hand, when price of the commodity falls, quantity supplied contracts.

It is known as contraction in supply and it is shown as a downward movement along the supply curve.

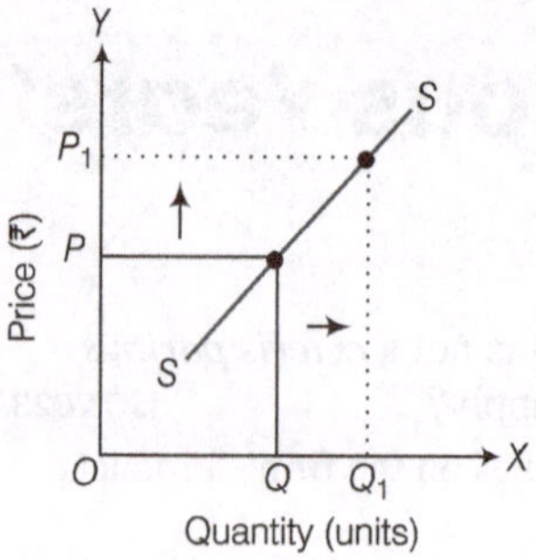

Extension

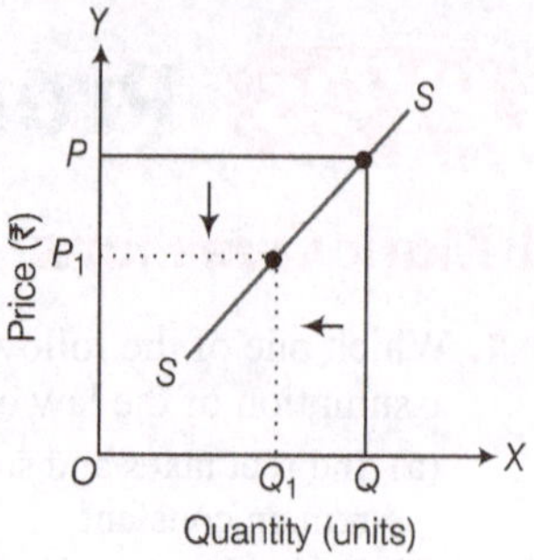

Contraction

4. State two significant difference between extension in supply and increase in supply. ***ISC 2009***

Ans Difference between extension in supply and increase in supply

Basis	Extension in supply	Increase in supply
Meaning	When supply of a commodity expands, keeping all other factors constant due to increase in price.	When supply of a commodity increases, keeping own price constant.
Cause	Increase in own price.	Decrease in price of substitute goods, fall in input prices, improvement in technology, etc.
Change in supply curve	An upward movement along the same supply curve.	Rightward shift in the supply curve.

3/4 Marks Questions

1. Briefly explain any two exceptions of law of supply. ***ISC 2023***

Or Discuss two exceptions of law of supply. ***ISC 2010, 2007***

Ans The two exceptions of law of supply are

(i) **Agricultural products** Agricultural produce (products) such as fruits, vegetables, etc do not follow law of supply, as there supply cannot be increased infinitely when their price increases, due to lack of resources and needed time.

Also with fall in price, there supply cannot be reduced as the goods are generally perishable in nature, hence supply curve for such goods is a vertical line parallel to the Y-axis.

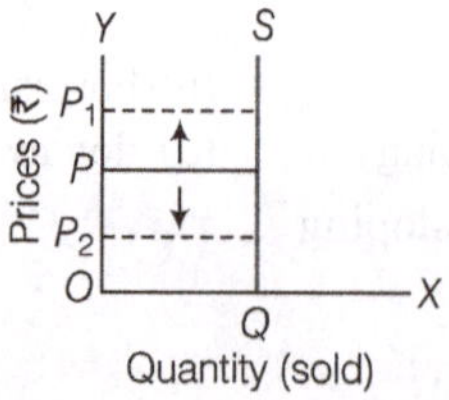

(ii) **Labour supply curve** Supply curve of labour is backward bending, indicating that less labour is supplied at a higher price (i.e. wages) and more labour is supplied at a lower price (wages). Hence, labour supply curve as well, does not follow law of supply.

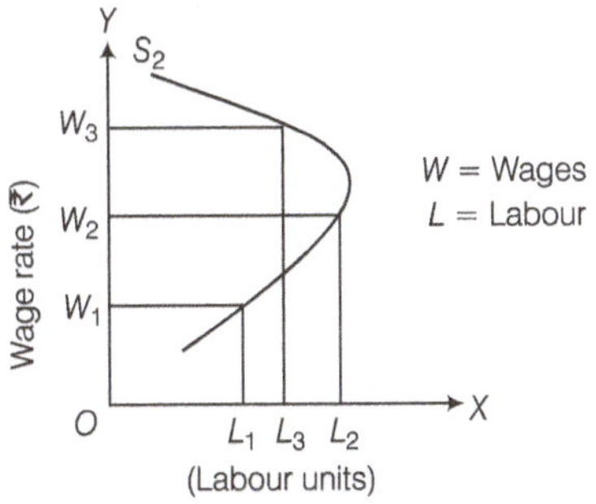

The Labour Supply Curve

Concept Enhancer Backward bending supply curve means that after a certain point of time, labour units doesn't increase with increase in wage rate.

2. Explain any two reasons for the supply curve to be positively sloped. **ISC 2020**

Or Explain any two reasons for the upward slope of the supply curve. **ISC 2016**

Ans Two reasons for the upward slope of the supply curve are

(i) **Profit motive** As price rises, supplier's profit margin also rises. This increased profit motivates a supplier to supply more with increase in price.

(ii) **Change in the number of firms** High prices generally imply a higher profit margin, as discussed above.

High margin of profit makes the particular business lucrative to new investors. As a result of this, the number of firms increases in the market, causing supply to rise simultaneously.

3. Discuss any three reasons for the leftward shift of a supply curve. **ISC 2019**

Ans Reasons for leftward shift of supply curve can be

(i) **Price of Related Goods** A rise in price of substitute goods or fall in price of complementary goods can cause decrease in supply, i.e. leftward shift in supply curve.

(ii) **Outdated Technology** Outdated technology causes lower output with the same inputs. Accordingly, producers are willing to supply less causing leftward shift in supply curve.

(iii) **Price of Inputs** A rise in prices of factors of productions causes lower profit margin, so the producer is willing to supply less thereby causing leftward shift in supply curve.

Reasons for Leftward shift of Supply Curve
- Price of Related Goods
- Outdated Technology
- Price of Inputs

4. "The supply curve of labour is an exception to the law of supply." Justify the statement, using a diagram. **ISC 2018**

Or Discuss how supply of labour is an exception to the law of supply. **ISC 2014**

Ans Law of supply does not hold true in case of labour supply. It has been observed that lesser labour is supplied when the wage rate (price of labour) is high and larger labour is supplied when wage rate is low.

A higher wage rate enables the workers to maintain his existing standard of living with less work.

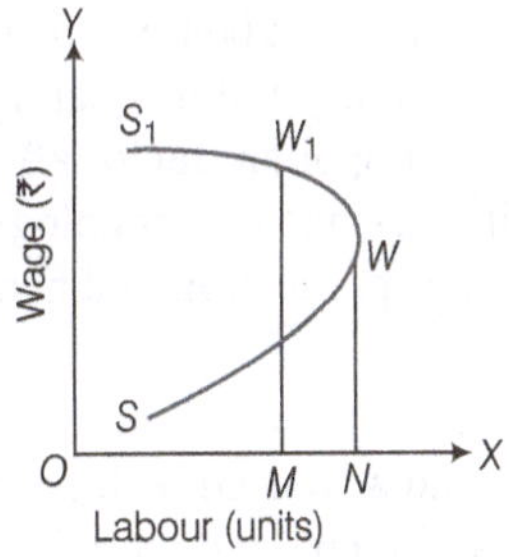

Hence, he would prefer to have more of leisure and less of work. The supply curve in such a situation becomes backward bending, as shown in the diagram. At *WN* wage rate, the supply of a labour is *ON*. But, beyond *NW* wage rate, the worker will reduce rather than increase his working hours. At MW_1, wage rate, the supply of labour is reduced to *OM*.

5. Differentiate with the help of diagrams, contraction in supply and decrease in supply. **ISC 2014**

Ans Difference between contraction in supply and decrease in supply

Basis	Contraction in supply	Decrease in supply
Meaning	When quantity supplied of a commodity contracts, keeping other things constant due to decrease in price.	When supply of a commodity falls due to change in other factors, keeping price constant.
Cause	It is caused by decrease in own price keeping all other factors constant.	It is caused by rise in the prices substitute goods, rise in input price, change in goal to profit maximisation.
Change in supply curve	Downward movement along the same supply curve shows contraction in supply.	In case of decrease in supply, supply curve shifts to the left.
Graphical representation	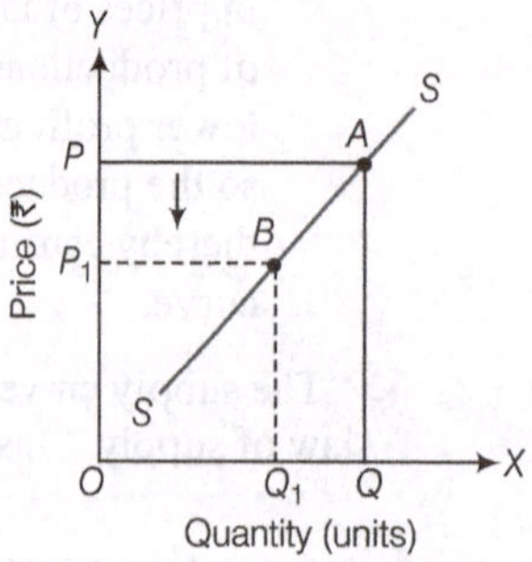	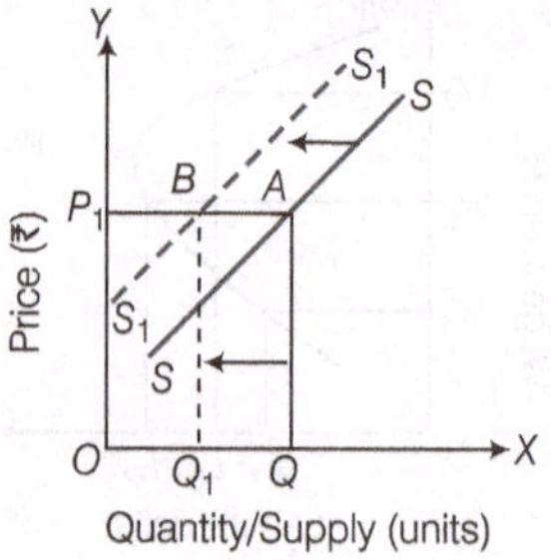

Value Points

For getting maximum marks, following value points can be included in the answer
- Add basis of differentiation.
- While using diagram, answer should be used to represent the situation.

6. State the law of supply. Discuss how change of technology affects the supply of a commodity. *ISC 2011*

Ans According to law of supply, keeping other factors constant, there is a direct/positive relationship between price of the commodity and its quantity demanded. Technology is an important factor affecting the supply of a commodity. Change in technology affects the input price/cost of production and hence, quantity supplied.

e.g. An improvement in technology, the invention of new machines and advanced techniques reduce the cost of production and increase the profit margin. Increased profitability induces the producers to produce more and it leads to increase in supply.

6 Marks Question

1. State and explain the law of supply with its assumptions. Discuss two exceptions of the law of supply. *ISC 2007*

Ans Law of supply states that keeping other factors constant, there exists a direct relationship between own price of the commodity and its quantity supplied.

According to the law, more quantity will be supplied at a higher price and less quantity at a lower price.

This can be explained using following schedule

Supply Schedule for Ice

Price (₹ per kg)	5	6	7	8	9
Supply (quintals)	20	21	22	23	24

The above schedule shows that as the price of ice is increasing from 5 to 6 and so on, the quantity supplied is also rising from 20 to 21 and so on.

Assumptions of law of supply The assumptions of law of supply are

(i) Input prices are constant.
(ii) Price of other goods are constant.
(iii) Goal of producer does not change.
(iv) Technique of production remains constant.
(v) Government policy does not change.

Exceptions of law of supply The two exceptions of law of supply are

(i) **Agricultural products** Agricultural produce (products) such as fruits, vegetables, etc do not follow law of supply, as there supply cannot be increased infinitely when their price increases, due to lack of resources and needed time. Also with fall in price, there supply cannot be reduced as the goods are generally perishable in nature, hence supply curve for such goods is a vertical line parallel to the *Y*-axis.

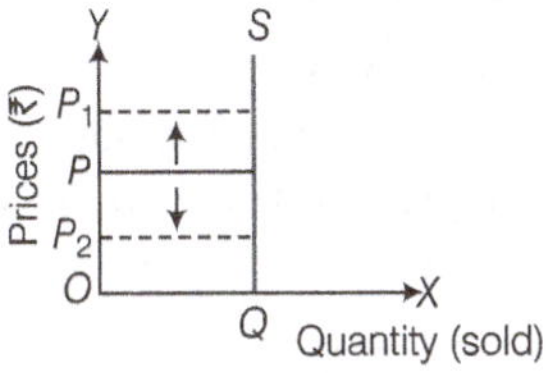

(ii) **Labour supply curve** Supply curve of labour is backward bending, indicating that less labour is supplied at a higher price (i.e. wages) and more labour is supplied at a lower price (wages). Hence, labour supply curve as well, does not follow law of supply.

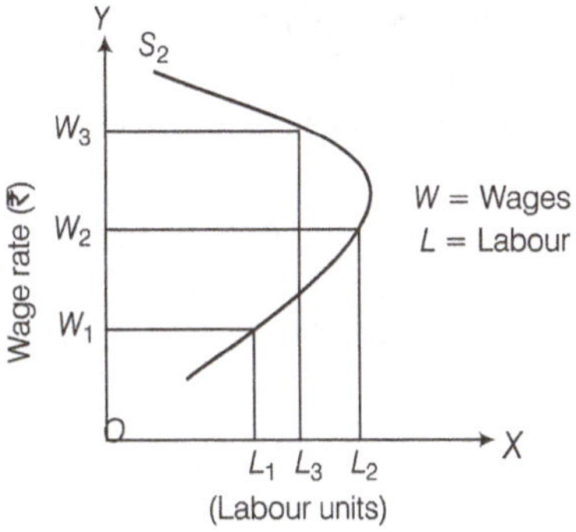

The Labour Supply Curve

TOPIC 3

Elasticity of Supply Meaning and Measurement

Price Elasticity of Supply

It measures the degree of responsiveness of the quantity supplied of a commodity to a change in its price. It measures the sensitivity of the quantity supplied to a change in price. It is calculated as

$$e_s = \frac{\text{Percentage Change in Quantity Supplied}}{\text{Percentage Change in Price}}$$

Measurement of Price Elasticity of Supply

There are two methods of measuring price elasticity of supply

(i) **Percentage change method or proportionate method** According to this method, elasticity of supply is the ratio between 'percentage change in quantity supplied' and 'percentage change in price' of the commodity.

$$e_s = \frac{\text{Percentage Change in Quantity Supplied}}{\text{Percentage Change in Price}}$$

$$or \quad \frac{\Delta Q}{\Delta P} \times \frac{P}{Q}$$

Here, e_s = Elasticity of Supply, Q = Initial Quantity
P = Initial Price
ΔQ = Change in Quantity Supplied
ΔP = Change in Price

(ii) **Geometric method** Geometrically, elasticity of supply depends on the 'origin' of the supply curve. Assuming the supply curve to be a straight line and positively sloped, we can conceive three possible situations of elasticity of supply.

$$e_s = \frac{\text{Intercept on } X\text{-axis}}{\text{Quantity at that Price}}$$

$e_s = 1$, When a straight line, positively sloped, supply curve starts from the origin 'O'.
$e_s > 1$, When a straight line positively sloped, supply curve starts from the Y-axis.
$e_s < 1$, When a straight line positively sloped, supply curve starts from the X-axis.

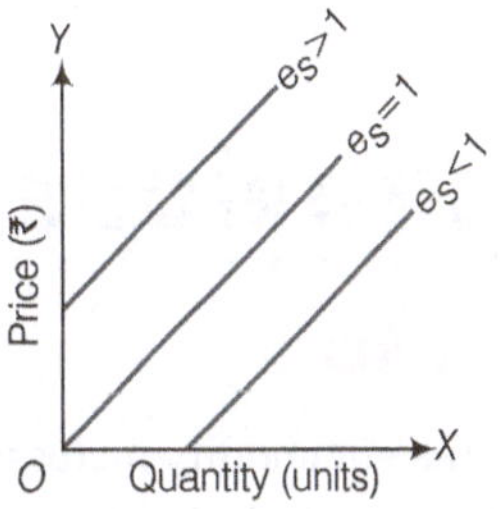

Degrees of Elasticity of Supply

There are five degrees of elasticity of supply which are as follows

1. Perfectly Inelastic Supply ($e_s = 0$)

When supply of a commodity does not change irrespective of any change in its price, it is called perfectly inelastic supply. In this condition, supply curve will be a straight line parallel to Y-axis. As in the case of agriculture products.

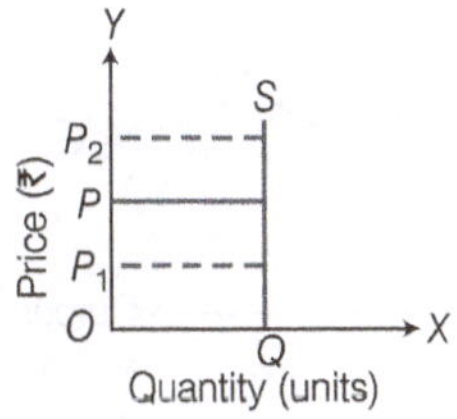

2. Perfectly Elastic Supply ($e_s = \infty$)

Supply of a commodity is said to be perfectly elastic when its supply expands or contracts to any extent at a given price.

It is assumed that supply will fall to 0 even with a slight fall in price. This is a imaginary condition. In this condition, supply curve will be a straight line parallel to *X*-axis.

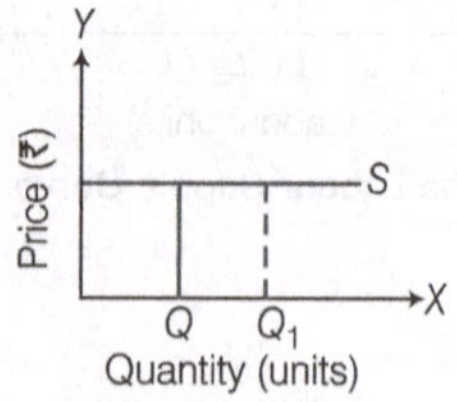

3. Unitary Elastic Supply ($e_s = 1$)

If percentage change in quantity supplied is equal to percentage change in price, it is called unitary elastic supply.

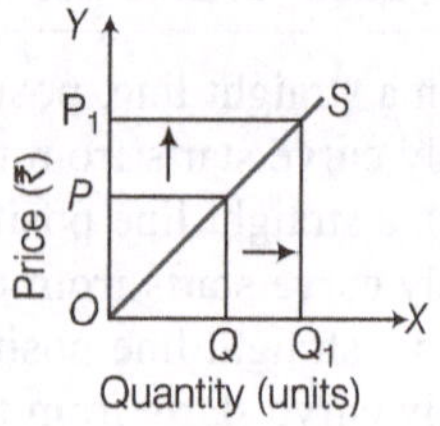

4. Inelastic or Less than Unitary Elastic Supply ($e_s < 1$)

When percentage change in quantity supplied is less than percentage change in price, it is called inelastic supply.

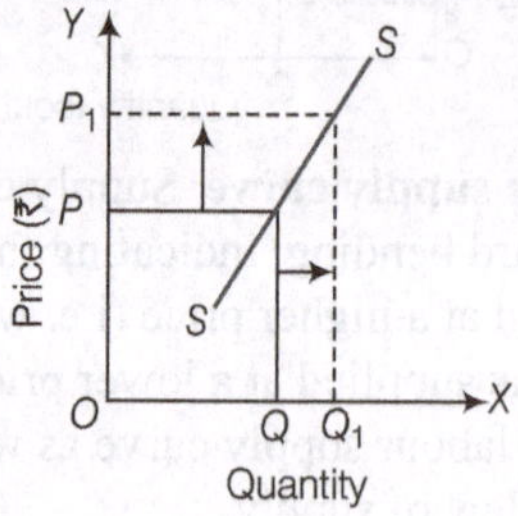

5. Elastic or More than Unitary Elastic Supply ($e_s > 1$)

When percentage change in quantity supplied is more than the percentage change in price, it is called more than unitary elastic supply.

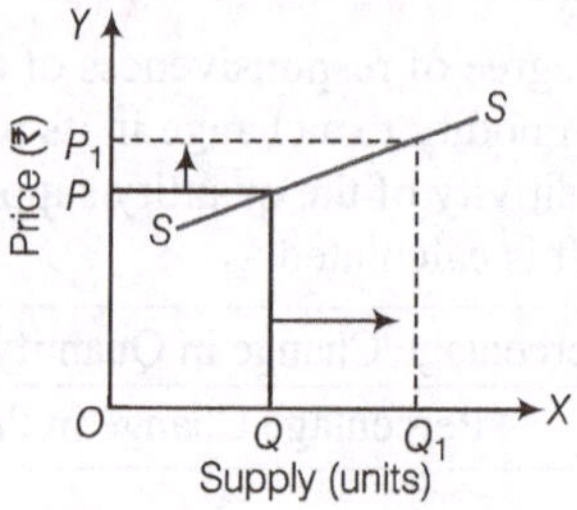

PYQs Previous Years' Questions

1 Mark Questions

1. When supply of a commodity increases by 24% following the rise in price by 8% supply curve will be ***ISC Specimen 2023***

(a) positively sloped with positive intercept
(b) positively sloped with negative intercept
(c) horizontal
(d) parallel to price axis

Ans (b) positively sloped with negative intercept

2. Based on the given diagram, choose the correct statements ***ISC Sem I 2021***

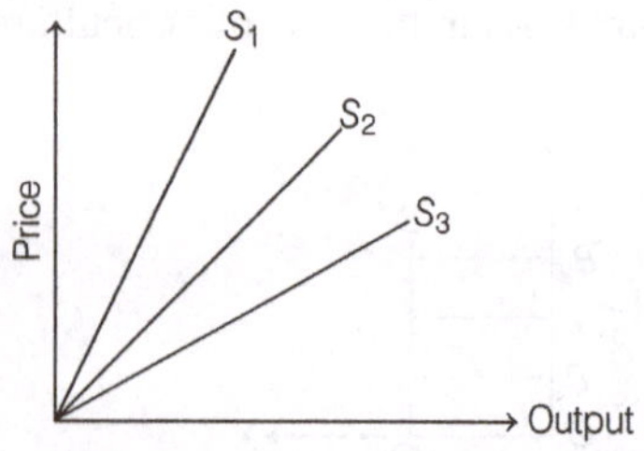

(a) S_1 is highly elastic, S_2 is unitary elastic and S_3 is highly inelastic
(b) S_1 is relatively elastic, S_2 is unitary elastic and S_3 is highly inelastic
(c) Both S_1 and S_2 are unitary elastic and S_3 is highly elastic
(d) S_1, S_2 and S_3 are unitary elastic

Ans (d) S_1, S_2 and S_3 are unitary elastic

Concept Enhancer When supply curve passes through the origin, the intercept remains same, so by geometric method, elasticity always become equal to 1.

3. Supply is elastic if ***ISC Sem I 2021***

(a) a 10% change in price causes a larger % change in quantity supplied
(b) the good in question is a normal good
(c) the slope of the supply curve is positive
(d) a 1% change in price causes a smaller % change in quantity supplied

Ans (a) a 10% change in price causes a larger % change in quantity supplied

4. The elasticity of supply is always positive because there is **ISC Sem I Specimen 2021**
(a) direct relation between supply and price
(b) inverse relation between demand and price
(c) Both (a) and (b) (d) Neither (a) nor (b)

Ans (b) inverse relation between demand and price

5.
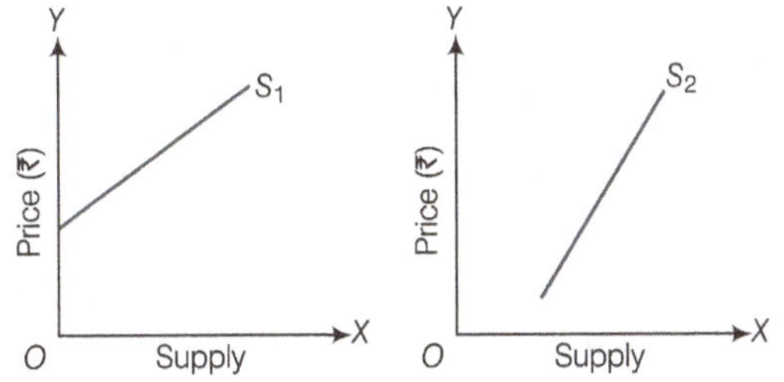

In figure **ISC Sem I Specimen 2021**
(a) S_1 supply curve indicates higher price elasticity of supply than S_2
(b) S_1 indicates relatively elastic supply and S_2 is for inelastic supply
(c) S_1 is for elastic supply and S_2 indicates relatively inelastic supply
(d) All of the above

Ans (d) All of the above

2 Marks Questions

1. The price of a mobile handset has risen in the market, but the dealers have not been able to increase the supply proportionately. What will be the price elasticity of supply for the mobile handsets? Draw the supply curve to indicate the type of elasticity. **ISC 2023**

Ans This case above indicates inelastic supply as the quantity supplied cannot be proportionately increased as much as price. In this case, supply curve will be steeper starting from *X*-axis.

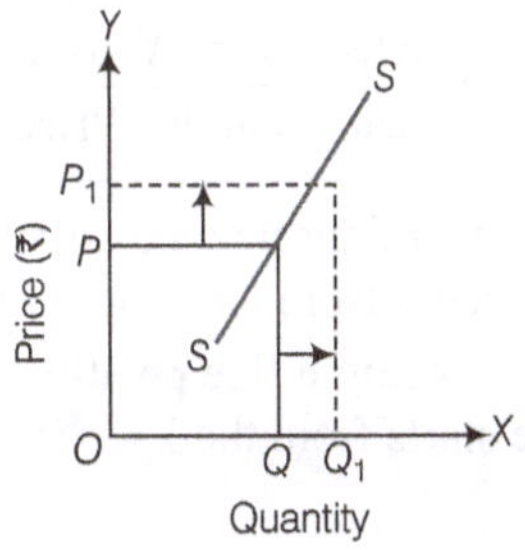

2. With the help of diagrams, show when the elasticity of supply is **ISC 2019**
(i) greater than one (ii) equal to one

Ans (i)
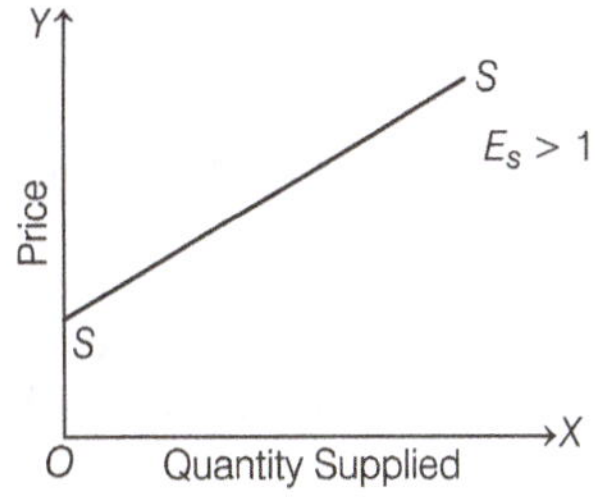

(ii)
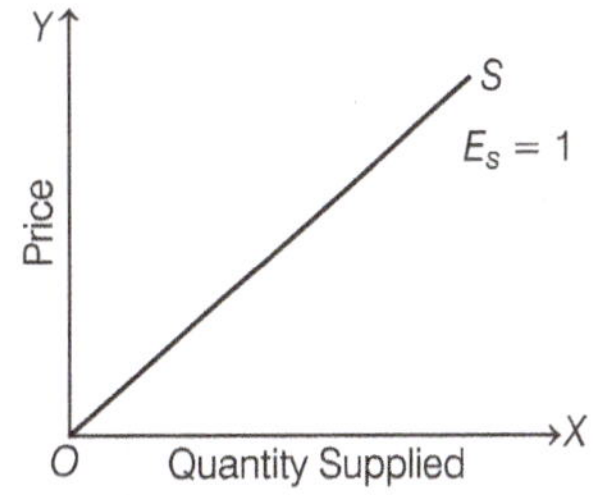

3. How is elasticity of supply different from supply of a commodity? **ISC 2017**

Ans Differences between elasticity of supply and supply of a commodity are

Basis	Elasticity of supply	Supply of a commodity
Meaning	It refers to the degree of responsiveness in quantity supplied when price of the concerned commodity changes.	It refers to the quantity of a good that the supplier is willing to sell at different prices.
Factors	Elasticity of supply is affected by the following factors Time period Nature of the commodity Nature of inputs used Technique of production Cost of production Natural factors	Supply of a commodity is affected by the following factors Price of the commodity Price of related goods Price of the factors of production State of technology Government's policy regarding indirect taxes Number of firms in the market

4. Draw the supply curve of a perishable commodity. Give a reason for the shape of supply curve. **ISC 2011**

Ans Supply curve for perishable goods is a vertical straight line and supply is completely inelastic. In case of most perishable goods (like fish, fruits, vegetables, etc), supply is perfectly fixed in the very short-run.

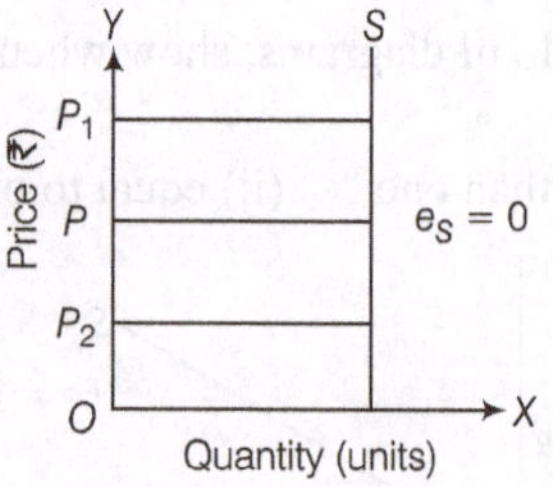

5. Draw two supply curves, the first one showing elasticity of supply greater than one and the second one showing elasticity of supply less than one. ***ISC 2010***

Ans The two supply curves showing elasticity are

(i) **Greater than one** (S_1) It is the supply curve showing elasticity greater than one.

(ii) **Lesser than one** (S_2) It is the supply curve showing elasticity lesser than one.

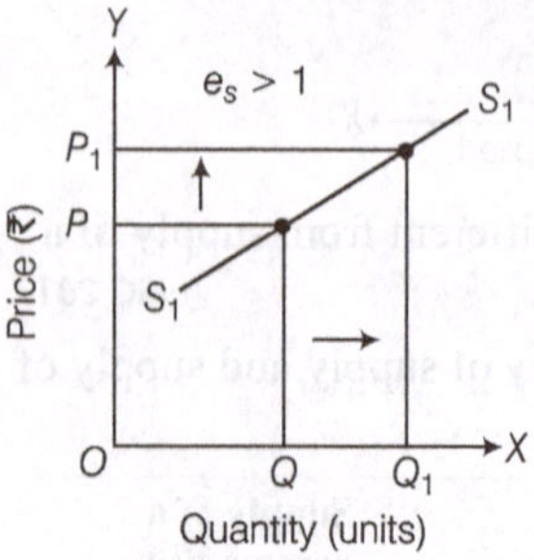

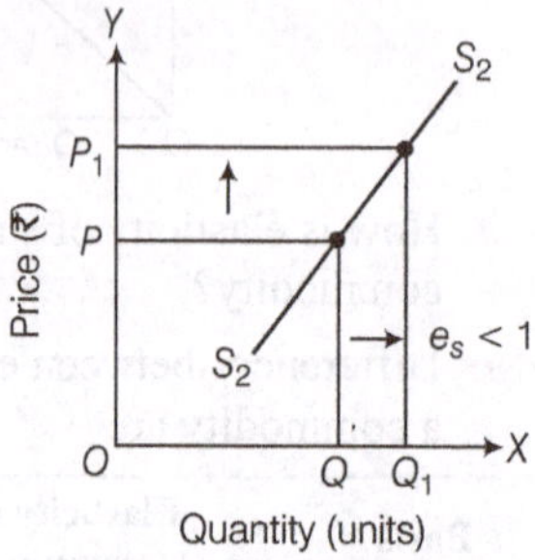

6. What is the price elasticity associated with a straight line supply curve passing through the origin? Explain with a diagram. ***ISC 2008***

KEY IDEA
When supply curve passes through the origin, intercept on X-axis and Y-axis remains the same.

Ans Elasticity of supply for any curve passing through the origin will have unitary elasticity i.e. $e_s = 1$.

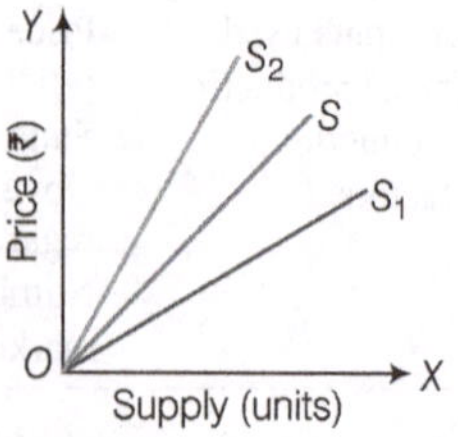

In other words, for any supply curve passing through the point of origin, percentage change in quantity supply will be equal to percentage change in price.

3/4 Marks Question

1. Define price elasticity of supply. Draw diagrams, when price elasticity of supply is

(i) Equal to one (ii) Greater than one ***ISC 2012***

Ans Price elasticity of supply measures the responsiveness of quantity supplied to change in price of the commodity.

Price Elasticity of Supply,

$$e_s = \frac{\text{Percentage Change in Quantity Supplied}}{\text{Percentage Change in Price}}$$

$$\text{or} \quad e_s = \frac{\Delta Q}{\Delta P} \times \frac{P}{Q}$$

Here, e_s = Elasticity of Supply, Q = Initial Quantity

P = Initial Price

ΔQ = Change in Quantity Supplied

P = Change in Price

For diagrams, when price elasticity of supply is equal to one and greater than one, refer to Q. No. 2 on page 57.

Common Mistake Students usually take minus sign only once in case of elasticity of supply. As supply and price changes in same direction, students should consider all minus signs.

6 Marks Questions

1. Explain the geometric method of calculating elasticity of supply. ***ISC 2020, 2015***

Ans Geometrically, elasticity of supply depends on the 'origin' of the supply curve. Assuming the supply curve to be a straight line and positively sloped, we can conceive three possible situations of elasticity of supply.

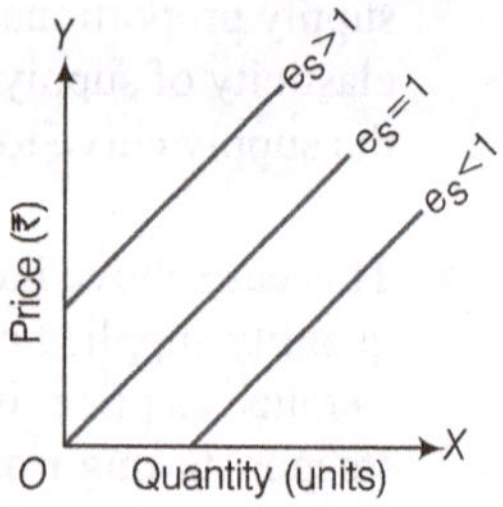

$$e_s = \frac{\text{Intercept on } X\text{-axis}}{\text{Quantity at that Price}}$$

$e_s = 1$, When a straight line, positively sloped, supply curve starts from the origin 'O'.

$e_s > 1$, When a straight line positively sloped, supply curve starts from the Y- axis.

$e_s < 1$, When a straight line positively sloped, supply curve starts from the X- axis.

Value Points

For getting maximum marks, following value points can be included in the answer

- While explaining the method, formula should be mentioned.
- Mention about all degrees of elasticity covered under this method.

2. Define price elasticity of supply. Draw a supply curve for each of the following situations

(i) When elasticity of supply is equal to zero.

(ii) When elasticity of supply is equal to infinity. ***ISC 2005***

Ans Elasticity of supply can be defined as a measure of the degree of responsiveness of quantity supplied to changes in the commodity's own price.

Price Elasticity of Supply,

$$e_s = \frac{\text{Percentage Change in Quantity Supplied}}{\text{Percentage Change in Price}}$$

$$= \frac{\frac{\Delta Q}{Q} \times 100}{\frac{\Delta P}{\Delta P} \times 100} = \frac{\Delta Q}{Q} \times \frac{P}{\Delta P} \ or \ \frac{\Delta Q}{\Delta P} \times \frac{P}{Q}$$

Where, e_s = Elasticity of Supply

P = Original Price

ΔP = Change in Price, Q = Original Quantity

ΔQ = Change in Quantity Demanded

(i) **Elasticity of supply is equal to zero**

($e_s = 0$) Elasticity of supply is said to be zero, when despite the change in price, quantity supplied does not change at all. Generally, in case of perishable goods or rare articles, supply behave in this manner. In this case, supply curve will be vertical parallel to Y-axis.

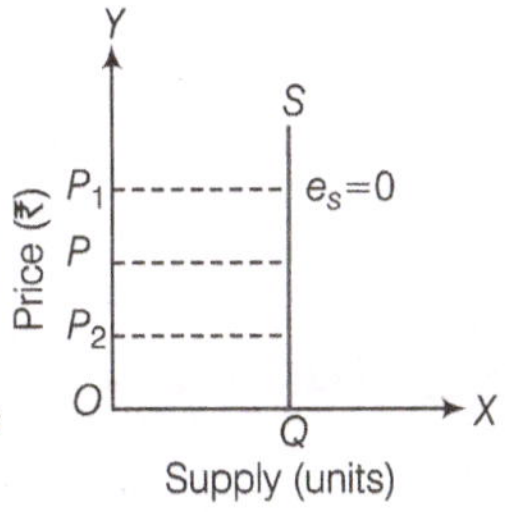

(ii) **Elasticity of supply is equal to infinity**

($e_s = \infty$) Elasticity of supply is said to be equal to infinity (or perfectly elastic), when quantity supplied changes infinitely, despite of no change in price or very small change in price. In such cases, supply curve will be horizontal parallel to X- axis. This is an imaginary condition.

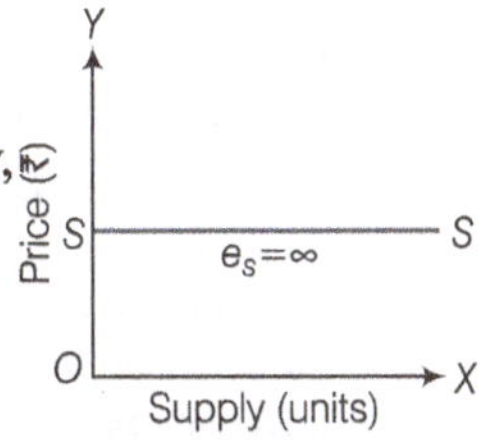

Common Mistake Students sometimes write the formula of elasticity incorrectly. Formula should be written keeping in mind alphabetical order of P followed by Q and then diagonal for ΔQ followed by ΔP. e.g. $\frac{P}{Q} \times \frac{\Delta Q}{\Delta P}$

Case Based Question

Case 1

During Covid pandemic, vegetables market price of essential vegetables like onion, tomatoes, potatoes, carrots were on a rise due to supply disruption. Items were stuck at store and not movable due to the lack of transportation and labour to lift stocks from wholesale markets, leading to disruptions in the movement of stocks from production centers to the retail level. Even prices of certain commodities like edible oils have been impacted because of a slowdown in production due to factory closures and labour shortage.

(i) Why does vegetable price increase during the pandemic?

Ans Due to the shortage of supply

(ii) What will be the impact on the supply curve of the above situation?

Ans In the above case, supply curve will shift to the left.

(iii) Briefly explain how the price of vegetables impacted by the interrupted supply?

Ans Following points highlight the impact

(a) Prices increased in India as supply of perishable goods falls because of disrupted transportation.

(b) Price of edible oil increased due to slowdown in production.

(c) World food price falls as demand falls due to economic recession. Purchasing power was low as people lost their job globally. Thus, low demand caused fall in oil prices.

(iv) How is wholesale price impacted by number of sellers in the market?

Ans Wholesale price of a commodity depends upon the number of sellers in the market. An increase in the number of seller, decreases the market price and *vice-versa*.

CHAPTER TEST

01 Mark Questions

1. The supply of a good refers to
(a) actual production of the good
(b) total existing stock of the good
(c) stock available for sale
(d) amount of the good offered for sale at a particular price per unit of time

2. Price elasticity of supply refers to the degree of responsiveness of supply of a good to changes in its
(a) demand (b) price
(c) cost of production (d) state of technology

3. Contraction of supply is the result of
(a) decrease in the number of producers
(b) decrease in the price of the goods concern
(c) increase in the prices of other goods
(d) decrease in the outlay of sellers

4. Supply is more elastic in case of
(a) very short period (b) short period
(c) long period (d) Both (b) and (c)

5. Slope of supply curve and elasticity of supply are inversely proportional. State true or false.

6. Change in the goal of producer from profit maximisation to sales maximisation leads to decrease in supply. State true or false.

7. Advancement in the technology of production leads to .... in supply curve.

8. .... refers to the specific quantities offered at a specific price.

9. As per geometric method of elasticity of supply, what will be the price elasticity of supply at a point below the mid-point of a linear supply curve?

10. How is the slope of supply curve calculated?

02 Marks Questions

11. According to the law of supply, in which direction supply of a commodity will move, when there is a change in price of the commodity? (Use diagram)

12. In which situation does the supply of a commodity fall at the same price?

13. A farmer grows wheat and rice, how will the supply curve of rice affected, if there is an increase in the price of wheat?

14. How does an increase in the number of firms affects the market supply of the commodity?

03/04 Marks Questions

15. The coefficient of elasticity of supply of a commodity is 0.4. What percentage change in supply will take place, if its price rises by 20%?

16. If nothing is supplied even at a marginally reduced price, what will be the elasticity of supply? Give reason.

17. Distinguish between individual supply curve and market supply curve.

18. Giving reason, state whether the following statement is true or false
"The supply curve of a good shift to the right when price of other goods rise."

06 Marks Questions

19. The price elasticity of supply of commodity Y is half the price elasticity of supply of commodity X. 16% rise in the price X result in a 40% rise in its supply. If the price of Y falls by 8%, calculate the percentage fall in its supply.

20. Examine the effect of
(i) rise in tax rate on good X, on the supply curve
(ii) fall in own price of good X use diagrams.

Answers

1. (d) amount of the good offered for sale at a particular price per unit of time
2. (b) price
3. (b) decrease in the price of the goods concern
4. (c) long period
5. True *6.* False
7. rightward shift *8.* Quantity supplied

04

Concept of Production

TREND ANALYSIS 5 YEARS

Average No. of Questions Across all Sets

	Types of Questions	2023	2020	2019	2018	2017
01 Production Function	1 Mark	1	—	—	—	—
	2 Marks	—	1	—	—	1
	3/4 Marks	1	—	1	—	1
	6 Marks	—	—	—	—	—
02 Law of Variable Proportion	1 Mark	—	—	—	—	—
	2 Marks	—	—	1	—	—
	3/4 Marks	—	—	—	—	1
	6 Marks	—	1	—	1	—

TOPIC 1

Production Function : Short-run and Long-run, Other Concepts of Production

Production

A producer or a firm acquires different inputs like labour, machines, land and raw materials, etc. After combining these inputs, we get an output. This is called the process of production.

Production is a process of value addition. In other words, production is defined as the transformation of input into output. In economics, production is defined as creation of utility for the consumers.

Production Function

Production function of a firm is a functional relationship between inputs used and output produced by the firm. It expresses the maximum quantity of output that can be produced with any given quantities of inputs.

A production function is defined for a given technology. It explains the functional relationship between factors of production (inputs) and physical output. Mathematically,

$$Q_X = f(f_1, f_2, f_3, \ldots\ldots\ldots\ldots f_n)$$

Here, Q_X = Production of Commodity X

$f(f_1, f_2 \ldots f_n)$ = Quantities of Different Inputs used to Produce the Commodity X

Short-run

It is the time period in which some factors of production cannot be changed (i.e. plant, machine, building, etc), hence, they are taken as fixed factors.

Therefore, production of commodity can be increased by increasing the use of only variable inputs like labour, raw material etc.

Long-run

It is the time period in which all the factors of production are variable, hence there is no fixed factor in long-run. Therefore, production of commodity can be increased by employing more of both variable and fixed inputs.

Types of Production Function

Production function is a tool of analysis used to explain the input-output relationship. Production functions are of two types

1. Short-run Production Function

It refers to the functional relation between input and output in which one factor of production is taken as fixed (i.e. capital) and other as variable (i.e. labour).

Mathematically, $Q_X = f(L, \bar{K})$

Here, Q_X = Production of a Commodity X, f = Function of, L = Labour, $\bar{K}$ = Capital, which is fixed

Returns to a factor The law relating to short-run production function is termed as the law of returns to factors or the law of variable proportions as given by the classical economist Professor Alfred Marshall.

There are three stages of operation of this law

(i) Increasing returns to factor
(ii) Diminishing returns to factor
(iii) Negative returns to factor

2. Long-run Production Function

It refers to the functional relation between input and output in which both the factors of production are variable.

Mathematically, $Q_X = f(L, K)$

Here, Q_X = Production of a Commodity X, f = Function of, L = Labour, K = Capital, which is variable

Returns to scale In the long-run, all factors of production are variable, no factor is fixed. Accordingly, the scale of production can be changed by changing the quantity of all factors of production.

According to **Koutsoyiannis**, "The term returns to scale refers to the changes in output as all factors change by the same proportion."

Returns to scale are of following types

(i) **Increasing returns to scale** Increasing returns to scale or diminishing cost refers to a situation where if all factors of production are increased, output increases at a higher rate.

(ii) **Diminishing returns to scale** Diminishing returns to scale or increasing cost refers to a situation where if all factors of production are increased, output increases at a lower proportion.

(iii) **Constant returns to scale** Constant returns to scale or constant cost refers to a situation in which output increases in the same proportion in which factors of production are increased.

Concepts Related to Production

There are mainly three concepts related to the process of production

1. Total Product (TP) or Total Physical Product (TPP)

It is the sum total of output produced by all units of labour alongwith other factors of production. It is also referred to as total physical product of the variable input.

$$TP = AP \times L \text{ or } \Sigma MP$$

Here, TP = Total Product; AP = Average Product
L = Units of Variable Factor

ΣMP signifies sum total of marginal product corresponding to all the units of a variable factor used.

2. Average Product (AP) or Average Physical Product (APP)

It is per unit production of the variable factor. It is obtained by dividing the total product by the number of units of variable input. The average product curve is hump shape or inverted 'U' shape.

$$AP = TP \div L$$

Here, AP = Average Product, TP = Total Product
L = Units of Variable Factor

3. Marginal Product (MP) or Marginal Physical Product (MPP)

It is the change in total product as a result of a unit change in the input of a variable factor. Marginal product is an addition made to the total product by employing an additional unit of variable input, keeping the other inputs unchanged.

$$MP_{nth} = TP_n - TP_{n-1} \text{ or } \Delta TP/\Delta L$$

Here, MP = Marginal Product
TP_n = Total Product at 'n' units
$TP_{(n-1)}$ = Total Product at $(n-1)$ units
Δ = Change, TP = Total Product
L = Units of Variable Factor

The marginal product thus, measures the, rate at which total product is changing as one factor varies. Labour is a variable factor, we consider symbol (L) for labour which is taken as a variable factor.

PYQs Previous Years' Questions

1 Mark Questions

1. When the marginal product turns negative, total product will *ISC 2023*

(a) fall (b) rise
(c) remain constant (d) be zero

Ans (a) fall

2. Which of the following equation is correct? *ISC Sem I 2021*

(a) $MP = TP_n - TP_{n-1}$ (b) $MP = \frac{AP}{L}$
(c) $MP = \frac{TP}{L}$ (d) $MP = TP - AP$

Ans (a) $MP = TP_n - TP_{n-1}$

3. If some inputs are variable and some inputs are fixed, then the functional relation is a case of *ISC Sem I 2021*

(a) short-run production function
(b) long-run production function
(c) law of variable proportions
(d) diminishing marginal utility

Ans (a) short-run production function

Concept Enhancer Functional relation indicates mathematical relationship between inputs and output.

4. When 50 hours of labour are spent, total output produced is 2,000 units and when 55 hours of labour are spent, total output produced is 2,250 units. In this case MP is *ISC Sem I 2021*

(a) 500 (b) 40
(c) 45 (d) 50

Ans (d) $MP = \frac{\Delta TP}{\Delta L} = \frac{2{,}250 - 2{,}000}{55 - 50} = \frac{250}{5} = 50$

5. Long-run production function studies the change in output when *ISC Sem I 2021*

(a) one input is variable (b) one input is fixed
(c) all inputs are variable (d) all inputs are fixed

Ans (c) all inputs are variable

6. How will you calculate the total product? *ISC Sem I Specimen 2021*

(a) Σ AP (b) Σ TP
(c) Σ MP (d) Any of these

Ans (c) Σ MP

7. The short-run refers to the period of time when output can be increased by increasing ...... while keeping ...... constant. *ISC Sem I Specimen 2021*

(a) capital, land
(b) labour, capital
(c) labour, land
(d) land, entrepreneur

Ans (b) labour, capital

2 Marks Questions

1. What is production function? *ISC 2020*

Or

Define production function. *ISC 2015*

Or

What is meant by production function? *ISC 2012 (M)*

Ans Production function explains the functional relationship between inputs of production (labour and capital) and output generated with a given state of technology. Production function is of two types

(i) Short-run production function, where
$Q_X = f(L, \bar{K})$

(ii) Long-run production function, where
$Q_X = f(L, K)$

Here, Q_X = Production of a Commodity X
L = Labour
$\bar{K}$ = Capital, which is fixed
K = Capital, which is variable

Concept Enhancer Production function doesn't exist in the very short-run (market period), as all factors are fixed.

2. What is short-run production function? Explain how is short-run production function different from long-run production function. *ISC 2017*

Ans Short-run production function refers to the functional relation between input and output in which one factor of production is taken as fixed (i.e. capital) and other as variable (i.e. labour). Mathematically,

$$Q_X = f(L, \bar{K})$$

Here, Q_X = Production of a Commodity X
f = Function of, L = Labour
$\bar{K}$ = Capital, which is fixed

Differences between short-run and long-run production function are

Basis	Short-run production function	Long-run production function
Meaning	It refers to the relationship between input and output in a situation, where one factor is fixed and other is variable.	It refers to the relationship between input and output in a situation, where all factors of production are variable.
Mathematical equation	$Q_X = f(L, \bar{K})$	$Q_X = f(L, K)$

3. What is meant by actual earning of a factor? **ISC 2010**

Ans The monetary payment or money income received by factors of production for providing their factor services is known as actual earnings of the factors.

4. Define average product. How can you get average product from total product? **ISC 2009**

> **KEY IDEA**
> AP indicates that on an average, how much a variable factor is producing.

Ans Average Product (AP) is defined as output (total product) per unit of variable factor (labour). It is obtained by dividing the total product by the number of units of variable inputs. It is calculated as

$$\text{Average Product (AP)} = \frac{\text{Total Product (TP)}}{\text{Units of Variable Factor (Labour)}}$$

5. What is meant by Marginal Physical Product (MPP)? **ISC 2007**

Ans Marginal Physical Product (MPP) or Marginal Product (MP) means the change in Total Physical Product (ΔTP) due to employment of an additional unit of Variable Factor (ΔL).

It is calculate as, $$\text{MP} = \frac{\Delta \text{TP}}{\Delta L}$$

or $$\text{MP}_n = \text{TP}_n - \text{TP}_{(n-1)}$$

6. What are the two types of production function? **ISC 2007**

Ans Two types of production functions are as follows

(i) Short-run production function where, $Q_X = f(L, \bar{K})$. It refers to relationship between input and output in a situation, where one factor is fixed and other is variable.

(ii) Long-run production function where, $Q_X = f(L, K)$. It refers to the relationship between input and output in a situation, where all factors of production are variable.

7. What is meant by short-run and long-run in production? **ISC 2006**

Ans **Short-run** It is the time period in which some factors of production are fixed and some are variable. Production can be changed only by changing variable factors.

Long-run It is the time period in which all the factors of production are variable, there is no fixed factor in long-run. Production can be changed by changing any factor of production.

3/4 Marks Questions

1. Give any two difference between returns to a factor and returns to scale. **ISC 2023**

Or Discuss two differences between returns to scale and returns to a variable factor. **ISC 2019**

Ans Difference between return to scale and return to variable factor are

Basis	Returns to scale	Returns to variable factor
Factors	It studies behaviour of output when all factors are variable.	It studies behaviour of output when more and more unit of variable is combined with fixed factor.
Time period	It is a long-run concept.	It is a short-run concept.

2. Fill the blanks in the table given below **ISC 2017**

Number of Workers	Total Product	Average Product	Marginal Product
1	…	150	…
2	230	…	…
3	…	…	120

Ans

Number of Workers	Total Product (TP)	Average Product (AP)	Marginal Product (MP)
1	**150**	150	**150**
2	230	**115**	80
3	**350**	**116.67**	120

$$\text{TP} = \text{AP} \times L = 150 \times 1 = 150$$

$$\text{MP} = \text{TP}_n - \text{TP}_{n-1};\ \text{MP} = \text{TP}_n - \text{TP}_{n-1} = 150 - 0 = 150$$

$$120 = \text{TP}_n - 230;\ \text{AP} = \frac{\text{TP}}{L} = \frac{230}{2} = 115,\ \text{TP}_n = 350$$

$$\text{MP} = \text{TP}_n - \text{TP}_{n-1} = 230 - 150 = 80$$

$$\text{AP} = \frac{\text{TP}}{L} = \frac{350}{3} = 116.67$$

*L = Labour or Number of Workers

> **Common Mistake** Students generally write TP and MP equal at 0 and 1 unit of labour. It should be remembered that when no factor is employed MP is not defined. It is equal only at the first level of output.

3. Differentiate between fixed factor of production and variable factor of production. **ISC 2016**

Or Distinguish between fixed factor and variable factor. **ISC 2007**

Ans Difference between fixed factor of production and variable factor of production

Basis	Fixed factor of production	Variable factor of production
Meaning	These factors of production do not change with the change in the level of output.	These factors of production change with the change in the level of output.
Relate to	Fixed factors of production relate to short-run.	Variable factors of production relate to short-run, as well as, long-run.
Examples	Land and machines	Material and labour

4. Differentiate between short-run production function and long-run production function. **ISC 2010 (M)**

Ans Difference between short-run and long-run production function are

Basis	Short-run production function	Long-run production function
Meaning	It refers to the relationship between input and output in a situation, where one factor is fixed and other is variable.	It refers to the relationship between input and output in a situation, where all factors of production are variable.
Mathematical equation	$Q_X = f(L, \overline{K})$	$Q_X = f(L, K)$
Law in operation	Returns to factors	Returns to scale
Stages	Increasing, diminishing, negative	Increasing, constant, diminishing

TOPIC 2

Law of Variable Proportioin (Returns to Factors)

This Law is only applicable in short-run with a combination of fixed and variable factors. In terms of marginal physical product, this law states that as more and more units of variable factors are employed (alongwith fixed factors), then marginal product initially rises, reaches its maximum point, then starts to fall and eventually becomes negative.

In terms of total physical product, according to this law, as more and more units of variable factors are employed (alongwith fixed factors), then total product initially rises at an increasing rate, then at a diminishing rate reaches its maximum and become constant and finally diminishes.

Assumptions of Law of Variable Proportion

Assumptions followed in the law of variable proportion are

(i) State of technology is given and it will remain constant.

(ii) This law is applied to short-run.

(iii) Input price remain unchanged.

(iv) All the units of variable factor are homogeneous and are equally efficient.

(v) It is assumed that labour is a single variable factor.

(vi) It is possible to change the proportion in which the factor units are combined.

Stages of Law of Variable Proportion

Generally, there are three stages of law of variable proportion

***Stage* I Stage of increasing returns** It is between *O* to *a* on the curve TP. In this zone, MP is increasing and TP is increasing at an increasing rate.

In this stage, increasing returns to a variable factor are obtained because greater use of the variable factors makes it possible to utilise the fixed indivisible factors fully and to introduce a greater degree of division of labour. In this stage, efficiency of the labour also increases due to increased competition and leads to optimum utilisation of resources at the initial stages.

***Stage* II Stage of diminishing returns** It is between *a* to *b*. In this zone, MP is decreasing but remains positive and TP is increasing at a decreasing rate.

In this stage, total product increases at decreasing rate. It means marginal product starts decreasing but remains positive. In this stage, diminishing returns to a factor is obtained because the proportion between the variable factor such as labour has less fixed factors to work on.

a is the point of inflexion, where TP stops increasing at an increasing rate and instead, starts increasing at a decreasing rate. A rational producer would like to operate in this stage.

***Stage* III Stage of negative returns** It is beyond point *b*. Now, TP starts declining because MP is negative. In this stage, the variable factors become too much relative to fixed factor, disturbing the production process due to which there is a fall in total product.

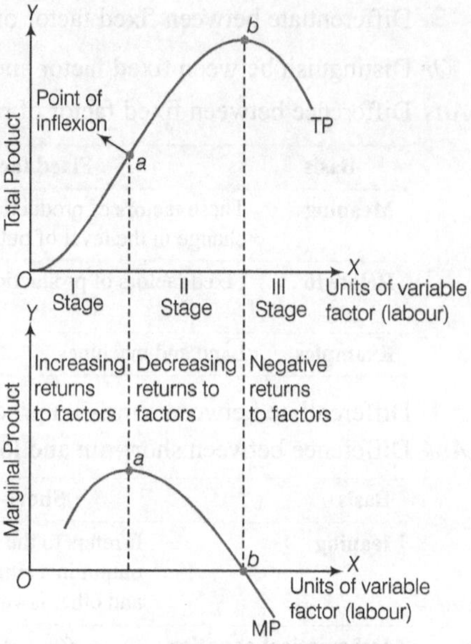

Law of Variable Proportion

Point of Inflexion

It is a point from where slope of TP curve changes, upto this point. TP has been increasing at the increasing rate. From this point onwards TP increases, but only at the diminishing rate.

Schedule of the Law of Variable Proportion

This law may be explained with the help of following schedule (based on hypothetical data)

Capital (Fixed)	Labour (Variable)	Total Product (TP)	Average Product (AP)	Marginal Product (MP)	Remark
1	0	0	–	–	
1	1	2	2	2	Increasing returns to factors
1	2	6	3	4	
1	3	12	4	6	
1	4	16	4	4	Decreasing returns to factors
1	5	18	3.6	2	
1	6	18	3	0	
1	7	14	2	(–) 4	Negative returns to factors
1	8	8	1	(–) 6	

Causes of Increasing Returns to a Factor

Increasing returns to a factor occur because of the following factors

(i) **Fuller utilisation of the fixed factor** In the initial stages, fixed factor remains underutilised. Its fuller utilisation is possible by adding additional units of the variable factor to total input and the marginal product of the variable factor tends to increase.

(ii) **Increased efficiency of the variable factor** Additional application of the variable factor causes process based division of labour that raises efficiency of the factor. Accordingly, marginal productivity of the factor tends to rise. It also results due to increase in competition.

(iii) **Better coordination between the factors** So long as fixed factor remains underutilised, additional application of the variable factor tends to improve the coordination. As a result, total output increases at the increasing rate.

Causes of Diminishing Returns to a Factor

Diminishing returns to a factor or the law of diminishing returns may be explained in terms of the following factors

(i) **Fixity of the factor** It is the principal cause behind the law of diminishing returns. As more and more units of the variable factors are combined with the fixed factor, the latter gets excessively utilised.

(ii) **Imperfect factor substitutability** Factors of production are imperfect substitutes of each other. e.g. More and more of labour cannot be continuously used in place of additional capital. Accordingly, diminishing returns to the variable factor becomes inevitable.

(iii) **Poor coordination between the factors** Continuously increasing application of the variable factor on the fixed factors beyond a point crosses the limit of ideal factor ratio. This results in poor coordination between the fixed and variable factors.

Causes of Negative Returns to a Factor

Negative returns to a factor occur due to following factors

(i) **Limitation of fixed factor** The fixed factor can be optimally used only upto a certain level.

(ii) **Decrease in efficiency of variable factor** As the variable factor is increased, the efficiency of it, tends to fall.

(iii) **Poor coordination between the fixed and the variable factors** As the variable factor is increased, it leads to a lack of coordination between the fixed and the variable factors leading to a fall in total product.

Postponement of the Law of Variable Proportion

Postponement of law of variable proportions is possible under two conditions given below

(i) When there is improvement in technology used in the process of production, so that greater output is achieved with the same inputs.

(ii) When some substitute of the fixed factor is discovered so that the constraint of fixity of the factor is removed.

Relationship between Average Product (AP) and Marginal Product (MP)

Relationship between AP and MP is stated below

(i) When average product is rising, marginal product is above average product i.e. MP >AP.

(ii) When average product is falling, marginal product is below average product i.e MP<AP.

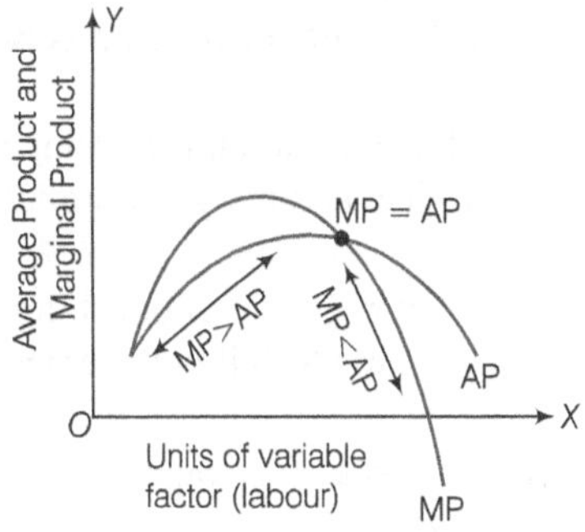

(iii) When average product reaches its maximum point, marginal product is equal to average product i.e. MP = AP.

(iv) Marginal product can become zero or negative, but average product cannot become zero or negative.

Relationship between Total Product (TP) and Marginal Product (MP)

Relationship between TP and MP is stated below

(i) When marginal product increases, total product increases at an increasing rate.

(ii) When marginal product decreases but positive, total product increases at a diminishing rate.

(iii) When marginal product becomes zero, total product reaches its maximum point and becomes constant.

(iv) When marginal product becomes negative, total product starts to fall.

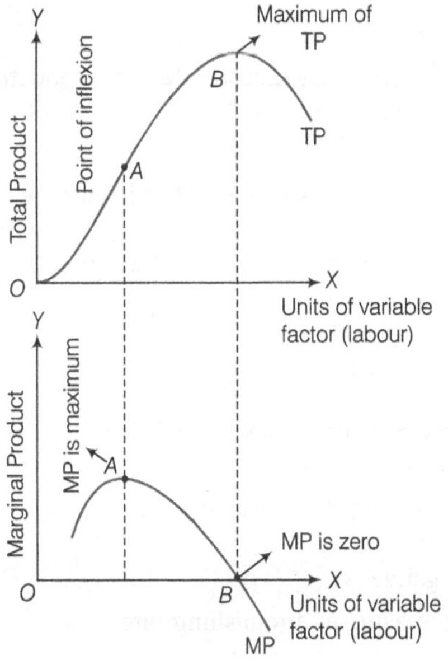

Relationship between Total Product (TP), Average Product (AP) and Marginal Product (MP)

Following points highlight the relationship between TP, AP and MP

(i) When total product rises at an increasing rate, both average product and marginal product rises.

(ii) When total product rises at a diminishing rate, marginal product starts to fall but average product still rises.

(iii) At the maximum point of average product, marginal product is equal to it.

(iv) Till the time total product rises at a diminishing rate, marginal product remains positive, though average product falls continuously after reaching its maximum point.

(v) When total product reaches its maximum point, average product falls and marginal product becomes zero.

(vi) When total product starts falling, marginal product becomes negative, average product falls but remains positive.

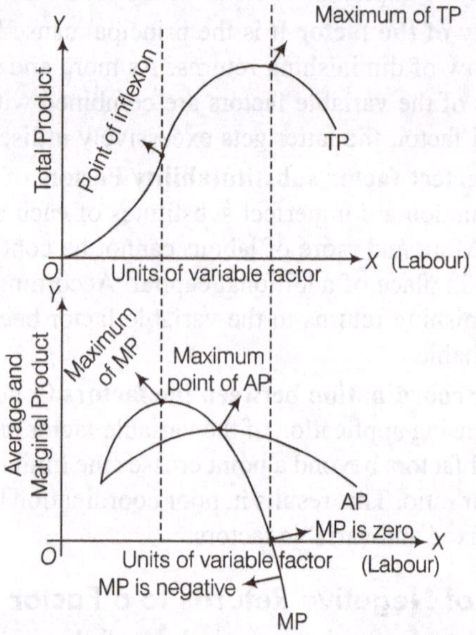

PYQs Previous Years' Questions

1 Mark Questions

1. A rational producer will operate in …… stage of law of variable proportions. **ISC Sem I 2021**

(a) Stage I (b) Stage II
(c) Stage III (d) Stage IV

Ans (b) Stage II

Concept Enhancer Second stage of production is also known as 'economic stage of production'.

2. If MP of labour is below AP of labour the **ISC Sem I 2021**

(a) MP is negative (b) MP = 0
(c) AP is falling
(d) AP is negative

Ans (c) AP is falling

3. When AP reaches maximum, TP is **ISC Sem I 2021**

(a) also maximum
(b) increasing at diminishing rate
(c) zero
(d) negative

Ans (b) increasing at diminishing rate

4. One of the reasons for negative returns to factor is **ISC Sem I 2021**

(a) imperfect substitutability
(b) overcrowding and management problems
(c) disturbance in optimum proportion
(d) indivisibility of factors

Ans (d) indivisibility of factors

5. The shape of MP curve is .... shape. **ISC Sem I 2021**

(a) U (b) inverse U
(c) inverse S
(d) S

Ans (b) inverse U

6. In the stage of diminishing returns of a variable factor **ISC Sem I 2021**

(a) TP is increasing, AP is increasing, MP is also increasing
(b) TP is constant, AP is decreasing, MP is also increasing
(c) TP is increasing, AP declines, MP is declining to become zero
(d) TP is decreasing, AP is decreasing, MP is negative

Ans (c) TP is increasing, AP declines, MP is declining to become zero

7. The law of variable proportion states *ISC Sem I 2021*

When variable factor is added to fixed factor, the total product increases at increasing rate and finally total product ....

(a) rises (b) falls
(c) remains the same (d) rises at diminishing rate

Ans (b) falls

8. In the case of the above law, diminishing returns to a factor occurs when, ... *ISC Sem I 2021*

(a) units of variable inputs are added to a fixed factor anti AP and MP fall
(b) units of variable inputs are added to fixed factor, AP increases
(c) size of the plant increases in the long run, and MP is constant
(d) quantity of the fixed factor increases and returns to variable input falls

Ans (a) units of variable inputs are added to a fixed factor anti AP and MP fall

9. Which of the given options shows the application of increasing returns? *ISC Sem I Specimen 2021*

(a) Specialisation (b) Efficiency of factors
(c) Indivisibility of factors (d) All of these

Ans (d) All of these

10. What is the basic reason for operation of the law of diminishing return? *ISC Sem I Specimen 2021*

(a) Scarcity of factors
(b) Imperfect substitution between factors
(c) Both (a) and (b)
(d) None of the above

Ans (c) Both (a) and (b)

11. Returns to a factor means *ISC Sem I Specimen 2021*

(a) quantity of only one factor is changed
(b) quantity of all factor inputs is changed
(c) fixed factors are changed but variable factors are kept constant
(d) fixed and variable both factors are changed in equal proportion

Ans (a) quantity of only one factor is changed

2 Marks Questions

1. Briefly explain why the producer is comfortable in the second stage of production. *ISC Specimen 2023*

Ans Second stage of production indicates diminishing returns to factor i.e. MP falls but remains positive and TP increases at a diminishing rate.

A rational producer will not produce beyond this stage, as at the end of second stage, MP becomes zero and then becomes negative.

2. With the help of a diagram, state the behaviour of MP when

(i) TP of the variable factor reaches maximum.
(ii) TP of the variable factor falls. *ISC 2019*

Ans (i) When TP of variable factor reaches maximum, MP is 0.

(ii) When TP of variable factor falls, MP is negative.

For figure, refer to text on page 66.

3. Give two assumptions of law of variable proportion. *ISC 2013*

Ans Two assumptions of law of variable proportion are

(i) State of technology is given and it remains constant.
(ii) It is assumed that all units of variable factor are homogeneous and are equally efficient.

4. What is meant by increasing returns to a variable factor? *ISC 2011*

Ans Increasing returns to a variable factor refers to the situation in which every additional unit of variable factor adds more than the previous one into the output i.e. when marginal product increases and hence total product increases at an increasing rate.

3/4 Marks Questions

1. Explain two causes of increasing returns to a factor. *ISC 2017*

Ans Two causes of increasing returns to a factor are explained below

(i) **Fuller utilisation of the fixed factor**
In the initial stages, fixed factor remains underutilised. Its fuller utilisation is ensured by increasing the units of the variable factor (labour) and the marginal product of the variable factor tends to increase leading to increasing returns to factor.

(ii) **Increased efficiency of the variable factor**
Additional application of the variable factor enables the firm to implement process based division of labour that raises efficiency of the factor. Accordingly, marginal productivity of the factor tends to rise resulting in increasing returns to factor.

2. According to the law of variable proportions, in which stage would a producer like to operate? Explain why? **ISC 2014**

Ans According to the law of variable proportions, as more and more units of variable factors are combined with fixed factors, marginal product initially rises, then falls and eventually becomes negative.

A rational producer would like to operate in the second stage i.e. diminishing returns to factor stage. In this stage though, marginal product falls but remains positive and hence, total product increases at a diminishing rate, while average product is also positive i.e. every unit of variable factor add something to the total product.

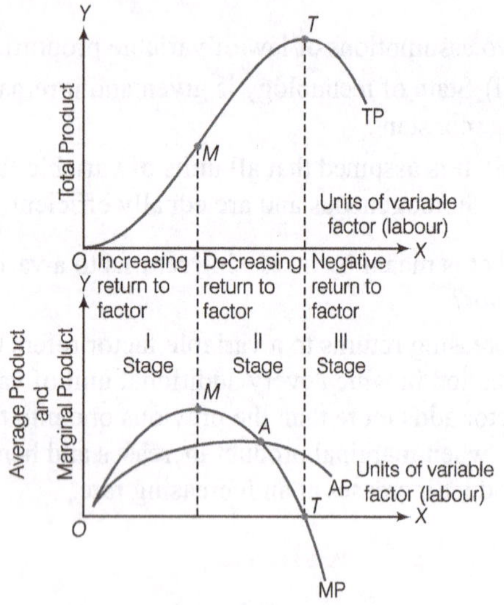

Law of Variable Proportion

Common Mistake Students generally intersects MP on the falling part of AP. However, MP should intersect AP at the maximum point of AP.

3. Explain returns to variable factor. **ISC 2012 (M)**

Ans Returns to variable factor explains short-run production function, in which one factor of production is taken as a fixed and other as variable. In other words, returns to variable factor measures change in total product (output) due to change in variable factor (labour) keeping fixed factor (capital) constant.

Assumptions followed in the law of variable proportion are

(i) State of technology is given and it will remain constant.

(ii) This law is applied to short-run.

(iii) Input price remain unchanged.

(iv) All the units of variable factor are homogeneous and are equally efficient.

(v) It is assumed that labour is a single variable factor.

(vi) It is possible to change the proportion in which the factor units are combined.

4. Draw a diagram to show the effect of total product on marginal product of a variable factor, when total product reaches its maximum. **ISC 2008**

Ans When Total Product (TP) reaches its maximum point, Marginal Product (MP) becomes zero. It is a situation of diminishing return to a factor. Under this stage, TP increases at decreasing rate and attains it maximum point at *B*. MP continues to fall and becomes zero at point *B*.

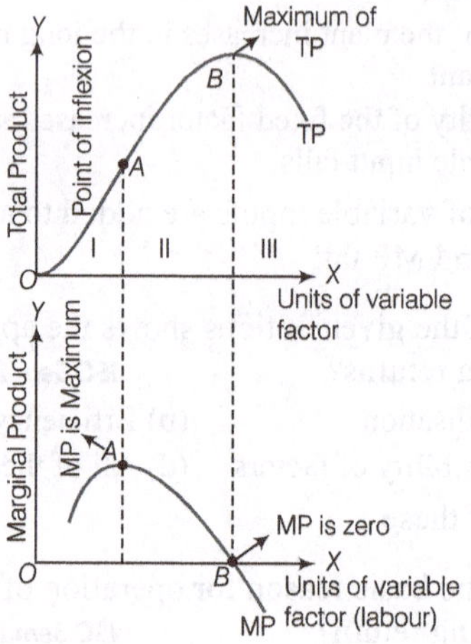

Value Points

For getting maximum marks, following value points can be included in the answer

- While explaining returns to a factor, stages should be shown in diagram.
- Draw both TP and MP curves.

6/8 Marks Questions

1. State the law of variable proportions. Explain its three stages by using a diagram. **ISC Specimen 2023**

Or Discuss the three stages of the law of variable proportions with the help of diagrams. In which stage will a rational producer like to operate? **ISC 2020**

Or Explain the law of variable proportions with the help of a diagram. **ISC 2015, 2005**

Ans This law states that as more and more of variable factors are employed (alongwith fixed factors), then marginal product initially rises, reaches its maximum point, then start to fall and eventually becomes negative or in other words, total product initially rises at a rising rate then at a decreasing rate and eventually starts falling.

Assumptions of the law are

(i) State of technology is given and it will remain constant.
(ii) This law is applied to short-run.
(iii) It is assumed that labour is the only variable input.
(iv) All the units of variable factor are homogeneous and equally efficient.

There are three stages in this law

(i) **Increasing returns to factor** TP increases at increasing rate while MP also increases and reaches its highest point.
(ii) **Diminishing returns to factor** TP increases at decreasing rate while MP fall. This stage comes to end when MP = 0 and TP is maximum.
(iii) **Negative returns to factor** TP falls while MP becomes negative.

Schedule and Diagram introducing the Law of Variable Proportion

Capital (Fixed)	Labour (Variable)	Total Product (TP)	Average Product (AP)	Marginal Product (MP)	Remarks
1	0	0	–	–	
1	1	2	2	2	Increasing returns to factors
1	2	6	3	4	
1	3	12	4	6	
1	4	16	4	4	Decreasing returns to factors
1	5	18	3.6	2	
1	6	18	3	0	
1	7	14	2	(–) 4	Negative returns to factors
1	8	8	1	(–) 6	

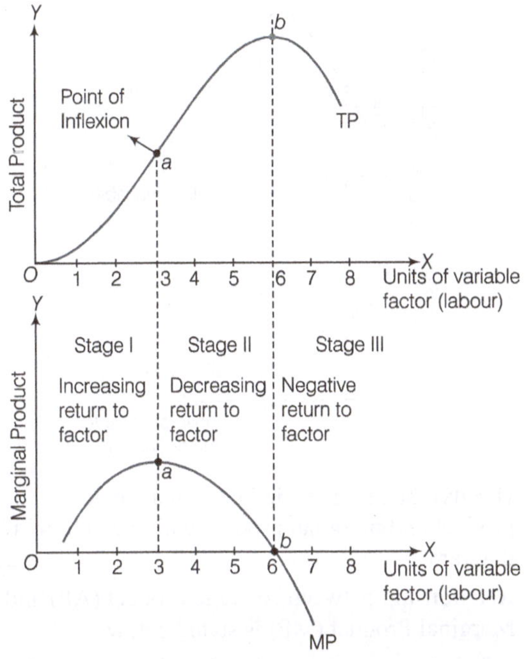

Law of Variable Proportion

From the given schedule and diagram, we can see that capital is taken as fixed and labour as variable factor. As more and more labour is employed initially till 3rd unit of labour, marginal product rises from 3rd unit onwards till 6th unit of labour, marginal product falls and thereafter, marginal product becomes negative.

Conclusion A rational producer would like to produce in the second stage where diminishing returns operates, as in this stage, marginal product falls but remains positive i.e. every additional labour is adding something to the output. He will not produce beyond this stage, as marginal product becomes negative thereafter.

2. If more variable factors are employed to fixed factors, the total product increases initially at increasing rate and finally it decreases. Explain this law with the help of a diagram. ***ISC 2018***

Or 'If more variable factors are employed with fixed factors, the total product increases at an increasing rate and finally it falls'. Explain the three stages of the law, with the help of TP, AP and MP curves. ***ISC 2010***

Ans According to the law of variable proportion, there are three stages of operation i.e. increasing returns to factors, decreasing returns to factors and negative returns to factors. Let us discuss the stages in detail

***Stage* I Increasing returns to factors** In this stage, total product increases at an increasing rate and hence marginal product increases, average product also increases in this stage. But remember that total product starts from origin but marginal product and average product cannot start from origin.

In the given diagram, it has been shown that till point M in total product curve, total product is increasing at an increasing rate, point M is known as point of inflexion, where marginal product reaches at its maximum point and hence Stage I comes to an end. In this stage, MP > AP.

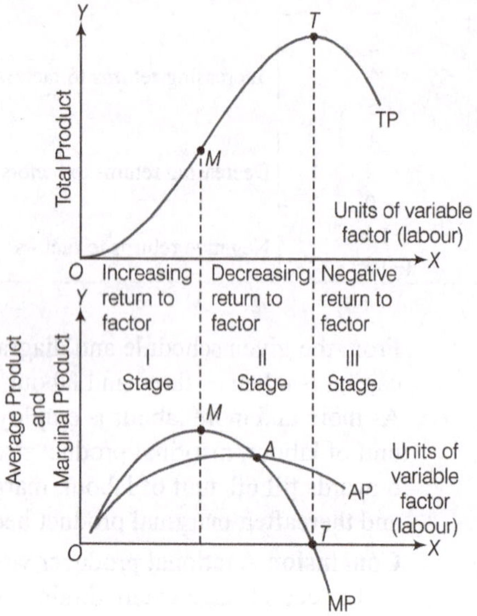

Law of Variable Proportion

***Stage* II Diminishing returns to factor** It starts from point *M* and continuous till point *T* where total product is maximum and marginal product becomes zero. In this stage, marginal product falls continuously, but remains positive while total product rises though at a diminishing rate.

If we look at average product curve in this stage, then we can find that average product is increasing till point *A* in this stage, where marginal product is equal to average product and eventually starts falling. Now, AP > MP.

***Stage* III Negative returns to factor** In this stage, total product starts falling and hence marginal product becomes negative, average product in this stage falls continuously but remains positive, again AP > MP.

3. Explain with the help of diagram, the relationship between total product and marginal product. ***ISC 2016, 2012, 2009***

Ans Relationship between Total Product (TP) and Marginal Product (MP) is stated below

(i) When marginal product increases, total product increases at an increasing rate.

(ii) When marginal product decreases, total product increases at a diminishing rate.

(iii) When marginal product becomes zero, total product reaches its maximum point.

(iv) When marginal product becomes negative, total product starts to fall.

It is clear from the given diagram that till point *A*, marginal product is rising, hence total product is increasing at an increasing rate.

Thereafter, till point *B*, marginal product falls but it is positive.

Hence, total product is rising at a diminishing rate. At point *B*, marginal product is zero and total product is maximum and constant and thereafter, marginal product becomes negative and total product starts falling.

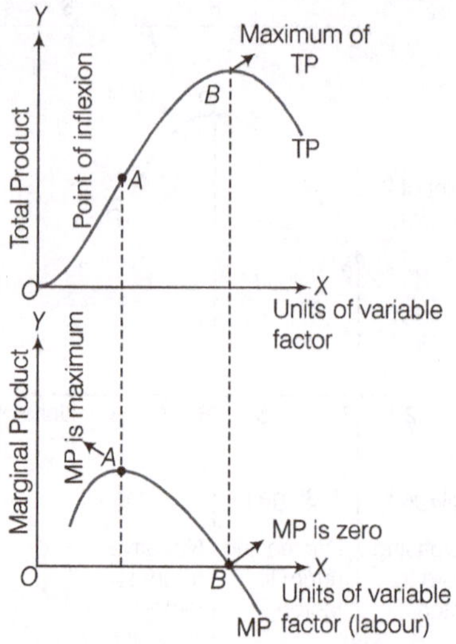

4. Discuss the relationship between average product and marginal product with the help of a diagram. ***ISC 2011***

Ans Relationship between Average Product (AP) and Marginal Product (MP) is stated below

(i) When average product is rising, marginal product is above average product, i.e. MP > AP.

(ii) When average product is falling, marginal product is below average product , i.e. MP < AP.

(iii) When average product reaches its maximum point, marginal product is equal to average product, i.e. MP = AP.

(iv) Marginal product can become zero or negative, but average product cannot become zero or negative.

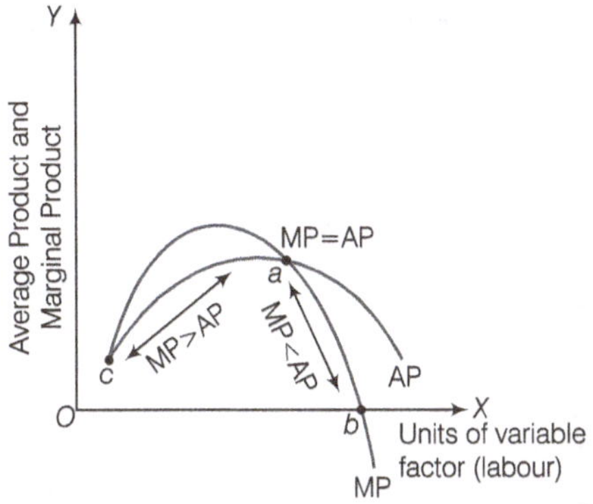

We can see in the adjacent diagram, Marginal Product (MP) and Average Product (AP) starts from same point *c*.

Between point *c* and point *a*, both marginal product and average product are rising, but marginal product lies above average product, after point *a* till point *b*, both marginal product and average product are falling, but marginal product lies below average product and after point *b*, marginal product becomes negative while average product falls continuously but remains positive throughout, because AP can never be negative.

5. Give one difference between increasing returns to factor and diminishing returns to factor. ***ISC 2008 (M)***

> **KEY IDEA**
> Diminishing returns indicate that the fixed factors are causing the productivity of variable factor to fall.

Ans **Increasing returns to factors** It refers to the situation in which total product increases at an increasing rate and marginal product increases, which means that every additional unit of variable factor (labour) adds more and more to the output level than the previous one.

Main reasons for increasing returns are

(i) Fuller and efficient utilisation of the fixed factors.
(ii) Increased efficiency of variable factors.
(iii) Better coordination between the factors.

Diminishing returns to factors It refers to the situation in which total product increases at a diminishing rate and marginal product diminishes but remains positive, which means that every additional unit of variable factor (labour) adds lesser and lesser to the total output than the previous one, but the additional labour is producing something.

Main reasons for diminishing returns are

(i) Fixity of the factors of production.
(ii) Imperfect factor substitutability.
(iii) Poor coordination between the factors.

Case Based Question

Case 1

A famous English economist believed that agricultural output would eventually stop growing, as more labour is added to land that was fixed in quantity. ***ISC Sem I Specimen 2021***

(i) Which law is applicable in the given context?
(a) Law of variable proportion
(b) Law of diminishing marginal utility
(c) Say's law
(d) None of these

Ans (a) Law of variable proportion

(ii) Which of the following statements is correct in the given context?
(a) This law is applicable when the state of technology is given and remains unchanged
(b) This law is applicable in long-run
(c) Variable factors are not equally efficient
(d) All inputs can vary

Ans (a) This law is applicable when the state of technology is given and remains unchanged

(iii) Which of the following is a variable factor in the context of the statement given above?
(a) Land
(b) Labour
(c) Capital
(d) Entrepreneur

Ans (b) Labour

CHAPTER TEST

01 Mark Questions

1. Which of the following statements accurately describe the relationship between AP and MP?
(a) No relationship exists
(b) AP and MP are always parallel to each other
(c) MP intersects AP at its maximum point
(d) AP is always rising when MP is falling and *vice-versa*

2. .... is the extension of "law of diminishing returns".
(a) Law of variable proportions (b) Law of demand
(c) Law of equi-marginal utility
(d) Law of diminishing marginal utility

3. The maximum possible output for a firm with two units of labour (L) and ten units of capital (K), if its production function is given as $5L + 2K$, is ....
(a) 0 units (b) 30 units (c) 200 units (d) 50 units

4. Identify the phase in which TP increases at an increasing rate and MP also increases.
(a) Increasing returns to a factor
(b) Diminishing returns to a factor
(c) Negative returns to a factor (d) None of the above

5. All factors become fixed factor in the long-run. State true or false.

6. Production function doesn't exist in the very short-run or market period. State true or false.

7. When output increases in the same proportion as increase in all factors of production, it is known as ....

8. Law of returns to scale is only applicable, in the .... time period.

9. What is the slope of total product called?

10. What is point of inflexion?

02 Marks Questions

11. When will total output be maximum? Use a diagram to explain it.

12. Can total product and average product curve become zero or negative? Why or why not?

13. What are the principal factors accounting for negative returns to factors?

14. Define marginal product.

15. 4 units of labour produce 100 units and 5 units of labour produce 120 units of output. Calculate MP of the 5th unit of labour.

16. As the variable input is increased by one unit, total output falls, what can you say about Marginal Physical Product (MPP) of variable factor.

17. Production function is always defined with respect to a given technology. Is the statement true or false?

03/04 Marks Questions

18. Complete the following table

Units of Labour	TPP	APP	MPP
1	...	...	24
2	...	...	20
3	...	...	16
4	...	...	12
5	...	...	8
6	...	...	0

19. State giving reasons whether the following statements are true or false.
(i) Average product falls only when marginal product is less than average product.
(ii) Average product will increase only when marginal product increases.

20. Why should MP of the variable factors increases at the first instance, when it must decline ultimately?

21. Identify the different stages of production in the given schedule

Units of Labour	1	2	3	4	5	6	7	8
Units of Output	2	6	12	16	18	18	14	8

06 Marks Question

22. Explain the behaviour of total product, under return to a factor with the help of schedule and diagram.

Answers

1. (c) MP intersects AP at its maximum point
2. (a) Law of variable proportions
3. (b) 30 units *4.* (a) Increasing returns to a factor
5. False *6.* True
7. constant returns to scale
8. long-run
9. Marginal product

05

Cost and Revenue

TREND ANALYSIS 5 YEARS

Average No. of Questions Across all Sets

	Types of Questions	2023	2020	2019	2018	2017
01 Concept of Cost	1 Mark	2	—	—	—	—
	2 Marks	1	—	—	1	1
	3/4 Marks	—	1	1	1	2
	6 Marks	—	—	—	—	—
02 Concept of Revenue	1 Mark	—	—	—	—	—
	2 Marks	—	—	—	—	—
	3/4 Marks	—	1	1	—	—
	6 Marks	—	—	—	—	—
03 Producer's Equilibrium	1 Mark	—	—	—	—	—
	2 Marks	—	—	—	—	—
	3/4 Marks	—	—	—	—	—
	6 Marks	—	—	1	1	1

TOPIC 1

Basic Cost Concept : Short-run and Long-run Costs, Relationship between Various Cost Concepts

Cost

It refers to the total expenditure incurred by a producer on the factor as well as non-factor inputs for producing a given amount of output in a given period of time. In economic sense, cost refers to all the monetary and non-monetary expenditures incurred by a producer for production of a particular good.

Basic Concepts of Cost

Costs can be divided into several types based on their concepts, which are as follows

(i) **Explicit cost and implicit cost** Explicit cost is the monetary expenditure incurred on hiring factor services from the outsiders, say wages to the labour, interest to the capital, rent to the land, etc. Whereas, implicit cost is the estimated cost of factors supplied by the owner himself, say imputed rent of own land, imputed interest on capital supplied by the owner. Sum of implicit and explicit cost is known as **'economic cost'**. It includes not only monetary transactions but also opportunity cost.

(ii) **Money cost or accounting cost** Money cost refers to the total money payment made to the outsiders for rendering their factor services. e.g. Salaries and wages of the labour, rent of the land, interest of capital and profit of entrepreneur.

Note The money cost is same as explicit cost.

(iii) **Opportunity cost** It is the cost of foregoing second best opportunity. e.g. In a piece of land either wheat or rice can be produced with yield of ₹ 500 and ₹ 600, respectively. If farmer opt for rice, then he has to forego the opportunity of producing wheat which is the second best alternative.

(iv) **Real cost** It is the efforts and sacrifices made by the owners of the factors of production used in the process of production.

(v) **Private and social cost** Private cost refers to the cost of an individual firm in producing a particular commodity. It includes both implicit as well as explicit costs. Whereas, social cost refers to the cost that a society has to pay/bear for production of a particular commodity.

e.g. A steel firm while taking production decision only considers the private cost but the pollution generated in operation has some additional cost, which the society has to bear.

Difference between Opportunity Cost and Accounting Cost

Basis	Opportunity cost	Accounting cost
Meaning	It is the cost of alternative opportunity sacrificed.	Accounting costs are explicit cost or actual cash payment made to outsiders.
Record	It is generally not recorded in book-keeping records.	It is recorded in book-keeping records.
Example	Rent of owned building proposed to be used for a new project and not used for own use.	Payment of salary/ wages, rent of building, etc.
Use	It is used for decision-making. It emphasises the problem of choice.	It is used for calculating profit.

Short-run Costs

We have already studied about the concept of short-run in the previous chapter, i.e. it is the time period where some factors are fixed, hence, the cost of fixed factors are termed as fixed cost and cost of variable factors are termed as variable cost.

Let us see these short-run costs in terms of a flow chart

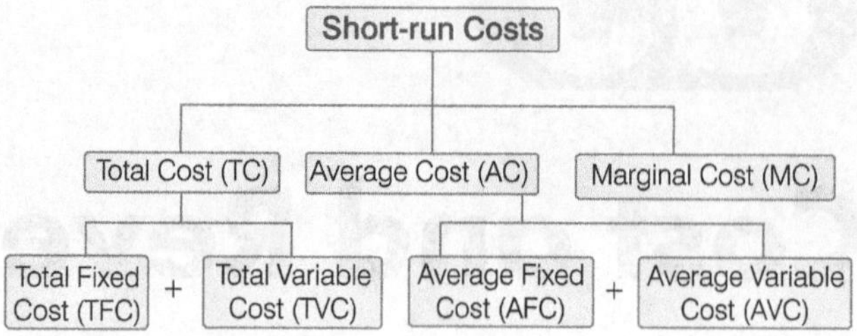

1. Total Cost (TC)

It refers to the sum total of costs incurred on all factors of production, including fixed and variable factors. i.e.

Total Cost = Total Fixed Cost + Total Variable Cost

or TC = TFC + TVC

Output (units)	Fixed Cost (₹)	Variable Cost (₹)	Total Cost (₹)
0	10	0	10
1	10	10	20
2	10	18	28
3	10	24	34
4	10	28	38
5	10	32	42

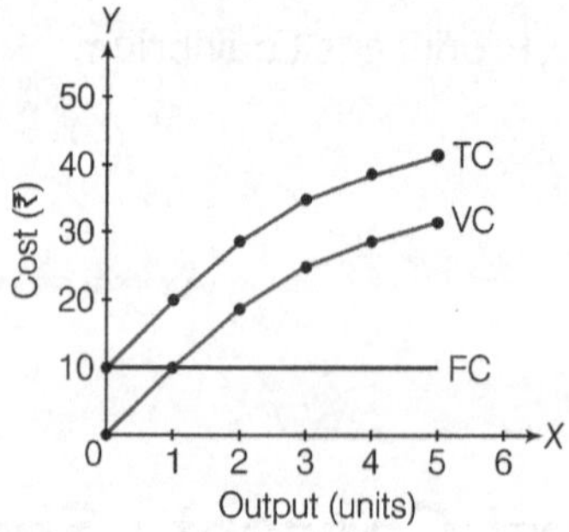

Note TC in the short-run is never zero.

Total cost may be classified into two types

(a) **Total Fixed Cost** (TFC) It refers to the sum total of costs incurred on fixed factors of production, say rent of the building, salary of permanent staff, etc. Total fixed costs do not vary with the level of output, it remains constant for all levels of output, including zero levels of output. They are overheads and are not identifiable with the product.

Total Fixed Cost = Total Cost − Total Variable Cost

or TFC = TC − TVC

Units of Output	Fixed Cost (₹)
0	10
1	10
2	10
3	10
4	10
5	10

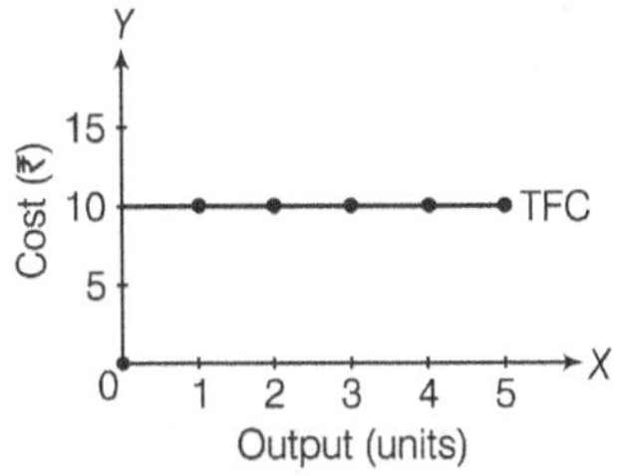

Fixed Cost Curve

(b) **Total Variable Cost** (TVC) It is the sum total of cost incurred on variable factors say, payment for raw material, salary of casual workers, etc. Total variable costs varies directly with the level of output. At zero level of output, variable cost is also zero. It is direct cost and is identifiable with the product.

Total Variable Cost = Total Cost – Total Fixed Cost

or TVC = TC – TFC *or* $TVC = \Sigma MC$

Units of Output	Variable Cost (₹)
0	0
1	10
2	18
3	24
4	28
5	32

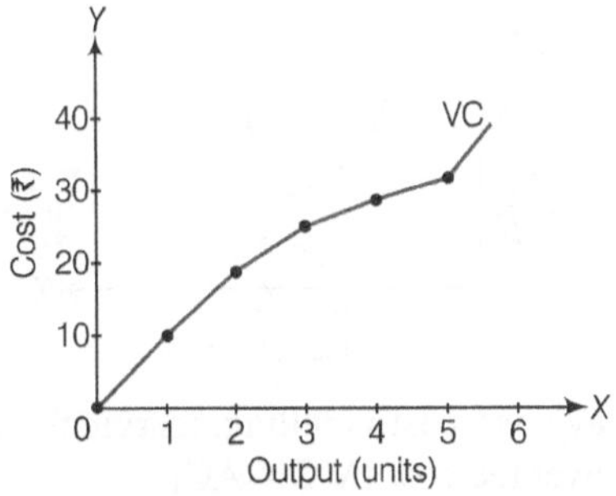

Variable Cost Curve

2. **Average Cost** (AC)

It is defined as per unit of total cost. It is calculated by dividing total cost with level of output (Q). Average cost curve is 'U' shaped.

$$\text{Average Cost} = \frac{\text{Total Cost}}{\text{Number of Units Produced}}$$

or

$$AC = \frac{TC}{Q}$$

Output (units)	**Average Cost** (₹)
1	10
3	8
5	6
6	6
7	7
10	10

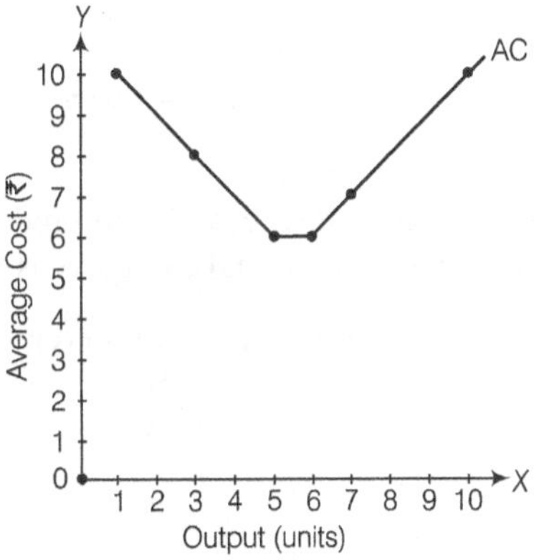

Average cost is classified into two types

(a) **Average Fixed Cost** (AFC) It refers to per unit of total fixed cost, it is calculated by dividing total fixed cost by the level of output (Q). Average fixed cost curve is also rectangular hyperbola.

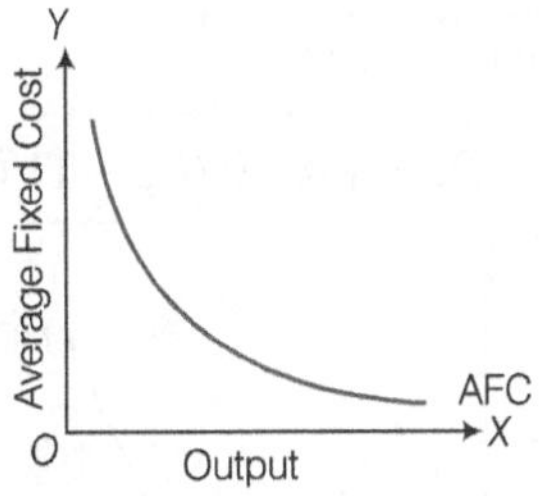

$$\text{Average Fixed Cost} = \frac{\text{Total Fixed Cost}}{\text{Number of Units Produced}}$$

or

$$AFC = \frac{TFC}{Q}$$

(b) **Average Variable Cost** (AVC) It is per unit of total variable cost, it is calculated by dividing total variable cost with the level of output (Q). Average variable cost curve is also 'U' shaped.

$$\text{Average Variable Cost} = \frac{\text{Total Variable Cost}}{\text{Number of Units Produced}}$$

or $$\text{AVC} = \frac{\text{TVC}}{\text{Q}}$$

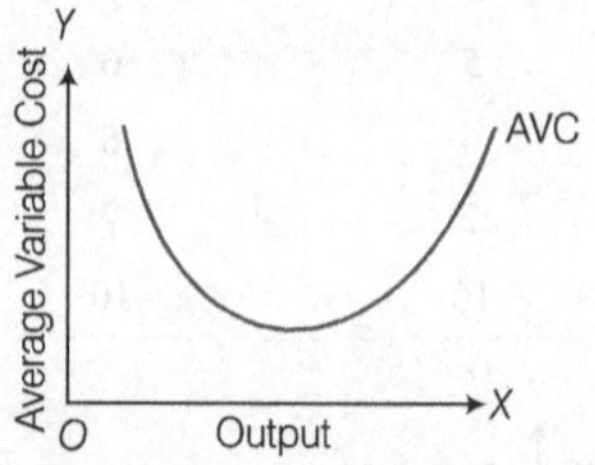

Average Variable Cost Curve

3. Marginal Cost (MC)

It is termed as change in total cost due to production of an additional unit of output. Marginal cost curve is 'U' shaped.

Output (units)	**Average Cost** (₹)
1	50
2	40
3	30
4	40
5	60

It can be calculated as

$$\text{Marginal Cost} = \frac{\text{Change in Total Cost/Change in Total Variable Cost}}{\text{Change in Output}}$$

or $$\text{MC} = \frac{\Delta\text{TC}}{\Delta\text{Q}} \text{ or } \frac{\Delta\text{TVC}}{\Delta\text{Q}}$$

or $$\text{MC} = \text{TC}_n - \text{TC}_{n-1} \text{ or } \text{TVC}_n - \text{TVC}_{n-1}$$

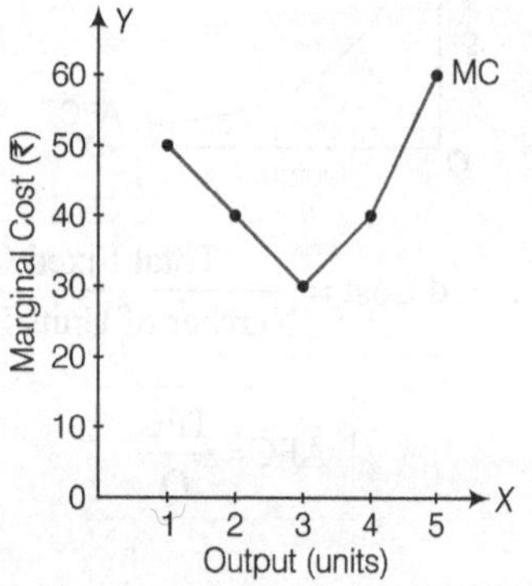

Note Generally, TVC is preferred for calculating MC.

Relationship between Total Cost (TC), Total Fixed Cost (TFC) and Total Variable Cost (TVC)

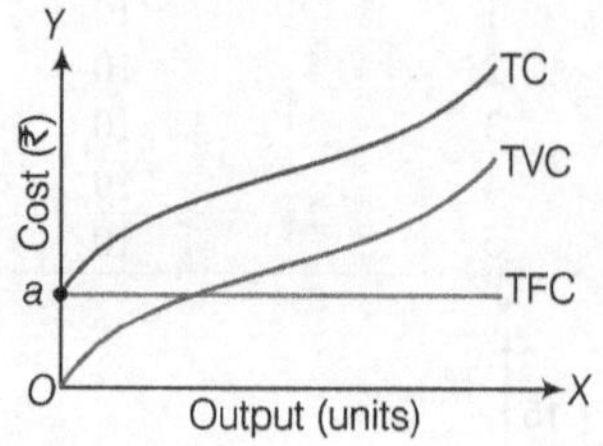

(i) Total Cost (TC) is the sum of Total Fixed Cost (TFC) and Total Variable Cost (TVC). i.e. TC= TFC+ TVC.

(ii) Difference between TC and TFC is TVC, while difference between TC and TVC is TFC.

(iii) TVC curve starts from origin, as TVC is zero when output is zero.

(iv) TC and TFC start from point *a*, which is above the origin, as TFC can never be zero, hence at zero level of output, TC = TFC.

(v) TC and TVC curves are parallel to each other, as there difference is TFC which remains fixed for all levels of output.

(vi) The gap between TC and TFC curves increases continuously, as TVC rises with level of output.

(vii) TC and TVC curves initially rise at a diminishing rate, then at an increasing rate, due to law of variable proportion.

Relationship between Average Cost (AC) and Marginal Cost (MC)

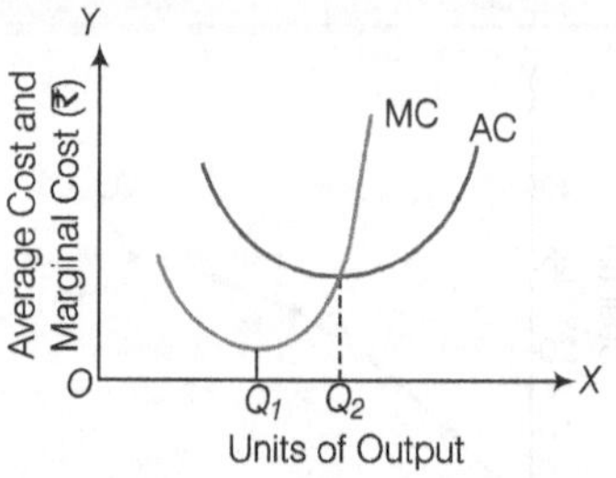

(i) When average cost is falling, marginal cost lies below average cost (MC < AC).

(ii) When average cost is rising, marginal cost lies above average cost (MC > AC).

(iii) When average cost is minimum and constant, marginal cost is equal to average cost (MC = AC).

(iv) Minimum point of marginal cost (Q_1) lies to the left of minimum point of average cost (Q_2).

(v) Both are calculated from total cost $AC = \frac{TC}{Q} \Rightarrow MC = TC_n - TC_{n-1}$.

(vi) The shape of AC and MC is similar to each other (i.e. U-shape) due to law of variable proportions.

Relationship between Average Variable Cost (AVC) and Marginal Cost (MC)

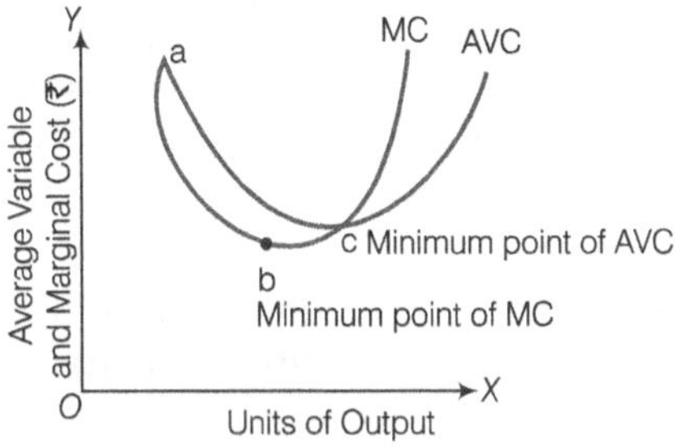

(i) Average variable cost (AVC) and Marginal Cost (MC) both are 'U' shaped and starts from the same point.

(ii) When MC is below AVC, AVC falls.

(iii) MC is equal to AVC at the minimum point of AVC (point c).

(iv) When MC is above AVC, AVC rises.

Relationship between Total Cost (TC) and Marginal Cost (MC)

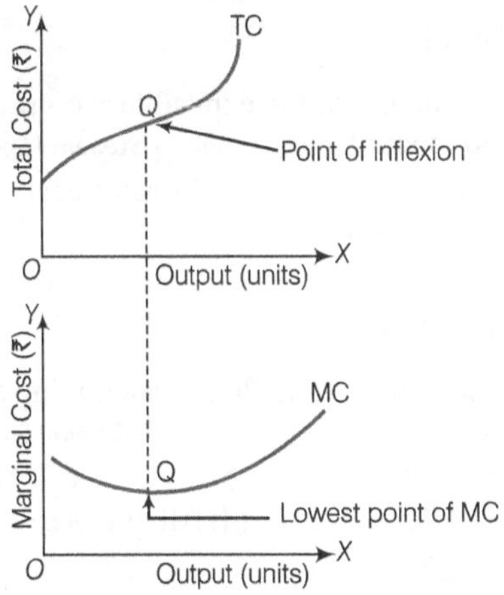

Diagrammatic representation of relationship between TC and MC

(i) MC is estimated as the difference between TC of two successive units of output. $MC_{nth} = TC_n - TC_{n-1}$

(ii) When MC is diminishing, TC increases at a diminishing rate.

(iii) When MC is risng, TC increases at an increasing rate.

(iv) When MC reaches its lowest point, TC stop increasing at a decreasing rate, it represents the point of inflexion of TC curve.

(v) Point Q on TC curve indicates point of inflexion.

Long-run Costs

In long-run, all the factors of production become variable, hence long-run cost is the least or minimum cost of producing each level of output.

Types of long-run cost indudes

1. Long-run Total Cost (LTC)

It refers to the minimum cost at which given level of output can be produced. LTC is always less than or equal to short-run total cost.

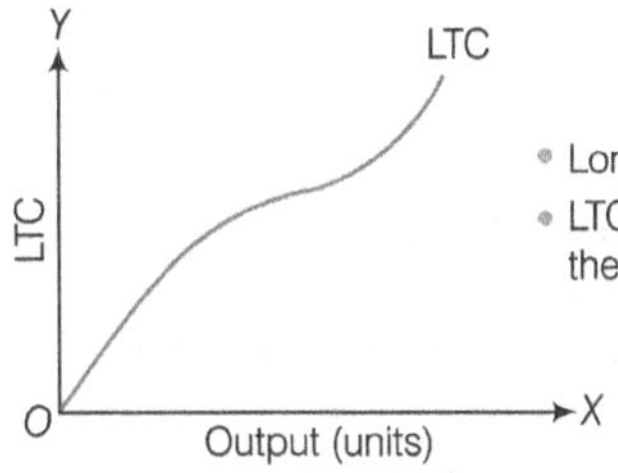

- Long-term total cost
- LTC starts from origin because there is no fixed cost in long-run

2. Long-run Average Cost (LAC)

It indicates the minimum per unit cost of production that can be incurred in the long-run.

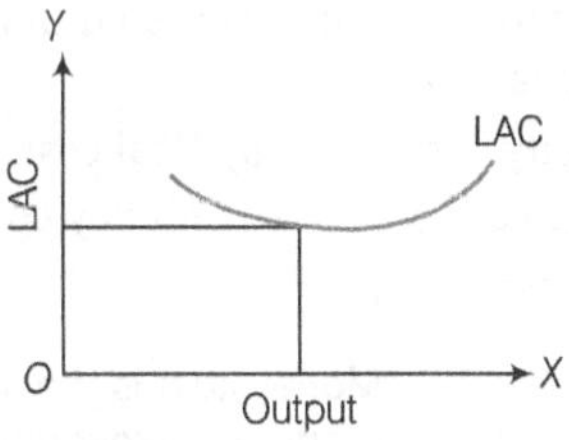

Long-run Average Cost Curve

3. Long-run Marginal Cost (LMC)

It is same as short-run Marginal Cost (MC) i.e. additional cost of producing an extra unit, however long-run marginal cost represents the minimum possible cost that needs to be incurred on production of each additional unit.

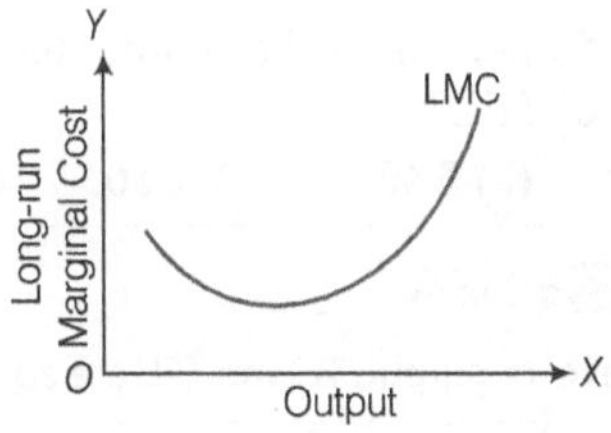

Long-run Marginal Cost Curve

PYQs Previous Years' Questions

1 Mark Questions

1. Why is AVC curve 'U-shaped'? *ISC 2023*

Ans AVC is 'U' shaped due to law of variable proportion.

2. What is meant by accounting cost? *ISC 2023*

Ans Accounting cost refers to monetary expenses paid to an outside factors for their services.

3. What is marginal cost of a firm? *ISC Specimen 2023*

Ans Marginal cost refers to the cost of hiring/producing an additional unit of output.

4. The shape of TVC is initially concave downwards and subsequently concave upwards because *ISC Sem I 2021*

(a) Initially TVC increases at decreasing rate and then increases at increasing rate.
(b) Initially TVC decreases at decreasing rate and then increases at diminishing rate.
(c) Initially increases at increasing rate and then increases at decreasing rate.
(d) Initially decreases at decreasing rate and then increases at decreasing rate.

Ans (a) Initially TVC increases at decreasing rate and then increases at increasing rate.

5. The type of cost that can be entered in the book of accountancy is *ISC Sem I 2021*

(a) Opportunity cost (b) Real cost
(c) Economic cost (d) Money cost

Ans (d) Money cost

Concept Enhancer Money cost is the actual monetary expenditure paid to factors of production.

6. Which of the following indicates fixed cost? *ISC Sem I 2021*

(a) Expenses on raw materials
(b) Salaries of casual workers
(c) Electricity bills (d) Interest on loans

Ans (d) Interest on loans

7. If TC = ₹ 50 at zero level of output then what will be the value of TFC? *ISC Sem I 2021*

(a) ₹ 30 (b) ₹ 40 (c) ₹ 50 (d) ₹ 60

KEY IDEA

At zero level of output, TC and TFC are equal as TVC is zero.

Ans (c) ₹ 50

8. Match the cost concepts in List I with their definitions in List II. *ISC Sem I 2021*

List I (cost concepts)	List II (description)
A. Explicit cost	(i) Change in total cost for a unit change in output.
B. Marginal cost	(ii) Value of inputs owned and used in production.
C. Implicit cost	(iii) Costs which a business incurs.

Codes

	A	B	C		A	B	C
(a)	(ii)	(i)	(iii)	(b)	(i)	(ii)	(iii)
(c)	(iii)	(i)	(ii)	(d)	(iii)	(ii)	(i)

Ans (c) (iii) (i) (ii)

9. Which of the following statements is true? *ISC Sem I 2021*

(a) MC is unaffected by variable cost
(b) MC is unaffected by fixed cost
(c) MC equals change in TR
(d) MC is unaffected by price

Ans (b) MC is unaffected by fixed cost

10. Cost of exertion, pains and sacrifices is known as *ISC Sem I Specimen 2021*

(a) Opportunity costs (b) Production costs
(c) Real costs (d) Explicit costs

Ans (c) Real costs

11. What is the nature of the expenditure on raw material, power and labour? *ISC Sem I Specimen 2021*

(a) Fixed cost (b) Variable cost
(c) Production costs
(d) Explicit cost

Ans (b) Variable cost

12. What is the correct formula for calculating the total variable cost? *ISC Sem I Specimen 2021*

(a) $TVC = \Sigma MC$ (b) $TVC = TC - TFC$
(c) $TVC = AVC \times Q$ (d) All of these

Ans (a) $TVC = \Sigma MC$

13. AVC and AC curves cannot intersect each other because *ISC Sem I Specimen 2021*

(a) MC starts falling
(b) $TC - TVC = TFC$ which is constant
(c) TC – does not increase
(d) None of the above

Ans (b) $TC - TVC = TFC$ which is constant

14. What is the reason for the U shape of short-run average cost curves? *ISC Sem I Specimen 2021*

(a) Law of demand (b) Law of DMU
(c) Law of variable proportions
(d) Law of supply

Ans (c) Law of variable proportions

15. Opportunity cost of a good is the .... *ISC Sem I Specimen 2021*

(a) Anticipated cost
(b) Next best alternative
(c) Upcoming cost
(d) Real cost

Ans (b) Next best alternative

16. Social cost is *ISC Sem I Specimen 2021*

(a) Implicit cost + Explicit cost
(b) Explicit cost + Opportunity cost
(c) Private cost + External cost
(d) Private cost + Real cost

Ans (c) Private cost + External cost

17. Economic cost refers to the sum of both explicit cost and implicit cost *ISC Sem I Specimen 2021*

(a) Including excess profit.
(b) Including normal profit.
(c) Including net profit.
(d) Including abnormal profit.

Ans (b) Including normal profit.

2 Marks Questions

1. Calculate total variable cost and marginal cost from the data given below *ISC 2023*

Output (Unit)	0	1	2	3
Total Cost (₹)	40	60	78	97

Ans

Output	TC	TVC	MC
0	40	0	—
1	60	20	20
2	78	38	18
3	97	57	19

Formulae used TVC = TC − TFC

TFC = 40

$MC = TVC_n = TVC_{n-1}$

2. Define implicit cost. How is it different from explicit cost? *ISC 2018, 2006*

Ans Implicit cost is the estimated cost of factors supplied by the owner himself, say rent of own land, interest on capital supplied by the owner.

Difference between implicit cost and explicit cost

Implicit costs are costs of self-owned and self-employed resources whereas explicit cost are those actual cost incurred on hiring factor services from the outsiders, say wages to labour, rent to land and interest to capital, etc.

Concept Enhancer If implicit cost is not considered in the total cost, it will underestimate cost and overestimate profit.

3. Explain the shape of MC curve. *ISC 2017*

Or Why is the marginal cost curve 'U' shaped? *ISC 2013*

Ans Marginal Cost (MC) is addition to the total variable cost due to production of an additional unit of output. Marginal Cost (MC) curve is 'U' shaped.

It is due to the operation of law of variable proportion, where initially increasing returns operates which causes marginal cost to fall and then diminishing returns set in leading to increases in marginal cost.

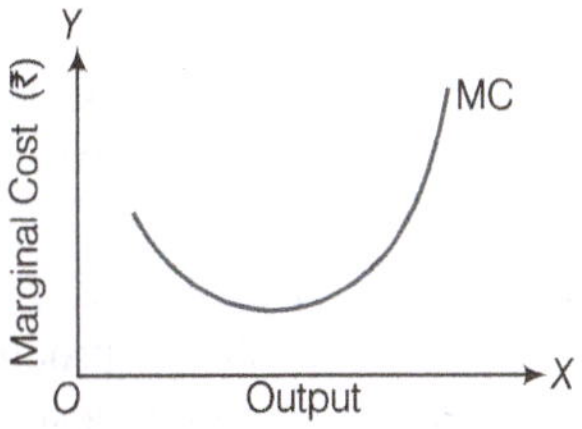

Hence, Marginal Cost (MC) first falls, then rises causing it to be a 'U-shaped' curve.

4. Explain the meaning of social cost with the help of an example. *ISC 2016*

Ans Social cost refers to the total cost of any activity. It includes private costs which fall directly on the firm producing a particular goods/services, as well as, external costs which fall on other people or firms i.e. the cost of chemical fertiliser will take into account not only the cost of producing that fertiliser but also the cost of pollution caused to the river in which waste materials from the factory are dumped.

5. Give one difference between accounting cost and opportunity cost. *ISC 2015*

Ans **Accounting cost** It refers to the total money payment made to the outsiders for rendering their factor services. e.g. Rent paid to landlord.

Opportunity cost It is the cost of the next best alternative foregone. e.g. A shopowner has two offers.'*X*' is offering him a rent of ₹ 8,000 per month and '*Y*' a rent of ₹ 10,000 per month. Then the opportunity cost of giving the shop to '*Y*' will be ₹ 8,000 per month.

Common Mistake Students generally gets confused between opportunity cost and implicit cost. These two types of cost should be considered seperately.

6. Explain the shape of Average Cost (AC) curve. **ISC 2014**

Ans Average Cost (AC) is defined as per unit of total cost. Average cost curve is 'U' shaped, i.e. it initially falls, reaches its minimum and starts to rise. This is due to the operation of law of variable proportion. Where initially the first stage of increasing returns to factors causes the AC to fall and when diminishing return, set in AC tends to rise.

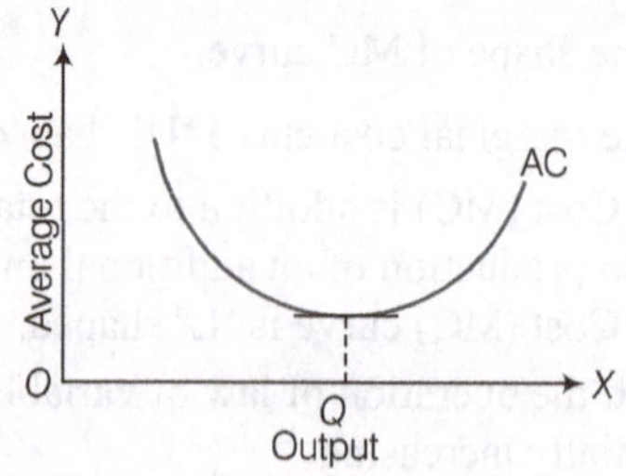

7. Define marginal cost. With the help of an example, show how marginal cost can be obtained from total cost. **ISC 2012**

Ans Marginal Cost (MC) is defined as addition to the Total Cost (TC) due to production of an additional unit of output. Marginal cost can be calculated in the following way

$$\text{Marginal Cost (MC)} = \frac{\text{Change in Total Cost}}{\text{Change in Output}} \text{ or } \frac{\Delta TC}{\Delta Q}$$

Output (Q)	TC	MC ($\Delta TC / \Delta Q$)
1	50	50
2	60	10
3	80	20

8. What is variable cost? Give two examples. **ISC 2011**

Ans Variable Cost (VC) is the cost incurred on hiring the services of the variable factors, which changes directly with output level.

Two examples of variable cost are

(i) Payment for raw material.

(ii) Payment for casual labour.

9. Identify whether the costs stated below are implicit costs or explicit costs. Justify your answer for each.

(i) Rent for self-owned land

(ii) Payment made for advertising. **ISC 2010**

Ans (i) Implicit cost, because this is supplied by the owner itself.

(ii) Explicit cost, because it is the money payment made to the outsiders.

10. Explain the shape of total variable cost with the help of a diagram. **ISC 2007**

Ans Total Variable Cost (TVC) refers to the cost incurred on the variable factors. The shape of TVC is inversely 'S' shaped, which starts from the origin. TVC curve initially rises at a diminishing rate and then at an increasing rate due to law of variable proportion.

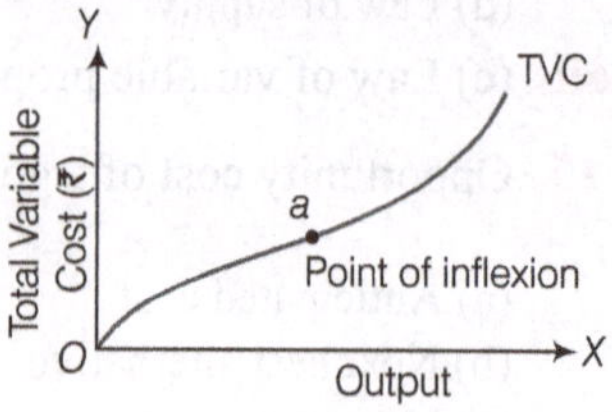

3/4 Marks Questions

1. Calculate total fixed cost, marginal cost and average cost from the following **ISC Specimen 2023**

Output (Unit)	0	1	2	3	4
Total Cost (₹)	100	240	360	540	620

Ans

Output (Units)	Total Cost (₹)	Total Fixed (₹)	Marginal Cost (₹)	Average Cost (₹)
0	100	100	–	–
1	240	100	140	240
2	360	100	120	180
3	540	100	180	180
4	620	100	80	155

Formulae Used

(i) TFC = TC at zero level of output and remains constant thereafter.

(ii) $MC = TC_n - TC_{n-1}$ (iii) $AC = TC/Q$

2. Give reasons for the following

(i) TC and TVC curves do not start from the same point.

(ii) ATC and AVC curves do not touch each other. **ISC 2020**

Ans (i) Refer to Q. No. 10 on page 85.

(ii) Both Average Total Cost (ATC) and Average Variable Cost (AVC) curves are 'U' shaped in general, though the gap between the curve falls continuously as the level of output rises but they can never intersect each other.

Because the difference between average total cost and average variable cost is average fixed cost which gradually falls but never becomes zero. Thus, ATC and AVC curves do not touch each other.

3. Study the cost function of a firm given below **ISC 2019**

Output (Units)	0	1	2	3
TC (₹)	30	90	110	120

Calculate

(i) AFC (ii) AC

(iii) MC

KEY IDEA

Here, TFC = ₹ 30 as it is the cost at zero level of output.

Ans

Output (Units)	**TC** (₹)	**AFC** (₹)	**AC** (₹)	**MC** (₹)
0	30	–	–	–
1	90	30	90	60
2	110	15	55	20
3	120	10	40	10

Formulae used

(i) $AFC = \frac{TFC}{Q}$ (ii) $AC = \frac{TC}{Q}$

(iii) $MC = TC_n - TC_{n-1}$

4. Explain the shapes of total fixed cost curve and average fixed cost curve. Give one reason each, to justify the shape of the two curve. **ISC 2018**

Ans **Shape of total fixed cost curve** Total Fixed Cost (TFC) refers to the sum total of costs incurred on fixed factors of production, say rent of the building, salary of permanent staff, etc. Total fixed costs do not vary with the level of output, it remains constant for all levels of output, including zero levels of output. They are overheads and are not identifiable with the product.

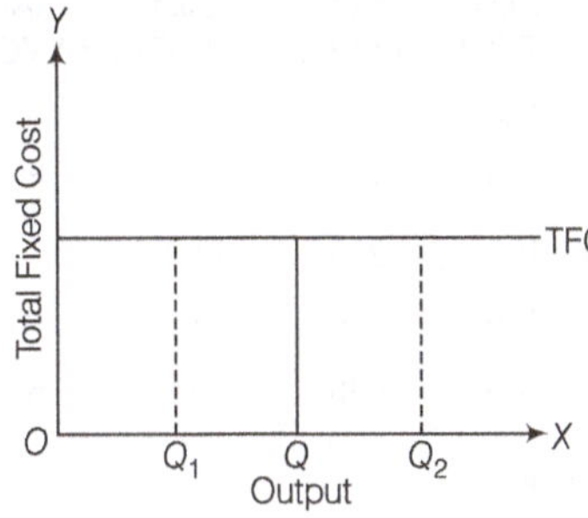

Total Fixed Cost Curve

Total Fixed Cost = Total Cost – Total Variable Cost

or

TFC = TC – TVC

Shape of average fixed cost curve Average Fixed Cost (AFC) is defined as per unit of Total Fixed Cost (TFC). AFC is a rectangular hyperbola shaped curve, i.e. AFC falls continuously, but it can never be equal to zero, as total fixed cost is always positive. Also, area below AFC curve remains constant (same).

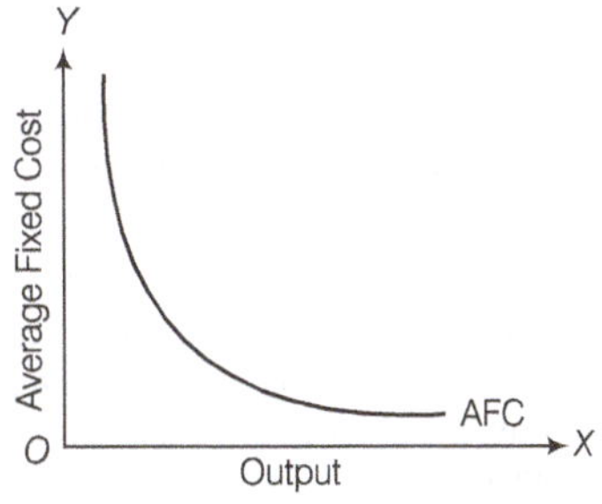

Average Fixed Cost Curve

Concept Enhancer AFC is rectangular hyperbola shaped as the area of rectangles under the curve are constant.

5. The difference between AC curve and AVC curve decreases with increase in output but the two curves never touch each other. Justify the statement with the help of a diagram. **ISC 2017**

Or Draw the average variable cost and average total cost curves. Do they intersect each other? Give one reason for your answer. **ISC 2010**

Ans Average Cost (AC) is the per unit of Total Cost (TC), calculated by dividing total cost by output level. Whereas, Average Variable Cost (AVC) is per unit total variable cost, calculated by dividing total variable cost by output level.

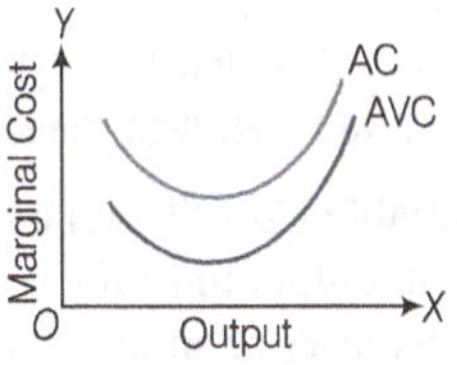

Average Cost and Average Variable Cost Curves

Both the curves are 'U' shaped in general. The gap between the curves fall continuously as the level of output rises but they never intersect each other.

It is because the difference between Average Cost (AC) and Average Variable Cost (AVC) is Average Fixed Cost (AFC) which gradually falls but never becomes zero.

6. Differentiate between real cost and money cost with the help of examples. ***ISC 2017***

Or Differentiate between money cost and real cost. ***ISC 2009***

Ans Difference between real cost and money cost are

Basis	Real cost	Money cost or Accounting cost
Meaning	It refers to the sacrifice made by the entrepreneur and his mental and physical efforts in manufacturing a good.	Money cost refers to the total payment made to the factors of production for rendering their factor services.
Example	An entrepreneur misses his child's birthday on account of an important meeting.	Salaries and wages to the labour, rent of the land, interest on capital and profit to entrepreneur.
Expression	These costs can not be expressed accurately in monetary terms.	These costs can be expressed accurately in monetary terms.

7. Explain the shape of the following ***ISC 2016***

(i) Total Fixed Cost Curve

(ii) Total Variable Cost Curve

Ans (i) Total Fixed Cost (TFC) curve is a straight line parallel to X-axis, indicating that total fixed cost is constant at all levels of output.

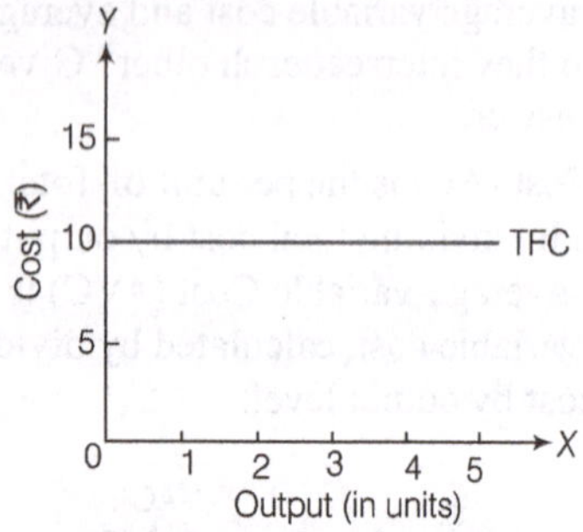

Fixed Cost (FC) Curve

(ii) Total Variable Cost (TVC) curve increases with increase in output initially at decreasing rate and finally increases at an increasing rate. It is positively sloped.

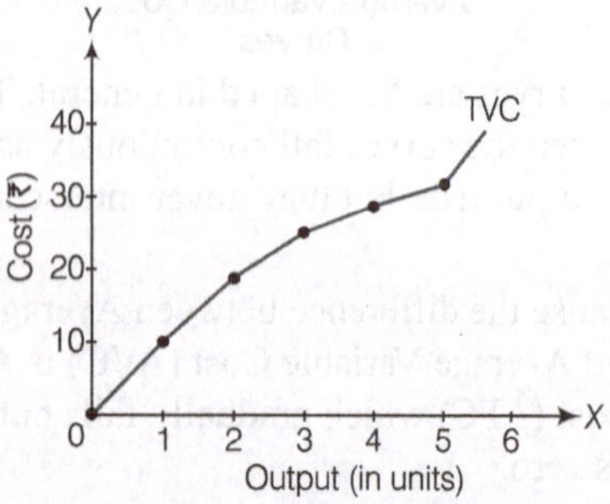

Variable Cost (VC) Curve

8. Classify the following into fixed cost and variable cost giving a reason for your answer ***ISC 2016***

(i) Expenses incurred on raw material

(ii) Interest on capital

(iii) Salaries to permanent employees

Ans (i) Expenses incurred on raw material is a Variable Cost (VC) as it depends on the level of output. As output increases, expenses incurred on raw material will also increase and *vice-versa*.

(ii) Interest on capital is a Fixed Cost (FC), as it is not dependent on the level of output. It would be required to be paid even if the output is zero.

(iii) Salaries to permanent employees is a fixed cost as it is a part of administrative expense and is not dependent on the level of output.

9. The cost function of a firm is given below

Output (units)	0	1	2	3	4
Total Cost (₹)	100	250	370	550	740

Calculate

(i) Average Fixed Cost (AFC)

(ii) Average Variable Cost (AVC)

(iii) Marginal Cost (MC) ***ISC 2015***

KEY IDEA

At zero level of output, TC and TFC are equal and TFC remains constant thereafter.

Ans

Output	Total Cost (TC)	Total Fixed Cost (TFC)	Total Variable Cost (TVC)	Average Fixed Cost (AFC)	Average Variable Cost (AVC)	Marginal Cost (MC)
0	100	100	0	—	—	—
1	250	100	150	100	150	150
2	370	100	270	50	135	120
3	550	100	450	33.33	150	180
4	740	100	640	25	160	190

Formulae used

(i) $TC = TFC + TVC$

(ii) $TFC = TC - TVC$

(iii) $TVC = TC - TFC$

(iv) $MC = TVC_n - TVC_{n-1}$

(v) $TC = TFC$ (at zero output level)

(vi) $AFC = TFC/Output$

(vii) $AVC = TVC/Output$

10. Why does the TC curve start from the Y-axis and TVC curve from the origin? **ISC 2013**

Or Why does the total cost curve starts from the Y-axis in the short-run? **ISC 2009**

Ans Total Cost (TC) is the sum of Total Fixed Cost (TFC) and Total Variable Cost (TVC). As we know that, total fixed cost remains positive and constant for all levels of output. Even if output level is zero, TFC still exist.

On the other hand, total variable cost varies directly with the level of output, TVC is zero when output is zero, hence, at zero level of output, total cost is equal to total fixed cost and total variable cost is zero.

Total Cost (TC) = Total Variable Cost (TVC) + Total Fixed Cost (TFC)

Total Cost (TC) = Total Fixed Cost (TFC) [When output = 0, TVC = 0]

As a result, TVC curve starts from origin and TC starts from Y-axis at the point equal to TFC.

We can explain it with the help of following schedule and diagram

Output (units)	**Fixed Cost** (₹)	**Variable Cost** (₹)	**Total Cost** (₹)
0	10	0	10
1	10	10	20
2	10	18	28
3	10	24	34
4	10	28	38
5	10	32	42

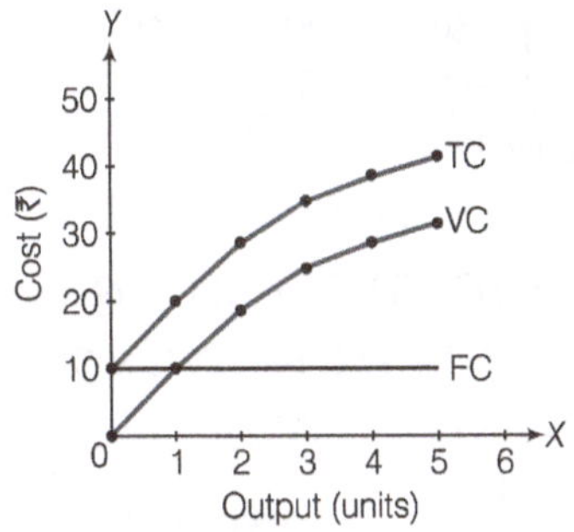

11. A cost function is given below

Output (units)	0	1	2	3	4
Total Cost (₹)	100	160	212	280	356

Calculate

(i) Total Fixed Cost

(ii) Total Variable Cost

(iii) Marginal Cost **ISC 2011**

Ans

Output (units)	**Total Cost** (TC) (₹)	**Total Fixed Cost** (TFC) (₹)	**Total Variable Cost** (TVC) (₹)	**Marginal Cost** (MC) (₹)
0	100	100	0	—
1	160	100	60	60
2	212	100	112	52
3	280	100	180	68
4	356	100	256	76

Formulae used,

(i) $TC = TFC + TVC$ (ii) $TFC = TC - TVC$

(iii) $TVC = TC - TFC$

(iv) $MC = TVC_n - TVC_{n-1}$

(v) $TC = TFC$ (at zero output level)

12. Discuss the shape of average fixed cost curve. **ISC 2011**

Ans Average Fixed Cost (AFC) is defined as per unit of Total Fixed Cost (TFC). AFC is a rectangular hyperbola shaped curve, i.e. AFC falls continuously. We know that TFC remains constant throughout all the output levels and as output increases, with TFC being constant so AFC falling.

But it can never be equal to zero, as total fixed cost is always positive. Also, area below AFC curve remains constant (same).

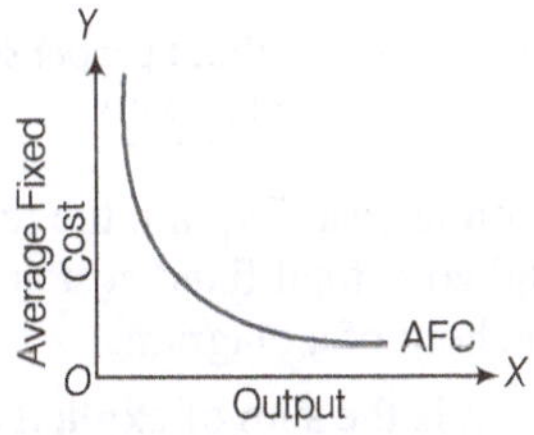

6 Marks Questions

1. Explain the relationship between AC and MC with the help of a diagram. **ISC 2014**

Or

Explain with the help of a diagram, the relationship between average cost and marginal cost. **ISC 2008**

Ans Average cost is the per unit of total cost i.e.

$$\text{Average Cost (AC)} = \frac{\text{Total Cost (TC)}}{\text{Output Level (Q)}}$$

Whereas, marginal cost is change in total cost due to production of an additional unit of output. i.e.

$$\text{Marginal Cost (MC)} = \frac{\text{Change in Total Cost } (\Delta TC)}{\text{Change in Output } (\Delta Q)}$$

Relationship between Average Cost (AC) **and Marginal Cost** (MC)

(i) When Average Cost (AC) is falling, Marginal Cost (MC) lies below average cost (MC < AC).

(ii) When Average Cost (AC) is rising, Marginal Cost (MC) lies above average cost (MC > AC).

(iii) When Average Cost (AC) is minimum and constant, Marginal Cost (MC) is equal to average cost (MC = AC).

(iv) Minimum point of Marginal Cost (MC) (Q_1) lies to the left of minimum point of average cost (AC) (Q_2).

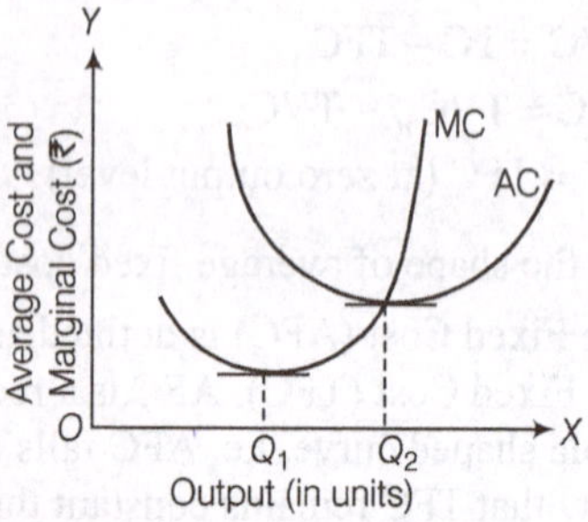

Value Points

For getting maximum marks, following value points can be included in the answer

- Both AC and MC curves should be shown in single graph.
- Curves can be drawn without proper scaling, but they must show all relationship points.

2. Define economic cost. Explain the relationship between total cost, total fixed cost and total variable cost with the help of a diagram. ***ISC 2012***

Ans Economic cost is the sum of explicit and implicit cost, i.e. total cost of hiring factor and non-factor services. Where, explicit cost is the cost of services hired from outsiders and implicit cost is the cost of services supplied by the owner itself.

Relationship between Total Cost (TC), **Total Fixed Cost** (TFC) **and Total Variable Cost** (TVC)

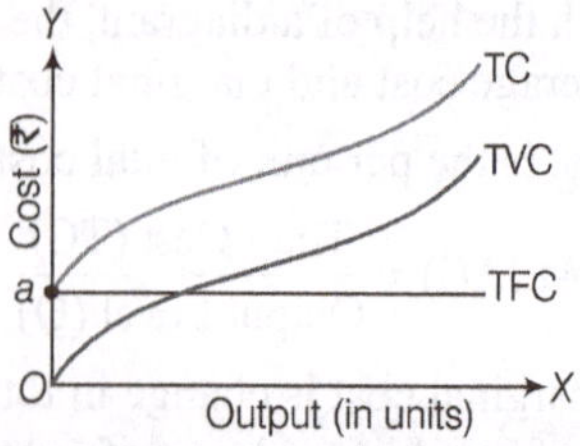

(i) Total cost is the sum total of Total Fixed Cost (TFC) and Total Variable Cost (TVC). i.e. TC = TFC + TVC.

(ii) Difference between TC and TFC is TVC, while difference between TC and TVC is TFC.

(iii) TVC curve starts from origin, as TVC is zero when output is zero.

(iv) TC and TFC curves start from point *a*, which is above the origin as TFC can never be zero and at zero level of output TC = TFC.

(v) TC and TVC curves are parallel to each other as their difference is TFC which remains fixed for all the levels of output.

(vi) The gap between TC and TFC curves increases continuously, as TVC rises with level of output.

(vii) TC and TVC curves initially rise at a diminishing rate, then at an increasing rate due to law of variable proportion.

3. The cost function of a firm is given below

Output (units)	0	1	2	3	4
Total Cost (₹)	60	80	100	111	116

Find

(i) Total Fixed Cost (ii) Total Variable Cost
(iii) Average Fixed Cost (iv) Average Variable Cost
(v) Marginal Cost ***ISC 2012***

Ans

Output (units)	Total Cost (TC) (₹)	Total Fixed Cost (TFC) (₹)	Total Variable Cost (TVC) (₹)	Average Fixed Cost (AFC) (₹)	Average Variable Cost (AVC) (₹)	Marginal Cost (MC) (₹)
0	60	60	—	—	—	—
1	80	60	20	60	20	20
2	100	60	40	30	20	20
3	111	60	51	20	17	11
4	116	60	56	15	14	5

Formulae used,

(i) TC = TFC + TVC

(ii) TFC = TC − TVC *or* AFC × Q

(iii) TVC = TC − TFC *or* AVC × Q

(iv) $\text{MC} = \text{TVC}_n - \text{TVC}_{n-1}$

(v) $\text{AFC} = \dfrac{\text{TFC}}{Q}$ (vi) $\text{AVC} = \dfrac{\text{TVC}}{Q}$

4. The cost function of a firm is given below ***ISC 2007***

Output (units)	0	1	2	3	4	5	6
Total Cost (₹)	40	80	110	125	128	135	180

Find

(i) Total Fixed Cost (ii) Total Variable Cost
(iii) Average Fixed Cost (iv) Average Variable Cost
(v) Average Total Cost (vi) Marginal Cost

Ans

Output (units)	Total Cost (TC) (₹)	Total Fixed Cost (TFC) (₹)	Total Variable Cost (TVC) (₹)	Average Fixed Cost (AFC) (₹)	Average Variable Cost (AVC) (₹)	Average Total Cost (ATC) (₹)	Marginal Cost (MC) (₹)
0	40	40	0	—	—	—	—
1	80	40	40	40	40	80	40
2	110	40	70	20	35	55	30
3	125	40	85	13.33	28.33	41.67	15
4	128	40	88	10	22	32	3
5	135	40	95	8	19	27	7
6	180	40	140	6.67	23.33	30	45

Formulae used,

(i) $TC = TFC + TVC$

(ii) $TFC = TC - TVC$ *or* $AFC \times Q$

(iii) $TVC = TC - TFC$ *or* $AVC \times Q$

(iv) $MC = TVC_n - TVC_{n-1}$

(v) $AFC = \frac{TFC}{Q}$

(vi) $AVC = \frac{TVC}{Q}$

5. Define average cost and marginal cost of production. Explain the shapes of the average cost curves. **ISC 2006**

Ans Average cost is defined as per unit of total cost i.e.

$$\text{Average Cost (AC)} = \frac{\text{Total Cost (TC)}}{\text{Number of Units Produced } (Q)}$$

Marginal cost is defined as incremental cost or addition cost of production which is incurred on production of an additional unit of output. i.e.

$$\text{Marginal Cost (MC)} = \frac{\text{Change in Total Cost}(\Delta TC)}{\text{Change in Output}(\Delta Q)}$$

Shapes of average cost curve There are three different average cost curves, which are as follows

(i) Average Fixed Cost (AFC)
(ii) Average Total Cost (ATC)
(iii) Average Variable Cost (AVC)

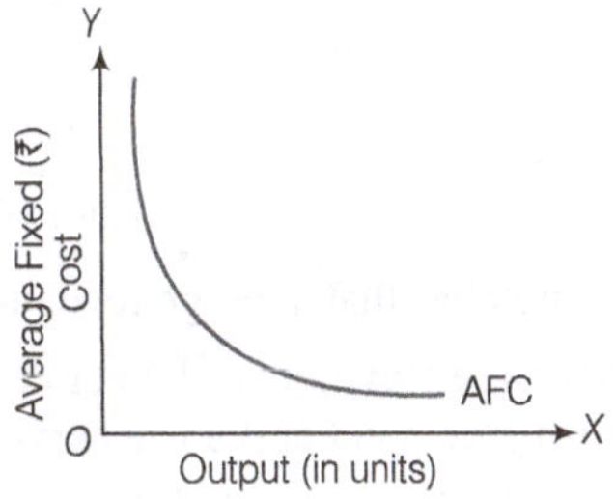

(i) **Average Fixed Cost** (AFC) It is defined as per unit total fixed cost. Average fixed cost is a rectangular hyperbola shape curve i.e. AFC falls continuously as total fixed cost remains constant and when divided with increasing level of output, it falls continuously, but it can never be equal to zero, as total fixed cost is always positive. Also the area below AFC remains constant.

(ii) **Average Total Cost** (ATC) It is the per unit of Total Cost (TC) calculated as total cost divided by output level.

(iii) **Average Variable Cost** (AVC) Average variable cost is per unit total variable cost calculated as total variable cost divided by output level.

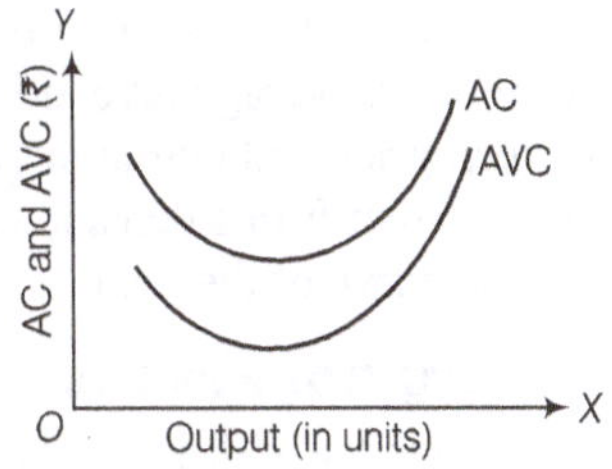

Both the AC and AVC curves are 'U' shaped in general, though the gap between the curves falls continuously as the level of output rises but they can never intersect each other. Because the difference between average total cost and average variable cost is average fixed cost which gradually falls but never becomes zero.

Value Points

For getting maximum marks, following value points can be included in the answer

- AFC is a rectangular hyperbola shape curve and can never be equal to zero.
- Vertical gap between AC and AVC must get narrower with rise in output.

TOPIC 2

Concepts of Revenue and Relation between Various Revenue Concepts

Revenue

It refers to money receipts of the producer from the sale of his output in a given period of time. Revenue is different from the profit. It can be calculated as

$$\text{Revenue} = \text{Costs} + \text{Profit}$$

Concepts of Revenue

Concepts of revenue has three variants, *viz* Total Revenue (TR), Average Revenue (AR) and Marginal Revenue (MR).

1. Total Revenue (TR)

It refers to the total amount of money income received by the firm from selling a given amount of his output. Total revenue is calculated by multiplying price with the quantity (units) sold. i.e.

$$\text{Total Revenue} = \text{Price} \times \text{Quantity Sold} \quad or \quad \text{TR} = P \times Q$$

2. Average Revenue (AR)

It refers to the revenue received (earned) per unit of output sold. It is calculated by dividing total revenue with units of output sold. i.e.

$$\text{Average Revenue} = \frac{\text{Total Revenue}}{\text{Units of Output Sold}} \quad or \; \text{AR} = \frac{\text{TR}}{\text{Q}}$$

Remember that average revenue is same as the price.

Average Revenue (AR) **curve is firm's demand curve** Firm's demand curve is a curve showing relationship between price of the products and its quantity demanded in the market. We know, for a firm, price is equal to average revenue and average revenue curve shows the relationship between price and output in the market. Accordingly, we can state that firm's demand curve is the same as average revenue curve of the firm.

3. Marginal Revenue (MR)

It measures the additional revenue that is generated by selling an extra unit of output. Marginal revenue can be calculated by dividing change in total revenue with change in units of output sold. i.e.

$$\text{Marginal Revenue} = \frac{\text{Change in Total Revenue}}{\text{Change in Units of Output Sold}}$$

$$or \qquad \text{MR} = \frac{\Delta\text{TR}}{\Delta Q}, \; \text{TR}_n - \text{TR}_{n-1}$$

Negative Marginal Revenue (MR) Negative marginal revenue is possible only when price is declining under monopoly or monopolistic competition.

It is not possible under perfect competition, where price remains constant.

Relationship between Average Revenue (AR) and Marginal Revenue (MR) under Perfect Competition

Under perfect competition, firms are able to sell their output only at a fixed price (i.e. industry is price maker and individual firm is price taker and individual firm cannot influence the market price).

As a result, average revenue and marginal revenue becomes equal. Both the curves are horizontal line parallel to *X*-axis. Average revenue also represents demand curve of the firm.

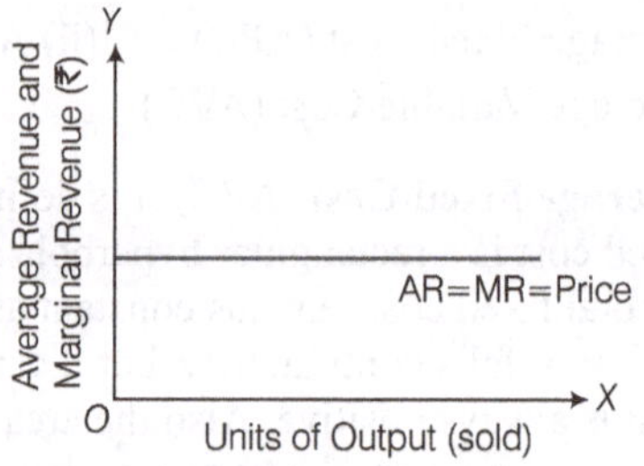

Relationship between Total Revenue (TR) and Marginal Revenue (MR) under Perfect Competition

As under perfect competition, price cannot be changed by the firms and hence, it remains constant. Marginal revenue is the rate of change of total revenue. As marginal revenue remains constant, total revenue increases but at a constant rate. i.e. it is a straight line from origin i.e. positively slope straight line.

Schedule

Output (units)	TR (₹)	AR (₹)	MR (₹)
1	10	10	10
2	20	10	10
3	30	10	10
4	40	10	10
5	50	10	10

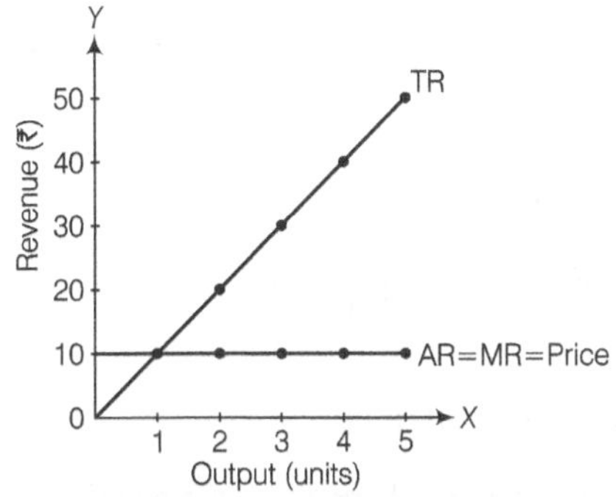

Relationship between Average Revenue (AR) and Marginal Revenue (MR) under Imperfect Competition

Under imperfect competition, firms can sell more only by lowering price of the commodity, as a result, both average revenue and marginal revenue are downward sloping.

Relationship between AR and MR under imperfect competition is stated below

Schedule

Output (units)	TR (₹)	AR (₹)	MR (₹)
1	15	15	15
2	28	14	13
3	36	12	8
4	36	9	0
5	35	7	–1
6	30	5	–5

(i) Marginal Revenue always lies below average revenue.
(ii) Slope of MR is half of slope of AR.
(iii) MR can become zero or even negative but AR cannot be, as AR is price.

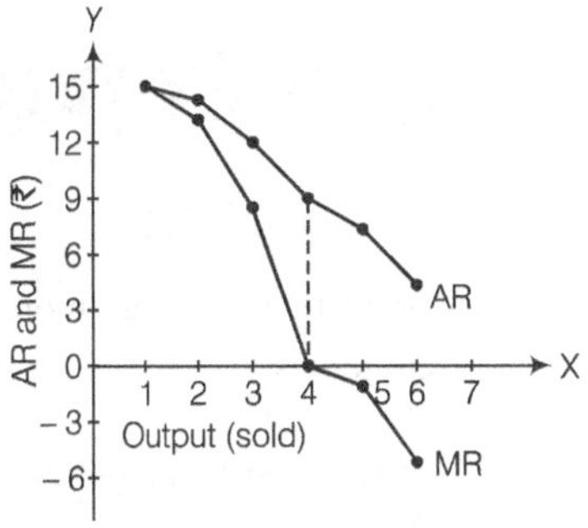

(iv) At the mid-point of AR curve, MR becomes equal to zero.
(v) Below the mid-point of AR, MR becomes negative.

Relationship between Total Revenue (TR) and Marginal Revenue (MR) under Imperfect Competition

As under imperfect competition, price does not remain constant, as a result, marginal revenue is also not constant, hence

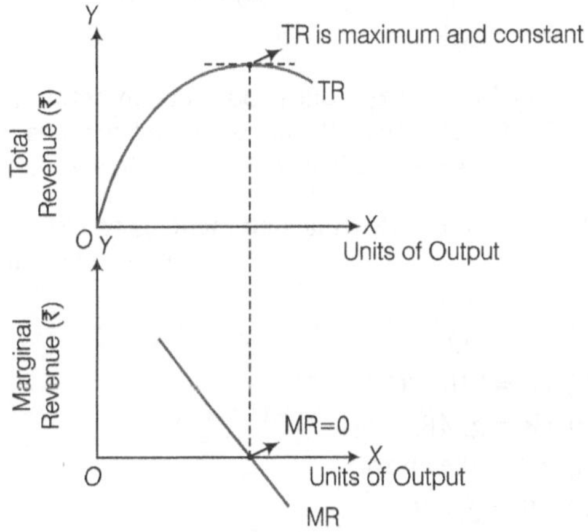

(i) When marginal revenue falls but remains positive, total revenue increases at a diminishing rate.
(ii) When marginal revenue reaches zero, total revenue reaches its maximum point and remains constant.
(iii) When marginal revenue becomes negative, total revenue falls.

PYQs Previous Years' Questions

1 Mark Questions

1. AR and MR curves are more elastic in **ISC Sem I 2021**
   (a) Oligopoly
   (b) Monopoly
   (c) Monopolistic Competition
   (d) Duopoly

Ans (c) Monopolistic Competition

2. When MR is perfectly elastic, TR is **ISC Sem I 2021**
   (a) Upward sloping (b) Downward sloping
   (c) Concave to origin (d) Convex to origin

Ans (a) Upward sloping

3. What is the relationship between AR and MR under perfect competition? **ISC Sem I Specimen 2021**
   (a) AR > MR (b) AR < MR
   (c) AR = MR (d) AR ≠ MR

Ans (c) AR = MR

Concept Enhancer Under perfect competition, as the price per unit remains the same, AR and MR becomes equal to each other.

4. Which of the following statements is true? **ISC Sem I Specimen 2021**
   (a) $AR = \frac{MR}{Q}$
   (b) $TR = MR \times Q$
   (c) $TR = \Sigma MR$
   (d) All of the above

Ans (c) $TR = \Sigma MR$

5. 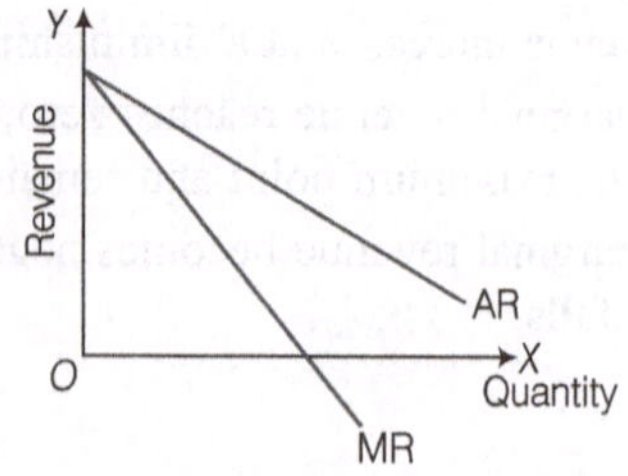

Figure

In figure, what is the slope of AR curve and MR curve? **ISC Sem I Specimen 2021**
   (a) AR = 2MR
   (b) MR = 2AR
   (c) Slope of AR = 2 × Slope of MR
   (d) Slope of MR = 2 × Slope of AR

Ans (d) Slope of MR = 2 × Slope of AR

6. Based on the data given in the table below, find the product pricing.

Output (Units)	0	1	2	3	4
TR (₹)	0	12	24	36	48

The product price facing the firm is **ISC Sem I Specimen 2021**
   (a) ₹ 6 (b) ₹ 8
   (c) ₹ 1 (d) None of these

Ans (d) None of these

Hint $AR = P = \frac{TR}{Q} = \frac{12}{1} = 12$

2 Marks Questions

1. Name the market where average revenue is equal to marginal revenue. Give a reason for your answer. **ISC 2015**

Ans Average revenue equals marginal revenue which is the same as the market price, in perfect competition market form. This is because a uniform price prevails in the market for a homogeneous product. This happens due to the main reason of infinitely large number of buyers and sellers under this frm of market.

2. Which revenue concept is also called 'price'? Justify your answer by giving a reason. **ISC 2012**

Ans Average Revenue (AR) is also known as 'price'. As average revenue refers to per unit of total revenue and it is calculated as total revenue divided by output sold. i.e.

$$\text{Average Revenue (AR)} = \frac{\text{Total Revenue (TR)}}{\text{Units of Output } (Q)}$$

$$= \frac{P \times Q}{Q} = \text{Price}$$

Hence, AR = Price. These two are always equal in economic sense.

3. Define marginal revenue. How can we get marginal revenue from total revenue? **ISC 2010**

Ans Marginal Revenue (MR) is defined as the additional revenue earned by selling an extra unit of output.

It is calculated as

Marginal Revenue (MR)

$$= \frac{\text{Change in Total Revenue } (\Delta TR)}{\text{Change in Units of Output } (\Delta Q)}$$

4. When can the AR = MR = Price? Give reason for your answer. **ISC 2009**

Ans Under perfect competition, AR = MR = Price. As under perfect competition, firms cannot change the market price, which remains constant and MR is the additional revenue which is also remains constant.

5. Why is the MR curve below the AR curve under imperfect competition? **ISC 2008**

Ans Under imperfect competition, firms can sell more only by lowering price. As we know that AR is also called price and MR is the additional revenue. Price falls continuously, hence, both are downward sloping and MR lies below AR curve.

3/4 Marks Questions

1. Explain with help of a diagram, the relationship betwen MR and TR under imperfect competition. **ISC 2020**

Ans Refer to text on page 89.

2. With the help of a diagram, explain the relationship between AR and MR of a firm under imperfect competition. **ISC 2019**

Ans Relationship between AR and MR under imperfect competition

(i) Both AR and MR curves slope downwards as firms can sell more only by lowering prices.
(ii) MR curve lies below AR curve, i.e. AR curve is more elastic as compared to MR curve.
(iii) Slope of MR is half of slope of AR.
(iv) At mid-point of AR curve, MR = 0
(v) Below mid-point of AR, MR becomes negative.
(vi) MR can be negative, but AR cannot.

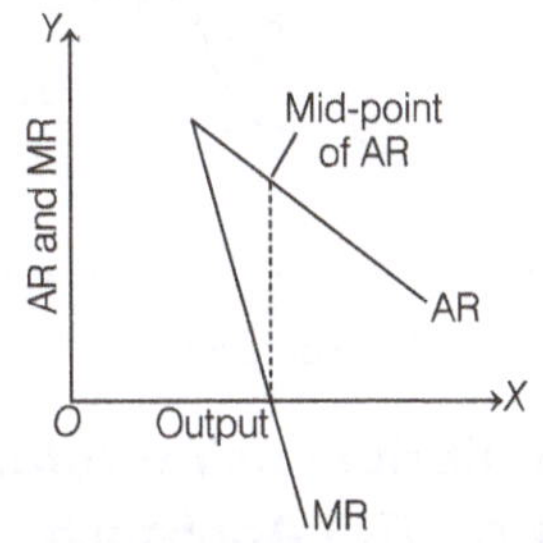

Relationship between AR and MR

Concept Enhancer AR curve is also the demand of the firm. Thus, at the mid-point of a downward sloping demand curve or AR, elasticity of demand is always equal to one.

3. Draw the TR and AR curves under perfect competition, with the help of a schedule. **ISC 2016**

KEY IDEA
In perfect competition, a uniform price prevails in the market. Producers can sell any quantity of a goods at that price.

Ans Schedule showing Total Revenue (TR) and Average Revenue (AR) of a firm operating in perfect competition market.

Schedule

Output	Price Per Unit (₹)	Average Revenue (₹)	Total Revenue (₹)
1	20	20	20
2	20	20	40
3	20	20	60
4	20	20	80
5	20	20	100
6	20	20	120

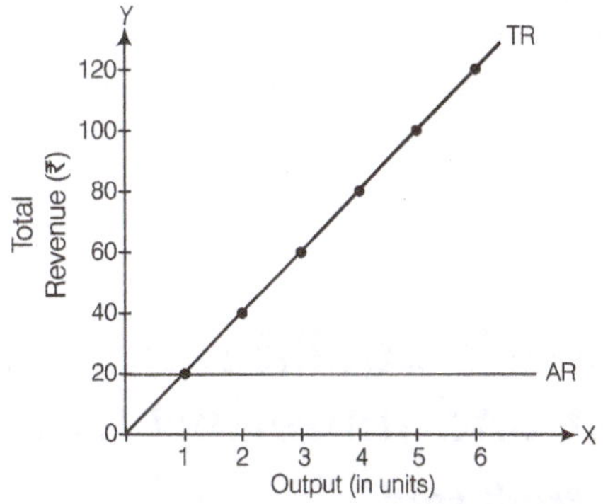

Graph depicting total revenue and average revenue curves.

4. Explain the nature of AR and MR curve under perfect and imperfect competition. **ISC 2013**

Ans **Nature of AR and MR curve under perfect competition** Under perfect competition, firms cannot influence the market price, which remains fixed. As a result, Average Revenue (AR) (price) becomes equal to Marginal Revenue (MR). Both AR and MR curves are horizontal line parallel to X-axis, i.e. both the curves are perfectly elastic.

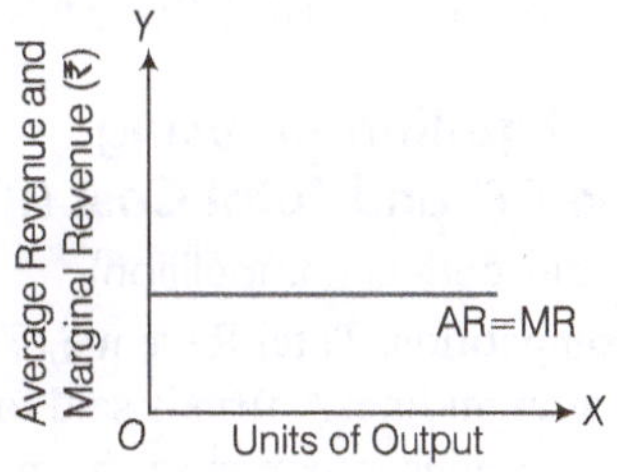

Nature of AR and MR curve under imperfect competition Under imperfect competition, firms have full or partial control over price and they can sell more output only by lowering the price.

As a result, both AR and MR curves slope downwards, wherein MR curve lies below AR curve, i.e. AR curve is more elastic as compare to MR curve.

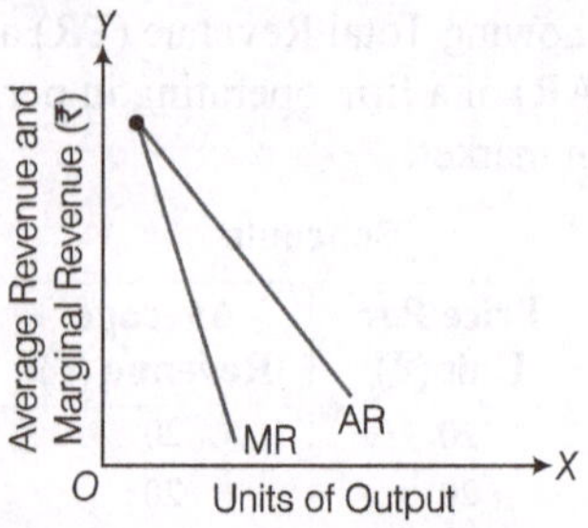

5. Using diagram, distinguish between the shapes of the total revenue curve under perfect and imperfect competition. ***ISC 2011***

Ans **Behaviour of total revenue under perfect competition** Total Revenue (TR) is the total money income received from sale of particular units of output.

Under perfect competition, price remains constant, as a result, AR is equal to MR and MR is the rate of TR, hence TR under perfect competition rises at a constant rate. i.e. it is a straight line from origin.

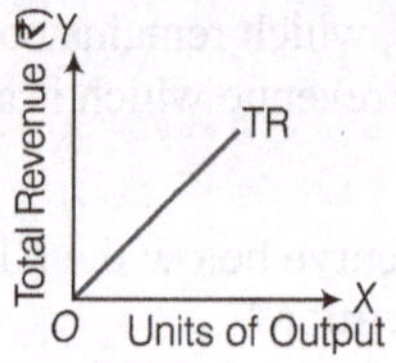

Behaviour of total revenue under imperfect competition Under imperfect competition, firms can influence the price, as a result, AR and MR are not constant, rather price falls with rise in output and MR lies below AR. Hence, TR initially increases though at a diminishing rate, reaches its maximum point and eventually starts to fall.

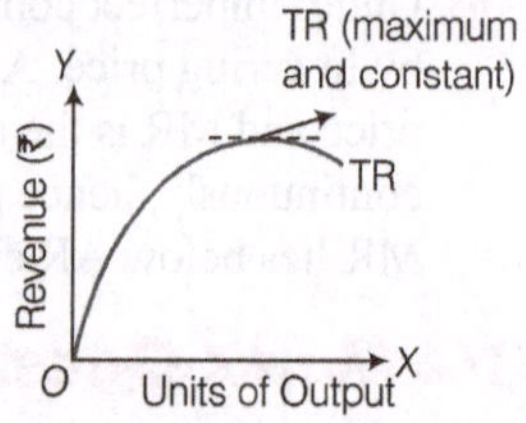

Common Mistake Students generally write TR as maximum. It should be written as maximum and constant.

TOPIC 3

Producer's Equilibrium Under Perfect and Imperfect Competition

Goal of Producers

Profit is the ultimate aim of all business firms. Therefore, all economic decisions of the firm generally targeted towards the maximisation of the firm's profit.

Producer's Equilibrium

Producer's equilibrium refers to a situation in which a rational producer maximises his profits or minimises his losses given his resources. It is also known as 'profit maximisation situation'.

There are two approaches of producer's equilibrium

(i) TR – TC approach (ii) MR – MC approach

1. Producer's Equilibrium using Total Revenue (TR) and Total Cost (TC) Approach (under perfect competition)

Under perfect competition, Total Revenue (TR) is an upward sloping straight line. A firm is said to be in equilibrium, when producer maximises his profit, i.e. Profit = TR – TC, is maximum. Producer will be in equilibrium at point a, a_1 where in the gap between TR and TC are maximum.

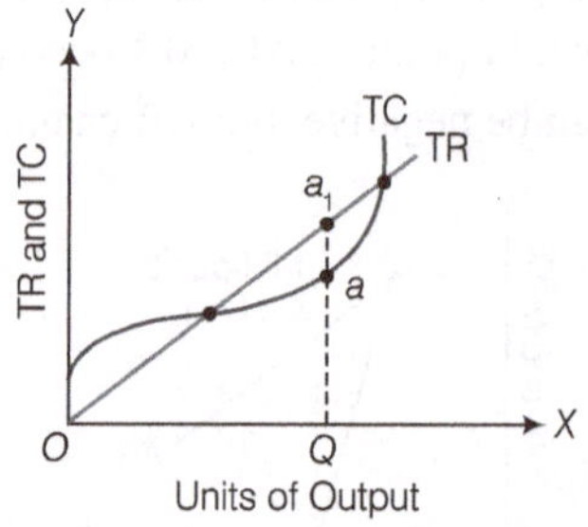

Producer's Equilibrium using Total Revenue (TR) and Total Cost (TC) Approach (under imperfect competition)

Under imperfect competition, TR initially increases and eventually falls, however, a firm under imperfect competition will be in equilibrium of the point, where producer maximises his profit given his cost.

Producer will be in equilibrium at point a to a_1, where he attains maximum profit.

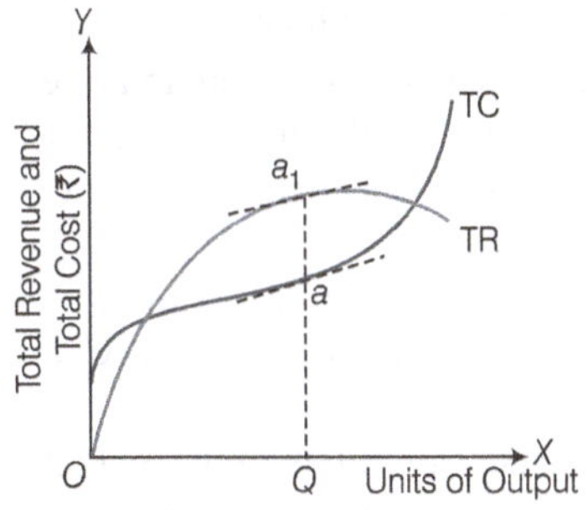

2. Producer's Equilibrium under Perfect Competition (MR – MC approach)

Under perfect competition, MR and AR are equal and they are horizontal line parallel to X-axis. Hence, there are two essential conditions for equilibrium, which are as follows

(i) MR = MC

(ii) MC should cut MR from below i.e. at equilibrium point, MC must be rising.

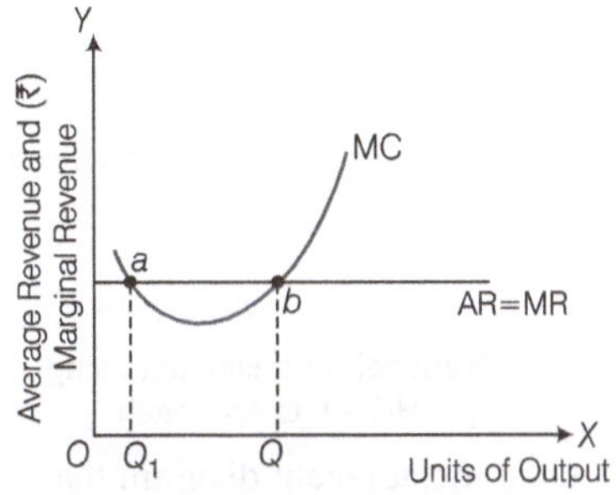

Although MC = MR is also satisfied at point a but it does not satisfy second condition (i.e. MC must be rising), so producer will be in equilibrium at point b, as both equilibrium conditions get satisfied at point b only and he will produce OQ quantity.

Producer's Equilibrium under Imperfect Competition (MR – MC approach)

Under imperfect competition, AR and MR curves are downward sloping, where MR lies below AR, producer equilibrium conditions are same as before that is

(i) MR = MC

(ii) MC should cut MR from below i.e. at equilibrium point, MC must be rising.

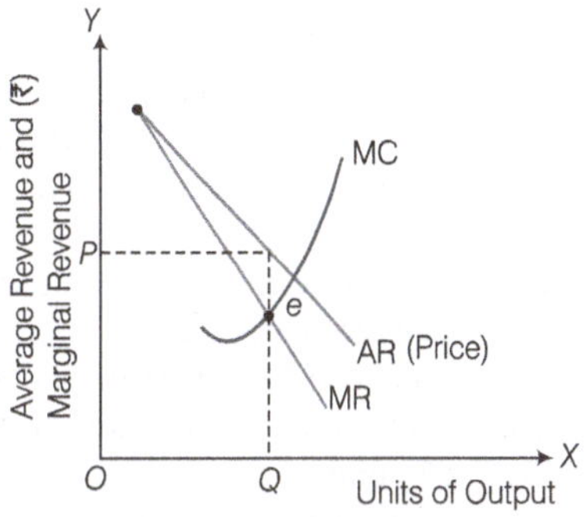

Hence, producer will be in equilibrium at point e, charging a price OP and selling quantity equal to OQ.

Perfectly competitive market is more efficient than imperfect competition, as under perfect competition, firms sell till P = MC, whereas, under imperfect competition, firms sell till MR = MC.

> Normal Profit – This exists when TR = TC, i.e. TR = TFC + TVC + Normal Profit. This situation is also known as break-even point.
>
> Super Normal Profit – If a firm makes more than normal profit, it is called 'Super Normal Profit' i.e. TR > TC
>
> Abnormal Loss – If a firm makes less revenue (TR) than cost (TC), it is called 'Super normal loss' or 'abnormal loss'.

PYQs Previous Years' Questions

1 Mark Questions

1. A firm produces its profit maximising level of output only when *ISC Specimen 2023*

(a) MR = AR (b) MR > MC

(c) AR < MR (d) MC = MR

Ans (d) MC = MR

2. A competitive firm will be in equilibrium when *ISC Sem I Specimen 2021*

(a) MR = MC and MC cuts MR from below

(b) AR = AC; AC cuts AR from above

(c) TR = TC (d) None of these

Ans (a) MR = MC and MC cuts MR from below

3. Firms maximise their profits by producing a level of output at which *ISC Sem I Specimen 2021*

(a) MC = AFC

(b) MC = MR

(c) P = ATC (d) MR = AVC

Ans (b) MC = MR

4. 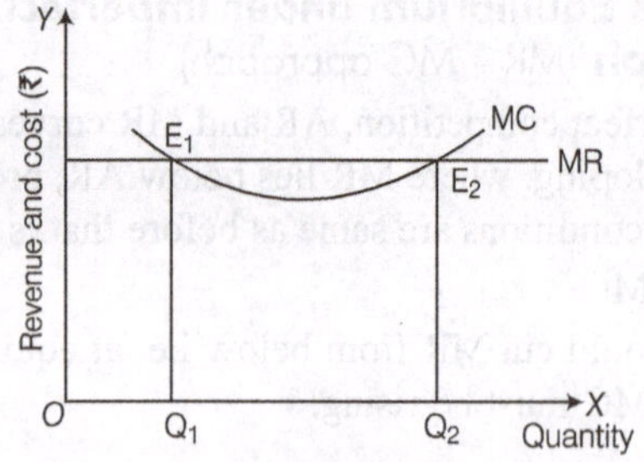

Figure

In figure, what is the condition of equilibrium?
ISC Sem I Specimen 2021

(a) Necessary condition of equilibrium has been satisfied at E_2 only.
(b) Necessary and sufficient conditions of equilibrium have been satisfied at E_2 only.
(c) Sufficient condition has been satisfied at E_1 only.
(d) Necessary and sufficient conditions have been satisfied at E_1 only.

Ans (b) Necessary and sufficient conditions of equilibrium have been satisfied at E_2 only.

2 Marks Questions

1. What is meant by super normal profit? ***ISC 2011***

Ans Super normal profit refers to the situation in which total revenue of a firm exceeds its total cost, i.e. Total Revenue (TR) > Total Cost (TC). In other words, market price is over and above what is required to cover the fixed cost and variable cost.

2. Is it possible to measure profits earned by a firm in the following diagram? Explain why. ***ISC 2008***

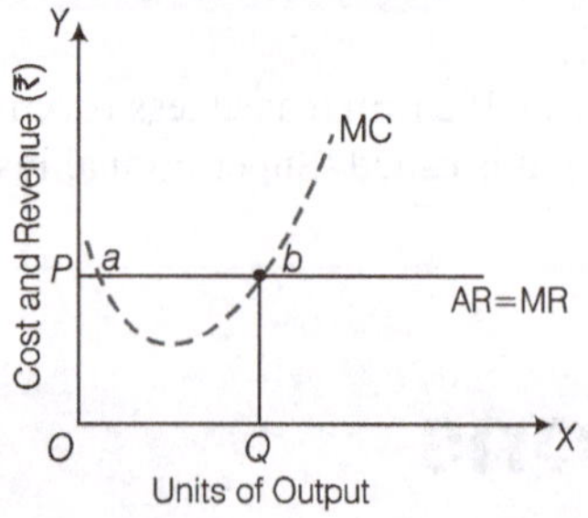

Ans No, it is not possible to measure the level of profit by only looking at the diagram. Profit per unit is the amount by which AR exceeds AC. Since, the diagram does not depict the AC of the firm. At best, we can just say that the producer will be in equilibrium at the point, where MC= MR and hence, profit will be maximum.

Common Mistake Students generally consider both points 'a' and 'b' as equilibrium. It should be remembered that equilibrium is attained only on rising part of MC.

6 Marks Questions

1. A producer is in equilibrium when MR = MC. Explain this statement with the help of a diagram. ***ISC 2019***

Or Discuss producer's equilibrium in perfect competition, using MR and MC approach. ***ISC 2017***

Or Explain how a producer can maximise profit by using MR and MC curves. ***ISC 2015***

Or How does a producer attain equilibrium under perfect competition through the MR and MC approach? ***ISC 2013***

Ans Perfect competition refers to the market situation in which firms are not in the position to change the market price, hence, price i.e. Average Revenue (AR) remains constant. In such a situation, the conditions for producer's equilibrium using MR – MC approach is as follows

(i) Marginal Revenue (MR) = Marginal Cost (MC)
(ii) MC should cut MR from below, i.e. MC should be rising beyond the point of equilibrium.

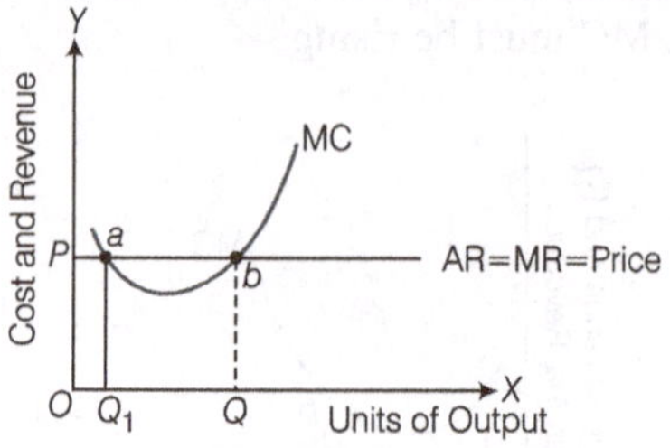

Producer's Equilibrium using MR – MC Approach

We can see in the adjacent diagram that AR curve and MR curve are one and the same are parallel to X-axis representing that price remains constant.

On the other hand, MC curve is 'U' shaped. It must be noted here, that MC and MR are equal at point *a* and point *b*, however point *a* could not be considered as point of equilibrium because beyond this point MC is falling.

Therefore, producer will be in equilibrium at point *b* because at this point both the conditions of equilibrium are fulfilled. He will be producing *OQ* level of output and charging *OP* price. Till point *b*, producer can increase profits by producing more because MR > MC. However, beyond point b, MC > MR. Hence, it can be concluded that point *b* is the point of equilibrium.

Concept Enhancer At the point of equilibrium a producer may earn super normal profit or suffer normal loss or even be at break-even.

2. Explain how a producer attains equilibrium using the TR and TC approach. *ISC 2018, 2014*

Ans Producer's equilibrium refers to a situation in which the producer either maximises his profits or minimises his losses. There are two approaches of producer's equilibrium i.e.

(i) TR – TC approach (ii) MR – MC approach

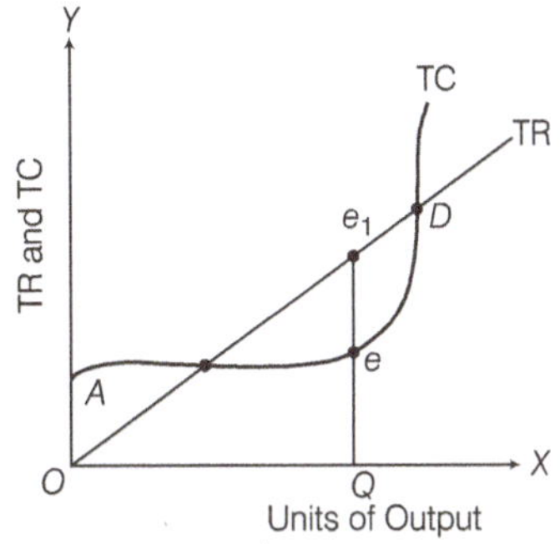

Producer's equilibrium using TR-TC approach

According to TR – TC approach, a producer will be at equilibrium at the point, where the gap between TR and TC i.e. profit is maximum.

The essential conditions for producer's equilibrium are as follows

(a) The difference between TR and TC is positively maximised.

(b) Total profit must fall, after equilibrium level of output.

In the diagram, we have shown producer's equilibrium using TR – TC by assuming, price as constant, hence, TR is a straight line starting from origin.

In the given diagram, TR and TC are equal at two points i.e *B* and *D*, these refer to the situation of normal profit (no profit-no loss situation).

The profit i.e. the difference between TR and TC is maximum at point ee_1, hence the producer will be in equilibrium at point ee_1, producing OQ_e level of output.

It must be noted that except ee_1, there could not be any other point of equilibrium, as only at this point, both the conditions of equilibrium get satisfied and to the left of point *B* and to the right of point *D*, there are losses.

Value Points

For getting maximum marks, following value points can be included in the answer

- Show the maximum profit using diagram.
- Conditions of the equilibrium must be stated poperly.

Case Based Questions

Case 1

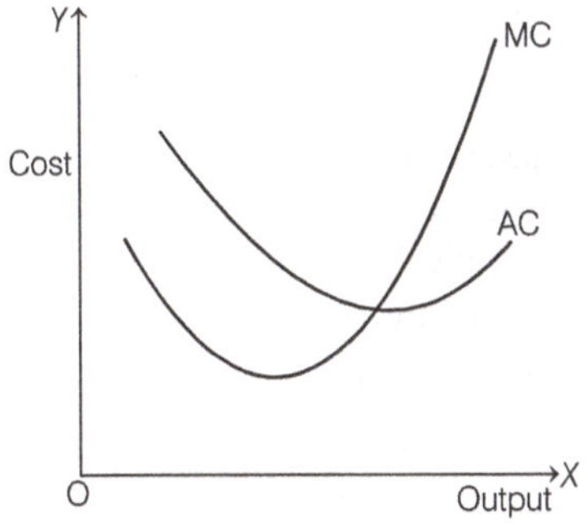

ISC Sem I 2021

(i) Choose the correct option

(a) When MC > AC, AC falls

(b) When MC < AC, AC rises

(c) When MC = AC, AC falls

(d) When MC > AC, AC rises

Ans (d) When MC > AC, AC rises

(ii) MC cuts AC at AC's .... point.

(a) Maximum point (b) Minimum point

(c) When AC is rising

(d) When AC becomes parallel to X-axis

Ans (b) Minimum point

Case 2

Choose the correct answer to fill the following table

ISC Sem I 2021

Output	Price	TR	AR
2	9		
3	7		

(i) The TR will be

(a) 18, 21 (b) 20, 27

(c) 15, 16 (d) 20, 21

Ans (a) 18, 21

Hint TR = Output × Price

(ii) The AR will be

(a) 9, 8 (b) 9, 7

(c) 10, 8 (d) 7, 9

Ans (b) 9, 7

Hint $AR = \frac{TR}{Output}$

Case 3

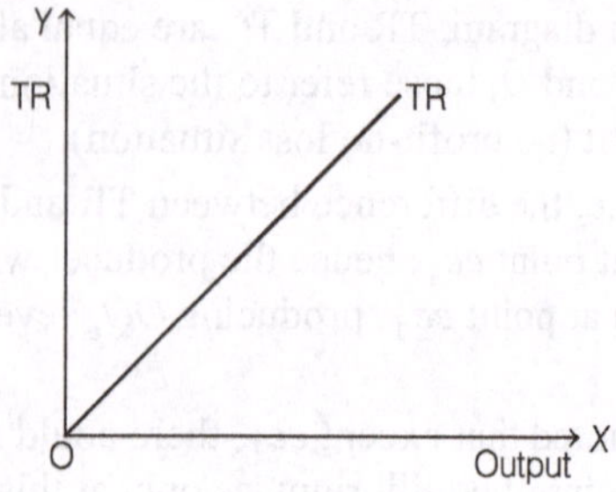

ISC Sem I 2021

(i) The TR curve in the above diagram belongs to

(a) Monopoly

(b) Monopolistic Competition

(c) Oligopoly

(d) Perfect Competition

Ans (d) Perfect Competition

(ii) The curve is a straight line because

(a) Price is increasing with output

(b) Price is decreasing with output

(c) Price remains constant

(d) Marginal revenue is increasing

Ans (c) Price remains constant

(iii) TR is calculated as

(a) Price × Output (b) AR × MR

(c) AC × MR (d) TC × Price

Ans (a) Price × Output

Case 4

Based on the data given in the table, calculate the AFC and AVC. ***ISC Sem I Specimen 2021***

Unit of Output	0	3	5
Total Cost (₹)	50	80	120

(i) AFC for 0, 3 and 5 units will be

(a) 0, 16.67, 10.00

(b) ∞, 16.00, 10.67

(c) 0, 16.00, 10.67

(d) ∞, 16.67, 10.00

Ans (d) ∞, 16.67, 10.00

Hint $TFC = 50$ and $AFC = \frac{TFC}{Q}$

(ii) AVC for 0, 3 and 5 units will be

(a) ∞, 10, 14

(b) 0, 10.1, 14.01

(c) ∞, 10.1, 14,01

(d) 0, 10, 14

Ans (d) 0, 10, 14

Hint $TVC = 0,\ 30,\ 70$ and $AVC = \frac{TVC}{Q}$

Case 5

Based on the data given in the table, calculate the TC and MC. ***ISC Sem I Specimen 2021***

Unit of Output	AC	TC	MC
1	20		
2	15		
3	30		

(i) TC will be

(a) 40, 60, 90 respectively

(b) 80, 60, 90 respectively

(c) 20, 30, 60 respectively

(d) 40, 60, 120 respectively

Ans (c) 20, 30, 60 respectively

Hint $TC = AC \times Q$

(ii) MC will be

(a) 0, 10, 20 respectively

(b) 20, 10, 30 respectively

(c) 10, 20, 30 respectively

(d) ∞, 10, 20 respectively

Ans (b) 20, 10, 30 respectively

Hint $MC = TC_n - TC_{n-1}$

CHAPTER TEST

01 Mark Questions

1. Assume that when price is ₹20, the quantity demanded is 9 units and when price is ₹19 the quantity demanded is 10 units. Based on this information, what is the marginal revenue resulting from an increase in output from 9 units to 10 units?
(a) ₹ 20 (b) ₹ 19
(c) ₹ 10 (d) ₹ 1

2. Average revenue is the revenue earned
(a) per unit of input
(b) per unit of output
(c) different units of input
(d) different units of output

3. Marginal revenue can be defined as the change in total revenue resulting from
(a) purchase of an additional unit of a commodity
(b) sale of an additional unit of a commodity
(c) sale of subsequent units of a product
(d) None of the above

4. When price remains constant at all level of output, total revenue
(a) increases at increasing rate
(b) increases at diminishing rate
(c) increases at constant rate
(d) None of the above

5. Social cost is only paid by the producer. State true or false.

6. At the point of equilibrium, a producer always earns super normal profit. State true or false.

7. Between the minimum point of MC and minimum point of AC, AC curve ....

8. Total cost is comprised of .... profit.

9. Define point of inflexion with respect to total variable cost curve.

10. What is the area of rectangles under AFC curve?

02 Marks Questions

11. If the total cost of producing 5 units of a commodity is ₹ 20 and that of producing 4 units is ₹ 15, what will be the Marginal Cost (MC)?

12. Why does Marginal Cost (MC) is equal to Average Cost (AC), only at its minimum point?

13. What will be the shape of AR and MR curves, when any output can be sold at the market price?

14. How are the total revenue of a firm, market price and quantity sold by the firm related to each other?

15. What is general profit maximising condition for a producer under MR – MC approach?

16. Can MR be zero or negative? Why?

03/04 Marks Questions

17. Complete the following table

Output	Total Cost (TC)	Average Cost (AC)	Marginal Cost (MC)
1	...	...	30
2	100	...	...
3	...	...	5
4	...	...	10
5	...	27	...
6	...	...	45

18. Explain the relationship between total revenue and marginal revenue with the help of a revenue schedule.

06 Marks Questions

19. Explain the relationship between AC, AVC and MC, using schedule and diagram.

20. Define producer's equilibrium. Explain the conditions of producer's equilibrium in terms of TC and TR (at falling prices). Use diagram.

Answers

1. (c) ₹ 10
2. (b) per unit of output
3. (b) sale of an additional unit of a commodity
4. (c) increases at constant rate
5. False *6.* False
7. rises
8. normal
10. Constant

06

Forms of Market and Application Tools of Demand and Supply

TREND ANALYSIS 5 YEARS

Average No. of Questions Across all Sets

	Types of Questions	2023	2020	2019	2018	2017
01 Main Market Forms	1 Mark	—	—	—	—	—
	2 Marks	1	—	1	2	1
	3/4 Marks	—	—	—	—	—
	6 Marks	1	1	1	1	1
02 Market Equilibrium under Perfect Competition	1 Mark	—	—	—	—	—
	2 Marks	2	—	—	—	—
	3/4 Marks	—	1	1	1	—
	6 Marks	1	1	—	1	—
03 Price Determination and Changes in Equilibrium	1 Mark	1	—	—	—	—
	2 Marks	—	1	—	1	—
	3/4 Marks	1	—	—	1	1
	6 Marks	—	1	1	—	—

TOPIC 1

Main Market Forms and their Features

Concept of Market

Market refers to the arrangement or mechanism by which buyers and sellers of a particular commodity are able to meet each other for having economic exchange, i.e. buying and selling at a particular price. In economics, it is a wide term not limited by geographical area, but relates to a product.

Forms of Market

On the basis of competition, market can be divided into two types

1. Perfect Competition

It refers to that form of market in which there are infinitely large number of buyers and sellers of a homogeneous product.

Note Perfect competition is basically an imaginary market form. It does not exist in reality.

The salient **features** of perfect competition are

(i) There are infinitely large number of buyers and sellers that no one can influence the price of commodity in market.

(ii) Firms sells homogeneous product i.e. identical so buyers are indifferent between sellers.

(iii) There are no barriers to entry or exit of firms, so all firms in industry will earn just normal profits in long-run.

(iv) The factors of production (i.e. land, labour, capital, entrepreneur, etc) are easily mobile from one line of production to another.

(v) Under perfect competition, no buyer will pay more than market price and no seller will charge less than market price. This is due to the assumption of perfect knowledge in the market.

(vi) There is no transportation cost because it is assumed that buyers and sellers are close to market.

(vii) There is zero advertisement cost because all products are identical.

(viii) Government does not interfere in the functioning of the market i.e. no intervention in form of taxes, subsidies, etc.

(ix) Price is determined by industry through market demand and supply, so firm is price taker while industry is price maker.

Note If only first three features are exhibited by a market, then it is known as 'pure competition'.

2. Imperfect Competition

It is a type of market structure showing some, but not all features of competitive market.

It may be classified into following types

(i) Monopolistic competition (ii) Oligopoly
(iii) Monopoly (iv) Monopsony

(i) Monopolistic Competition

Under this form of market, there are large number of buyers and sellers of differentiated products. Firm under this market has partial control over price.

Features of monopolistic competition are

(a) The number of firms in monopolistic competition is large but less than perfect competition. Buyers are assumed to be very large in size.

(b) Product differentiation is important feature of this market. Each firm produce a product that is atleast slightly different from those of other sellers.

(c) Firm can enter or exit the industry without restriction.

(d) Firm have partial control over price due to product differentiation.

(e) There is imperfect knowledge about product price, quality of product among buyers in the market.

(f) Under this market, products are differentiated and these differences are made known to the buyers through advertisement.

(g) Firms compete on the basis of brand, product quality, advertisement, etc.

(ii) Oligopoly

It is the form of the market in which there are a few big sellers of a commodity and a large number of buyers. Each seller has a significant share of the market. e.g. There are few auto producers in Indian market like Maruti, Tata, Ford and GM.

There are two main forms of oligopoly market

(a) Collusive oligopoly and Non-collusive oligopoly

(b) Pure and impure oligopoly.

The main **features** of oligopoly market are

(a) Few big firms dominating the market enjoy an important control over the price of the product.

(b) Perfect or pure oligopoly produces homogeneous product i.e. steel industry; imperfect or impure oligopoly produces differentiated products i.e. automobile companies.

(c) Under oligopoly, every firm remains alert to the actions of other firms and keep plan for counterattack. Therefore, there is a complete interdependence among firms.

(d) The firms can easily exit from the industry whenever it want but entry of new firm is difficult due to government licence, patents, high capital requirement, competition from existing firms, etc.

(e) Under this market, firms try to increase their market share through advertisement and other sales promotion techniques.

(iii) Monopoly

It refers to the market form in which there is only a single seller/producer and large number of buyers of a commodity which has no close substitute. Indian Railways is the example of monopoly.

Features of monopoly market are

(a) There is single seller in market i.e. no difference between firm and industry. Number of buyers is assumed to be large.

(b) The product produced by a monopolist firm has no close substitute.

(c) There exist strong barriers (i.e. licence, patents, cartel, natural resources, etc) to entry of new firm.

(d) Monopolist is a price maker and fixes its own market price because he has complete control over the industry output.

(e) A monopolist can charge different prices for his product from different persons and in different markets, known as 'price discrimination'.

(f) There is less advertisement expenditure due to single seller in market.

(iv) Monopsony

It refers to the market situation, in which there is a single buyer of the product who is not in competition with other buyers for the product which he purchases.

The main **features** of monopsony market are

(a) The word 'monopsony' actually translates as 'one buyer'. As the single buyer, he control the demand side of the market completely.

(b) There is a specialised product i.e. government is a single buyer for military procurement and military products are specialised in nature.

(c) Mobility of labour is very much limited either geographically or in terms of skills of offer.

(d) Often monopsony demands lower pricing from the suppliers. So, we may say that he is price maker.

Nature of Demand Curve under Different Market Forms

Demand curve under different market forms are given below

1. **Under perfect competition** It is horizontal straight line parallel to X-axis (i.e. perfectly elastic).

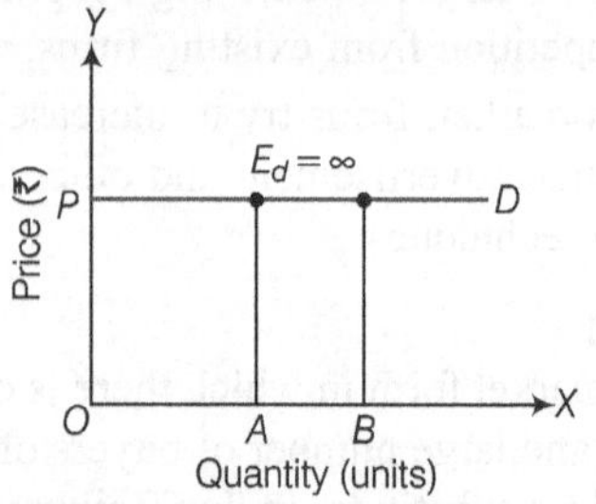

Demand Curve under Perfect Competition

2. **Under monopolistic competition** Demand curve is downward sloping but more elastic in nature because of the presence of large number of substitutes.

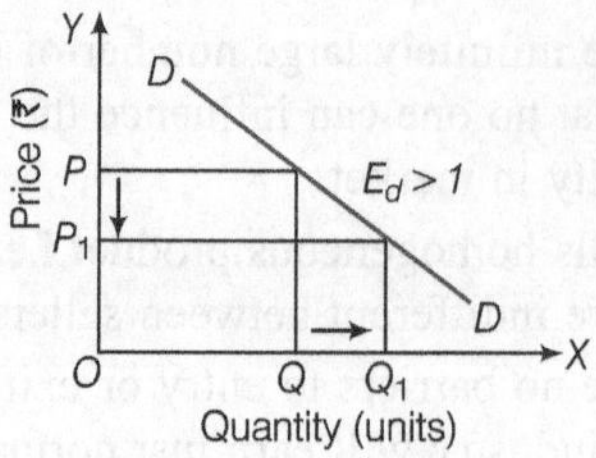

Demand Curve under Monopolistic Competition

3. **Under monopoly** Demand curve would be downward sloping but less elastic in nature because the product does not have close substitute, but consumers will buy more only at reduced price.

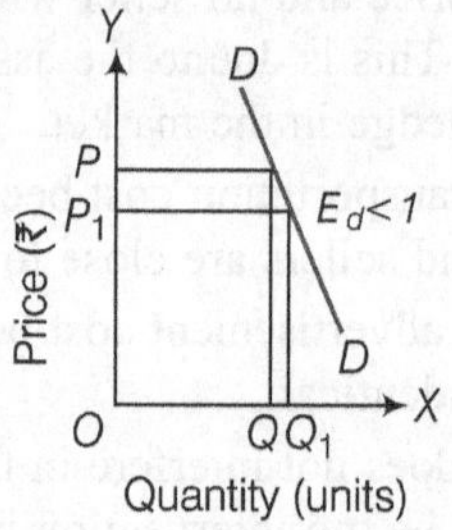

Demand Curve Under Monopoly

4. **Under oligopoly market** Demand curve cannot be determined or kinked shaped demand curve is drawn as propounded by Professor Paul Sweezy.

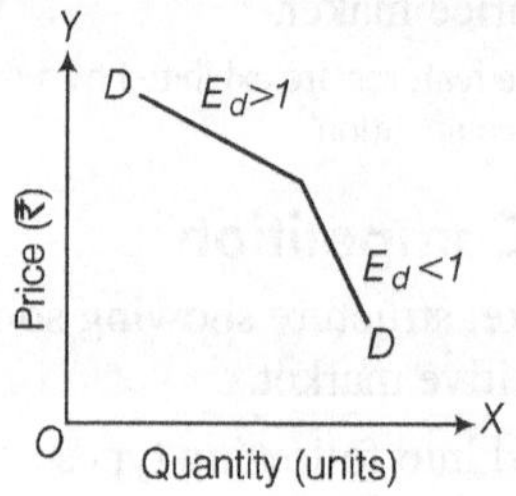

5. **Under monopsony market** Demand curve is downward sloping because buyer would buy more at less price.

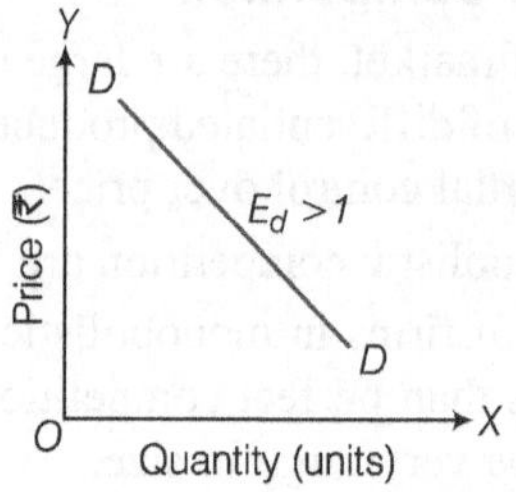

PYQs Previous Years' Questions

1 Mark Questions

1. An oligopolist has an indeterminate demand curve. What is the reason for this feature of oligopoly? *ISC Specimen 2023*

Ans This is due to the interdependence between firms under oligopoly market.

2. A monopoly market has *ISC Sem I 2021*
   (a) no barriers to entry (b) many substitutes
   (c) many suppliers (d) one seller

Ans (d) one seller

Concept Enhancer Number of buyers are large in all market except monopsony, it is only the number of seller that varies.

3. Selling cost is not required in *ISC Sem I 2021*
   (a) perfect competition and monopolistic competition
   (b) oligopoly and monopolistic competition
   (c) monopoly and oligopoly
   (d) monopoly and perfect competition

Ans (d) monopoly and perfect competition

4. Which of the following is not a characteristic of a price taker firm? *ISC Sem I 2021*
   (a) $TR = P \times Q$ (b) AR = Price
   (c) AR = MR = Price
   (d) Negatively sloped demand curve

Ans (d) Negatively sloped demand curve

5. In the context of monopolistic competition, which of the following is correct? *ISC Sem I 2021*
   (a) Firm has full control over price
   (b) Horizontal straight line in demand curve of the firm
   (c) Freedom of entry and exit
   (d) Selling cost do not exist

Ans (c) Freedom of entry and exit

6. In a perfectly competitive market, who decides the price? *ISC Sem I Specimen 2021*
   (a) A firm (b) An industry
   (c) Both (a) and (b) (d) None of these

Ans (b) An industry

7. Monopolistic competition is a form of market in which there are large number of sellers of a particular product, with each seller selling *ISC Sem I Specimen 2021*
   (a) homogenous products
   (b) differentiated products which are entirely distinct from each other
   (c) perfect substitutes
   (d) differentiated products which are close substitutes to the product

Ans (d) differentiated products which are close substitutes to the product

8. The demand curve for the firm operating under perfect competition is *ISC Sem I Specimen 2021*
   (a) upward sloping to the right
   (b) downward sloping to the right
   (c) perfectly horizontal line (d) perfectly vertical line

Ans (c) perfectly horizontal line

2 Marks Questions

1. State any two features of oligopoly. *ISC 2023*

Ans Features of oligopoly includes
   (i) Few sellers and large number of buyers
   (ii) Homogenous and heterogenous goods sold.

2. What is meant by intense competition under oligopoly? *ISC Specimen 2023*

Ans There are few firms under oligopoly market but each seller is very large in size. Thus, there exist interdependency between firms. No firm can take decision without considering the probable reaction of its competitors. This situation is referred to as intense or cut-throat competition.

3. Explain any two features of perfect competition. *ISC* *ISC Specimen 2023*

Ans Features of perfect competition are as follows
   (i) **Large number of buyers and sellers** Under perfect competition, there are very large number of buyers and sellers that each individual agent becomes negligable.
   (ii) **Firms are price taker** Under perfect competition, firms become price taker as all sellers sell homogenous goods.

4. What is meant by product differentiation in monopolistic competition? *ISC 2019*

Ans In product differentiation, products are similar but still differentiated in terms of quantity, quality, size, shape, colour etc. This is a distinguishing feature in monopolistic competition. e.g. Soaps and detergent.

Common Mistake Students generally gets confused between product differentiation and price discrimination. Price discrimination is a feature under monopoly market.

5. What is meant by price discrimination in monopoly market? *ISC 2018*

Ans Price discrimination is a very important characteristic of the monopoly market. It means that the monopolist charges different prices for the same product from different groups of consumers.

e.g. Railways charge different tariffs for passengers and goods.

6. Why is price per unit equal to AR and MR under perfect competition? *ISC 2018*

Or Why is price per unit equal to average revenue and marginal revenue of a firm under perfect competition? *ISC 2006*

Ans Price and Average Revenue (AR) are same in all market forms however, under perfect competition, AR is also equal to MR, as each individual firm is so small according to the market that they cannot influence the price, which remains constant.

Also, in this market form, it is assumed that the firms can sell any amount of output at this uniform price, i.e. to increase demand, it is not required to reduce price. Because of this, $P = \text{AR} = \text{MR}$ in perfect competition.

7. Explain one main feature of each *ISC 2017*

(i) Monopsony market (ii) Monopoly market

Ans (i) Monopsony market possesses the following distinct feature

Single buyer and large number of sellers A monopsony market is one in which there is a single buyer of a good which is produced by a large number of sellers. e.g. Ink and paper required for printing currency can be purchased only by the government.

(ii) Monopoly market possesses the following distinct feature

Single seller and a large number of buyers Under monopoly, there is a single seller for selling the product. However, there are a large number of buyers. In monopoly, a single firm constitutes the whole industry, making the firm and industry as one and the same.

8. What is the reason for an indeterminate demand curve under oligopoly? *ISC 2015*

Ans Demand curve under oligopoly is indeterminate because of a high degree of interdependence among firms. So, if a firm lowers its price, then it does not necessarily lead to an increase in demand for its products, because rival firms may also lower their prices, on the other hand, if a seller raises his price, rivals may not follow.

9. Justify the following as price-takers/price-makers

(i) An oligopoly market

(ii) A perfectly competitive market *ISC 2014*

Ans (i) An oligopoly market is the form of the market in which there are a few big sellers of a commodity and a large number of buyers. Each seller has a singnificant share of the market e.g. There are few auto producers in Indian market. Maruti, Tata, Ford and GM are some well known brand name.

Oligopoly is a price-maker, because each firm has a substantial share in the market and therefore, can exercise control over market supply, thereby affecting the price of the product.

(ii) A perfectly competitive market is a price taker, as there are very large number of buyers and sellers, hence a few of them are so small according to the market that they cannot influence the market price and also because the consumer has knowledge about the market and the prevailing price, that he cannot be cheated. Also, all sellers are selling a homogeneous product.

10. What is the significance of freedom of entry and exit of firms under perfect competition? *ISC 2012*

Ans Freedom of entry and exit signifies that firms can enter the market any time they wish, if they think that they could make profits. On the other hand, loss-making firms can leave the market anytime. Due to this unique feature of perfect competition, firms under this form earn only normal profit in the long-run.

Concept Enhancer This feature is common in perfect competition and monopolistic competition.

11. Identify the type of market which has a characteristics of perfect substitutes. Give one reason for your answer. *ISC 2011*

Ans Perfect competitive market has the feature of perfect substitutes, because all firms in the market sell homogeneous product. They charge a uniform price set by the market forces of demand and supply.

12. Mention two similarities between perfect competition and monopolistic competition. *ISC 2010, 2008*

Ans Two similarities between perfect competition and monopolistic competition are

(i) Large number of buyers and sellers.

(ii) Freedom of entry and exit.

13. Define the market which has product differentiation as a distinguishing characteristic. *ISC 2009*

Ans Monopolistic competition has the feature of product differentiation, wherein large number of sellers sell similar, but still differentiated (in some aspect) products in the market, e.g. Soaps and detergents.

14. What is product differentiation? *ISC 2006*

Ans Product differentiation means similar products but still differentiated in terms of quantity, quality, size, shape, colour, etc. This is an important feature of monopolistic competition. e.g. Soaps, toothpaste, detergents, etc.

15. Define oligopoly. *ISC 2006*

Ans An oligopoly market is the form of market in which there are a few big sellers of a commodity and a large number of buyers. Each seller has a significant share of the market e.g. There are few auto producers in Indian market. Maruti, Tata, Ford and GM are some well known brand name.

16. State essential requisites of pure competition. *ISC 2005*

Ans Essential requisites of pure competition are

(i) Very large number of buyers and sellers.

(ii) Homogeneous products.

(iii) Freedom of entry and exit.

17. What is meant by monopolistic competition? *ISC 2005*

Ans Under this form of market, there are large number of buyers and sellers of differentiated product. Firms under this market has partial control over price.

3/4 Marks Questions

1. Discuss two features of monopoly. *ISC 2015*

Ans Two features of monopoly are

(i) **One seller and large number of buyers**
Monopoly is a market situation where there is only one seller of a commodity. Since, there is only one seller, any change in the amount of output produced by the monopolist has significant influence over the market price.
However, the number of buyers of the product is large. So, no buyer can influence the price of the product under monopoly.

(ii) **No close substitutes** An essential condition for the existence of monopoly is that no close substitutes should be available for the product or service that the monopolist offers. Monopoly is a market devoid of competition.

2. Highlight any three differences between monopolistic competition and oligopoly. *ISC 2014*

Ans Difference between monopolistic competition and oligopoly (any three)

Basis	Monopolistic competition	Oligopoly
Meaning	It refers to that market structure in which there are large number of sellers selling differentiated products.	It refers to the market structure in which there are few large firm selling homogeneous as well as differentiated products.
Entry of firm	Freedom of entry.	Barriers to entry.
Nature of demand curve	Downward sloping demand curve (more elastic).	Kinked demand curve.
Nature of product	Differentiated product.	Homogeneous and differentiated product.

Concept Enhancer Monopolistic competition and oligopoly, both are the types of imperfect competition.

3. Identify the market where a firm is not required to reduce the price to sell more. Explain the behaviour of TR and MR. *ISC 2014*

Ans Under perfect competition, firm is not required to reduce the price to sell more, as each firm is selling homogeneous products with no control over price of the products. Under this form of market, TR is an upward sloping straight line starting from origin, whereas, MR is horizontal straight line parallel to *X*-axis and equal to AR or price.

4. Distinguish between monopoly and perfect competition on the basis of

(i) AR curve (ii) Control over price *ISC 2012*

Ans (i) AR curve also specifies price or demand curve. Demand curve under perfect competition is horizontal straight line parallel to *X*-axis i.e. perfectly elastic. On the other hand, demand curve of monopoly firm is downward sloping curve but relatively less elastic in nature.

(ii) Perfectly competitive firms do not have any control over the price. They have to accept the price set by the industry, i.e. each firm is a price taker. On the other hand, monopoly firm is price maker, as being a single seller, he has full control over price.

5. What is selling cost? Which kind of market does not need selling cost and why? **ISC 2011**

Ans Selling cost refers to the additional cost which is incurred by the firms to promote sales. These expenditures may include advertisement cost, promotional offer's cost, offering rebates or discounts, etc. This cost becomes important in those market forms where products are differentiated, hence this cost has no importance in perfectly competitive markets as the products under this market form are homogeneous i.e. identical. As a result, no additional cost is needed to promote sales, firms can sell any quantity of output at the existing market price.

6/8 Marks Questions

1. Discuss any four difference between monopoly and monopolistic competition. **ISC 2023**

Or Distinguish between monopoly and monopolistic competition on the basis of average revenue curves and entry of firms. **ISC 2010**

Ans Difference between monopoly and monopolistic competition are

Basis	Monopoly	Monopolistic competition
Average revenue curve or demand curve	Downward sloping but less elastic.	Downward sloping but relatively more elastic.
Diagram	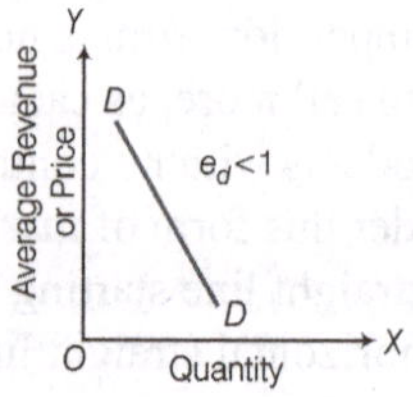	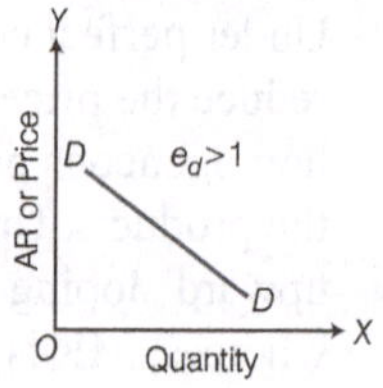
Entry of firms	Restriction on entry of new firms.	Freedom of entry and exit of new firms.
Selling cost	Very less selling cost is incurred.	Huge selling cost.
Nature of product	No close substitute available.	Differentiated product (substitutes are available).
Control over price	Full control over price.	Partial control over price.

Value Points

For getting maximum marks, following value points can be included in the answer

- Difference should be given alongwith basis in each point.
- Diagrams can be used to distinguish between demand curves of both market forms.

2 Differentiate between perfectly competitive market and monopolistically competitive market on the basis of the following **ISC 2020**

(i) Nature of the product (ii) Price influence
(iii) Relationship of AR and MR
(iv) Demand curve

Ans Difference between perfectly competitive market and monopolistically competitive market are

Basis	Perfectly competitive market	Monopolistically competitive market
Nature of product	The product is homogeneous. It is identical in all respect.	Products are differentiated on the basis of brand, size, colour, shape, etc.
Price influence	Firm is a price-taker as price is determined by the industry.	Firm has partial control over price due to product differentiation.
Relationship of AR and MR	AR is equal to MR, i.e. AR = MR.	AR is greater than MR, i.e. AR > MR.
Demand curve	It has perfectly elastic demand curve.	It's demand curve is relatively more elastic.

3. Discuss any four features of monopoly market. **ISC 2019**

Or Define monopoly market. Discuss four main features of monopoly market. **ISC 2008**

Ans Monopoly refers to that market form under which there is only a single seller selling a product which has no close substitutes available, hence have full control over market price. e.g. Indian Railways.

Features of monopoly market are

(i) **One seller and large number of buyers** Under monopoly, there is a single producer of a commodity. He may be alone or there may be a group of partners or a joint stock company or a state. However, there are a large number of buyers of the product.

Features of Monopoly
- One seller and large number of buyers
- Restrictions on the entry of new firms
- No close substitutes
- Full control over price

(ii) **Restrictions on the entry of new firms** Under monopoly, there are some restrictions on the entry of new firms into the monopoly industry. Generally, there are patent rights or exclusive control over a technique or raw material.

(iii) **No close substitutes** A monopoly firm produces a commodity that has no close substitutes.

(iv) **Full control over price** Being a single seller of the product, a monopolist has full control over its price. A monopolist thus, is a price-maker. He can fix whatever price he wishes to charge for his product.

4. Explain any four features of perfect competition. *ISC 2018*

Or Enumerate four characteristics of perfect competition. *ISC 2009*

Or Explain briefly the necessary conditions for perfect competition in the market. *ISC 2005*

Ans Four features/characteristics of perfect competition are as follows

(i) **Large number of buyers and sellers** No individual buyer or seller can influence the price of the commodity in the market as there are large number of buyers and sellers.

(ii) **Homogeneous product** Firms in the market produce a homogeneous product. Homogeneity of a product implies that one unit of the product is a perfect substitute for another.

Features of Perfect Competition
- Large number of buyers and sellers
- Homogeneous product
- Free entry or exit of firms
- Perfect knowledge

(iii) **Free entry or exit of firms** In a perfectly competitive market, there are no barriers to entry or exit of firms.

Entry or exit may take time, but firms have freedom of movement in and out of an industry with no government's restrictions.

(iv) **Perfect knowledge** Firms have all the knowledge about the product market and the factor market. Buyers also have perfect knowledge about the product market and the prevailing price.

5. Explain any four features of oligopoly market. *ISC 2017*

Or Discuss four features of oligopoly. *ISC 2011*

Ans Features of oligopoly market are

(i) **Few large firms and large number of buyers** A few firms, but large in size dominate the market for a commodity. Each firm commands a significant share of the market which can impact market price of the product. There are a large number of buyers of a commodity. The number is so large that no individual buyer can influence market price of the product.

(ii) **Barriers to entry** There are various barriers to the entry of new firms. These barriers are almost similar to those under monopoly. Entry of the new firm is extremely difficult, if not impossible.

(iii) **Non-price competition** Under oligopoly, firms tend to avoid price competition. e.g. In India both Coke and Pepsi drinks sell at the same price. However, in order to enhance its share of the market, each firm tries to resort to non-price competition, i.e. by giving discounts, etc. This feature is more visible in collusive oligopoly.

Features of Oligopoly
- Few large firms and large number of buyers
- Barriers to entry
- Non-price competition
- Nature of product

(iv) **Nature of product** Nature of the products sold under oligopoly could be homogeneous or differentiated. Based on the nature of product differentiation, oligopoly market can be classified into pure oligopoly and imperfect or differentiated oligopoly. Firms providing services of cooking gas is a good example of pure oligopoly, whereas, automobile industry is an example of differentiated oligopoly.

6. Discuss four differences between perfect competition and monopolistic competition. *ISC 2016*

Ans Difference between perfect competition and monopolistic competition are

Basis	Perfect competition	Monopolistic competition
Number of sellers	There are very large number of sellers and no individual seller has control over market supply.	There are large number of sellers. So, a firm does not have much impact on the market supply.
Nature of product	The product is homogeneous. It is identical in all respect.	Products are differentiated on the basis of brand, size, colour, shape, etc.
Entry and exit	There is freedom of entry and exit. It leads to absence of abnormal profits and losses in long-run.	There is freedom of entry and exit. So, a firm earns only normal profits in the long-run.
Price	Firm is a price-taker as price is determined by the industry.	Firm has partial control over price due to product differentiation.

7. Explain the features of an oligopoly market. How is an oligopoly market different from a monopoly market? *ISC 2007*

Ans **Features of Oligopoly** Refer to Q.No. 5 on page 105.

Difference between oligopoly and monopoly are

Basis	Oligopoly	Monopoly
Number of sellers	Few large sellers.	Single seller.
Entry of new firm	Barrier to entry.	Entry is restricted for new firms.
Nature of demand curve	Kinked demand curve.	Downward sloping demand curve but relative less elastic.
Nature of product	Homogeneous anddifferentiated products are sold.	Product has no close substitute.

8. Explain any four features of monopolistic competition. ***ISC 2006***

Ans Monopolistic competition refers to that market form under which there are large number of sellers selling similar but differentiated products, having partial control over prices. Features of monopolistic competition are

(i) **Product differentiation** The products of the sellers are differentiated, but are close substitutes of one another.

Product differentiation can be real or artificial. Its effect is that sellers has partial control over its price.

(ii) **Free entry or exit of firms** Firms can freely move in and out of a 'group'. There are no government's restrictions on entry of new firms or exit of existing firms.

(iii) **Imperfect knowledge** Buyers and sellers do not have perfect or complete knowledge of the market condition.

Buyer's preferences are guided by advertising and other selling activities undertaken by the sellers.

(iv) **Selling cost** A firm under monopolistic competition incurs huge selling costs which are the cost of promoting the demand for its product.

Examples of selling costs are advertisement, window displays, salesman salaries, etc.

Features of Monopolistic Competition
- Product differentiation
- Free entry or exit of firms
- Imperfect knowledge
- Selling cost

TOPIC 2

Market Equilibrium Under Perfect Competition, Short-run & Long-run and the Concept of Shut Down Point

Price and Output Determination

Under perfect competition, each firm has a very negligible share in the market, hence price and output is determined by the market forces in the open market by the interaction of industry's demand and supply.

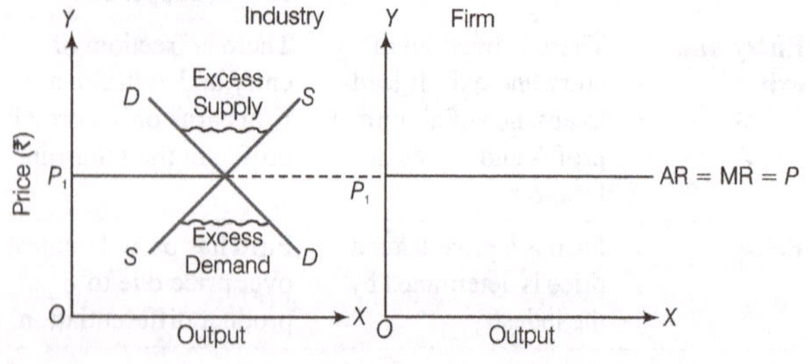

Industry's Demand and Supply   Firm's Demand Curve

Short-run Equilibrium of Individual Firm

In short-run, every individual firm attains equilibrium at the point where the following two conditions get satisfied

(i) AR (P) = MR = MC

Where, AR (P) = Average Revenue (Price), MR = Marginal Revenue, MC = Marginal Cost

(ii) MC should cut MR from below, i.e. MC should be rising at the point of equilibrium.

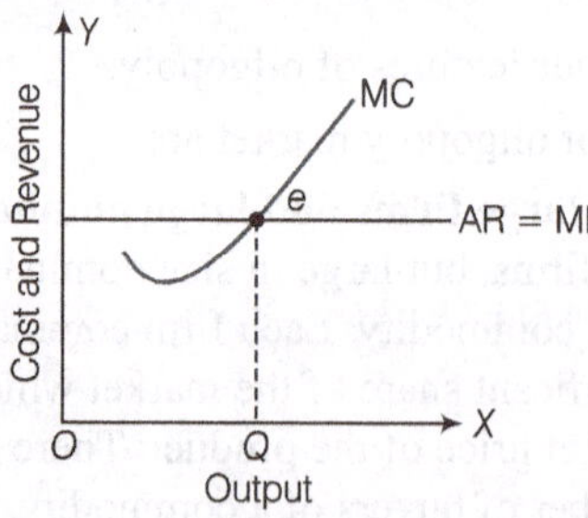

Short-run Profit
(Super normal profit) **of Individual Firm**

In short-run, individual firms may earn super normal profits. To know about profit/loss in short-run, Average Revenue (AR) and Average Cost (AC) are compared at the point of equilibrium.

If AR > AC, there will be super normal profit.

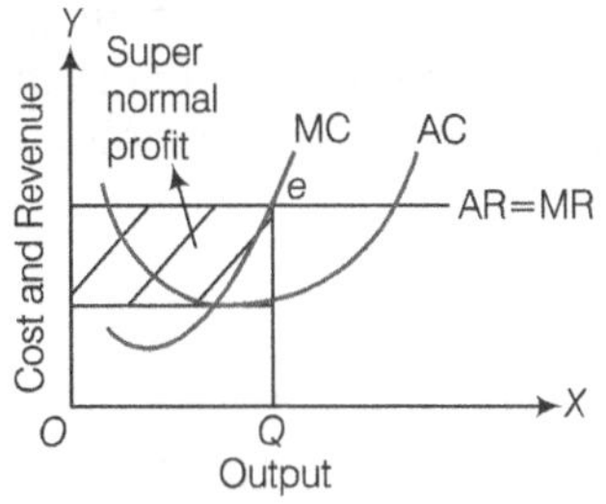

Short-run Losses of Individual Firms

In short-run, firms may even suffer from losses, if AR < AC at the point of equilibrium then firm would be suffering from losses (Super normal loss).

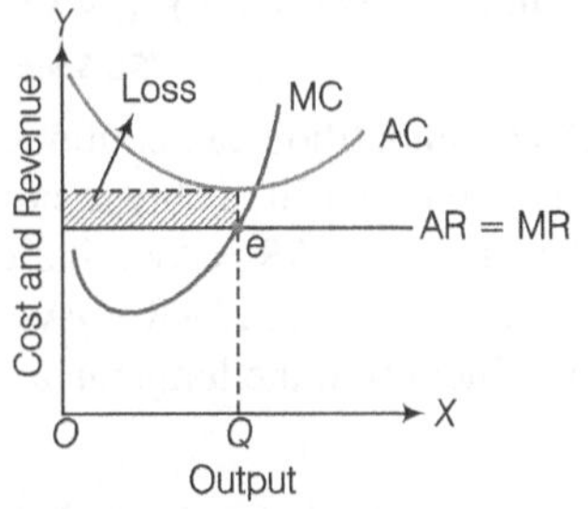

• MC and AC at minimum point

Firms Earning Normal Profits in Short-run

Firms are said to be earning normal profit when AR = AC at the point of equilibrium, i.e. a situation of no profit-no loss, but it should be remembered that normal profit is an element of cost.

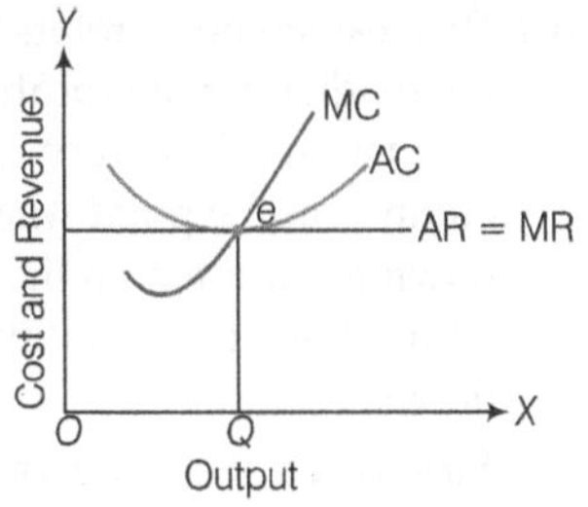

Break-even Point

Break-even point refers to the situation in which a firm neither earns profit nor suffer from loss, i.e. a situation of normal profit, where AR = AC or Price = AC.

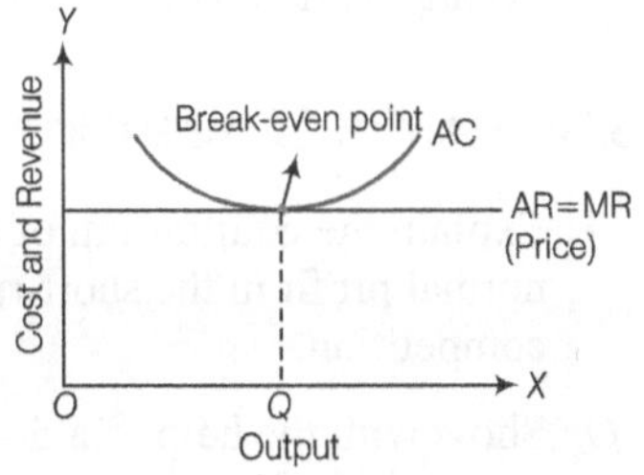

Short-run Supply Curve of Individual Firms

The short-run supply curve of individual firms is rising portion of MC curve from the minimum point of AVC curve, as the rising portion signifies direct relation with price and quantity.

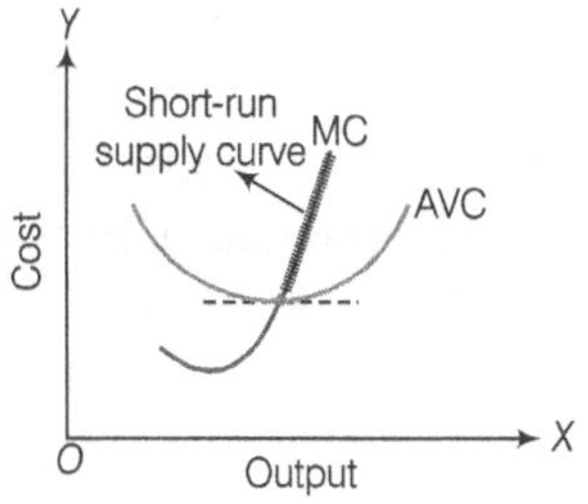

Where, AVC = Average Variable Cost

Shut Down Point

In short-run, when an individual firm suffers from loss, then it has to decide that whether to operate in long-run or not. If the firm earns sufficient revenue to cover its variable cost, then it may operate in long-run, however if it can't then the firm will shut down. Hence, shut down point is the point beyond which a firm does not operate.

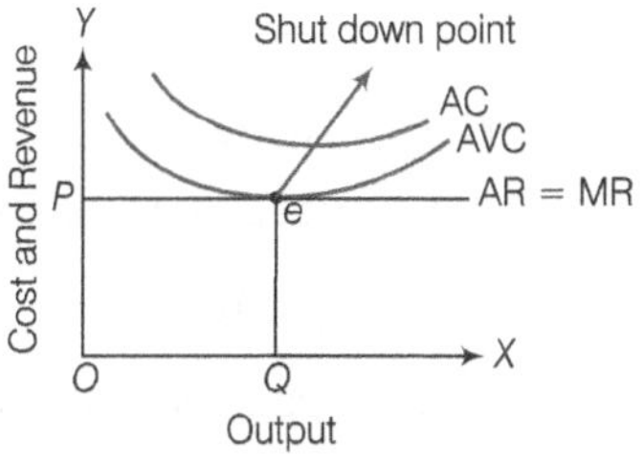

Shut down point: Price < AVC or AR < AVC

Any price below *OP*, it pays the firm to close down as it minimises its loss.

Long-run Equilibrium of Individual Firm

Firms under perfect competition earn only normal profit (AR = AC) in the long-run. Any profit (super normal profit) in the short-run will be wiped out due to entrance of new firms, while any loss in short-run will be eliminated due to exit of some firms. However, the condition for long-run equilibrium is as follows

(i) *P* (AR) = LAC (Normal profit)
Where, LAC = Long-run Average Cost

(ii) LMC = MR and LMC should cut MR from below
Where, LMC = Long-run Marginal Cost.
Under perfect competition, long-run equilibrium condition becomes, LMC = MR = AR = LAC.

Long-run Equilibrium of the Industry

In long-run, industry would be in equilibrium when following two conditions get satisfied

(i) Market Demand = Market Supply

(ii) Industry is neither expanding nor contracting i.e. it has stabilised.

PYQs Previous Years' Questions

1 Mark Questions

1. Why is AR = MR = *P* a horizontal straight line under perfect oition in the short-run? **ISC Specimen 2023**

Ans Under perfect competition, there are very large number of sellers selling homogenous goods, thus demand becomes perfectly elastic.

2. If revenue equals cost, then firm earns only **ISC Sem I 2021**

(a) normal profit (b) pure profit
(c) economic profit (d) supernormal profit

KEY IDEA
Normal profit is the break-even point.

Ans (a) normal profit

3. Shut down point is a situation where the firm covers **ISC Sem I 2021**

(a) only fixed cost (b) only variable cost
(c) Both fixed and variable cost
(d) Neither fixed nor variable cost

Ans (b) only variable cost

Concept Enhancer At the shut down point, firms suffer a loss equal to their fixed cost.

4. Normal profit is defined as that amount of profit that is high enough so that firms in the industry are induced to remain in the industry, yet low enough so that **ISC Sem I Specimen 2021**

(a) new firms will want to enter the industry
(b) new firms will not want to enter the industry
(c) old firms will want to expand their operations
(d) old firms will not want to expand their operations

Ans (b) new firms will not want to enter the industry

2 Marks Questions

1. Under perfect competition, a firm will enjoy normal profit in the long-run even if it enjoys super normal profit in the short-run. Explain. **ISC 2023**

Or Why do firms earn normal profit in the long-run under perfect competition? **ISC Specimen 2023**

Ans There is freedom of entry and exit of firms under perfect competition. If a firm enjoys super normal profit in the short-run, it will attract new firms to join the market leading to rise in market supply and fall in market price.

Further this will wipe out the short-run profit and firms will only enjoy normal profit in the long-run.

2. What is meant by break-even point? Draw a well labelled diagram to show the break-even point. **ISC 2023**

Ans Break-even point refers to the situation in which a firm neither earns profit nor suffer from loss, i.e. a situation of normal profit, where AR = AC or Price = AC.

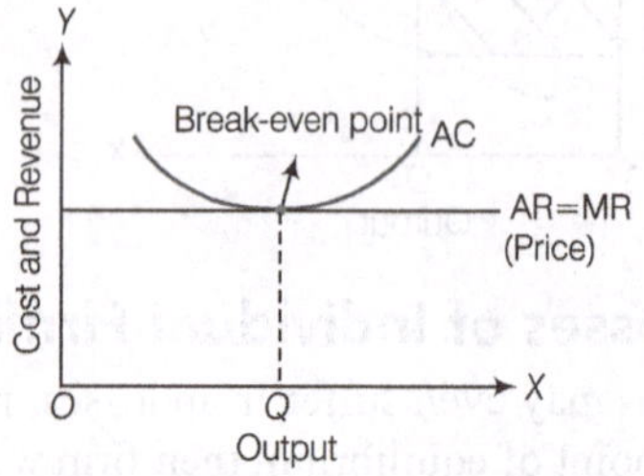

3. In the short-run under perfect competition, a firm should produce if and only if P for AR ≥ AVC. Justify. **ISC Specimen 2023**

Ans A firm under perfect competition can continue to produce in the long-run only if it is able to cover the variable cost in the short-run. AR = AVC indicates shut down point in the short-run. If AR > AVC, firms will continue its production in the long-run and *vice-versa*.

4. Differentiate between-break even point and shut down point. **ISC 2008**

Ans Break-even point refers to the situation in which firms are neither earning profits nor suffering from loss i.e. a situation of no profit-no loss. Break-even point is attained at the point where AR = AC whereas shut down point refers to the situation, beyond which firms do not operate or continue production i.e. they shut down.

Firm reaches shut down point when price is less than AVC i.e. price or AR are not sufficient to cover average variable cost.

3/4 Marks Questions

1. Explain the equilibrium of a firm when it enjoys super normal profit in the short-run under perfect competition. **ISC Specimen 2023**

Or Show with the help of a diagram, how a perfectly competitive firm earns super normal profit in short-run equilibrium. **ISC 2018, 2015**

Or How does a perfectly competitive firm earn super normal profits in the short-run equilibrium? Explain it with the help of a diagram. **ISC 2012**

Or Explain how is short-run equilibrium attained by a competitive firm earning super normal profits. **ISC 2005**

Ans A perfectly competitive firm will earn super normal profits at the point where average revenue is more than the average cost, i.e. AR > AC.

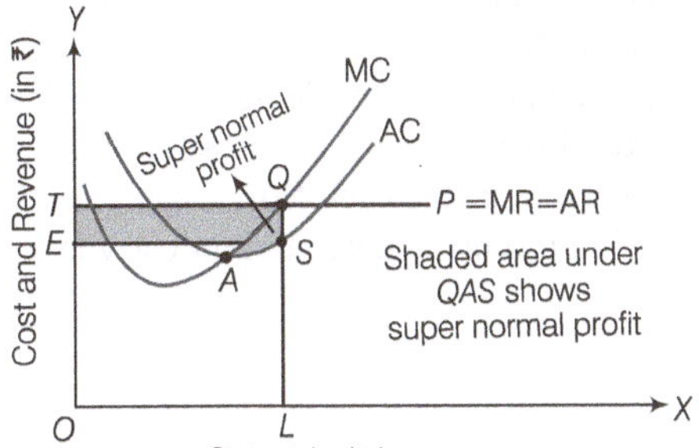

Super Normal Profit

In the above figure, point *Q* is the point of equilibrium, because at this point

(i) Marginal revenue is equal to marginal cost, and

(ii) Marginal cost curve cuts the marginal revenue curve from below.

At this point, average revenue exceeds the average cost. So, the shaded region *TESQ* represents the super normal profits earned by the firm. However, a firm will be able to earn such profits only in the short-run. In the long-run, the firm would be able to earn only normal profits.

Common Mistake Students generally marks the profit area incorrectly. Profit is the area between AR and AC curve.

2. Show with the help of a diagram, how a perfectly competitive firm earns normal profit in short-run equilibrium. **ISC 2019, 2015, 2013, 2010**

Ans A firm under perfect competition attains its short-run equilibrium at the point where following two conditions gets satisfied

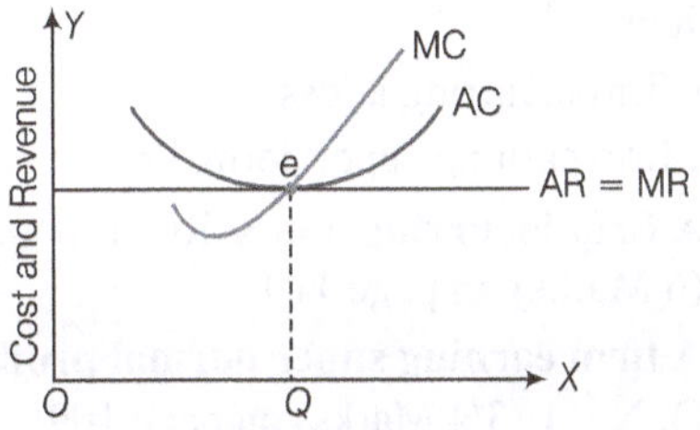

(i) MR = MC

Here, MR = Marginal Revenue

MC = Marginal Cost

However, as AR and MR are equal only under perfect competition, hence the first condition can be re-written as Price = MC (As, AR = Price = MR).

(ii) MC should cut MR from below

At the point of equilibrium profit/loss is checked by comparing AR and AC curves.

Normal profit refers to situation of no profit-no loss i.e. AR = AC.

In the given diagram, firm attains its equilibrium at point *e*, where MR = MC. However, at the equilibrium point, AR and AC curves are also equal, which represent the situation of normal profits.

6 Marks Questions

1. Explain the short-run equilibrium of a firm facing losses under perfect competition. **ISC 2023**

Or Explain how a firm in perfect competition incurs loss, in short-run equilibrium. **ISC 2018**

Or Explain how a perfectly competitive firm in equilibrium incurs losses in short-run. Show the same with the help of a diagram. **ISC 2011**

Ans A perfectly competitive firm is in equilibrium under two conditions

(i) MR = MC

Here, MR = Marginal Revenue

MC = Marginal Cost

(ii) MC should cut MR from below

At the point of equilibrium, we need to compare AC and AR to check profit or loss. If at equilibrium level of output AC is greater than AR, then firm suffer from loss.

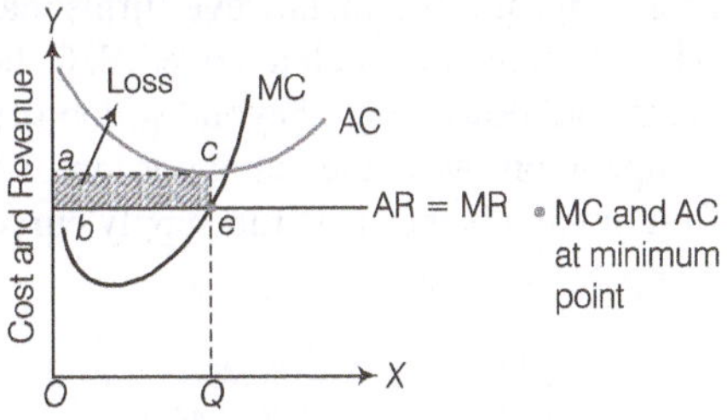

It can be seen from the above diagram that the firm is in equilibrium at point *e* where MR = AR = Price = MC, selling a level of output equal to *OQ* at price *Ob*. However, at the point of equilibrium, AC is equal to *Oa* which is greater than AR (*Ob*), hence firm is suffering from losses equal to the area *abec*.

2. Using diagrams, explain the concepts of
(i) Shut down point
(ii) Break-even point of a firm in perfect competition under short-run. **ISC 2020**

Ans (i) Refer to text 'Shut Down Point' on page 107.
(ii) Refer to text 'Break-even Point' on page 107.

Value Points

For getting maximum marks, following value points can be included in the answer
- In diagram, mark the points properly.
- Mention the situation/condition of each case clearly.

3. A perfectly competitive firm can continue producing even if it is incurring losses in short-run equilibrium. Justify the given statement with the help of a diagram. **ISC 2014**

Ans Perfectly competitive market structure is characterised by large number of sellers selling homogeneous product. As a result, individual firms are not in the position to influence market price. They attain their equilibrium at the point where MR or AR or price equals MC.

At the point of equilibrium, in short-run, firms may earn profit or may suffer from loss.

At equilibrium, if a firm suffer from loss (AR < AC), then it may or may not operate in long-run. Let us discuss the case in which firm will operate in long-run despite of losses in short-run. In case of loss in short-run, firms need to check for operating profit i.e. whether the revenue is sufficient to cover variable cost or not, if price i.e. AR is greater than AVC, then firm operates in long-run.

We can see in the above diagram that, firms are suffering from losses equal to the area *abce* at short-run equilibrium, however firms may operates if AR is sufficient enough to cover AVC, hence point *e* is the shut down point, beyond which firms will stop its operation. Also, the rising portion of MC curve from point *e* is the short-run supply curve of the competitive firms.

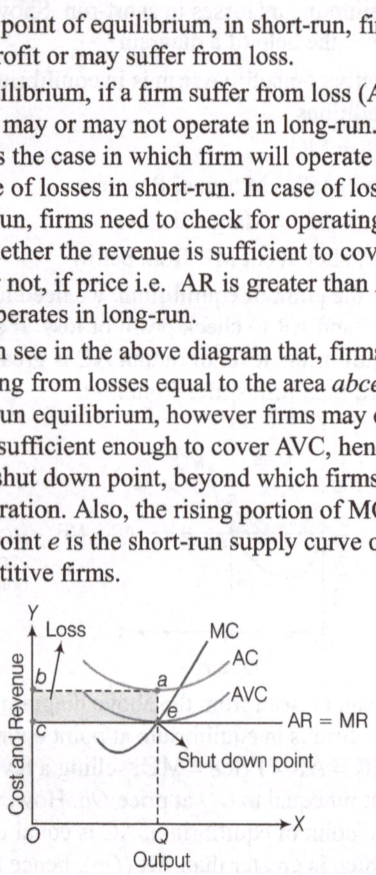

4. Discuss how under perfect competition, a firm is a price taker and an industry a price maker. **ISC 2011**

Ans Under perfect competition, there are large number of buyers and sellers in the market, who sell homogeneous or identical product.

As a result of which, the market share of each individual firm is so small that they cannot nfluence the market price by changing their output decision.

They can sell any quantity of output at a price set by the market forces of demand and supply i.e. price set by the industry, hence each firm under perfect competition is a price-taker and industry is price-maker.

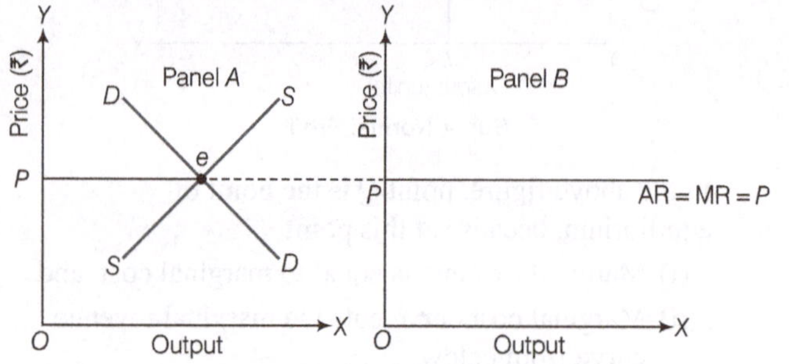

Industry's demand and supply **Firms' demand curve**

Above we have drawn two diagram, in panel *A* we have shown the determination of price in the industry by the market forces of demand and supply, price determined at the point where demand curve (*DD*) intersects supply curve (*SS*), given the price equal to *OP*.

On the right side (in Panel *B*), we have shown individual firms demand curve which is horizontal straight line parallel to *X*-axis, indicating that individual firms are not in the position to influence the market price, hence the demand curve is perfectly elastic.

5. Discuss how is short-run equilibrium attained by a perfectly competitive firm under the following situations
(i) A firm incurring a loss
(ii) A firm earning super normal profit **ISC 2009**

Ans (i) **A firm incurring a loss** Refer to Q. No. 3 (6 Marks) on page 110.
(ii) **A firm earning super normal profit** Refer to Q. No. 1 (3/4 Marks) on page 109.

TOPIC 3

Determination of Price and Output in the Open Market, Changes in Equilibrium and Simple Applications of Demand and Supply

Price and Output Determination/Market Equilibrium

It is a situation of the market in which demand for a commodity is exactly equal to its supply corresponding to a particular price. This is also known as market equilibrium.

The price at which the amount of quantity demanded and quantity supplied are equal to each other, is known as **equilibrium price**. The quantity demanded and supplied at an equilibrium price is known as **equilibrium quantity**.

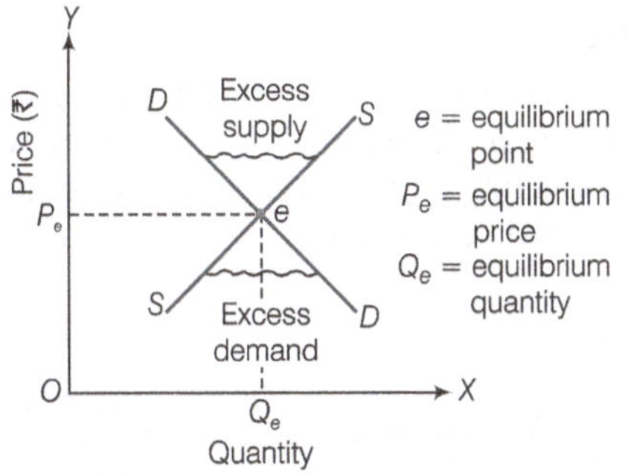

Determination of Equilibrium Price

The following assumptions of equilibrium are

(i) Demand curve should always have a negative slope.

(ii) Supply curve should have a positive slope.

(iii) If demand increases at a faster rate than the supply, the price will increase.

(iv) If supply increases at faster rate than the demand, the price will fall.

In the graph given alongside

DD = Demand Curve, SS = Supply Curve

e = Equilibrium Point ($DD = SS$)

$$\left.\begin{array}{l}\text{Excess Supply}: DD < SS\\ \text{Excess Demand}: DD > SS\end{array}\right\}\text{Disequilibrium}$$

Change in Demand and its Effects on Equilibrium Price

(i) **Increase in demand** When demand increases, demand curve shifts to the right, with no change in supply, price rises and quantity increases.

(ii) **Decrease in demand** When demand decreases with no change in supply, demand curve will shift to the left and as a result, equilibrium price and quantity will fall.

Change in Supply and its Effects on Equilibrium Price

(i) **Increase in supply** When supply increases with no change in demand, supply curve shifts to the right, as a result equilibrium price falls and quantity increases.

(ii) **Decrease in supply** When supply decreases, supply curve shifts to the left, with no change in demand, price will increase and quantity will fall.

Effect of Simultaneous Increase in Demand and Supply on Equilibrium

When there is simultaneous increase in demand and supply, three different cases may be obtained, which are as follows

(i) Increase in Demand > Increase in Supply

Effect Equilibrium price and quantity rises.

(ii) Increase in Demand < Increase in Supply

Effect Equilibrium price falls, quantity increases.

(iii) Increase in Demand = Increase in Supply

Effect No change in equilibrium price, quantity increases.

Effect of Simultaneous Decrease in Demand and Supply on Equilibrium

When demand and supply decreases simultaneously, three cases can be obtained

(i) Decrease in Demand > Decrease in Supply

Effect Equilibrium price and quantity will fall.

(ii) Decrease in Demand < Decrease in Supply

Effect Equilibrium price rises, quantity falls.

(iii) Decrease in Demand = Decrease in Supply

Effect No change in equilibrium price, quantity falls.

Effect of Change in Supply on Equilibrium when Demand is Perfectly Elastic

When demand curve is perfectly elastic, it is horizontal straight line parallel to X-axis. In such situation, due to change in supply, equilibrium price does not change, only quantity increases when supply increases and *vice-versa*.

Effect of Change in Supply on Equilibrium when Demand is Perfectly Inelastic

When demand is perfectly inelastic, it is vertical straight line parallel to *Y*-axis. In this case, equilibrium quantity does not change when supply changes, but price increases when supply falls and *vice-versa*.

Effect of Change in Demand on Equilibrium when Supply is Perfectly Elastic

When supply is perfectly elastic, it is a horizontal curve. In this case, price does not change due to change in demand, but equilibrium quantity increases with increase in demand and *vice-versa*.

Effect of Change in Demand on Equilibrium when Supply is Perfectly Inelastic

Supply curve will be vertical when supply is perfectly inelastic. In this case, equilibrium quantity does not change with change in demand, but price increases when demand increases and *vice-versa*.

Price Control

When market mechanism fails to attain desirable result, then government fixes the price on its own rather than allowing market forces to determine prices, this situation is known as price control.

This is considered as the 'Direct Action' taken by the government by entering into the market mechanism.

There are two cases of price control

(i) Price ceiling

(ii) Price floor

Price Ceiling

It refers to the maximum price that a seller can charge for a particular product from the buyers. Generally, government fixes this price below the market price to benefit the poorer sections of society.

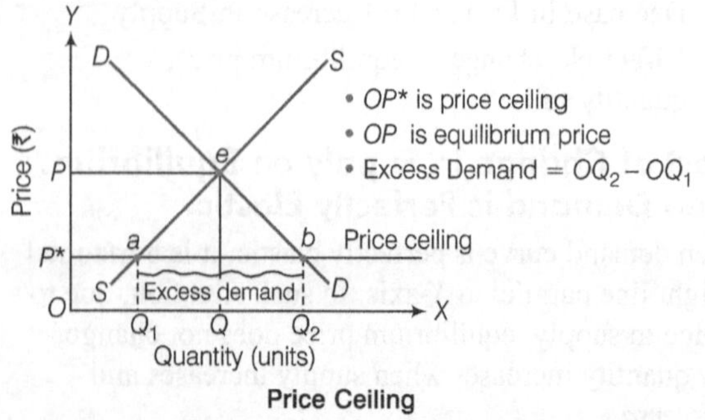

Price Ceiling

Price Floor

It means the minimum price fixed by the government for a commodity in the market. Generally, it is fixed to protect the producer from losses. This price is fixed above the market or equilibrium price.

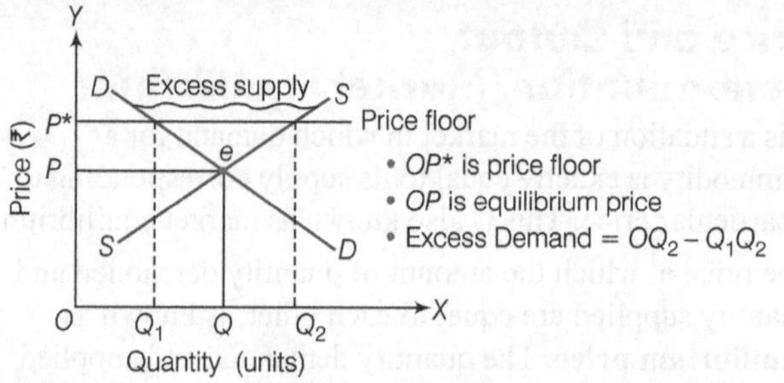

Price Floor

Rationing

It is the most effective way of controlling excess demand that arises due to price ceiling. It is a system of distribution of specified quantity of a commodity at a specified price to maximum possible consumers.

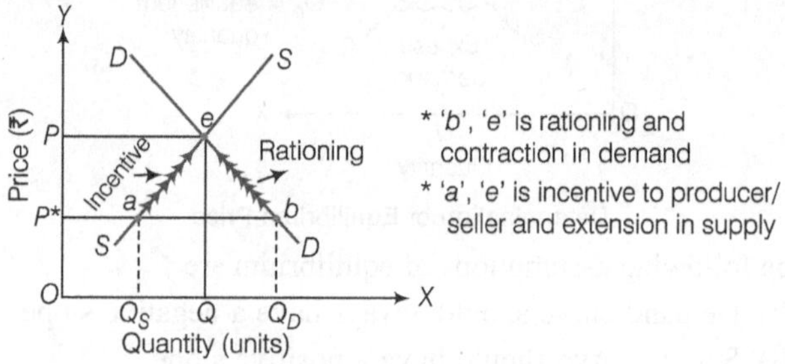

Rationing

Viable Industry

An industry is said to be viable in condition if corresponding to the minimum price, there is some demand in the market. For an industry to be viable, demand and supply curve should intersect in the first quadrant (positive axis).

Non-viable Industry

A non-viable industry is one which will not produce the product in an economy, may be due to very high cost of production. e.g. Commercial aircraft industry in India. In this case, supply curve lies about the demand curve.

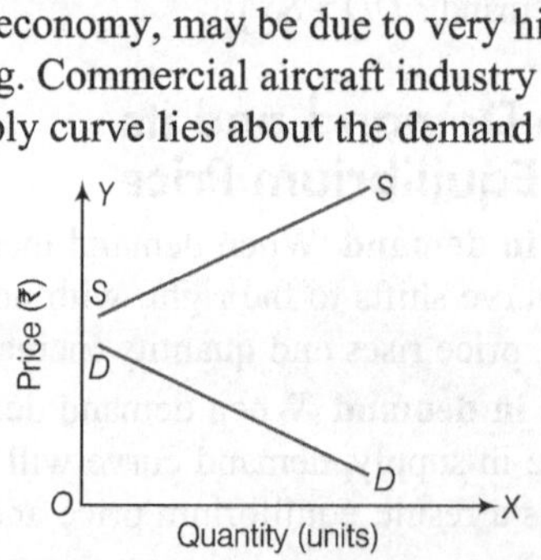

PYQs Previous Years' Questions

1 Mark Questions

1. Which one of the following will cause a rise in the equilibrium price of rice when the demand for rice remains the same? **ISC 2023**
   (a) Government subsidy to rice farmers
   (b) Successful advertising campaign for rice
   (c) Improved rice farming methods
   (d) Poor weather conditions

Ans (d) Poor weather conditions

2. Indian Railways charges lower freight rates for transporting essential products like food, coal etc, as compared to freight charges for other products like T.V., air coolers etc. This is an example of **ISC Specimen 2023**
   (a) price ceiling (b) price discrimination
   (c) price control (d) floor pricing

Ans (a) price ceiling

Concept Enhancer Price ceiling is opted by the government to protect the interest of the buyers.

3. What will be the effect on equilibrium price if supply is decreased without any change in demand? **ISC Sem I 2021**
   (a) No change (b) It will fall
   (c) It will rise
   (d) It will move in circular manner

Ans (b) It will fall

4. What will be the effect on equilibrium price when increase in demand equals increase in supply? **ISC Sem I 2021**
   (a) Equilibrium price remains constant
   (b) Equilibrium price rises (c) Equilibrium price falls
   (d) Equilibrium price rises and falls respectively

Ans (a) Equilibrium price remains constant

5. What would the price ceiling lead to, when maximum price is fixed below the equilibrium price? **ISC Sem I 2021**
   (a) Excess demand (b) Excess supply
   (c) Deficient demand (d) No change at all

Ans (a) Excess demand

6. Which of the following is an example of agricultural support price? **ISC Sem I 2021**
   (a) Price ceiling (b) Floor price
   (c) Equilibrium price (d) Product price

Ans (b) Floor price

7. What is determined at the point where market demand and market supply curves intersect each other? **ISC Sem I Specimen 2021**
   (a) Equilibrium price
   (b) Equilibrium quantity
   (c) Both (a) and (b)
   (d) None of the above

Ans (c) Both (a) and (b)

8. What will be the effect upon equilibrium price, when an increase in demand is more than increase in supply? **ISC Sem I Specimen 2021**
   (a) Equilibrium price remains constant
   (b) Equilibrium price rises
   (c) Equilibrium price falls (d) None of these

Ans (b) Equilibrium price rises

9. What does floor price refer to? **ISC Sem I Specimen 2021**
   (a) Controlled price (b) Maximum ceiling price
   (c) Minimum support price (d) Any of these

Ans (c) Minimum support price

2 Marks Questions

1. Show with the help of a diagram, a situation when change in supply will keep the equilibrium quantity of the commodity unchanged. **ISC 2020**

Ans When the demand is inelastic, the equilibrium quantity will remain constant with change in supply.

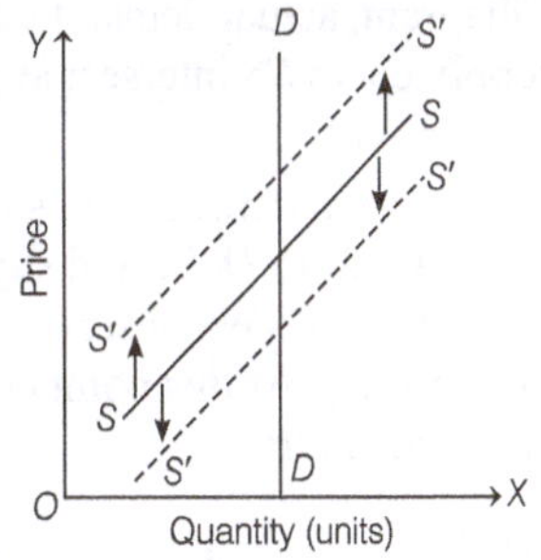

Concept Enhancer In this situation, quantity demanded can only change if demand itself shifts either to the right or to the left.

2. With the help of diagrams, show how equilibrium price and quantity of a commodity are affected when
   (i) Demand is perfectly elastic and supply decreases.
   (ii) Supply is perfectly elastic and demand increases.
   ISC 2018

Ans (i) Demand is perfectly elastic and supply decreases

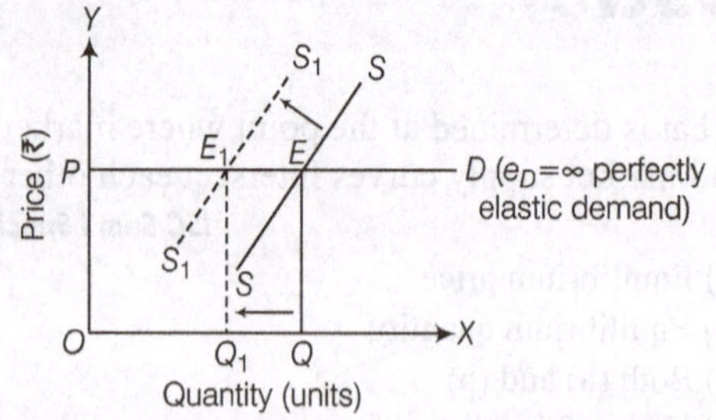

(ii) Supply is perfectly elastic and demand increases

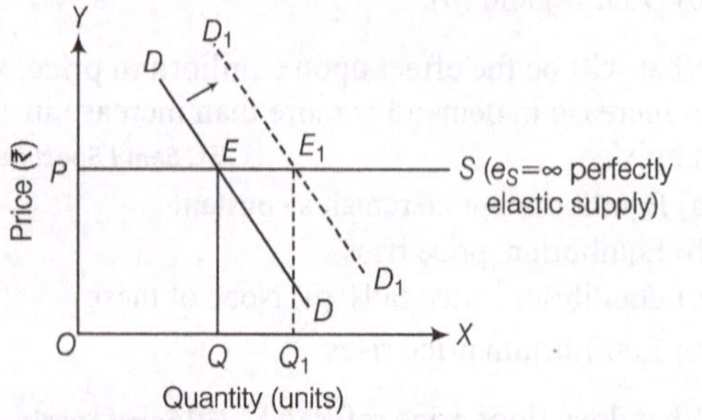

Concept Enhancer In this case, price can change only if demand curve shifts upwards or downwards.

3. With the help of a diagram, show how the equilibrium price can remain unchanged even after a rightward shift of the demand curve. **ISC 2016**

Ans Equilibrium price will remain unchanged even after a rightward shift of demand curve, if the supply also increases in the same proportion, as is illustrated in the diagram given below

In the given diagram, actual demand curve *DD* and actual supply curve *SS* intersect at point *E* (i.e. equilibrium point).

Now, due to increase in demand and supply, demand curve shifts rightwards to D_1D_1 and supply curve shifts rightwards to S_1S_1. We observe that the new equilibrium point is E_1. At this point equilibrium price remains unchanged at *OP*.

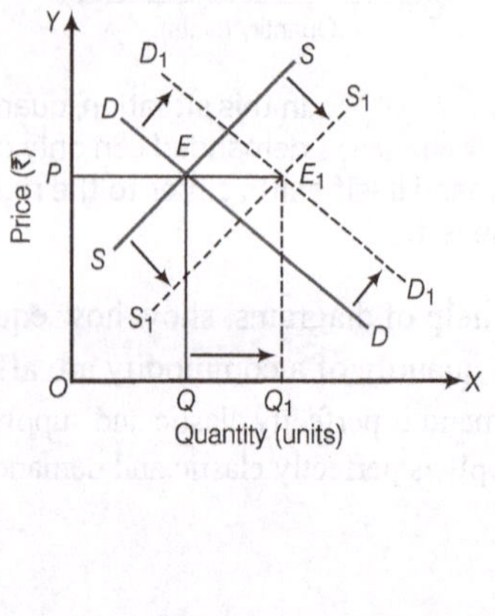

Common Mistake Most of the time, students draw the free handed curve and get the change in price incorrectly. In this situation, proper margin should be taken to keep price constant.

4. Explain the meaning of price ceiling with the help of a diagram. **ISC 2013**

Ans Ceiling means maximum limit. Price ceiling means maximum price of a commodity that the sellers can charge from the buyers. Often the government fixes this price much below the equilibrium market price of a commodity, so that it becomes within the reach of the poorer sections of the society.

Equilibrium Price $= OP$,

Equilibrium Quantity $= OQ$

Ceiling Price $= OP^*$,

Excess Demand $= ab = Q_1Q_2$

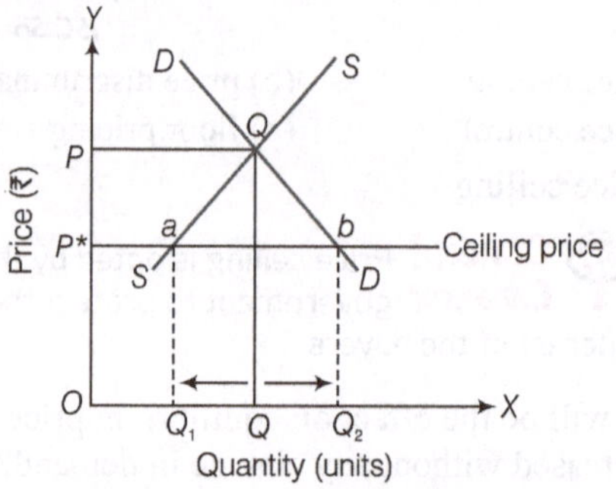

5. When does the equilibrium quantity in a market remain unchanged with a change in demand? Show it with the help of a diagram. **ISC 2012**

Or Show with the help of a diagram the effect of change in demand on equilibrium price, when supply is perfectly inelastic. **ISC 2007**

Ans Equilibrium quantity remains unchanged when supply is perfectly inelastic, in this case, supply curve will be a vertical line parallel to *Y*-axis, as a result, quantity will not change even if demand increases or decreases.

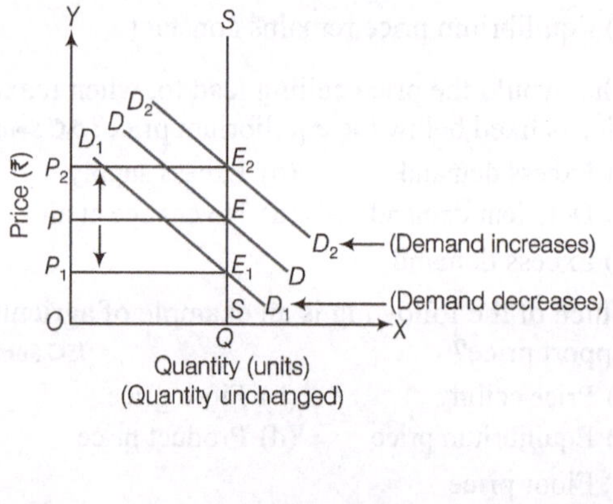

3/4 Marks Questions

1. Explain price ceiling with the help of a diagram. **ISC 2023**

Or

Explain the concept of maximum price legislation with the help of a diagram. **ISC 2018**

Ans Price ceiling refers to the maximum price that a seller can charge for a particular product from the buyers. Generally, government fixes this price below the market price to benefit the poorer sections of society.

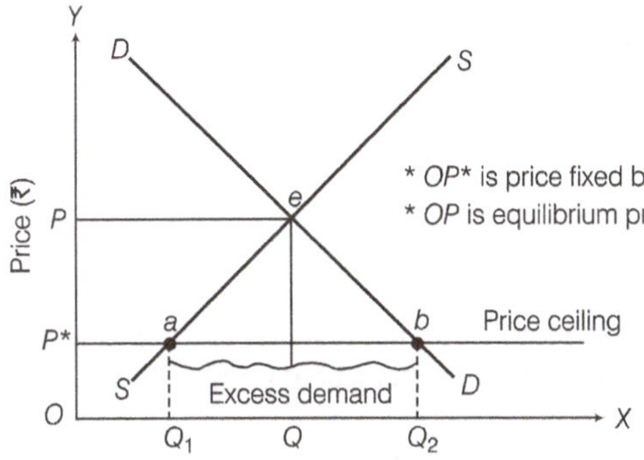

Price Ceiling

2. What is meant by floor price? Explain its impact on producers. **ISC 2017**

Ans Floor price refers to the minimum price of a commodity which is fixed by the government and which should be paid to the producers for their goods. It is fixed above the equilibrium price, as is depicted in the given diagram.

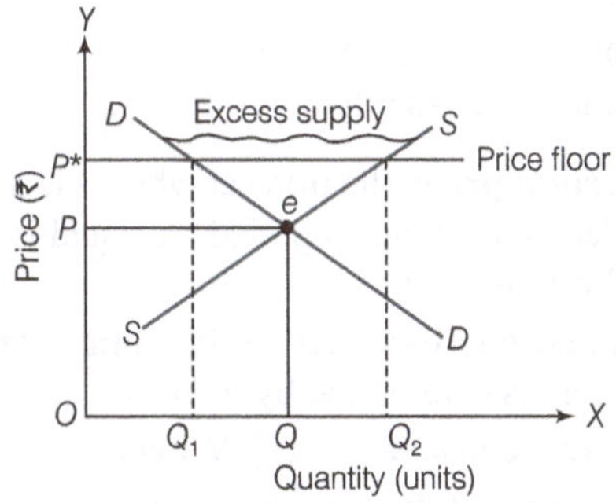

Price Floor

In the above diagram, equilibrium price is *OP* but the floor price has been fixed at *OP*.

Impact on producers The floor price helps the producers to get a fair price for their goods.

It help them to earn profits, even when supply is excess, as in case of agriculture produce.

3. Show with the help of diagrams, the effect on equilibrium price and quantity when
   (i) There is fall in price of substitute goods.
   (ii) There is a rise in prices of inputs. **ISC 2015**

Ans (i) **When there is fall in price of substitute goods** It will lead to a decrease in demand for the concerned good. Accordingly, demand curve shifts towards the left. Supply remaining unchanged, it causes equilibrium price and quantity to fall, as is depicted in the diagram. Equilibrium price falls from OP to OP_1 and equilibrium quantity falls from OQ to OQ_1.

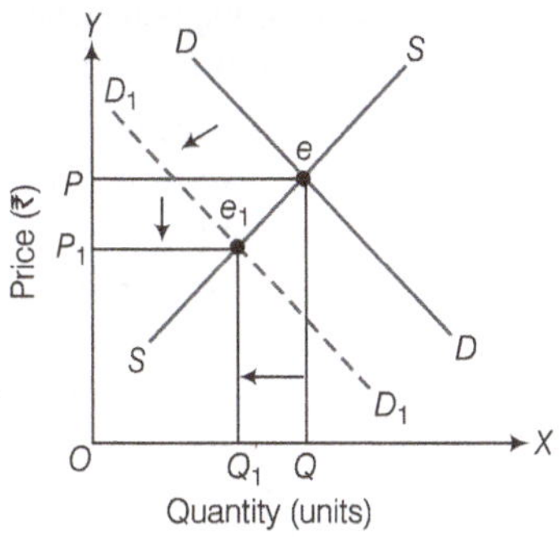

(ii) **When there is a rise in the price of inputs** Rise in the price of inputs leads to a decrease in supply, causing supply curve to shift leftwards. Demand remaining unchanged, this will lead to an increase in equilibrium price and decrease in equilibrium quantity, as is depicted in the given diagram. Equilibrium price rises from OP to OP_1 and equilibrium quantity falls from OQ to OQ_1.

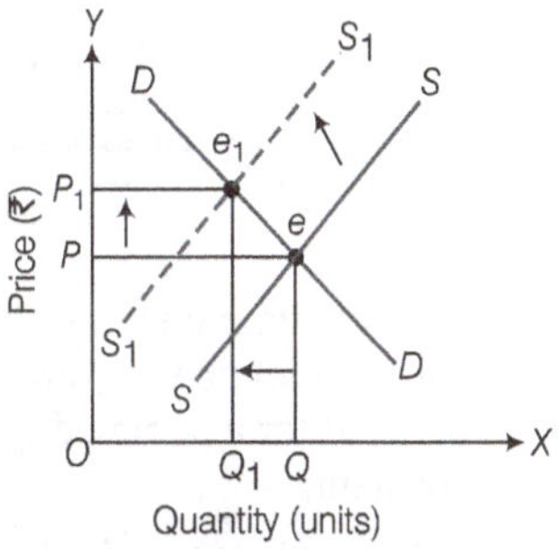

4. Study the diagram given below and answer the questions that follow
   (i) P_e is the equilibrium price. What would prompt the government to fix the price at P_1?
   (ii) What would be the effect of fixing the price at P_1? **ISC 2014**

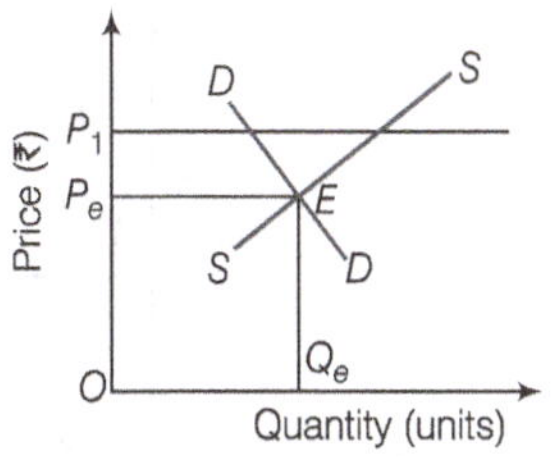

Ans (i) P_e is the equilibrium price, however P_1 is the price above the market price which is known as price floor. Government generally set price floor to protect the producers from losses in the situation of excessive production.

(ii) The effect of setting high price would be excess supply at that price, i.e. supply will exceed the demand at price P_1. The government would buy the entire surplus of the farmers produce which they fail to sell in the open market at floor price.

5. Explain what happens when the market price is less than the equilibrium price. **ISC 2013**

Ans When market price is less than the equilibrium price, there will be excess demand i.e. demand would be greater than supply.

The immediate effect of this will be increase in market price. Due to increase in market price, there will be expansion in supply (upward movement along supply curve) and contraction in demand (upward movement along demand curve), this process will continue till the time market again reaches the equilibrium point.

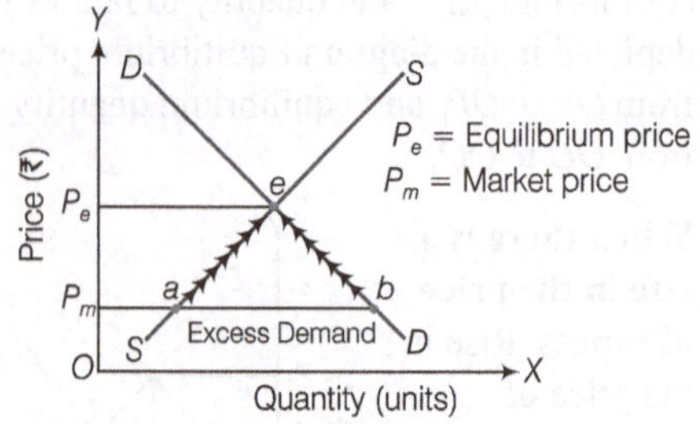

6. Explain diagrammatically how equilibrium price and equilibrium quantity are affected by changes in the demand for a commodity, with the supply remaining constant. **ISC 2012**

Ans **Effect of increase in demand on equilibrium price and quantity** Supply curve remaining unchanged, if there is increase in demand, demand curve and equilibrium point will shift to the right. As a result of it, equilibrium quantity and equilibrium price both will increase.

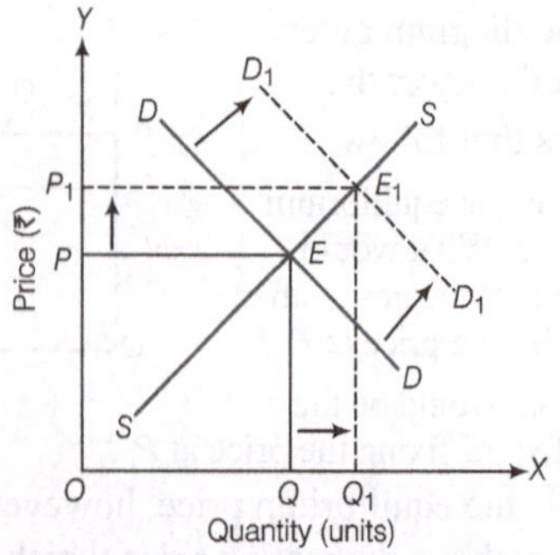

In the given diagram, actual demand curve DD and actual supply curve SS intersect at point E (i.e. equilibrium point).

OP is equilibrium price and OQ is equilibrium quantity. Now, with increase in demand, new demand curve becomes D_1D_1. So, equilibrium point shifts from E to E_1 and OP_1 is new equilibrium price and OQ_1 is new equilibrium quantity.

Effect of decrease in demand on equilibrium price and quantity Supply curve remaining unchanged, if there is decrease in demand, demand curve and equilibrium point will shift to the left.

As a result of it, equilibrium quantity and equilibrium price both will decrease.

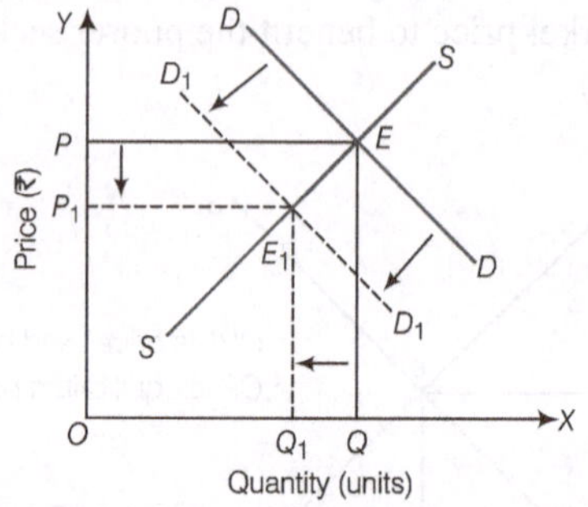

In the above diagram, actual demand curve DD and actual supply curve SS intersect at point E (i.e. equilibrium point).

At this point, the price is OP and quantity demanded is OQ. Due to decrease in demand, new demand curve D_1D_1 is formed.It shows that price declines to OP_1 because the demand has decreased from OQ to OQ_1.

6 Marks Questions

1. Briefly explain how equilibrium price is determined with the help of demand and supply. **ISC 2020**

Or Explain how equilibrium price can be determined with the help of

(i) Demand and supply schedule

(ii) Demand and supply curves **ISC 2016**

Ans **Equilibrium price** The price at which the amount demanded and amount supplied are equal is known as equilibrium price.

Determination of market equilibrium Market equilibrium is determined by forces of

(i) Market demand (ii) Market supply

Market demand It refers to the sum total of demand of a commodity by all the buyers in the market.

Market supply It refers to the sum total of supply of a commodity by all the firms in the market.

In a purely competitive market, the equilibrium price is determined by the interaction of the demand and supply curves in the market.

This has been explained with the help of an imaginary schedule and diagram

Price (in ₹)	**Demands** (units)	**Supply** (units)	
1	500	100	Excess demand
2	400	200	
3	300	300	Equilibrium (D = S)
4	200	400	Excess supply
5	100	500	

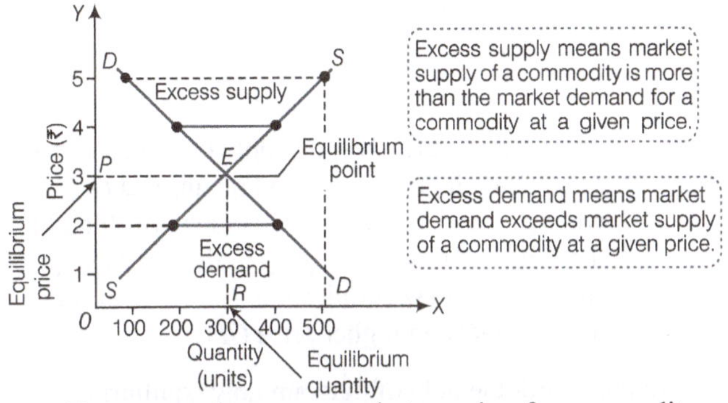

Excess supply means market supply of a commodity is more than the market demand for a commodity at a given price. It will cause the price to fall.

When market demand exceeds market supply of a commodity at a given price, it is known as excess demand. It will cause the price to rise.

Thus equilibrium price can be determined by the interaction of both supply and demand.

Value Points

For getting maximum marks, following value points can be included in the answer

- Define equilibrium price
- Use proper schedule and diagram
- Explain the situations of excess demand and excess supply

2. Explain with the help of diagrams how equilibrium price changes when there is simultaneous increase of both, demand and supply. ***ISC 2019***

Ans When both demand and supply increase, different cases are

(i) **Increase in demand is same as increase in supply** In this case, equilibrium price will remain same but equilibrium output will increase. OP is initial equilibrium price and OQ is initial equilibrium output. Initial equilibrium is at E.

When demand and supply shifts, new equilibrium is established at E_1. Since, both demand and supply increase in same proportions, price remains same but equilibrium quantity increases to OQ_1.

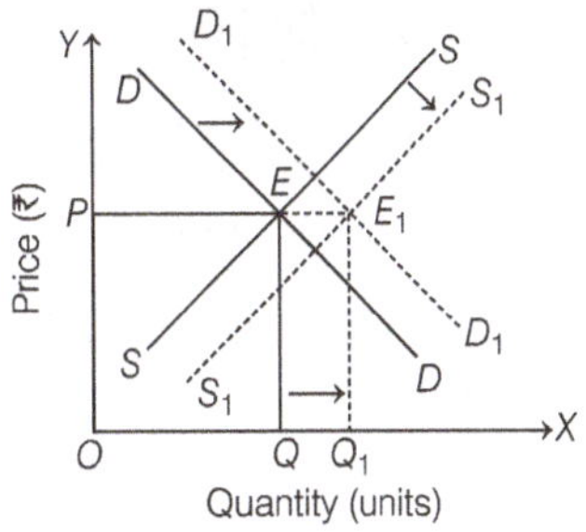

(ii) **Increase in demand is more than increase in supply** In this case, equilibrium price and equilibrium quantity will increase. OP is initial equilibrium price and OQ is initial equilibrium output. Initial equilibrium is at E.

When demand and supply shifts, new equilibrium is established at E_1. Equilibrium price rises to OP_1 because increase in demand is more than that of supply. Equilibrium quantity demanded and supply will increase to OQ_1.

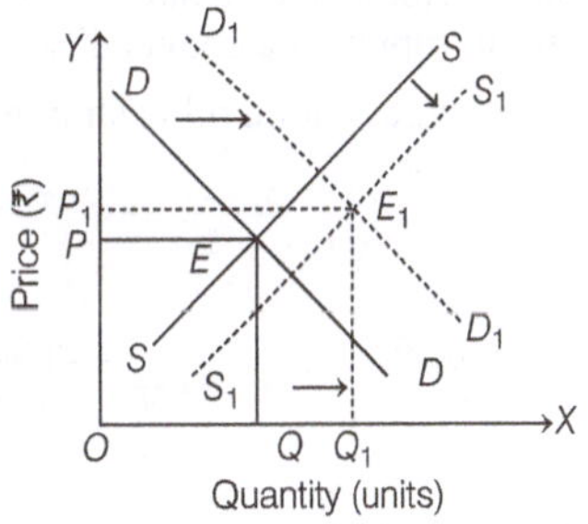

(iii) **Increase in demand is less than increase in supply** In this case, equilibrium price will decrease but equilibrium quantity will increase. OP is initial equilibrium price and OQ is initial equilibrium output.

Initial equilibrium is at E. When demand and supply shifts, new equilibrium is established at E_1.

Equilibrium price falls to OP_1 because increase in demand is less than that of supply.

Equilibrium quantity demanded and supply will increase to OQ_1.

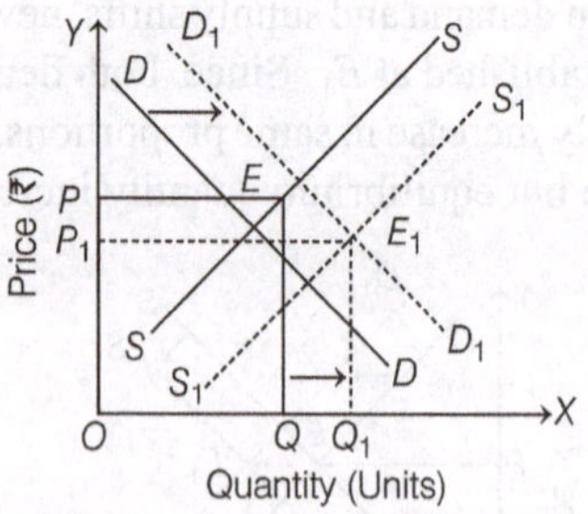

3. In the graph below, DD is the demand curve and SS is the market supply curve.

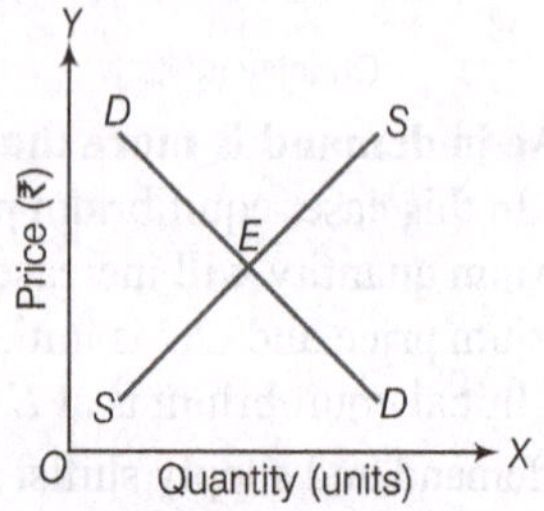

(i) On the Y-axis, mark any price P, showing excess demand.

(ii) How will equilibrium be restored from a situation of excess demand?

(iii) Show how equilibrium price will be affected when the increase in demand is equal to the decrease in supply of a commodity. **ISC 2011**

Ans (i) Situation of excess demand is shown in figure below

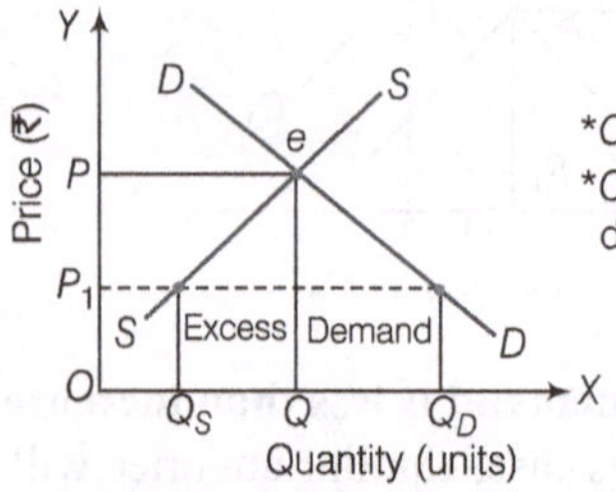

*OP is equilibrium price
*OP_1 is market price where demand is more than supply

(ii) Due to excess demand, price will increase, as a result of increase in price, there will be contraction in demand (upward movement along the demand curve) and expansion in supply (upward movement along supply curve), this process will continuous till the time, the gap between demand and supply exist and again the equilibrium point E will be attained.

(iii) **Effect on equilibrium when increase in demand is equal to decrease in supply**

When demand increases by the same proportion as decrease in supply, equilibrium quantity will not change, however equilibrium price will increase owing to decrease in supply and increase in demand.

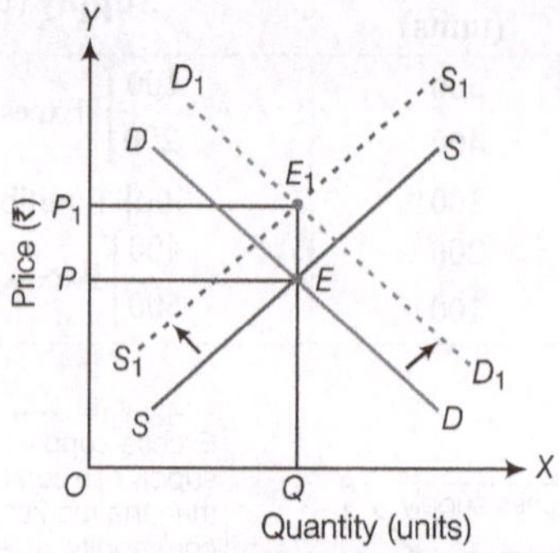

Initial demand (DD) and supply (SS) intersect at point E, with price at OP and quantity at OQ, when demand increases, demand curve shifts to the right to D_1D_1 and supply to the left S_1S_1 (as supply fall), new equilibrium is at E_1 with same quantity OQ and higher price OP_1.

4. Explain with the help of diagram how equilibrium price and quantity changes when both demand and supply decreases. **ISC 2009**

Ans When both demand and supply decrease, three different cases arise

(i) Decrease in Demand = Decrease in Supply

(ii) Decrease in Demand > Decrease in Supply

(iii) Decrease in Demand < Decrease in Supply

Let us discuss these cases one by one

(a) **If both demand and supply decrease in the same proportion** When decrease in supply is equal to decrease in demand, equilibrium price will remain the same but equilibrium output will decrease.

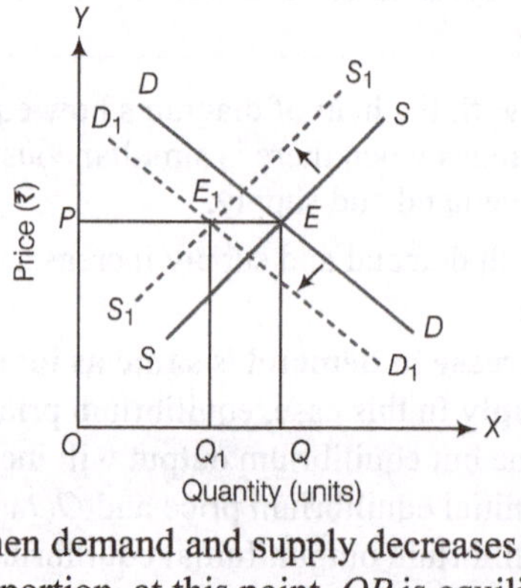

When demand and supply decreases in the same proportion, at this point, OP is equilibrium price and OQ is equilibrium quantity.

Demand decreases to D_1D_1 and supply decreases to S_1S_1. The new curves intersect each other at point E_1. It shows that equilibrium price remains constant because both demand and supply have decreased in the same proportion. However, equilibrium quantity decreases to OQ_1.

(b) **When decrease in demand is more than the decrease in supply** If decrease in demand is more than the decrease in supply, the equilibrium price will fall.

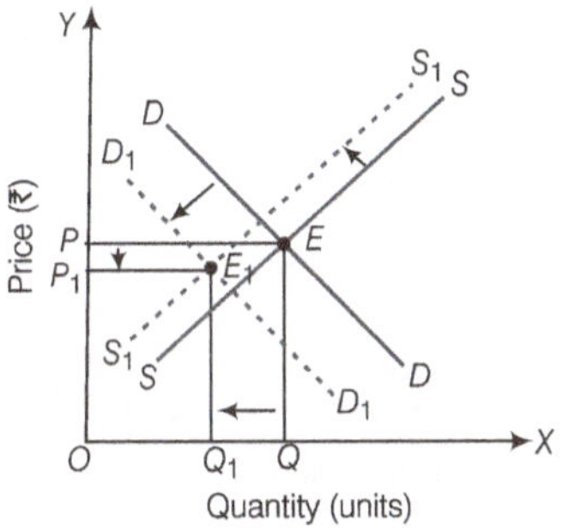

At this point, OP is equilibrium price and OQ is equilibrium quantity. Demand decreases to D_1D_1 and supply decreases to S_1S_1. The new curves intersect each other at point E_1, which is the new equilibrium point.

Thus, the equilibrium price reduces to OP_1 because decrease in demand is more than that of supply. Equilibrium quantity demanded and supplied will decrease to OQ_1.

(c) **When decrease in demand is lesser than decrease in supply** From the figure, it is clear that the leftward shift in demand curve from DD to D_1D_1 is proportionately less than the leftward shift in supply curve from SS to S_1S_1. The new equilibrium point is E_1. Equilibrium price increases from OP to OP_1 and equilibrium quantity decreases from OQ to OQ_1.

Decrease in quantity is greater than increase in price.

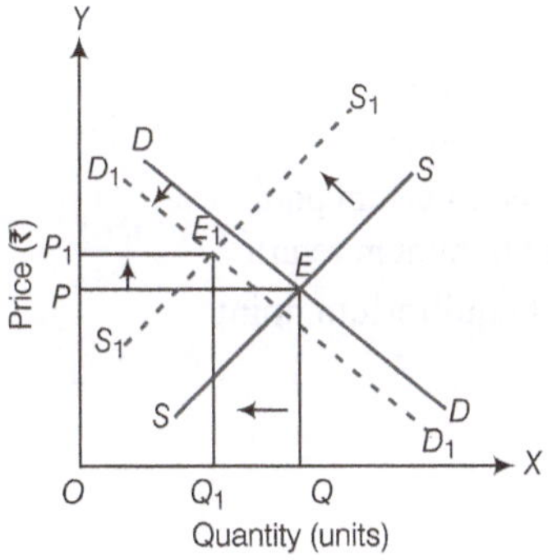

5. Explain graphically, the impact on equilibrium price and on quantity in the following situations

(i) An increase in the consumer's income.

(ii) A decrease in the price of inputs.

(iii) An improvement in technology.

(iv) An increase in the price of complementary goods.

ISC 2008

Ans (i) **An increase in the consumer's income** When consumer's income increases, demand will also increase. As a result, demand curve will shift to the right, leading to increase in equilibrium price and quantity.

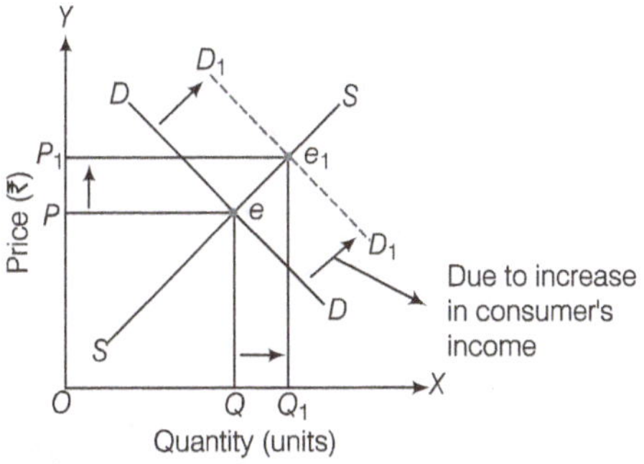

We can see from the given diagram, that initial equilibrium was at point e with price OP and quantity OQ.

Now, due to increase in income of the consumer demand curve shifts to the right to D_1D_1 and new equilibrium is attained at point e_1 with higher price OP_1 and greater quantity OQ_1.

(ii) **A decrease in the input prices** When input price falls, the goods become more profitable hence its supply will increase, resulting in fall in equilibrium price and rise in quantity.

It can be seen from the given diagram that, due to fall in input price supply will increase and supply curve would shift to the right to S_1S_1 from SS. As a result, equilibrium price falls form OP to OP_1 and quantity increases from OQ to OQ_1.

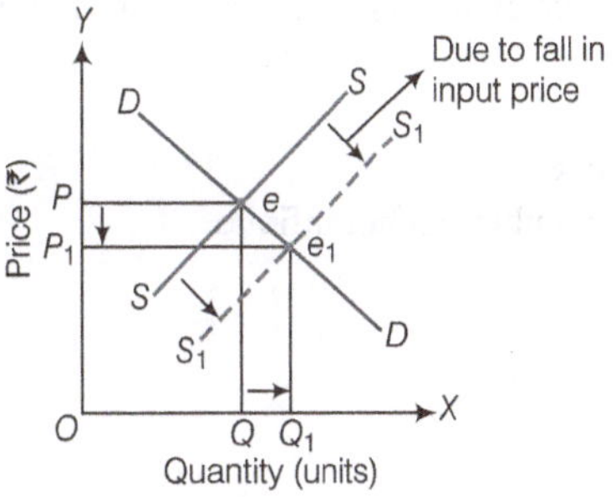

(iii) **An improvement in technology** When there is an improvement in technology, it reduces the cost of input. As a result, supply will increase and hence equilibrium price will fall and quantity will increase.
We can see from the given diagram that due to improvement in technology, supply will shift to the right to S_1S_1, as a result, equilibrium price falls to OP_1 and quantity expands to OQ_1.

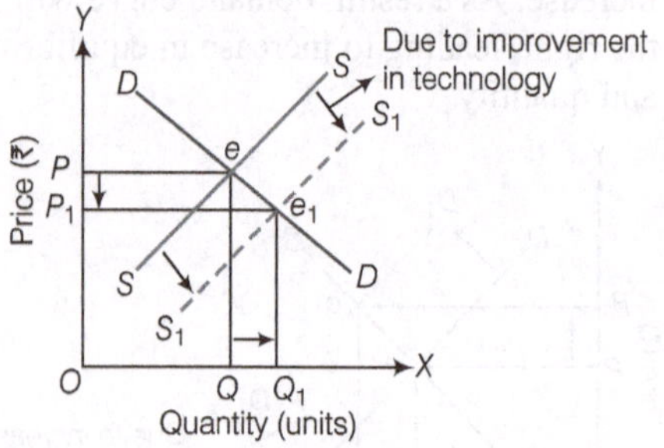

(iv) **An increase in the prices of complementary goods** When the prices of complementary goods rise, it leads to fall in demand, resulting in leftward shift in demand curve hence, price falls and quantity also falls. Given diagram shows that due to rise in price of complementary goods, demand curve shifts to the left from DD to D_1D_1. As a result, equilibrium also moves to e_1 from e and price falls to OP_1 while quantity falls to OQ_1 from OQ.

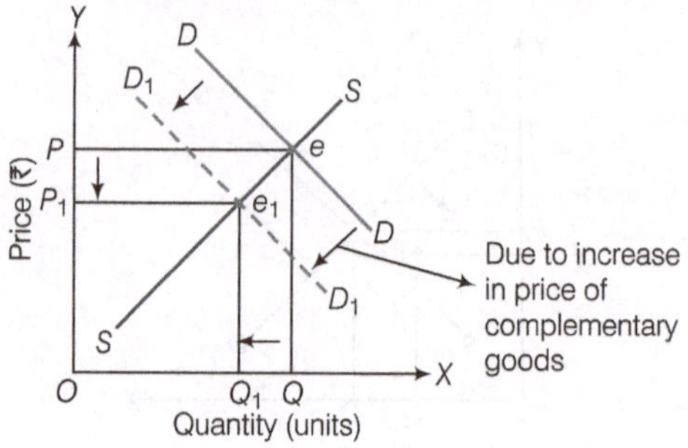

Case Based Questions

Case 1

When a soft drink company A roped in a Hollywood star for its endorsement in India, the soft drink company B went in for a Hollywood star as a competitor. ***ISC Sem I 2021***

(i) This is a feature of
(a) differentiated products
(b) non-price competition
(c) interdependence and non-price competition among firms
(d) price discrimination

Ans (c) interdependence and non-price competition among firms

(ii) Name the kind of market
(a) Monopoly
(b) Perfect competition
(c) Oligopoly
(d) Monopolistic competition

Ans (c) Oligopoly

(iii) The number of sellers in this kind of market are
(a) infinite
(b) few
(c) only one
(d) large number but not infinite

Ans (b) few

Case 2

Study the diagram given below

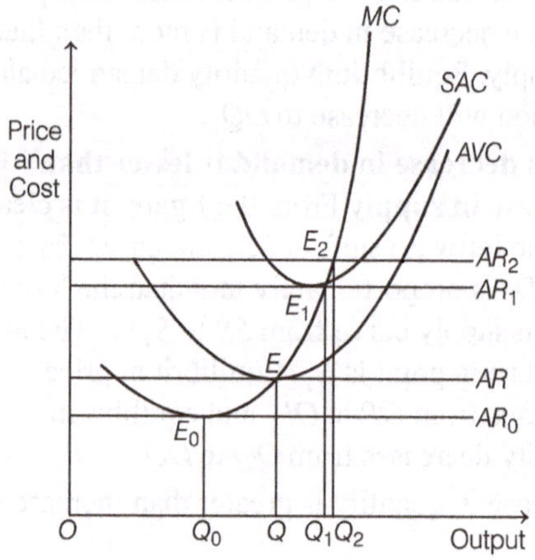

ISC Sem I 2021

(i) Point E is
(a) shut down point
(b) break-even point
(c) market equilibrium point
(d) point of minimum return

Ans (c) market equilibrium point

(ii) Point E_1 is
  (a) shut down point (b) break-even point
  (c) market equilibrium point
  (d) point of maximum return

Ans (a) shut down point

(iii) At E_0
  (a) firm may stop producing
  (b) firm must stop producing
  (c) firm may continue production
  (d) firm must continue production

Ans (c) firm may continue production

(iv) Point E_2 indicates
  (a) normal profit
  (b) loss
  (c) supernormal profit
  (d) Neither loss nor profit

Ans (b) loss

Case 3

Pre COVID, an oxygen cylinder could be refilled for ₹ 300. During the second wave of the pandemic, the people bought oxygen cylinder and stored it. Hence, the price of one refill went up to ₹ 2,000. **ISC Sem I 2021**

(i) The reason for the price increased was
  (a) the demand for oxygen increased and supply for oxygen remained the same
  (b) the demand for oxygen and the supply for oxygen both increased simultaneously
  (c) the demand for oxygen and the supply for oxygen decreased simultaneously
  (d) the demand for oxygen and the supply for oxygen remained unchanged

Ans (a) the demand for oxygen increased and supply for oxygen remained the same

(ii) It is a case of .... in demand curve
  (a) leftward shin of demand curve
  (b) upward movement along the demand curve
  (c) downward movement along the demand curve
  (d) rightward shift of demand curve

Ans (d) rightward shift of demand curve

(iii) People bought oxygen cylinder and stored it
  (a) The above is a case of price ceiling
  (b) The above is a case of hoarding
  (c) It is a case or floor price
  (d) It is n case or rationing

Ans (b) The above is a case of hoarding

Case 4

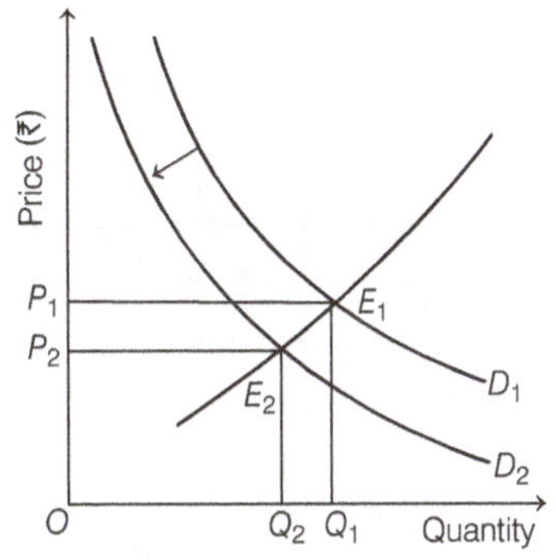

ISC Sem I 2021

As per the diagram given above

(i) Equilibrium price his shifted from
  (a) OP_1 to OP_2
  (b) E_1 to E_2
  (c) OQ_1 to OQ_2
  (d) OP_2 to OP_1

Ans (a) OP_1 to OP_2

(ii) Equilibrium quantity has shifted from
  (a) OP_2 to OP_1 (b) E_2 to E_1
  (c) OQ_1 to OQ_2 (d) D_1 to D_2

Ans (c) OQ_1 to OQ_2

(iii) The new equilibrium point is
  (a) E_2 (b) E_1
  (c) P_1 (d) Q_1

Ans (a) E_2

Case 5

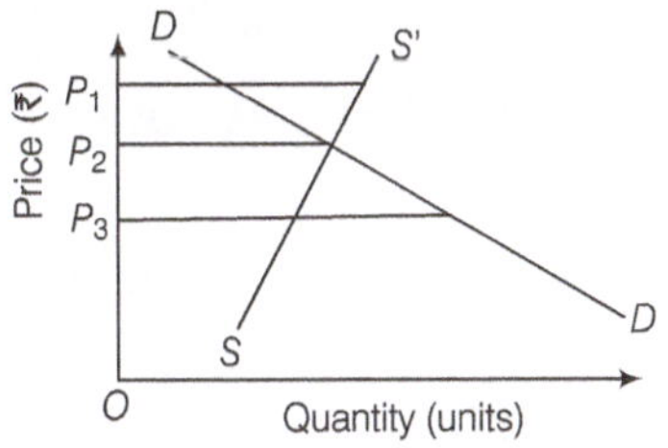

ISC Sem I Specimen 2021

(i) In figure, the floor price is
  (a) OP_1 (b) OP_2
  (c) OP_3 (d) (d) None of these

Ans (a) OP_1

(ii) In figure, ceiling price is
  (a) OP_1 (b) OP_2
  (c) OP_3 (d) None of these

Ans (c) OP_3

Case 6

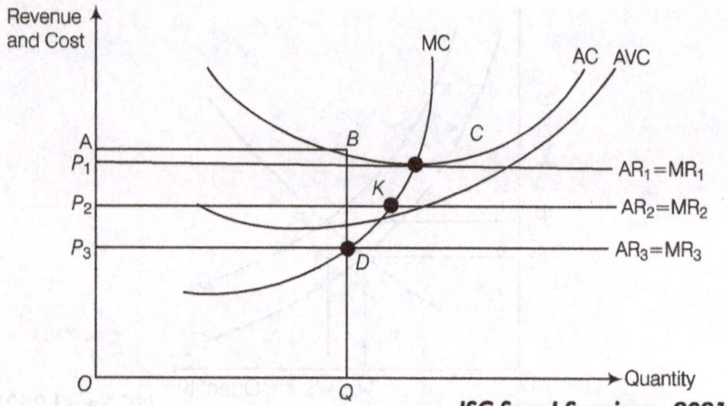

ISC Sem I Specimen 2021

(i) In figure,

(a) C is an equilibrium point, but D is not
(b) C is shut down point, D is break-even point
(c) C is break-even point, D is shut down point
(d) None of the above

Ans (c) C is break-even point, D is shut down point

(ii) In figure,

(a) firm enjoys normal profit at point C
(b) firm enjoys normal profit at point D
(c) firm enjoys supernormal profit at B
(d) firm enjoys supernormal profit at K

Ans (a) firm enjoys normal profit at point C

(iii) In figure,

(a) area $ABDP_3$ represents loss
(b) area P_3DBA represents total fixed cost
(c) area OP_3DQ represents total variable cost
(d) All of the above

Ans (b) area P_3DBA represents total fixed cost

Case 7

Ramu is a sole producer and a seller of AC. He sells the product at a high price in Delhi and at a low price in Mussoorie. **ISC Sem I Specimen 2021**

(i) What kind of a market structure is this?

(a) Monopolistic competition (b) Oligopoly
(c) Monopoly (d) Monopsony

Ans (c) Monopoly

(ii) He is able to sell the product at a higher price in Delhi because

(a) demand is elastic (b) demand is inelastic
(c) unit elastic (d) None of these

Ans. (a) demand is elastic

(iii) The characteristic of this market is

(a) Price discrimination (b) Product differentiation
(c) None of these (d) Both (a) and (b)

Ans (a) Price discrimination

CHAPTER TEST

01 Mark Questions

1. In which kind of market, a firm is a price taker?
(a) perfect competition (b) monopoly
(c) monopolistic competition
(d) oligopoly

2. A firm can sell more only at the lower price. To which market would you relate this statement?
(a) Perfect competition (b) Monopolistic competition
(c) Monopoly (d) Duopoly

3. In case of perfect competition
(a) firm is able to charge higher price
(b) firm is able to charge uniform price
(c) firm is able to sell products at different price to different people
(d) Both (b) and (c)

4. Charging different prices from different buyers for the same good is called
(a) price extension (b) price contraction
(c) price discrimination (d) price flooring

5. A monopolist can earn super normal profit in the long-run as well. State true or false.

6. When demand is perfectly elastic, there will be no impact on the equilibrium quantity with change in supply. State true or false.

7. Under ……… industries, demand and supply never intersects in the positive axis.

8. At the shut down point, firms suffers a loss equal to ……… .

9. What is price discrimination?

10. Under which form of market(s) firms sells homogenous goods?

02 Marks Questions

11. Explain why the demand curve of monopolistic market is more elastic than demand curve of monopoly market?

12. Why firms under perfect competition do not incur selling cost?

13. What do you mean by price discrimination? In which form of market, price discrimination is practised?

14. What is the impact of interdependence of firms under oligopoly market?

15. A severe drought results in a drastic fall in the output of wheat. Analyse how it will affect the market price of wheat?

03/04 Marks Questions

16. 'The demand curve under oligopoly is indetermined'. Comment.

17. 'A day without selling cost is nearly impossible'. Comment.

18. 'Demand curve facing a monopoly firm is a constraint for the monopolist'. Do you agree?

19. Explain the concept of viable industry with an example.

20. 'Demand and supply are like two blade pair of scissors'. Present your view.

06 Marks Questions

21. Suppose the demand and supply functions are given as $QD = 1000 - P$ and $QS = 700 + 2P$
(i) Find out equilibrium price and quantity.
(ii) Now suppose that the price of an input used to produce the good has increased. So the new supply function is $QS = 400 + 2P$. How equilibrium price and quantity will change?
(iii) Suppose government has imposed a tax of ₹ 50 per unit on sales. How it will affect the equilibrium?

22. Discuss the nature of demand curve under
(i) Perfect competition
(ii) Monopoly
(iii) Monopolistic competition
(iv) Monopsony

Answers

1. (a) perfect competition
2. (b) Monopolistic competition
3. (b) firm is able to charge uniform price
4. (c) price discrimination
5. True
6. False
7. non-viable
8. fixed cost
9. Perfect competition and pure oligopoly

07

Theory of Income Determination

TREND ANALYSIS 5 YEARS

Average No. of Questions Across all Sets

	Types of Questions	2023	2020	2019	2018	2017
01 Aggregate Demand and Aggregate Supply	1 Mark	3	—	—	—	—
	2 Marks	—	—	—	—	1
	3/4 Marks	—	—	1	1	1
	6 Marks	—	1	—	—	—
02 Short-run Equilibrium and Multiplier	1 Mark	—	—	—	—	—
	2 Marks	—	1	1	—	—
	3/4 Marks	1	1	—	1	—
	6 Marks	—	—	1	—	1
03 Deficient and Excess Demand	1 Mark	1	—	—	—	—
	2 Marks	—	—	—	1	—
	3/4 Marks	—	—	1	—	1
	6 Marks	—	1	—	1	—

TOPIC 1

Aggregate Demand (AD), Aggregate Supply (AS) and Related Concepts

Aggregate Demand (AD)

The total demand for all the goods and services by all sectors in an economy during a period of time is termed as Aggregate Demand (AD) of the economy. Mathematically, it can be calculated as

$$\boxed{AD = C + I + G + (X - M)}$$

Where, C = Consumption Expenditure by Household

I = Investment Expenditure by Firms

G = Government Expenditure

NX = Net Exports (Exports – Imports)

Components of Aggregate Demand

Broadly, there are four components of aggregate demand

(i) **Consumption expenditure by household** (C) Total demand for all goods and services by the household in an economy during an accounting year, is termed as consumption expenditure. It is determined by the level of personal disposable income of the consumer.

$$C = f(Y^d)$$

Here, Y^d = Disposable income or income after tax

(ii) **Investment expenditure by firms** (I) It refers to planned expenditure by private firms on creation of new capital assets like machines, buildings and raw materials. It is determined by the market rate of interest.

(iii) **Government's expenditure** (G) It includes total expenditure of government on the purchase of consumption goods and investment expenditure. There is a significant difference between government and private investments.

Private investments are done on the considerations of profit and termed as induced investment.

Government investment expenditure is done on the consideration of social welfare and termed as autonomous investment.

(iv) **Net exports** ($X - M$) Net exports refer to the difference between the value of exports and imports of goods and services i.e.

Net Exports ($X - M$) = Exports (X) − Imports (M).

> **Aggregate Demand in Two Sector Economy**
> Aggregate demand function in a two sector model
> $$\text{AD} = C + I = \bar{C} + bY^d + \bar{I}$$
> (assuming investment to be only autonomous investment)
> *or* $$\text{AD} = \bar{A} + bY^d$$
> ($\bar{A} = \bar{C} + \bar{I}$; b = MPC; Y^d = Disposable income)

Concept of Ex-ante Demand and Ex-post Demand

Ex-ante aggregate demand It can be defined as planned/desired amount of goods and services demanded in the economy at a given overall price level and in a given period of time.

Ex-post aggregate demand It refers to the actual amount of goods and services purchased in the economy at a given overall price level and in a given period of time. It is also called 'effective demand'.

Aggregate Supply (AS)

It refers to the total quantity of goods and services produced by all the producers in an economy during a period of time. In other words, it is the total cost of production of goods and services produced in a country.

Components of Aggregate Supply

Keynes has regarded only two main constituents of aggregate supply *viz*, consumption and saving. Hence, according to Keynes,

$$\text{Aggregate Supply} = \text{Consumption} + \text{Saving}$$

Propensity to Consume

It refers to the ratio between consumption (C) and income (Y). It shows the level of consumption (C) with respect to a given level of income (Y). It has two aspects

(i) **Average Propensity to Consume** (APC) It refers to the ratio between the consumption expenditure and income. i.e.

$$\text{Average Propensity to Consume (APC)} = \frac{C}{Y}$$

Where, C = Consumption Expenditure
Y = Income Level

(ii) **Marginal Propensity to Consume** (MPC) It refers to the ratio of change in consumption expenditure with the change in income. In other words, it indicates how much of the additional income is spent on consumption.

$$\text{Marginal Propensity to Consume (MPC)} = \frac{\Delta C}{\Delta Y}$$

Where, ΔC = Change in Consumption
ΔY = Change in Income

Propensity to Save

It refers to the ratio between saving (S) and income (Y) with respect to given level of income. It has two aspects

(i) **Average Propensity to Save** (APS) It refers to the ratio between total savings and total income in an economy. i.e.

$$\text{Average Propensity to Save (APS)} = \frac{S}{Y}$$

Where, S = Savings, Y = Income Level

(ii) **Marginal Propensity to Save** (MPS) It is the ratio of change in savings with change in income. In other words, it indicates how much of the changed income is spent on savings.

$$\text{Marginal Propensity to Save (MPS)} = \frac{\Delta S}{\Delta Y}$$

Where, ΔS = Change in Savings
ΔY = Change in Income

Relationship between APC and APS

$$APC + APS = 1 \text{ or } APC = 1 - APS$$

and $APS = 1 - APC$ or $Y = C + S$

By dividing both sides by Y,

$$\frac{Y}{Y} = \frac{C}{Y} + \frac{S}{Y}, \quad 1 = APC + APS$$

Relationship between MPC and MPS

$$\Delta Y = \Delta C + \Delta S$$

By dividing both sides by ΔY,

$$\frac{\Delta Y}{\Delta Y} = \frac{\Delta C}{\Delta Y} + \frac{\Delta S}{\Delta Y}, \quad 1 = MPC + MPS$$

or $\quad MPC = 1 - MPS$

and $\quad MPS = 1 - MPC$

Consumption Function

The relationship between the consumption expenditure and income is known as 'consumption function'.

$$C = f(Y) \text{ or } C = \overline{C} + cY^d$$

Where, C = Consumption Expenditure

$\overline{C}$ = Autonomous Consumption i.e. consumption when income level is zero

c = Marginal Propensity to Consume (MPC)

Y^d = Disposable Income, Y = Income Level

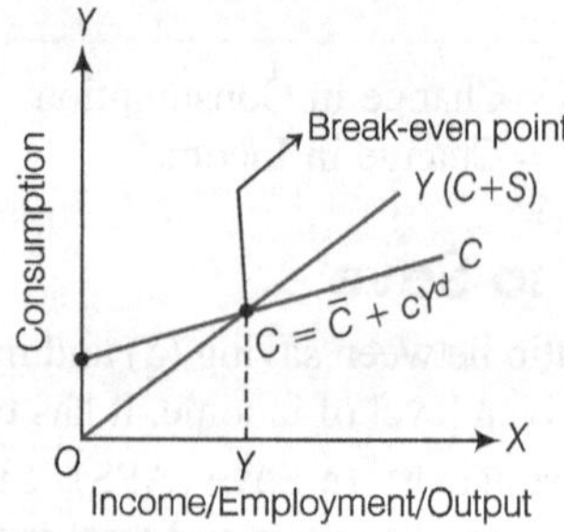

Saving Function

The relationship between savings and income is known as 'saving function'.

$$S = f(Y)$$

Where, S = Saving, Y = Income

Saving is also referred to as the excess of income over consumption, i.e. $S = Y - C$

Where, S = Saving, Y = Income Level, C = Consumption

Algebraically, saving function can be expressed as

$$S = -\overline{S} + sY^d$$

Where, S = Saving,

$\overline{S}$ = Autonomous Saving i.e. saving when income is zero,

s = Marginal Propensity to Save (MPS)

and Y^d = Disposable Income

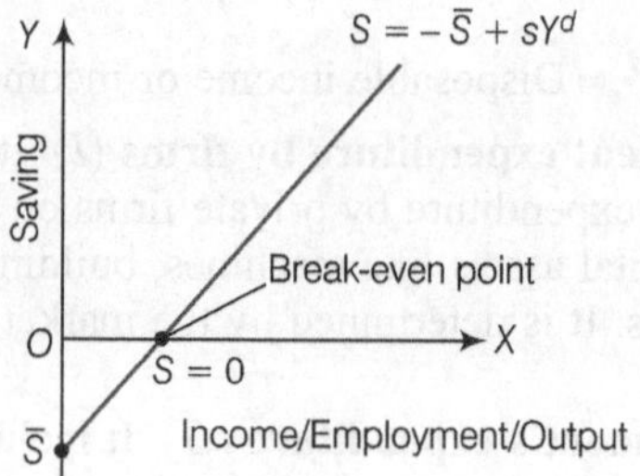

Saving Curve

Influence of Income over Induced and Autonomous Investment

Induced Investment

It is positively related to the level of income in an economy. At higher levels of national income, consumption expenditure tends to increase. Increased consumption expenditure or the increased level of aggregate demand raises expected profitability of the producers, who accordingly are induced to make greater investment.

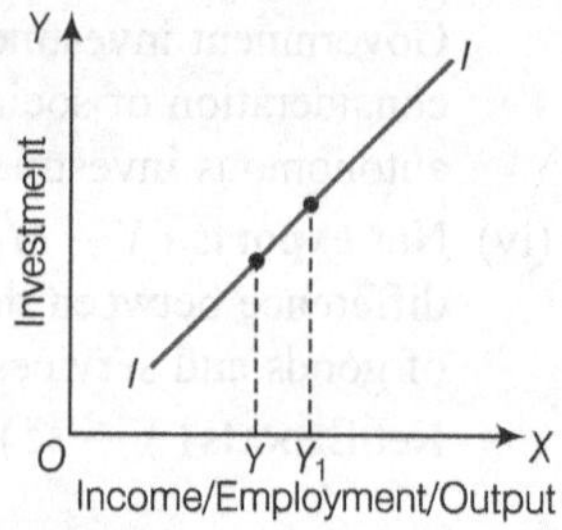

Induced Investment

Determinants of Induced Investment

The main determinants of induced investment are

(i) The prospective yield from the capital i.e. marginal efficiency of capital.

(ii) The supply price of the capital i.e. cost of capital.

(iii) The market rate of interest.

Autonomous Investment

An investment which is not influenced by expected profitability or level of income is called autonomous investment.

In fact, it is an investment expenditure incurred by the government, with a view to promote the level of aggregate demand in the economy.

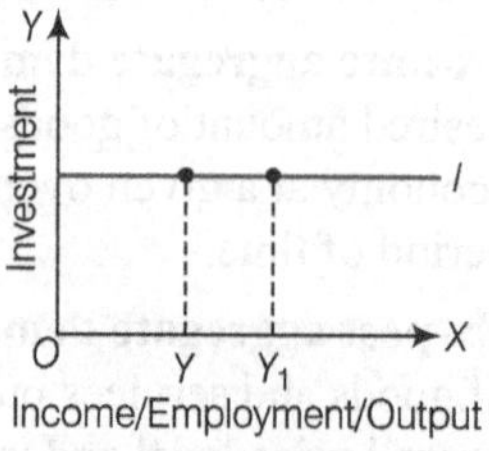

Autonomous Investment

Relationship between Marginal Efficiency of Capital (MEC) and Investment (I)

There is an inverse relationship between Marginal Efficiency of Capital (MEC) and investment i.e. as investment increases, MEC falls and *vice-versa*.

PYQs Previous Years' Questions

1 Mark Questions

1. Induced investment expenditure refers to **ISC 2023**
   (a) the investment made by a firm
   (b) the expenditure made by a firm, that remains constant
   (c) the investment made in the economy that remains unaltered
   (d) total investment expenditure which changes with change in national income

Ans (d) total investment expenditure which changes with change in national income

2. Complete the following table **ISC 2023**

Income (Y)	Saving (S)	APC
0	(–) 12	—
20	6	—

Ans

Income (Y)	Saving (S)	APS (S/Y)	APC (1–APS)
0	(–) 12	—	—
20	6	0.3	0.7

3. Why is effective demand also known as ex-post demand? **ISC 2023**

Ans Ex-post demand means actual level of demand that is actually consumed at the end of the period. For this reason, it is also known as effective demand.

4. Complete the following table **ISC Specimen 2023**

Income (Y) (₹)	Consumption (C) (₹)	MPC (₹)	MPS (₹)
8,000	6,800	—	—
10,000	8,000	—	—

Ans $MPC = \frac{1{,}200}{2{,}000} = 0.6,\ MPS = 1 - 0.6 = 0.4$

Formula used, $MPC = \frac{\Delta C}{\Delta Y}$ and $MPS = 1 - MPC$

5. What does $0 < C < 1$ signify? **ISC Specimen 2023**

Ans The above equation indicates that MPC always varies between 0 and 1.

6. What is meant by autonomous consumption? **ISC Specimen 2023**

Ans Autonomous consumption is the minimum basic level of consumption that remains constant at all levels of income including zero.

7. The type of investment which is affected by a change in the level of output or income is called. **ISC Sem II 2022**

Ans Induced investment

Concept Enhancer Induced investment is positively related with level of income and negatively related with rate of interest.

8. Aggregate supply is equal to **ISC Sem II Specimen 2022**
   (a) $C+I$ (b) $C+S$
   (c) $I+C$ (d) S_1+S_2

Ans (b) $C+S$

9. A consumer spending on purchase of goods regardless of the income in possession, is an example of .... consumption. **ISC Sem II Specimen 2022**

Ans autonomous

2 Marks Questions

1. Complete the following schedule **ISC Sem II Specimen 2022**

Y	C	APC	MPC
100	90	—	—
120	108	—	—

Ans

Y	C	APC	MPC
100	90	0.9	—
120	108	0.9	18/20 = 0.9

Formula used, $APC = \frac{C}{Y}$, $MPC = \frac{\Delta C}{\Delta Y}$

Common Mistake Students generally tries to calculate the very first value of MPC. It always remain not defined as the change is not known.

2. What is meant by ex-ante demand and ex-post demand? **ISC 2017**

Ans **Ex-ante demand** It refers to the amount of goods that consumers want to buy during a particular time period. In other words, it is anticipated demand.

Ex-post demand It refers to the amount of the goods that the consumer actually purchases during a specific time period. In other words, it is actual demand.

3. What is meant by propensity to consume? **ISC 2015**

Ans Propensity to consume shows the level of consumption (C) with respect to a given level of income (Y). It has two aspects

(i) Average propensity to consume

(ii) Marginal propensity to consume

3/4 Marks Questions

1. What is meant by average propensity to consume? Explain its relationship with average propensity to save. **ISC 2019**

Ans Average Propensity to Consume (APC) refers to the ratio between consumption expenditure and income, i.e.

Average Propensity to Consume (APC)

$$= \frac{\text{Total Consumption Expenditure}}{\text{Income}}$$

or $$APC = \frac{C}{Y}$$

Relationship between Average Propensity to Consume (APC) and Average Propensity to Save (APS)

$$APC + APS = 1 \text{ or } APC = 1 - APS$$

or $$APS = 1 - APC$$

Here, we know $Y = C + S$

Where, $S = S$ Savings

By dividing both sides by Y,

$$\frac{Y}{Y} = \frac{C}{Y} + \frac{S}{Y}$$

We get $\Rightarrow 1 = APC + APS$

Concept Enhancer APC tends to fall with rise in level of income while APS tends to rise with rise in level of income.

2. Complete the following table **ISC 2018**

Income (Y) (₹)	Consumption (C)	APS	MPS
0	40	—	—
50	70	—	—
100	100	—	—
150	120	—	—

Ans

Income (Y) (₹)	Consumption (C) (₹)	Saving (S) (₹)	APS $\left(\frac{S}{Y}\right)$	MPS $\left(\frac{\Delta S}{\Delta Y}\right)$
0	40	– 40	—	—
50	70	– 20	– 0.4 [– 20/50]	0.4 [20/50]
100	100	0	0	0.4 [20/50]
150	120	30	0.2 [30/150]	0.6 [30/50]

3. Define marginal propensity to consume. How is it different from marginal propensity to save? **ISC 2017**

Ans **Marginal Propensity to Consume** (MPC) It refers to the amount of changed income which is consumed. It is calculated as the ratio of change in consumption (ΔC) with change in income (ΔY),

i.e. $$MPC = \frac{\Delta C}{\Delta Y}$$

Marginal Propensity to Save (MPS) It refers to the amount of the changed income which is saved. It is calculated as the ratio of change in saving (ΔS) with change in income (ΔY),

i.e. $$MPS = \frac{\Delta S}{\Delta Y}$$

So, it can be concluded that MPC measures change in consumption due to change in income, whereas MPS measures change in savings due to change in income.

4. Show the relationship between APC and APS. **ISC 2016**

Ans Refer to Q. No. 1 on page 128.

5. Explain the difference between induced investment and autonomous investment. **ISC 2016**

Ans **Induced investment** It is positively related to the level of income in an economy. At higher levels of income, consumption expenditure tends to increase. Increased consumption expenditure or the increased level of demand raises expected profitability of the producers who accordingly are induced to make greater investment, leading to rise in the level of investment.

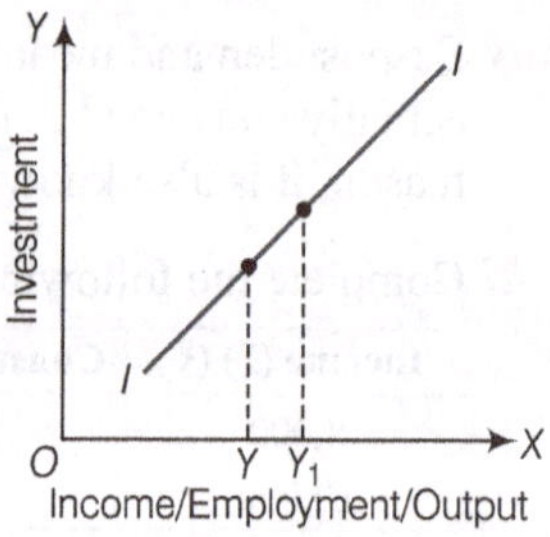

Induced Investment

Autonomous investment An investment which is not influenced by expected profitability or level of income is called 'autonomous investment'. In fact, it is an investment expenditure incurred by the producers with a view to continue production at its present level.

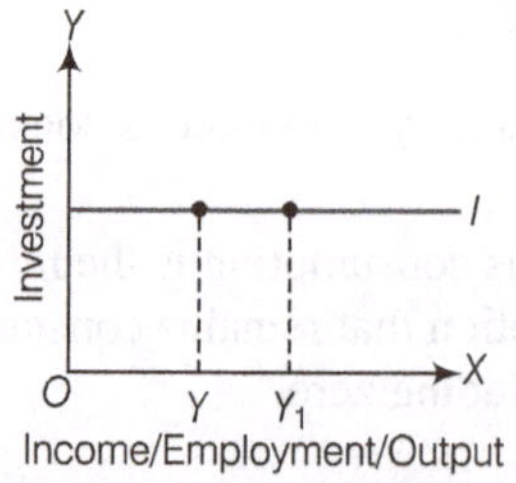

Autonomous Investment

6. What is meant by autonomous consumption? Explain with the help of a diagram. **ISC 2015**

Ans Autonomous consumption ($\bar{C}$) means consumption at zero level of income. Even when income is zero, a typical household will have some minimum amount of consumption expenditure which can be financed through borrowings or past savings.

This minimum consumption is termed as autonomous consumption. Since, it is not dependent on the level of income, therefore it is represented by a vertical straight line parallel to X-axis.

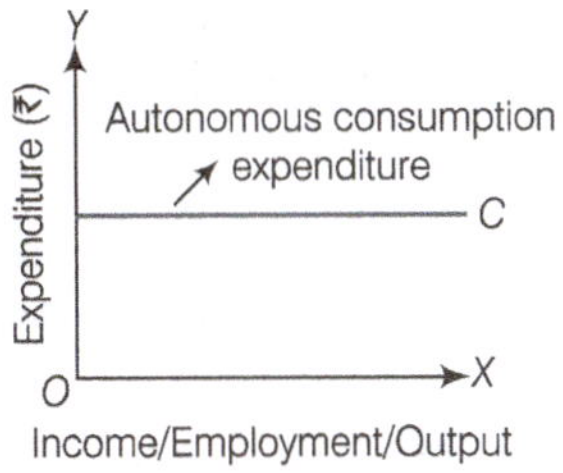

7. Distinguish between Marginal Propensity to Consume (MPC) and Marginal Propensity to Save (MPS). What is the relationship between the two? **ISC 2014**

Ans **Marginal Propensity to Consume** (MPC) It refers to the amount of changed income which is consumed. It is calculated as the ratio of change in consumption (ΔC) with change in income (ΔY),

i.e. $\text{MPC} = \dfrac{\Delta C}{\Delta Y}$

Marginal Propensity to Save (MPS) It refers to the amount of the changed income which is saved. It is calculated as the ratio of change in saving (ΔS) with change in income (ΔY),

i.e. $\text{MPS} = \dfrac{\Delta S}{\Delta Y}$

Relationship between MPC and MPS

$$\Delta Y = \Delta C + \Delta S$$

By dividing both sides by ΔY,

we get $\dfrac{\Delta Y}{\Delta Y} = \dfrac{\Delta C}{\Delta Y} + \dfrac{\Delta S}{\Delta Y}$

$1 = \text{MPC} + \text{MPS}$ *or* $\text{MPC} = 1 - \text{MPS}$

and $\text{MPS} = 1 - \text{MPC}$

8. Calculate MPC, MPS and APC from the following data **ISC 2013**

Income (Y)	Consumption (C)	($Y-C$) S
100	95	5
110	104	6

KEY IDEA

For the first level of income (₹ 100 in this case) MPC and MPS are not defined.

Ans $\text{MPC} = \dfrac{\Delta C}{\Delta Y} = \dfrac{104 - 95}{110 - 100} = \dfrac{9}{10} = 0.9$;

$\text{MPS} = \dfrac{\Delta S}{\Delta Y} = \dfrac{6 - 5}{110 - 100} = \dfrac{1}{10} = 0.1$

$\text{APC} = \dfrac{C}{Y} = \dfrac{95}{100} = 0.95$

$\text{APC} = \dfrac{C}{Y} = \dfrac{104}{110} = 0.94545$

Formulas used, $\text{MPC} = \dfrac{\Delta C}{\Delta Y}$; $\text{MPS} = \dfrac{\Delta S}{\Delta Y}$; $\text{APC} = \dfrac{C}{Y}$

Savings = Income − Consumption

Here, MPC = Marginal Propensity to Consume

APS = Average Propensity to Save

APC = Average Propensity to Consume

ΔC = Change in Consumption

ΔY = Change in Income

ΔS = Change in Savings

C = Consumption, Y = Income

6 Marks Question

1. Briefly discuss the components of aggregate demand in an economy. **ISC 2020**

Or Discuss the main components of aggregate demand in an economy with the help of a diagram. **ISC 2016**

Ans The components of aggregate demand in a four-sector economy are

(i) **Household consumption demand or expenditure** (C) It refers to total expenditure to be incurred by all households on purchase of goods and services, e.g. Households demand for food, clothing, housing, etc. It is also called 'private consumption expenditure'.

It is determined by the level of personal disposable income in the economy. Higher the level of personal disposable income, higher the private consumption expenditure.

(ii) **Investment expenditure by firms** (I) It refers to planned expenditure by private entrepreneurs on creation of new capital assets like machines, buildings and raw materials. An economy grows through investment. Increase in capital assets through investment is called 'capital formation'.

It is also called 'private investment expenditure'. Private investment expenditure comprises of investment in fixed assets and inventory stock. It is determined by the market rate of interest.

Higher the market rate of interest, lower the investment expenditure as rate of interest is considered as cost of borrowings.

(iii) **Government expenditure or demand for goods and services** (G) It refers to government planned expenditure on purchase of consumer and capital goods to fulfil common needs of the society.

These include provision for schools, transport, hospitals, roads, parks, etc.

Components of Aggregate Demand

- Household consumption demand or expenditure (C)
- Investment expenditure by firms (I)
- Government expenditure or demand for goods and services (G)
- Net export ($X - M$)

(iv) **Net export** ($X - M$) It is defined as the aggregate of demand for our goods and services by foreign countries over our country's demand for foreign countries' goods and services.

It depends upon foreign exchange rate, terms of trade, trade policy, etc.

Thus, aggregate demand can also be written as

$$AD = C + I + G + (X - M)$$

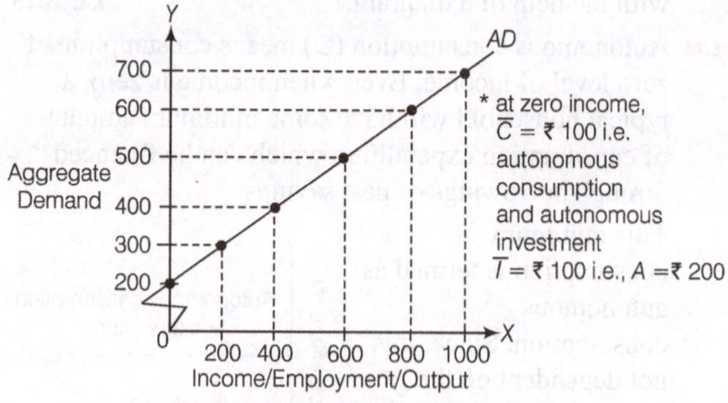

Curve Showing Aggregate Demand

Value Points

For getting maximum marks, following value points can be included in the answer

- There are four components of aggregate demand, explain all of them.
- Use diagram of aggregate demand considering the autonomous consumption.

TOPIC 2

Short-run Equilibrium and Multiplier

Short-run

According to **J.M. Keynes**, "A period of time during which, level of output is determined exclusively by the level of employment in the economy is termed as short-run".

There are two approaches of determination of the equilibrium level of output/income

1. AD = AS Approach

According to this approach, equilibrium output is determined by the equality of aggregate demand and aggregate supply. In other words, equilibrium is attained at the point where desired output level equals to the desired expenditure.

Desired Output (AS) = Desired Expenditure (AD),
$C + S = C + I$ or $Y = C + I$

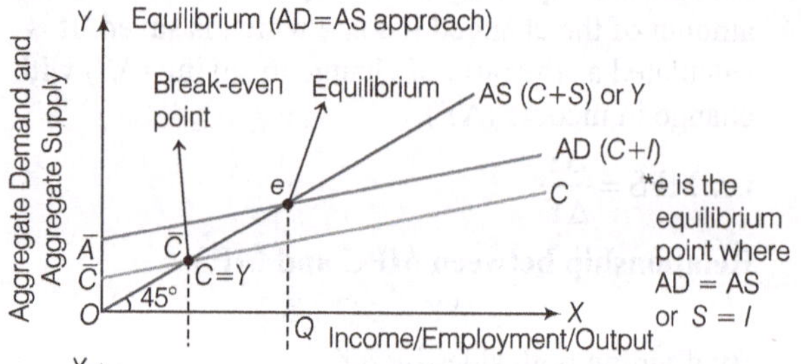

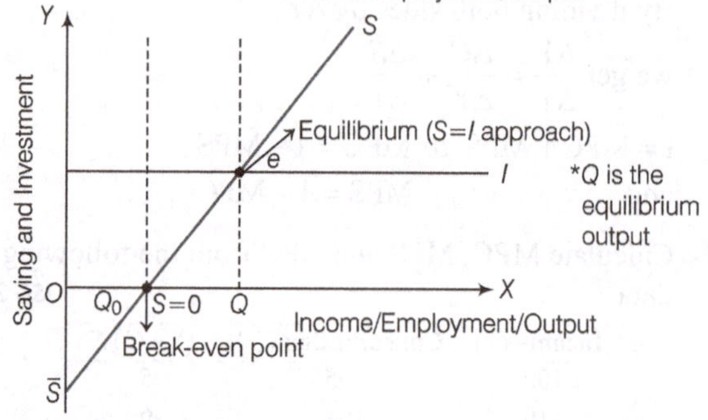

2. S = I Approach

According to this approach, equilibrium output level will be attained at the point where planned investment is equal to planned savings.

Planned Savings (S) = Planned Investment (I)

Note Only autonomous investment is to be considered under this approach.

***Shift in equilibrium** In an economy, the flow of income shifts due to introduction of additional investment (injections) and withdrawals i.e. savings (leakages) in the circular flow of income. Injections boost the flow of income, whereas leakages reduce the flow of income.

Types of Equilibrium

Broadly there are three types of equilibrium

(i) Full employment equilibrium
(ii) Over full employment equilibrium
(iii) Under full employment equilibrium

Meaning of Investment Multiplier

The investment multiplier refers to the amount by which income will change due to change in investment expenditure, it is the ratio between the change in income and change in investment. It is denoted by K, i.e.

$$K = \frac{\Delta Y}{\Delta I} \quad or \quad K = \frac{1}{1 - \text{MPC}} \quad or \quad K = \frac{1}{\text{MPS}}$$

Where, ΔY = Change in Income

ΔI = Change in Investment

* Value of K lies between 1 to infinity.

Mechanism (Process) of Investment Multiplier

Mechanism of investment multiplier can be explained with the help of a numerical example.

Suppose, government makes a new investment of ₹ 1,000 crore and MPC is assumed to be 0.75, which means 75% of the new income generated, will be consumed. Hence, due to increase investments, consumption will increase by ₹ 750 crore (i.e. $\Delta C = \text{MPC} \times \Delta Y$).

In the second round, when output and employment increase to meet this demand by ₹ 750 crore, then this increased income of ₹ 750 crore leads to further income, due to increase in consumption expenditure in the third round, equal to MPC × ΔY i.e. 0.75 × ₹ 750 = ₹ 562.5 crore, this process will continue and in every round income will get multiplied by MPC, at the end, total amount of income that will generate, equals ₹ 4,000 crore.

$$K = \frac{1}{1 - \text{MPC}}$$

or

$$K = \frac{1}{1 - 0.75} = \frac{1}{0.25} = 4$$

$$K = \frac{\Delta Y}{\Delta I} \quad or \quad 4 = \frac{\Delta Y}{1{,}000}$$

$$\Delta Y = ₹\ 4 \times 1{,}000$$

$$= ₹\ 4{,}000 \text{ crore}$$

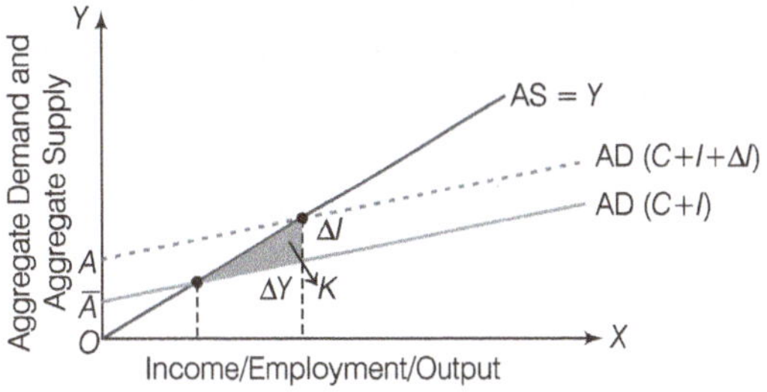

Relationship between Multiplier (K) and Marginal Propensity to Consume (MPC)

There is a direct relationship between multiplier and MPC. Higher the value of MPC, higher the multiplier and *vice-versa*.

Infact, multiplier is estimated using the following equation

$$K = \frac{1}{1 - \text{MPC}}$$

This equation establishes a direct relationship between MPC and K.

Relationship between Multiplier (K) and Marginal Propensity to Save (MPS)

There is an inverse relationship between multiplier and MPS. Higher the value of MPS, lower the multiplier and *vice-versa*.

Infact, multiplier is estimated using the following equation

$$K = \frac{1}{\text{MPS}}$$

This equation establishes an inverse relationship between MPS and K.

Paradox of Thrift

It implies that if all the consumers increase the proportion of income they save, then the total volume of savings in that economy will not increase. Total savings will either decrease or remain same.

PYQs Previous Years' Questions

2 Marks Questions

1. What is meant by investment multiplier?
ISC Specimen 2023, 2019

Ans Investment multiplier (K) refers to the amount by which income will increase in investment expenditure. It is calculated as

$$K = \frac{\text{Change in Income}}{\text{Change in Investment}} = \frac{\Delta Y}{\Delta I}$$

or $$K = \frac{1}{1-\text{MPC}} = \frac{1}{\text{MPS}}$$

Common Mistake Students in most cases, writes the equation of multiplier incorrectly. It is always the change in income due to change in investment.

2. If the initial increase in autonomous investment is ₹ 100 crore and MPC = 0.8, calculate the increase in income.
ISC Sem II 2022

Ans Equilibrium income is calculated as $Y = C + I$ and investment multiplier is equal to $\frac{1}{1-\text{MPC}}$

$$\therefore \quad K = \frac{1}{1-0.8} = \frac{1}{0.2} = 5$$

As per question $\Delta I =$ ₹ 100 crore

and, Investment multiplier $= \frac{\Delta Y}{\Delta I}$

$$\Rightarrow \quad 5 = \frac{\Delta Y}{100}$$

$\therefore$ $\Delta Y =$ ₹ 500 crore

3. What is meant by MPS? How is MPS related to investment multiplier?
ISC 2020

Ans Marginal Propensity to Save (MPS) is the ratio of change in savings with change in income. i.e.

$$\text{MPS} = \frac{\text{Change in Savings } (\Delta S)}{\text{Change in Income } (\Delta Y)}$$

There is an inverse relationship between investment multiplier and MPS. i.e. Higher the value of MPS, lower will be the investment multiplier and *vice-versa*.

4. If the value of MPC is 0.9, find the value of multiplier.
ISC 2016

Ans Given that, Marginal Propensity to Consume (MPC) = 0.9

We know that, Multiplier $(K) = \frac{1}{1-\text{MPC}} = \frac{1}{1-0.9}$

$$= \frac{1}{0.1} = 10$$

$\therefore$ Value of Multiplier $(K) = 10$

5. If the value of multiplier is 4, what will be the value of MPC and MPS?
ISC 2014

KEY IDEA
Sum of MPC and MPS is always equal to unity.

Ans $K = 4$ (Given)

$$K = \frac{1}{\text{MPS}} \quad or \quad 4 = \frac{1}{\text{MPS}}, \quad \text{MPS} = \frac{1}{4}$$

$\therefore$ MPS = 0.25

MPC = 1 − MPS = 1 − 0.25

MPC = 0.75

Here, K = Investment Multiplier

MPS = Marginal Propensity to Save

MPC = Marginal Propensity to Consume

6. Calculate the value of multiplier, if MPC is equal to MPS.
ISC 2013

Ans MPC + MPS = 1

MPC = MPS = x

$x + x = 1$

$2x = 1, x = 0.5$

$\therefore$ MPS = 0.5

We know that multiplier,

$$K = \frac{1}{\text{MPS}}, \quad K = \frac{1}{0.5}, \quad K = 2$$

Here, MPC = Marginal Propensity to Consume

MPS = Marginal Propensity to Save

K = Investment

3/4 Marks Questions

1. Explain the concept of investment multiplier using a diagram. **ISC 2023**

Or Discuss the mechanism of investment multiplier with the help of a numerical. **ISC Sem II Specimen 2022**

Or Briefly explain the mechanism of the investment multiplier with the help of a schedule. Take initial increase in autonomous investment as ₹ 1,000 crores and MPC as 0.8. **ISC 2020**

Or Discuss the mechanism of investment multiplier with the help of a numerical example. **ISC 2018, 2014**

Ans Investment multiplier refers to the amount by which income will increase, due to increase in investment. It is measured as $K = \frac{\Delta Y}{\Delta I}$, where K = Multiplier,

ΔY = Change in income, ΔI = Change in investments

$$\text{Also, } K = \frac{1}{1-\text{MPC}} \text{ or } \frac{1}{\text{MPS}}$$

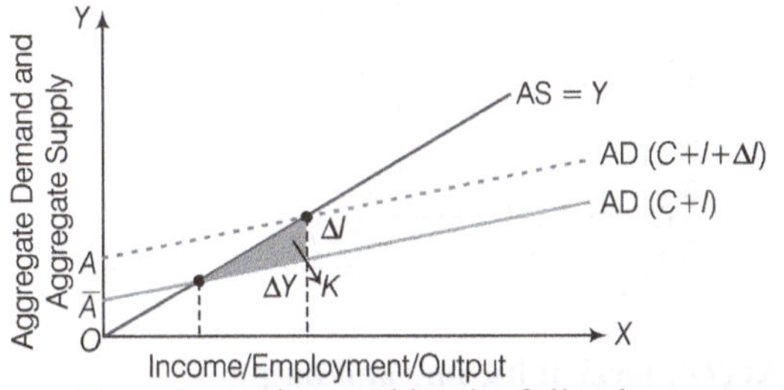

It can be understood by the following example

Rounds of Income Generation	Increase in Investment (ΔI)	Increase in Income (ΔY) (crores)	Increase in Consumption (ΔC) (crores)
Round 1	1,000	1,000 →	800 (0.8 × 1,000)
Round 2	—	800 →	640 (0.8 × 800)
Round 3	—	640 →	512 (0.8 × 640)
Round 4	—	512 →	409.6 (0.8 × 512)
Round 5	—	409.6	...
...	—	...	...
Last Round	—	...	0.00
Total		5,000	

Total increase in income (ΔY) can also be calculated using following formula

$$K = \frac{1}{1-\text{MPC}}$$

$$\Rightarrow \frac{1}{1-0.8} \Rightarrow \frac{1}{0.2} \Rightarrow 5$$

Now, $K = \frac{\Delta Y}{\Delta I}$

$\Rightarrow 5 = \frac{\Delta Y}{1{,}000}$

$\Rightarrow \Delta Y = 1{,}000 \times 5$

$\Rightarrow$ ₹ 5,000 crore

Value Points

For getting maximum marks, following value points can be included in the answer

- Show the formula and calculation of multiplier.
- In tabular example, mention at least four steps before summing up.

2. Find the value of additional investment made by the government, when MPC is 0.5 and increase in income (ΔY) is ₹1,000. **ISC 2015**

Ans Investment Multiplier $(K) = \frac{1}{1-\text{MPC}}$

$\therefore \quad K = \frac{1}{1-0.5} = \frac{1}{0.5} = 2$

Also, $K = \frac{\Delta Y}{\Delta I}$

$\therefore \quad 2 = \frac{1{,}000}{\Delta I}$

or $\Delta I = \frac{1{,}000}{2} = 500$

(where ΔI = Additional Investment)

Therefore, the value of additional investment made by government is ₹ 500.

6 Marks Questions

1. Explain the equilibrium level of income and output determination by aggregate demand and aggregate supply approach with the help of a diagram. **ISC Specimen 2023**

Or Explain how equilibrium level of income can be determined with the help of aggregate demand curve and aggregate supply curve. **ISC 2017**

Or Explain how the equilibrium level of income can be determined by aggregate demand and aggregate supply. **ISC 2013**

Ans **Determination of equilibrium output** We have two approaches to study the determination of equilibrium output/income *viz*, AS = AD approach and $S = I$ Approach. The determination of income and employment under AS = AD approach depends on the level of aggregate demand and aggregate supply.

AS = AD Approach

According to the modern theory of income and employment determination, in any economy at any given time, income and employment are determined at that level where, aggregate demand is equal to aggregate supply. It can be illustrated with the help of given diagram.

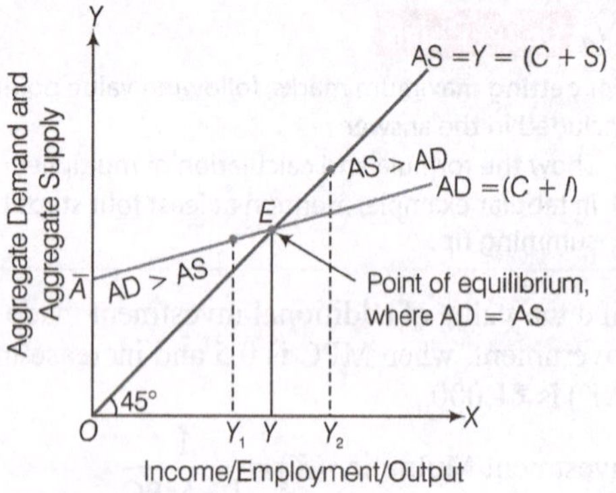

What happens if AS > AD?

When AS is greater than AD (AS > AD), flow of goods and services in the economy tends to exceed their demand. As a result, some of the goods would remain unsold. To clear unwanted stocks, the producers would plan a cut in production. Consequently, AS would reduce to become equal to AD. This is how AS adapts itself to AD.

What happens if AS < AD?

When AS is less than AD (AS < AD), flow of goods and services in the economy tends to be less than their demand. As a result, the existing stock of the producers would be sold out.

To rebuild the desired stocks, the producers would plan greater production. AS would increase to become equal to AD. This is how AS converges with AD.

Hence, the equilibrium will be stable at point *E*, where AD and AS are equal to each other.

Value Points

For getting maximum marks, following value points can be included in the answer

- Explain equlibrium with reference to the diagram.
- Explain situations when AD > AS and AD < AS.

2. What is meant by equilibrium income? How is it determined by using saving and investment approach? ***ISC Sem II Specimen 2022***

Or Explain how equilibrium level of income can be determined with the help of saving and investment approach. ***ISC 2019***

Or Explain the determination of equilibrium level of output with the help of saving and investment curves. If savings exceed planned investment, what changes will bring about equality between them? ***ISC 2014***

Ans **Equilibrium level of income and output** It refers to that level, at which planned savings and planned investments are equal. Actual saving and actual investment are always equal but planned saving and planned investments are equal only at the point of equilibrium. Following diagram shows equilibrium level of income and output with savings and investment

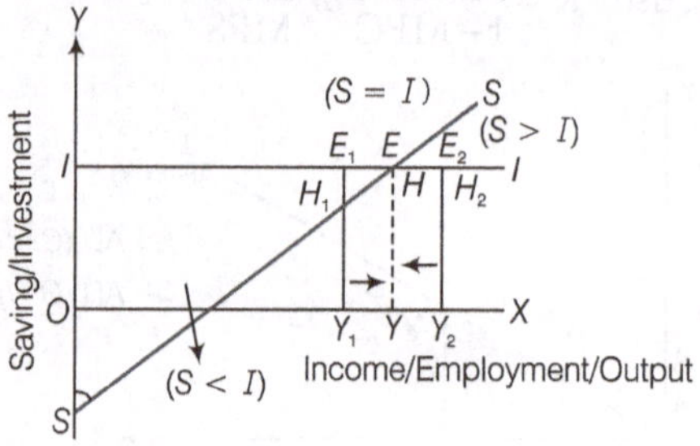

At OY_2 level of income and output

Planned savings $= E_2Y_2$

Planned investments $= H_2Y_2, S > I$ (H_2E_2 amount)

This means that household's aggregate expenditure is less than output. As a result, inventories increase. Firms, seeing a build up of unplanned inventories, start cutting production and hence output falls.

At OY_1 level of income and output

Planned savings $= H_1Y_1$

Planned investments $= E_1Y_1, S < I$ (H_1E_1 amount)

This means that aggregate expenditure is more than output. Firms, seeing a depletion of planned inventories step up production, leading to increase in income and output level. This process will continue till planned saving and planned investments become equal at OY equilibrium level of income and output.

TOPIC 3

Concept of Deficient Demand and Excess Demand and its Remedies

Important Terms

Full employment equilibrium In an economy, when equilibrium is attained alongwith fuller utilisation of available resources, is known as full employment equilibrium.

Under employment equilibrium In an economy, when equilibrium is reached without fuller utilisation of resources, is known as under employment equilibrium.

Full employment A situation when all those persons who are willing and able to work at the existing wage rate are getting work. Full employment does not signify zero unemployment, there may be voluntary unemployment.

Voluntary unemployment Voluntary unemployment means, when some people are not willing to work at all, at the existing wage rates.

Involuntary unemployment Involuntary unemployment means, when some people are willing to work at the prevailing wage rate but are not getting employment.

Deficient Demand

A situation when the aggregate demand falls short of aggregate supply in an economy, at the full employment level of output, is termed as deficient demand.

Deflationary Gap

When there is involuntary unemployment in the economy, there is a short fall in aggregate demand from the level required to maintain full employment equilibrium. This short-fall is termed as deflationary gap, as it leads to fall in prices.

Deflationary Gap = Deficient Demand

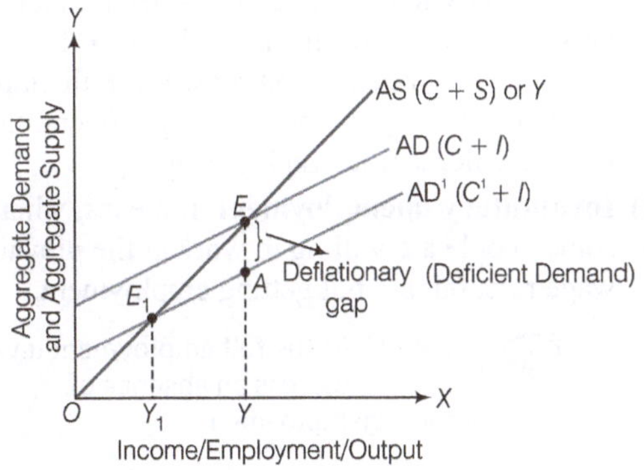

Measures to Correct Deficient Demand

Broadly, there are three measures to reduce deficient demand

(i) Fiscal policy (ii) Monetary policy

(iii) Export promotion

1. Fiscal Policy Measures

Fiscal policy is the government's revenue and expenditure policy. Components of fiscal policy measures which help in solving the problem of deficient demand are

(i) **Public expenditure** Increase in government's expenditure and investment.

(ii) **Taxes** Reduction in taxes to increase the disposable income of the people.

(iii) **Transfer payments** Increase in transfer payments and subsidies.

(iv) **Deficit financing** More use of deficit financing to increase the flow of money.

(v) **Public debts** Repayment of public debts.

2. Monetary Policy Measures

Monetary policy is the policy of Central Bank to regulate and control supply of credit and money in the economy. Components of monetary policy which help in reducing the problem of deficient demand are

(i) **Bank rate** Central Bank reduces the bank rate to make credit cheaper.

(ii) **Open market operation** Central Bank buys securities from the open market and releases funds for the banks.

(iii) **Cash Reserve Ratio** (CRR) Central Bank reduces the CRR and it will increase the cash reserves with the banks which can be offered for credit.

(iv) **Statutory Liquidity Ratio** (SLR) Central Bank lowers SLR to increase availability of credit.

(v) **Margin requirement** Central Bank reduces margin requirement which encourage borrowing.

(vi) **Moral suasion** Central Bank persuades, appeals or advices its member banks to expand credit facilities.

Note Monetary policy is broadly divided into two sub-tools i.e. quantitative tools and qualitative tools. In the above case, point (i) to (iv) are quantitative tools and point (v) and (vi) are qualitative tools.

3. Export Promotion

In the situation of deficient demand, government should take measures to increase exports by giving subsidies or tax benefits, so that demand for domestic goods increases.

Excess Demand

The situation of an economy, when aggregate demand is more than the aggregate supply corresponding to full employment, it is termed as excess demand.

Inflationary Gap

The excess of demand above the level required to maintain equilibrium under full employment situation in an economy, is termed as inflationary gap, as it leads to rise in the general price level.

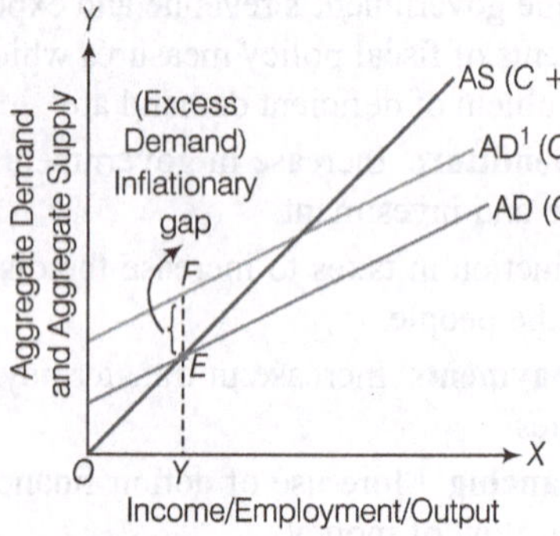

Measures to Reduce Inflationary Gap or Excess Demand

Broadly, there are four ways of controlling the problems of excess demand

(i) Fiscal policy (ii) Monetary policy
(iii) Increasing imports (iv) Increase in output

1. Fiscal Policy

Fiscal policy can control excess demand in the following ways

(i) **Public expenditure** Reduce in government's expenditure and investment.

(ii) **Taxes** Increase in taxes to decrease the disposable income of the people.

(iii) **Transfer payments** Decrease in transfer payments and subsidies.

(iv) **Deficit financing** Less use of deficit financing to decrease the flow of money.

(v) **Public debts** Increase in public borrowings.

2. Monetary Policy

Monetary policy can help in reducing excess demand in the following ways

(i) **Bank rate** Central Bank increases the bank rate which makes credit costlier.

(ii) **Open market operation** Central Bank sells the securities to commercial banks and reduces their capacity to offer loan.

(iii) **Cash Reserve Ratio** (CRR) Central Bank raises the CRR and it will reduce the cash deposits left with commercial banks to be loaned out.

(iv) **Statutory Liquidity Ratio** (SLR) Central Bank raises the SLR to reduced availability of credit.

(v) **Margin requirement** Central Bank increases the margin requirement which discourage borrowings.

(vi) **Moral suasion** Central Bank persuades, appeals or advices its member banks to restrict credit.

3. Increasing Imports

Excess demand can also be reduced by increasing imports, which will increase the supply of goods and services in the economy.

4. Increase in Output

Excess demand can be reduced by increasing output level in the economy. However, this policy cannot be applied in short-run, but in long-run, this could prove out to be a good measure.

PYQs Previous Years' Questions

1 Mark Question

1. Give the meaning of deficit demand. *ISC 2023*

Ans It refers to the shortage of aggregate demand over aggregate supply at the full employment level.

2 Marks Questions

1. Explain the meaning of the following
   (i) Full employment
   (ii) Involuntary unemployment *ISC 2018*

Ans (i) **Full employment** A situation when all those persons who are willing and able to work at the existing wage rate are getting work. Full employment does not signify zero unemployment, there may be voluntary unemployment.

(ii) **Involuntary unemployment** It means, when some people are willing to work at the prevailing wage rate, but are not getting employment.

Concept Enhancer At the full employment level, there is an absence of involuntary unemployment.

2. What is meant by fiscal policy? Name any two instruments of fiscal policy. *ISC 2016*

Ans Fiscal policy is the revenue and expenditure policy of the government, focussing on growth and stability of the economy. The two instruments of fiscal policy are

(i) Public revenue (revenue policy)
(ii) Public expenditure (expenditure policy)

3/4 Marks Questions

1. Discuss any two fiscal measures to correct a situation of deficient demand in an economy. *ISC 2019*

KEY IDEA
Fiscal measures are the government policy measures using taxes and public debts.

Ans Fiscal measures used to correct the situation of deficient demand in an economy are

(i) **Decrease in taxes** The government reduces the rate of taxes at the time of deficient demand. This increases disposable income of people and leads to increase in aggregate demand, thus helping in solving problem of deficient demand.

(ii) **Public debts** At times of deficient demand, government repays the public debt. This increase disposable income and consequently aggregate demand increases. This solves the problem of deficient demand to some extent.

2. Explain how fiscal policy measures can be used to reduce excess demand in an economy. *ISC 2017*

Ans Fiscal policy measures can be used to reduce excess demand in an economy in the following ways

(i) **Surplus budget policy** It is necessary that government's expenditure should be less than its income in order to correct the situation of excess demand.

(ii) **Increase in taxes** The government should levy new taxes and enhance the rate of the existing ones. This will reduce disposable income of the people and would lead to reduction in aggregate demand.

(iii) **Increase in domestic borrowings** Government's borrowings from public can help in reducing the problems of excess demand. It enables government to meet its expenditures and hence, reduces the need for deficit financing, which again results in fall in the purchasing power of the individuals.

3. Discuss the fiscal measures used to solve the situation of deficient demand. *ISC 2013*

Ans Fiscal measures used to solve the problem of deficient demand are

(i) Increase in government's expenditure and investment.
(ii) Increase in transfer payments and subsidies.
(iii) Reduction in taxes to increase the disposable income of the people.
(iv) More use of deficit financing to increase the flow of money.
(v) Repayment of public debts.

6 Marks Questions

1. Explain the concept of deflationary gap with the help of a diagram. Discuss any two monetary measures to reduce the gap. *ISC 2020*

Ans **Deflationary gap** The extent to which current aggregate demand falls short of the actual aggregate demand required for full employment level, is termed as deflationary gap. Deflationary gap is equal to the difference between the actual level of aggregate demand and the level of aggregate demand to establish full employment equilibrium.

It measures the size of deficient demand.

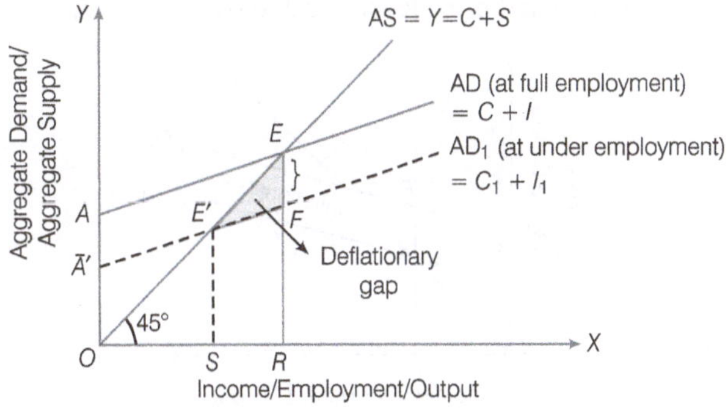

Curve Showing Deflationary Gap

Deflationary gap causes the economy's income, output, employment and prices to decline, hence pushing the economy into under employment equilibrium.

Two monetary measures to control deflationary gap (Deficient Demand)

(i) **Role of bank rate in correcting deficient demand** The rate at which the Central Bank lends money to commercial bank is termed as bank rate. In case of deficient demand, the Central Bank decreases the bank rate to increase money supply in the economy.

Decrease in bank rate, increases the money creation of power of commercial banks and reduces the market rate of interest which encourages public to borrow loans. The aggregate demand goes up and the deficient demand is corrected.

(ii) **Role of open market operations in correcting excess demand** Open market operations refer to sale and purchase of government securities by the Central Bank in open market. In case of deficient demand, the Central Bank buys the securities from public. It increases the money supply and also increases the credit creation power of commercial banks. In this way, the aggregate demand of economy goes up and the problem of deficient demand is corrected.

Common Mistake Students generally marks the deflationary gap to the left of full employment level of income. Deflationary gap should always be marked at the full employment level.

2. Explain the concept of inflationary gap with the help of a diagram. Discuss two monetary measures to correct it. **ISC 2018**

Ans Inflationary gap occurs when AD > AS corresponding to full employment level. This inflationary gap i.e. excess of aggregate demand causes inflation in the economy and price levels tend to rise.

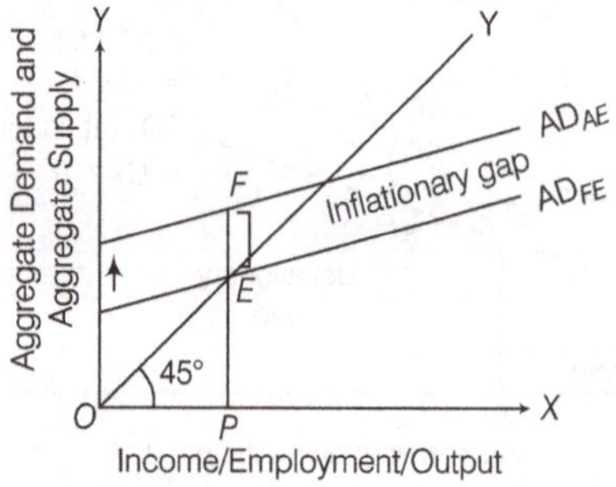

In the above figure,

AD_{FE} = AD at full employment level

AD_{AE} = AD above full employment level

The point *E* is the equilibrium point where AD = AS. But the excess demand (current) of AD_{AE}, aggregate demand *FP* is more than the aggregate supply in the economy.

This difference of actual aggregate demand and aggregate supply i.e. *EF* is the inflationary gap.

Inflationary Gap = Excess Demand

$= AD_{AE} - AD_{FE}$

$= EF$

Two monetary measures to control inflationary gap (Excess Demand)

(i) **Role of bank rate in correcting excess demand** The rate at which the Central Bank lends money to commercial bank is termed as bank rate. In case of excess demand, the Central Bank increases the bank rate to decrease the supply of money in the economy.

Increase in bank rate reduces the money creation power of commercial banks and also increases the market rate of interest which discourages public to borrow loans. The aggregate demand comes down and the excess demand is corrected.

(ii) **Role of open market operations in correcting excess demand** Open market operations refer to sale and purchase of government securities by the Central Bank in open market. In case of excess demand, the Central Bank sells the securities to public. It reduces the supply of money and also reduces the credit creation power of commercial banks. In this way, the aggregate demand of economy comes down and the problem of excess demand is corrected.

3. Explain the concept of deficient demand with the help of aggregate demand and aggregate supply curves. Discuss one fiscal and one monetary measure to correct it. **ISC 2015**

Ans Deficient demand is defined as the amount by which aggregate demand falls short of the aggregate supply, at full employment level. The concept of deficient demand is explained with the help of the given figure.

In the given figure, the aggregate demand curve intersects the 45° aggregate supply curve originating from origin at *E*. This is the level of full employment equilibrium.

Now, suppose due to a fall in government expenditure, aggregate demand falls to AD_1, the new equilibrium point is *A*. So, the deficient demand at the full employment income level is *EA*.

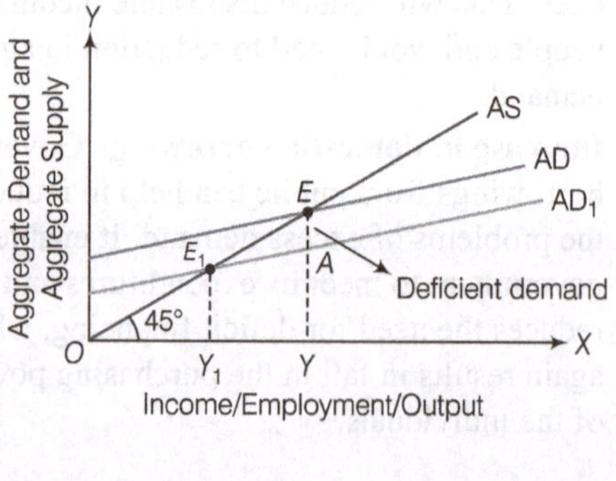

One fiscal measure to correct deficient demand is

Public expenditure The most important and direct mean of overcoming deficient demand is increase in public expenditure. Government should undertake huge investments in construction of roads, dams, railway lines, etc.

Also, government should initiate various welfare measures like unemployment allowance, old-age pension, etc. These measures will help increase aggregate demand in the economy.

One monetary measure to correct deficient demand is

Bank rate The Central Bank of the country should reduce bank rate to overcome the situation of deficient demand in the economy. A decrease in bank rate will lower the cost of credit. This will increase the credit borrowed by consumers leading to an increase in the level of aggregate demand.

4. Define fiscal policy. Explain how excess demand can be controlled through fiscal measures? *ISC 2008*

Ans Fiscal policy refers to the policy undertaken by the government of a country through its tools like taxes, government expenditure, public borrowing, etc. Let us first discuss the problem of excess demand.

It refers to the situation when Aggregate Demand (AD) is in excess of Aggregate Supply (AS) corresponding to full employment in the economy. i.e. AD > AS.

Excess demand gives rise to inflation

The extent to which current aggregate demand becomes higher than the aggregate demand required for full employment, it is termed as inflationary gap. In other words, inflationary gap is equal to the difference between the actual level of aggregate demand and the level of the aggregate demand required to establish full employment equilibrium.

Inflationary gap measures the size of excess demand.

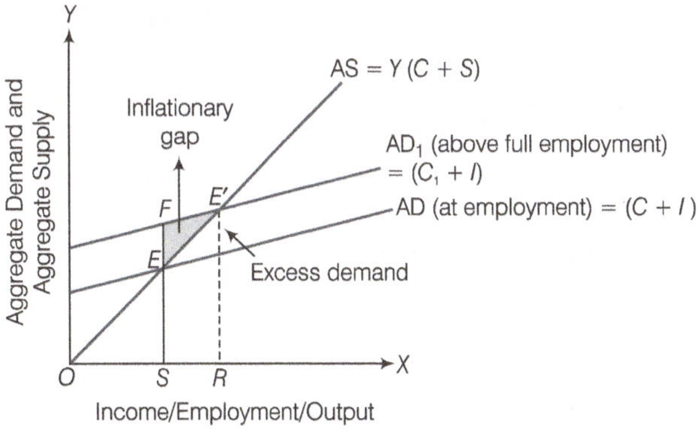

Inflationary gap causes a rise in price level or inflation because full employment has already been attained, hence output and income level cannot be increased, hence, increased consumption demand would end up by raising prices in the economy.

Fiscal measures to correct excess demand

(i) **Surplus budget policy** It is necessary that government's expenditure should be less than its income in order to correct the situation of excess demand.

(ii) **Increase in taxes** The government should levy new taxes and enhance the rate of the existing ones. This will reduce disposable income of the people and hence reduction in aggregate demand.

(iii) **Increase in domestic borrowings** Government's borrowings from public can help in reducing the problems of excess demand.

It enables government to meet its expenditures and hence, reduces the need for deficit financing, which again results in fall in the purchasing power of the individuals.

Case Based Question

Case 1

The Great Depression of 1930s proved that without the government's intervention, the economy cannot create employment opportunities. In India, MGNREGA programmes are based on Keynesian aggregate demand strategy of direct job creation by the government. MGNREGA increases the purchasing power of those individuals whose MPC is the highest. *ISC Sem II 2022*

(i) What is meant by MPC?

Ans MPC measures the change in consumption due to change in income. Mathematically, MPC $= \Delta C / \Delta Y$.

(ii) State the components of aggregate demand.

Ans Components of aggregate demand are

(a) Consumption expenditure (C)

(b) Investment expenditure (I)

(iii) How is MPS obtained from MPC?

Ans MPS $= 1 -$ MPC

CHAPTER TEST

01 Mark Questions

1. Which of the following is not a component of aggregate demand?
   (a) Consumption expenditure
   (b) Investment expenditure
   (c) Speculative expenditure
   (d) Government expenditure

2. Consumption expenditure is a function of ....
   (a) Gross National Income (b) Net National Income
   (c) Disposable Income (d) All of these

3. Consumption at zero level of income is financed by which of the following?
   (a) Dis-savings
   (b) Borrowings
   (c) Both (a) and (b)
   (d) Neither (a) nor (b)

4. What will be the value of APC at the break-even point?
   (a) Zero
   (b) One
   (c) Infinity
   (d) Between zero and one

5. At the full employment level, there is zero unemployment. State true or false.

6. Under full employment equilibrium indicates under employment in an economy. State true or false.

7. When consumption exceeds income, the value of APS will be ....

8. Rise in MPS leads to ...... in investment multiplier.

9. Define break-even point using average propensity to save.

10. Why over full employment equilibrium is not attainable?

02 Marks Questions

11. The consumption is given as $C = 40 + 0.6Y$. Derive saving function, autonomous consumption and MPC.

12. 'There is minimum level of consumption, even at zero level of income'. Do you agree?

13. An increase of ₹ 100 crore in investment, leads to rise in National Income by ₹ 500 crore. Calculate multiplier.

14. How should bank rate change to check inflation?

15. What is the difference between excess demand and deficient demand?

03/04 Marks Questions

16. Distinguish between 'average propensity to save' and 'marginal propensity to save'. How they are calculated?

17. Does a situation of increasing aggregate demand imply a situation of excess demand? Discuss.

18. What is the basic difference between fiscal and monetary policy and what is common objective of these policies?

19. Explain the effect of sale and purchase of government's securities by the Central Bank, on availability of credit.

06 Marks Questions

20. 'The size of multiplier varies directly with the size of MPC'. Do you agree? Why or why not?

21. When and how would you use the various instruments of (i) Fiscal Policy and (ii) Monetary Policy to control the problem of deficient demand?

22. How can changes in budget deficits control excessive demand and deficient demand? Explain.

Answers

1. (c) Speculative expenditure
2. (c) Disposable Income
3. (c) Both (a) and (b)
4. (b) One
5. False
6. True
7. less than zero
8. fall

08

Money and Banking

TREND ANALYSIS 5 YEARS

Average No. of Questions Across all Sets

	Types of Questions	2023	2020	2019	2018	2017
01 Money, its Functions and Supply of Money	1 Mark	1	—	—	—	—
	2 Marks	—	—	1	—	—
	3/4 Marks	1	2	1	1	1
	6 Marks	—	—	—	—	—
02 Banks : Commercial Banks and Central Bank	1 Mark	1	—	—	—	—
	2 Marks	1	—	—	1	1
	3/4 Marks	—	1	1	1	1
	6 Marks	—	1	1	1	1

TOPIC 1

Meaning, Functions of Money and Supply of Money

Money

It is defined as a thing or object that is commonly accepted as a medium of exchange. It is an intermediate good which is acceptable to both the parties to settle transactions.

Stages in Evolution of Money

The main stages in the evolution of money are

(i) **Commodity money** All sorts of commodities like pearls, sea shells, salt, etc have been used as a medium of exchange.

(ii) **Metallic money** Money made from some metals like gold, silver, copper, etc was called 'metallic money'.

(iii) **Paper money** Money made by paper is known as 'paper money' or 'currency notes'.

(iv) **Deposit** (credit) **money** It refers to the deposits made by the people with banks which they can withdraw at any time they like or transfer it to someone else through a bank cheque.

(v) **Plastic money** The most modern form of money is plastic money in the form of debit and credit cards.

(vi) **Digital money** Any means of payment that exists purely in electronic form e.g. Paytm.

Kinds of Money

Some important kinds of money are

(i) **Fiat money** The money issued by the authority of the government or an economy, such as coins and notes, are termed as fiat money.

(ii) **Fiduciary money** The form of money which is backed by the trust between the two parties, i.e. payer and payee, is termed as fiduciary money. e.g. Cheques issued by one party to another, promissory note, etc.

(iii) **Full bodied money** The money in terms of coins whose commodity value is equal to the money value as and when these are issued, is termed as full bodied money.

(iv) **Credit money** The form of money whose commodity value is less than the money value, is termed as credit money.

(v) **Legal tender** It is money backed by the order of the government of a country. It is further of two types

(a) **Limited legal tender** It is money in which payment upto a certain limit is only acceptable. In India, coins are limited legal tender as one cannot make a payment of more than ₹ 1,000 using coins as per Indian Coinage Act.

(b) **Unlimited legal tender** It is money in which payments upto any amount are acceptable. In India, currency notes are unlimited legal tender.

(vi) **Token money** Its face value is significantly greater than its intrinsic (commodity) value.

Functions of Money

Functions of money can be classified into three different groups

1. Primary Functions

There are two primary functions of money

(i) **Medium of exchange** It is a very important and main function of money. Any commodity can be purchased or sold through the medium of money. In other words, money becomes the representative of general purchasing power.

It is the function of money which has made the work of exchange easy. In other words, medium of exchange means that money acts as an intermediary for the goods and services in an exchange transaction.

(ii) **Measure of value** Money serves as a common measure of value or a standard of value. Value of all goods and services are expressed in terms of money. e.g.The price of a pen as ₹ 5, the price of a book as ₹ 10, etc.

2. Secondary Functions

Secondary functions of money are derivatives of the primary functions.

There are three secondary functions of money

(i) **Store of value** Wealth can be conveniently stored in the form of money because value of money remains relatively stable compared to other commodities and storage of money does not need much space.

In other words, everybody saves some part of his income and purchasing power to fulfil the various objectives of the future, it is known as 'store of value'.

(ii) **Standard of deferred payments** Money serves as the measure by which the value of future payments are regulated. In modern economic system, loans are generally given and taken and the repayment is generally postponed for a future date. Future payments cannot be made in terms of physical goods. Money is, therefore used as a standard of deferred payments.

(iii) **Transfer of value** With money, purchasing power can be transferred from one person to another person and from one place to another, upto any amount, due to general acceptability.

3. Contingent Functions

Money performs certain other functions also which are as follows

(i) **Distribution of national income** (Employment of factor inputs) Money facilitates the distribution of National Income among various factor of productions e.g. Wages to labour.

(ii) **Maximum satisfaction** A consumer and a producer measures the utilities of different goods and factors of production with the help of money and try to get maximum satisfaction.

(iii) **Basis of credit** Banks create credit with the help of deposits money of the people.

(iv) **Liquidity** A person by keeping his wealth in the form of money makes it more liquid.

Supply of Money

Money supply refers to the stock of money held by the banks and public at a particular point of time as a means of payment and store of wealth.

Components of Money Supply

The different components of money supply includes

(i) Currency held by the public

(ii) Demand deposits of banks

(iii) Time deposits of banks

(iv) Savings account deposits

(v) Time and savings deposits with post office

(vi) Other deposits of RBI

Measures of Money Supply in India

There are five measures of money supply followed in India

(i) M_0 = Currency in circulation + Bank's deposits with RBI + Other deposits.

(ii) M_1 = Currency Notes and Coins with Public (C) + Demand Deposits with Commercial Banks (DD) + Other Deposits with RBI (OD) i.e. ($C + DD + OD$).

(iii) $M_2 = M_1$ + Post office saving deposits.

(iv) $M_3 = M_1$ + Time deposits with commercial banks.

(v) $M_4 = M_3$ + Total post office deposits excluding NSCs.

High Powered Money

It is referred to as money base on which overall money supply depends i.e. the amount money issued by the Central Bank (RBI) i.e. High Powered Money (H) = Currency in Circulation + Currency Deposits of Commercial Banks with RBI + Other Deposits of RBI

PYQs Previous Years' Questions

1 Mark Questions

1. With reference to money, which one of the following statements is correct? *ISC 2023*

(a) All paper currency is inconvertible money

(b) Cheque is also a fast money

(c) Money cannot transfer value from one person to another

(d) $M_2 = C + DD + OD$

Ans (a) All paper currency is inconvertible money

2. RBI has adopted four measures of money supply. In this, M_3 comprises *ISC Sem II 2022*

(a) M_1 + Saving deposits of post office.

(b) M_1 + Net time deposits with banks.

(c) M_2 + Total deposits with post office saving.

(d) Cash + Demand deposits + other deposits.

Ans (b) M_1 + Net time deposits with banks.

Concept Enhancer M_3 is also known as broad money or monetary base as the central bank uses M_3 to check the quantity of money supply in the economy.

3. Medium of exchange and measure of value are

(a) Primary functions of money *ISC Sem II Specimen 2022*

(b) Secondary functions of money

(c) Tertiary functions of money

(d) Contingent functions of money

Ans (a) Primary functions of money

2 Marks Questions

1. What is meant by high powered money? *ISC 2019*

Or What is high powered money? *ISC 2014*

KEY IDEA
High powered money is comprised of liquid components and non-liquid components of money.

Ans High powered money is the monetary base, on which overall supply of money depends. In other words, it is the total amount of money issued by the Central Bank (RBI), i.e.

High Powered Money (H) = Currency in Circulation + Currency Deposits of Commercial Banks with RBI + Other Deposits of RBI.

2. Explain the meaning of M_1 and M_4 supply of money. *ISC 2016*

Ans The M_1 and M_4 measures of supply of money are explained below

M_1 = Currency Notes and Coins with Public (C) + Demand Deposits with Commercial Banks (DD) + Other Deposits with RBI.

$M_4 = M_1$ + Time Deposits with Commercial Banks + Total Post Office Deposits excluding NSCs.

This measure of money supply is a broad measure and includes every form of deposit within its purview.

Concept Enhancer M_1 is also known as 'Narrow money' as it is the most liquid measure of money supply.

3. What is unlimited legal tender? *ISC 2013*

Ans Unlimited legal tender simply means money, which is backed by the legal promise of the central authority and hence, has a general acceptance upto any limit.

3/4 Marks Questions

1. State any two secondary functions of money. *ISC 2023, 2019, 2015*

Ans Two secondary functions of money are

(i) **Store of value** Wealth can be conveniently stored in the form of money because value of money remains relatively stable compared to other commodities and storage of money does not need much space.

In other words, everybody saves some part of his income and purchasing power to fulfil the various objectives of the future, it is known as 'store of value'.

(ii) **Standard of deferred payments** Money serves as the measure by which the value of future payments are regulated. In modern economic system, loans are generally given and taken and the repayment is generally postponed for a future date.

Future payments cannot be made in terms of physical goods. Money is, therefore used as a standard of deferred payments.

2. Mention the components of M_1, M_2 and M_3 measures of money supply by RBI. *ISC 2020*

Ans Refer to text on page 143.

3. Briefly explain any one primary function of money. *ISC 2020*

Or Explain the primary functions of money. *ISC 2016*

Ans Primary functions of money are

(i) **Medium of exchange** It is a very important and main function of money. Any commodity can be purchased or sold through the medium of money.

In other words, money becomes the representative of general purchasing power. It is the function of money which has made the work of exchange easy because money has the merit of general acceptability.

(ii) **Measure of value** It refers to monetary expression of the market value of goods and services.

Money serves as a common measure of value or a standard of value. Value of all goods and services are expressed in terms of money.

e.g. The price of a pen as ₹ 5, the price of a book as ₹ 10, etc. It is also referred to as unit of account function of money.

Common Mistake Students most of time gets confused between the primary and secondary function of money. Primary functions are basic functions and secondary functions are advance/ additional functions.

4. Explain the following terms *ISC 2018*

(i) Fiat money (ii) Deposit money

(iii) Token money

Ans (i) **Fiat money** The money issued by the authority of the government or an economy, such as coins and notes, are termed as fiat money.

(ii) **Deposit money** The money includes cheques, letters of credit, etc that circulate and are payable on demand.

(iii) **Token money** The money whose face value exceeds its cost of production. Most modern coins and notes in circulation are token money.

Concept Enhancer It is Illegal to deny payments using fiat money in a country.

5. Explain the following contingent functions of money

(i) Employment of factor inputs.

(ii) Basis of credit system. *ISC 2017*

Or Discuss two contingent functions of money. *ISC 2014*

Ans Two contingent functions of money are

(i) **Employment of factor inputs** Evolution of money has facilitated easy distribution of income among factors of production, thus facilitating their employment. Production in an outcome of collective or combined efforts of factors of production.

Therefore, a firm needs to employ a number of factor inputs. The factor inputs will be willing to work only when reward is given in terms of money.

(ii) **Basis of credit system** Every business and commercial activity depends upon credit and credit has gained its importance due to the presence of money. In other words, banks create credit with the help of deposits money of people.

6. Explain the following functions of money *ISC 2013*

(i) Medium of exchange

(ii) Store of value

Ans (i) **Medium of exchange** Refer to Q. No. 3 on page 144.

(ii) **Store of value** Refer to Q. No. 1 on page 143.

TOPIC 2

Banks : Commercial Banks and Central Bank (RBI)

Bank

Bank is an institution which receives funds from the public which is repayable on demand and can be withdrawn by mean of cheques, drafts order, etc and gives loans and advances to those who need them.

Types of Banks

(i) Commercial Banks
(ii) Development Banks (like ICICI, IDBI)
(iii) Cooperative Banks (iv) Land Development Banks
(v) Regional Rural Banks
(vi) Export Import (EXIM) Bank
(vii) Foreign Banks (viii) Merchant Banks

Commercial Banks

A financial institution which accepts chequeable and non-chequeable deposits from the people and offer different kinds of loans for the purpose of consumption or investment, is termed as commercial bank.

Functions of Commercial Banks

The main functions of commercial banks are

(i) **Accepting deposits** Accepting deposits from the public in the form of demand deposits, saving deposits as well as time deposits.

(ii) **Advancing of loans** Advancing of loans to the public, which include

(a) **Cash credit** The bank advances cash loan upto a specified limit against securities.

(b) **Overdraft** Banks advance loans to current account customers' upon a certain amount and charge interest.

(c) **Bill discounting** Banks discount bills of exchange before its maturity and give short-term loans and advances.

(d) **Outright loans** It refers to the lumpsum amount of money that the borrower intended to use for sure out of the limit granted by the banks.

(iii) **Credit creation** It refers to the power of commercial banks to expand deposits through loans and advances is known as 'credit creation'.

(iv) **Transfer of funds** Banks provide facility of economical and easy remittance of funds from one to another.

(v) **Facilitation of payments** Banks have provided a very convenient system of payment in the form of cheques.

(vi) **Agency functions** Bank performs various agency functions like transfer and collection of funds, purchase and sale of securities and foreign exchange, etc.

(vii) **Other miscellaneous services** Providing lockers facility, issuing travellers cheque, etc.

Credit Creation Process by Commercial Banks

Commercial banks maintain the supply of money in an economy by credit creation. The process of credit creation is an outcome of its two primary functions, i.e. advancement of loans and acceptance of deposits.

The banks issue loans out of their cash reserves with the confidence on their historical experience that all depositors will not withdraw their funds at the same time. In this way, commercial banks create credit many more times than their initial cash reserves and contributes to increased money supply in the economy.

Main Determinants of Credit Creation

There are two main determinants of credit creation, which are

(i) Initial level of deposits with the commercial banks.

(ii) Legal Reserve Ratio (i.e. sum of CRR and SLR) and money multiplier $\left(\frac{1}{LRR}\right)$.

Assumptions of Credit Creation Process

(i) Entire banking system is taken as a single unit and referred as 'Bank'.

(ii) All transactions in the economy are routed through 'Bank'.

Legal Reserve Ratio (LRR)

It is the total amount of deposit that each commercial bank must keep with the Central Bank and with itself and includes Cash Reserve Ratio (CRR) and Statutory Liquidity Ratio (SLR).

Money Multiplier

It refers to the fraction which indicates the quantum of money creation by the commercial banks.

It is calculated by the following formula

$$\text{Money Multiplier} = \frac{1}{\text{Legal Reserve Ratio (LRR)}}$$

Money created = Initial deposits × Money multiplier

Limitations of Credit Creation

(i) Amount of cash possessed by the banks.
(ii) Banking habits of the people like use of cash or cheque.
(iii) Minimum legal reserve ratio prescribed by Central Bank.
(iv) Leakages like cheque received but not deposit in bank account.
(v) Economic conditions exist in the country.
(vi) Monetary policy changes by Central Bank.

Central Bank

It is an apex body or institution which controls and regulates the entire banking structure of a country. Reserve Bank of India (RBI) works as Central Bank in India.

Regulatory Role of Central Bank (RBI)

The RBI regulates the Indian banking and financial system by issuing broad guidelines and instructions.

Objectives of RBI Regulations

(i) Controlling money supply in the economy.
(ii) Maintaining people's confidence in banking and financial system.
(iii) Helping customers' through 'Banking Ombudsman'.
(iv) Monitoring different key indicators like GDP and inflation.

Functions of Central Bank

Following are the functions of Central Bank

(i) **Issue of currency** Central Bank has authority of issuing currency notes.
(ii) **Banker to government** As a banker to both State and Central Governments, it carries out their banking business.
(iii) **Banker of banks** As a banker of other commercial banks, Central Bank grants loan to commercial banks to fulfil their needs of funds and accepts their deposits.
(iv) **Lender of last resort** Central Bank provides financial accommodation to commercial banks, if they fail to get it from any where.
(v) **Custodian of foreign exchange reserves** Central Bank is the custodian of nation's foreign exchange reserve.
(vi) **Clearing house** It provides facilities to banks to come together everyday and set off their chequing claims.
(vii) **Controller of credit** It acts as controller of credit and money supply through issuing monetary policy.
(viii) **Collection and publication of data** Central Bank publishes economic and statistical information.
(ix) **Supervision of banks** Central Bank is authorised to carry out periodical inspection of the commercial banks.

Inflation

Inflation can be defined as a situation of appreciable increase in the general price level in an economy at a given period as compared to base year.

It is considered as the gradual loss of buying power of a particular currency. A quantitative estimate of the rate at which buying power declines can be expressed in the growth of an economy's average price level of a basket of selected goods and services over time.

A rise in the overall level of prices, commonly stated as a percentage, signifies that a unit of money buys less than it did previously.

Demand-pull Inflation

Inflation that originates from the demand forces is called demand-pull inflation. It occurs when the aggregate demand in the economy exceeds the overall supply.

Cost-pull inflation occurs when aggregate demand stays constant, but aggregate supply falls owing to external causes that cause price levels to rise.

Cost-push Inflation

Cost-push inflation occurs when the aggregate supply of goods and services declines due to increased production costs. Cost-push inflation means prices are 'pushed up' by rises in the cost of any of the four production components, i.e., labour, capital, land, or entrepreneurship or it may be caused by the rise in price of non-factor inputs like raw materials, etc.

Credit Control Policy of Central Bank

By credit control, we mean flow of credit can be regulated in such a way that they may rise or fall according to the needs of an economy. This is done by the Central Bank by using two types of methods which are as discussed below

1. Quantitative Methods

The methods which affect the overall supply of credit in the economy are quantitative methods.

Following instruments are used

(i) **Bank rate policy** The bank rate is the minimum rate at which the Central Bank of a country is prepared to give credit to the commercial banks.

The increase in bank rate increases the rate of interest and credit becomes dear or expensive. Accordingly, the demand for credit is reduced and *vice-versa*.

(ii) **Open market operations** It refers to the sale and purchase of securities in open market by the Central Bank (RBI). By selling the securities, the Central Bank withdraws cash balances from within the economy and by buying the securities, the Central Bank contributes cash balances in economy.

Thus, through open market operations, if cash balances are increased through purchase of securities, flow of credit increases and if cash balances are reduced through sale of securities, the flow of credit decreases. So, open market operations pump in or pump out money from circulation.

(iii) **Cash Reserve Ratio** (CRR) It refers to the minimum percentage of a bank's total deposits required to be kept with the Central Bank. Commercial banks have to keep with the Central Bank a certain percentage of their deposits in the form of cash reserves as a matter of law. Increase in CRR will reduce credit supply and *vice-versa*.

(iv) **Statutory Liquidity Ratio** (SLR) Every bank is required to maintain a fixed percentage of its assets in the form of cash or other liquid assets, called 'SLR'. Increase in SLR will reduce credit supply and *vice-versa*.

(v) **Repo rate** It is the rate of interest at which commercial banks can raise short-term loans from the Central Bank. Increase in repo rate will reduce the credit supply and *vice-versa*.

(vi) **Reserve repo rate** It is the rate of interest at which commercial banks can park their surplus funds with the Central Bank, for short period of time. Increase in reserve repo rate will reduce the credit supply and *vice-versa*.

2. Qualitative Methods

These methods focus on the alternative uses of credit in the economy or seek to influence the quality of credit. These methods are as follows

(i) **Marginal requirements** It refers to the limit which is deducted from the value of security provided by the borrower before granting them loan. So, if margin requirement is 20%, then borrowers can get only upto 80% of loan of the value of security that the borrower has provided.

The Reserve Bank of India (RBI) increases the margin requirements when it wants to reduce credit in the economy and *vice-versa*. At present, the RBI fixes minimum margins to be maintained by commercial banks in respect of their advances against foodgrains, oil seeds, vegetable oils, cotton, sugar, cotton textile, etc.

(ii) **Rationing of credit** It refers to fixation of credit quotas for different business activities. Rationing of credit is introduced when the flow of credit is to be checked particularly for speculative activities in the economy.

(iii) **Direct action** The Central Bank may initiate direct action against the member banks, in case these do not comply with its directives.

(iv) **Moral suasion** By this measure, Central Bank requests bank to lend more or not to lend in some cases. The Central Bank is empowered to issue directives to member banks. Such direct orders are in the form of directional control, prohibiting loans of particular type or giving advice to grant loan to priority sectors.

PYQs Previous Years' Questions

1 Mark Questions

1. State whether the following is true or false.

"Rate of interest on savings account is more than that on recurring account". *ISC 2023*

Ans False. Rate of interest on savings account is less than that an recurring account.

2. The Central Bank provides, direct or indirect, financial assistance to the Commercial bank when the latter is facing severe liquidity problem. Hence, Central Bank *ISC Sem II 2022*

(a) has a monopoly of note issue.
(b) acts as banker to the government.
(c) acts as controller of credit.
(d) acts as lender of the last resort.

Ans (d) acts as lender of the last resort.

Concept Enhancer This function of central bank ensures that the banking system remains stable and commercial banks doesn't fail overtime.

2 Marks Questions

1. Explain open market operations as a measure to control inflation. ***ISC 2023***

Ans Open market operations refers to buying and selling of securities in the open market by the Central Bank. In case of inflation, Central Bank conducts open market sales, this leads to falls in income and hence demand, leading to fall in general price (inflation) level.

2. What is meant by inflation? Mention the types of inflation. ***ISC Specimen 2023***

Ans Inflation refers to the persistant rise in the prices of the current period compared with the base year. There are two types of inflation

(i) Demand pull inflation (ii) Cost-push inflation

3. Explain the role of repo rate in controlling inflation. ***ISC Specimen 2023***

Ans Repo rate refers to the rate at which central bank lends to commercial banks for short-term needs. In the situation of inflation, central bank increases the repo rate making it expensive for the commercial banks, this leads to fall in money supply and *vice-versa* in case of deflation.

4. Differentiate between demand pull and cost push inflation. ***ISC Sem II 2022***

Ans Refer to text on page 146.

5. Differentiate between CRR and SLR. ***ISC Sem II Specimen 2022***

Or Distinguish between CRR and SLR. ***ISC 2013***

Ans Cash Reserve Ratio (CRR) is the fraction of total deposits that each commercial bank must keep with the Central Bank (i.e. RBI). While Statutory Liquidity Ratio (SLR) is the fraction of total deposits that each commercial bank must keep with themselves in liquid assets like gold or government securities.

Concept Enhancer The Central Bank doesn't pay any interest on the amount of deposits kept by commercial banks under CRR or SLR.

6. Differentiate between cash credit and outright loans. ***ISC Sem II Specimen 2022***

Ans Cash credit refers to the loans and advances granted by the commercial banks to their customers against securities. On the other hand, outright loans refers to a lumpsum of money that the borrower intended to use for sure.

7. What is meant by the following functions of central bank? ***ISC Sem II Specimen 2022***

(i) Clearing house (ii) Lender of last resort

Ans Refer to text on page 146.

8. Explain the overdraft facility given by banks. ***ISC 2018***

Ans Overdraft facility is given to the depositors maintaining a current account. It is a credit facility under which a customer is allowed to withdraw more amount that what he has deposited upto a previously agreed limit.

It is short-term credit facility and very populat with the Indian businessmen.

9. Give two differences between time deposit and demand deposit. ***ISC 2017***

Ans Differences between time deposit and demand deposit are

Basis	Time deposit	Demand deposit
Repayability	Time deposits are repayable at the end of a specified time period.	Demand deposits are repayable as and when demanded by the depositors.
Rate of interest	A higher rate of interest is offered on time deposits.	A very low rate of interest is offered on demand deposits.

10. Explain 'discounting bills of exchange' as one of the functions of the banks. ***ISC 2015***

Ans Discounting bills of exchange is a function of commercial banks through which they grant short term loans and advances. The holder of a trade bill may sell the bill to a bank, at a discount, before its maturity. This is termed as 'discounting of bills of exchange'.

11. Why is Central Bank considered to be 'lender of last resort'? ***ISC 2013***

Ans Central Bank is considered as the lender of last resort because it assists the commercial banks in need, with money when commercial banks fail to raise money by any other source.

12. Define the 'custodian of foreign exchange' function of Central Bank. **ISC 2004**

Ans Central Bank is the custodian of nation's foreign exchange reserve. The Central Bank maintains foreign exchange reserves in order to promote international trade and stabilise exchange rate.

13. Give two important factors limiting the volume of credit creation by commercial banks. **ISC 2004**

Ans Two important factors which limits the process of credit creation are

(i) Greater initial amount of deposits, greater would be the money creation and *vice-versa*.

(ii) Legal reserve ratio, which is the sum of CRR and SLR, higher the LRR, lower would be the money creation and *vice-versa*.

3/4 Marks Questions

1. Explain any two types of deposits of commercial bank. **ISC Sem II 2022**

Ans The deposits may be in the form of

(i) **Saving deposits** A person can open a saving deposits account by depositing a small sum of money. He can withdraw money from his account and make additional deposits at will, but their is a certain restriction on the number of withdrawls.

(ii) **Fixed deposits** A fixed deposit is repayable after the expiry of the specified period, which may range from 6 months to 5 years. Deposits for more than one year are known as term deposits. These deposits are not repayable on demand and carry a high rate of interest.

2. Explain the following functions of the Central Bank

(i) Custodian of foreign exchange reserves.

(ii) Lender of the last resort. **ISC 2020**

Ans (i) Central Bank is the custodian of nation's foreign exchange reserve. The Central Bank maintains foreign exchange reserves in order to promote international trade and stabilise exchange rate. By the sale and purchase of foreign currencies in the market, Central Bank can bring the external value of the currencies at par with their internal values and helps the government to pursue a coordinated policy towards balance of payment situation in country.

(ii) Central Bank is considered as the lender of last resort because it assists the commercial banks in need, with money when commercial banks fail to raise money by any other source.

By offering loan to commercial banks in situations of emergency, the Central Bank ensures that the banking system of the country does not suffer from any set back and money market remains stable.

3. Discuss any two limitations of credit creation by commercial banks. **ISC 2019**

Ans Limitations of credit creations are as follows

(i) Leakages like cheque received but not deposited in bank account causes disruption. This is a major drawback of credit creation by commercial banks especially when economic conditions changes in the country.

(ii) Banking habits of the people whose pattern of usage of cash or cheque can't be predicted proves to be a limitation in the process of credit creation.

4. Explain any two functions of the Reserve Bank of India. **ISC 2018**

Or Explain the following functions of the Reserve Bank of India **ISC 2016**

(i) Banker to the government

(ii) Issue of currency notes

Ans Two functions of Reserve Bank of India are

(i) **Bankers to the government** The Central Bank acts as a banker to the government, both Central and State Governments. It carries out banking business of the government and the government keeps its cash balances on current account with the Central Bank.

(ii) **Issue of currency** The first and foremost important function of Central Bank is to issue currency notes. It has its various departments, which issue currency notes and coins for the public of a country.

5. What is meant by repo rate and reverse repo rate? **ISC 2017**

Ans **Repo rate** It is the rate of interest at which commercial banks can raise short-term loans from the Central Bank. Increase in repo rate will reduce the credit supply and *vice-versa*.

Reverse repo rate It is the rate of interest at which commercial banks can park their surplus funds with the Central Bank, for short period of time. Increase in reverse repo rate will reduce the credit supply and *vice-versa*.

Common Mistake Students generally get confused between repo rate and bank rate. Under repo rate, central bank grants short-term credits while under bank rate, central bank grants long-term credits to the commercial banks.

6. Discuss two qualitative methods of credit control. **ISC 2015**

Ans Two qualitative methods of credit control are

(i) **Marginal requirements** At present, the RBI fixes minimum margins to be maintained by commercial banks in respect of their advances against foodgrains, oil seeds, vegetable oils, cotton, sugar, cotton textile, etc.

(ii) **Rationing of credit** It refers to fixation of credit quotas for different business activities. Rationing of credit is introduced when the flow of credit is to be checked particularly for speculative activities in the economy.

7. Explain the role of the Reserve Bank of India with respect to **ISC 2014**

(i) Custodian of foreign exchange reserve
(ii) Promotional and developmental functions

Ans (i) **Custodian of foreign exchange reserve** Central Bank is the custodian of nation's foreign exchange reserve. The Central Bank maintains foreign exchange reserves in order to promote international trade and stabilise exchange rate.

(ii) **Promotional and developmental functions** It includes, the responsibility of the Central Bank to build a strong banking system in the country (specially in developing countries), to achieve the same, it gives several concessions to the commercial banks. It also helps in the development of money and capital market in the country.

8. Explain how bank rate and open market operations can be used by the Central Bank to control credit? **ISC 2013**

Ans **Bank rate policy** The bank rate is the minimum rate at which the Central Bank of a country is prepared to give credit to the commercial banks. The increase in bank rate increases the rate of interest and credit becomes dear or expensive. Accordingly, the demand for credit is reduced or *vice-versa*.

Open market operations It refers to the sale and purchase of securities in open market by the Central Bank (RBI). By selling the securities, the Central Bank withdraws cash balances from within the economy and by buying the securities, the Central Bank contributes cash balances in economy. Cash balances are high powered money.

Thus, through open market operations, if cash balances are increased, flow of credit increases and if cash balances are reduced, the flow of credit decreases. So, open market operations pump in or pump out money from circulation.

6 Marks Questions

1. Illustrate the process of credit creation by commercial banks with the help of a numerical example. **ISC Specimen 2023**

Or How do commercial banks create credit? Explain with the help of an example. **ISC 2018, 2013**

Or Explain the mechanism of credit creation by commercial banks with the help of an example. **ISC 2016**

Ans One of the important functions of commercial banks is money creation or credit creation in an economy. By the historical experience of commercial banks, they know that the depositors would not be withdrawing all of their funds at a particular time.

That is why, they create credit in the form of much higher demand deposits than their cash reserves. Commercial banks issue loans on the basis of their demand deposits even if a fraction of the amount is with them as cash reserves.

In this way, they contribute to increase the flow of money in an economy by the process of credit creation.

Main determinants of credit creation There are two main determinants of credit creation, which are

(i) Initial level of deposits with the commercial banks.

(ii) Legal Reserve Ratio (i.e. sum of CRR and SLR) and money multiplier $\left(\frac{1}{LRR}\right)$.

Legal Reserve Ratio (LRR) It is the total amount of deposit that each commercial bank must keep with the Central Bank and with itself and includes Cash Reserve Ratio (CRR) and Statutory Liquidity Ratio (SLR).

Money multiplier It refers to the fraction which indicates the quantum of money creation by the commercial banks. It is calculated by the following formula

$$\text{Money Multiplier} = \frac{1}{\text{Legal Reserve Ratio (LRR)}}$$

e.g. Suppose a bank has a cash reserve of ₹ 1,500 and demand deposits of ₹ 12,000.

If the withdrawals are 12.5% of the deposits i.e. LRR = 12.5% hence, the bank needs to keep only 12.5% of its total deposits as cash in the form of LRR.

$$\text{Here, Demand Deposits} = \frac{1}{\text{LRR}} \times \text{Cash Reserves}$$

or Demand Deposits $= \frac{1}{12.5\%} \times 1{,}500 = ₹\ 12{,}000$

Now, the bank can issue loans to its customers on the basis of these demand deposits. As loans are never offered in cash, but only as demand deposits in favour of the customers. Suppose, the bank issues loan of ₹ 10,500 to its customers keeping ₹ 1,500 as cash reserve.

Now, this loan is also with the bank as demand deposit. Again, the bank keeps 12.5% of this ₹ 10,500 and can give ₹ 9,188 to its customers as loan. Thus, the money goes on multiplying and creates new flow of money in the economy.

The total credit creation by this bank can be obtained by the following formula

$$\text{Total Credit Money Creation} = \text{Initial Deposit} \times \frac{1}{\text{LRR}}$$

$$= 12{,}000 \times \frac{1}{12.5\%} = ₹\ 96{,}000$$

Value Points

For getting maximum marks, following value points can be included in the answer

- Mention the main determinants of credit creation.
- Explain the process in own words before explaining through illustration.

2. How does central bank control credit by using qualitative methods? ***ISC Specimen 2023***

Or Discuss four qualitative measures of the Central Bank to control credit in the economy. ***ISC 2017***

Or Explain four important measures of selective credit control by Central Bank. ***ISC 2004***

Ans Refer to the text on page 147.

3. Discuss the different ways in which commercial bank extend loans to their customers. ***ISC 2020***

Ans Different ways in which commercial banks extend loans to their customers

(i) **Cash credit** The bank advances cash loan upto a specified limit against securities. It is basically a facility to withdraw money from a current bank account without having credit balance, but limited to the extent of borrowing limit fixed by the commercial bank.

(ii) **Overdraft** Banks advance loans to current account customers' upon a certain amount and charge interest. It does not require any written formalities and customers use overdraft to meet urgent needs.

(iii) **Bills discounting** Banks discount bills of exchange before its maturity and give short-term loans and advances, i.e. a bank discounts a bill of exchange by providing money immediately to the holder of the bill, after deducting an interest for the loan period.

Ways of Extending Loans
- Cash credit
- Overdraft
- Bills discounting

4. Discuss any two qualitative methods and any two quantitative methods of credit control used by the Central Bank. ***ISC 2019***

Ans Qualitative methods to control credit are

(i) **Marginal requirements** RBI fixes minimum margin to be maintained by commercial banks in respect of their advances against foodgrains, oil seeds, vegetable oils, cotton, sugar, cotton textile etc.

(ii) **Rationing of credit** It refers to fixation of credit quotas for different business activities. Rationing of credit is introduced when flow of credit is to be checked particularly for speculative activities in the economy.

Quantitative methods to control credit are

(i) **Bank rate policy** The bank rate is minimum rate at which Central Bank is prepared to give credit to commercial bank.

The increase in bank rate increases rate of interest and credit becomes expensive. Accordingly, demand for credit is reduced and *vice-versa.*

(ii) **Open market operations** It refers to sale and purchase of securities in open market by Central Bank (RBI) with a purpose of releasing or soaking liquidity in economy.

Through open market operations, cash balances are increased through purchase of securities to increase flow of credit and *vice-versa.*

5. Explain four major functions of Reserve Bank of India. ***ISC 2003***

Or Explain any four functions of a Central Bank. ***ISC 2002***

Ans Main functions of Central Bank are

(i) **Issue of currency** The first and foremost important function of Central Bank is to issue currency notes. It has its various departments which issue currency notes and coins for the public of a country.

(ii) **Bankers to the government** The Central Bank acts as a banker to the government, both Central and State Governments. It carries out banking business of the government and the government keeps its cash balances on current account with the Central Bank.

(iii) **Banker of banks** A Central Bank is a bank of government and also of other commercial banks of the country. It grants loans to the commercial banks to fulfil their needs of funds. It is not for the common people of the country.

(iv) **Lender of last resort** It means that if a commercial bank fails to get financial accommodation from anywhere, it approaches the Central Bank as a last resort.

Central Bank advances loan to such bank against approved securities. By offering loan to the commercial banks in situations of emergency, the Central Bank ensures

(a) That the banking system of the country does not suffer from any set bank and
(b) Money market remains stable.

Functions of Central Bank
- Issue of currency
- Bankers to the government
- Banker of banks
- Lender of last resort

6. Write a note on the quantitative credit control measures of RBI. *ISC 2001*

Ans Refer to the text on page 147.

7. Explain the main functions of commercial banks. *ISC 2001*

Ans Main functions of commercial banks are

(i) **Accepting deposits** Commercial banks accept deposits of public under saving account, current account and fixed deposits.

They play a role of custodian of money. In monetary analysis, deposits are classified as demand deposits and time deposits.

(ii) **Providing loans** Commercial bank is advancing loans to the public to fulfil their needs of money. Loan may be granted in the form of cash credits, ordinary loans, overdraft, discounting of bills, short-term loans, consumer credits, etc.

(iii) **Credit creation** It refers to the creation of demand deposits with the commercial banks on the basis of their cash reserves. Often the deposits are created many times more than the cash reserve.

This is based on the historical experience of the banks that cash withdrawal of funds is only a small percentage of the total demand deposits.

(iv) **Facilitation of payments through cheques** Banks have provided a very convenient system of payment in the form of cheques. The cheque is the principal method of payment in business in recent time.

It is convenient, cheap and safe means of making payments.

Functions of Commercial Banks
- Accepting deposits
- Providing loans
- Credit creation
- Facilitation of payments through cheques

Case Based Question

Case 1

Mr. X wanted to buy an expensive motorcycle for his son but he did not have sufficient money to buy it. He approached a public sector commercial bank for the loan. The bank asked Mr. X to deposit 20% cash of the loan amount and rest 80% of the loan amount was given by the bank. *ISC Sem II Specimen 2022*

(i) Briefly explain a commercial bank.

Ans A commercial bank is a banking institution that works for the motive of earning profits.

(ii) What is the regulation of consumer credit in selective credit control?

Ans The regulation of consumer credit is an example of selective credit control as it does not impacts the quantity of money supply directly in the economy at a given point of time.

(iii) Name the bank which controls all the commercial banks and financial institutions in the country.

Ans Central Bank or RBI.

CHAPTER TEST

01 Mark Questions

1. Which of the following is not a secondary function of money?
(a) Store of value
(b) Unit of value
(c) Standard of deferred payment
(d) Both (a) and (c)

2. Cash amount granted to an individual consumer by the commercial bank is known as
(a) Overdraft (b) Credit card
(c) Cash credit (d) None of thes

3. Which of the following banks is known as the apex bank of the country?
(a) Central Bank of India
(b) Reserve Bank of India
(c) State Bank of India
(d) Both (a) and (b)

4. Which of the following is a contingent function of commercial bank?
(a) Accepting deposits
(b) Distribution of income in the market
(c) Granting loans and advance
(d) All of the above

5. Central bank fixes the lending rate charged by the commercial banks from the customers. State true or false.

6. In cost-push inflation, the inputs of production become expansive. State true or false.

7. Increase in CRR leads to ……… in money supply.

8. Open market operations are comprised of ……… and ………. .

9. What is meant by overdraft facility?

10. Why commercial banks offer higher rate of interest on fixed deposits as compared to saving deposits?

02 Marks Questions

11. Write the equations of M_1 and M_2.

12. What is meant by standard of deferred payments?

13. Explain the meaning of money.

14. Write two advantages of 'sole authority of note issue' with RBI.

03/04 Marks Questions

15. Write a short note on supply of money.

16. Briefly explain the measures of money supply.

17. Differentiate between commercial banks and central bank.

18. Explain the significance of the store of the value function of money.

06 Marks Questions

19. Differentiate between qualitative and quantitative instruments of monetary policy.

20. Describe the evolution of money.

Answers

1. (b) Unit of value
2. (c) Cash credit
3. (b) Reserve Bank of India
4. (b) Distribution of income in the market
5. False
6. True
7. decrease
8. open market purchases and open market sale

09

Balance of Payments and Exchange Rate

TREND ANALYSIS 5 YEARS

		Average No. of Questions Across all Sets				
	Types of Questions	2023	2020	2019	2018	2017
01 BoP and its Components	1 Mark	—	—	—	—	—
	2 Marks	—	1	—	—	1
	3/4 Marks	—	—	—	—	—
	6 Marks	—	—	1	1	—
02 Disequilibrium in BoP	1 Mark	—	—	—	—	—
	2 Marks	—	—	—	—	—
	3/4 Marks	—	—	—	—	—
	6 Marks	—	1	—	—	1
03 Foreign Exchange Rate	1 Mark	—	—	—	—	—
	2 Marks	—	—	1	—	—
	3/4 Marks	—	—	—	—	—
	6 Marks	1	—	—	1	—

TOPIC 1

Balance of Payments : Meaning and Components

Balance of Payments (BoP)

It is a systematic accounting record of all economic transactions between the residents of one country and residents of rest of the world during a given period of time. It is based on double entry system of accounting.

The two aspects of balance of payments are

(i) **Debit aspects** When payments are made by a domestic country's residents to the resident of other countries, it is called debit aspect or these transactions are recorded on the debit side of balance of payments accounts.

(ii) **Credit aspects** When amount is received by a resident of a domestic country from the residents of other countries, it is called credit aspect or these transactions are recorded on the credit side of balance of payments accounts.

Components of Balance of Payments

Main components of BoP are as follows

1. Current Account

Transactions relating to trade in goods and services and transfer payments constitute the current account. These transactions do not impact assets or liabilities of the country.

The main components of a current account are discussed below

(i) **Export and import of visible items** Current account includes export and import of visible items or goods like wheat, rice, machine, etc.

(ii) **Export and import of invisible items** Current account also includes export and import of invisible items or services like shipping, insurance, banking, etc.

(iii) **Unilateral transfers** These are transfers between residents and non-residents. These can be private as well as public which include gifts, donations, etc or official transfers including donations, grants in cash, etc.

(iv) **Income receipts and payments from and to abroad** It includes factor incomes in the form of wages, interest, rent, profit, etc.

2. Capital Account

It covers all transactions between resident of a country and rest of the world which causes a change in the assets or liability status of the residents of a country or its government. The main components of a capital account are discussed below

(i) **Foreign investment** It includes foreign direct investment and foreign institutional investment or portfolio investment by the residents of the country in abroad or by rest of the world in domestic country.

(ii) **Borrowings** It includes commercial borrowing by the government or private sector from rest of the world and external assistance to or by a country.

(iii) **Official international reserve** It includes the changes in gold and foreign exchange reserve with the Central Bank.

Balance of Trade (BoT)

It refers to the merchandise/goods portion of balance of payments, meaning that it is the value of exported merchandise minus the value of imported merchandise. Merchandise means goods i.e. only visible items.

Thus, Balance of Trade (BoT) = Export of Merchandise − Import of Merchandise

Difference between Balance of Trade (BoT) and Balance of Payments (BoP)

Basis	Balance of Trade (BoT)	Balance of Payments (BoP)
Meaning	It is the difference between the money value of exports and imports of merchandise (i.e. goods).	It is a systematic record of all economic transactions between residents of a country and residents of other countries during a given period.
Nature of transactions	It does not record transactions of capital nature.	It records transactions of capital nature.
Scope	It is a narrow concept because it is only one part of BoP account.	It is a wider concept because it includes BoT, balance of services, balance of unilateral transfers and balance of capital transactions.
Forms/Types	It may be favourable, unfavourable or in equilibrium.	It always remains in balance in accounting sense because receipt side is always made equal to payment side.
Treatment of deficit	Deficit in BoT can be met by BoP.	Deficit in BoP cannot be met through BoT.

Autonomous Items in Balance of Payment (BoP)

These refer to international economic transactions that take place due to some economic motives like earning of income and profit maximisation. Such transactions are independent of the state of country's balance of payments. These items are generally called 'above the line item' in balance of payment and they are recorded in both current as well as capital account of BoP.

The main autonomous items are as follows

(i) Autonomous exports and imports of goods

(ii) Autonomous exports and imports of services

(iii) Autonomous unilateral transactions

(iv) Autonomous capital transactions

Accommodating Items in Balance of Payment (BoP)

These refer to transactions that take place to cover deficit or surplus in the autonomous transactions. In other words, accommodating items are taken to maintain balance in Balance of payment account. These items are also called 'below the line items' and these are recorded only in capital account of BoP.

The main accommodating items are as follows

(i) Which are not related to the such transaction which are determined by consideration of profit.

(ii) Which are conditioned by the positive or negative BoP status of the country.

Difference between Autonomous Capital Flows and Accommodating Capital Flows of Balance of Payments

Basis	Autonomous capital flows	Accommodating capital flows
Meaning	These refer to international economic transactions that take place due to some economic motives like earning of income and profit maximisation.	These refer to transactions that take place to cover deficit or surplus in the autonomous transactions.
Effect in BoP	Such transactions are independent of the state of country's Balance of Payments (BoP).	Such items are taken to maintain balance in BoP account.
Nature of transactions	These involve the movement of goods across borders.	These involve only the movement of money (i.e. official reserves).
Alternate names	These transactions are known as 'above the line' transactions.	These transactions are known as 'below the line' transactions.
Recording of account	Recorded in both current and capital accounts of BoP.	Recorded only in capital account of BoP.

PYQs Previous Years' Questions

2 Marks Questions

1. Differentiate between autonomous capital flow and accommodating capital flow. ***ISC 2020***

Or Distinguish between autonomous and accommodating capital flows in Balance of Payments (BoP). ***ISC 2008, 02***

Ans Difference between autonomous and accommodating capital flows

Basis	Autonomous capital flows	Accommodating capital flows
Meaning	These refer to international economic transactions that take place due to some economic motives like earning of income and profit maximisation.	These refer to transactions that take place to cover deficit or surplus in the autonomous transactions.
Effect in BoP	Such transactions are independent of the state of country's Balance of Payments (BoP).	Such items are taken to maintain balance in BoP account.

2. Write any two differences between balance of trade and balance of payment. ***ISC 2017, 05***

KEY IDEA
BoT is only one component of BoP which includes only visible trade.

Ans Differences between Balance of Trade (BoT) and Balance of Payments (BoP)

Basis	Balance of Trade (BoT)	Balance of Payments (BoP)
Meaning	It is the difference between the money value of exports and imports of merchandise (i.e. goods).	It is a systematic record of all economic transactions between residents of a country and residents of other countries during a given period.
Nature of transactions	It does not record transactions of capital nature.	It records transactions of capital nature.

3. What is meant by balance of current account? ***ISC 2007***

Ans Balance of current account is the balance of exports and imports of goods and services (including income flows) and international transfer payments. The balance of current account may not be in equilibrium. It can show a surplus or deficit.

In short, Balance of Current Account = Balance of Trade + Balance of Invisibles + Balance of Transfers

4. Mention two invisible items of the balance of payments of a country. ***ISC 2004***

Ans Two invisible items of balance of payments of a country are

(i) Shipping services (ii) Financial services

3/4 Marks Question

1. Balance of Payments (BoP) always balances in the accounting sense. Explain briefly. *ISC 2011*

Ans In the accounting sense, balance of payments is always in balance or equilibrium.

Balance of payments is kept in standard double entry book keeping system, under which an international economic transaction undertaken by residents of a country is shown on both sides, which results in debit and credit of equal amount.

e.g. An export is credit for the movement of goods, the payment for that export in form of receipt of foreign currency or gold or investment made abroad out of this export is shown as a debit. So, the recorded amount of both the product sold and the foreign currency received is exactly the same, keeping balance of payments always in balance.

Concept Enhancer BoP always balances in accounting sense. In actual/ economic sense, there is either a surplus or deficit in BoP.

6 Marks Questions

1. Discuss the components of the balance of payments in the current account. *ISC Sem II 2022*

Or Explain the components of the current account of the balance of payments. *ISC 2015, 2010*

Ans The main components of the current account of BoP are

(i) **Export and import of goods** (Merchandise) This includes all types of tangible goods exported or imported. Exports of goods appears as a credit items in BoP, whereas, imports of goods are shown as a debit item in BoP.

(ii) **Export and import of invisible items** It includes those items which are intangible and can't be seen. These invisible items are classified into three group

(a) **Non-factor services** It includes a large variety of non-factor services sold to and purchased by the residents of a country from rest of the world. e.g. Banking, shipping, tourism, etc.

(b) **Unilateral transfers** Those receipts and payments which take place without any services rendered in return, in the current period, are included in unilateral transfers. e.g. Gifts, donations, indemnity payments, etc given or received at private and government level.

(c) **Income receipts and payments from and to abroad** It includes factor incomes in the form of wages, interest, rent, profit, etc.

Common Mistake Students get confused between BoT and BoP. BoT is only one component of BoP as it considers only visible items.

2. Discuss briefly the various components of balance of payment. *ISC 2019*

Or Discuss the components which are included in the balance of payments of a country. *ISC 2006*

Or State the items included in the balance of payments of a country. *ISC 2003*

Or What are the items that enter into a country's balance of payments? *ISC 2000*

Ans The items included in the balance of payments are called components of balance of payments. Balance of payments account of a country has two sides i.e. credit (receipts) and debit (payments).

Any item that enables a country to acquire foreign currency is recorded as a credit item and any item that gives rise to use or spending of the foreign currency, is recorded as debit item in the balance of payments.

Various items in the balance of payments are generally categorised into two main groups as given below

(i) **Current account transactions** It covers broadly the following main categories

(a) **Export and import of goods or services** This category includes all types of tangible goods, exported and imported.

(b) **Invisible items** These are the items which are not tangible and cannot be seen. These items are classified into three groups, such as

- Services (e.g. Shipping, banking and insurance services, etc)
- Unilateral transfers (e.g. Gifts, donations, etc)
- Incomes (e.g. Interest, dividends, profits, etc)

(ii) **Capital account transactions** It is a record of short-term and long-term capital transactions, both private and official.

The main components of capital account are as follows

(a) **Foreign investment** It includes foreign direct investment and foreign institutional investment or portfolio investment by the residents of the country in abroad or by rest of the world in domestic country.

(b) **Borrowings** It includes commercial borrowing by the government or private sector from rest of the world and external assistance to or by a country.

(c) **Official international reserve** It includes the changes in gold and foreign exchange reserve with the Central Bank.

Value Points

For getting maximum marks, following value points can be included in the answer

- Mention what is recorded on credit and debit side of BoP.
- Mention sub-point of each component of BoP.

3. Differentiate between current account and capital account of balance of payment. *ISC 2018, 2016*

Or

Discuss four differences between balance of current account and balance of capital account. *ISC 2008*

Ans Difference between balance of current account and balance of capital account

Basis	Balance of current account	Balance of capital account
Meaning	It records movements of foreign exchange resulting from flow of goods, services, unilateral transfers, etc.	It records all such transactions between residents of a country and the rest of the world, which cause a change in assets and liabilities.
Components	Its main components are (i) Export and import of visible items, (ii) Export and import of invisible items, (iii) Transfer receipts and payments.	Its main components are (i) Portfolio investment, (ii) Foreign Direct Investment (FDI), (iii) Other capital transactions.
Scope	It does not show change in the assets and liability status.	It shows the change in the assets and liability status.
Flow and stock concept	It shows flow items, expressed over a period of time.	Capital account transactions show change in stock magnitude.

TOPIC 2

Balance of Payments Disequilibrium : Causes and Remedies

Disequilibrium in Balance of Payments (BoP)

It means there is either deficit or surplus in balance of payments. If outflow of foreign exchange is more than inflow of foreign exchange, deficit in balance of payment occurs reflecting disequilibrium in balance of payments.

Causes of Disequilibrium in BoP

Disequilibrium in Balance of Payments (BoP) is caused by a number of factors, which are broadly categorised as below

(i) **Economic factors** Main economic factors that cause a disequilibrium in BoP are

(a) **Inflation** Changes in price and cost structure of a country's export industries affect the volume of export and the balance of payments position. Increase in price due to higher wages, higher prices of raw material make production costlier and results in deficit in BoP.

(b) **Expenditure on developing relations** Newly independent countries, in order to develop relations with other countries have to spend huge amount of money on ambassadors, missions, etc. This has adverse effect on BoP.

(c) **Fall in exports** When the demand for the countries goods falls in the foreign market, exports reduce and results in adverse BoP.

(d) **Rise in imports** Underdeveloped countries import capital and other services from developed countries. This results deficit in BoP.

(e) **Devaluation of the currency** If the currency of a country is devalued, then its goods and services become cheaper leading to increase in exports and a surplus in BoP.

(ii) **Social factors** In changing times, people of underdeveloped countries try to imitate the consumption pattern of the people of developed countries.Therfore, due to demonstration effect, their import increases and results in disequilibrium in balance of payments.

(iii) **Political factors** Political instability of a country has an adverse effect on balance of payments of a country. Further, partition or unification of a country also affects the balance of payments of a country.

Note A regular balance of payments leads to degrading of economy internationally. Disequilibrium in balance of payments can be corrected by various methods like promoting exports, reducing imports, depreciation, devaluation and exchange control, etc.

Remedies for Correcting BoP Disequilibrium

Various remedies for correcting BoP disequilibrium are discussed below

(i) **Depreciation** (in case of flexible exchange rate regime) Depreciation of currency means rise in the price of foreign currency or fall in the price of domestic currency.

(ii) **Devaluation** (in case of fixed exchange rate regime) It refers to reduction in the external value of a country's currency as a conscious policy measure adopted by the Central Bank of a country to correct the deficit in its balance of payments.

(iii) **Import control** Imports may be kept in check through the adoption of a wide variety of measures such as quotas and tariffs and quantity restrictions.

(iv) **Export promotion** The government may pursue various export promotion measures to stimulate exports.

These measures may be as follows

(a) The government may reduce export duties, so as to encourage exports.

(b) Cash assistance and subsidies can be given to exporters to stimulate exports.

(c) Various facilities like quality control, provision of market information and arranging exhibitions of exportable goods in foreign countries, can be provided to promote exports.

(d) Special Economic Zones (SEZ's) may be set-up to provide for tax concessions for export oriented units.

(v) **Exchange control** The government may try to hold complete control over all dealings in foreign exchange by directing all the exporters to sell their foreign exchange earnings to the Central Bank and all the importers to buy foreign exchange from the Central Bank.

(vi) **Production of import substitutes** Steps may be taken to encourage the production of import substitutes. This will save foreign exchange in the short-run, by replacing the use of imports with domestically produced goods.

(vii) **Monetary policy** (by the Central Bank) A tight monetary policy can be used effectively to reduce expenditure and thereby, correct deficits in the balance of payments.

(viii) **Fiscal policy** (by the Central Government) A restrictive fiscal policy can also be successfully used to wipe out balance of payments deficit by reducing the total expenditure in the economy. Increase in tax rates, decrease in government expenditure, will reduce the demand for imported goods.

(ix) **Capital import** A country can also attract short-run private capital from abroad by raising the domestic rate of interest and offering certain tax concessions to foreign investors.

PYQs Previous Years' Questions

2 Marks Questions

1. Briefly explain two reasons for the adverse BoP in any economy. ***ISC Sem II Specimen 2022***

Or Explain any two causes of disequilibrium in the balance of payments. ***ISC 2016***

Or Explain any two causes of disequilibrium in the balance of payments in an economy. ***ISC 2014, 2011, 2000***

Ans The disequilibrium in the balance of payments is caused by the following factors

(i) **Economic factor** Huge development expenditure by the government owing to which, there are large scale imports. It may cause a deficit BoP equilibrium.

(ii) **Social factor** At times people of underdeveloped countries try to imitate the consumption pattern of the people of developed countries.

Therefore, due to demonstration effect, their import increases and results in disequilibrium in balance of payments.

2. What is meant by unfavourable balance of payments? ***ISC 2011***

Ans Unfavourable balance of payments means adverse balance of payments or a deficit in the balance of payments.

It arises because of excess of imports over exports made in an accounting year.

6 Marks Questions

1. Discuss any two export promotion measures undertaken to correct the disequilibrium in the balance of payments. **ISC Sem II 2022**

Or Explain four measures to correct disequilibrium in the balance of payment. **ISC 2017**

Or Discuss four methods of correction of adverse Balance of Payments (BoP) of a country. **ISC 2004**

Or Explain any four methods of correcting the disequilibrium in the balance of payments of a country. **ISC 2002**

Ans The methods of correction of adverse balance of payments of a country have been discussed below

(i) **Depreciation** Depreciation of the country's currency will itself wipe out deficits in the balance of payments. Depreciation of currency means rise in the price of foreign currency or fall in the price of domestic currency. Depreciation will make imports costlier in terms of domestic currency.

As a result, prices of imports will rise and thereby imports will fall. On the other hand, exporters can afford to reduce the prices of exports because they are earning more in terms of domestic currency. Exports will become cheaper, as a result of which, BoP will improve.

Methods of Correcting Adverse BoP
- Depreciation
- Devaluation
- Import control
- Monetary policy

(ii) **Devaluation** A country can devalue its currency to wipe out deficit in the balance of payments. This makes imports expensive to domestic consumers and its exports cheaper in foreign countries.

If demand and supply elasticities are fairly high, this will definitely lead to fall in imports and a rise in exports and thereby, an elimination or reduction of balance of payments deficit.

(iii) **Import control** Imports may be kept in check through the adoption of a wide variety of measures such as quotas and tariffs. Quotas limit the volume of imports by applying quantitative restrictions.

The government may also increase the import duties or tariffs. This will raise the prices of imported goods and reduce the imports. Although, this can lead to an emergence of a black market, but balance of payments deficit is reduced.

(iv) **Monetary policy** A tight monetary policy can be used effectively to reduce expenditure and thereby, correct deficits in the balance of payments.

The Central Bank can reduce the volume of credit by raising the bank rate, by selling the approved securities in the open market and by raising cash reserve ratio and statutory liquidity ratio.

As it becomes more expensive to borrow money, due to increase in interest rate and as the availability of credit decreases, consumers and producers will borrow and invest less. A decrease in investment will lead to a decrease in income and fall in imports thereby improving the BoP.

2. Discuss any four causes of adverse balance of payments of a country. **ISC 2020**

Or

Define balance of payments. Discuss any four causes of disequilibrium in the balance of payments. **ISC 2009**

Or

Explain any four causes of disequilibrium in the balance of payments of a country. **ISC 2005, 01**

Ans Balance of Payments (BoP) of a country is a systematic record of all economic transactions between the residents of one country and residents of rest of the world, during a given period. It is based on double entry book keeping system of accounting and has two aspects. One is debit and other is credit.

Causes for disequilibrium in balance of payment

Disequilibrium in balance of payments means there is either deficit or surplus in balance of payment.

If outflow of foreign exchange is more than inflow of foreign exchange, deficit in balance of payments occurs reflecting disequilibrium in balance of payment and *vice-versa* will result in surplus.

The main causes for disequilibrium in balance of payments are explained below

(i) **Inflation** Changes in price and cost structure of a country's export industries affect the volume of export and the balance of payments position.

Increase in price due to higher wages, higher prices of raw material make export costlier and it results in deficit in balance of payments.

Causes of Disequilibrium
- Inflation
- Expenditure on developing relations
- Fall in demand
- Import services

(ii) **Expenditure on developing relations** Newly independent countries, in order to develop relations with other countries have to spend huge amount of money on ambassadors, missions, etc. This has adverse effect on balance of payments.

(iii) **Fall in demand** When the demand for the country's goods fall in the foreign market, exports reduce and results in adverse balance of payments.

(iv) **Import services** Underdeveloped countries import capital and other services from developed countries. This results in deficit in BoP.

TOPIC 3

Foreign Exchange Rate and Determination of Exchange Rate

Foreign Exchange

It refers to foreign currencies and claims on them in the form of bank deposits, cheques, etc payable in those currencies or in other words, foreign exchange is the reserve of foreign currencies with the country.

Terms of Trade

The 'terms of trade' refers to the rate at which country's exports are exchanged against its imports. It relates to the quantity of imported goods that can be obtained per unit of goods exported or the quantity of the country's exports that must be given in exchange of per unit of imported goods.

Meaning of Foreign Exchange Rate

It refers to the rate at which one unit of currency of a country can be exchanged for the number of units of currency of another country. In other words, it is the price paid in domestic currency in order to get one unit of foreign currency, e.g.

$$1\,\$ = ₹\,60 \quad or \quad ₹\,1 = \frac{1}{60}\text{ dollar}$$

Types of Foreign Exchange Rate

Foreign exchange rate is of two types

1. Fixed Exchange Rate

It is the rate which is officially fixed by the monetary authority on daily or monthly basis. It has two important variants

(i) **Gold standard system of exchange rate** Under this system, each country was to define value of its currency in terms of gold.

Accordingly, value of one currency in terms of the other currency was fixed considering gold value of each currency.

e.g. If UK pound = 4 gm of gold and US dollar = 2 gm of gold, then, 1 UK pound = 2 US dollar

Exchange rate between UK pound and US dollar = 1 : 2

(ii) **Bretton Woods system of exchange rate or adjustable peg system of exchange rate** Bretton Woods system is named after United Nations Monetary Financial Conference held at Bretton Woods (USA) in 1944.

Bretton Woods system, even when it was a fixed system of exchange rate, allowed some adjustments. So, it was called 'adjustable peg system of exchange rate'.

2. Flexible Exchange Rate

It is that rate which is determined by the demand for and supply of different currencies in the foreign exchange market. In other words, it is determined by the market forces of demand and supply, like the price of any other commodity.

It can be of two types

(i) **Pure floating rate** Under this, Central Bank stands aside completely and allows exchange rate to be freely determined in the open market.

(ii) **Managed floating rate** Under this, Central Bank intervenes from time to time to buy and sell foreign currencies in an attempt to influence the exchange rate. This is also known as dirty floating.

Difference between Fixed Exchange Rate and Flexible Exchange Rate

Basis	Fixed exchange rate	Flexible exchange rate
Meaning	It refers to the rate of exchange as fixed by the Central Bank.	It is that rate, which is determined by the demand for and supply of different currencies in the foreign exchange market.
Determination	Gold exchange rate and adjustable peg system of exchange rate are the two important types of determining fixed exchange rate.	It is determined by the market forces of demand and supply, like the price of any other commodity.
Intervention	There is complete RBI intervention.	There is no or partial RBI intervention.

Determination of Exchange Rate in a Free Market

The exchange rate of a currency (like price of a commodity) is determined by forces of demand and supply of foreign exchange in the foreign exchange market. Alternatively, exchange rate is determined at a level, where demand and the supply of foreign exchange are equal. The factors determining exchange rate can be grouped under following two heads

(i) Factors determining demand for foreign exchange.
(ii) Factors determining supply of foreign exchange.

Sources of Demand for Foreign Exchange

Foreign exchange is demanded for the following purposes

(i) Purchase of foreign goods by domestic residents, i.e. imports.
(ii) Payments of international loans.
(iii) Gifts and grants to the rest of the world.
(iv) Investments in the rest of the world.
(v) Tourism to abroad.

Note Demand curve for foreign exchange is downward sloping.

Sources of Supply of Foreign Exchange

Supply of foreign exchange depends on the following factors

(i) Purchases of domestic goods by the foreigners, i.e. exports.
(ii) Foreign direct investment as well as portfolio investment from rest of the world.
(iii) Speculative purchases of foreign exchange.
(iv) Tourism and remittances from abroad.
(v) Transfer of foreign exchange by the residents of the country abroad.

Note Supply curve of foreign exchange is upward sloping.

Equilibrium Rate of Exchange

At any particular time, the price at which demand for foreign currency (say, US dollar) equals its supply is called equilibrium rate of exchange.

It has been shown in the following diagram

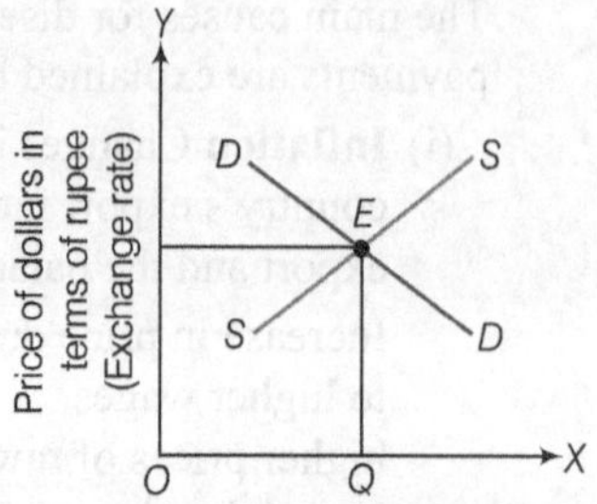

Note *E* is the equilibrium rate of exchange which is obtained at the intersection of Demand Curve (*DD*) and Supply Curve (*SS*), of foreign exchange (US$).

Change in Exchange Rate

(i) **Depreciation** (in case of flexible exchange rate)
Depreciation of a currency means fall in the value of domestic currency in terms of foreign currency.
e.g. If value of rupee in terms of US dollar falls, say from ₹ 60 to ₹ 64 a dollar, it will be a case of depreciation of Indian rupee because more rupees are required now to buy one US dollar. It takes place in flexible exchange rate system.

(ii) **Appreciation** (in case of flexible exchange rate)
Appreciation of a currency is the increase in value of domestic currency in terms of foreign currency. It makes the domestic currency more valuable indicating less of it is required to buy the foreign currency.
e.g. If the value of a rupee in terms of US dollar increases, say from ₹ 60 to ₹ 58 to a dollar, it will be called appreciation of Indian currency.

(iii) **Devaluation** (in case of fixed exchange rate)
Devaluation means reduction in the external value of a country's currency as a conscious policy measure adopted by the Central Bank of a country. In other words, we make our currency cheaper in terms of foreign currency.
This makes our goods cheaper for foreign buyers and foreign goods costlier to our buyers. Hence, exports increase, imports fall, reducing the deficit in balance of payments. It takes place in fixed exchange rate system.

(iv) **Revaluation** (in case of fixed exchange rate)
It refers to an action undertaken by the Central Bank to raise the value of domestic currency relative to other currencies under a system of fixed exchange rates.

PYQs Previous Years' Questions

1 Mark Question

1. If at present \$ 1 = ₹ 95 and later \$ 1 = ₹ 80, it is a case of *ISC Sem II 2022*
   (a) appreciation of currency (b) devaluation of currency
   (c) depreciation of currency (d) supply of currency

Ans (a) appreciation of currency

Common Mistake Students generally gets confused between rise in price of foreign exchange and rise in the value of foreign exchange. There exist an indirect relation between price of foreign exchange and value of foreign exchange.

2 Marks Questions

1. How is devaluation of currency different from depreciation of currency? Give two differences. *ISC Sem II Specimen 2022*

Or Distinguish between depreciation and devaluation. *ISC 2019*

Or Distinguish between 'devaluation' and 'depreciation' of a currency. *ISC 2003*

Ans Difference between depreciation and devaluation of a currency

Basis	Depreciation of currency	Devaluation of currency
Meaning	It means fall in value of domestic currency in terms of foreign currency due to the free forces of demand and supply of foreign currency in the foreign exchange market.	It refers to reduction in the external value of a country's currency as a conscious policy measure adopted by the government of a country to correct the deficit in its balance of payments.
Occurrence	It occurs in flexible exchange rate regime.	It takes place in fixed exchange rate regime.

2. Differentiate between revaluation of currency and appreciation of currency. *ISC 2015*

Ans Difference between revaluation and appreciation of currency

Basis	Revaluation	Appreciation
Meaning	It refers to an action undertaken by the Central Bank to raise the value of domestic currency, relative to other currencies under a system of fixed exchange rates.	It refers to an increase in the value of domestic currency in terms of foreign currency, as determined by the market forces of demand and supply.
Occurrence	It takes place in fixed exchange rate regime.	It occurs in flexible exchange rate regime.

3. Give one difference between flexible exchange rate and fixed exchange rate. *ISC 2012*

Ans Difference between flexible exchange rate and fixed exchange rate

Basis	Flexible exchange rate	Fixed exchange rate
Meaning	It is that rate which is determined by the demand for and supply of different currencies in the foreign exchange market. In other words, it is determined by the market forces, like the price of any other commodity.	It refers to rate of exchange as fixed by the government. Historically, it has two important variants (i) Gold standard system (ii) Bretton Woods system of exchange rate.

4. What is meant by foreign exchange rate? *ISC 2007*

Ans Foreign exchange rate refers to the rate at which one unit of currency of a country can be exchanged for the number of units of currency of another country. In other words, it is the price paid in domestic currency in order to get one unit of foreign currency.

e.g. $1\ \$ = ₹\,60 \quad \text{or} \quad ₹1 = \frac{1}{60}\ \text{dollar}$

5. Define terms of trade. *ISC 2003, 2001*

Ans The 'terms of trade' refers to the rate at which country's exports are exchanged against its imports. It relates to the quantity of imported goods that can be obtained per unit of goods exported or the quantity of the country's exports that must be given in exchange of per unit of imported goods.

3/4 Marks Question

1. Mention one difference between devaluation and depreciation of currency. How can depreciation of a currency be a measure to correct disequilibrium of balance of payments? *ISC 2010*

Ans **Difference between devaluation and depreciation of a currency** Refer to Q. No. 1 (2 Marks) on page 163.

Depreciation of the country's currency will itself wipe out deficits in the balance of payments.

Depreciation of currency means rise in the price of foreign currency or fall in the price of domestic currency. Depreciation will make imports costlier in terms of domestic currency. As a result, prices of imports will rise and thereby, imports will fall.

On the other hand, exporters can afford to reduce the prices of exports because they are earning more in terms of domestic currency. Exports will become cheaper, as a result of which, exports will be stimulated. These mechanisms will help to correct disequilibrium in BoP.

6 Marks Question

1. How is the rate of exchange determined in a flexible exchange rate system? **ISC Sem II Specimen 2022**

Or Show with the help of a diagram how exchange rate is determined under flexible exchange rate system. **ISC 2018**

Or Discuss how exchange rate is determined under flexible exchange rate system. **ISC 2014**

Ans At any particular time, the price at which demand for foreign currency (say, dollar) equals its supply, is called the equilibrium exchange rate.

The exchange rate of a currency (like price of a commodity) is determined by forces of demand and supply of foreign exchange in the foreign exchange market.

The determination of exchange rate has been shown in the following diagram

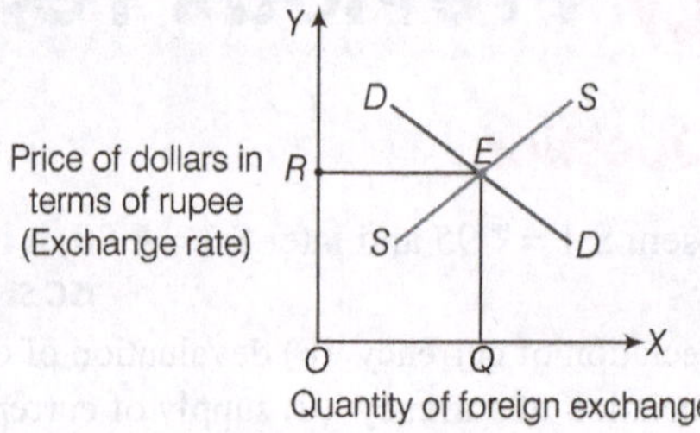

Expressed graphically, the intersection of demand and supply curves determines the equilibrium exchange rate and equilibrium quantity of foreign currency. In this diagram, price on the vertical axis is stated in terms of domestic currency (say, rupee).

The horizontal axis measures quantity demanded or supplied of foreign exchange (i.e. dollars). The Demand Curve (*DD*) is downward sloping due to inverse relationship between foreign exchange rate and its demand. The Supply Curve (*SS*) is upward sloping which implies that supply of foreign exchange rises as the exchange rate increase.

Demand Curve (*DD*) and Supply Curve (*SS*) of dollar intersect each other at point *E* which implies that at exchange rate of *OR* (*QE*), quantity demanded and supplied are equal (both being equal to *OQ*). Hence, equilibrium exchange rate is *OR* and equilibrium quantity is *OQ*.

Case Based Questions

Case 1

A change in the rupee-dollar exchange rate represents the change in external value of rupee. The value of rupee, in terms of dollar, has been falling continuously over a period of time. Since rupee-dollar exchange rate is determined by the demand for and supply of dollars, it is possible that the value of rupee slides further if appropriate measures are not taken.

The Reserve Bank of India, in change of both internal and external value of rupee, has repeatedlly emphasised on maintaining stability in the foreign exchange market. **ISC 2023**

(i) What kind of exchange rate system is being referred to in the passage?

Ans Managed floating exchange rate.

(ii) The value of rupee in terms of dollar, has been falling continuously over a period of time. Give the economic term for this phenomenon.

Ans This phenomenon is known as depreciation of domestic currency (INR).

(iii) How would this phenomenon affect balance of payments?

Ans Depreciation of domestic currency leads to decrease in the external price of domestic goods. This further leads to rise in exports and thus inflow of foreign exchange.

(iv) Explain the role of Reserve Bank of India, as a custodian of foreign exchange.

Ans Central Bank maintains the reserve of foreign currencies in order to promote international trade and stabilise exchange rate to an agreed limit.

(v) Suggest two measures to correct adverse balance of payments.

Ans Measures to control adverse BoP

(a) Promotion of exports for domestic country.

(b) Control over imports to domestic country.

Case 2

India is predominantly an agriculture based country. It is the second largest producer of wheat in the world and wheat export is also an important component in its international business transactions.

Recently, Indian Government put a ban on the export of wheat to other countries to control inflation in the country. This decision of Indian Government may decrease the flow of foreign exchange in credit side of the balance of payments of our country in comparison to the debit side of it.

This may affect the balance of payment as India has been following flexible exchange rate system, to some extent, since 1991-92. ***ISC Specimen 2023***

(i) What is meant by balance of payments?

Ans Balance of payments refers to the accounting record of all economic transactions between the residents of home country and residents of rest of the world.

(ii) State any two causes of adverse balance of payments.

Ans Cause of adverse BoP

(a) Increase in imports (b) Decrease in exports

(iii) In the context of international business relations, what does flexible exchange rate system mean?

Ans Flexible exchange rate system is the system where the foreign exchange rate is determined by the demand for foreign exchange and supply of foreign exchange in the foreign exchange market.

(iv) What is meant by net exports?

Ans Net exports refers to the excess of exports over imports of both goods and services. Mathematically,

Net Exports = Exports – Imports

(v) What economic variables are measured along x-axis and y-axis for the determination of foreign exchange rate?

Ans While determination of exchange rate, quantity of foreign exchange is taken on x-axis and foreign exchange rate is taken on y-axis.

CHAPTER TEST

01 Mark Questions

1. Import of machinery will be recorded in which sub-account of BoP?
(a) Capital account
(b) Current account
(c) Both (a) and (b)
(d) Neither (a) nor (b)

2. Increase in foreign exchange reserves with the Central Bank is recorded on .... side of capital account.
(a) credit
(b) debit
(c) Both (a) and (b) (d) None of the above

3. Under which of the following exchange rate systems, foreign exchange rate is maintained in a fixed band by the Central Bank?
(a) Fixed exchange rate
(b) Floating exchange rate
(c) Managed floating exchange rate
(d) Both (b) and (c)

4. Depreciation of domestic currency leads to
(a) increase in exports
(b) increase in imports
(c) decrease in imports
(d) Both (a) and (c)

5. Fixed exchange system is also known as pegging exchange rate. State true or false.

6. Rise in imports leads to favourable BoP. State true or false.

7. BoT is a .... concept compared to BoP.

8. .... account of BoP impacts the assets and liabilities of a country.

9. What are accommodating transaction of BoP?

10. Write two social factors responsible for BoP disequilibrium.

02 Marks Questions

11. Why are exports entered as positive items in balance of payments accounts?

12. If balance of trade deficit is ₹ 5,000 crore and value of imports is ₹ 9,000 crore. What is the value of exports?

13. What will be the treatment of furniture purchased from abroad in the capital account of BoP?

14. What will be the impact of appreciation of currency on exports and imports of the domestic country?

15. What is the basic difference between 'crawling peg and managed float' exchange rate?

03/04 Marks Questions

16. If inflation is higher in country *A* than in country *B* and the exchange rate between the countries is fixed, what will the impact on the balance of trade of the two countries?

17. Are the concepts of demand for domestic goods and domestic demand for goods the same? Explain.

18. What are unilateral transaction? How they are treated in BoP accounts?

19. Balance of payments always balances. Does it mean a situation of zero net financial obligations for a country?

06 Marks Question

20. How Bretton Woods system is different from gold standard system of exchange rate?

Answers

1. (b) Current account
2. (b) debit
3. (c) Managed floating exchange rate
4. (d) Both (a) and (c)
5. True
6. False
7. narrow
8. capital

10

Public Finance

TREND ANALYSIS 5 YEARS

	Average No. of Questions Across all Sets					
	Types of Questions	2023	2020	2019	2018	2017
01 Fiscal Policy and Public Revenue	1 Mark	1	—	—	—	—
	2 Marks	—	1	1	—	1
	3/4 Marks	—	—	—	1	—
	6 Marks	—	—	—	—	—
02 Public Expenditure, Public Debt and Debt Financing	1 Mark	1	—	—	—	—
	2 Marks	1	—	—	1	—
	3/4 Marks	—	1	1	—	1
	6 Marks	—	—	—	—	—
03 Government Budget and Budget Deficit	1 Mark	—	—	—	—	—
	2 Marks	1	—	—	—	—
	3/4 Marks	—	1	1	1	1
	6 Marks	—	—	—	—	—

TOPIC 1

Fiscal Policy and Public Revenue

Public Finance

Public finance is the branch of knowledge which is concerned with the income and expenditure of public authorities and with the adjustment of one with another.

Fiscal Policy

It is the revenue and expenditure policy of the government, focusing on growth and stability of the economy.

Objectives of Fiscal Policy

Following are the main objectives of fiscal policy

(i) **Economic stability** It requires that the cyclical fluctuations, i.e. booms and depression are checked.

(ii) **To achieve full employment** Attainment of the objective of full employment means that the economy is able to produce the maximum level of output with the available resources.

(iii) **Economic growth** It enables the economy to produce more goods and services and thereby, raise the standard of living of the people.

(iv) **Price stability** It is needed because it keeps the value of money stable, eliminates economic fluctuations, brings stability in the economy and promotes economic welfare.

(v) **Reducing inequalities of income and wealth** Through levying taxes on rich people and granting subsidies to the poor.

Instruments of Fiscal Policy

Instruments of fiscal policy are

(i) Public revenue (revenue policy)
(ii) Public expenditure (expenditure policy)
(iii) Public borrowings (debt policy)

Public Revenue (Revenue Policy)

Income of the government from all its sources is called 'public revenue'.

The sources of public revenue can be grouped into following categories

1. Revenue Receipts

These receipts of government neither reduce the assets nor increase the liability of the government.

These receipts are of two types

(i) Tax Revenue

Tax is a compulsory payment to the government by an individual, household or a firm without reference to anything in return.

Types of Taxes

Two types of taxes are there, which are as follows

(a) **Direct tax** A direct tax is the one whose incidence and impact falls on the same person i.e. burden of these taxes cannot be shifted to others. Direct tax is levied on the income and property of a person. e.g. Personal income tax, corporation tax, wealth tax, etc.

Merits of direct tax are

- Economical
- Certainty of payment
- Promotes equity
- Elastic in nature

Demerits of direct tax are

- Unpopular
- Possibility of tax evasion
- Inconvenient
- Non-economical
- Narrow in scope

(b) **Indirect tax** An indirect tax, is the one whose incidence and impact falls on different persons i.e. burden of these taxes can be shifted to others, indirect taxes are levied on expenditure. e.g. GST.

Merits of indirect taxes are

- Convenient
- Elastic
- Wide coverage
- Equality
- Less chances of tax evasion

Demerits of indirect taxes are

- Regressive
- Non-economical
- Inflationary impact
- Uncertainty of payment
- Lack of civil consciousness

Difference between Direct Tax and Indirect Tax

Basis	Direct tax	Indirect tax
Meaning	When incidence to pay tax and the burden of that tax falls on the same person, the tax is called a 'direct tax'.	When incidence to pay tax is on one person and the burden of that tax falls on some other person, the tax is called an 'indirect tax'.
Shift of burden	It is not possible here.	It is possible to shift the burden on to others.
Nature of tax	These are generally considered progressive taxes because they are based on the ability to pay.	These are generally regressive taxes as greater burden is on the poorer section of the society.
Examples	(i) Income tax (ii) Wealth tax (iii) Corporate tax	(i) GST (ii) Value Added Tax (VAT) (iii) Sales tax

Classification of Taxes Tax may be classified as follows

- **Proportional tax** A tax is called 'proportional' when the rate of taxation remains same as the income of the tax payer increases. i.e. same tax rate for all income groups.
- **Progressive tax** A tax is called 'progressive' when the rate of taxation increases as the tax payer's income increases. i.e. higher tax for higher income groups.
- **Regressive tax** It is one in which the rate of taxation decreases as the tax payer's income increases. i.e. lower tax for higher income groups.
- **Degressive tax** It is one in which the rate of progression in taxation does not increase in the same proportion, as the increase in income.

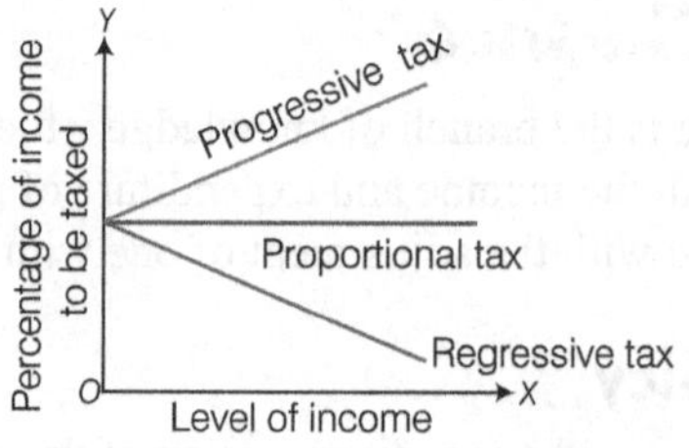

Graphical Presentation of Taxes

(ii) Non-tax Revenue

Those receipts which are received from sources other than taxes are known as 'non-tax revenue' receipts.

It includes following items

(a) Fees (i.e. land registration fee, passport fee, etc)
(b) Fines (due to disobeying law and order)

(c) Grants/Donations (in the events of earthquake, floods, famines, etc)
(d) Profits of Public Sector Undertakings (PSUs)
(e) Escheat (income from forfeiture of property of individuals without a legal hier)

Concepts of Taxation

- **Impact of taxation** It refers to the immediate burden of the tax.
- **Incidence of taxation** It is the settlement of the tax burden on the final (ultimate) tax payer.
- **Vertical sharing of tax proceeds** It is a system of sharing of financial resources between the centre and the state.
- **Horizontal sharing of tax proceeds** It refers to the system of sharing of financial resources among the states.

2. Capital Revenue

It is the sources of government revenue which creates liability for government or reduces assets. It includes

(i) **Borrowings** It creates liability for the government.
(ii) **Recovery of loans** Recovery of loans from State Governments, public sector undertakings and Foreign Governments.
(iii) **Disinvestment** The process of selling off the shares of public sector enterprises of the government to private sector is known as 'disinvestment'. Disinvestment may take two forms
   (a) **Minority sale** (only a small part is sold i.e. upto 24% of equity).
   (b) **Strategic sale** (major portion is sold i.e. upto 51% of equity).

PYQs Previous Years' Questions

1 Mark Questions

1. Mention any one difference between impact of tax and incidence of tax. *ISC 2023*

Or What is the difference between the impact and incidence of taxation? *ISC 2001*

Ans Difference between the impact and incidence of taxations

Basis	Impact of taxation	Incidence of taxation
Meaning	It refers to the immediate burden of the tax.	It is the settlement of the tax burden on the ultimate tax-payer.

2. Which one of the following is a pair of direct taxes? *ISC Specimen 2023*

(a) Excise duty and wealth tax
(b) Services tax and income tax
(c) Excise duty and service tax
(d) Wealth tax and income tax

Ans (d) Wealth tax and income tax

3. State one difference between progressive tax and regressive tax. *ISC Sem II 2022*

Ans A tax is called progressive when the rate of taxation increases as the tax payer's income increases while regressive tax is one in which the rate of taxation decreases as the tax payer's income increases.

Concept Enhancer Income tax in India is progressive in nature while it is regressive in nature in the USA.

2 Marks Questions

1. Give one difference between a direct tax and indirect tax. *ISC Sem II Specimen 2022*

Or Distinguish between direct tax and indirect tax. *ISC 2004*

Ans Difference between direct tax and indirect tax

Basis	Direct tax	Indirect tax
Meaning	When liability to pay a tax and the burden of that tax falls on the same person, the tax is called a 'direct tax'.	When liability to pay a tax is on one person, and the burden of that tax falls on some other person, the tax is called an 'indirect tax'.

2. What is progressive tax? *ISC 2020*

KEY IDEA
It helps in reducing income inequalities.

Ans A tax is called progressive when taxation rate increases with the increase in tax payer's income, i.e. higher tax for higher income groups. In this type of tax, the real burden of the tax is more on the rich and less on the poor.

3. Give two examples of each of the following *ISC 2019*

(i) Revenue receipts of the government.
(ii) Revenue expenditure of the government.

Ans (i) Revenue receipts – Tax revenue and non-tax revenue.
(ii) Revenue expenditure – Interest payments and payments of salaries.

4. What is direct tax? ***ISC 2017***

Ans A direct tax is one whose incidence and impact falls on the same person i.e. burden of these taxes cannot be shifted to others. Direct tax is levied on the income and property of a person. e.g. Personal income tax, corporation tax, wealth tax, etc.

5. What is meant by fiscal policy? Name any two instruments of fiscal policy. ***ISC 2016***

Ans Fiscal policy is the revenue and expenditure policy of the government, focusing on growth and stability of the economy. The two instruments of fiscal policy are

(i) Public revenue (revenue policy)

(ii) Public expenditure (expenditure policy)

6. Define proportional tax and show it graphically. ***ISC 2010***

Ans A tax is called 'proportional' when the rate of taxation remains same, as income of the tax payer increases. In this tax system, all incomes are taxed at a single uniform rate irrespective of whether tax payer's income is high or low.

In the given diagram, the horizontal line parallel to the X-axis shows proportional tax.

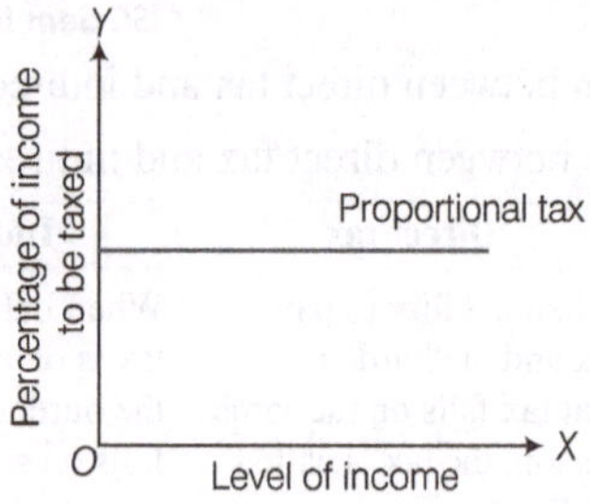

7. Mention two non-tax sources of revenue of Central Government. ***ISC 2009***

Ans Non-tax sources of revenue of Central Government are

(i) **Fees** A fee is a payment to the government for the services that it renders to the people. e.g. Passport fees.

(ii) **Fines** Those payments which are made by the law breakers to the government by way of economic punishment.

8. Give two sources of revenue for the Central Government. ***ISC 2004***

Ans Two sources of revenue for Central Government are

(i) Tax revenue (i.e. income tax and service tax, etc)

(ii) Non-tax revenue (i.e. fees, fines and grants, etc)

9. How can indirect taxes be made progressive? ***ISC 2004, 2002***

Ans Indirect taxes can be made progressive if these are levied on those goods and services which are consumed by the rich people. In this way, by taxing on luxury items and by exempting items of necessary consumption from taxation, indirect taxes can be made progressive.

Concept Enhancer In Indian context, indirect taxes are proportional in nature.

10. Distinguish between a tax and a fee. ***ISC 2003***

Ans Difference between tax and fee

Basis	Tax	Fee
Meaning	A tax is a compulsory payment made by an individual, household or a firm to the government without reference to anything in return. e.g. Income tax, sales tax, etc.	A fee is a payment to the government for the services that it renders to the people. e.g. Land registration fees, passport fees, etc.

11. Give any two weaknesses of the Indian tax structure. ***ISC 2001***

KEY IDEA
Tax evasion means when people avoid paying necessary taxes.

Ans Two weaknesses of Indian tax structure are

(i) No certainty of tax payment by individuals.

(ii) It lacks transparency and people try to evade taxes.

12. Give two differences between a tax and a subsidy. ***ISC 2001***

Ans Difference between tax and subsidy

Basis	Tax	Subsidy
Meaning	It is a compulsory payment made by an individual, household or a firm to the government.	It is a special relief given by the government to the enterprise or individuals.
Concept type	It is a main source of income for the state.	It is an expenditure for the state.

13. What do you mean by vertical and horizontal sharing of tax proceeds? ***ISC 2000***

Ans Vertical sharing of tax proceeds is a system of sharing of financial resources between the centre and the state. Horizontal sharing refer to the system of sharing of financial resources among the states.

14. Explain one merit and one demerit of progressive taxation. *ISC 2000*

Ans **Merit** Progressive taxes are elastic because the revenue of the government increases substantially with increase in tax rate.

Demerit Progressive taxation is regarded as entirely imaginary, since there is no rational basis for determining the rates of tax.

3/4 Marks Questions

1. State any two differences between a direct tax and an indirect tax. *ISC Specimen 2023*

Or What is an indirect tax? How is it different from a direct tax? *ISC 2018*

Ans **Indirect tax** An indirect tax, is the one who's incidence and impact falls on different persons i.e. burden of these taxes can be shifted to others, indirect taxes are levied on expenditure. e.g. VAT, Goods and Service Tax (GST), etc.

Difference between direct tax and indirect tax are

Basis	Direct tax	Indirect tax
Meaning	When liability to pay a tax and the burden of that tax falls on the same person, the tax is called a 'direct tax'.	When liability to pay a tax is on one person and the burden of that tax falls on some other person, the tax is called an 'indirect tax'.
Example	Income tax	Goods and services tax

2. Highlight two differences between sales tax and income tax. *ISC 2015*

Ans Difference between sales tax and income tax

Basis	Sales tax	Income tax
Levied on	It is levied on interstate sale and purchase of goods.	It is levied on the personal income of an individual.
Form of tax	It is an indirect form of tax, as burden is shifted to the final consumer.	It is a direct form of tax, because burden cannot be shifted.

3. Differentiate between degressive taxation and regressive taxation. *ISC 2014*

Ans Difference between degressive taxation and regressive taxation

Basis	Degressive taxation	Regressive taxation
Meaning	The rate of tax which decreases when the amount being taxed increases is called 'degressive taxation'.	Taxation that taxes a larger percentage of a lower income and a smaller percentage of a higher income.
Example	Tax on income of the tax assessee.	Tax on the basic necessities.

4. What is disinvestment? *ISC 2003*

Ans The process of selling off the shares of public sector enterprises of the government to private sector is known as 'disinvestment'. It involves transfer of ownership of public sector enterprises to the private entrepreneurs. It is also called 'privatisation'.

6 Marks Questions

1. Explain any two objectives of the fiscal policy in a developing economy. *ISC 2013*

Or Discuss how equity, stability and growth can be achieved through the fiscal policy. *ISC 2006*

Or Discuss four objectives of fiscal policy. *ISC 2004*

Ans Main objectives of fiscal policy in a developing country are

(i) **Economic stability** It means that the level of economic activity is maintained at a stable level, so that there are no fluctuations in output and employment. Economic stability requires that the cyclical fluctuations, i.e. booms and depression are checked.

Situation of booms are undesirable because they lead to sharp rise in prices. Periods of depression need to be averted because they lead to situation of severe unemployment in the economy.

(ii) **To achieve full employment** Full employment refers to a situation when all those persons, who are willing and able to work at the existing wage rate, are able to get work. Full employment is a leading objective of fiscal policy. Attainment of the objective of full employment means that the economy is able to produce the maximum level of output with the available resources. If the economy is not operating at full employment, then it means that it is operating below the Production Possibility Curve (PPC).

(iii) **Economic growth** It is defined as the process whereby, the real per capita income of a country increases over a long period of time. Economic growth enables the economy to produce more goods and services and thereby, raise the standard of living of the people. Moreover, higher rate of economic growth helps in solving the problems of poverty and unemployment in the developing countries like India.

(iv) **Price stability** Another objective of fiscal policy in a developing economy is to achieve price stability. Price stability does not mean that prices remain absolutely stable. It means that price changes are kept within a modest range. Large fluctuations in prices bring uncertainty and instability in the economy. Therefore, price stability is needed because it keeps the value of money stable, eliminates economic fluctuations, brings stability in the economy and promotes economic welfare.

Common Mistake Students generally consider full employment as zero unemployment. However, full employment only indicates zero involuntary unemployment.

2. Define tax. Explain four differences between direct tax and indirect tax. *ISC 2008, 2004*

Ans **Tax** A tax is a compulsory payment made by an individual, household or a firm to the government without reference to anything in return.

Difference between direct tax and indirect tax

Basis	Direct tax	Indirect tax
Meaning	When liability to pay a tax and the burden of that tax falls on the same person, the tax is called a 'direct tax'.	When liability to pay a tax is on one person and the burden of that tax falls on some other person, the tax is called an 'indirect tax'.
Shift of burden	It is not possible here.	It is possible to shift the burden on to others.
Nature of tax	These are generally considered progressive taxes because they are based on the ability to pay.	These are generally regressive taxes as greater burden is on the poorer sections of the society.
Examples	(i) Income tax (ii) Wealth tax (iii) Corporate tax	(i) Excise duty (ii) Service tax (iii) Value Added Tax (VAT)

3. Explain four merits of direct taxes. *ISC 2003*

Ans Merits of direct taxes are

(i) **Reducing inequalities** Direct taxes are more equitable than indirect tax. Richer people are subjected to a higher rate of taxation, as compared to poor people. Hence, these taxes can be used for reducing inequalities of income and wealth in the economy.

(ii) **Certainty** The cannon of certainty is found in direct taxation.

(iii) **Elasticity** Direct taxes are elastic, as the government revenue can be increased by raising the tax rates in times of crisis.

Merits of Direct Tax
- Reducing inequalities
- Certainty
- Elasticity
- Productivity

(iv) **Productivity** Direct taxes are an important source of government revenue and also their collection charges are low. Hence, these are productive.

4. Discuss the characteristics of a good tax system. *ISC 2002*

Ans Characteristics of a good tax system are

(i) **Compulsory payment** A tax is a compulsory payment made by an individual, household or a firm to the government. No one can escape himself from taxation. Whether, a person is buying goods or services, manufacturing goods and services or generating income from jobs or business, everybody has to pay the taxes according to the laws prevailing in the country.

Characteristics of Good Tax System
- Compulsory payment
- Personal obligation
- Common benefits
- No consideration

(ii) **Personal obligation** The person who is liable to pay the taxes, has the personal responsibility to make payment of due taxes to the government in order to avoid himself from conflict.

(iii) **Common benefits** No person can take direct benefit of the taxes paid by him to the government. All the taxes collected by the government are allocated to various projects, programmes and schemes according to the requirements of the state. The society commonly takes benefit of the taxes paid to the government.

(iv) **No consideration** There is no quid pro quo (i.e. something in return) promised by the government to the tax payer. A tax payer does not receive any definite or direct benefit when he pays the taxes.

5. Discuss briefly the various sources of revenue of the Central Government. *ISC 2001*

Ans Income of the government from all its sources is called 'public revenue'.

It comprises of income by way of taxes and receipts from non-tax revenue sources like fees, fines, grants or donations, etc.

Sources of revenue of the Central Government are

(i) **Revenue receipts sources** These are those money receipts which do not create a liability for the government and do not lead to reduction in assets of the government. Types of revenue receipts sources are

(a) **Tax revenue** Collection by way of taxes by the government from individuals, households, firms, etc. e.g. Income tax, corporate tax, excise duty, sales tax, etc.

(b) **Non-tax revenue** The collections of the government from sources other than taxes are known as 'non-tax revenue' sources. e.g. Fees like passport fees, fines, grants and donations in case of famines, earthquakes, etc.

(ii) **Capital receipts sources** These are those money receipts which either create a liability for the government or causes a reduction in its assets. In India, capital receipts are often classified as

(a) Recovery of loans
(b) Borrowings
(c) Disinvestment

Value Points

For getting maximum marks, following value points can be included in the answer

- Meaning/Difference in revenue and capital receipt sources
- Types of revenue and capital receipt sources

TOPIC 2

Public Expenditure, Public Debt and Deficit Financing

Public Expenditure

It refers to the government expenditure. The expenditure incurred by public authorities like Central, State and Local Governments to satisfy the collective needs of the people is known as 'public expenditure'.

Importance/Need of Public Expenditure

Public expenditure accelerates economic growth and ensures economic stability. It has great need/importance for an economy as it

(i) Promotes rapid economic development.
(ii) Promotes trade and commerce.
(iii) Promotes rural development.
(iv) Promotes balanced rural growth.
(v) Develops agricultural and industrial sectors.
(vi) Efficiently uses mineral resources like coal, minerals and oil.
(vii) Provides collective wants and maximises social welfare.
(viii) Promotes full employment and maintains price stability.

Causes of Increase in Public Expenditure

Public expenditure is increasing due to following causes

(i) Growing population
(ii) Huge defence expenditure
(iii) Interest payments (iv) Subsidies
(v) Social security measures
(vi) Inflation
(vii) Rural development
(viii) Development of agriculture and industry
(ix) Poverty alleviation programmes

Types of Public Expenditure

Broadly there are two types of public expenditures

(i) Planned and non-planned expenditures
(ii) Developmental and non-developmental expenditure

Effects of Public Expenditure

Effects of public expenditure are

(i) **On production** Public expenditure on education, medical services, sanitation and cheap housing facilities increases the productive efficiency of the people at large, which leads to increase in production and income of the people.

(ii) **On economic growth** Public expenditure promotes and stimulate economic development directly and indirectly by establishing capital goods industries, by providing education, training and research facilities.

(iii) **On economic stability** Public expenditure can be used as a balancing factor in order to maintain economic stability, i.e. stability of income, output and employment. Such expenditures may be increased during the period of depression and reduced during the boom period.

Public Debt (Borrowing)

It refers to government debt i.e. borrowings of government from individuals, financial institutions, organisations and foreign countries. If revenue collected through taxes and other sources is not adequate to cover government expenditure, the government may resort to borrowings.

Why Public Debt?

The government may borrow for the following reasons

(i) To meet budget expenditure.
(ii) To finance development plans.
(iii) To check recession.
(iv) To meet unexpected/unseen expenses.
(v) To finance expenditures of public enterprises.
(vi) To meet defence expenditure.
(vii) To provide foreign exchange.

Methods of Debt Redemption (Payment)

Following are the methods of debt redemption

(i) **Debt refusal** Sometimes, government may refuse to pay a public debt. It is called 'repudiation of debt'. When the government repudiates public debt, it does not recognise its obligation to pay the loan.

(ii) **Debt refunding** Government may as an alternative to the above method, take a fresh loan to repay an old debt. In this case, the money burden of the debt is not liquidated, but is postponed to some future date.

(iii) **Debt conversion** Under this method, there is no repayment made for old debt, but the form of debt is altered or charged.

(iv) **Instalment redemption method** Under this method, the government pays back the debt in equal annual instalments including interest component.

(v) **Budgetary surplus** The government may use the budgetary surplus to purchase its own bonds and securities from the open market. Consequently, there is automatic liquidation of the debt liability of the government.

(vi) **Capital levy** The imposition of heavy taxes on wealth and property of the peoples is known as 'capital levy'. It is a quick and equitable method of debt repayment.

(vii) **Export surplus** (to repay external debt) External borrowings need to be repaid normally in foreign currency. It can be facilitated by creating an export surplus. The repayment of debt would be easy, when the foreign loans are invested in those industries which produce exportable goods.

(viii) **Terminal annuities** The government pays the debt in equal annual instalments which include interest as well as the amount of debt.

Deficit Financing (or monetisation of budget deficit)

When Central Government expenditure exceeds government revenue and government is unable to reduce its expenditure, then it borrows from Central Bank. This is done by selling security bills (i.e. treasury bills) to Central Bank which creates new currency notes for the purpose. This is called 'deficit financing' or 'monetisation of budget deficit'.

Effects of Deficit Financing

Various effects of deficit financing are

(i) Inflationary rise in price (ii) Forced savings
(iii) Unequal distribution of income
(iv) Change in investment pattern

PYQs Previous Years' Questions

1 Mark Questions

1. What is meant by 'Sinking fund'? *ISC 2023*

Ans A sinking fund is a fund containing money set aside or saved to pay off a debt or bond.

2. ...... is the creation of new currency to fill the gap between government revenue and government expenditure of the country. *ISC Sem II Specimen 2022*

Ans Deficit financing

2 Marks Questions

1. What is public expenditure? How does public expenditure on social security schemes enhance production in an economy? *ISC 2023*

Ans Public expenditure refers to the expenditure incurred by authorities for public welfare. Social security schemes like provident fund, helps people post retirement and thus encourage to work more at present. Thus, it helps to increase production.

2. What is deficit financing? *ISC Sem II 2022*

Or Define deficit financing. *ISC 2018*

Ans Deficit financing is one of the methods of debt redemption. When Central Government expenditure exceeds government revenue and government is unable to reduce its expenditure, then it borrows from Central Bank.

This is done by selling security bills (i.e. treasury bills) to Central Bank which creates new currency notes for the purpose. This is called 'deficit financing' or 'monetisation of budget deficit'.

> **Concept Enhancer** The Central Bank is independent of central government. Thus under the above situation, Central Bank is requested to print/issue new currency by the central government.

3. How can an increase in public expenditure create more employment in the country? *ISC 2011*

Ans Causes of more employment due to increase in pubic expenditure are

(i) Public expenditure on non-developmental activities such as defence, administration, etc creates demand for various goods and services and thereby, increases employment.

(ii) Public expenditure on the development of basic and key industries like capital goods industries increases output in the economy, leading to generation of more jobs.

4. Mention two compulsive reasons for deficit financing in India. *ISC 2007*

Ans Compulsive reasons for deficit financing in India are

(i) **Slow increase in taxes** Taxable capacity of the people in India is very low, which provides insufficient funds to the government.

(ii) **Increase in public expenditure** Fund requirement for development projects is very large and unavoidable since India is a developing economy.

5. Distinguish between 'development' and 'non-development' expenditures of the government. *ISC 2003*

Ans Difference between development expenditure and non-development expenditure

Basis	Development expenditure	Non-development expenditure
Definition	It refers to expenditure on activities which are directly related to economic and social development of the country.	It refers to the government expenditure incurred on providing essential general services of routine nature like defence, public administration, etc.
Example	Expenditure incurred on education, health, housing, agriculture, social welfare, etc.	Expenditure on police, judiciary, defence, tax collection, subsidies, etc.

3/4 Marks Questions

1. Refunding and debt conversion are two methods of debt redemption. Briefly explain these two methods of debt redemption. *ISC Specimen 2023*

Or Discuss two methods of redemption of public debt in on economy. *ISC 2020*

Or Discuss the following methods of debt redemption *ISC 2017*

(i) Refunding (ii) Debt conversion

Ans (i) **Refunding** It is the process by which the government raises new bonds to pay-off the maturing bonds. Thus, the government takes a fresh loan to repay an old debt.

Usually, this method is adopted, when the government is not in a position to repay its outstanding loans at present.

(ii) **Debt conversion** Conversion of public debt means exchange of new debt for the old debt. In this method, the loan is actually not repaid, but the form of debt is changed.

e.g. converting a high interest debt into a low interest debt. This helps the government to reduce the burden of interest payments.

2. Discuss how public expenditure can be used as an important tool to attain *ISC Sem II 2022*

(i) Regional equality (ii) Economic growth

Ans (i) **Regional equality** Government through its budget tries to bring equality between various regions/states of the country, as economic development is incomplete without regional balance. In order to do so, government provides special packages etc as and when required.

(ii) **Economic growth** Refer to text 'Effects of public expenditure' point (ii) on page 173.

Concept Enhancer Regional equality is key for economic development.

3. Explain the following methods of redemption of public debt *ISC Sem II Specimen 2022*

(i) Debt conversion (ii) Sinking fund

Ans (i) Refer to Q. No. 1 (ii) (3/4 Marks) on page 175.

(ii) A skinking fund is a fund containing money set aside or saved to pay off a debt or bond. A company that issues debt will need to pay-off the debt in the future. In the same manner, government keeps aside some money from its revenue to pay off the debt in future.

4. Explain how public expenditure can be used as an instrument of fiscal policy to solve the problem of *ISC 2019*

(i) Income inequality

(ii) Inflation

Ans (i) To combat income inequality, government uses public expenditure. Here, it provides free education and healthcare for people living in object poverty. For economical weaker sections, it offers subsidies on foodgrains and other necessities. These measures help in solving problem of income inequality to some extent.

(ii) Government reduces expenditure during inflation. When expenditure is lowered, aggregate demand is reduced due to lack of liquidity which helps to solve the problem of inflation.

5. Public expenditure helps in increasing the production of an economy. In this context, discuss any two points of importance of public expenditure. *ISC 2016*

Ans Public expenditure on education, medical services, sanitation and cheap housing facilities increases the productive efficiency of the people at large, which leads to increase in production and income of the people.

This further leads to

(i) **Economic growth** Public expenditure promotes and stimulate economic development directly and indirectly by establishing capital goods industries, by providing education, training and research facilities.

(ii) **Economic stability** Public expenditure can be used as a balancing factor in order to maintain economic stability, i.e. stability of income, output and employment.

Such expenditures may be increased during the period of depression and reduced during the boom period.

6. Explain how public expenditure can be used as a tool to attain economic stability? *ISC 2014*

Ans Economic stability is a characteristic or a feature of free market economy. These economies have been suffering from business cycles, characterised by alternating periods of booms and depressions.

Public expenditure policy can be effectively used as an anti-cyclical instrument for bringing about economic stability. Such expenditure may be increased during the period of depression and reduced during the boom period to bring about economic stability.

6 Marks Questions

1. Explain four ways of redemption of public debt. *ISC 2015*

Or Discuss four methods of repayment of public debt. *ISC 2011, 2009, 2004, 2002*

Ans The main ways of redemption of public debt are

(i) **Refunding** It is the process by which the government raises new bonds to pay-off the maturing bonds. Thus, the government takes a fresh loan to repay an old debt. Usually, this method is adopted, when the government is not in a position to repay its outstanding loans at present.

Four Ways of Public Debt Redemption
- Refunding
- Debt conversion
- Budgetary surplus
- Terminal annuities

(ii) **Debt conversion** Conversion of public debt means exchange of new debt for the old debt. In this method, the loan is actually not repaid, but the form of debt is changed. The process of converting a high interest debt into a low interest debt, the government is able to reduce the burden of debt thereby.

(iii) **Budgetary surplus** A policy of surplus budget may be followed annually for paying off public debt gradually.

The government may use the budgetary surplus to purchase its own bonds and securities from the market. As a result, there is automatic liquidation of the debt liability of the government.

(iv) **Terminal annuities** Under this method, the government pays its debt in equal annual instalments, which include interest as well as the principal amount of debt.

The government is not required to repay the entire debt at a time, but the burden of debts is reduced every year. Thus, it is the method of repayment of loans in instalments.

2. Discuss four reasons for the internal borrowing by the government. *ISC 2012*

Ans Four reasons for the internal borrowings by the government are

(i) **To meet budgetary deficit** Many a time, the yield from taxation and other sources of revenue, may fall short of its current expenditure. In such cases, the government requires loans for short period to cover the gap between the current revenue and expenditure.

(ii) **Financing development plans** The government has to incur huge expenditure to undertake various development projects. The government in underdeveloped countries cannot resort to heavy taxation because of the low taxable capacity of the people. Under such circumstances, public loans are the only way out.

(iii) **To check recession** The government in the developing countries have been borrowing to control recession, so as to prevent the possibility of occurrence of depression. Recession arises because of a fall in private consumption and investment expenditure.

In such a situation, the government can raise loans, so as to increase public expenditure.

(iv) **Meeting unforseen expenses** Sometimes, the country has to face some unforeseen contingencies like floods, famines, epidemics, etc. It is required to undertake huge expenditure to meet such situations of crisis in the economy. Thus, the government raises loans to meet large expenditure arising therefrom.

Reasons for Internal Borrowing
- To meet budgetary deficit
- Financing development plans
- To check recession
- Meeting unforseen expenses

TOPIC 3

Government Budget and Budget Deficit

Concept of Government Budget

Government budget is a statement of the estimates of the government's expected receipts and expenditure during the financial year or fiscal year which runs from 1st April to 31st March. In India, Article 112 of the Constitution requires the Central Government to prepare 'Annual Financial Statement' for the country as a whole. This is called 'Budget of the Central Government'. Article 202 of the Constitution requires every State Government to prepare 'Annual Financial Statement' for the concerned state. This is called 'Budget of the State Government'.

Union Budget

It is the budget prepared by the Central Government and it relates to the whole country. It is a summarised presentation of anticipated income and anticipated expenses of the Central Government.

State Budget

It is the budget prepared by the State Government and it relates to a particular state. It is a summarised presentation of anticipated income and anticipated expenses of the State Government.

Objectives of Government Budget

Following are the objectives of government budget

(i) **Reallocation of resources** The government, through its budgetary policy reallocate resources, so that social and economic objectives can be met.

(ii) **Redistribution of income and wealth** Government through fiscal tools of taxation and transfer payment brings fair distribution of income. Equitable distribution of income and wealth is a way to bring social justice.

(iii) **Economic stability** The government tries to prevent business fluctuations and maintain price and employment stability.
Economic stability stimulates inducement to invest and increases the rate of growth and development.

(iv) **Economic growth** The growth rate of a country depends on the rate of savings and investment. Therefore, the roles that are assigned to budgetary policy in this regard are to create conditions for increase in savings and investment.

(v) **Managing public enterprises** Public sector enterprises are owned and governed by the government through budgetary policy.

Components of the Budget

It has two broad components

1. Budget Receipts

These refer to estimated money receipts of the government from all sources during the fiscal year.

Broadly, the budget receipts are classified as

(i) **Revenue receipts** The money receipts
(a) which do not create a liability for the government.
(b) which do not lead to reduction in assets of the government.
Revenue receipts have following two sources
- **Tax receipts** i.e. direct tax like income tax, corporate tax, etc. Indirect tax like VAT, GST, etc.
- **Non-tax receipts** i.e. fees, fines, grants and donations, etc.

(ii) **Capital receipts** The money receipts
(a) which either create a liability for the government.
(b) or cause a reduction in its asset.
In India, capital receipts are often classified as under
- Recovery of loans.
- Borrowings (from public, Central Bank and external sources)
- Disinvestment (selling off shares to private sector)

2. Budget Expenditure

These refer to estimated expenditure of the government relating to its development as well as non-development programmes during the fiscal year (budget year).

All expenditures of the government are broadly classified as

(i) **Revenue expenditure** All those expenditure which neither create any financial and physical assets nor reduce any liability.

(ii) **Capital expenditure** All those expenditure of the government which either leads to creation of physical and financial assets or reduction of liabilities.

Features of Government Budget

Main features of government budget are

(i) Budget is presented in two parts i.e. revenue budget and capital budget.

(ii) Budget is presented in the Lok Sabha and a copy of budget is also laid on the table of Rajya Sabha.

(iii) Budget is discussed in the Parliament in two stages i.e. for general discussion stage and the voting stage.

(iv) Budget reflects receipts and expenditures of the government for three consecutive years. It gives details of
(a) Actual receipts and expenditure for preceding year.
(b) Revised estimate for the current year.
(c) Budget estimates for the coming year.

Types of Budget

Budget may be classified in following three types

(i) **Balanced budget** When budget receipts are equal to the budget expenditure, it is called 'balanced budget'.
i.e. Budget Receipts = Budget Expenditure
$\Rightarrow$ Balanced Budget

(ii) **Deficit budget** When budget expenditure exceeds budget receipts, the budget is called 'deficit budget'.
i.e. Budget Expenditure > Budget Receipt
$\Rightarrow$ Deficit Budget

(iii) **Surplus budget** When budget receipts are more than budget expenditure, it is called 'surplus budget'.
i.e. Budget Receipts > Budget Expenditure
$\Rightarrow$ Surplus Budget

Concept of Budget Deficit
(or government deficit)

There are three important types of budget deficit

(i) **Revenue deficit** It refers to the situation in which revenue expenditure of government exceeds the revenue receipts.
i.e. Revenue Expenditure > Revenue Receipts
Mathematically, Revenue Deficit
= Revenue Expenditure – Revenue Receipts

Main **implications** of revenue deficit are

(a) **Reduction of assets** (i.e. disinvestment) It implies that government has to make up revenue deficit from capital receipts i.e. through disinvestment.

(b) **Inflationary situation** Use of capital receipts for meeting extra consumption expenditure leads to an inflationary situation in the economy.

(c) **Increased tax burden** A revenue deficit gives a signal to the government to increase taxes.

(d) **Inefficiency** of **government** It implies the inability of the government to meet its regular and recurring expenditure.

(ii) **Fiscal deficit** It is defined as excess of total budget expenditure over total budget receipts excluding borrowings during a fiscal year.

i.e. Total Expenditure > Total Revenue (excluding borrowings)

Mathematically, Fiscal Deficit = Total Expenditure – Total Receipts (net of borrowings)

Implications of fiscal deficit are

(a) **Debt trap** Repayment of loan together with interest further increases fiscal deficit, which creates debt trap.

(b) **Wasteful expenditure** Fiscal deficit generally leads to wasteful and unnecessary expenditure by the government.

(c) **Inflationary pressure** Printing of new currency increases the money supply in the economy and creates inflationary pressure.

(d) **Foreign dependence** Generally, government borrows from foreign countries in case of fiscal deficit.

(e) **Retards future growth** Government borrowings increase the financial burden for future generations.

(iii) **Primary deficit** It is the difference between fiscal deficit and interest payment.

Mathematically, Primary Deficit = Fiscal Deficit – Interest Payments on Previous Loans

Implications of primary deficit are

(a) It indicates how much government borrowing is going to meet expenses other than interest payments.

(b) It is used as a basic measure of fiscal irresponsibility.

PYQs Previous Years' Questions

1 Mark Questions

1. Mention any two sources of receipts from tax revenue of government budget. *ISC Specimen 2023*

Ans Income tax and GST.

2. Fiscal defict – Primary deficit = ... *ISC Sem II 2022*

Ans Interest payment

2 Marks Questions

1. How are revenue receipts different from capital receipts in a budget? Give one example of each receipt. *ISC 2023*

Ans

Basis	Capital receipts	Revenue receipts
Meaning	It refers to the receipts of the government that either increases liabilities or reduces assets of the government.	It refers to the receipts of the government that neither increases liabilities or reduces assets of the government.
Example	Borrowings.	Tax receipts.

2. What is meant by government budget? *ISC Sem II 2022*

Ans Government budget is a statement of the estimates of the government receipts and government expenditure during the period of a financial year. It reveals fiscal policy (budgctary policy) of the government for the coming year.

3. What is meant by revenue deficit? Explain its implication. *ISC 2015*

Ans Revenue deficit refers to the situation in which revenue expenditure of the government exceeds its revenue receipts. i.e.

Revenue Expenditure > Revenue Receipts

Main implication of this deficit is that it leads to reduction in assets through the process of disinvestment to cover the deficit.

4. What is meant by a balanced budget? *ISC 2010*

Ans A government budget is said to be a balanced budget when government's estimated receipts are shown equal to government's estimated expenditure.

Balanced Budget ⇒ Estimated Government Receipts = Government Expenditure

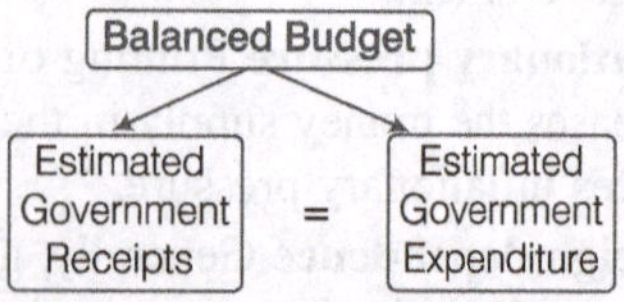

5. Discuss any one importance of a budget. ***ISC 2009***

Ans **Re-allocation of resources** To re-allocate resources in line with social and economic objectives, government provides more resources into socially productive sectors where private sector is not coming forward e.g. Sanitation, water supply, rural development, health, etc.

6. Differentiate between fiscal deficit and primary deficit. ***ISC 2009***

Ans Difference between fiscal deficit and primary deficit

Basis	Fiscal deficit	Primary deficit
Meaning	It is the difference between the total expenditure and total receipts excluding borrowing.	It is the difference between fiscal deficit and interest payments.
Indication	It is the key indicator of budgetary deficit.	It indicates the real position of the government.

7. What is fiscal deficit? ***ISC 2008***

Ans Fiscal deficit is the excess of total expenditure (revenue + capital) over total receipts (revenue + capital other than borrowings).

It is calculated as under

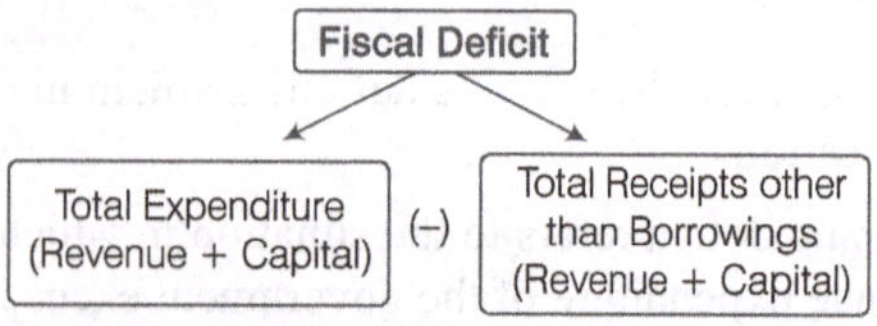

or

Fiscal Deficit = Borrowings

Common Mistake Students generally get confused while writing the fiscal deficit formula. In fiscal deficit, instead of total receipts only revenue receipts and non-debt creating capital receipts are included.

8. What is the difference between a plan budget and performance budget? ***ISC 2002***

Ans Difference between plan budget and performance budget

Basis	Plan budget	Performance budget
Meaning	It is a document which shows the budgetory provisions for important projects, programmes and schemes included in the central plan.	It is a document which monitors the progress of the projects, programmes and schemes in terms of their actual physical achievements against the given target.
Stage of preparation	It is prepared before executing projects, programmes and schemes.	It is prepared during and after completing the projects, programmes and schemes.

3/4 Marks Questions

1. How is fiscal deficit different from primary deficit? Explain one implication of fiscal deficit. ***ISC 2020***

Ans For difference between fiscal deficit and primary deficit, refer to Q.No. 6 on page 180.

One implication of fiscal deficit is

Debt trap It refers to a situation in which government borrows new funds to pay previous loan or to pay interest on previous loans, this creates a trap for the government and burden of future payments mount sup.

2. Differentiate between the revenue and capital components of the union budget. ***ISC 2019***

Ans Following is the difference between revenue and capital budget

Basis	Revenue budget	Capital budget
Meaning	This refers to the current receipts of the government and related expenditure.	This refers to the capital receipts of government and related expenditures.
Implications	This does not cause any change in assets or liabilities of the government.	This leads to creation or reduction in asset or liability of the government.
Examples	Tax receipts, interest payments.	Disinvestment, expenditure on construction of building.

3. Differentiate between fiscal deficit and revenue deficit. *ISC 2018*

Ans Difference between fiscal deficit and revenue deficit are

Basis	Fiscal deficit	Revenue deficit
Meaning	It is the difference between total expenditure and total receipts excepts borrowings.	It results when revenue receipts are less than the revenue expenditure.
Indicator	It is an indicator of the total borrowings needed by the government.	It indicates the dependency on loans in near future.
Arises	It arises due to hikes in capital expenditure.	It arises when the government actual net receipts is lower than the projected receipts.

4. What is meant by budget of the government? Give two differences between revenue expenditure and capital expenditure. *ISC 2017*

Ans Government budget is a statement of the estimates of the government receipts and government expenditure during the period of a financial year. It reveals fiscal policy (budgetary policy) of the government for the coming year.

Two differences between revenue expenditure and capital expenditure are

Basis	Revenue expenditure	Capital expenditure
Definition	It refers to estimated expenditure of the government in a fiscal year, (i) which neither create assets or (ii) nor cause a reduction in liabilities.	It refers to the estimated expenditure of the government in a fiscal year, (i) which create assets or (ii) causes a reduction in liabilities.
Purpose	It is incurred for normal running and maintenance of government departments.	It is incurred for acquisition of capital assets or repayment of liability.

5. What is meant by *ISC 2015*

(i) Union budget

(ii) State budget

KEY IDEA

Budget is prepared by both Central and State government to balance their receipts and expenditures.

Ans (i) **Union budget** It is the budget prepared by the Central Government and it relates to the whole country. It is a summarised presentation of anticipated income and anticipated expenses of the Central Government.

(ii) **State budget** It is the budget prepared by the State Government and it relates to a particular state. It is a summarised presentation of anticipated income and anticipated expenses of the State Government.

6. What is primary deficit and fiscal deficit in a government budget? What is the implication of the primary deficit on the economy? *ISC 2013*

Ans **Primary deficit** It is the difference between fiscal deficit and interest payment.

It is calculated as

Primary Deficit = Fiscal Deficit – Interest Payment on Previous Loans

Fiscal deficit It is the excess of total expenditure (revenue + capital) over total receipts (revenue + capital other than borrowings).

It is calculated as

Fiscal Deficit = Total Expenditure (Revenue expenditure + Capital expenditure) – Total Receipts (Revenue receipts + Capital receipts other than borrowings)

Implications of primary deficit on economy

(i) It indicates how much government borrowing is going to meet expenses other than interest payments.

(ii) It is used as basic measure of fiscal irresponsibility.

7. Differentiate between revenue expenditure and capital expenditure. *ISC 2011*

Ans Difference between revenue expenditure and capital expenditure are

Basis	Revenue expenditure	Capital expenditure
Definition	It refers to estimated expenditure of the government in a fiscal year, (i) which does not create assets or (ii) cause a reduction in liabilities.	It refers to the estimated expenditure of the government in a fiscal year, (i) which create assets or (ii) causes a reduction in liabilities.

Basis	Revenue expenditure	Capital expenditure
Purpose	It is incurred for normal running of government departments and maintenance.	It is incurred for acquisition of capital assets or repayment of liability.
Time period	It is a short-period expenditure.	It is generally a long-period expenditure.
Examples	(i) Wage bill of the government (ii) Interest payments	(i) Expenditure on land and buildings (ii) Purchase of shares

8. Explain two effects of deficit financing. **ISC 2010**

Ans Two effects of deficit financing are

(i) **Inflationary rise in price** Deficit financing may result in inflationary rise in prices. An increase in money supply resulting from deficit financing, increases the demand for goods and services. In the absence of corresponding increase in aggregate supply of goods and services in the short-run, prices tend to rise.

(ii) **Unequal distribution of income** Profits tend to rise while the purchasing power of the fixed income group is reduced on account of rise in prices. Therefore, deficit financing tends to redistribute income and wealth in favour of producers group. Hence, inequalities in the distribution of income and wealth are widened, as a result of deficit financing.

9. Explain four important features of a government budget. **ISC 2004, 2000**

Ans Four important features of government budget are

(i) The budget is presented in two parts i.e. revenue budget and capital budget. Revenue budget shows revenue receipts of the government and the expenditure met from these receipts. Likewise, capital budget comprises capital receipts and capital expenditure of the government.

(ii) The budget is presented in the Lok Sabha on such a day, as the President of India may direct. However, by convention, the budget is presented on the last working day of February. Simultaneously, a copy of the budget is laid on the table of Rajya Sabha.

(iii) The budget is discussed in the Parliament in two stages. In the first stage, there is general discussion about the budget in both the houses of Parliament. In the second stage, the budget is submitted to vote and the voting on the demand for grant is taken.

(iv) It set forth receipts and expenditures of the government for three consecutive years. It gives details for the actual receipts and expenditures for the preceding year, revised estimates for the current year and the budget estimates for the coming year.

6 Marks Questions

1. Define fiscal deficit, primary deficit and revenue deficit. Discuss their implications with reference to India. **ISC 2016**

Ans **Revenue deficit** It is defined as the excess of government's revenue expenditure over revenue receipts.

The revenue deficit includes only such transactions that affect the current income and expenditure of the government.

It is calculated as Revenue Deficit

= Revenue Expenditure – Revenue Receipts

Implications of Revenue Deficit for India

In developing countries like India, often the situation arises when the government has to incur huge expenditure on administration and maintenance and it is difficult to force the people to pay high taxation.

This situation means that the government will have to borrow not only to finance its investment but also for its consumption requirements leading to a high revenue deficit.

This will lead to build up stock of debt and interest liabilities and force the government, eventually, to cut expenditure.

Since, a major part of revenue expenditure is committed expenditure, it cannot be reduced. Often the government reduces productive capital expenditure or welfare expenditure. This would mean lower growth and adverse welfare implications.

Fiscal deficit It is the difference between the government's total expenditure and total receipts, excluding borrowings.

It is calculated as

Fiscal Deficit = Total Budget Expenditure – Total Budget Receipts (Excluding borrowings)

or Fiscal Deficit = Total Budget Expenditure – (Revenue Receipts + Non-debt Creating Capital Receipts)

Implications of Fiscal Deficit for India

Implications of fiscal deficit for India are as under

(i) It determines total borrowing requirements of the government.

(ii) It is always injurious to the economy and leads to financial unsoundness.

(iii) Repayment of loan together with interest further increases fiscal deficit, which creates debt trap.

(iv) It increases the liability of the government.

(v) It increases foreign dependence.

Primary deficit It is equal to fiscal deficit reduced by interest payments. It is calculated as

Primary Deficit = Fiscal Deficit – Interest Payments on Previous Loans.

Implications of Primary Deficit It indicates borrowing requirements of the government to meet fiscal deficit net of interest payments. It enables us to see the way, how the government is currently conducting its financial affairs.

Concept Enhancer A zero primary deficit is not desirable as it indicates that the present borrowings are due to the burden of interest payments.

2. Explain the various components of the budget. *ISC 2014*

Ans Structure of the budget refers to the components of budget. It has two broad components

(i) **Budget receipts** These refer to estimated money receipts of the government from all sources during the fiscal year. Broadly, the budget receipts are classified as

(a) **Revenue receipts** Those money receipts which do not create a liability for the government and do not lead to reduction in assets of the government.

Revenue receipts are further classified as tax receipts i.e. receipts from income tax, sales tax, etc and non-tax receipts such as fees, fines, grants, etc.

(b) **Capital receipts** Those money receipts which either create a liability for the government or causes a reduction in its assets.

In India, capital receipts are often classified as recovery of loans, borrowings and disinvestment.

(ii) **Budget expenditures** These refer to estimated expenditure of the government relating to its development as well as non-development programmes during the fiscal year.

All expenditures of the government are broadly classified as

(a) **Revenue expenditure** It refers to estimated expenditure of the government in a fiscal year which does not create assets or cause a reduction in liabilities. e.g. Interest payments, expenditure on subsidies, etc.

(b) **Capital expenditure** It refers to the estimated expenditure of the government in a fiscal year which creates assets or causes a reduction in liabilities. e.g. Expenditure on land and building, purchase of shares, etc.

3. Define deficit financing. Explain four reasons as to why the governments expenditure has increased in recent year. *ISC 2009*

Ans Deficit financing is used to denote the excess of total government expenditure over total revenue comprising current revenue and public borrowings. The government may cover the deficit, either by running down its accumulated cash balances or by borrowing from the Central Bank.

In recent years, government expenditure has increased due to the act of development, which needs higher imports of capital goods.

Also increasing demand of foreign goods was contributing towards the expenditure of the government. Also, India being a developing economy with high level of poverty, illiteracy and unemployment, government has to incur large amount for the same. Again, the debt burden of previous years due to balance of trade crisis, decrease in world orders and other wasteful expenditures on interest payments, subsidies, etc has lead to increase government expenditure in recent years.

Factors responsible for rise in public expenditure in India

(i) Rapid population growth

(ii) Huge expenditures on defence

(iii) Urbanisation

(iv) State welfare activities

(v) Expenditure on infrastructure development

(vi) Maintenance of economic stability

(vii) Expenditure on subsidies

4. Discuss four issues that highlight the need and importance of the central budget. **ISC 2000**

Ans Need and importance of central budget is stated below

(i) **Planned system** In order to meet the increasing budgeted expenditures, government has to plan the budgeted revenue/receipts accordingly. It can be possible only, by way of making comprehensive planning of the future course of action of the economy. Thus, budgets are made for proper estimation of future receipts and expenditures.

Need of Central Budget
- Planned system
- Instrument of economic policy
- Influencing economic activities
- Allocation of resources

(ii) **Instrument of economic policy** A budget is a powerful instrument for implementing various economic and social objectives of government. Budget helps in promoting economic development, reducing inequalities of income and social welfare.

(iii) **Influencing economic activities** The functioning of the economy is affected by the budgetary activities of the government. e.g. The level and structure of taxes influence the allocation of resources among various sectors as well as distribution of income among different classes.

(iv) **Allocation of resources** Government uses budgetary policy in order to allocate resources in accordance with the economic and social priorities of the economy. The government can encourage the private sector through tax concessions and subsidies to undertake the production of goods required in public interest.

5. Explain any four effects of deficit financing on economic growth. **ISC 2000**

Ans Four effects of deficit financing on economic growth are

(i) **Inflationary rise in prices** Deficit financing may result in inflationary rise in prices. An increase in money supply resulting from deficit financing, rises the demand for commodities.

In the absence of corresponding increase in aggregate supply of commodities in the short-run, prices tend to rise.

(ii) **Forced savings** The effect of forced saving may fall more on fixed income earners rather than on the higher income groups.

Effects of Deficit Financing
- Inflationary rise in prices
- Forced savings
- Distribution of income
- Change in pattern of investment

(iii) **Distribution of income** Profits tend to rise while the purchasing power of the fixed income group is reduced on account of rise in prices.

Therefore, deficit financing tends to redistribute income and wealth in favour of producers group.

(iv) **Change in pattern of investment** Deficit financing may lead to distortion of investment.

It may encourage types of investments which are not desirable for a developing economy, such as hoarding, speculation and construction.

Case Based Question

Case 1

India's fiscal deficit touched 115% of the budgeted target in the first half of 2020-21 as the Covid-19 pandemic continued to hurt government's receipts while expenditure remained close to the same level of last year. The gap between revenue and expenditure stood at ₹ 9.14 lakh crore during April-September, according to data on the website of the Controller General of Accounts.

(i) How is fiscal deficit measured?

Ans Fiscal Deficit = Total Expenditure – Total Receipts excluding Borrowings.

(ii) Which receipts of the government leads to increase in liabilities?

Ans Capital receipts

(iii) State and give formula of other two types of deficit.

Ans Revenue Deficit = Revenue Expenditure – Revenue Receipts

Primary Deficit = Fiscal Deficit – Interest Payments on Previous Borrowings

(iv) Briefly explain the implications of fiscal deficit.

Ans This reduces the availability of funds in the money market for private firms. A lower supply of money leads to a higher interest rate.

This increased interest rate will discourage private firms from undertaking investment projects, thus 'crowding-out' investment.

CHAPTER TEST

01 Mark Questions

1. Which of the following is not a debt creating capital receipt?
(a) Borrowings (b) Disinvestment
(c) Recovery of loans (d) Both (b) and (c)

2. Budget is prepared by
(a) Union government (b) State government
(c) Local government bodies
(d) All of the above

3. Monetising public debt is known as
(a) deficit financing (b) deficit funding
(c) deficit refunding (d) None of these

4. Which of the following is a type of government budget?
(a) Surplus budget (b) Deficit budget
(c) Balanced budget (d) All of these

5. Revenue deficit is always equal to the borrowings of the government State true or false.

6. Government uses the fiscal tools like tax and subsidies to achieve the objective of reducing income inequalities in the economy. State true or false.

7. Escheat is a ……….. revenue of the government.

8. Minority sale includes ……….. equity of public sector undertakings.

9. Is fiscal deficit necessarily inflationary?

10. What is reallocation of resources?

02 Marks Questions

11. Why borrowings are treated as capital expenditures?

12. A government budget shows a primary deficit of ₹ 4,400 crore. The revenue expenditure on interest payments is ₹ 500 crore. How much is the fiscal deficit?

13. What do you mean by non-developmental expenditures?

14. Which of the following is/are capital expenditures?
(i) Interest payments
(ii) Purchase of machinery
(iii) Payment of pension
(iv) Purchase of land

03/04 Marks Questions

15. Distinguish between progressive, regressive and proportional taxes.

16. What is the basic difference between planned and non-planned expenditures of government budget?

17. Can 'surplus budget' be a useful tool for curbing inflation?

18. Briefly discuss the sources of fiscal deficit.

06 Marks Questions

19. 'Balanced budget is helpful in raising the level of aggregate demand in the economy'. Do you agree? Why or why not?

20. Explain the role of taxation policy in reducing income inequalities.

Answers

1. (d) Both (b) and (c)
2. (d) All of the above
3. (a) deficit financing
4. (d) All of these
5. False *6.* True
7. non-tax
8. less than 50 percent

11

National Income

TREND ANALYSIS 5 YEARS

Average No. of Questions Across all Sets

	Types of Questions	2023	2020	2019	2018	2017
01 Circular Flow of Income	1 Mark	—	—	—	—	—
	2 Marks	—	—	—	—	—
	3/4 Marks	1	1	1	—	1
	6 Marks	—	—	—	—	—
02 Basis Concepts of National Income Accounting	1 Mark	—	—	—	—	—
	2 Marks	—	—	—	1	—
	3/4 Marks	2	1	1	—	1
	6 Marks	—	—	—	—	—
03 Measurement of National Income	1 Mark	—	—	—	—	—
	2 Marks	1	1	1	—	1
	3/4 Marks	—	—	—	1	—
	6 Marks	2	1	1	1	1

TOPIC 1

Circular Flow of Income

Circular Flow of Income

It refers to continuous circular flow of money, income and flow of goods among different sectors of an economy. It is circular in nature because it moves in a circle coming back to the starting point. Four sectors are considered in circular flow of income

(i) Household sector (ii) Firms

(iii) Government

(iv) Rest of the world

Principles in Circular Flow of Income

The main principles in circular flow of income are

(i) The seller/firm receives the same amount which the buyer/consumer spends.

(ii) Goods and services flow in one direction and the money payments to acquire them flow in the opposite direction giving rise to a circular flow.

Types of Circular Flow of Income

Following are the types of circular flow of income

(i) **Real flow** The flow of goods and services between firm sector and household sector are called 'real flows'. Such flows are continuous and there is no starting or end point in these flows.

(ii) **Money flow** These refer to flow of money in the form of factor payments and consumption expenditure. In other words, flows of money between firm sector and household sector are called 'money flows'.

Circular Flow of Income and Economic Models

Circular flow of income can be studied under following models

1. Circular Flow in Two Sector Economy Model

It can be studied under two heads

(i) Two Sector Without the Presence of Capital Market

The firms hire factor services from households, for producing goods and services and pays them compensation in the form of money for rendering the productive services. Thus, money income flows from firms to the households.

With this money, the households purchase from the firms, manufactured goods and services to satisfy their wants, with the result, the same money flows back from household to the firms. Thus, entire income of economy come back to firms in the form of sales revenue.

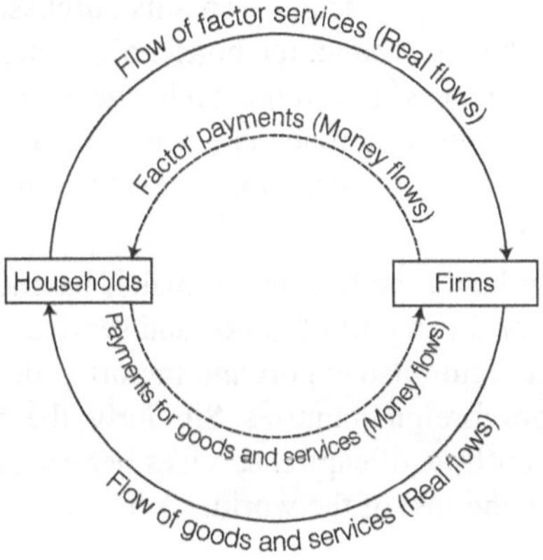

Circular Flow Diagram : Two Sector Simple Model (without capital markets)

Assumptions of this model are

(a) There are only two sectors involved namely, household sector and firm sector.
(b) There are no exports or imports.
(c) No saving and investments are involved.
(d) Two types of market exist *viz*, product market and factor market.

(ii) Two Sector Model with Capital Markets

In this model, we bring the role of capital market consisting of financial institutions. Financial institutions are primary intermediaries between savers (or lenders) and investors (or borrowers). Household and firms save part of their income and deposit in the capital market leading to money flows from households and firms to capital market.

This constitutes a leakage from the circular flow of money. Firms also borrow for purposes of investment. This becomes injection in circular flow.

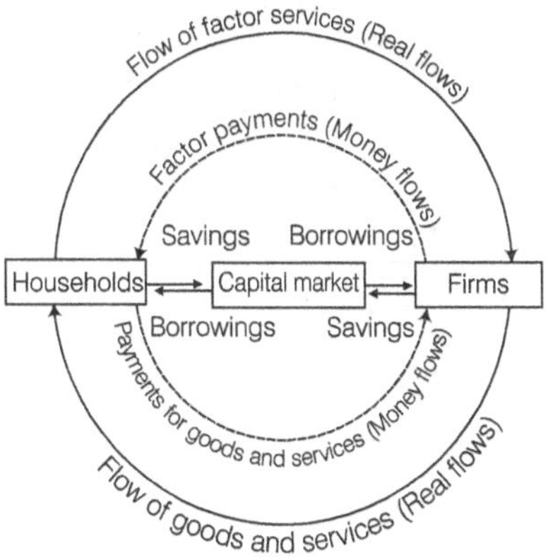

Circular Flow Diagram: Two Sector Model (with capital markets)

Assumptions of this model are

(a) Only two sectors, *viz* household sector and firm sector are present.
(b) There are no exports or imports.
(c) There are savings as well as investments, because of the presence of capital market.
(d) There are two types of market, *viz* product and factor market.

Leakages

A leakage is the amount of money which is withdrawn from the flow of income. e.g. Savings, taxes by households and firms, etc.

Injections

These are the amount of money which are added to the flow of income in the economy. e.g. Investment, government expenditure, etc.

2. Circular Flow in Three Sector Economy Model

By adding government sector to the two sector model of household and firm sector, we obtain three sector model. Government purchases goods from firms and labour services from households.

It collects corporate taxes from firms and personal taxes like income tax, wealth tax, etc from households. Government makes transfer payments like scholarships, old age pensions, etc to households and grants subsidies to firms. All these cause flow of money which are shown in the given diagram.

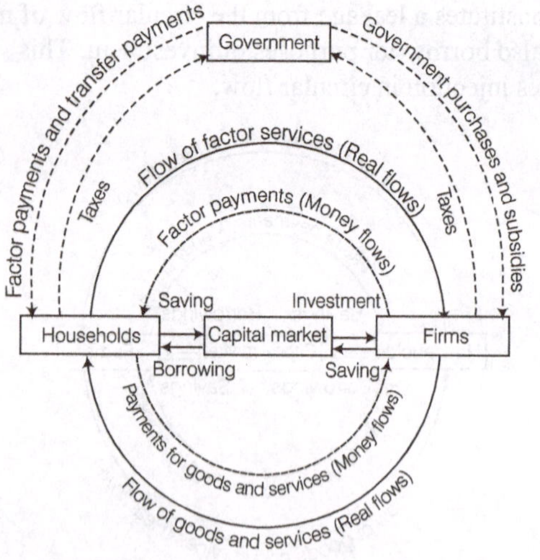

Circular Flow Diagram: Three Sector Model

3. Circular Flow in Four Sector Economy Model

Four sector economy model is an open economy model. An open economy is one who freely trade its goods and services with the economies of rest of the world. Thus, 'rest of the world' sector must be included in our models to make it a realistic model. We can say, that a four sector model will consists of

(i) Households sector
(ii) Firms (producer) sector
(iii) Government sector
(iv) Rest of the World (RoW) sector

Circular flow of income in an open economy is explained in the given diagram.

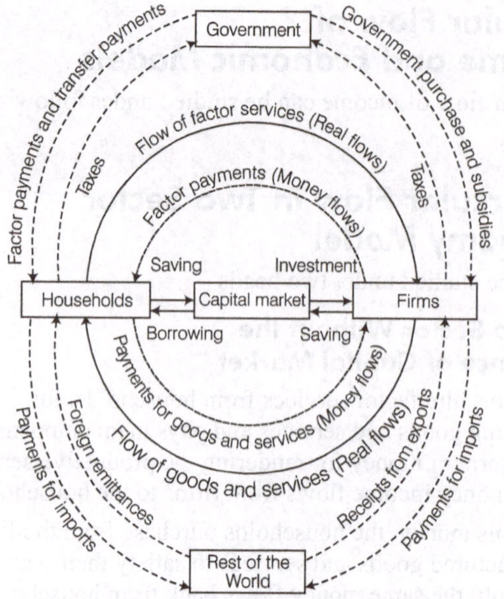

Circular Flow Diagram : Four Sector Model

In the diagram, the household sector purchases goods from abroad and makes payment towards its purchases to abroad. On the other hand, the household sector receives 'foreign remittances' in foreign exchange by selling some of the factor services abroad. The firms export goods and services to foreign countries and receive payment against their exports.

On the other hand, the firm sector makes payment to the foreign sector for import of goods and services. Likewise, government sector also export and import goods and services from foreign countries. Similarly, there is an inflow and outflow of capital services between the government and rest of the world.

PYQs Previous Years' Questions

1 Mark Question

1. Which one of the following is not an example of leakage in the circular flow of income? **ISC Sem II 2022**

(a) Taxation (b) Import (c) Investment (d) Saving

Ans (c) Investment

2 Marks Questions

1. Differentiate between money flow of income and real flow of income. **ISC 2007**

Ans Difference between money flow of income and real flow of income

Basis	Money flow	Real flow
Meaning	Fldow of money in the form of factor payments and consumption expenditure are called money flows.	Flow of goods and services between firm sector and household sector are called real flows.

Basis	Money flow	Real flow
Presentation	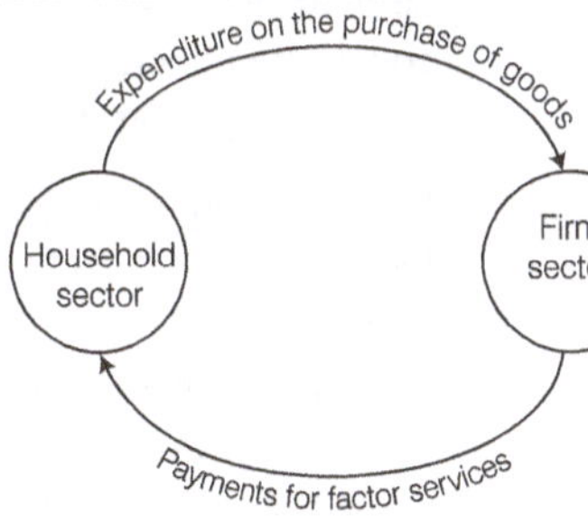	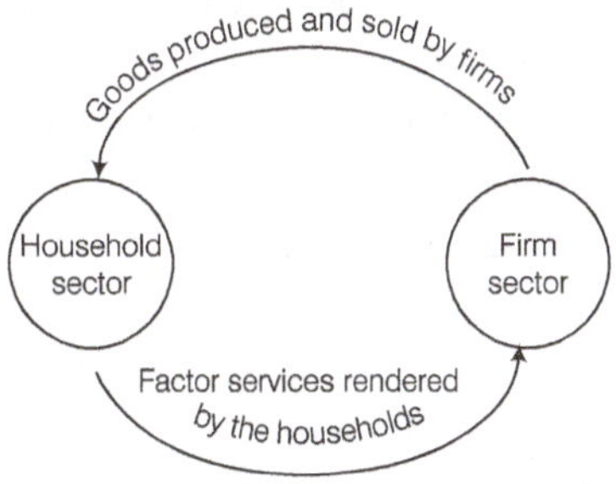

2. Draw a diagram to show the real flow and money flow of income under a two sector model of circular flow. **ISC 2006**

Ans

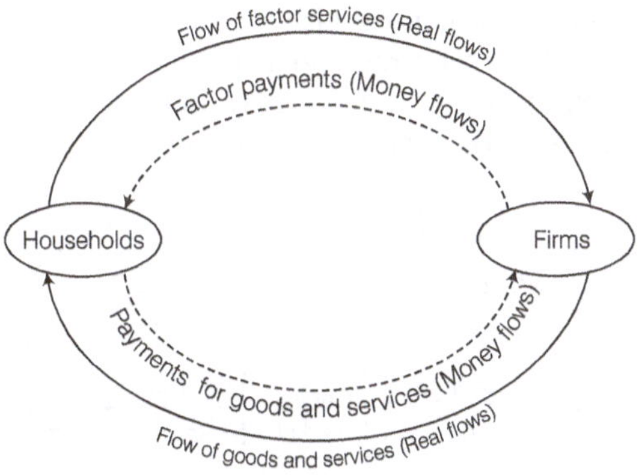

Common Mistake Students generally don't mention the real flow and money flow in the diagram. It should always be mentioned.

3/4 Marks Questions

1. With the help of a diagram, show the circular flow of income in a two sector model with saving and investment. **ISC 2023**

Or Draw a well labelled diagram of two sector model of circular flow of income including financial sector. **ISC Sem II Specimen 2022**

Or Draw a well labelled diagram to show a circular flow of income in a two sector model. What happens to the flow of income when savings equals investment? **ISC 2019**

Or Draw a diagram to show the circular flow of income in a two sector model with leakage and injection. **ISC 2017**

Or Show the circular flow of income in a two sector model with leakages and injections. **ISC 2010**

Ans Circular flow of income explains the flow of money and goods and services between various sectors. In a two sector model, only household and firms are included, wherein household provides factor services and in return get compensation in form of money or goods and services. Also in this model, we bring the role of capital market consisting of financial institutions. Financial institutions are primary intermediaries between savers (or lenders) and investors (or borrowers).

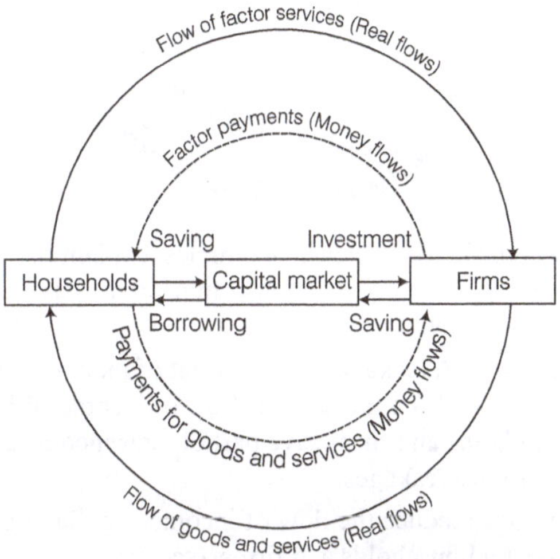

Circular Flow Diagram : Two Sector Model with Capital Markets

Household and firms save part of their income and deposit in the capital market leading to money flows from households and firms to capital market. This constitutes a leakage from the circular flow of money. Firms also borrow for purposes of investment. This comes as an injection in circular flow. It has been shown in the given diagram.

2. Draw a well labelled diagram to explain briefly the circular flow of income in a three sector model. **ISC Sem II 2022**

Or With the help of a well labelled diagram, show the circular flow of income in a three sector model. **ISC 2011**

Ans By adding government sector to the two sector model of household and firm sector, we obtain three sector model. Government purchases goods from firms and labour services from households. It collects corporate taxes from firms and personal taxes like income tax, wealth tax, etc from households.

Government makes transfer payments like scholarships, old age pensions, etc to households and grants subsidies to firms.

All these cause flow of money which has been shown in the given diagram.

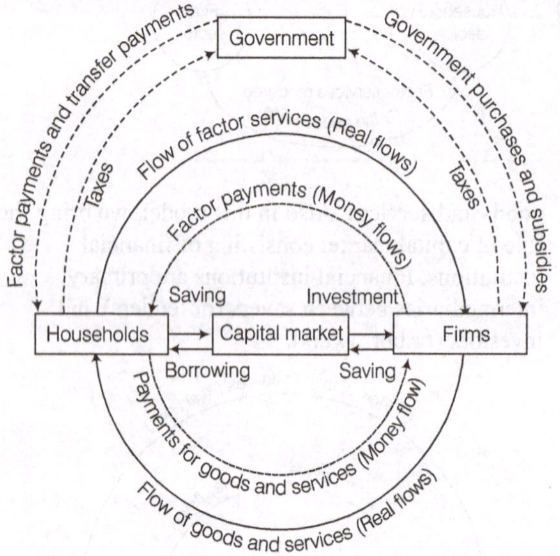

3. With the help of relevant examples, explain the meaning of leakages and injections in the circular flow of income. **ISC 2020**

Ans **Leakages** A leakage is the amount of money which is withdrawn from the circular flow of income. When households and firms save part of their incomes, it constitutes leakages.

Leakages reduce the flow of income. e.g. Savings, taxes by households and firms, etc.

Injections It means introduction of income into the circular flow. When households and firms borrow, they constitute injections. Injections increase the flow of income. e.g. Investment, government expenditure, etc.

4. With the help of a diagram, show the circular flow of income in a two sector model with savings and investment. **ISC 2015**

Ans **Circular flow of income in two sector model with saving and investment** In a two sector economy, there are only two sectors in an economy namely, households and firms. Households supply factors services to the firms and firms hire factor services from households. Households spend their income on consumption. Firms sell what is produced from services of the households with the presence of financial market, firms and households save a portion of their income as well and may borrow from financial market, whenever required.

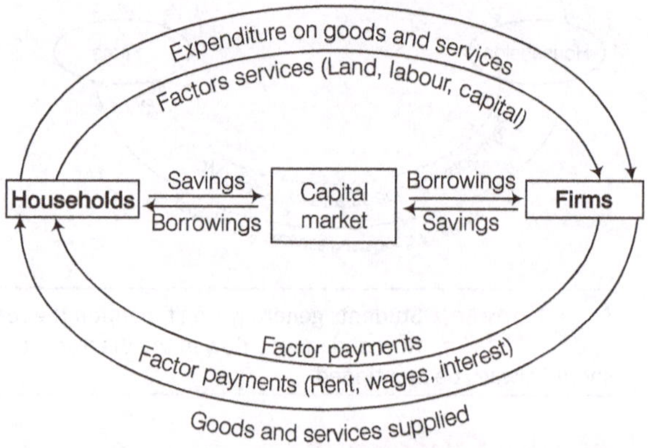

Circular Flow with Capital Market

TOPIC 2

Basic Concepts of National Income Accounting

National Income

National income refers to the total factor income earned by all residents of a country during a period of one year.

It can also be defined in three ways as mentioned below

(i) **From production point of view** National Income is the sum total of money value of net flow of all the final goods and services produced by normal residents within and outside the country during an accounting year.

(ii) **From income point of view** National Income is the sum total of factor incomes earned by normal residents of a country in the form of rent, wages, interest and profit in an accounting year.

(iii) **From expenditure point of view** National product is the net output of commodities flowing during the year from the country's productive system into the hands of final consumers or into the net addition to the country's capital goods.

Measurement of National Income

National Income can be measured in terms of money in two ways

(i) **National income at current prices** (Nominal National Income) It is the money value of all the final goods and services measured at current prices, i.e. prices prevailing in that particular accounting year.

e.g. When goods and services produced during the year 2017-18 are valued at prices of the same year i.e. 2017-18, it will be called National Income at current prices.

(ii) **National income at constant prices** (Real National Income) It is the money value of all the final goods and services produced in a year measured at fixed prices i.e. prices of the base year.

e.g. If goods and services produced during the year 2017-18 are valued at the prices of the base year (i.e. 2011-12)*, it will be called National Income at constant prices.

Note ***Base year** A base year is a carefully chosen year which is a normal year free from price fluctuations. In India, at present, 2011-12 is treated as base year.

Types of Goods

There are two types of goods

(i) **Intermediate goods** These goods which are purchased by one firm from the other for purpose of

(a) Resale

(b) Using them as raw material

e.g. Flour, sugar, milk, etc purchased by a confectioner for producing biscuits are intermediate goods.

(ii) **Final goods** Those goods which are used by final consumer for their end use and not purchased for resale are called final goods.

e.g. Biscuits consumed by a household is treated as final good, as it is available to final consumer for its end use.

All goods that are purchased by a consumer are final goods. On the other hand, any good that is purchased by a producer can be either final good (capital good/ investment) or intermediate good.

Domestic Territory of a Country

Domestic territory is the geographical territory administered by a government within which persons, goods and capital circulate freely. It includes

(i) Territory lying within the political frontiers of a country.

(ii) Ships and aircrafts owned and operated by the resident between two or more countries.

(iii) Fishing vessels, oil and natural gas rigs and floating platforms operated by the residents of a country in the international waters.

(iv) Embassies, consulates and military establishments of the country located abroad.

(v) Territorial waters upto 12 nautical miles (i.e. 22.2 km).

Normal Residents

These are those residents who ordinarily reside within the country for a period of more than one year and whose centre of economic interest also lies in that country. It includes both individuals as well as institutions.

Transfer Payments

These are payments for which no service is rendered in return. These include gifts, family pension, old age pension, unemployment allowance, etc.

Aggregates Related to National Income

Following are the aggregates related to National Income

(i) **Gross Domestic Product at Market Price** (GDP_{MP}) It refers to the sum total of value added by all producing units within the domestic territory of a country during an accounting year, inclusive of depreciation and estimated at market price.

(ii) **Net Domestic Product at Market Price** (NDP_{MP}) It refers to market value of the final goods and services produced by all the producing units within the domestic territory of a country during an accounting year, exclusive of depreciation.

Formula for NDP_{MP} is,

$$NDP_{MP} = GDP_{MP} - \text{Depreciation}$$

(iii) **Gross Domestic Product at Factor Cost** (GDP_{FC}) It refers to the sum total of factor incomes (rent, wages, interest and profits) generated within the domestic territory of a country in an accounting year, alongwith depreciation.

Formula for GDP_{FC} is,

$$GDP_{FC} = GDP_{MP} - \text{Net Indirect Taxes}$$

Where, Net Indirect Taxes = Indirect Tax – Subsidy

(iv) **Net Domestic Product at Factor Cost** (NDP_{FC}) It refers to the sum total of factor incomes generated within the domestic territory of a country during an accounting year. NDP_{FC} is also known as 'domestic factor income'.

Formula for NDP_{FC} is,

$$NDP_{FC} = GDP_{MP} - \text{Depreciation} - \text{Net Indirect Tax}$$

(v) **Gross National Product at Market Price** (GNP_{MP}) GNP_{MP} is the sum total of market value of the final goods and services produced within the domestic territory of a country during an accounting year and also includes net factor income from abroad.

Formula for GNP_{FC} is,

$$GNP_{MP} = GDP_{MP} + \text{Net Factor Income from Abroad}$$

(vi) **Net National Product at Market Price** (NNP_{MP}) It is the sum total of market value of the final goods and services produced within the domestic territory of a country during an accounting year, exclusive of depreciation and inclusive of net factor income from abroad.

Formula for NNP_{MP} is,

$$NNP_{MP} = GDP_{MP} - \text{Depreciation} + \text{Net Factor Income from Abroad}$$

(vii) **Gross National Product at Factor Cost** (GNP_{FC}) It is the sum total of factor cost of final goods and services produced within the domestic territory of a country during an accounting year, inclusive of depreciation and net factor income from abroad.

Formula of GNP_{FC} is,

$$GNP_{FC} = GDP_{MP} + \text{Net Factor Income from Abroad} - \text{Net Indirect Taxes}$$

(viii) **Net National Product at Factor Cost** (NNP_{FC}) It is the sum total of factor cost of final goods and services produced within the domestic territory of a country during an accounting year, exclusive of depreciation and calculated at factor cost and includes net factor income from abroad. It is also known as 'National Income'.

Formula for NNP_{FC} (National Income) is,

$$NNP_{FC} = GDP_{MP} - \text{Depreciation} - \text{Net Indirect Tax} + \text{Net Factor Income from Abroad}$$

(ix) **National disposable income** It is the income from all sources (earned income as well as transfer payments from abroad) available to residents of a country for consumption expenditure or for saving during a year. It is calculated as gross or net.

Formula of NNDI is,

Net National Disposable Income
= National Income + Net Indirect Taxes + Net Current Transfers from Abroad

Formula for GNDI is,

Gross National Disposable Income
= Net National Disposable Income + Depreciation

(x) **Factor income from net domestic product accruing to private sector** It is that part of NDP_{FC} which accrues to the private sector.

Formula

Factor Income from Net Domestic Product Accruing to Private Sector
= NDP_{FC} − Income from Property and Entrepreneurship Accruing to the Government Departmental Enterprises– Savings of Non-departmental Enterprises

(xi) **Private income** It is the total of factor income from all sources and current transfers from the government and abroad to private sector.

Formula for private income is,

Private Income = Factor Income from Net Domestic Product Accruing to Private Sector + Net Factor Income from Abroad + Interest on National Debt + Current Transfers from Government + Current Transfers from Abroad

Note Private income includes both factor income as well as transfer income, but National Income only includes factor income.

(xii) **Personal income** It is the income actually received by the individuals and households from all sources in the form of factor income and current transfers.

Formula for personal income is,

Personal Income = Private Income − Corporate Saving (or undistributed profits) − Corporate Tax

(xiii) **Personal disposable income** It is personal income remaining with individuals after paying direct personal taxes like income tax and house tax and other fees and fines to the government administrative departments.

Formula for PDI is,

Personal Disposable Income
= Personal Income − Direct Personal Tax − Miscellaneous Receipts of the Government Administrative Departments (i.e. fees and fines)

Some More Concepts of National Income

Following are the some more concepts of National Income

(i) **Per capita income** (Real) It is the average income of the normal residents of a country in a particular year measured at constant prices.

In other words, real per capita income is the average availability of goods and services per person during a year.

$$\text{Real Per Capita Income} = \frac{\text{Real National Income}}{\text{Total Population}}$$

Note Real per capita income is generally taken as an index of economic welfare.

(ii) **Per capita income** (Nominal) It may be defined as the income per head of population in an economy.

$$\text{Nominal Per Capita Income} = \frac{\text{National Income (Nominal)}}{\text{Total Population}}$$

Real GDP and Nominal GDP

Read GDP When GDP is valued at base year (i.e. 2011-12) prices or constant prices. It changes only by change in production not by change in price level. It is better measure of economic well being than the nominal GDP.

Nominal GDP When GDP is valued at current year (i.e. 2017-18) prices. It is influenced by change in both production and price level in the economy. It is not considered as true indicator of economic development.

GDP and Welfare

Welfare means sense of material well-being among the people. It depends on

(i) Economic factor like GDP, consumption level, etc.

(ii) Non-economic factors like law and order, environment, etc.

In other words, when GDP rises, it shows great availability of goods and services to the people which is an indicator of high standard of living in economy. It increases economic welfare.

GDP as an Indicator of Economic Welfare

GDP may be a good indicator of economic growth but is not considered as a good measure of economic welfare because of the following reasons

(i) With every increase in the level of GDP, distribution of GDP is getting more unequal, welfare level of the society may not rise.

(ii) Composition of GDP may not be welfare oriented even when the level of GDP tends to rise. i.e. rise in GDP may be concentrated in few hands.

(iii) Because of non-monetary transactions, GDP remains under estimated and therefore, there is no proper index of welfare.

(iv) Impact of externalities (positive or negative impact of an activity) is not accounted in the index of social welfare in terms of GDP.

Difference between Factor Payment and Transfer Payment (or factor income and transfer income)

Basis	Factor payment	Transfer payment
Meaning	Payment made to a factor of production in return for rendering factor services is called factor payment (or factor income).	Payment which is received without rendering any service or good in return is called transfer payment (or transfer income).
Concept	It is an earned income (earning concept).	It is an unearned income (receipt concept).
Nature	Bilateral payment.	Unilateral payment.
Relation with national income	It is included in National Income.	It is not included in National Income.
Example	Retirement pension.	Old age pension.

Three Golden Rules

(i) To change from gross to net, subtract depreciation and *vice-versa*.

(ii) To change from domestic to national, add net factor income from abroad and *vice-versa*.

(iii) To change from market price to factor cost, subtract net indirect taxes and *vice-versa*.

PYQs Previous Years' Questions

1 Mark Questions

1. Which one of the following is included in the calculation of national income? *ISC Specimen 2023*
   (a) Transfer earnings
   (b) Sale proceeds of shares and bonds
   (c) Black money
   (d) None of the above

Ans (d) None of the above

2. State whether the following statement is true or false. Give one reason for your answer.
   Undistributed profits are not a part of domestic factor income. *ISC Specimen 2023*

Ans False. There are three sub-components of profit *viz.* corporate tax, dividend and undistributed profits.

3. $NNP_{FC} = NDP_{FC} + \ldots\ldots$ *ISC Sem II 2022*

Ans NFIA

4. Transfer earning in national income refers to *ISC Sem II Specimen 2022*
   (a) transfer of income from one person to another.
   (b) income received by selling goods.
   (c) unilateral payment received not related to any production
   (d) earning received by offering services

Ans (c) unilateral payment received not related to any production

2 Marks Questions

1. Differentiate between personal income and national income. *ISC Specimen 2023*

Ans Personal income refers to the sum total of income earned by the household and firms from all sources including factor and trasfer income. National income, entire other hand, refers to the sum total of all factor incomes earned by the residents of a country during a year.

2. Explain two differences between factor income and transfer income. *ISC 2018*

Ans Difference between factor income and transfer income

Basis	Factor income	Transfer income
Meaning	Payment made to a factor of production in return for rendering factor services is called 'factor payment' or 'factor income'.	Payment which is received without rendering any services or goods in return is called 'transfer payment' or 'transfer income'.
Concept	It is an earned income (earning concept)	it is an unearned income (receipt concept)
Nature	Bilateral payment.	Unilateral payment.
Example	Wages to labours.	Old age pension.

3. How can Gross Domestic Product at Factor Cost (GDP_{FC}) be obtained from Gross National Product at Market Price (GNP_{MP})? *ISC 2015*

Ans From Gross National Product at Market Price (GNP_{MP}), we can obtain Gross Domestic Product at Factor Cost (GDP_{FC}) by deducting Net Factor Income from Abroad (NFIA) and Net Indirect Taxes (NIT), i.e. $GDP_{FC} = GNP_{MP} - NFIA - NIT$.

4. Define GNP at factor cost. How is it different from National Income? *ISC 2013*

Ans GNP at Factor Cost (GNP_{FC}) is the sum total of factor cost of final goods and services produced within the domestic territory of a country during an accounting year (inclusive of depreciation and Net Factor Income from Abroad) and GNP_{FC} is different from National Income in such a manner that former includes depreciation allowance while the later does not include depreciation allowance.

5. Difference between national income at current and constant prices. *ISC 2012, 2003*

Ans Difference between national income at current and constant prices

Basis	National income at current price	National income at constant price
Meaning	It is the money value of all the final goods and services measured at current prices (i.e. prices prevailing in that particular year).	It is the money value of all the final goods and services produced in a year measured at base year prices (i.e. constant prices).
Other name	It is also called nominal National Income.	It is also called real National Income.

6. How is personal income calculated from private income? *ISC 2011*

Ans In order to get personal income, we have to deduct corporate (profit) tax and corporate savings or undistributed profits out of private income.

i.e. Personal Income = Private Income – Corporate Tax – Corporate Savings

7. How is net national product at factor cost obtained from net national product at market price? *ISC 2010*

Ans From net national product at market price, we obtain net national product at factor cost by deducting net indirect taxes i.e. $NNP_{FC} = NNP_{MP}$ – Net Indirect Tax

8. What do you mean by transfer payment? Give one example. *ISC 2009*

Ans Payment which is received without rendering any service or good in return is called transfer payment. These are unilateral payments which have no obligation of any return. e.g. Old age pension.

9. When is the national product of a country higher than domestic product? *ISC 2008*

Ans National product will be higher than domestic product of a country only when there is positive inflows from rest of the world in the form of positive net factor income earned from abroad.

10. What is national product minus domestic product equal to? *ISC 2004*

Ans National product minus domestic product is equal to net factor income from abroad.

11. Differentiate between personal income and personal disposable income. *ISC 2004*

Ans Difference between personal income and personal disposable income

Basis	Personal income	Personal disposable income
Meaning	It is the income actually received by the households from all sources in the form of current transfer payment and factor income.	It is the personal income remaining with individuals after paying personal taxes like income tax and house tax and other fees and fines to the government administrative departments.
Formula	Personal Income = Private Income – Corporate Saving – Corporate Tax	Personal Disposable Income = Personal Income – Direct Personal Tax – Miscellaneous Receipts of the Government Administrative Departments in the form of fees and fines.

12. How is National Income different from GNP at market price? *ISC 2003*

Ans National Income is the aggregate of factor payments of all final goods and services produced by nationals of country during a year, but after making allowance for depreciation (i.e. NNP_{FC}).

Whereas, Gross National Product at Market Price (GNP_{MP}) is the aggregate of market value of all final goods and services produced by nationals of a country during a year, but it does not make allowance for depreciation, i.e. it includes depreciation and it is valued at market price while National Income is valued at factor cost.

13. Define National Income. *ISC 2002*

Ans National Income is the sum total of factor incomes earned by normal residents of a country in the form of rent, wages, interest and profit in an accounting year. It is denoted as net national product at factor cost.

14. Why are pure exchange transaction excluded in the calculation of National Income? *ISC 2002*

Ans While calculating National Income, pure exchange transactions are excluded because nothing new is produced from it during the current accounting year.

15. Differentiate between GNP_{MP} and NDP_{FC}. *ISC 2002*

Ans Difference between Gross National Product at Market Price (GNP_{MP}) and Net Domestic Product at Factor Cost (NDP_{FC})

Basis	Gross National Product at Market Price (GNP_{MP})	Net Domestic Product at Factor Cost (NDP_{FC})
Meaning	It is defined as the aggregate market value of all final goods and services produced by the nationals of a country during a year including depreciation.	It is the estimate of the domestic product in terms of earning of factor of production within the domestic territory of a country excluding depreciation.
Scope	It is a wider concept as it includes net factor income earned from abroad.	It is a narrow concept as it does not include net factor income earned from abroad.

16. Why has the GDP measure been higher than the GNP measure in India? *ISC 2000*

Ans The GDP measure in India has been higher than the GNP measure because of the negative value of net factor income earned from abroad.

3/4 Marks Questions

1. With the help of appropriate example, briefly discuss Real GDP and Nominal GDP. *ISC 2023*

Ans GDP of a country can be estimated in two ways i.e., at the prices of the current year and at the prices of the base year. When the GDP is estimated at the current year's price, it is known as Nominal GDP while the GDP at the base year's price is known as Real GDP.

This helps in estimating the actual change in quantity produced over the base year and current year. If the base year price is ₹ 100 and quantity is 1,000 units while the price in current year is ₹ 120 and quantity is 1,000, the Nominal GDP will be ₹ 1,20,000 while Real GDP will be ₹ 1,00,000. Further this shows that there is no change in the quantity produced in the current year.

2. Per capita is not considered a good indicator of the economic welfare. Explain this statement by giving any two reasons. ***ISC 2023***

Or The growth of gross domestic product is not a real indicator of economic welfare. Discuss two reasons to justify the given statement. ***ISC 2015***

Ans Increase in national income or increase in per capita income does not necessarily lead to an increase in the economic welfare of a country because Nominal National Income is not considered to be an appropriate measure of economic welfare due to the reasons mentioned below

(i) **Increasing disparity of income** Increase in nominal National Income does not mean equitable distribution of income. The increase may be concentrated in the hands of few, thereby increasing disparity of income and reducing economic welfare.

(ii) **Externalities** Externalities are benefits/losses for which payment is not received or fine is not levied. So, negative as well as positive externalities are ignored while calculating National Income. This leads to either under or overestimation of National Income, therefore affecting its credibility as a measure of economic welfare.

3. How can you obtain

(i) National income from GDP_{MP}.

(ii) Personal disposable income from personal income. ***ISC 2020***

Ans (i) National income is Net National Income at Factor Cost (NNP_{FC}). To calculate NNP_{FC} from GDP_{MP}, following formula is used

$NNP_{FC} = GDP_{MP}$ – Depreciation (Consumption of fixed capital) + Net Factor Income from Abroad (NFIA) – Net Indirect Taxes (Taxes – Subsidies)

(ii) It is a personal income remaining with individuals after paying direct personal taxes like income tax and house tax and other fees and fines to the government administrative departments.

It can be calculated as

Personal Disposable Income
= Personal Income – Direct Personal Tax
– Miscellaneous Receipts of the Government Administrative Departments

4. What is meant by economic welfare? Explain how GDP is an indicator of economic welfare. ***ISC 2019***

Ans Economic welfare is the sense of material well-being among the people of a country or economy. It depends on

(i) Economic factors like GDP, consumption level etc.

(ii) Non-economic factors like law and order, environment etc.

GDP as an Indicator of Economic Welfare

When real GDP increases, it means increase in level of output of economy. Other things remaining constant, it implies greater availability of goods and services to the people which is an indicator of high standard of living in economy. It increases economic welfare.

Concept Enhancer Estimation of GDP excludes factor that doesn't have a market value or non-marketable services, like services of housewife, etc.

5. Distinguish between real GDP and nominal GDP. Which of these is a better indicator of economic welfare and why? ***ISC 2017***

Ans Differences between real GDP and nominal GDP are

Basis	Real GDP	Nominal GDP
Meaning	It is the money value of all the final goods and services produced in a year at base year prices (i.e. constant prices).	It is the money value of all the final goods and services measured at current prices (i.e. prices prevailing in that particular year).
Other name	It is also referred to as National Income at constant price.	It is also referred to as National Income at current price.

The per capita real income is considered to be a better index of economic welfare than Gross Domestic Product (GDP) due to the following reasons

(i) The average availability of goods and services is indicated by per capita real income rather than Gross Domestic Product (GDP). Higher GDP, need not result in increased availability of goods and services on average if the rise in GDP in due to rise in price. Thus, per capita real income is a better index than GDP.

(ii) Rise in real per capita income means rise in the level of economic activity in terms of rise in level of production.

6. Distinguish between private income and personal income. *ISC 2016*

Ans Difference between private income and personal income

Basis	Private income	Personal income
Meaning	It is the income which accrues to the private sector, from all sources.	It is the sum total of income actually received by a person from all sources, including factor income and transfer income.
Formulae	Private Income = Domestic Income Accruing to Private Sector + Net Factor Income From Abroad + Interest on National Debt + Current Transfers from Government + Net Current Transfers from Rest of the World.	Personal Income = Private Income – Corporation Tax – Corporation Savings.
Concept	It is a comparatively broader concept.	It is a narrow concept.

7. Discuss two reasons why the per capita real income is considered to be a better index of economic welfare than gross domestic product. *ISC 2013*

Ans The per capita real income is considered to be a better index of economic welfare than gross domestic product due to following reasons

(i) The average availability of goods and services is indicated by per capita real income rather than Gross Domestic Product (GDP). Higher GDP, need not result in increased availability of goods and services on average if the rise in GDP is due to rise in price. Thus, per capita real income is better index than GDP.

(ii) Rise in real per capita income means rise in the level of economic activity in terms of rise in level of production.

8. Discuss two differences between intermediate goods and final goods. *ISC 2012*

Ans Difference between intermediate goods and final goods

Basis	Intermediate goods	Final goods
Meaning	Those goods which are purchased by one firm from the other for the purpose of (i) resale or (ii) using them as raw material.	Those goods which are used by final consumer for their final consumption and not purchased for resale.
Inclusion in national product	These goods are not included in the estimation of national product.	These goods are included in the estimation of national product.

Common Mistake Students generally consider specific goods as final good or intermediate goods. However, no good is a final or intermediate good only, it depends on its end use.

9. Distinguish between *ISC 2012*

(i) Gross domestic product at market price and net national product at factor cost.

(ii) Personal income and personal disposable income.

Ans (i) Difference between gross domestic product at market price and net national product at factor cost

Basis	Gross domestic product at market price	Net national product at factor cost
Meaning	It refers to market value of the final goods and services produced by all the producing units within the domestic territory of a country during the period of an accounting year, inclusive of depreciation.	It refers to the sum total of (i) Market value of final goods and services produced within the domestic territory of a country during an accounting year excluding depreciation. (ii) Net factor income from abroad.
Net Factor Income from Abroad	It does not include Net Factor income from abroad.	It includes the net factor income from abroad.

(ii) **Difference between personal income and personal disposable income** Refer to Q. No. 11. (2 Marks).

6 Marks Question

1. Does an increase in national income necessarily lead to an increase in economic welfare? Discuss. *ISC 2002*

Ans No, increase in national income does not necessarily lead to an increase in the economic welfare of a country. As we know, that there are two methods of measuring National Income

(i) **Nominal national income** which is calculated at current year prices.

(ii) **Real national income** which is calculated at base year prices.

Of the above two measures, nominal national income is not considered to be an appropriate measure of economic welfare due to the reasons mentioned below

(a) **Increasing disparity of income** Increase in nominal National Income does not mean equitable distribution of income.
The increase may be concentrated in the hands of few, thereby increasing disparity of income and reducing economic welfare.

(b) **Externalities** Externalities are benefits/ drawbacks for which payment is not received or fine is not levied. So negative as well as positive externalities are ignored while calculating national income. This leads to either under or over estimation of national income, therefore affecting its credibility as a measure of economic welfare.

(c) **Increase in national income due to rise in prices** Sometimes, it may so happen that the increase in national income is due to an increase in the general price level and not due to an increase in the quantum of production. This increase will not lead to an increase in economic welfare, rather it will decrease it.

So, we can say that increase in nominal national income does not mean increase in the level of economic welfare. Real national income is a more reliable measure of economic welfare.

Value Points

For getting maximum marks, following value points can be included in the answer

- National income is not a measure of welfare, so both the aspects, i.e. real and nominal national income, should be mentioned.
- Mention about other components like externalities and price level.

TOPIC 3

Measurement of National Income

Methods of Measuring National Income

Methods of measurement of National Income originate from three different phases in circular flow of income as discussed in the previous topic. Corresponding to these phases, there are three methods of measuring National Income, as described below

1. Value Added Method

It is the method, in which National Income is measured in terms of value addition by each producing enterprise in the economy during an accounting year. It is also known as product method.

Steps Involved in Value Added Method

Value added method involves following steps

(i) First of all, the production units/entities have to be identified which are located in the domestic economy.

(ii) Secondly, the net final output or net value added by production units is estimated by subtracting the value of intermediate consumption from the value of output to get GDP_{MP}.

(iii) Thirdly, estimating net domestic output.

(iv) Finally, estimate net factor income from abroad and add it to domestic income for deriving National Income (Net National Product at Factor Cost).

Using product method (or value added method), formula for GDP_{MP} is

GDP_{MP} = Value of Output – Value of Intermediate Consumption

Where, Value of Output = Sales + Change in Stock (Closing stock – Opening stock) + Goods Produced for Self-consumption

Value of Intermediate Consumption
= Cost of Raw Materials Purchased + Fuel and Labour Charges + Other Manufacturing Expenses

National Income/NNP_{FC} = (Sales + Change in Stock + Goods Produced for Self-consumption) – Intermediate Consumption – Depreciation – Net Indirect Taxes + Net Factor Income from Abroad

Note Value of output will be equal to sales if entire output is sold with in the same year.

Precautions in Value Added Method

Following are the precautions to be followed in value added method

(i) **Items to be included in national income**
   (a) Imputed rent of owner occupied houses.
   (b) Value of own account production of goods and services.
   (c) Brokerage or commission on sale of second hand goods.

(ii) **Items to be excluded from national income**
   (a) Sales and purchases of second hand goods (as these are not part of current year production).
   (b) Sale of bonds, shares, etc (these are merely financial transactions or paper claims).
   (c) Income from illegal activities like smuggling, gambling, etc.

2. Income Method

Under this method, National Income is calculated by adding up factor incomes generated by all the producing units located within the domestic economy during an accounting year.

Steps Involved in Income Method

Various steps involved in income method are

(i) Identify enterprises which employ factors of production (i.e. land, labour, capital and entrepreneur).
(ii) Classify factor payments into various categories like rent, wages, interest and profits.
(iii) Estimate amount of factor payments made by each enterprise.
(iv) Sum up all factor payments made within domestic territory to get domestic income (Net Domestic Product at Factor Cost).
(v) Estimate net factor income from abroad which is added to domestic income to derive National Income.

National Income by Income Method = Compensation of Employees + Operating Surplus + Mixed Income of Self-employed + Net Factor Income from Abroad

Components of Compensation of Employees

It is the reward paid in cash or in kind by producers to their employees in the form of wages and salaries, social security benefits and retirement benefits. No matter employee is part time or full time, casual or regular, skilled or unskilled. Every kind of compensation to employees from its employers are considered under it.

Compensation of employees has the following main components

(i) **Wages and salaries** Every employee gets periodic (say monthly/daily) payments from their employers in consideration of the services rendered by them. It is known as wages and salaries. It includes basic pay, bonus, commission, dearness allowance, house rent allowance, free meals, free clothing, etc.

   The above does not include the following
   (a) Claim received to an injured worker from insurance company.
   (b) Interest free loan to staff.
   (c) Travelling allowance.

(ii) **Employer's contribution of social security** It refers to payments towards provident fund, insurance schemes which are for the benefits or social security of the employees. The contributions made towards provident fund can be made by both employer as well as employee. But, contribution from employees are not considered under it.

(iii) **Retirement pension** It refers to pension payments as a part of the 'service-contract' between the employer and the employees.

Note Old age pension is different from retirement pension and hence, not considered in compensation of employees, as old age pension is transfer payment.

Operating Surplus

The sum of income from property and income from entrepreneurship is known as operating surplus. In simple terms, operating surplus is the sum total of rent, royalty, interest and profit.

Mixed Income of Self-employed

It refers to the incomes of the self-employed persons using their own labour, land, capital and entrepreneurship to produce goods and services.

Precautions in Income Method

Precautions to be taken in income method are

(i) All types of transfer income like old age pension, scholarships, etc are to be excluded.
(ii) Sale and purchase of second hand goods are excluded since, they are not part of current year production but commission paid on sale of second hand good is included, as it is reward for rendering productive services.
(iii) Income from illegal activities like smuggling, gambling, etc are excluded.
(iv) Income from windfall sources (i.e. gains from lotteries) are excluded.

3. Expenditure Method

Under this method, National Income is calculated first by adding up all the items of final consumption expenditure and final investment expenditure within domestic territory during a year. Then, by subtracting depreciation and net indirect taxes from the sum and adding net factor income from abroad, we obtain National Income.

Steps Involved in Expenditure Method

Expenditure method involves following steps

(i) Identifying the economic units incurring final expenditure i.e. household sector, firm sector or producer sector, government sector and rest of the world sector.

(ii) Classifying final aggregate expenditure into following components

(a) Private final consumption expenditure

(b) Government final consumption expenditure

(c) Gross domestic fixed capital formation

(d) Change in stocks

(e) Net exports (exports – imports)

By summing up all the five components, we get Gross Domestic Product at Market Price (GDP_{MP}).

(iii) By deducting depreciation and net indirect taxes from GDP_{MP}, we get Net Domestic Product at Factor Cost (NDP_{FC}) or domestic income.

(iv) Estimation of net factor income from abroad, which is added to NDP_{FC} (domestic income) to obtain NNP_{FC} (National Income).

National Income/NNP_{FC}
= Private Final Consumption Expenditure
+ Government Final Consumption + (Gross Domestic Fixed Capital Formation
+ Change in Stock) + Net Exports
− Depreciation − Net Indirect Tax
+ Net Factor Income from Abroad

Precautions in Expenditure Method

While using expenditure method, items included or excluded in calculation of National Income are

(i) Only final expenditure is to be taken into account to avoid error of double counting.

(ii) Expenditure on second hand goods is not to be included, because value of second hand goods has already been accounted for during the year of their production.

(iii) Expenditure on shares and bonds is not to be included in total expenditure, as these are mere paper claims and are not related to the production of final goods and services.

(iv) Expenditure on transfer payments by the government is not to be included.

(v) Imputed value/estimated value of expenditure on goods produced for self-consumption should be taken into account, as these goods are reflected in the estimation of GDP.

Difficulties in Measuring National Income

Following are the problems faced during measuring National Income

(i) **Non-availability of data** A significant part of every economy is engaged in the services of regular nature and operating their works in an unorganised way. Persons like electricians, plumbers, small shopkeepers, street hawkers, etc do not keep their accounts and they don't have correct information about their income. It is very difficult to calculate the income of such a group. Consequently, National Income figure estimation becomes difficult.

(ii) **Problem of double counting** While computing the National Income, there is always the danger of double or multiple counting. Double counting means counting value of the same commodity more than once in calculating National Income. If care is not taken in estimating the National Income, the cost of the commodity is likely to be counted twice or more and due to which, National Income will be overestimated.

(iii) **Own-account production** (or production for self-consumption) In developing countries, a significant part of the output is not exchanged for money in the market.

It is either consumed directly by producers or bartered for other goods. This unorganised and non-monetised sector makes calculation of National Income difficult.

(iv) **Price level changes** National Income is measured in money terms. The measuring rod of money itself does not remain stable. This means that National Income can change without any change in output.

(v) **Conceptual difficulties** There may be problem in interpreting new products like new chemical fertilizer as it did not exist in the base year, so problem arises in estimating them at constant prices.

Factors Determining the Size of National Income

Factors determining the size of National Income are

(i) The state of factors of production

(ii) Labour

(iii) State of technical knowledge

(iv) Political stability

PYQs Previous Years' Questions

1 Mark Question

1. Firm A sells flour to Firm B for ₹ 100 and Firm B sells biscuits to the wholesaler C for ₹ 160 and Firm C sells biscuits to consumers for ₹ 200. Hence, the gross value added is *ISC Sem II Specimen 2022*
(a) ₹ 460
(b) ₹ 305
(c) ₹ 244
(d) ₹ 200

Ans (d) Gross value added is measured as the value of final goods consumed by the consumers as it includes the value of all other intermediate goods.

2 Marks Questions

1. Briefly discuss any two precautions to be taken while calculating national income by value added method. *ISC 2023*

Ans Two precautions to be taken while calculating national income by value added method are
(i) Imputed rent of owner occupied houses to be included in national income.
(ii) Sale and purchase of second hand goods to be excluded from national income.

2. What is the difference between GDP_{MP} and NNP_{FC}? *ISC Specimen 2023*

Ans

Basis	GDP_{MP}	NNP_{FC}
Meaning	Gross value of all final goods produced in domestic territory.	Net value of all final goods produced by the normal residents.
Value of depreciation	Includes depreciation.	Excludes depreciation.

3. State the components of compensation of employees. Given one example of any one of the components. *ISC Sem II 2022*

Ans It is the total remuneration payable to employees, whether in cash or in kind and includes the following
(i) Wages and salaries in cash
(ii) Payment in kind
(iii) Employer's contribution to social security schemes (e.g. Contribution towards provident fund)
(iv) Pension on retirement

4. State whether the following will be included or not in the National Income Accounting. Give one reason for each.
(i) Interest paid on a loan taken to buy consumer durable good.
(ii) Food grain grown by a farmer for self consumption. *ISC Sem II 2022*

Ans (i) It will not be included as the loan is taken for cosumption purposes and does not add to the current flow of production.
(ii) It will be included. It is a part of goods produced for self consumption.

Common Mistake Students generally get confused between factors to be included in domestic income and national income. Income earned by normal residents is included in national income while income earned within domestic territory is included in domestic income.

5. What is meant by operating surplus? *ISC 2020*

Ans Operating surplus refers to income from property and entrepreneurship. It includes rent, royalty, interest and profit.

6. Explain any two precautions to be taken while calculating National Income by Income method. *ISC 2019*

Ans Precautions while calculating National Income by income method
(i) Transfer earnings like scholarships, old age pensions etc is to be excluded.
(ii) Imputed rent of owner's house is to be included.

7. Explain with the help of an example, the problem of double counting while calculating national income. *ISC 2017*

Ans While computing the National Income, there is always the danger of double or multiple counting. Double counting means counting value of the same commodity more than once in calculating National Income. If care is not taken in estimating the National Income, the cost of the commodity is likely to be counted twice or more and due to which, National Income will be overestimated.
e.g. Steel is the end product of Tata Steel. It is used to manufacture Maruti cars. So, the cost of Maruti cars is inclusive of the cost of steel. If it is not deducted from the cost of car, then it will be counted twice.

8. State whether each of the items given below is included in estimating National Income. Give a reason in each case to justify your answer.

(i) Expenditure on the construction of Express Highway.

(ii) Expenditure on the purchase of an old house.

ISC 2016

Ans (i) Expenditure on the construction of Express Highway 'will be included' in estimating National Income as a part of Gross Domestic Capital Formation. It is a form of Public Investment.

(ii) Expenditure on the purchase of an old house 'will not be included' in estimating National Income. National Income represents the value of final goods and services produced during the year. So, goods produced in the previous year cannot be included while computing the National Income for the current year.

9. How are the following treated in National Income calculation

(i) Pension

(ii) Income from sale of an old television set. *ISC 2009*

Ans (i) **Pension** It is a part of compensation of employees and is included in National Income as compensation of employees is one of the main component by income method.

(ii) **Income from sale of an old television set** It does not form a part of National Income as it had been earlier considered while production of goods and services by output method in the year, it was produced.

Concept Enhancer Pension is of two types i.e. old age pension and retirement pension.

10. Mention the components of domestic factor income.

ISC 2008

Ans Components of domestic factor income are

(i) Compensation of employees

(ii) Operating surplus

(iii) Mixed income of self-employed

11. Why are the following not included in the estimation of the National Income? *ISC 2006*

(i) Sale of an old car (ii) Winning a lottery

Ans (i) **Sale of an old car** It is not included in estimation of the National Income because it had been earlier counted in the production by output method in the year it was produced.

(ii) **Winning a lottery** It is a wind fall gain, thus, not taken while estimating National Income.

Concept Enhancer Any brokerage/commission charged on buying/selling of second hand goods is included in national income.

12. What is double counting? *ISC 2004*

Or What is double counting and what does it lead to?

ISC 2001

Ans Double counting means counting value of the same commodity more than once in calculating National Income. It leads to over estimation of National Income.

3/4 Marks Questions

1. Explain the steps involved in calculation of National Income by expenditure method. *ISC Sem II 2022*

Or Explain clearly the expenditure method of calculating National Income. *ISC 2001*

Ans Under expenditure method, National Income is calculated first by adding up all the items of final consumption expenditure and final investment expenditure within the domestic economy during a year. Then by subtracting depreciation and net indirect taxes from the sum calculated earlier and adding to it net factor income from abroad, we get National Income or NNP_{FC}.

Expenditure method involves the following steps

(i) Identifying the economic units incurring final expenditure i.e. household sector, firm sector or producer sector, government sector and rest of the world sector.

(ii) Classifying final aggregate expenditure into following components

(a) Private final consumption expenditure

(b) Government final consumption expenditure

(c) Gross domestic fixed capital formation

(d) Change in stocks

(e) Net exports

By summing up all the five components, we get Gross Domestic Product at Market Price (GDP_{MP}).

(iii) By deducting depreciation and net indirect taxes from GDP_{MP}, we get Net Domestic Product at Factor Cost (NDP_{FC}) or domestic income.

(iv) Net factor income from abroad is added to NDP_{FC} (Domestic Income) to obtain NNP_{FC} (National Income).

Precautions

(i) Government expenditure on all transfer payment such as scholarship, unemployment allowance, old age pension, etc is excluded because no productive services are rendered by the receipients in exchange.

(ii) Expenditure on purchase of shares or bonds is excluded because it is not payment for goods or services currently produced. It shows only transfer of property from one person to another.

2. Explain how the following are treated in estimating National Income *ISC 2018*

(i) Wheat grown by a farmer for self-consumption.

(ii) Earnings of the shareholders from the sale of shares.

(iii) Services rendered by family members to each other.

Ans (i) It is addition to the current flow of good in the economy no matter, it is used for self-consumption. So, imputed value of wheat will be included in national income.

(ii) It will not be included in national income because shares are just paper titles in economics which do not contribute in production of goods and services.

(iii) This is an example of self consumption of services (i.e. non-economic production that are not meant to sold nor is there any market for them, nor do they have a market price). So, service rendered by family member to each other will not be included in National Income.

3. Explain the following components of domestic factor income *ISC 2016*

(i) Compensation of employees

(ii) Operating surplus

KEY IDEA

Operating surplus is the sum total of income earned by factors other than labour.

Ans (i) **Compensation of employees** It is the total remuneration payable to employees, whether in cash or in kind and includes the following

(a) Wages and salaries in cash

(b) Payment in kind

(c) Employer's contribution to social security schemes

(d) Pension on retirement

(ii) **Operating surplus** It refers to income from property and entrepreneurship.

It includes the following items

(a) Rent and royalty

(b) Interest (c) Profit

4. Classify the following as final and intermediate goods. Give reasons for your answer *ISC 2013*

(i) A car purchased by a company for business purposes.

(ii) Pen or paper purchased by a consumer.

Ans (i) It is an intermediate good because it is used by the company as input in producing a good which is sold to the consumer.

(ii) It is final good because pen or paper is purchased for final consumption by the consumer.

5. Define compensation of employees and mention its components. *ISC 2011*

Or Explain the components of compensation of employees for calculation of National Income by income method. *ISC 2010*

Or Explain the components of compensation of employees. *ISC 2007*

Ans Income from work is known as 'compensation of employees'. It is the reward paid in cash or in kind by producers to their employees in the form of wages and salaries, social security benefits and retirement benefits.

Compensation of employees has the following main components

(i) **Wages and salaries** Every employee gets periodic (say monthly/daily) payments from their employers in consideration of the services rendered by them. It is known as wages and salaries.

It includes basis pay, bonus, commission, dearness allowance, house rent allowance, free meals, free clothing, etc.

(ii) **Employer's contribution to social security** It refers to payments towards provident fund, insurance schemes which are for the benefits or social security of the employees. But, contribution from employees are not considered under this head.

(iii) **Retirement pension** It refers to pension payments as a part of the 'service contract' between the employer and the employees.

6. Discuss the problem of double counting in the estimation of National Income. *ISC 2010*

Ans Double counting means counting value of the same commodity more than once in calculating National Income.

According to output method of calculating national income, value of only final goods and services produced by all the production units in the economy during a year should be taken.
In other words, value of intermediate goods should not be taken into account. But in actual practice, value of intermediate goods which have entered as inputs in production of final goods also gets included separately because every producer treats sale of its commodity as final product irrespective of what happens to it after sale.
As a result, there occurs double counting leading to overestimation of National Income.

There are two ways to avoid problem of double counting. These are

(i) Value of only final goods be included in estimating National Income.

(ii) Value added method be used in estimating National Income.

7. Estimate operating surplus from the following data **ISC 2009**

	₹ (in crores)
Profit before Tax	320
Royalty	30
Corporate Tax	100
Interest	415
Rent	327
Mixed Income	510
Dividend	200
Indirect Tax	180

Ans Operating Surplus = Profit before Tax + Royalty + Interest + Rent

= 320 + 30 + 415 + 327 = ₹ 1,092 crore

8. Calculate the operating surplus from the following data **ISC 2008**

	₹ (in crores)
Gross Value Added at Market Price	5,550
Wages and Salaries	1,200
Employer's Contribution to Social Security	250
Net Indirect Taxes	100
Consumption of Fixed Capital	75
Mixed Income	300

Ans As we know, Gross Domestic Product at Market Price (GDP_{MP}) is calculated by Income Method as

GDP_{MP} = Compensation of Employees + Operating Surplus + Mixed Income + Consumption of Fixed Capital + Net Indirect Taxes

Therefore, GDP_{MP} = 1,450 + 3,625 + 300 + 75 + 100 = ₹ 5,550 crore

Compensation of Employees = Wages and Salaries + Emloyer's Contribution of Social Security

= 1,200 + 250 = ₹ 1,450 crores

GDP_{MP} = (1,450 + Operating surplus + 300 + 75 + 100

5,550 − 1,925 = Operating surplus (As, GDP = ₹ 5,550 crore)

∴ Operating Surplus = ₹ 3,625 crore

9. Calculate the compensation of employees from the following data **ISC 2007**

	₹ (in crores)
Wages and Salaries Received by the Employees	125
Dearness Allowance	75
Medical Expenses on Employees	5
Life Insurance Premium Paid by Employees	2
Contribution to Provident Fund by Employer	10

Ans Calculation of Compensation of Employees

= Wages and Salaries Received by the Employees + Dearness Allowance + Medical Expenses on Employees + Contribution to Provident Fund by Employer

= 125 + 75 + 5 + 10 = ₹ 215 crore

Note Life insurance premium paid by employees is not a component of compensation of employees as it is expenditure incurred by employee.

10. Calculate the operating surplus from the following data **ISC 2006**

	₹ (in crores)
Compensation of Employees	1,000
Dividends	15,400
Rent	2,250
Interest	150
Undistributed Profits	2,400
Corporate Tax	300
Personal Income Tax	200

Ans Operating Surplus = Rent + Interest + Profits (Corporate tax + Undistributed profits + Dividends)

= 2,250 + 150 + (300 + 2,400 + 15,400) crore

= 2,250 + 150 + 18,100 crore = ₹ 20,500 crore

11. Explain any four major difficulties in calculating national income of a country. **ISC 2003**

Ans The measurement of national income is a complicated problem with the following difficulties

(i) **Non-availability of data** A significant part of every economy is engaged in the services of regular nature and operating their works in an unorganised way.

Persons like electricians, plumbers, small shopkeepers, street hawkers, etc do not keep their accounts and they have no correct information of their income. It is very difficult to calculate the income of such a group, consequently, National Income figure estimation becomes difficult.

(ii) **Danger of double counting** While computing the National Income, there is always the danger of double or multiple counting. Double counting means counting value of the same commodity more than once in calculating National Income. If care is not taken in estimating the income, the cost of the commodity is likely to be counted twice or more and due to which National Income will be overestimated.

(iii) **Own-account production** (or production for self-consumption) In developing countries, a significant part of the output is not exchanged for money in the market. It is either consumed directly by producers or bartered for other goods. This unorganised and non-monetised sector makes calculation of National Income difficult.

(iv) **Price level changes** National Income is measured in money terms. The measuring rod of money itself does not remain stable. This means that National Income can change without any change in output.

Difficulties in Calculating National Income
- Non-availability of data
- Danger of double counting
- Own-account production
- Price level changes

6 Marks Questions

1. Calculate GDP_{MP} and NNP_{FC} by value added method from the following data *ISC 2023*

S. No.	Items	₹ (in crores)
(i)	Net value added at factor cost in primary sector	6,000
(ii)	Net value added at factor cost in secondary sector	4,000
(iii)	Net value added at factor cost in tertiary sector	4,500
(iv)	Net factor income from abroad	(–)50
(v)	Net indirect tax	150
(vi)	Intermediate consumption	2,500
(vii)	Depreciation	500

Ans $GDP_{MP} = \text{(i)} + \text{(ii)} + \text{(iii)} + \text{(vii)} + \text{(v)}$

$= 6{,}000 + 4{,}000 + 4{,}500 + 500 + 150$

$=$ ₹ 15,150 crores

$NNP_{FC} = GDP_{MP} - \text{(vii)} - \text{(v)}$

$= 15{,}150 - 500 - 150$

$=$ ₹ 14,500 crore

2. Calculate national income and operating surplus from the following data *ISC 2023*

S. No.	Items	₹ (in crores)
(i)	Government final consumption expenditure	900
(ii)	Net factor income from abroad	210
(iii)	Private final consumption expenditure	1,000
(iv)	Net domestic capital formation	300
(v)	Profits	320
(vi)	Rent	190
(vii)	Net exports	(–)75
(viii)	Interest	200
(ix)	Net indirect taxes	265

Ans $NNP_{FC} = \text{(i)} + \text{(iii)} + \text{(iv)} + \text{(vii)} + \text{(ii)} - \text{(ix)}$

$= 900 + 210 + 300 + (-75) + 210 - 265$

$=$ ₹ 1,280 crore

Operating Surplus $= \text{(vi)} + \text{(viii)} + \text{(v)}$

$= 190 + 200 + 320$

$=$ ₹ 710 crore

3. Calculate domestic income and national income from the following information *ISC Specimen 2023*

S. No.	Items	₹ (in crores)
(i)	Rent	120
(ii)	Interest	15
(iii)	Profits	45
(iv)	Wages and salaries	330
(v)	Consumption of fixed capital	150
(vi)	Factor income earned abroad	30
(vii)	Factor income paid abroad	60
(viii)	Mixed income of self-employed	360
(ix)	Employer's contribution to social security schemes	30

Ans $NDP_{FC} = \text{(iv)} + \text{(ix)} + \text{(i)} + \text{(ii)} + \text{(iii)} + \text{(viii)}$

$= 330 + 30 + 120 + 15 + 45 + 360$

$=$ ₹ 900 crore

$NNP_{FC} = NDP_{FC} + (\text{vi} - \text{vii})$

$= 900 + (30 - 60)$

$=$ ₹ 870 crore

4. Calculate the GNP_{MP} and NPD_{FC} from the following data *ISC Specimen 2023*

S. No.	Items	₹ (in crores)
(i)	Government final consumption expenditure	800
(ii)	Net factor income earned from abroad	(–)10
(iii)	Import	300
(iv)	Export	250
(v)	Net indirect taxes	70
(vi)	Private final consumption expenditure	1,200
(vii)	Net domestic capital formation	385
(viii)	Consumptioin of fixed capital	85

Ans $GNP_{MP} = (vi) + (i) + (vii) + (viii) + (iv - iii) + (ii)$

$= 1{,}200 + 800 + 385 + 85 + (250 - 300) + (-10)$

$=$ ₹ 2,410 crore

$NDP_{FC} = GNP_{MP} - (viii) - (ii) - (v)$

$= 2{,}410 - 85 - (-10) - 70$

$=$ ₹ 2,265 crore

5. Explain the steps involved in calculating the national income by income method. *ISC Sem II Specimen 2022*

Or Explain the income method of measuring National Income. State two precautions taken while calculating National Income by the income method. *ISC 2008*

Ans According to this method, National Income is measured in terms of factor payments (wages, rent, interest and profit) to the owners of factors of production (labour, land, capital and enterprise) during an accounting year.

The main steps involved in estimating National Income by income method are

(i) Identify enterprises which employ factors of production (i.e. land, labour, capital and entrepreneur).

(ii) Classify factor payments into various categories like rent, wages, interest and profits.

(iii) Estimate amount of factor payments made by each enterprise.

(iv) Sum up or factor payments made within domestic territory to get domestic income (Net Domestic Product at Factor Cost).

(v) Estimate net factor income from abroad which is added to domestic income to derive National Income.

Precautions For accurate National Income by income method, following precautions need to be taken

(i) Sale and purchase of second hand goods are excluded since they are not part of production of current year, but commission paid on sale of second hand goods is included as it is reward for rendering productive services.

(ii) Income from illegal activities like smuggling, black marketing, etc as well as windfall gains (e.g. Gains from lotteries) are not included in National Income.

6. From the following data, calculate GNP_{FC}, NDP_{FC} and national income. *ISC 2020*

S. No.	Items	₹ (in crores)
(i)	Private final consumption expenditure	950
(ii)	Gross domestic fixed capital formation	370
(iii)	Consumption of fixed capital	20
(iv)	Government final consumption expenditure	410
(v)	Closing stock	300
(vi)	Subsidy	80
(vii)	Net exports	(–)50
(viii)	Wages and salaries	780
(ix)	Net factor income from abroad	(–)40
(x)	Indirect tax	180
(xi)	Opening stock	150
(xii)	Profit before tax	200

Ans (i) Gross Domestic Product at Market Price (GDP_{MP})

= Private final consumption expenditure + Government final consumption expenditure + Gross domestic capital formation (Gross domestic fixed capital formation + Change in stock) + Net exports (Exports – Imports)

$= 950 + 410 + [370 + (300 - 150)] + (-50)$

$=$ ₹ 1,830 crore

Now, $GNP_{FC} = GDP_{MP}$ + Net factor income from abroad – Net indirect taxes

$= 1{,}830 + (-40) - [180 - 80] =$ ₹ 1,690 crore

(ii) $NDP_{FC} = GDP_{MP}$ – Consumption of fixed capital – Net indirect taxes

$= 1{,}830 - 20 - [180 - 80] =$ ₹ 1,710 crore

(iii) National Income (NNP_{FC}) $= GDP_{MP}$ – Consumption of fixed capital + Net factor income from abroad – Net indirect taxes

$= 1{,}830 - 20 + (-40) - (180 - 80) =$ ₹ 1,670 crore

Common Mistake Students get confused when net exports are given as negative. When net exports are negative, they are treated as net imports.

7. From the following data, calculate National Income by output method and income method *ISC 2019*

S. No.	Items	₹ (in crores)
(i)	Value of output	2,500
(ii)	Value of intermediate consumption	1,300
(iii)	Subsidies	40
(iv)	Rent	110
(v)	Employer's contribution to social security	30
(vi)	Profit	50
(vii)	Wages and salaries	340
(viii)	Interest	10
(ix)	Mixed income of self-employed	360
(x)	Indirect tax	180
(xi)	NFIA	(–)30
(xii)	Consumption of fixed capital	160

Ans (i) **By Output Method**

GDP_{MP} = Value of output – Value of intermediate consumption

$= 2{,}500 - 13{,}00 = ₹ 1{,}200$ crore

National Income (NNP_{FC}) = GDP_{MP} – Consumption of fixed capital + Net factor income from abroad – Net indirect tax

$= 1{,}200 - 160 + (-30) - (180 - 40)$

$= 1{,}200 - 160 - 30 - 140$

$= ₹ 870$ crore

(ii) **By Income Method**

NDP_{FC} = Compensation of employees + Operating surplus + Mixed income

= (Employer's contribution to social security + Wages and interest) + (Rent + Interest + Profit) + Mixed income

$= (30 + 340) + (110 + 10 + 50) + 360$

$= 370 + 170 + 360$

$= ₹ 900$ crore

National Income (NNP_{FC}) = NDP_{FC} + Net factor income from abroad

$= 900 + (-30)$

$= ₹ 870$ crore

Value Points

For getting maximum marks, following value points can be included in the answer

- Mention all formulae to be used in numerical.
- Mention the units.

8. From the following data, calculate National Income by income method and expenditure method *ISC 2018*

		₹ (in crores)
(i)	Compensation of Employees	700
(ii)	Government Final Consumption Expenditure	750
(iii)	Net Factor Income from Abroad	(–) 10
(iv)	Net Exports	(–) 15
(v)	Profits	600
(vi)	Net Indirect Taxes	60
(vii)	Mixed Income of Self-employed	350
(viii)	Rent	200
(ix)	Interest	310
(x)	Private Final Consumption Expenditure	1,100
(xi)	Net Domestic Capital Formation	385
(xii)	Consumption of Fixed Capital	65

Ans (i) National Income (Income Method)

National Income = (i) + (v) + (viii) + (ix) + (vii) + (iii)

$= 700 + 600 + 200 + 310 + 350 + (-10)$

$= ₹ 2{,}150$ crore

(ii) National Income (Expenditure Method)

National Income = (ii) + (x) + (xi) + (iv) – (vi) + (iii)

$= 750 + 1{,}100 + 385 + (-15) - 60 + (-10)$

$= ₹ 2{,}150$ crore

9. Calculate GNP at FC from the following data by using income method and expenditure method *ISC 2017*

		₹ (in crores)
(i)	Operating Surplus	600
(ii)	Exports	30
(iii)	Imports	60
(iv)	Private Final Consumption Expenditure	1,000
(v)	Net Indirect Tax	60
(vi)	Compensation of Employees	900
(vii)	Mixed Income of Self-employed	160
(viii)	Gross Domestic Capital Formation	330
(ix)	Depreciation	30
(x)	Net Factor Income from Abroad	(–20)
(xi)	Government Final Consumption Expenditure	450

Ans **Gross National Product at Factor Cost** (GNP_{FC}) **by Income Method** = Compensation of Employees + Operating Surplus + Mixed Income of Self Employed + Depreciation + Net Factor Income from Abroad (NFIA)

$= 900 + 600 + 160 + 30 + (-20) = ₹ 1{,}670$ crores

Gross National Product at Factor Cost (GNP_{FC}) **by Expenditure Method** = Government Final Consumption Expenditure + Private Final Consumption Expenditure + Gross Domestic Capital Formation + (Exports − Imports) − Net Indirect Taxes + Net Factor Income from Abroad

$= 450 + 1{,}000 + 330 + (30 - 60) - 60 + (-20)$

= ₹ 1,670 crores

10. From the following data calculate GNP_{MP} and National Income by using Value Added Method

ISC 2016

		₹ (in crores)
(i)	Gross Value of Output in Primary Sector (at FC)	950
(ii)	Gross Value of Output in Secondary Sector (at FC)	470
(iii)	Gross Value of Output in Tertiary Sector (at FC)	500
(iv)	Value of Intermediate Goods in Primary Sector	360
(v)	Value of Intermediate Goods in Secondary Sector	200
(vi)	Value of Intermediate Goods in Tertiary Sector	175
(vii)	Depreciation	20
(viii)	Indirect Tax	35
(ix)	Subsidy	10
(x)	Net Factor Income from Abroad	4

KEY IDEA

In this case, gross output is given in FC but by value added method, the aggregate we get is in MP. So, NIT needs to be adjusted.

Ans Gross National Product at Market Price (GNP_{MP})

= Gross Values of output in Primary Sector (at FC) + Gross Values of Output in Secondary Sector (at FC) + Gross Values of Output in Tertiary Sector (at FC) − Value of Intermediate Goods in Primary Sector − Value of Intermediate Goods in Secondary Sector − Value of Intermediate Goods in Tertiary Sector + Indirect Tax − Subsidy

$= 950 + 470 + 500 - 360 - 200 - 175 + 35 - 10$

= ₹1,210 crore

National Income or Net National Product at Factor Cost (NNP_{FC})

= GNP_{MP} − Depreciation + Net Factor Income from Abroad − Indirect Tax + Subsidy

$= 1{,}210 - 20 + 4 - 35 + 10$

= ₹1,169 crore

11. From the following data, calculate GNP_{MP} and NNP_{FC} by expenditure method

		₹ (in crores)
(i)	Mixed Income of Self-employed	450
(ii)	Compensation of Employees	550
(iii)	Private Final Consumption Expenditure	1,000
(iv)	Net Factor Income from Abroad	(−)20
(v)	Net Indirect Taxes	150
(vi)	Consumption of Fixed Capital	170
(vii)	Net Domestic Capital Formation	380
(viii)	Net Exports	(−)30
(ix)	Profits	400
(x)	Rent	150
(xi)	Interest	200
(xii)	Government Final Consumption Expenditure	550

ISC 2015

Ans **Computation of GNP_{MP} and NNP_{FC} by expenditure method**

GNP_{MP} = Government Final Consumption Expenditure + Private Final Consumption Expenditure + Net Domestic Capital Formation + Depreciation + Net Exports + Net Factor Income form Abroad

$= 550 + 1{,}000 + 380 + 170 + (-30) + (-20)$

= ₹ 2,050 crore

NNP_{FC} = GNP_{MP} − Depreciation − Net Indirect Taxes

= 2,050 − 170 − 150 = ₹ 1,730 crore

12. Calculate National Income and operating surplus from the following data

ISC 2014

	₹ (in crores)
Government Final Consumption Expenditure	800
Net Factor Income Earned from Abroad	(−) 110
Private Final Consumption Expenditure	900
Net Domestic Capital Formation	200
Profits	220
Rent	90
Net Exports	(−) 25
Interest	100
Net Indirect Taxes	165

Ans Calculation of National Income is as under

= Government Final Consumption Expenditure + Private Final Consumption Expenditure + Net Domestic Capital Formation + Net Exports + Net Factor Income Earned from Abroad − Net Indirect Taxes

$= 800 + 900 + 200 + (-25) + (-110) - 165$

= ₹ 1,600 crore

Calculation of operating surplus is as under

Rent + Profits + Interest = 90 + 220 + 100 = ₹ 310 crore

13. Calculate National Income and GDP_{MP} by the income method using the following information *ISC 2013*

	₹ (in crores)
Private Final Consumption Expenditure	1,300
Net Factor Income Earned from Abroad	50
Mixed Income of the Self-employed	500
Subsidies	100
Indirect Taxes	200
Consumption of Fixed Capital	1,000
Operating Surplus	5,000
Compensation of Employees	1,500

Ans National Income = Mixed Income of the Self-employed + Operating Surplus + Compensation of Employees + NFIA

= 500 + 5,000 + 1,500 + 50 = ₹ 7,050 crore

GDP_{MP} = National Income − Net Factor Income Earned from Abroad + Net Indirect Taxes + Consumption of Fixed Capital

= 7,050 − 50 + 100 (200 − 100) + 1,000

= ₹ 8,100 crore

14. Calculate National Income and Net Domestic Product at Market Price by income method from the following data *ISC 2012*

	₹ (in crores)
Value of Output	800
Value of Intermediate Consumption	400
Subsidies	10
Indirect Taxes	60
Factor Income Received from Abroad	10
Factor Income Paid Abroad	20
Mixed Income of Self-employed	120
Rent and Royalty	40
Interest and Profit	20
Wages and Salaries	110
Consumption of Fixed Capital	50
Employer's Contribution to Social Security	10

Ans Net Domestic Product at Market Price

= Mixed Income of Self-employed + Rent and Royalty + Interest and Profit + Wages and Salaries + Employer's Contribution to Social Security + Indirect Taxes − Subsidies

= 120 + 40 + 20 + 110 + 10 + 60 − 10 = 350 crore

National Income = NDP_{MP} + Factor Income Received from Abroad − Factor Income Paid Abroad − Net Indirect Taxes

= 350 + 10 − 20 − (60 − 10)

= 290 crore

15. Explain briefly the steps involved in calculating National Income by expenditure method. Mention any two precautions which are required to be taken while calculating National Income by this method. *ISC 2009*

Ans Refer to Q. No. 1 (3/4 Marks).

16. Describe the steps involved in estimating the National Income by the value added method. *ISC 2007*

Or Discuss briefly the production method of estimating National Income of a country. *ISC 2003*

Ans National Income of a country by production method (or value added method) can be calculated by the following steps

(i) First of all, the production units/entities have to be identified which are located in the domestic economy and then classify them into three industrial sectors such as primary, secondary and tertiary sectors. Primary sector consists of agriculture and animal husbandry activities, fishing, etc.

Secondary sector produces manufactured goods by converting one type of commodity into another type of commodity, e.g. Hotel businesses, construction, factories, etc. Tertiary sector includes services like educational, medical, banking, etc.

(ii) Secondly, we calculate Net Value Added at Factor Cost (NVA_{FC}) by each producing unit. It can be estimated as under

NVA_{FC} = Value of Output − Value of Intermediate Consumption − Depreciation − Net Indirect Taxes

(iii) Thirdly, calculate net value added of each industrial sector by summing up Net Value Added at Factor Cost of all producing units falling in each industrial sector.

(iv) Fourthly, compute domestic income by adding up Net Value Added at Factor Cost of all industrial sectors.

(v) Finally, estimate Net Factor Income from Abroad and add it to domestic income for deriving National Income (Net National Product at Factor Cost).

The methodology for finding National Income (NNP_{FC}) can be briefed in following manner

Value of Output of Primary Sector		...
Value of Output of Secondary Sector		...
Value of Output of Tertiary Sector		...
Gross Value of Output		...
(–) Value of Intermediate Consumption of		
(i) Primary Sector	...	
(ii) Secondary Sector	...	
(iii) Tertiary Sector	...	(...)
Gross Value Added at Market Price (GVA_{MP})		...
(–) Depreciation		(...)
(–) Net Indirect Taxes		(...)
Domestic Income (Net Domestic Product at Factor Cost)		...
(+) Net Factor Income from Abroad		...
National Income (NNP_{FC})		...

17. Define the terms mixed income of self-employed and operating surplus. ***ISC 2006***

Ans **Mixed income of self-employed** It refers to the income of the self-employed persons using their own labour, land, capital and entrepreneurship to produce goods and services.

In other words, income of own account workers like farmers, barbers, etc and uncorporated enterprises like small shopkeepers, retailers, etc is known as mixed income. They do not maintain proper books of accounts. Also, the income they earn is not attributable to any one head.

Operating surplus The sum of income from property and income from entrepreneurship is known as operating surplus. In simple terms, operating surplus is the sum total of rent, royalty, interest and profit. The components of operating surplus are briefly explained below

(i) **Rent** It is the factor income earned from lending the services of land and building.

(ii) **Royalty** It is the income received by landlord for granting leasing rights of subsoil assets.

(iii) **Interest** It is the payment which the borrower makes to the lender of the capital for using his capital for a certain period of time.

(iv) **Profit** It is the reward that entrepreneur gets for being in business and undertaking the risk involved therein. It can be taken as sum of corporate tax, dividends and undistributed profits.

Concept Enhancer Royalty is generally paid on intellectual properties.

18. Explain four problems faced in the calculation of the National Income in underdeveloped countries. ***ISC 2005***

Or

Discuss four problems faced in computing National Income of various countries. ***ISC 2001***

Ans Refer to Q. No. 11 (3/4 Marks).

19. Estimate compensation of employees from the following data relating to a firm ***ISC 2005***

	₹ (in thousands)
Wages and Salaries Received by the Staff	1,000
Value of Free Medical Facilities	105
Travelling Allowances Paid to Staff	70
Employer's Contribution to Employees' State Insurance Fund	40
Commission Received by Workers in Sales Department	30
Interest Free Loans Given to Staff	201
Value of Subsidised Food	52

KEY IDEA
Commission received is a factor income.

Ans **Calculation of Compensation of Employees**

= Wages and Salaries + Free Medical Facilities + Employer's Contribution to Employees State Insurance Fund + Commission Received + Value of Subsidised Food

= ₹ (1000 + 105 + 40 + 30 + 52) = ₹ 1,227 thousand

20. Explain four factors that determine the size of national income. ***ISC 2000***

Ans The determinants (or factors) which influence the size of national income are as follows

(i) **The stock of factors of production** One of the very important factor which influences the size of the National Income is the quality and quantity of the country's stock of factors of production. The factors are land, labour capital and entrepreneurship. Land supplies man with gifts of nature. It provides him with agricultural goods and raw material for production. The production of land depends upon fertility of soil, climate and irrigation system in the country.

Factors Influencing Size of National Income
- The stock of factors of production
- Labour
- State of technical knowledge
- Political stability

If the land is fertile, the size of the National Income will be quite large and if the quality of land is poor, the size of National Income will be small. In a similar way, other factor also affect the level of National Income in the economy.

(ii) **Labour** The size of the National Income greatly depends upon the quality and quantity of labour in the country. If labour is efficient and its size is consistent, the size of the National Income will be large and if the labour is underfed, underclothed, unskilled and has no ambition to rise, the size of the National Income will be small.

(iii) **State of technical knowledge** If the state of technical knowledge is poor in the country, the size of the National Income will be small, but if advance technical knowledge is available, then the size of the National Income will be large.

(iv) **Political stability** Political instability greatly hampers economic progress. If there is political stability in the country, the production can be maintained at the highest level. The size of National Income will be large. In case of political instability, the production will be adversely affected and so the size of the National Income will be small.

Case Based Question

Case 1

There are only two kinds of producers in the economy. They are the wheat producers (or the farmers) and the bread makers (the bakers). The wheat producers grow wheat and they do not need any input other than human labour. They sell a part of the wheat to the bakers. The bakers do not need any other raw materials besides wheat to produce bread.

Let us suppose that in a year the total value of wheat that the farmers have produced is ₹ 100. Out of this, they have sold ₹ 50 worth of wheat to the bakers. The bakers have used this amount of wheat completely during the year and have produced ₹ 200 worth of bread.

If we follow the simple way of aggregating the values of production of the sectors, we would add ₹ 200 (value of production of the bakers) to ₹ 100 (value of production of farmers).

(i) What is the value of total production in the economy?

Ans ₹ 300

(ii) Intermediate goods are used .... the production process.

Ans within

(iii) How can we avoid the problem of double counting in the above situation?

Ans There are two alternative ways of avoiding double counting

(a) Take value of final output.

(b) Take value added of each firm.

(iv) Briefly explain the process of calculating value added by a firm.

Ans Value added is defined as the gross receipts of a firm minus the cost of goods and services purchased from other firms. Value added includes wages, salaries, interest, depreciation, rent, taxes and profit.

(v) Differentiate between intermediate goods and final goods.

Ans

Intermediate goods	Final goods
Used as inputs in the production process, meaning they are used to create other goods and services. They are not directly consumed by the final user, but are included in the value of the final product.	Not used as inputs in the production process, meaning they are the final products that are ready to be consumed or used by the final user. They are not included in the value of any other product and are directly consumed by the final user.
Examples of intermediate goods include raw materials, components and parts used in the production of final goods.	Examples of final goods include finished products such as consumer goods and durable goods like cars, appliances and furniture. They are not only used for personal consumption but also for capital formation.

CHAPTER TEST

01 Mark Questions

1. National income is a
   (a) Hypothetical concept (b) Non-economic concept
   (c) Stock concept (d) Flow concept

2. Money flow is the flow of
   (a) Goods (b) Factor payments
   (c) Services (d) Goods and services

3. Which of the following is a part of profit?
   (a) Dividend (b) Undistributed profit
   (c) Corporate tax (d) All of these

4. Which of these is not included while calculating national income?
   (a) Mixed income (b) Royalty
   (c) Income tax (d) None of these

5. NDP_{FC} is equal to NDP_{MP} less net indirect tax. State true or false.

6. Double counting can be avoided by summing up total output of firms. State true or false.

7. ...... refers to the income of the household that they can spend on consumption expenditure.

8. Subsidies are an example of .... payments.

9. What is gross national disposable income?

10. Under what circumstances, domestic income can exceed national income?

02 Marks Questions

11. Why transfer incomes are not included while estimating National Income?

12. 'Machine purchased' is always a final good. Do you agree?

13. Write the formula to calculate national disposable income.

14. If compensation of employees in a firm, constitutes 55% of Net Value Added at Factor Cost of a firm, find the proportion of operating surplus.

15. Write two examples of intermediate consumption.

03/04 Marks Questions

16. Interest on public debt is treated as an intermediate consumption. Why?

17. Calculate GNP_{FC}

	₹ (in crores)
NDP_{MP}	25,000
Depreciation	5,000
Indirect Taxes	130
Subsidies	30
Factor Income from Abroad	400
Factor Income to Abroad	600

18. Explain the concept of 'normal resident'.

19. 'Sum of value added' is equal to 'sum of factor income'. Do you agree? Why or why not?

06 Marks Questions

20. Why are exports included in the estimation of domestic product by the expenditure method? Can gross domestic product be greater than gross national product? When?

21. How will you treat the following while estimating National Income?
    (i) Salary received by Russian's in Indian Embassy in Russia.
    (ii) Profit earned by a Foreign Bank in India.
    (iii) Wealth tax received by the government.

Answers

1. (d) Flow concept
2. (d) Goods and services
3. (d) All of these
4. (d) None of these
5. True
6. True
7. Personal disposable income
8. transfer

Assertion/Reasoning Based MCQs

Chapter 1 Theory of Consumer Behaviour and Demand

Direction (Q. No. 1 to 5) *There are two statements marked as Assertion (A) and Reason (R). Read the statements and choose the appropriate option from the options given below*

(a) Both Assertion (A) and Reason (R) are true and Reason (R) is the correct explanation of Assertion (A)
(b) Both Assertion (A) and Reason (R) are true, but Reason (R) is not the correct explanation of Assertion (A)
(c) Assertion (A) is true, but Reason (R) is false
(d) Both Assertion (A) and Reason (R) are false

1. **Assertion** (A) Different persons derive different levels of utility from consumption of similar types of commodities.

Reason (R) The want satisfying power of any commodity is known as its utility, which is measured in 'utils' under cardinal approach.

Ans (b) Different consumers getting different utility from same good makes the utility subjective in nature i.e., depends upon the user of the good.

2. **Assertion** (A) Consumer equilibrium occurs when the marginal utility per rupee spent is equal for all goods.

Reason (R) At consumer equilibrium, the consumer maximises his/her total utility by allocating his/her budget in a way that the marginal utility derived from the last rupee spent on each good is the same.

Ans (a) Both Assertion (A) and Reason (R) are true and Reason (R) is the correct explanation of Assertion (A)

3. **Assertion** (A) When consumers make choices about the quantity of goods and services to consume, it is presumed that their objective is to maximise total utility.

Reason (R) In maximising total utility, the consumer faces a number of constraints, the most important of which are the consumer's income and services that the consumer wishes to consume.

Ans (b) Both Assertion (A) and Reason (R) are true, but Reason (R) is not the correct explanation of Assertion (A)

4. **Assertion** (A) Higher IC represents higher satisfaction due to monotonic preferences.

Reason (R) A consumer always prefers more units of a good over fewer units.

Ans (a) Both Assertion (A) and Reason (R) are true and Reason (R) is the correct explanation of Assertion (A)

5. **Assertion** (A) Veblen goods are an exception to the law of demand.

Reason (R) Veblen goods are luxury goods for which demand increases as the price increases, contrary to the law of demand.

Ans (c) Veblen goods are luxury goods that exhibit an upward sloping demand curve, contrary to the downward sloping demand curve predicted by the law of demand.

Chapter 2 Elasticity of Demand

Direction (Q. No. 1 to 5) *There are two statements marked as Assertion (A) and Reason (R). Read the statements and choose the appropriate option from the options given below*

(a) Both Assertion (A) and Reason (R) are true and Reason (R) is the correct explanation of Assertion (A)
(b) Both Assertion (A) and Reason (R) are true, but Reason (R) is not the correct explanation of Assertion (A)
(c) Assertion (A) is true, but Reason (R) is false
(d) Both Assertion (A) and Reason (R) are false

1. **Assertion** (A) Demand for durable goods has higher elasticity of demand.

Reason (R) Demand for durable goods can be postponed once they are demanded at present.

Ans (a) Both Assertion (A) and Reason (R) are true and Reason (R) is the correct explanation of Assertion (A)

2. **Assertion** (A) Perfectly inelastic demand implies that quantity demanded does not change regardless of price changes.

Reason (R) Perfectly inelastic demand occurs rarely in the real world. Close examples might include rare medicines or fresh water in a time of drought. Regardless of any price changes, these products will remain in demand.

Ans (b) Both Assertion (A) and Reason (R) are true, but Reason (R) is not the correct explanation of Assertion (A)

3. **Assertion** (A) Unitary elastic demand occurs when the percentage change in quantity demanded is equal to the percentage change in price.

Reason (R) The unit elasticity of demand is a dividing line to distinguish between relatively elastic demand and relatively inelastic demand.

Ans (b) Both Assertion (A) and Reason (R) are true, but Reason (R) is not the correct explanation of Assertion (A)

4. **Assertion** (A) Cross elasticity of demand helps to determine whether two goods are substitutes or complements.

Reason (R) Cross elasticity of demand measures the responsiveness of quantity demanded of one good to changes in the price of another good, indicating whether the goods are substitutes or complements.

Ans (a) Both Assertion (A) and Reason (R) are true and Reason (R) is the correct explanation of Assertion (A)

5. **Assertion** (A) A commodity which can be put to several uses, is price inelastic.

Reason (R) As price of such commodities falls, number of buyers decreases in the market.

Ans (d) Goods which can be put to several uses have elastic demand. Also, as price of such commodities falls, number of buyers increases in the market.

Chapter 3 Supply and Elasticity of Supply

Direction (Q. No. 1 to 5) *There are two statements marked as Assertion (A) and Reason (R). Read the statements and choose the appropriate option from the options given below*

(a) Both Assertion (A) and Reason (R) are true and Reason (R) is the correct explanation of Assertion (A)
(b) Both Assertion (A) and Reason (R) are true, but Reason (R) is not the correct explanation for Assertion (A)
(c) Assertion (A) is true, but Reason (R) is false
(d) Both Assertion (A) and Reason (R) are false

1. **Assertion** (A) An individual supply curve slope upwards.

Reason (R) There exists a positive relationship between price and quantity supplied.

Ans (a) Both Assertion (A) and Reason (R) are true and Reason (R) is the correct explanation of Assertion (A)

2. **Assertion** (A) Contraction in supply leads to a downward movement along the same supply curve.

Reason (R) Downward movement along the same supply curve occurs due to an increase in price of the commodity, other factors remaining constant.

Ans (c) There is a direct relationship between own price of a commodity and its quantity supplied.

3. **Assertion** (A) Supply is that part of stock which a seller is ready to sell at a certain price during a certain period of time.

Reason (R) Supply depends on stock and price in market.

Ans (b) Both Assertion (A) and Reason (R) are true, but Reason (R) is not the correct explanation of Assertion (A)

4. **Assertion** (A) In the case of perfectly inelastic supply, the supply curve is a vertical straight line supply curve.

Reason (R) In case of $E_s = 0$, supply does not change with change in price.

Ans (a) Both Assertion (A) and Reason (R) are true and Reason (R) is the correct explanation of Assertion (A)

5. **Assertion** (A) Inelastic supply occurs when the percentage change in quantity supplied is less than the percentage change in price.

Reason (R) Inelastic supply implies that changes in price result in proportionately smaller changes in quantity supplied due to the limited responsiveness of producers to price fluctuations.

Ans (b) Both Assertion (A) and Reason (R) are true, but Reason (R) is not the correct explanation of Assertion (A)

Chapter 4 Concept of Production

Direction (Q. No. 1 to 5) *There are two statements marked as Assertion (A) and Reason (R). Read the statements and choose the appropriate option from the options given below*

(a) Both Assertion (A) and Reason (R) are true and Reason (R) is the correct explanation of Assertion (A)
(b) Both Assertion (A) and Reason (R) are true, but Reason (R) is not the correct explanation of Assertion (A)
(c) Assertion (A) is true, but Reason (R) is false
(d) Both Assertion (A) and Reason (R) are false

1. **Assertion** (A) Production refers to the process of transforming inputs into output to satisfy human wants.

Reason (R) The main objective of production is to create goods and services that fulfill the needs and desires of individuals.

Ans (a) Both Assertion (A) and Reason (R) are true and Reason (R) is the correct explanation of Assertion (A)

2. **Assertion** (A) Factors of production are the resources required for the production process.

Reason (R) Factors of production include land, labour, capital and entrepreneurship, which are essential for producing goods and services.

Ans (a) Both Assertion (A) and Reason (R) are true and Reason (R) is the correct explanation of Assertion (A)

3. **Assertion** (A) The law of variable proportion explains the relationship between the quantity of a variable input and the quantity of output.

Reason (R) According to the law of variable proportion, as more units of a variable input are added to a fixed input, the marginal product initially increases but eventually diminishes.

Ans (b) Both Assertion (A) and Reason (R) are true, but Reason (R) is not the correct explanation of Assertion (A)

4. **Assertion** (A) A rational producer always seeks to operate in phase II of law of variable proportions.

Reason (R) In phase II of law of variable proportions, marginal product is negative.

Ans (c) In stage II, marginal product starts decreasing but remains positive.

5. **Assertion** (A) In phase I of law of variable proportions, there are increasing returns to scale.

Reason (R) At this stage, greater use of variable factors makes it possible to utilise the fixed indivisible factors fully and to introduce a greater degree of division of labour.

Ans (a) Both Assertion (A) and Reason (R) are true and Reason (R) is the correct explanation of Assertion (A)

Chapter 5 Cost and Revenue

Direction (Q. No. 1 to 5) *There are two statements marked as Assertion (A) and Reason (R). Read the statements and choose the appropriate option from the options given below*

(a) Both Assertion (A) and Reason (R) are true and Reason (R) is the correct explanation of Assertion (A)
(b) Both Assertion (A) and Reason (R) are true, but Reason (R) is not the correct explanation of Assertion (A)
(c) Assertion (A) is true, but Reason (R) is false
(d) Both Assertion (A) and Reason (R) are false

1. **Assertion** (A) Fixed costs are expenses that do not change with the level of output.

Reason (R) Fixed costs are incurred by a firm regardless of the quantity of output produced.

Ans (a) Both Assertion (A) and Reason (R) are true and Reason (R) is the correct explanation of Assertion (A)

2. **Assertion** (A) Variable costs are expenses that change with the level of output.

Reason (R) Variable costs increase or decrease in direct proportion to the quantity of output produced.

Ans (a) Both Assertion (A) and Reason (R) are true and Reason (R) is the correct explanation of Assertion (A)

3. **Assertion** (A) Average fixed cost decreases as output increases.

Reason (R) Average fixed cost is calculated by dividing total fixed cost by the quantity of output produced, resulting in a declining average as output expands.

Ans (a) Both Assertion (A) and Reason (R) are true and Reason (R) is the correct explanation of Assertion (A)

4. **Assertion** (A) When price remains the same at all levels of output, then the Total Revenue (TR) curve is a positively sloped straight line.

Reason (R) In the case of constant prices, MR is constant, i.e., TR increases at a constant rate.

Ans (a) Both Assertion (A) and Reason (R) are true and Reason (R) is the correct explanation of Assertion (A)

5. **Assertion** (A) Total revenue is calculated by multiplying the quantity of output sold by the price per unit.

Reason (R) Total revenue represents the overall income generated by selling a specific quantity of output at a given price level.

Ans (a) Both Assertion (A) and Reason (R) are true and Reason (R) is the correct explanation of Assertion (A)

Chapter 6 Forms of Market and Application Tools of Demand and Supply

Direction (Q. No. 1 to 5) *There are two statements marked as Assertion (A) and Reason (R). Read the statements and choose the appropriate option from the options given below*

(a) Both Assertion (A) and Reason (R) are true and Reason (R) is the correct explanation of Assertion (A)
(b) Both Assertion (A) and Reason (R) are true, but Reason (R) is not the correct explanation of Assertion (A)
(c) Assertion (A) is true, but Reason (R) is false
(d) Both Assertion (A) and Reason (R) are false

1. **Assertion** (A) A monopoly firm has significant barriers to entry, restricting the entry of new firms into the market.

Reason (R) Monopoly firm often possess exclusive rights, patents or control over scarce resources, making it difficult for new firms to enter the market and compete.

Ans (a) Both Assertion (A) and Reason (R) are true and Reason (R) is the correct explanation of Assertion (A)

2. **Assertion** (A) Price discrimination refers to a strategy where a firm charges different prices for the same product by different customers or markets.

Reason (R) Price discrimination allows firms to maximise their profits by segmenting the market and charging higher prices to customers with a higher willingness to pay.

Ans (a) Both Assertion (A) and Reason (R) are true and Reason (R) is the correct explanation of Assertion (A)

3. **Assertion** (A) Producer surplus is the difference between the price a producer receives for a good and the minimum price he/she is willing to accept.

Reason (R) Producer surplus represents the additional benefit or profit gained by producers when they receive a price higher than their cost of production.

Ans (a) Both Assertion (A) and Reason (R) are true and Reason (R) is the correct explanation of Assertion (A)

4. **Assertion** (A) Firm under perfect competition earn only normal profit in the long-run.

Reason (R) Under this market, any super normal profit in the short-run will be eliminated due to entrance of new firms, while any loss in short-run will be eliminated due to exit of some firms.

Ans (a) Both Assertion (A) and Reason (R) are true and Reason (R) is the correct explanation of Assertion (A)

5. **Assertion** (A) Under oligopoly, every firm remains alert to the actions of other firms and keep plan for counterattack.

Reason (R) Under this market, firms try to increase their market share through advertisement and other sales promotion techniques.

Ans (b) Both Assertion (A) and Reason (R) are true, but Reason (R) is not the correct explanation of Assertion (A)

Chapter 7 Theory of Income Determination

Direction (Q. No. 1 to 5) *There are two statements marked as Assertion (A) and Reason (R). Read the statements and choose the appropriate option from the options given below*

(a) Both Assertion (A) and Reason (R) are true and Reason (R) is the correct explanation of Assertion (A)
(b) Both Assertion (A) and Reason (R) are true, but Reason (R) is not the correct explanation of Assertion (A)
(c) Assertion (A) is true, but Reason (R) is false
(d) Both Assertion (A) and Reason (R) are false

1. **Assertion** (A) Consumption curve makes an intercept on the Y-axis, at some point above the origin.

Reason (R) People need certain basic goods and services to sustain themselves, even if income is zero.

Ans (a) Both Assertion (A) and Reason (R) are true and Reason (R) is the correct explanation of Assertion (A)

2. **Assertion** (A) The sum of APC and APS is equal to one.

Reason (R) Income is either used for consumption or for saving.

Ans (a) Both Assertion (A) and Reason (R) are true and Reason (R) is the correct explanation of Assertion (A)

3. **Assertion** (A) Rich people have a lower propensity to consume as compared to poor people.

Reason (R) Consumption can never be zero even if the national income is zero.

Ans (b) Both Assertion (A) and Reason (R) are true, but Reason (R) is not the correct explanation of Assertion (A)

4. **Assertion** (A) Induced investment expenditure refers to the total investment expenditure which changes with change in national income.

Reason (R) Induced investment expenditure is made in the economy that remains unaltered.

Ans (c) Assertion (A) is true, but Reason (R) is false

5. **Assertion** (A) During excess demand, there is no change in the level of employment.

Reason (R) At the time of excess demand, there is no involuntary unemployment.

Ans (a) Both Assertion (A) and Reason (R) are true and Reason (R) is the correct explanation of Assertion (A)

Chapter 8 Money and Banking

Direction (Q. No. 1 to 5) *There are two statements marked as Assertion (A) and Reason (R). Read the statements and choose the appropriate option from the options given below*

(a) Both Assertion (A) and Reason (R) are true and Reason (R) is the correct explanation of Assertion (A)
(b) Both Assertion (A) and Reason (R) are true, but Reason (R) is not the correct explanation of Assertion (A)
(c) Assertion (A) is true, but Reason (R) is false
(d) Both Assertion (A) and Reason (R) are false

1. **Assertion** (A) Plastic money is becoming more popular these days.

Reason (R) It is considered as safe method and enables to avoid carrying each.

Ans (a) Both Assertion (A) and Reason (R) are true and Reason (R) is the correct explanation of Assertion (A)

2. **Assertion** (A) RBI is known as issuing authority.

Reason (R) It has the monopoly power of issuing currency.

Ans (a) Both Assertion (A) and Reason (R) are true and Reason (R) is the correct explanation of Assertion (A)

3. **Assertion** (A) Currency notes and coins are called fiat money.

Reason (R) Fiduciary money is backed by the trust between the two parties, i.e. payer and payee.

Ans (b) Both Assertion (A) and Reason (R) are true, but Reason (R) is not the correct explanation of Assertion (A)

4. **Assertion** (A) Commercial banks play a crucial role in providing financial services to individuals and businesses.

Reason (R) Commercial banks offer various services like deposit accounts, loans and payment mechanisms to facilitate economic transactions.

Ans (a) Both Assertion (A) and Reason (R) are true and Reason (R) is the correct explanation of Assertion (A)

5. **Assertion** (A) Statutory liquidity ratio is the ratio of demand deposits of a commercial bank which, it has to keep with itself in the form of specified liquid assets.

Reason (R) Statutory liquidity ratio is a component of legal reserve ratio, which affects the credit creation in the economy.

Ans (b) Both Assertion (A) and Reason (R) are true, but Reason (R) is not the correct explanation of Assertion (A)

Chapter 9 Balance of Payments and Exchange Rate

Direction (Q. No. 1 to 5) *There are two statements marked as Assertion (A) and Reason (R). Read the statements and choose the appropriate option from the options given below*

(a) Both Assertion (A) and Reason (R) are true and Reason (R) is the correct explanation of Assertion (A)
(b) Both Assertion (A) and Reason (R) are true, but Reason (R) is not the correct explanation of Assertion (A)
(c) Assertion (A) is true, but Reason (R) is false
(d) Both Assertion (A) and Reason (R) are false

1. **Assertion** (A) When the price of foreign currency rises, the demand for foreign currency will fall.

   Reason (R) There exists an inverse relation between foreign exchange rate and demand for foreign currency.

Ans (a) Both Assertion (A) and Reason (R) are true and Reason (R) is the correct explanation of Assertion (A)

2. **Assertion** (A) Managed floating exchange rate system is an amalgamation of fixed exchange rate and flexible exchange rate.

   Reason (R) Central bank can manipulate the flexible exchange rate.

Ans (c) A flexible exchange rate regime is one where the government or the central bank does not intervene in the foreign exchange market and lets the market forces of supply and demand determine the value of the domestic currency in relation to other currencies.

3. **Assertion** (A) A company located in India receives a loan from a company located abroad. This will be recorded on the debit side of BoP account.

   Reason (R) It is because it results in outflow of foreign exchange.

Ans (d) Inflow of foreign exchange is recorded as a credit item in BoP.

4. **Assertion** (A) Accommodating transactions are undertaken to make equilibrium in BoP account.

   Reason (R) In accounting sense, BoP account should always be balanced.

Ans (a) Both Assertion (A) and Reason (R) are true and Reason (R) is the correct explanation of Assertion (A)

5. **Assertion** (A) Autonomous transactions are independent of the state of the BoP account.

   Reason (R) Autonomous items are also known as above-the-line items.

Ans (b) Both Assertion (A) and Reason (R) are true, but Reason (R) is not the correct explanation of Assertion (A)

Chapter 10 Public Finance

Direction (Q. No. 1 to 5) *There are two statements marked as Assertion (A) and Reason (R). Read the statements and choose the appropriate option from the options given below*

(a) Both Assertion (A) and Reason (R) are true and Reason (R) is the correct explanation of Assertion (A)
(b) Both Assertion (A) and Reason (R) are true, but Reason (R) is not the correct explanation of Assertion (A)
(c) Assertion (A) is true, but Reason (R) is false
(d) Both Assertion (A) and Reason (R) are false

1. **Assertion** (A) A developing country like India prepares a deficit budget, i.e., its expenditure is more than its receipts.

   Reason (R) A developing country generally has to spend more on infrastructural projects.

Ans (a) Both Assertion (A) and Reason (R) are true and Reason (R) is the correct explanation of Assertion (A)

2. **Assertion** (A) Public goods are non-rivalrous.

   Reason (R) The benefit of such goods can be enjoyed by all and are not restricted to any one person.

Ans (a) Both Assertion (A) and Reason (R) are true and Reason (R) is the correct explanation of Assertion (A)

3. **Assertion** (A) Fiscal deficit indicates the total borrowing requirements of the government from all sources.

   Reason (R) Fiscal deficit is financed through borrowings. From the financing side,

   Fiscal deficit = Net borrowing at home + Borrowing from RBI + Borrowing from abroad

Ans (a) Both Assertion (A) and Reason (R) are true and Reason (R) is the correct explanation of Assertion (A)

4. **Assertion** (A) Direct taxes have limited reach.

   Reason (R) Direct taxes do not reach to all the sections of the economy.

Ans (a) Both Assertion (A) and Reason (R) are true and Reason (R) is the correct explanation of Assertion (A)

5. **Assertion** (A) Repayment of loans by the government is the capital expenditure of the government.

Reason (R) Capital expenditure of government leads to the creation of assets or reduction in liabilities.

Ans (a) Both Assertion (A) and Reason (R) are true and Reason (R) is the correct explanation of Assertion (A)

Chapter 11 National Income

Direction (Q. No. 1 to 5) *There are two statements marked as Assertion (A) and Reason (R). Read the statements and choose the appropriate option from the options given below*

(a) Both Assertion (A) and Reason (R) are true and Reason (R) is the correct explanation of Assertion (A)
(b) Both Assertion (A) and Reason (R) are true, but Reason (R) is not the correct explanation of Assertion (A)
(c) Assertion (A) is true, but Reason (R) is false
(d) Both Assertion (A) and Reason (R) are false

1. **Assertion** (A) Income earned by foreigner bank in India is a part of domestic income.

Reason (R) It is included in gross domestic income because foreign bank is located within the domestic territory of the country.

Ans (a) Both Assertion (A) and Reason (R) are true and Reason (R) is the correct explanation of Assertion (A)

2. **Assertion** (A) Undistributed profits are part of domestic factor income.

Reason (R) There are three sub-components of profit, i.e. corporate tax, dividend and undistributed profits.

Ans (a) Both Assertion (A) and Reason (R) are true and Reason (R) is the correct explanation of Assertion (A)

3. **Assertion** (A) Real GDP is a better indicator of economic growth.

Reason (R) It is not affected by changes in general price level.

Ans (a) Both Assertion (A) and Reason (R) are true and Reason (R) is the correct explanation of Assertion (A)

4. **Assertion** (A) GDP, as an index of welfare, may underestimate or overestimate the welfare.

Reason (R) It does not consider the non-monetary exchanges and does not take into consideration the positive or negative aspects associated with economic activity.

Ans (a) Both Assertion (A) and Reason (R) are true and Reason (R) is the correct explanation of Assertion (A)

5. **Assertion** (A) Depreciation is also termed as consumption of fixed capital.

Reason (R) Depreciation refers to that value of fixed capital that is used up in the process of production.

Ans (a) Both Assertion (A) and Reason (R) are true and Reason (R) is the correct explanation of Assertion (A)

ISC

Examination Paper 2024

Time : 3 hrs
Marks : 80

Economics XII

General Instructions

1. Candidates are allowed additional 15 minutes for only reading the paper. They must not start writing during this time.
2. Answer all questions in Section A, Section B and Section C.
3. Section A consists of objective/very short answer questions.
4. Section B consists of short answer questions.
5. Section C consists of long answer questions.
6. The intended marks for questions or parts of questions are given in brackets [ ].

Section A

(16 Marks)

1. (i) If the price elasticity of demand for a commodity is 2 and the percentage change in price is 5, the percentage change in quantity demanded will be **[1]**

(a) 3 (b) 2.5
(c) 10 (d) 7

(ii) **Assertion** (A) An increase in public expenditure during recession can help to control the situation.
Reason (R) Government reduces subsidies to overcome its budget deficit. **[1]**
Alternatives
(a) Both Assertion (A) and Reason (R) are true and Reason (R) is the correct explanation of Assertion (A)
(b) Both Assertion (A) and Reason (R) are true, but Reason (R) is not the correct explanation of Assertion (A)
(c) Assertion (A) is true, but Reason (R) is false
(d) Assertion (A) is false, but Reason (R) is true

(iii) At the point of inflexion, ... is maximum. **[1]**
(a) total product
(b) total cost
(c) average product
(d) marginal product

(iv) In which one of the following types of market, are average revenue curve and market demand curve the same? **[1]**
(a) Monopoly
(b) Oligopoly
(c) Perfect competition
(d) Monopolistic competition

(v) The diagram given below shows the change in price of cotton shirts. Which one of the following causes the equilibrium price to move from P_1 to P_2? **[1]**

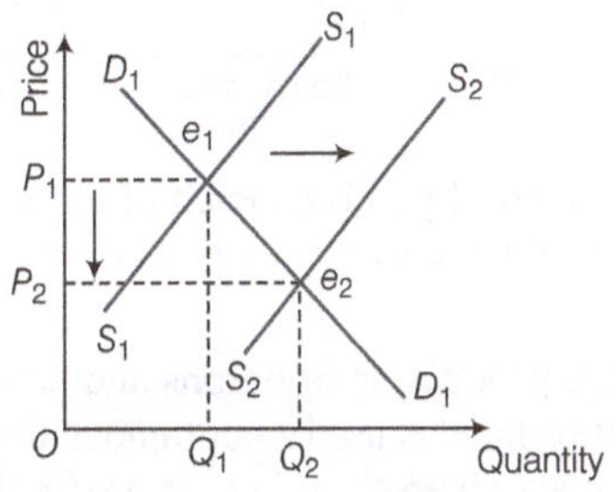

(a) Increase in excise duty on raw cotton
(b) Expected fall in future price of cotton shirts
(c) Fall in the price of synthetic shirts
(d) Increase in wage rate

(vi) Refer to the diagram given below and choose the incorrect statement. [1]

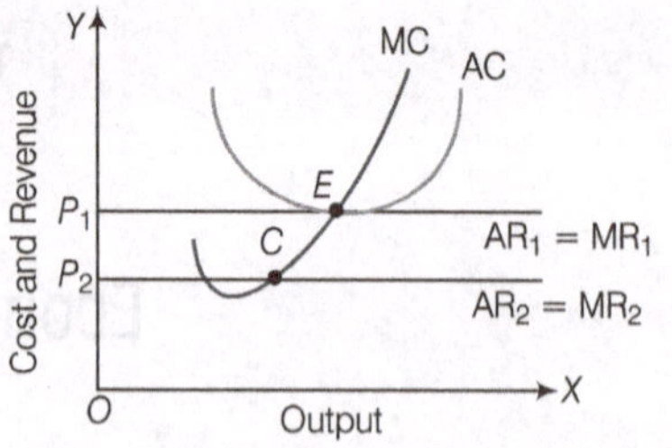

(a) E is the equilibrium point
(b) The diagram shows a situation of normal profit
(c) C is the shut down point
(d) E is the break-even point

(vii) Government of India purchased Raffle aircrafts from France in recent times.
Which one of the following market forms is applicable for this product in India? [1]
(a) Monopsony
(b) Monopoly
(c) Oligopoly
(d) Monopolistic competition

(viii) Revenue receipts in the government's budget [1]
(a) create liability
(b) reduce liability and create assets
(c) reduce assets
(d) keep liability and assets unaltered

(ix) If S > I, it will lead to [1]
(a) excess demand (b) deficient demand
(c) notional demand (d) actual demand

(x) An increase in the number of firms in the market causes a rightward shift in the market supply curve, but the individual supply curve may shift leftwards. Justify the statement. [1]

(xi) State whether the following is true or false. Give a reason for your answer.
TVC is an avoidable cost. [1]

(xii) Mention any one difference between induced investment and autonomous investment. [1]

(xiii) Why is the demand curve for foreign exchange negatively sloped? [1]

(xiv) Mention any one difference between balance of trade and balance of payments. [1]

(xv) How is APS obtained from APC? [1]

(xvi) With reference to simple Keynesian model, give the meaning of ex-ante demand. [1]

Section B (32 Marks)

2. (i) Milk is used for making curd, sweets and chocolates. What type of demand does milk have? Give a reason. [1]

(ii) Figures (A), (B) and (C) given below represent different types of demand curves.

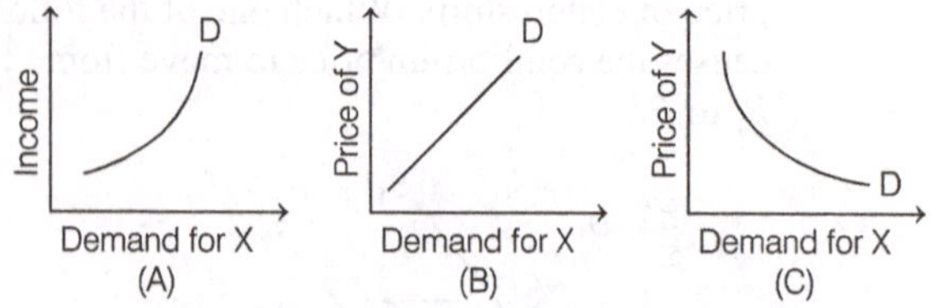

What kind of goods do each of these demand curves represent? Give a reason for each of the curves. [3]

3. (i) A huge production of onions and lack of storage facilities have caused a continuous fall in its price. This may adversely affect the production of onions in the subsequent year. With the help of a diagram, briefly explain the measure that the government should adopt to combat this situation. [2]

(ii) Draw and explain average fixed cost curve. [2]

4. With the help of a diagram, explain the relationship between average product and total product under the law of variable proportions. [4]

5. (i) Briefly discuss the implication of 'freedom of entry and exit' under perfect competition. [2]

(ii) Per unit price of electricity is higher in the commercial sector as compared to the domestic sector. Identify and briefly describe this phenomenon. Name the market in which it is applicable. [2]

Or

(i) Briefly discuss the importance of selling cost under oligopoly market.

(ii) There are many manufacturers of pencils in the market who produce pencils in different designs and colours to attract children. Which market form is referred to here? Briefly explain the feature of this market form indicated in the given situation.

6. (i) What is meant by autonomous consumption expenditure? Show it on a diagram. [2]

(ii) When national income rises from ₹ 600 crore to ₹ 1,000 crore the consumption expenditure increases from ₹ 500 crore to ₹ 800 crore. Calculate MPC and hence the value of investment multiplier. **[2]**

7. (i) A large amount of fiscal deficit proves to be counter productive. Give any two reasons in support of this statement. **[2]**

(ii) What is meant by *no quid pro quo* of a tax? Name any two direct taxes. **[2]**

8. (i) Categorise the following items into current account or capital account of balance of payment of India.

(a) Acquisition of land in India by an American firm.

(b) Use of transport by Indian tourists in Dubai.

(c) Dividend paid to foreigners on their investment in shares in India.

(d) Loan taken by India from International Monetary Fund (IMF) to cover its BoP deficit. **[2]**

(ii) Briefly explain the effect the following on the balance of payment of a country.

(a) Inflationary pressure in the economy.

(b) Appreciation in domestic exchange rate. **[2]**

Or

(i) Suppose the exchange rate was \$1 = ₹ 80 and later changed to \$1= ₹ 92. What will be its effect on the following?

(a) Export of cotton garments by Indian to the USA.

(b) Export of technical knowledge by the USA to India.

(c) Import of wheat by India from the USA.

(d) Import of gold jewellery by the USA from India.

(ii) Briefly discuss the fixed exchange rate system of determining foreign exchange rate.

9. Draw a well-labelled diagram and explain the circular flow of income in a four sector model. **[4]**

Section C

(32 Marks)

10. (i) How is total revenue under perfect competition different from total revenue under imperfect competition? Give two points to show the difference. **[2]**

(ii) Explain the short-run equilibrium of a perfectly competitive firm earning super normal profit with the help of a diagram. **[6]**

11. (i) Draw a straight line demand curve joining both the axes. Indicate the following on the demand curve.

(a) Elasticity of demand is equal to zero.

(b) Elasticity of demand is greater than one. **[2]**

(ii) Observe the graph given below and answer the questions that follow.

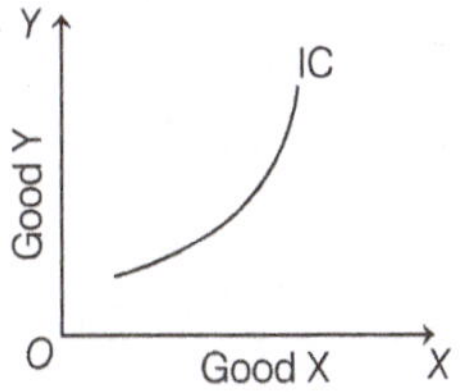

(a) Give a reason to explain if the graph shown above can be a common phenomenon or not. **[2]**

(b) What is an indifference map? Draw its diagram. **[2]**

(c) State any two differences between cardinal utility and ordinal utility. **[2]**

Or

(i) Give two differences between intended supply and actual supply.

(ii) Refer to the diagram given below and answer the questions that follow.

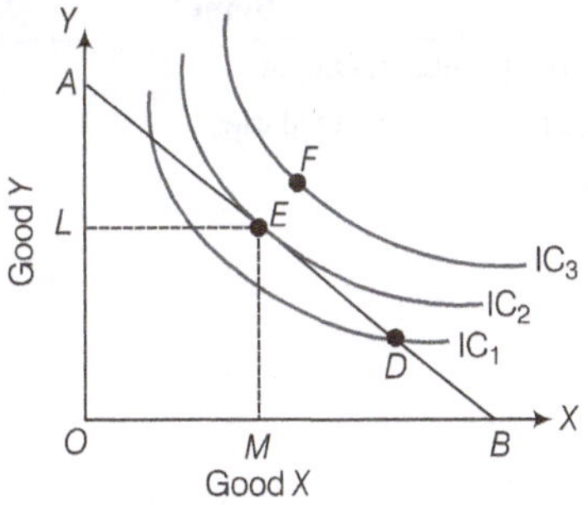

(a) What does the line *AB* represent? Why is the line *AB* negatively sloped?

(b) At which one of the given points, *D*, *E* and *F*, will the consumer attain equilibrium? Explain.

(c) Briefly explain why the consumer is not in equilibrium at the other two points.

12. (i) State whether the following items will be included in the estimation of national income or not. Give reason for your answer.

(a) Government expenditure on street lighting.

(b) Profit earned by State Bank of India in a foreign country. **[2]**

(ii) Calculate GNP_{MP} and NNP_{FC} from the following data by expenditure method. **[6]**

S.No.	Items	₹ (in crores)
(i)	Mixed Income of Self-employed	550
(ii)	Private Final Consumption Expenditure	1,100
(iii)	Net Factor Income from Abroad	(–) 120
(iv)	Net Indirect Taxes	250
(v)	Consumption of Fixed Capital	270
(vi)	Net Domestic Capital Formation	480
(vii)	Net Exports	(–)130
(viii)	Interest	300
(ix)	Government Final Consumption Expenditure	650

Or (i) State whether the following items will be included in the estimation of national income or not. Give a reason for your answer.

(a) Fresh tomatoes used by a food processing company.

(b) Wooden cupboard purchased by a family.

(ii) Calculate national income using income method and output method.

S.No.	Items	₹ (in crores)
(i)	Value of Output	1,200
(ii)	Wages and Salaries	165
(iii)	Rent	60
(iv)	Subsidies	15
(v)	Mixed Income of Self-employed	180
(vi)	Employer's Contribution to Social Security	15
(vii)	Value of Intermediate Consumption	600
(viii)	Interest	7
(ix)	Factor Income Earned from Abroad	15
(x)	Indirect Taxes	90
(xi)	Profits	23
(xii)	Depreciation	75
(xiii)	Factor Income Paid Abroad	30

13. Read the passage given below and answer the questions that follow.

The Monetary Policy Committee (MPC) increased the repo rate, at which RBI lends short-term funds to the commercial banks, from 6.25 percent to 6.50 percent. This increase in repo rate is based on the increase in the key rate by 250 bps. The committee also decided to continue the withdrawal of money supply in the economy.

Source *(Edited) The Economics Times 8th February, 2023.*

(i) Which function of central bank is hinted at, in the passage given above? **[1]**

(ii) In which situation does central bank adopt the measure given in the above passage? **[1]**

(iii) Explain any two monetary measures that can be used to accomplish a similar objective, other than the one given in the above passage. **[4]**

(iv) Differentiate between Reserve Bank of India and commercial banks by giving any two points. **[2]**

Answers

1. (i) (c) $E_d = \frac{\text{Percentage Change in Quantity Demanded}}{\text{Percentage Change in Price}}$

2 = Percentage Change in Quantity Demanded/5

∴ Percentage Change in Quantity Demanded = 10

(ii) (b) Both Assertion (A) and Reason (R) are true, but Reason (R) is not the correct explanation of Assertion (A)

(iii) (d) marginal product

(iv) (c) Perfect competition

(v) (c) Fall in the price of synthetic shirts

(vi) (c) C is the shut down point

(vii) (a) Monospony

(viii) (d) keep liability and assets unaltered

(ix) (b) deficient demand

(x) Market supply curve is the sum total of individual supply curves. An increase in number of firms will increase the market supply even though there may be decline in supply an individual supplier.

(xi) False. TVC can be avoided by suspending production as it varies directly with output.

(xii) Induced investment depends upon the level of income while autonomous investment is independent of the level of income.

(xiii) Demand curve foreign exchange is downward sloping or negatively sloped due to the inverse relationship between the exchange rate and the demand for foreign exchange.

(xiv) Difference between Balance of Trade (BoT) and Balance of Payments (BoP)

Basis	Balance of Trade (BoT)	Balance of Payments (BoP)
Nature of transactions	It does not record transactions of capital nature.	It records transactions of capital nature.

(xv) APS = 1 – APC

(xvi) Ex-ante demand refers to the amount of goods that consumers want to buy during a particular time period. In other words, it is anticipated demand.

2. (i) It is referred to as 'composite demand' as milk has multiplie uses.

(ii) The demand curves show the following goods

Figure (A) shows upward sloping non-linear demand curve.

In this situation, the slope is not constant. This curve represents the direct relation between price and quantity demanded. The demand curve for giffen goods is upward sloping.

Figure (B) shows upward sloping linear demand curve. In this situation, the slope is constant. This curve represents the direct relation between price and quantity demanded. The demand curve for giffen goods is upward sloping.

Figure (C) shows a downward sloping non-linear demand curve. In this situation, the slope is not constant. This curve represents the indirect relation between price and quantity demanded. The demand curve for normal goods is downward sloping.

3. (i) A surplus production of crops and lack of storage facilities will lead to a fall in the market price of onions and make the producer suffer losses. To deal with the situation, government can intervene in the market and set the minimum price of onions (price floor).

Also, to avoid the market price falling further, government may opt for the purchase of crops and maintain buffer stock.

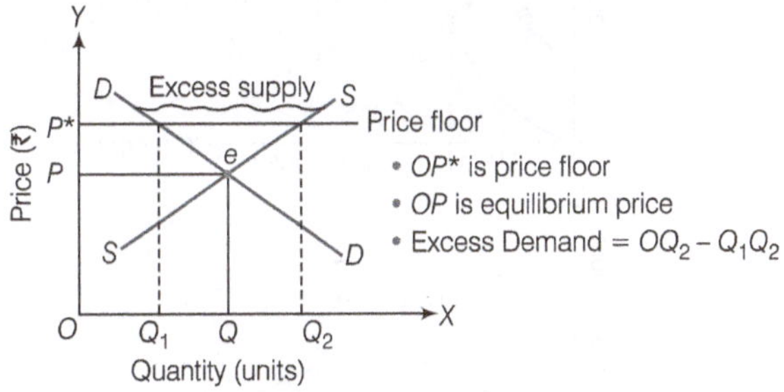

Price Floor

(ii) Average Fixed Cost (AFC) is defined as per unit of Total Fixed Cost (TFC). AFC is a rectangular hyperbola shaped curve, i.e. AFC falls continuously, but it can never be equal to zero, as total fixed cost is always positive. Also, area below AFC curve remains constant (same).

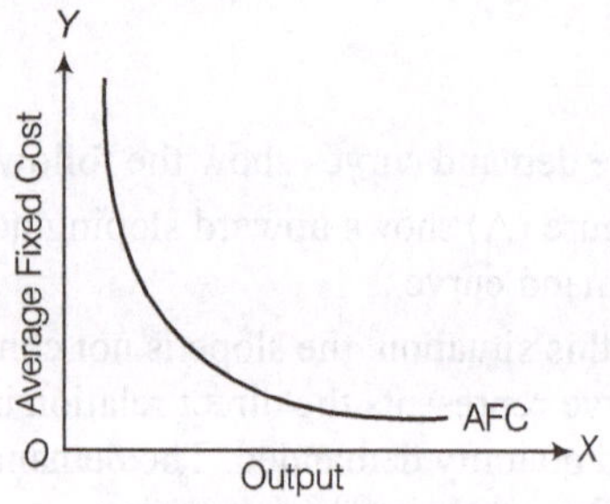

Average Fixed Cost Curve

4. **Relationship between Total Product** (TP) and **Average Product** (AP)

Following points highlight the relationship between TP and AP

(i) When total product rises at an increasing rate, average product rises.

(ii) When total product rises at a diminishing rate, average product still rises.

(iii) Till the time total product rises at a diminishing rate, average product falls continuously after reaching its maximum point.

(iv) When total product reaches its maximum point, average product continues to fall.

(v) When total product starts falling, average product falls but remains positive.

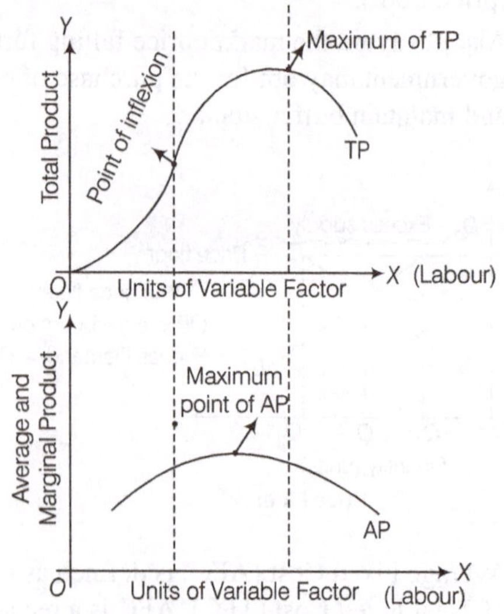

5. (i) Freedom of entry and exit signifies that firms can enter the market any time they wish, if they think that they could make profits. On the other hand, loss making firms can leave the market anytime. Due to this unique feature of perfect competition, firms under this form earn only normal profit in the long-run.

(ii) The practice of charging different prices of electricity from the commercial sector and the domestic sector is known as 'price discrimination'. This is applicable mainly under the monopoly market.

Or (i) Selling cost refers to the additional cost which is incurred by the firms to promote sales. Under oligopoly market, there is interdependence between firms and each firm in the market is large in size (in terms of market share) selling either homogeneous or heterogeneous goods.

Firms cannot change the selling price very often in the fear of price war. So, they rely on selling cost in form of advertising, after sales service, etc. to increase their sales in the market.

(ii) The form of the market indicated in the question is monopolistic competition.

The feature indicated in the given situation is product differentiation.

Product differentiation means similar products but still differentiated in terms of quantity, quality, size, shape, colour, etc. This is an important feature of monopolistic competition. e.g. Soaps, toothpaste, detergents, etc.

6. (i) Autonomous consumption ($\bar{C}$) means consumption at zero level of income. Even when income is zero, a typical household will have some minimum amount of consumption expenditure which can be financed through borrowings or past savings.

This minimum consumption is termed as autonomous consumption. Since, it is not dependent on the level of income, therefore it is represented by a vertical straight line parallel to *X*-axis.

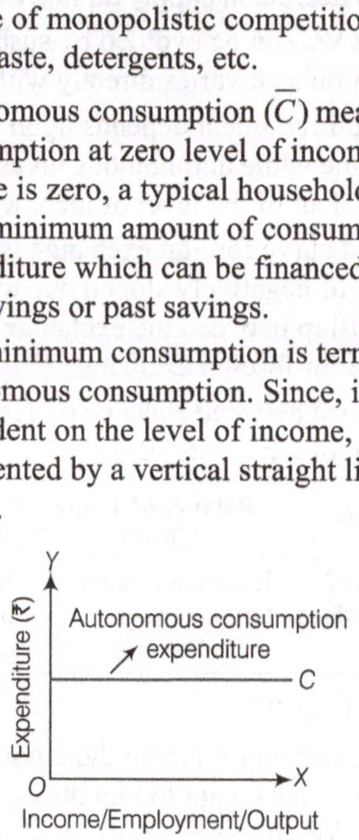

(ii) Y = ₹ 600 crore, Y_1 = ₹ 1,000 crore

∴ ΔY = ₹ 400 crore

C = ₹ 500 crore

C_1 = ₹ 800 crore

∴ Δ C = ₹ 300 crore

Now, $MPC = \Delta C/\Delta Y = 300/400 = 3/4$

Now, $K = \frac{1}{1-MPC} = \frac{1}{1-\frac{3}{4}} = \frac{1}{\frac{1}{4}} = 4$

7. (i) A large fiscal deficit can indeed be counter productive due to several reasons

(a) **Increased borrowing costs** When a government runs a large fiscal deficit, it typically finances the shortfall by borrowing from the market or issuing government bonds. As the deficit grows, the government's borrowing requirements increase, which can lead to higher demand for credit in the financial markets.

(b) **Crowding out private investment** A large fiscal deficit can crowd out private investment. When the government increases its borrowing to finance its deficit, it competes with private borrowers for available funds in the financial markets.

(ii) '*No quid pro quo*' in the context of taxes means that there is no direct correlation between the taxes paid by an individual or entity and the specific benefits or services they receive from the government in return. In other words, taxpayers are not receiving a direct exchange or compensation for the taxes they pay.

Examples of direct tax are income tax and corporate tax.

8 (i) (a) Capital account

(b) Current account

(c) Current account

(d) Capital account

(ii) (a) Inflationary situation in the domestic country will lead to an increase in demand for imports, hence the outflow of foreign exchange.

(b) Appreciation of domestic currency will lead to an increase in imports and a decrease in exports.

Or

(i) (a) Export will increase

(b) Import to India will decrease

(c) Import to India will decrease

(d) Export from India will increase

(ii) It is the rate which is officially fixed by the monetary authority on daily or monthly basis. It has two important variants

(a) **Gold standard system of exchange rate** Under this system, each country was to define value of its currency in terms of gold.

(b) **Bretton woods system of exchange rate or adjustable peg system of exchange rate** Bretton Woods system, even when it was a fixed system of exchange rate, allowed some adjustments. So, it was called 'adjustable peg system of exchange rate'.

9. Circular flow in a four sector economy

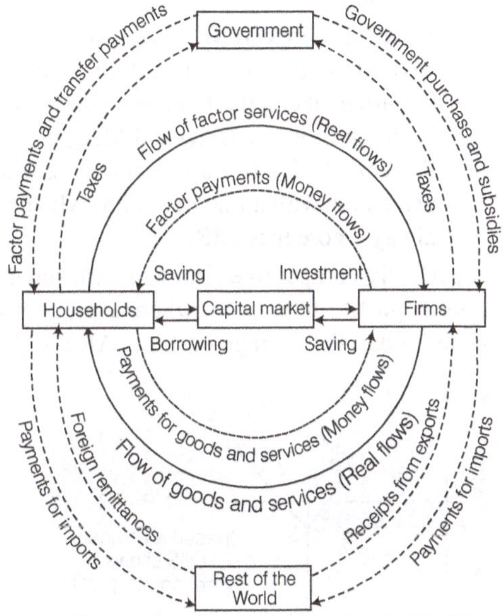

Circular Flow Diagram : Four Sector Model

In the diagram, the household sector purchases goods from abroad and makes payment towards its purchases to abroad. On the other hand, the household sector receives 'foreign remittances' in foreign exchange by selling some of the factor services abroad. The firms export goods and services to foreign countries and receive payment against their exports.

On the other hand, the firm sector makes payment to the foreign sector for import of goods and services. Likewise, government sector also export and import goods and services from foreign countries.

Similarly, there is an inflow and outflow of capital services between the government and rest of the world.

10. (i) Total Revenue (TR) under perfect competition and imperfect competition differs in two significant ways

(a) **Shape of the total revenue curve** Under perfect competition, the total revenue curve is a straight line with a positive slope. Under imperfect competition (such as monopolistic competition or oligopoly), the total revenue curve initially increases at a diminishing rate, reaches its maximum and eventually falls.

(b) **Relation between price and marginal revenue** In perfect competition, since firms are price takers, the price is equal to both Average Revenue (AR) and Marginal Revenue (MR). In imperfect competition, as price falls with a rise in output, AR (price) is always more than MR.

(ii) A perfectly competitive firm will earn super normal profits at the point where average revenue is more than the average cost, i.e. AR > AC.

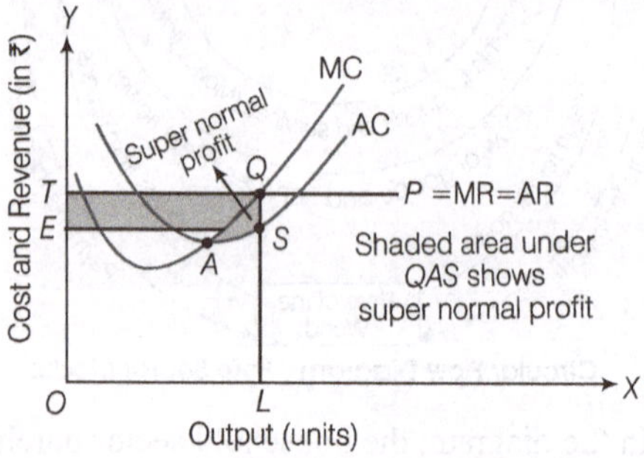

Super Normal Profit

In the above figure, point *Q* is the point of equilibrium, because at this point

(a) Marginal revenue is equal to marginal cost and

(b) Marginal cost curve cuts the marginal revenue curve from below.

At this point, average revenue exceeds the average cost. So, the shaded region *TESQ* represents the super normal profits earned by the firm. However, a firm will be able to earn such profits only in the short-run. In the long-run, the firm would be able to earn only normal profits.

11. (i)

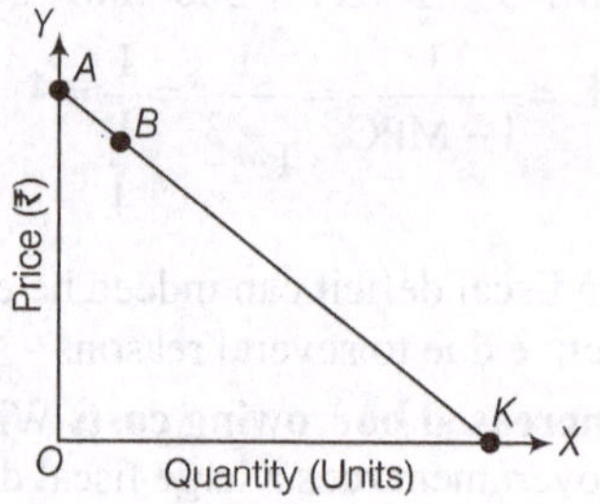

(a) At point *K*, elasticity of demand $= \frac{0}{KA} = 0$

(b) At point *B*, elasticity of demand $= \frac{BK}{BA}$

$\Rightarrow \quad e_d > 1$

(ii) (a) The above shown indifference curve is not a common phenomenon. The shown IC is concave to the origin i.e. it has an increasing slope. The ideal indifference curve is convex to the origin.

(b) The set of indifference curves showing different combination of two goods is called indifference map.

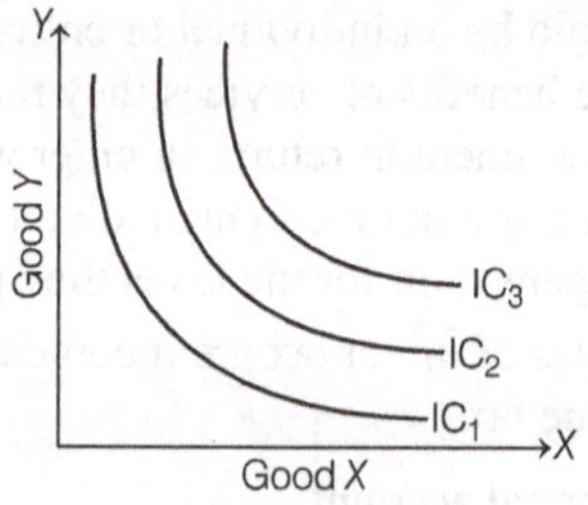

Indifference Map

(c) Difference between cardinal utility and ordinal utility

Basis	Cardinal utility	Ordinal utility
Meaning	This approach to utility assumes that utility is measurable in terms of numbers such as 1, 2, 3, etc. The unit of measurement under this approach is 'utils'.	This approach to utility refers to the measurement of utility in terms of psychological satisfaction on consuming one good in comparison to other.
Example	A basket of oranges offers 10 utils of utility to a consumer.	A pizza offers greater satisfaction to a consumer than a chapati.

Or

(i) Difference between intended supply (stock) and actual supply (supply)

Basis	Intended supply	Actual supply
Meaning	It refers to total amount of the commodity that can be supplied in market.	It refers to the quantity that are actually supplied in the market for sale.
Dependence	It depends on output.	It depends on stock and price in market.

(ii) (a) The line *AB* represents the budget line. It slopes downwards as the consumption of one good can be increased only by reducing the consumption of other good to remain on the same budget line.

(b) Consumer will attain equilibrium at point *E*. The condition of equilibrium is satisfied at this point only.

The condition for consumer's equilibrium under ordinal approach is as follows

- $MRS_{XY} = P_X/P_Y$

  i.e. Slope of Indifference Curve = Slope of Budget Line

  Here, MRS_{XY} = Marginal Rate of Substitution between Goods *X* and *Y*

  P_X/P_Y = Price Ratio between Goods *X* and *Y*

- **MRS continuously falls** The indifference curve must be convex to the origin at the point of equilibrium. Consumer is equilibrium at point *E* where the IC is tangent to the budget line.

  The consumer is attaining maximum satisfaction at this point within his given income.

(c) Consumer is not in equilibrium at points *D* and *F*

- At point *D*, the consumer derives lesser satisfaction as it appears on a lower IC.
- At point *F*, it is an unattainable combination as it is beyond the consumer's income.

12. (i) (a) It will be included as it is part of government final consumption expenditure.

(b) It will be included as it is a factor income received from abroad.

(ii) GNP at MP = Private Final Consumption Expenditure + Government Final Consumption Expenditure + Gross Domestic Capital Formation + Net Exports + Net Factor Income from Abroad

= 1,100 + 650 + (480 + 270) + (–130) + (– 120)

= ₹ 2,250 crore

Note Gross Domestic Capital Formation = Net Domestic Capital Formation + Consumption of Fixed Capital

NNP at FC = GNP at MP – Consumption of Fixed Capital – Net Indirect Taxes

= 2,250 – 270 – 250

= ₹ 1,730 crore

Or (i) (a) It will not be included as it is an intermediate cost.

(b) It will be included as it is a final expenditure (part of private final consumption expenditure).

(ii) **National income by income method**

NNP at FC = Wages and Salaries + Employer's Contribution to Social Security + Rent + Interest + Profits + Mixed Income of Self-employed + Net Factor Income from Abroad

= 165 + 15 + 60 + 7 + 23 + 180 + (15 – 30)

= ₹ 435 crore

Note NFIA = Factor Income Earned from Abroad – Factor Income Paid Abroad

National income by output method

NNP at FC = Value of Output – Value of Intermediate Consumption – Depreciation + Net Factor Income from Abroad – Net Indirect Taxes

= 1,200 – 600 – 75 + (–15) – (90 –15)

= ₹ 435 crore

Note Net Indirect Taxes = Indirect Taxes – Subsidies

13. (i) Controller of credit function is indicated in the passage above.

(ii) Central bank increases the repo rate during excess demand or inflation.

(iii) **Bank rate policy** The bank rate is the minimum rate at which the central bank of a country is prepared to give credit to the commercial banks.

The increase in bank rate increases the rate of interest and credit becomes dear or expensive. Accordingly, the demand for credit is reduced or *vice-versa*.

Open market operations It refers to the sale and purchase of securities in open market by the Central Bank (RBI). By selling the securities, the central bank withdraws cash balances from within the economy and by buying the securities, the central bank contributes cash balances in economy. Cash balances are high powered money.

Thus, through open market operations, if cash balances are increased, flow of credit increases and if cash balances are reduced, the flow of credit decreases. So, open market operations pump in or pump out money from circulation.

(iv) Difference between central bank and commercial bank

Basis	Central bank	Commercial bank
Meaning	Central bank is an apex body that controls, operates, regulates and directs the entire banking and monetary structure of the country.	Commercial bank is an institution which performs the functions of accepting deposits, granting loans and making investments with the objective of earning profits.
Number of banks	There is only one central bank that oversees the entire banking operation.	There are several commercial banks in a country with many branches.

ISC

Examination Paper 2025

Time : 3 hrs
Marks : 80

Economics XII

General Instructions

1. Candidates are allowed additional 15 minutes for only reading the paper. They must not start writing during this time.
2. There are thirteen questions in the paper. All questions are compulsory.
3. This paper is divided into three Sections A, B and C.
4. Section A has sixteen subparts which are very short answer questions. Each question carries 1 mark.
5. Section B has eight questions which are short answer questions. Each question carries 4 marks.
6. Section C has four questions which are long answer questions. Each question carries 8 marks.
7. Internal choices have been provided in two questions in Section B and in one question in Section C.
8. The intended marks for questions are given in brackets [ ].

Section A

(16 Marks)

1. (i)

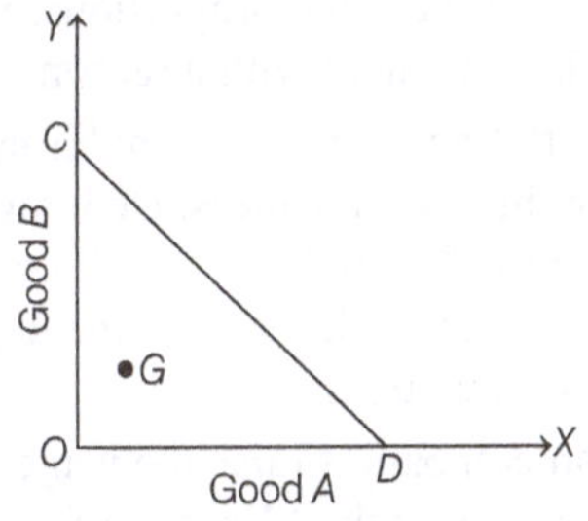

In the diagram given above, CD is the budget line. What does the point G represent? **[1]**

(a) Combination of two goods on which a consumer spends her entire money income
(b) Combination of two goods on which a consumer spends less than her money income
(c) Combination of two goods on which a consumer spends greater than her money income
(d) Consumer spends her entire money income either on Good A or Good B

(ii) Abhinav derives total utility of 11 utils after consuming 4 mangoes and 9 utils after consuming 6 mangoes.

What is his marginal utility on consuming the 6th mango? **[1]**

(a) 1 util (b) 21 utils
(c) 10 utils (d) –1 util

(iii) Law of variable proportions is not applicable when **[1]**

(a) all factor inputs increase in the same proportion
(b) the time period is short
(c) all the units of variable input are equally efficient
(d) technology remains constant

(iv) Refer to the diagram given below and choose the correct statement **[1]**

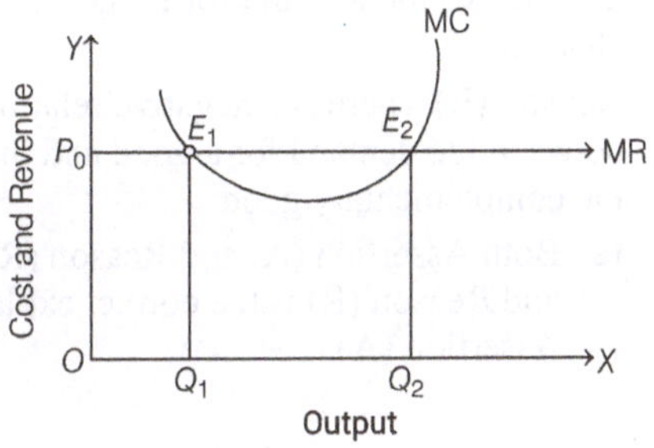

(a) E_1 is the equilibrium point as $MR = MC$
(b) E_1 and E_2 are equilibrium points as $MR = MC$
(c) E_2 is the equilibrium point because $MC > MR$ beyond this point
(d) E_2 is the equilibrium point because $MC < MR$ beyond this point

(v) Identify the correct statement with reference to the measures of money supply. [1]
(a) M_3 includes M_2
(b) M_3 includes time deposits with commercial banks
(c) M_1 includes time deposits with commercial banks
(d) M_2 includes national saving certificates

(vi) Suppose the total receipts are ₹ 1,045 crore and total payments are ₹ 1,526 crore in the balance of payments account of India.
In the above context, which one of the following can improve the balance of payments of India? [1]
(a) Indian tourists buying souvenirs in the foreign countries
(b) Foreign Institutional Investor (FII) buying shares of Indian companies
(c) Indian students joining foreign universities for higher education
(d) Value of the US dollar falling against the Indian rupee

(vii) Which one of the following scenarios correctly represents a Degressive tax system? [1]
(a) Ruhi paid income tax in three consecutive years at the rate of 10% on her income of ₹ 10,000, 15% on her income of ₹ 20,000 and 15% on her income of ₹ 30,000.
(b) Goods and Service tax on gold ornaments is 3% and 18% on fine dining in restaurants.
(c) Roshan was promoted to the position of senior manager and received a raise in his income. But he continued paying 10% of his income as tax.
(d) Suhana paid TDS at a higher rate on her increased interest income in the current year as compared to the previous year.

(viii) **Assertion** (A) Rise in price of burger at Burger Bliss raises the demand for burgers at Burger Heaven.
Reason (R) There is a negative relationship between the demand for a good and the price of the complementary good. [1]
(a) Both Assertion (A) and Reason (R) are true and Reason (R) is the correct explanation of Assertion (A).
(b) Both Assertion (A) and Reason (R) are true but Reason (R) is not the correct explanation of Assertion (A)
(c) Assertion (A) is true and Reason (R) is false
(d) Both Assertion (A) and Reason (R) are false

(ix) **Assertion** (A) Commercial banks can deposit their surplus funds with RBI.
Reason (R) A high reverse repo rate enables the commercial banks to earn an income. [1]
(a) Both Assertion (A) and Reason (R) are true and Reason (R) is the correct explanation of Assertion (A).
(b) Both Assertion (A) and Reason (R) are true but Reason (R) is not the correct explanation of Assertion (A)
(c) Assertion (A) is true and Reason (R) is false
(d) Both Assertion (A) and Reason (R) are false

(x) With the help of a diagram, illustrate the effect of an increase in the price of the product shown in **Image A** on the demand for the product shown in **Image B.** [1]

Image A Image B

(xi) The long run average cost curve is U shaped due to the law of variable proportions. Defend or refute the statement with a reason. [1]

(xii) Amit withdrew ₹ 50,000 from his savings to invest in his own business. He bought a Xerox machine for ₹ 30,000 for his office the same day. Identify the explicit cost and the implicit cost in the above situation. [1]

(xiii) If Indian companies raise the wages in accordance with the Minimum Wage Act, it will lead to cost push inflation. Give a reason to support this statement. [1]

(xiv) Sagarika wants to buy a car worth ₹ 10 lakhs. She has only ₹ 3 lakhs and plans to borrow the remaining amount from the bank.
Name and briefly explain the selective credit control measure that enables Sagarika to get maximum loan from the bank. [1]

(xv) Why does the supply of foreign exchange increase with an increase in the foreign exchange rate? [1]

(xvi) What is meant by primary deficit? [1]

Section B

(32 Marks)

2. (i) Ibrahim works as a mechanic and earns ₹ 5000 per month. To increase his family income, his wife and parents also begin to work. Over a period of time when his income increases to ₹ 20,000, Ibrahim asks his family members not to work and enjoy leisure.

The phenomenon indicated in this situation does not conform to the law of supply. Give a reason to support this statement. Draw the supply curve based on the given situation. **[2]**

(ii) When the price of potato chips falls from ₹ 40 to ₹ 20 per unit, its demand increases by 20 units. If the price elasticity of demand is (–) 0.5, calculate the quantity demanded of potato chips at ₹ 20. **[2]**

3. (i) Study the schedule given below and explain the relation between average revenue and marginal revenue by giving a suitable reason. **[2]**

Units	Price	TR	AR	MR
1	15	15	15	15
2	14	28	14	13
3	13	39	13	11

(ii) With the help of a diagram, illustrate the effect of a simultaneous and proportional decrease in demand and supply on equilibrium price and quantity. **[2]**

4. (i) Why is fixed cost a short run phenomenon? Draw the total fixed cost curve.

(ii) How do total product, average product and marginal product behave under the law of increasing returns to a factor? Briefly explain one reason for the operation of this law. **[2]**

5. (i) Laxman & Sons is a leading producer of perfume among many other firms. Recently, it introduced a new fragrance and offered gift vouchers to the customers who bought this product.

Identify the form of market and explain the feature implied in this situation. **[2]**

(ii) Briefly discuss the situations when a perfectly competitive firm continues to produce even after facing losses in the short run. **[2]**

Or (i) The main occupation of the villagers in a village is beekeeping. The villagers sell their produce only to Firm X.

(a) Identify the type of market prevalent here.

(b) Is it a buyer's market or a seller's market? Give a reason.

(ii) Monopolistic competition is a blend of perfect competition and monopoly. Discuss the statement by giving two reasons.

6. Aditi deposits ₹ 1,000 in a bank which leads to an increase in money supply in the economy to the extent of ₹ 4,000. Name and explain the process of this increase in money supply. **[4]**

7. (i) The Indian rupee fell 14 paisa to 83.91 against the US dollar on Wednesday amid outflow of foreign capital and volatile domestic equity markets.

Source*(edited) The Pioneer, New Delhi, 22nd August, 2024*

The above situation would lead to a surplus in balance of payments account of India. Defend or refute the statement by giving a reason. **[2]**

(ii) The government initiated the 'Make in India' programme to attract global investment in the Indian economy. Explain the impact of this programme on the balance of payments account of India. **[2]**

Or (i) In July 2024, India's retail inflation rate was 3.54%, though it is falling yet it continues to persist.

Explain how this would affect India's balance of payments.

(ii) Tata Motor's purchase of iconic British luxury car maker Jaguar Land Rover ($2.3 billion) has proved to be a master stroke.

Source *(edited) https://economictimes.indiatimes.com*

State whether the above transaction will be recorded under the debit side or the credit side of balance of payments. Give a reason.

8. (i) With reference to government budget, classify the following as revenue receipt or capital receipt. Give a valid reason for each. **[2]**

(a) Financial help from a Multinational Corporation (MNC) for victims in a flood affected area.

(b) Sale of shares of a Public Sector Undertaking (PSU) to a private company.

(ii) Budget 2024 outlined the sources of government revenue which comprised 19% from income tax, 18% from goods and service tax and the remaining from borrowings.

Source *(edited) Business Standard, New Delhi*

Categorise the two types of taxes mentioned above. State any one difference between them. **[2]**

9. (i) Under the Gruha Lakshmi Scheme in Karnataka, the State Government provides ₹ 2,000 monthly assistance to head female member in each family.

Will this receipt be a part of national income accounting? Explain. **[2]**

(ii) State whether the following are true or false. Give a reason for each. **[2]**

(a) In a closed economy, GDP is always equal to GNP.

(b) Money received by an Indian cricketer as man of the match does not contribute to the national income of India.

Section C

(32 Marks)

10. (i) The price of chocolates increased during the valentine week in February leading to an increase in the supply at a greater rate. Identify the price elasticity of supply and illustrate it on a diagram. **[2]**

(ii) Robert consumes commodities X and Y. The price of commodity X is ₹ 2 and the price of commodity Y is ₹ 1. He has decided to spend ₹ 11 on these two commodities.

(a) Using the following schedule, identify the combination of the two commodities X and Y that gives maximum satisfaction to Robert. **[4]**

Units	1	2	3	4	5	6
MU_x	16	14	12	10	8	6
MU_y	10	9	8	7	6	5

(b) State the underlying law related to the schedule given above. Mention the equilibrium condition. **[2]**

11. (i) What is investment multiplier? Briefly explain how it is related to Marginal Propensity to Consume (MPC). **[2]**

(ii) Refer to the diagram given below and answer the questions that follow.

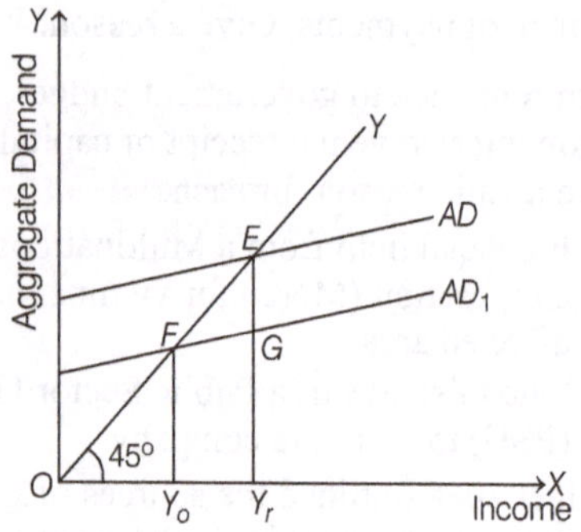

(a) What does the gap *EG* represent? Explain. **[2]**

(b) Recommend any two fiscal measures and any two monetary measures to combat the situation referred to in subpart (a). **[4]**

12. (i) Discuss the problem of double counting with the help of an example. How can it be solved? **[4]**

(ii) Calculate NDP_{FC} and NNP_{FC} on the basis of the following information **[4]**

S. No.	Items	₹ (in crores)
(a)	Value of output of primary sector	1300
(b)	Value of output of other sectors	700
(c)	Raw materials purchased by primary sector	800
(d)	Raw materials purchased by the other sectors	600
(e)	Consumption of fixed capital	85
(f)	Subsidies	40
(g)	Indirect taxes	120
(h)	Factor income paid to the rest of the world	30
(i)	Factor income received from rest of the world	15

Or (i) Discuss two reasons for not considering GDP a true indicator of economic welfare.

(ii) Calculate GDP_{MP} and National Income from the following information.

S. No.	Items	₹ (in crores)
(a)	Net fixed capital formation	500
(b)	Change in stock	60
(c)	Private final consumption expenditure	2500
(d)	Rent	250
(e)	Interest	200
(f)	Net indirect taxes	500
(g)	Net exports	30
(h)	Government final consumption expenditure	700
(i)	Net factor income from abroad	(–) 30
(j)	Consumption of fixed capital	120

13. Read the passage given below and answer the questions that follow

In May 2016, the Ministry of Petroleum and Natural Gas (MOPNG), introduced the 'Pradhan Mantri Ujjwala Yojana (PMUY)' as a flagship scheme with an objective to make clean cooking fuel such as LPG available to the rural and deprived households. Under the union budget for the financial year 2021–22, provision for release of additional 1 crore LPG connections was made. In this phase, special facility was given to migrant families.

LPG belongs to a market form where small number of competitors produce a relatively homogenous product and are aware of one another's presence. To survive in the market, they have to match one another's marketing strategy which sometimes influences the prices of their own products.

Source *(edited) www.myscheme.gov.in*

(i) Identify the form of market referred to in the above passage. Name any two industries which come under the same market form. **[2]**

(ii) Explain any two important features of the market form referred to in the passage. **[2]**

(iii) Briefly discuss the nature of demand curve in this form of market. **[2]**

(iv) Distinguish between perfect competition and imperfect competition on the following basis **[2]**

(a) Nature of product

(b) Nature of demand curve

Answers

1. (i) (b) Combination of two goods on which a consumer spends less than her money income

(ii) (d) −1 util

(iii) (a) all factor inputs increase in the same proportion

(iv) (c) E_2 is the equilibrium point because $MC > MR$ beyond this point

(v) (b) M_3 includes time deposits with commercial banks.

(vi) (b) Foreign Institutional Investor (FII) buying shares of Indian companies

(vii) (c) Roshan was promoted to the position of senior manager and received a raise in his income. But he continued paying 10% of his income as tax.

(viii) (b) Both Assertion (A) and Reason (R) are true but Reason (R) is not the correct explanation of Assertion (A)

(ix) (a) Both Assertion (A) and Reason (R) are true and Reason (R) is the correct explanation of Assertion (A)

(x) Due to increase in price of image A, there will be rise in demrand for image B, as these are substitute goods.
Increase in price of one substitute good leads to increase in the demand for other substitute good.

(xi) Refute the statement as law of variable proportions applies in short run. It is U-shaped not due to law of variable proportions, but due to economies and diseconomies of scale.

(xii) Explicit cost - ₹ 30,000 (Xerox Machine)
Implicit cost - ₹ 50,000 (Savings)

(xiii) Yes, raising wages in accordance with the Minimum Wage Act can lead to cost-push inflation because higher wages increase the production costs for businesses.

(xiv) The selective credit control measure applicable in this case is the 'margin requirement'.

Margin requirement refers to the limit which is deducted from the value of security provided by the borrower before granting them loan. A lower margin requirement set by the central bank allows borrowers like Sagarika to obtain a higher loan amount, reducing the portion they need to pay upfront.

(xv) The supply of foreign exchange increases with an increase in the foreign exchange rate because a higher exchange rate makes domestic goods and services cheaper for foreigners, encouraging more inflows (through exports, investments, etc.) of foreign currency into the country.

(xvi) Primary deficit is the difference between fiscal deficit and interest payment.

Mathematically, primary deficit = fiscal deficit − interest payments on previous loans

2. (i) Law of supply does not hold true in this case of labour supply. It has been observed that lesser labour is supplied when the wage rate (price of labour) is high and larger labour is supplied when wage rate is low.

A higher wage rate enables the workers to maintain his existing standard of living with less work.

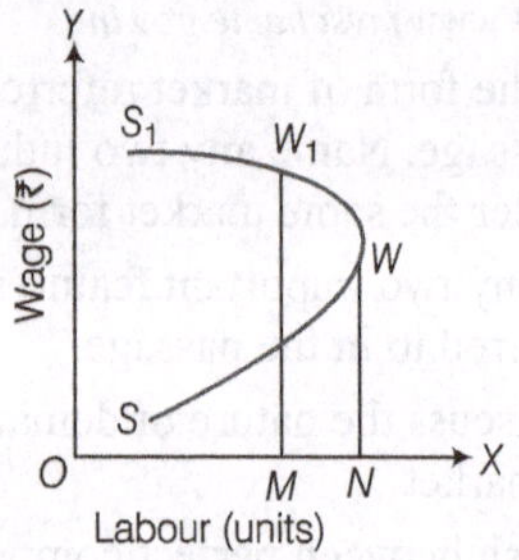

Hence, he would prefer to have more of leisure and less of work. The supply curve in such a situation becomes backward bending, as shown in the diagram.

At *WN* wage rate, the supply of a labour is *ON*. But, beyond *NW* wage rate, the worker will reduce rather than increase his working hours. At MW_1, wage rate, the supply of labour is reduced to *OM*.

(ii) The formula for price elasticity of demand (E_d) is

$$E_d = \frac{\%\text{ change in Q.D}}{\%\text{ change in price}} = \frac{\Delta Q}{\Delta P} \times \frac{P}{Q}$$

$$0.5 = \frac{20}{20} \times \frac{40}{Q}$$

$Q = 80$ units

Thus, the quantity demanded at new price is

$$Q_2 = Q_1 + 20 = 80 + 20$$
$$= 100 \text{ units}$$

3. (i) Under imperfect competition, firms can sell more only by lowering price of the commodity, as a result, both average revenue and marginal revenue are downward sloping.

Relationship between AR and MR under imperfect competition

(a) Both AR and MR curves slope downwards as firms can sell more only by lowering prices.

(b) MR curve lies below AR curve, i.e. AR curve is more elastic as compared to MR curve.

(c) Slope of MR is half of slope of AR.

(d) At mid-point of AR curve, MR = 0.

(e) Below mid-point of AR, MR becomes negative.

(f) MR can be negative, but AR cannot.

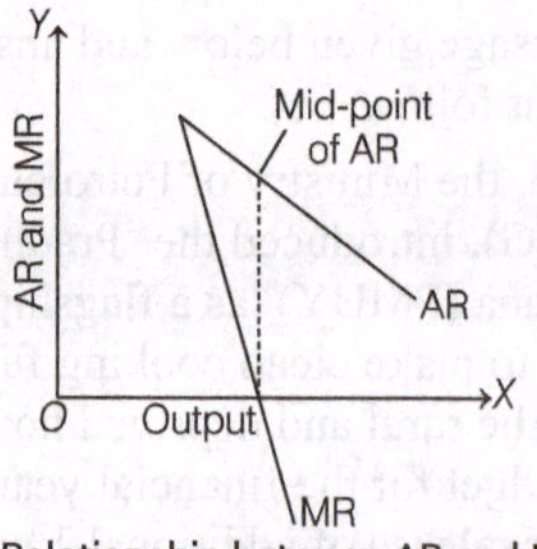

Relationship between AR and MR

(ii) **If both demand and supply decrease in the same proportion** When decrease in supply is equal to decrease in demand, equilibrium price will remain the same but equilibrium output will decrease.

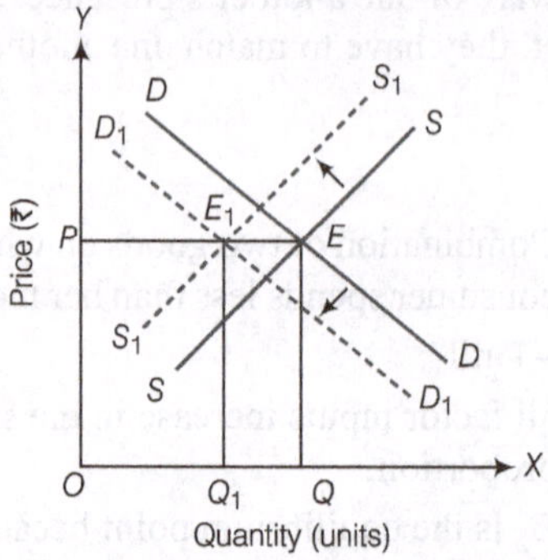

When demand and supply decreases in the same proportion, at this point, *OP* is equilibrium price and *OQ* is equilibrium quantity.

Demand decreases to D_1D_1 and supply decreases to S_1S_1. The new curves intersect each other at point E_1. It shows that equilibrium price remains constant because both demand and supply have decreased in the same proportion. However, equilibrium quantity decreases to OQ_1.

4. (i) Fixed cost is a short-run phenomenon because fixed costs do not vary with the level of output, it remains constant for all levels of output, including zero level of output. They are overheads and are not identifiable with the product.

Total fixed cost curve

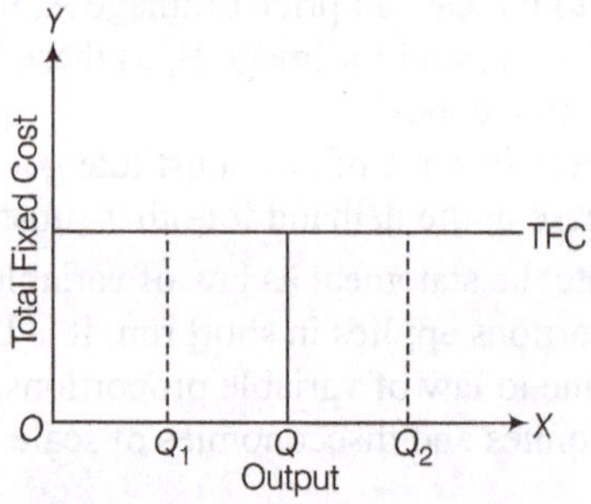

(ii) **Increasing returns to factors** In this stage, total product increases at an increasing rate and hence marginal product increases, average product also increases in this stage. But remember that total product starts from origin but marginal product and average product cannot start from origin.

Reason

Fuller utilisation of the fixed factor In the initial stages, fixed factor remains underutilised. Its fuller utilisation is possible by adding additional units of the variable factor to total input and the marginal product of the variable factor tends to increase.

5. (i) The form of market in this situation is 'monopolistic competition'.

Feature implied is 'product differentiation'.

Product differentiation means similar products but still differentiated in terms of quantity, quality, size, shape, colour, etc. This is an important feature of monopolistic competition which leads to non-price competition.

Instead of competing solely on price, firms in monopolistic competition often use advertising, promotions and other strategies to differentiate their products. Offering gift vouchers is a classic example of non-price competition to attract customers and build brand loyalty.

(ii) If P > AVC but P < ATC, then the firm continues to produce in the short-run, making economic losses. However, if P < AVC, then the firm stops producing as the price is not sufficient enough to cover the variable cost and the firm incurs its fixed costs.

Or

(i) (a) Type of market highlighted is monopsony.

(b) It is a buyer's market as firm X is a single buyer and as a single buyer, he control the demand side of the market completely.

(ii) Monopolistic competition is a blend of perfect competition and monopoly, as it combines the features of both, i.e.

(a) Large number of sellers like in case of perfect competition.

(b) Product differentiation like monopoly.

6. The process that leads to an increase in the money supply is called the credit creation process by commercial banks.

Explanation

Aditi deposits ₹ 1,000 in a bank, which will be primary deposits for the bank and total money supply is ₹ 4,000.

This means money multiplier = 4 and hence, reserve ratio is 25%.

Now, if primary deposits = ₹ 1,000 and RR = 25%, i.e. 1,000 × 25/100 = ₹ 250 will be kept as reserve and now 1,000 – 250 = ₹ 750 can be used to give loans. Loans are never offered in cash, but only as demand deposits in favour of their customers.

Now, this loan will again be with the banks as demand deposits and the process will again start.

Thus, the money goes on multiplying and creates new flow of the economy.

7. (i) The given statement is defended.

Depreciation will make imports costlier in terms of domestic currency.

As a result, prices of imports will rise and thereby imports will fall. On the other hand, exporters can afford to reduce the prices of exports because they are earning more in terms of domestic currency. Exports will become cheaper, as a result of which, BoP will improve.

(ii) The 'Make in India' programme aims to attract global investment and boost domestic manufacturing which can positively impact India's Balance of Payments (BoP) account in the following way

Increase in capital inflows Foreign Direct Investment (FDI) and Foreign Institutional Investment (FII) inflows rise as global companies invest in Indian industries. This improves the capital account surplus.

Or (i) A persistent retail inflation rate of 3.54% in India, even though declining, can impact India's Balance of Payments (BoP) in the following ways

(a) **Reduction in exports** Inflation increases the cost of production, making Indian goods and services less competitive in global markets. This will reduce exports and widen the current account deficit.

(b) **Increase in imports** If domestic prices rise, consumers and businesses may increase imports of cheaper foreign goods, further worsening the trade balance.

(ii) Tata Motors' purchase of Jaguar Land Rover (JLR) for $2.3 billion will be recorded on the debit side of India's Balance of Payments (BoP).

Reason This transaction represents an outflow of foreign exchange from India to the UK, as Tata Motors is making a payment to acquire a foreign company. Such capital outflows are recorded as debits in the capital account of the BoP.

8. (i) **Classification of Government Receipts**

Transaction	Type of Receipt	Reason
(a) Financial help from an MNC for flood victims	Revenue receipt	It neither create any liability nor reduce government assets. It is a non-recurring income for the government.
(b) Sale of shares of a Public Sector Undertaking (PSU) to a private company	Capital receipt	It reduces assets of the government.

(ii) **Categorisation of Taxes**

(a) Income tax – Direct tax

(b) Goods and Services Tax (GST) – Indirect tax

Direct Tax	Indirect Tax
The burden of the tax cannot be shifted; it is paid directly by the individual or entity on whom it is levied.	The burden of the tax can be shifted from one person to another, usually from producers to consumers.

9. (i) No, this monthly assistance provided under the Gruha Lakshmi Scheme will not be a part of national income accounting.

Reason This payment is a transfer payment, as it is provided by the government without any productive activity in return. This has not lead to the production of goods or services.

(ii) (a) True, in a closed economy, there are only two sectors, households and firms and there is no external sector, so, there are no international transactions (no exports, imports or foreign investments). Since Net Factor Income from Abroad (NFIA) is zero, Gross Domestic Product (GDP) equals Gross National Product (GNP).

(b) True, the money received by an Indian cricketer as man of the match does not contribute to the national income of India because it is considered a transfer payment. National income accounts focus on the value of goods and services produced within a country, and transfer payments (such as prizes, grants, or subsidies) do not reflect production.

10. (i) The situation describes a scenario where the supply of chocolates increases at a greater rate in response to a price increase during valentine week. This suggests that the price elasticity of supply is greater than 1, meaning the supply is highly elastic.

Here is a graphical representation

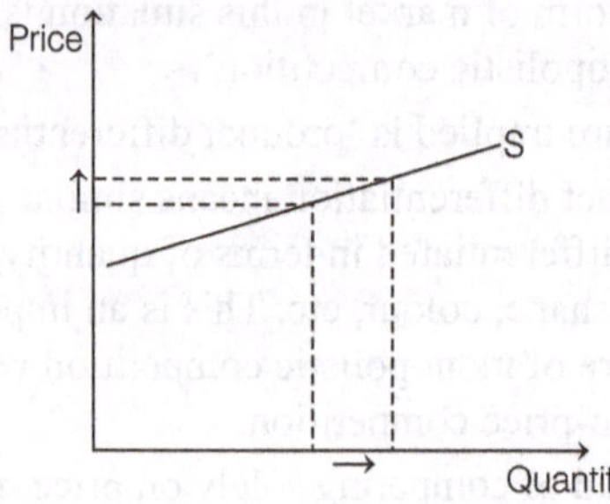

(ii) (a) Robert should allocate his budget according to the law of equi-marginal utility, which states that utility is maximised when

$$\frac{MU_x}{MU_y} = \frac{P_x}{P_y}$$

Given

- Price of X (P_x) = ₹ 2
- Price of Y (P_y) = ₹ 1,
- Budget = ₹ 11

We calculate the Marginal Utility per Rupee (MU/P) for each unit

Units	MU_X	MU_X/P_X (MU_X/2)	MU_Y	MU_Y/P_Y (MU_Y/1)
1	16	8	10	10
2	14	7	9	9
3	12	6	8	8
4	10	5	7	7
5	8	4	6	6
6	6	3	5	5

Allocation of ₹ 11 for maximum satisfaction

- Buy 3 units of X → Cost = 3 × 2 = ₹ 6
- Buy 5 units of Y → Cost = 5 × 1 = ₹ 5
- Total expenditure = 6 + 5 = ₹ 11

So, if Robert will buy 3 units of X and 5 units of Y, he will be in equilibrium.

(b) The schedule follows the law of equi-marginal utility, which states that a consumer achieves equilibrium when the ratio of marginal utility to price is equal for all goods

$$\frac{MU_x}{MU_Y} = \frac{P_X}{P_Y}$$

At equilibrium, the consumer distributes expenditure in such a way that the last rupee spent on each commodity gives equal marginal utility.

11. (i) The investment multiplier (K) measures the effect of an initial increase in investment on the overall national income. It is given by the formula

$$k = \frac{1}{1 - MPC}$$

There exists a direct relation between MPC and multiplier. The higher the value of MPC, the higher the value of the multiplier.

(ii) (a) The gap *EG* represents a deflationary gap. The deflationary gap is the gap showing a deficient of current aggregate demand over aggregate supply at the level of full employment. It is called deflationary because it leads to deflation.

(b) **Fiscal measures**

- **Decrease in taxes** To curb the deflationary gap, the government may decrease the taxes. This may increase the purchasing power in the hands of the people which in turn may increase the aggregate demand in the economy to bring it equal to the aggregate supply.
- **Increase in government expenditure** To curb the deflationary gap, the government may increase its expenditure. It increases the money income of the people. This may again increase the purchasing power in the hands of the people which in turn may increase the aggregate demand in the economy to bring it equal to the aggregate supply.

Monetary measures

- **Bank rate** In case of deflation, the central bank reduces the bank rate to increase the supply of money in the economy. Reduction in bank rate increases the money creation power of commercial banks and also decreases the market rate of interest which induces the public to borrow more. The aggregate demand increases and the deflation is corrected.
- **Open market operations** In a situation of deficient demand leading to deflation, the central bank purchases government securities and bonds from a commercial bank. With the purchase of these securities, the power of commercial bank of giving loans increases, which will control deficient demand.

12. (i) Double counting occurs when the value of intermediate goods is included in the calculation of national income along with the final goods, leading to an overestimation of Gross Domestic Product (GDP).

Example Suppose a farmer sells wheat to a flour mill for ₹ 10, the mill sells flour to a baker for ₹ 20 and the baker sells bread to the final consumer for ₹ 30. If we count all transactions, the total value would be 10 + 20 + 30 = ₹ 60, which is incorrect because the value of intermediate goods (wheat and flour) is being counted multiple times. The correct value of production should be only ₹ 30, the price paid by the final consumer.

Double counting can be avoided by the following ways

(a) **Final goods approach** Only count the value of final goods and services in GDP. In the above example, only the bread's value (₹ 30) should be included.

(b) **Value-added method** Include only the additional value added at each stage of production

- Farmer ₹ 10
- Flour mill ₹ 10 (20 – 10)
- Baker ₹ 10 (30 – 20)
- Total GDP = ₹ 30

By using these methods, we can avoid double counting and ensure an accurate measurement of national income.

(ii) Calculation of NDP at Factor Cost (NDP_{FC}) and NNP at Factor Cost (NNP_{FC})

GDP_{MP} = value of output –raw materials purchased
= 2,000 – 1,400 = ₹ 600 crore

$NDP_{FC} = GDP_{MP}$ – consumption of fixed capital – NIT

$= 600 - 85 - 80$
$= ₹ 435$ crore

$NNP_{FC} = NDP_{FC} + NFIA$
$= 435 - (15 - 30)$
$= ₹ 420$ crore

Or

(i) (a) **Exclusion of non-market activities** GDP only accounts for goods and services traded in the market, ignoring unpaid work such as household chores, volunteer services and caregiving.

These activities contribute significantly to societal well-being but are not reflected in GDP calculations.

(b) **Externalities** Economic activities that increase GDP may also lead to pollution, deforestation and resource depletion. While GDP rises, environmental damage can reduce the quality of life, making it an incomplete measure of economic welfare.

(ii) Calculation of GDP_{MP} and National Income

GDP_{MP} = Private Final Consumption Expenditure + Government Final Consumption Expenditure + Gross Investment + Net Exports (Gross Investment = Net Fixed Capital Formation + Change in Stock + Consumption of Fixed Capital)

$GDP_{MP} = 2{,}500 + 700 + (500 + 60 + 120) + 30$
$= 2{,}500 + 700 + 680 + 30$
$= ₹ 3{,}910$ crore

Calculation of National Income (NNP_{FC})

$NNP_{FC} = GDP_{MP}$ − Net Indirect Taxes + Net Factor Income from Abroad − Consumption of Fixed Capital

$NNP_{FC} = 3{,}910 - 500 + (-30) - 120$
$= 3{,}910 - 500 - 30 - 120 = ₹ 3{,}260$ crore

13. (i) The market form referred to in the passage is 'oligopoly'. Two industries that operate under an oligopoly market structure are

(a) Automobile industry (e.g., Maruti Suzuki, Hyundai, Tata Motors)

(b) Telecommunication industry (e.g., Jio, Airtel, Vodafone-Idea)

(ii) Two important features of oligopoly are

(a) **Few large firms** A small number of firms dominate the market and each firm's actions influence others.

(b) **Interdependence** Firms closely monitor competitors' pricing and marketing strategies and often respond accordingly.

(iii) **Nature of the demand curve in oligopoly** The demand curve in an oligopoly is kinked due to price rigidity. If a firm increases its price, competitors may not follow, leading to a loss of market share. However, if it lowers its price, competitors may also reduce theirs, resulting in a price war. This creates a kink at the current market price, with a steeper demand curve above it and a flatter one below.

(iv) Difference between perfect competition and imperfect competition is as follows

Basis	Perfect Competition	Imperfect competition
Nature of product	Homogeneous (identical) products with no differentiation.	Differentiated or heterogeneous products (branding, quality variations, etc.).
Nature of demand curve	Perfectly elastic (horizontal) demand curve; firms are price takers.	Downward sloping demand curve; firms have some control over price.

ISC

SAMPLE PAPER 01

Time : 3 hrs
Marks : 80

Economics XII

General Instructions

1. Candidates are allowed additional 15 minutes for only reading the paper. They must not start writing during this time.
2. There are thirteen questions in the paper. All questions are compulsory.
3. This paper is divided into three Sections A, B and C.
4. Section A has sixteen subparts which are very short answer questions. Each question carries 1 mark.
5. Section B has eight questions which are short answer questions. Each question carries 4 marks.
6. Section C has four questions which are long answer questions. Each question carries 8 marks.
7. Internal choices have been provided in two questions in Section B and in one question in Section C.
8. The intended marks for questions are given in brackets [ ].

Section A

(16 Marks)

1. (i) The figure given below shows the relation between the quantity demanded for the good X and the price of the good Z. What type of goods are X and Z? **[1]**

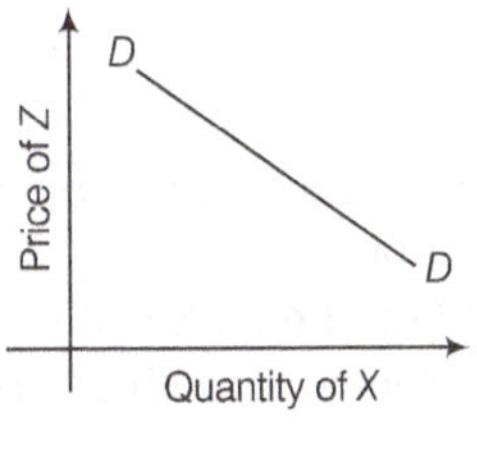

(a) Unrelated goods
(b) Substitute goods
(c) Complementary goods
(d) Giffen goods

(ii) When the percentage change in quantity demanded is equal to percentage change in price, the elasticity of demand will be equal to **[1]**

(a) Unity
(b) More than one
(c) Less than one
(d) Infinity

(iii) Elasticity of supply is not affected by which one of the following? **[1]**

(a) Nature of good
(b) State of technology
(c) Market expenditure
(d) All of the above

(iv) What is the nature of demand curve shown in the image below? **[1]**

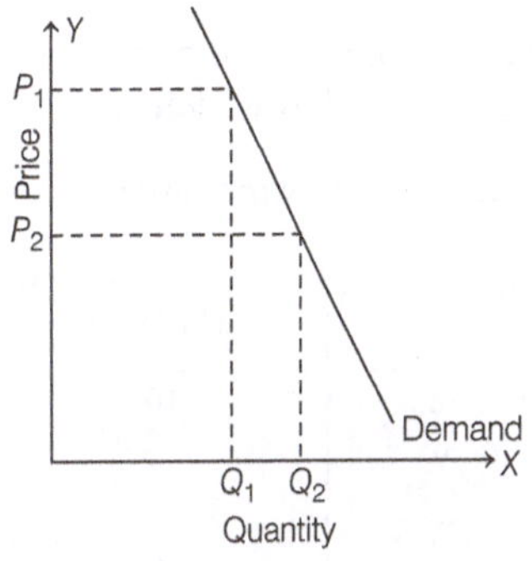

(a) Inelastic demand
(b) Elastic demand
(c) Unit elastic demand
(d) Perfectly elastic demand

(v) If at present \$ 1 = ₹ 95 and later \$ 1 = ₹ 80, it is a case of [1]
(a) appreciation of currency
(b) devaluation of currency
(c) depreciation of currency (d) supply of currency

(vi) Depreciation of domestic currency leads to [1]
(a) increase in exports (b) increase in imports
(c) decrease in imports (d) Both (a) and (c)

(vii) What will be the value of MPC in the given saving function, $S = -100 + 0.3Y$? [1]
(a) 0.3 (b) 0.7
(c) 0.8 (d) Can's be determined

(viii) **Assertion** (A) Commercial banks play a crucial role in providing financial services to individuals and businesses.
Reason (R) Commercial banks offer various services like deposit accounts, loans and payment mechanisms to facilitate economic transactions. [1]
Alternatives
(a) Both Assertion (A) and Reason (R) are true and Reason (R) is the correct explanation of Assertion (A)
(b) Both Assertion (A) and Reason (R) are true, but Reason (R) is not the correct explanation of Assertion (A)
(c) Assertion (A) is true, but Reason (R) is false
(d) Both Asserton (A) and Reason (R) are false

(ix) **Assertion** (A) RBI is known as issuing authority.
Reason (R) It has the monopoly power of issuing currency. [1]
Alternatives
(a) Both Assertion (A) and Reason (R) are true and Reason (R) is the correct explanation of Assertion (A)
(b) Both Assertion (A) and Reason (R) are true, but Reason (R) is not the correct explanation of Assertion (A)
(c) Assertion (A) is true, but Reason (R) is false
(d) Both Asserton (A) and Reason (R) are false

(x) Give two examples of direct taxes. [1]

(xi) State whether the following statement is true or false
"Legal reserve ratio is the sum of CRR and SLR." [1]

(xii) Identify and explain the function of the central bank shown in the image below. [1]

(xiii) What is deficit financing? [1]

(xiv) Define full employment. [1]

(xv) What are the components of aggregate demand in an open economy? [1]

(xvi) What is explicit cost? [1]

Section B

(32 Marks)

2. (i) An increase in income affect the quantity demanded of an inferior commodity. Why? [2]

(ii) Giving example explain how 'emergencies' are an exception to the law of demand? [2]

3. (i) Complete the following table [2]

Output (units) (Q)	Price (₹) (P)	Marginal Revenue (MR) (₹)	Total Revenue (TR) (₹)
1	...	10	...
2	9	...	...
3	...	...	24
4	...	4	...

(ii) What will be the behaviour of Total Product (TP), when Marginal Product (MP) falls? [2]

4. Explain the implications of the following features of perfect competition.
(i) Large number of buyers and sellers. [2]
(ii) Freedom of entry and exit of firm. [2]

5. (i) Write any two differences between balance of trade and balance of payment. [2]
(ii) Mention two invisible items of the balance of payments of a country. [2]

Or Balance of Payments (BoP) always balances in the accounting sense. Explain briefly. [4]

6. (i) Why National Saving Certificates (NSCs) are not included in the money supply? [2]
(ii) "Money has overcome the problem of barter system." Give two reasons to support your answer. [2]

7. (i) The savings function of an economy is $S = -200 + 0.25Y$. The economy is in equilibrium when income is equal to ₹ 2,000. Calculate

(a) Investment expenditure at equilibrium level of income (I)

(b) Autonomous consumption $(\overline{C})$ **[2]**

(ii) What is meant by ex-ante demand and ex-post demand? **[2]**

8. State whether the following will be included in national income or not. Give reasons for your answer.

(i) Dividend received by an Indian from his investment in some foreign company. **[2]**

(ii) Compensation of employees paid to an Indian resident working in Japan Embassy in India. **[2]**

Or

Differentiate between national income and private income.

9. (i) "An increase in public expenditure create more employment in the country." Justify this statement. **[2]**

(ii) Giving reasons, classify the following into direct and indirect tax

(a) Wealth Tax

(b) Goods and Services Tax **[2]**

Section C

(32 Marks)

10. (i) Under perfect competition, a firm will enjoy normal proft in the long-run even if it enjoys super normal profit in the short-run. Explain. **[4]**

(ii) Explain the implications of the following features of oligopoly market.

(a) Few firms **[2]**

(b) Barriers to the entry of firms **[2]**

11. (i) Following diagram shows the supply curve of two different commodities. Give their price elasticities. **[2]**

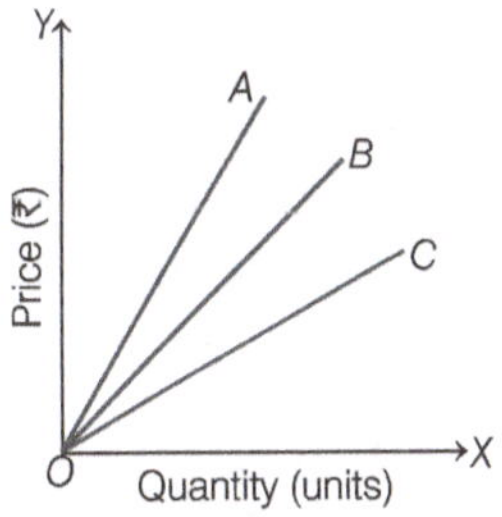

(ii) How is price elasticity of demand affected by

(a) number of substitute available for the good

(b) nature of good **[6]**

12. (i) Distinguish between factor income and transfer income. **[4]**

(ii) From the following data, calculate national income by income method and expenditure method. **[4]**

S. No.	Items	₹ (in crores)
(i)	Compensation of employees	700
(ii)	Government final consumption expenditure	750
(iii)	Net factor income from abroad	(–)10
(iv)	Net exports	(–) 15
(v)	Profits	600
(vi)	Net indirect taxes	60
(vii)	Mixed income of self-employed	350
(viii)	Rent	200
(ix)	Interest	310
(x)	Private final consumption expenditure	1,100
(xi)	Net domestic capital formation	385
(xii)	Consumption of fixed capital	65

Or (i) What do you mean by appreciation of domestic currency? How it affects exports?

(ii) Calculate net national product at factor cost.

S. No.	Items	₹ (in crores)
(i)	Private final consumption expenditure	8,000
(ii)	Government final consumption expenditure	1,000
(iii)	Exports	700
(iv)	Imports	120
(v)	Annual allowance for wear and tear	60
(vi)	Fixed business investment	300
(vii)	Residential investment	200
(viii)	Change in stock	100
(ix)	Factor income to abroad	40
(x)	Factor income from abroad	90
(xi)	Net product taxes	400
(xii)	Net production taxes	250

13. Read the passage given below and answer the questions that follow

India's current account may turn surplus in the June quarter after a gap of 12 years, the finance ministry said, as a stringent coronavirus lockdown squeezed domestic economic activity and crimped imports.

The last time India's current account turned positive was in the March quarter of 2006-07 at $4.2 billion.

However, for the full year, current account was positive for three consecutive years from 2001-02 to 2003-04. Data for the March quarter is expected to be released by this month end.

(i) Briefly explain the components of current account of BoP. **[2]**

(ii) Differentiate between current account and capital account of BoP. **[2]**

(iii) Did the imports increase or decrease during the coronavirus lockdown and why? **[2]**

(iv) State whether the following transaction is recorded in the current or capital account. "Shipping services by an Indian company to a foreign company."

What happen to BoP if the inflows on account of BoP exceeds the outflows? **[2]**

Answers

1. (i) (c) Complementary goods

(ii) (b) More than one

(iii) (c) Market expenditure

(iv) (a) Inelastic demand

(v) (a) appreciation of currency

(vi) (d) Both (a) and (c)

(vii) (b) 0.7

(viii) (a) Both Assertion (A) and Reason (R) are true and Reason (R) is the correct explanation of Assertion (A)

(ix) (a) Both Assertion (A) and Reason (R) are true and Reason (R) is the correct explanation of Assertion (A)

(xi) True

3. (i) Price – 10, 8, 7; MR = 8, 6

TR = 10, 18, 28

7. (i) (a) ₹ 300 (b) ₹ 200

12. (ii) ₹ 2,150 crore (both methods)

Or

(ii) ₹ 9,920 crore

ISC

SAMPLE PAPER 02

Time : 3 hrs
Marks : 80

Economics XII

General Instructions

1. Candidates are allowed additional 15 minutes for only reading the paper. They must not start writing during this time.
2. There are thirteen questions in the paper. All questions are compulsory.
3. This paper is divided into three Sections A, B and C.
4. Section A has sixteen subparts which are very short answer questions. Each question carries 1 mark.
5. Section B has eight questions which are short answer questions. Each question carries 4 marks.
6. Section C has four questions which are long answer questions. Each question carries 8 marks.
7. Internal choices have been provided in two questions in Section B and in one question in Section C.
8. The intended marks for questions are given in brackets [ ].

Section A

(16 Marks)

1. (i) Balance of trade includes which of the following items? **[1]**

(a) Export and import of visible goods
(b) Export and import of invisible goods
(c) Both (a) and (b)   (d) Neither (a) nor (b)

(ii) Increase in the value of domestic currency by the central bank is referred to as **[1]**

(a) devaluation   (b) revaluation
(c) depreciation   (d) appreciation

(iii) Identify the reason of shift in the supply curve given below. **[1]**

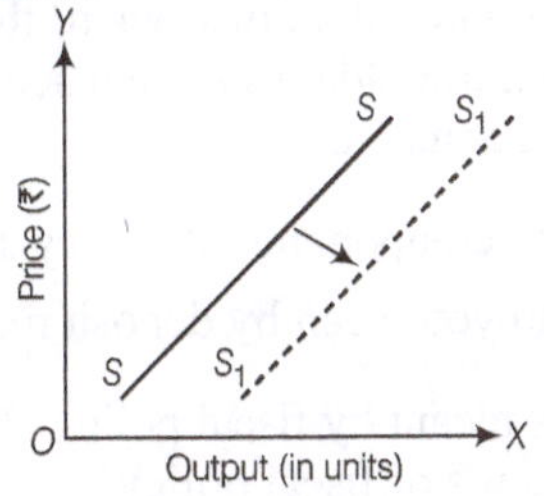

(a) Change in the price of the commodity
(b) Increase in input prices
(c) Increase in the price of substitute goods
(d) Improvement in technology

(iv) Identify the type of good from the demand curve shown below. **[1]**

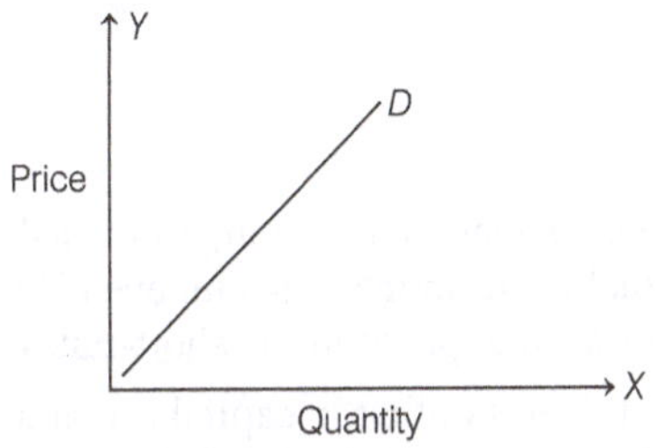

(a) Normal good
(b) Inferior good
(c) Giffen good
(d) None of the above

(v) During the covid lockdown period, government fixed the maximum price of sanitizers. This action is referring to as **[1]**

(a) price ceiling
(b) price flooring
(c) price regulation
(d) None of the above

(vi) A rational producer prefers to produce in which phase of the law of variable proportion? **[1]**

(a) First phase (b) Second phase
(c) Third phase (d) At the end of second phase

(vii) In the simple aggregate demand function, investment is assumed to be [1]
(a) autonomous investment
(b) induced investment
(c) sum of autonomous and induced investment
(d) None of the above

(viii) **Assertion** (A) Statutory liquidity ratio is the ratio of demand deposits of a commercial bank which, it has to keep with itself in the form of specified liquid assets.

Reason (R) Statutory liquidity ratio is a component of legal reserve ratio, which affects the credit creation in the economy. [1]

Alternatives
(a) Both Assertion (A) and Reason (R) are true and Reason (R) is the correct explanation of Assertion (A)
(b) Both Assertion (A) and Reason (R) are true, but Reason (R) is not the correct explanation of Assertion (A)
(c) Assertion (A) is true, but Reason (R) is false
(d) Both Asserton (A) and Reason (R) are false

(ix) **Assertion** (A) Public goods are non-rivalrous.

Reason (R) The benefit of such goods can be enjoyed by all and are not restricted to any one person. [1]

Alternatives
(a) Both Assertion (A) and Reason (R) are true and Reason (R) is the correct explanation of Assertion (A)
(b) Both Assertion (A) and Reason (R) are true, but Reason (R) is not the correct explanation of Assertion (A)
(c) Assertion (A) is true, but Reason (R) is false
(d) Both Asserton (A) and Reason (R) are false

(x) Mention the fiscal tools used by the government to meet the objectives of reducing inequalities of income and wealth in the economy. [1]

(xi) Commercial banks acts as the 'lender of last resort' for the general public. State true or false. [1]

(xii) Observe the image given below carefully and identify the value of investment multiplier for the same. [1]

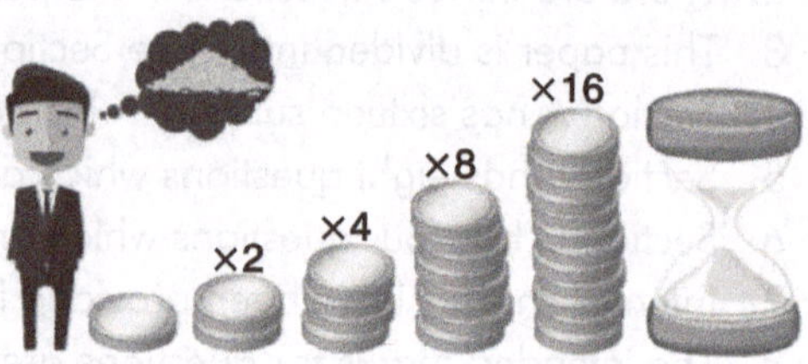

(xiii) Define revenue receipts of government budget. [1]

(xiv) What is inflationary gap? [1]

(xv) Write the formula to calculate MPS. [1]

(xvi) What are accommodating transactions of BoP? [1]

Section B

(32 Marks)

2. (i) Under perfect competition, a firm will enjoy normal profit in the long-run even if it enjoys super normal profit in the short-run. Explain. [2]

(ii) What does a deficit in capital account of Balance of Payments (BoP) indicate? [2]

3. (i) From the schedule provided below calculate the total revenue. [2]

Quantity	1	2	3	4	5	6	7	8	9
Marginal Revenue	10	6	2	2	2	0	0	0	−5

(ii) Why does Total Variable Cost (TVC) increases at a diminishing rate at initial levels of output? [2]

4. Discuss. How under perfect competition, a firm is a price-taker and an industry a price-maker? [4]

5. (i) What is the implication of imperfect knowledge under monopoly market? [2]

(ii) Why is the average revenue curve of a firm under perfect competition parallel to x-axis and negatively sloped under monopoly? [2]

Or There are certain situations where the law of demand does not hold true. Identify and discuss two exceptions to the law of demand. [4]

6. (i) State the components of money supply. [2]

(ii) What do you mean by deposit money? [2]

7. (i) What is meant by fiscal policy? Name any two instruments of fiscal policy. [2]

(ii) The consumption is given as $C = 40 + 0.6Y$. Derive saving function, autonomous consumption and MPC. [2]

8. "India's GDP is expected to expand around 7.5% in 2022-23: World Bank." Does the given statement mean that welfare of people in India increases at the same rate? Comment with reason. **[4]**

Or Why should the aggregate final expenditure of an economy be equal to the aggregate factor payments? Explain.

9. (i) A government budget shows a primary deficit of ₹ 6,000 crore. The revenue expenditure on interest payment is ₹ 350 crore. How much is the fiscal deficit? **[2]**

(ii) Balanced budget is an achievement to the government. Why or why not? **[2]**

Section C

(32 Marks)

10. (i) Price per unit is equal to average revenue and marginal revenue of a firm under perfect competition. Justify this statement, give reason to support your answer. **[2]**

(ii) Explain the determination of equilibrium price and quantity under competitive market using suitable diagram. **[6]**

11. (i)

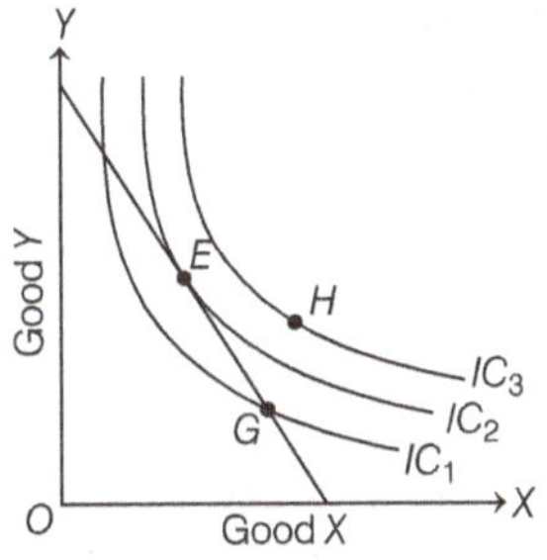

(i) Identify the point of consumer equilibrium in the above diagram and also state the conditions of consumer equilibrium under ordinal approach. **[2]**

(ii) Explain the following

(a) Why is an indifference curve convex to the origin? **[2]**

(b) Why does a higher indifference curve represents a higher level of satisfaction? **[4]**

12. (i) Is it possible for an individual to be a citizen of more than two countries at one point of time? **[4]**

(ii) Calculate national income by (a) Product method and (b) Expenditure method. **[4]**

Items	₹ (in crores)
Gross value added at market price by primary sector	300
Private final consumption expenditure	750
Consumption of fixed capital	150
Net indirect taxes	120
Gross value added at market price by secondary sector	200
Net domestic fixed capital formation	220
Change in stock	(–)20
Gross value added at market price by tertiary sector	700
Net import	50
Government final consumption expenditure	150
Net factor income from abroad	20

Or (i) When does NDP_{MP} is less than NDP_{FC}?

(ii) From the following data estimat to (a) National income and (b) Personal income.

S. No.	Items	₹ (in crores)
(i)	Net national product at market price	1,015
(ii)	Income from property and entrepreneurship accuring to government administrative departments	25
(iii)	Indirect taxes	150
(iv)	Subsidies	20
(v)	Saving of non-departmetnal entcrprieses	5
(vi)	National debt interest	10
(vii)	Current transfers from government	25
(viii)	Current transfer from rest of the world	10
(ix)	Saving of private corporate sector	15
(x)	Corporate profit tax	10

13. Read the passage given below and answer the questions that follow

The case is about the shift in India's electricity demand and supply due to changes in the macro environment. In 2019, India's annual electricity demand increased by 1.1%, the smallest rise since 2013. For the month of December 2019, power demand dropped to 100.81 billion units from 101.28 billion units a year earlier, representing the fifth straight month of decline in the year.

Electric supply in the country also fell for the fifth consecutive month in December 2019. Power supply fell to 101.92 billion units in December 2019, down 1.1% from 103.04 billion units the previous year.

The economic slowdown, lower demand from the industrial sector, losses made by the power distribution companies, and energy efficiency measures were some of the factors responsible for the fall in power demand and supply.

(i) What is the nature of elasticity of demand for electricity and why? **[2]**

(ii) How will be the demand for electricity impacted if government imposes a tax on electricity consumption? **[2]**

(iii) Briefly explain any two other factors that impacts elasticity of demand. **[2]**

(iv) How is elasticity of demand measured using percentage method? Why is demand said to be highly elastic? **[2]**

Answers

1. (i) (a) Export and import of visible goods

(ii) (b) revaluation

(iii) (d) Improvement in technology

(iv) (c) Giffen good

(v) (a) price ceiling

(vi) (b) Second phase

(vii) (a) autonomous investment

(viii) (b) Both Assertion (A) and Reason (R) are true, but Reason (R) is not the correct explanation of Assertion (A)

(ix) (a) Both Assertion (A) and Reason (R) are true and Reason (R) is the correct explanation of Assertion (A)

(xi) False

9. (i) ₹ 6,350 crore

12. (ii) (a) ₹ 950 crore

(b) ₹ 950 crore

Or (ii) (a) ₹ 885 crore

(b) ₹ 875 crore

ISC

SAMPLE PAPER 03

Time : 3 hrs
Marks : 80

Economics XII

General Instructions

1. Candidates are allowed additional 15 minutes for only reading the paper. They must not start writing during this time.
2. There are thirteen questions in the paper. All questions are compulsory.
3. This paper is divided into three Sections A, B and C.
4. Section A has sixteen subparts which are very short answer questions. Each question carries 1 mark.
5. Section B has eight questions which are short answer questions. Each question carries 4 marks.
6. Section C has four questions which are long answer questions. Each question carries 8 marks.
7. Internal choices have been provided in two questions in Section B and in one question in Section C.
8. The intended marks for questions are given in brackets [ ].

Section A

(16 Marks)

1. (i) Demand for a good depends upon which of the following? **[1]**

(a) Willingness to buy (b) Ability to buy
(c) Price of the good (d) All of these

(ii) Which property of indifference curves is being violated in the following figure? **[1]**

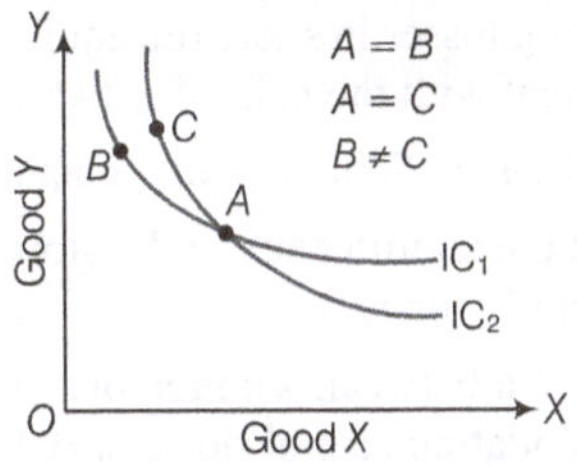

(a) An IC slope downward from left to the right
(b) An IC is convex to the origin
(c) Higher IC yeilds higher satisfaction
(d) Indifference curves never intersect each other

(iii) Movement along the supply curve is caused by **[1]**

(a) Change in other factors keeping price constant
(b) Change in price keeping other factors constant
(c) Both (a) and (b)
(d) Neither (a) nor (b)

(iv) What will be the elasticity of demand for the curve shown in the image below? **[1]**

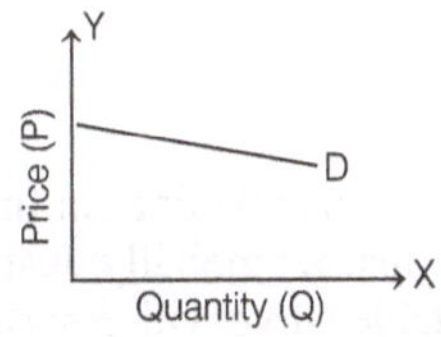

(a) Elastic demand (b) Inelastic demand
(c) Unit elastic demand (d) Perfectly elastic demand

(v) Indian Railways charges lower freight rates for transporting essential products like food, coal etc, as compared to freight charges for other products like TV, air coolers, etc. This is an example of **[1]**

(a) price ceiling (b) price discrimination
(c) price control (d) floor pricing

(vi) Law of returns to scale is applicable in which of the following time period? **[1]**

(a) Short-run (b) Medium-run
(c) Long-run (d) Both (a) and (c)

(vii) Under which of the following exchange rate systems, foreign exchange rate is maintained in a fixed band by the central bank? **[1]**

(a) Fixed exchange rate (b) Floating exchange rate
(c) Managed floating exchange rate
(d) Both (b) and (c)

(viii) **Assertion** (A) Plastic money is becoming more popular these days.

Reason (R) It is considered as safe method and enables to avoid carrying each. **[1]**

Alternatives

(a) Both Assertion (A) and Reason (R) are true and Reason (R) is the correct explanation of Assertion (A)

(b) Both Assertion (A) and Reason (R) are true, but Reason (R) is not the correct explanation of Assertion (A)

(c) Assertion (A) is true, but Reason (R) is false

(d) Both Asserton (A) and Reason (R) are false

(ix) **Assertion** (A) Commercial banks play a crucial role in providing financial services to individuals and businesses.

Reason (R) Commercial banks offer various services like deposit accounts, loans and payment mechanisms to facilitate economic transactions. **[1]**

Alternatives

(a) Both Assertion (A) and Reason (R) are true and Reason (R) is the correct explanation of Assertion (A)

(b) Both Assertion (A) and Reason (R) are true, but Reason (R) is not the correct explanation of Assertion (A)

(c) Assertion (A) is true, but Reason (R) is false

(d) Both Asserton (A) and Reason (R) are false

(x) State any two objectives of government budget. **[1]**

(xi) The central bank of the country functions as the "Custodian of foreign exchange reserves." State true or false. **[1]**

(xii) Observing the image given below carefully, identify and explain the objective that government should pursue to deal with this situation. **[1]**

(xiii) Fiscal deficit is always equal to borrowings. Why? **[1]**

(xiv) What is point of inflexion? **[1]**

(xv) Explain open market operations as a measure to control inflation. **[1]**

(xvi) In which market AR and MR coincides with each other? **[1]**

Section B

(32 Marks)

2. (i) Due to Russia and Ukraine conflict, petroleum prices are impacted globally. Justify the statement using a suitable curve with respect to the supply of petroleum. **[2]**

(ii) As price falls from ₹ 5 to ₹ 4 per unit, total expenditure on the commodity increases from ₹ 300 to ₹ 600. Find out the Elasticity of Demand (E_d) using percentage method. **[2]**

3. (i) Complete the table given below **[2]**

Output	0	1	2	3	4	5
TC	20	38	54	74	104	144
AFC						

(ii) Can total product and marginal product become zero or negative? Why? **[2]**

4. Explain, why demand curve for a monopolistic firm is more elastic than demand curve for a monopoly firm. **[4]**

5. (i) In the short-run under perfect competition, a firm should produce if and only if P for AR ≥ AVC. Justify the given statement. **[2]**

(ii) Distinguish between break-even point and shut down point. **[2]**

Or A perfectly competitive firm can continue producing even if it is incurring losses in short-run equilibrium. Justify the given statement with the help of a diagram. **[4]**

6. (i) Define money. Write its components. **[2]**

(ii) Explain the significance of the store of the value function of money. **[2]**

7. (i) Distinguish between autonomous and accommodating capital flows in Balance of Payments (BoP). **[2]**

(ii) Balance of Payments (BoP) always balances in the accounting sense. Explain briefly. **[2]**

8. Explain the importance of normal residents while calculating national income. Use appropriate example. **[4]**

Or Write the precautions of value added method while calculating national income.

9. (i) Are fiscal deficit necessarily inflationary? **[2]**

(ii) Why do developing countries like India prepare a deficit budget? **[2]**

Section C

[32 Marks]

10. (i) In a certain market, a firm is not required to reduce the price to sell more. Identify the market and explain the behaviour of TR and MR. **[2]**

(ii) Differentiate between perfect competition and monopolistic competition. **[6]**

11. (i)

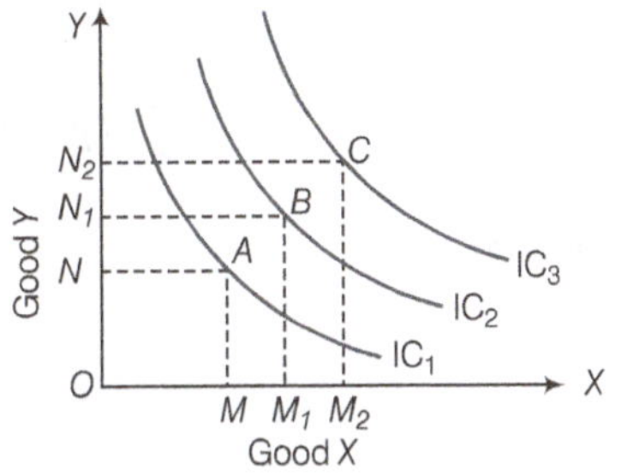

Identify and explain the property of IC being depicted in the figure above. **[2]**

(ii) (a) Define an indifference map. **[2]**

(b) Explain why an indifference curve to the right shows higher utility level. **[4]**

12. (i) Is depreciation different from capital loss? Explain briefly. **[4]**

(ii) Calculate Net National Product at Market Price (NNP_{MP}) by

(a) Income method (b) Expenditure method

From the following data **[4]**

Items	(₹ in crores)
Net indirect tax	200
Net factor income to abroad	30
Profit	230
Bonus	43
Compensation of employees	600
Net domestic capital formation	200
Government final consumption expenditure	300
Rent	120
Interest	130
Net imports	100
Private final consumption expenditure	900
Royalty on land	20

Or

(i) Write the steps of calculating personal disposable income from National Income (NI).

(ii) Find Net Value Added at MP.

S. No.	Items	₹ (in crores)
(i)	Output sold (units)	1,000
(ii)	Price per unit of output	30
(iii)	Excise	1,600
(iv)	Import duty	400
(v)	Net change in stock	(–) 500
(vi)	Depreciation	2,000
(vii)	Intermediate cost	8,000

13. Read the passage given below and answer the questions that follow

Aggregate demand for petroleum products, including auto and industiral fuels, rose for the first time in seven months, as India's economy limped out of a pandemic-induced consumption slowdown. Consumption of petroleum and related products rose 2.5% year-on-year to 17,777 thousand metric tonnes in October, according to data from the Petroleum Planning and Analysis Cell.

That's the first increase since March. The combined consumption of petrol, diesel, liquefied petroleum gas, naphtha and pet coke, among others, was 84.1% of last year's level in April-October. That reflects the prolonged impact of one of the harshest lockdowns in the world to contain the pandemic.

(i) What do you mean by aggregate demand? Write down the components of aggregate demand. **[2]**

(ii) What is the equation of consumption? Explain its components. **[2]**

(iii) What is the slope of consumption curve? How it impacts the shape of the same? **[2]**

(iv) Explain the relation the APC and APS using suitable numerical example. **[2]**

Answers

1. (i) (d) All of these

(ii) (d) Indifference curves never intersect each other

(iii) (b) Change in price keeping other factors constant

(iv) (a) Elastic demand

(v) (a) price ceiling (vi) (c) Long-run

(vii) (c) Managed floating exchange rate

(viii) (a) Both Assertion (A) and Reason (R) are true and Reason (R) is the correct explanation of Assertion (A)

(ix) (a) Both Assertion (A) and Reason (R) are true and Reason (R) is the correct explanation of Assertion (A)

(xi) True

2. (ii) E_d will be more than 1.

12. (ii) (a) ₹ 1,270 crore

(b) ₹ 1,270 crore

Or (ii) NVA_{MP} = ₹ 19,500

ISC

Latest ISC Specimen Paper

Time : 3 hrs
Marks : 80

Economics XII

General Instructions

1. Candidates are allowed additional 15 minutes for only reading the paper. They must not start writing during this time.
2. There are 13 questions in the paper. All questions are compulsory.
3. This paper is divided into three Sections : A, B and C.
4. Section-A consists of sixteen subparts which are objective/very short answer type questions carrying 1 mark each.
5. Section-B consists of eight questions which are short answer type questions carrying 4 marks each.
6. Section-C consists of four questions which are long answer type questions carrying 8 marks each.
7. Internal choices have been provided in two questions in Section-B and in one question in Section-C.
8. The intended marks for questions or parts of questions are given in brackets [ ].

Section A

(16 Marks)

1. (i)

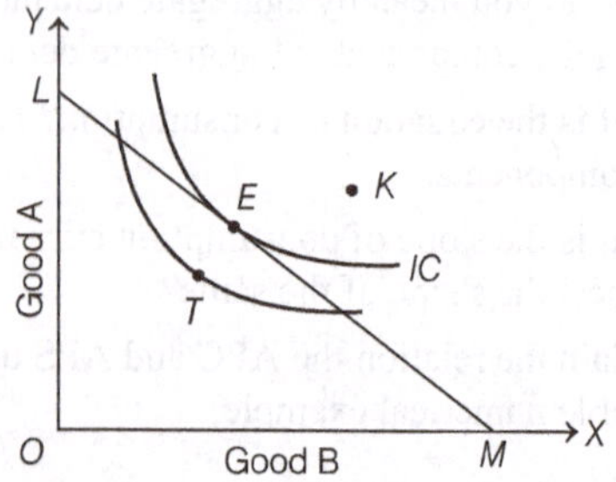

Points *K* and *T* will not be attained by the consumer. Select the reason from the options given below. **(Understanding) [1]**

(a) *K* does not lie on any IC and entire money is not spent at *T*

(b) *K* is beyond the financial capacity of the consumer and *T* provides a lower level of satisfaction

(c) Equilibrium should be unique and that is point *E*

(d) *K* gives more of both the goods A and B and *T* gives less B

(ii) Utility maximising consumers would like to decrease the consumption when **(Understanding) [1]**

(a) $MU_x = P_x$
(b) $MU_x > P_x$
(c) $MU_x < P_x$
(d) $MU_x = P_Y$

(iii)

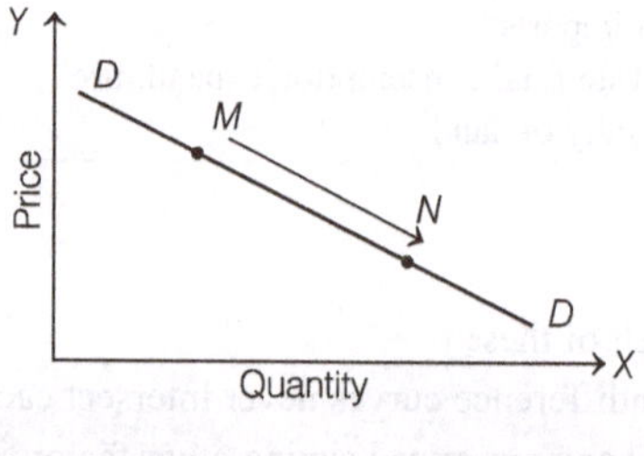

With reference to the diagram shown above, select the reason for the movement from point *M* to *N* from the following options. **(Analysis) [1]**

(a) Increase in the real income of the consumer and rise in relative price of the commodity

(b) Increase in the real income of the consumer and fall in relative price of the commodity

(c) Decrease in the real income of the consumer and rise in relative price of the commodity
(d) Decrease in the real income of the consumer and fall in relative price of the commodity

(iv) Naseer is planning to buy a car for his family. Observe the image shown below and select the most rational reaction of Naseer. **(Application) [1]**

(a) Naseer will not change his decision to buy a car
(b) He will postpone his plan to buy a car
(c) Naseer will become indecisive
(d) He will decide to purchase two cars instead of one

(v) Which one of the following statements is correct with reference to government budget? **(Application) [1]**
(a) Interest paid on government's borrowing reduces liability of the government
(b) Financial aid received from the World Bank for cyclone affected areas is revenue receipt
(c) Grants given by the central government to the state government is capital expenditure
(d) Profits of BHEL, a PSU, increases the assets of the government

(vi) If the value of US Dollar increases continuously in terms of Yen, it will result in **(Understanding) [1]**
(a) more import from USA by Japan
(b) more import from Japan by USA
(c) more export of USA to Japan
(d) less export of Japan to USA

(vii) Sometimes, a firm considers the action and reaction of its rival firms while determining its price and output levels.
Which market form does such firm belong to? **(Recall) [1]**
(a) Perfect competition
(b) Monopoly
(c) Monopolistic competition
(d) Oligopoly

(viii) **Assertion** (A) A firm is able to sell more quantity of a commodity by reducing its price.
Reason (R) As it sells additional units of the commodity at a lower price, the firm's marginal revenue will be less than its average revenue. **(Analysis) [1]**

Alternatives
(a) Both Assertion (A) and Reason (R) are true and Reason (R) is the correct explanation of Assertion (A)
(b) Both Assertion (A) and Reason (R) are true, but Reason (R) is not the correct explanation of Assertion (A)
(c) Assertion (A) is true, but Reason (R) is false
(d) Both Assertion (A) and Reason (R) are false

(ix) **Assertion** (A) GST is a kind of proportional tax.
Reason (R) The tax rate remains same irrespective of the level of income of the people. **(Analysis) [1]**

Alternatives
(a) Both Assertion (A) and Reason (R) are true and Reason (R) is the correct explanation of Assertion (A)
(b) Both Assertion (A) and Reason (R) are true, but Reason (R) is not the correct explanation of Assertion (A)
(c) Assertion (A) is true, but Reason (R) is false
(d) Both Assertion (A) and Reason (R) are false

(x) Oligopoly differs from monopolistic competition on the basis of number of sellers.
State any other difference between these two market forms. **(Recall) [1]**

(xi) APC can be greater than one, but MPC is always less than one. Give a reason to justify this phenomenon. **(Understanding) [1]**

(xii) If aggregate demand exceeds aggregate supply in a situation of full employment, what will be its impact on the economy? **(Understanding) [1]**

(xiii) If autonomous payments are higher than autonomous receipts, how can BoP be brought into balance? **(Understanding) [1]**

(xiv) Monopsony is regarded as a buyers' market. Do you agree? Give a reason. **(Evaluate) [1]**

(xv) Illustrate that investment multiplier is inversely proportional to MPS. **(Understanding) [1]**

(xvi) Cite one measure to overcome a deflationary gap. **(Recall) [1]**

Section B (32 Marks)

2. (i) Prices of air conditioners and refrigerators have shot up in the new year as consumer durables makers pass on the impact of rising raw material costs and higher freight charges to customers, while home appliances like washing machines may witness 5-10 per cent price hike later this month or by March.

Source *The Economic Times*

Explain the behaviour of supply of this consumer durable. Illustrate the same in a diagram. **(Understanding) [2]**

(ii) If the price hike in the market is about 10% and this leads to the fall in the quantity demanded by 12%, calculate the price elasticity of demand. Mention the degree of price elasticity of demand. **(Application) [2]**

3. (i) Union Finance Minister Mrs. Nirmala Sitharaman announced during her budget speech that the centre would reduce its fiscal deficit to 5.1% of gross GDP in 2024-25.

(The present fiscal deficit is 5.8% of GDP.)

Source *Union budget 2024-25*

What would be the impact of this decision on government borrowing? Why? **(Understanding) [2]**

(ii) It is believed that increase in public expenditure leads to inflation. Under what circumstances, may a government consider it prudent to increase public expenditure to control inflation? **(Understanding) [2]**

4. (i) Given that fixed cost is ₹ 30. Calculate TVC and TC from the following data. **(Application) [2]**

Output (Units)	0	1	2	3
Marginal cost	0	10	15	25

(ii) Cite any two differences between returns to factor and returns to scale. **(Understanding) [2]**

Or

(i) Draw a well-labelled diagram to show AFC and AC curves. State the nature of each curve. **(Understanding)**

(ii) Study the data given below and identify the laws followed in the production of A and B depicted in the Table I and Table II.

Justify your answer with a reason for each. **(Analysis)**

Table I			**Table II**		
Machines	**Labour**	**Output of A** (Units)	**Machines**	**Labour**	**Output of B** (Units)
5	10	1,000	5	10	400
5	11	1,150	10	20	800
5	12	1,310	15	30	1,200

5. (i) A perfectly competitive firm always enjoys normal profit in the long-run irrespective of the situation it faces in the short-run. Discuss the statement in brief. **(Understanding) [2]**

(ii) A car company 'W' hired an international cricket player for its endorsement in India while two other car companies' 'Y' and 'R' hired two famous bollywood film stars for this purpose. Explain the feature of the competitive market indicated above. **(Understanding) [2]**

6. (i) A firm under perfect competition is a price taker but the industry is the price maker. Defend or refute this statement by giving a reason. **(Evaluate) [2]**

(ii) Normal profits for a firm imply that the firm is breaking even. Explain. **(Understanding) [2]**

7. (i) India has been operating on a managed floating exchange rate regime since March 1993. Explain the statement. **(Understanding) [2]**

(ii) List different components of balance of payment on current account and capital account. **(Recall) [2]**

8. (i) With the help of a reason, explain why the following are included in calculation of national income.

(a) Goods supplied free of cost by the government

(b) Own account production **(Understanding) [2]**

(ii) Outline any two precautions that should be taken in estimation of national income by expenditure method. **(Understanding) [2]**

Or (i) Differentiate between personal income and private income. **(Understanding)**

(ii) Why are net exports added in the total expenditure in measuring national income by expenditure method? **(Understanding)**

9. With the help of a diagram, determine the equilibrium level of output and income by using aggregate demand and aggregate supply approach. **(Understanding) [4]**

Section C

(32 Marks)

10. (i) What are average product and marginal product? With the help of a suitable diagram, discuss the relationship between average product and marginal product. **(Understanding) [6]**

(ii) Which stage of the law of variable proportions will be the best for the producer? Explain with a reason. **(Understanding) [2]**

11. (i) Will you defend or refute the case depicted in the following diagram? Provide a rationale in support of your view. **(Evaluate) [2]**

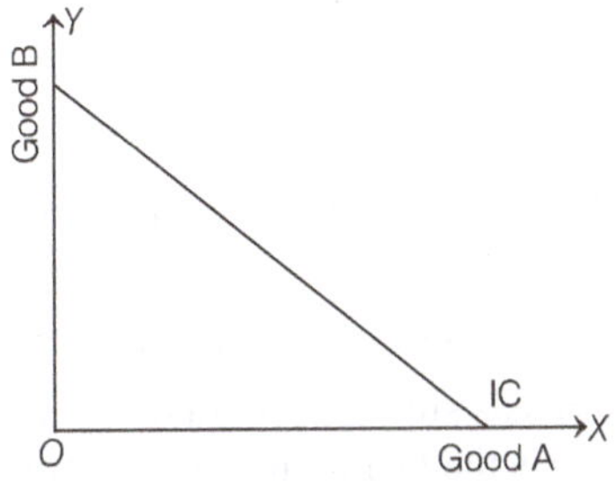

(ii) Name the law which deals with the behaviour of marginal utility when the consumer consumes a commodity continuously at a given time. Explain this law with the help of a diagram. **(Understanding) [6]**

12. (i) Discuss the categories of factor income considered in calculating the national income by income method. **(Understanding) [4]**

(ii) Calculate GDP_{MP} and NNP_{FC} from the following data **(Application) [4]**

S. No.	Items	₹ (in crores)
(i)	Wages and salaries	170
(ii)	Rent	10
(iii)	Interest	20
(iv)	Profits	25
(v)	Dividend	12
(vi)	Royalty	5
(vii)	Employer's contribution to social security	30
(viii)	Net factor income from abroad	(–) 3
(ix)	Consumption of fixed capital	34
(x)	Net indirect tax	38

Or (i) Explain the different components of final expenditure in calculating the national income by expenditure method. **(Understanding)**

(ii) Calculate GNP_{MP} using income method and expenditure method from the following data **(Application)**

S. No.	Items	₹ (in crores)
(i)	Private final consumption expenditure	800
(ii)	Net exports	20
(iii)	Rent	40
(iv)	Interest	60
(v)	Government final consumption expenditure	200
(vi)	Profit	120
(vii)	Net domestic capital formation	100
(viii)	Compensation of employees	800
(ix)	Net indirect taxes	100
(x)	Consumption of fixed capital	20
(xi)	Net factor income from abroad	(–)30

13. Read the passage given below and answer the questions that follow

In India, fixed deposits have long been a favourite investment choice of people especially senior citizens as it promises steady returns.

It attracts those people who are seeking a stable income.

But it's an illusion in the period of inflation. Inflation is the rate at which the general level of prices for goods and services rises, subsequently eroding the purchasing power of money. In simple terms, what money could buy today, it might not a few years down the line. Fixed deposits are financial instruments offered by banks where you deposit a lump sum amount for a fixed period at a pre-determined rate of interest.

Consider an investment of ₹ 1 crore in a fixed deposit at a 6% annual interest rate and the annual rate of inflation is 5%.

By the 10th year your pre-inflation return is 1.79 crore, but post inflation it's just 1.10 crore. The nominal value of investment in fixed deposits may appear to grow, inflation significantly diminishes their real value and purchasing power over time.

HOW INFLATION IMPACTS YOUR FD INVESTMENT

Year	Beginning Amount (in ₹ crore)	Interest Earned (in ₹ crore)	End of Year Total (in ₹ crore)	Adjusted for Inflation (in ₹ crore)
1	1	0.06	1.06	1.01
10	1.69	0.10	1.79	1.10
20	3.03	0.18	3.21	1.21

Assumptions: i. FD at a 6 percent annual interest rate
ii. Annual inflation rate of 5 percent

Source *https://www.linkedin.com*

(i) What is the theme of the extract? **(Interpretation) [2]**

(ii) Differentiate between demand pull and cost push inflation. **(Understanding) [2]**

(iii) What are the demand deposits and time deposits? **(Recall) [2]**

(iv) Since 1998, RBI has been using new measures of money supply, M_0, M_1, M_2 and M_3. Which one of these measures incorporates fixed deposit as one of its components? Mention the other components of that measure. **(Understanding) [2]**

Answers

1. (i) (b) *K* is beyond the financial capacity of the consumer and *T* provides a lower level of satisfaction.

(ii) (c) $MU_x < P_x$

(iii) (b) Increase in the real income of the consumer and fall in relative price of the commodity

(iv) (b) He will postpone his plan to buy a car

(v) (b) Revenue receipts are those which neither create any liability nor reduce the assets of the government.

(vi) (b) more import from Japan by USA

(vii) (d) Oligopoly

(viii) (b) Both Assertion (A) and Reason (R) are true, but Reason (R) is not the correct explanation of Assertion (A)

(ix) (a) Both Assertion (A) and Reason (R) are true and Reason (R) is the correct explanation of Assertion (A)

(x) Difference between monopolistic competition and oligopoly is as follows (any one)

Basis	Monopolistic Competition	Oligopoly
Type of product	Firms sell differentiated products.	Firms sell homogeneous or differentiated products.
Entry and exit	There is a free entry of firms.	Entry of firms is restricted.
Control over market price	Every firm has fairly large control over price of its own product.	Each firm exercises substantial control over price.

(xi) When $C > Y$, $APC = C / Y > 1$, but MPC is always less than 1 because increase in consumption expenditure is always less than increase in income as a part of increased income is used for saving as well.

(xii) It will generate inflationary gap or will lead to inflation.

(xiii) Through accommodating capital receipt.

(xiv) As there is a single buyer in the market, the buyer influences the market in determination of price of the product. So it's regarded as buyers' market for the dominance of buyer.

(xv) Investment multiplier $(K) = \frac{1}{MPS}$. Higher MPS reduces *K* and lower MPS raises *K*.

(xvi) Measures to overcome a deflationary gap are (any one)

(a) Direct tax rate is to be reduced.

(b) Government can increase its expenditure.

(c) Policy of deficit financing can be followed.

(d) Central bank can reduce bank rate, repo rate, CRR and SLR.

2. (i) Supply will decrease as the same supply will be at higher price (or lower supply at the same price) due to an increase in the cost of production and transportation.

Therefore, supply curve will shift leftwards as shown below

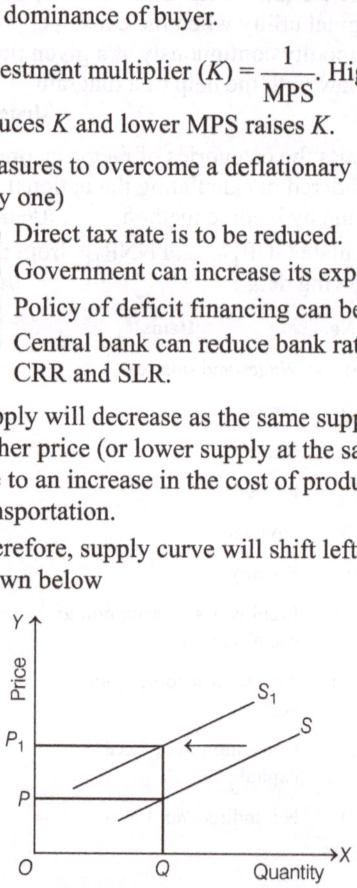

(ii) $E_P = \frac{\text{\% Change in quantity demanded}}{\text{\% Change in price}} = \frac{12}{10} = 1.2$

Here $E_P > 1$. Therefore, demand is (relatively) elastic.

3. (i) Decision of reduction of fiscal deficit will lead to a decrease in government borrowing because

Fiscal Deficit = Total Expenditure of the Government – (Revenue receipt + Recoveries of loan + Other receipts of the government)
= Borrowing and Other Liabilities of the Government.

Therefore, reduction of fiscal deficit will lead to reduction of borrowing.

(ii) In the situation of emergency, like natural calamity, pandemic (Covid-19), etc. government can provide subsidies to the sellers or producers of the basic necessities to control the upward pressure on prices of these commodities. In this situation, government has to increase its expenditure for providing this subsidy.

4. (i)

Output	Marginal cost	TVC	TC
0	0	0	30
1	10	10	40
2	15	25	55
3	25	50	80

(ii) Differences between returns to factor and returns to scale are

Basis	Returns to factor	Returns to scale
Law	It means or indicates a change in the level of output due to change in any one factor, keeping other factors constant.	It means or indicates a change in the level of output due to change in all the factors of production at a particular rate.
Variability of factors	Here factor proportion, i.e. K/L, changes.	In this case, factor proportion, i.e. K/L, remains constant.
Types of returns	Three possible returns to a factor are, increasing return, constant return and diminishing return to a factor.	There are three types of returns to scale, like increasing returns to scale, constant returns to scale and decreasing returns to scale.
Applicability	It is applicable in the short-run.	It is applicable in the long-run.

Or

(i) AFC curve is a rectangular hyperbolic curve or it is asymptotic.

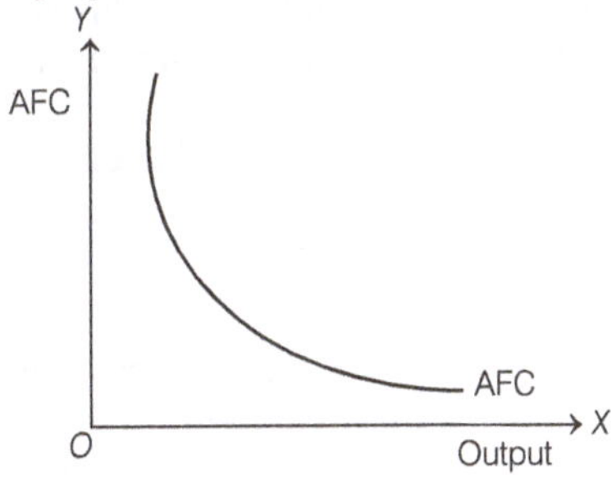

AC curve is a 'U' shaped curve.

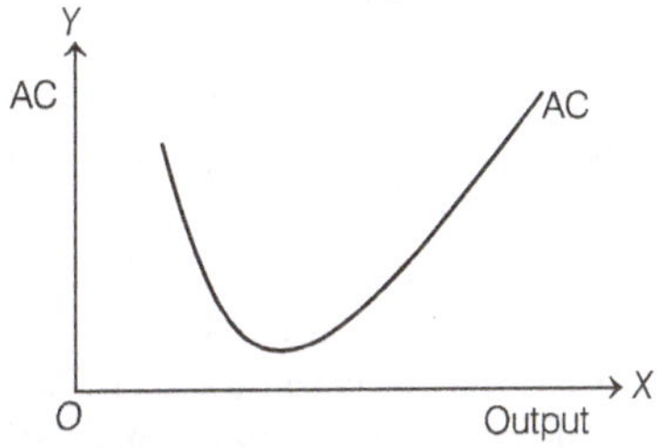

(ii) Table I depicts the law of variable proportions. Here, output increases due to change in K/L ratio, i.e. due to change in labour only while machine remains constant.

Table II depicts the law of returns to scale as $K/L = 1/2$ i.e. constant. Here, output increases due to change in labour and machine at the same rate.

5. (i) If firms enjoy supernormal profit in the short- run, new firms will enter the industry in the long-run which will cause an increase in the market supply. This will lead to a fall in price of the commodity till it becomes equal to AC and each firm enjoys normal profit.

If firms face loss in the short-run, they will exit the industry in the long-run which will cause a decrease in the market supply. This will lead to a rise in price of the commodity till it becomes equal to AC and each firm enjoys normal profit.

(ii) It is a sales promotion measure in view of intense competition and interdependence of firms under oligopoly. Every firm under this market form enjoys a large market share due to small number of firms.

Every firm's action affects its rival firms. So, while taking decision a firm has to take into account the impact on and reaction of its rivals. This phenomenon has been reflected in the example.

6. (i) Price of the commodity is determined by the interaction of market demand and market supply. So, market or the industry is the price maker. But no individual firm under this industry can influence this price for its insignificant market share.
It only has to accept the market determined price and can sell any amount of the commodity. So, firm is the price taker. Therefore, the statement is to be defended.

(ii) Normal profit is the minimum profit which is required by the organiser to continue the production. This is a part of total cost of production of a firm. Break-even point is the point where TR=TC, i.e. neither loss nor profit. A firm enjoys normal profit when the total revenue of the firm is enough to cover its cost only since normal profit is a part of total cost.

7. (i) India has been following flexible exchange rate system for many decades, where foreign exchange rate is determined by the forces of demand for and supply of foreign exchange. Since 1993, RBI has been intervening to purchase and sell foreign currencies when foreign exchange rate is very low or high, i.e. India is now following the managed floating exchange rate system for controlling the fluctuation of foreign exchange rate.

(ii) Components of current account are as follows
(a) Export of goods and import of goods.
(b) Export of services and import of services.
(c) Unilateral transfer receipts and unilateral transfer payments.
Components of capital account are capital receipt and capital payment, which include
(a) Borrowing and lending to and from abroad.
(b) Investments to and from abroad.
(c) Change in foreign exchange reserve.

8. (i) (a) Because it is a part of government's final consumption expenditure.
(b) Because it constitutes a portion of current production of the economy.

(ii) Precautions is that should be taken in estimation of national inome by expenditure method are (any two)
(a) All final products irrespective of whether these are marketed or not, are to be included.
(b) Expenditure on intermediate goods is to be excluded.
(c) Expenditure on second hand goods is to be excluded.
(d) Expenditure on financial assets is to be excluded.
(e) Government expenditure on transfer payments is to be excluded.

Or (i) Differences between personal income and private income are

Personal income	Private income
It is the income which individuals actually receive from all the sources.	It is the income accruing to the private sector from all the sources.
Corporate savings and corporate taxes remain excluded from personal income.	Both corporate savings and corporate taxes are the parts of private income.

(ii) Exports represent the expenditure by foreigners on the goods and services exported by the country. It is to be added to get GDP because goods and services exported are the part of domestic product. Again, imports represent the expenditure made by the residents of the country on imported goods and services.
It should be subtracted from the total expenditure as the goods and services imported are not the part of domestic production of the country. Hence, it cannot be a part of GDP. Therefore, (Exports– Import) i.e. net export is a part of GDP and hence of national income.

9. Equilibrium income refers to the level of real income or the level of output for which aggregate demand and aggregate supply become equal. Therefore, the equilibrium condition is stated as, AS = AD i.e. $Y = C + I$.

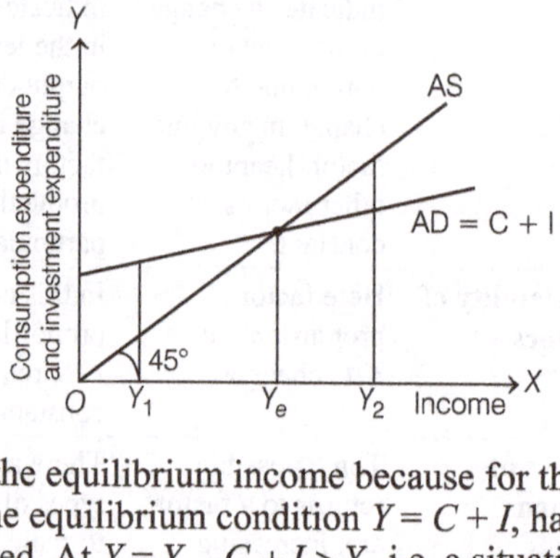

Y_e is the equilibrium income because for this level of income equilibrium condition $Y = C + I$, has been satisfied. At $Y = Y_1$, $C + I > Y$, i.e. a situation of excess demand which induces the producers to produce more and this leads to rise in Y until $Y = C + I$ i.e. equilibrium is restored.
Again, at $Y = Y_2$, $C + I < Y$ i.e. a situation of excess supply which induces the producers to reduce the current production and this leads to fall in Y until $Y = C + I$ i.e. equilibrium is restored.

10. (i) Average product is the production per unit of a factor, such as labour. It is expressed as $AP_L = TP/L$ or Q/L.
Marginal product is the change in production for one unit change in variable factor, say labour. It is expressed as, $MPL = \Delta Q/\Delta L$.

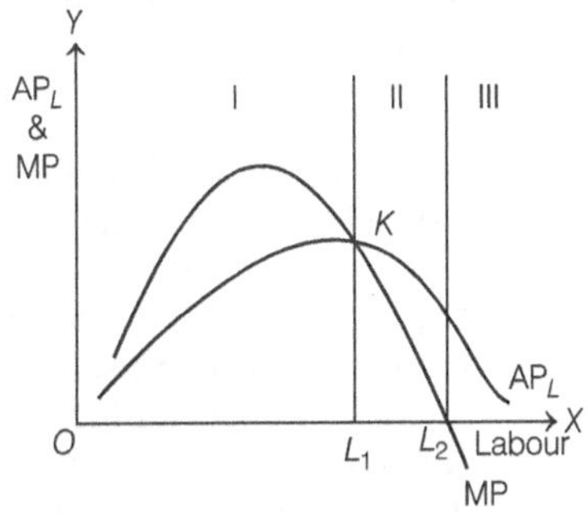

In Stage I (Under law of increasing return) When AP rises, MP > AP. MP curve lies above AP curve in the above diagram when later slopes positively. At the end of the Stage I, When AP is maximum for L_1 of labour, MP = AP and MP curve intersects AP curve at its maximum point, K.

In Stage II (Under law of diminishing return) When AP falls, MP < AP and MP curve lies below AP curve and intersects labour axis, i.e. MP = 0, for L_2 level of labour at the end of the stage II.

In Stage III (Under law of negative return) AP continues to fall, but never becomes zero for positive labour. MP< 0 and the curve lies under labour axis.

(ii) Producer will take the decision of his operation, among these three stages, through the process of elimination. Stage III will be eliminated as MP< 0. If producer operates at any point in Stage I before it ends, he won't be able to enjoy the full advantage of maximum productivity as AP is continuously rising over the entire stage. Therefore, a rational producer will operate only in Stage II.

11. (i) The diagram shows a straight line indifference curve which is to be refuted. IC cannot be a straight line in general for imperfect substitute goods. Here, always a same amount of good B is sacrificed for every additional unit of good A, i.e. MRS is constant. But the concept of indifference curve, in general, is based on the assumption of DMRS. Therefore, the case depicted in the diagram should be refuted on the ground of violation of the assumption of DMRS.

(ii) The law of diminishing marginal utility states that with continuous increase in consumption of a commodity, total utility increases at a diminishing rate, i.e. marginal utility declines.

Assumptions

(a) Utility is measured cardinally.
(b) Every unit of the commodity is homogeneous.
(c) Law of satiety holds.
(d) Consumption is continuous.

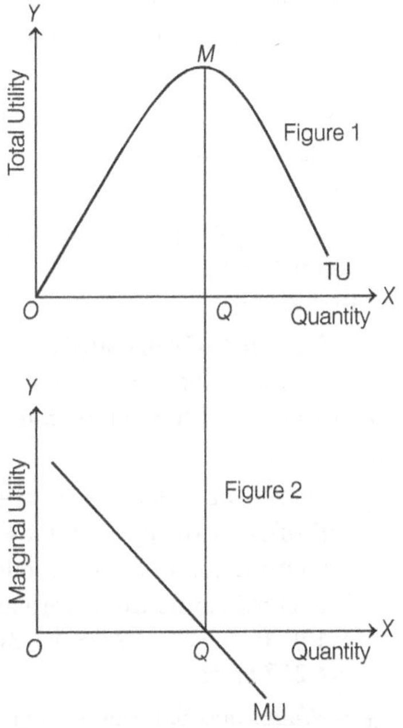

Figure 1, shows that TU curve slopes positively till point M indicating rising TU with increase in consumption up to Q and it becomes maximum at M. Beyond it, TU curve slopes negatively, i.e. beyond the satiation point TU decreases with further increase in consumption. TU curve is concave to the horizontal axis as TU increases at diminishing rate. MU curve slopes negatively in Figure 2.
It indicates that MU falls continuously with increase in consumption of the commodity.
As consumer fails to derive any additional utility from consumption of additional unit of commodity at the point of saturation, MU becomes zero and MU curve intersects the quantity axis for OQ level of consumption.
Beyond Q, MU becomes negative with further increase in consumption.

12. (i) Broad categories of factor income are

(a) **Compensation of employees** It comprises all types of payment made by the employers for their employees.

It includes the following

- Wages and salaries in cash inclusive of bonus, DA, LTC, house rent allowance, etc.
- Payment in kind, like free medical facilities, rent-free accommodation, subsidised food, etc.
- Supplementary labour income in form of employer's contribution toward social security benefit such as group insurance, provident fund, gratuity, etc.

(b) **Operating surplus** It is the income earned from the ownership of capital and entrepreneurship. It comprises rent, interest, profit and royalty.

(c) **Mixed income of self-employed** It covers total income of the own account workers and the profits generated in the unincorporated enterprises.

(ii) NNP_{FC} = Wages and Salaries + Rent + Interest + Profits + Royalty + Employer's contribution to Social Security + Net Factor Income from Abroad

= 170 + 10 + 20 + 25 + 5 + 30 + (–) 3

= ₹ 257 crore

GDP_{MP} = Wages and Salaries + Rent + Interest + Profits + Royalty + Employer's contribution to Social Security + Consumption of Fixed Capital + Net Indirect Tax

= 170 + 10 + 20 + 25 + 5 + 30 + 34 + 38

= ₹ 332 crore

Or

(i) The components of final expenditure are as follows

(a) Private final consumption expenditure

(b) Gross investment expenditure (inclusive of government investment expenditure)

(c) Government final consumption expenditure

(d) Net exports

(ii) By income method

GNP_{MP} = Rent + Interest + Profit + Compensation of Employees + Net Indirect Taxes + Compensation of Fixed Capital + Net Factor Income from Abroad

= 40 + 60 + 120 + 800 + 100 + 20 + (–) 30

= ₹ 1,110 crore

By expenditure method

GNP_{MP} = Private Final Consumption Expenditure + Net Exports + Government Final Consumption Expenditure + Net Domestic Capital Formation + Compensation of Fixed Capital + Net Factor Income from Abroad

= 800 + 20 + 200 + 100 + 20 + (–) 30

= ₹ 1,110 crore

13. (i) The theme of the extract is fixed deposit is a myth during the time of inflation. As inflation is a continuous rise in price level in the economy, it causes a decline in the purchasing power of money and hence the real value of return from the fixed deposit.

(ii) Demand pull inflation originates from demand forces, i.e. when aggregate demand rises and exceeds aggregate supply of goods and services, it will lead to rise in price level in the economy.

Cost push inflation refers to the continuous increase in price level due to increase in cost of production caused by increase in wage rate, profit margin, etc.

(iii) **Demand deposits** These are the deposits in bank account where the deposited money can be withdrawn by cheques at any time. Current account deposits and saving account deposit are the demand deposits.

Time deposits These are the deposits in bank account where the deposited money cannot be withdrawn before the time of its maturity. Cheque is not issued on this deposit. Fixed deposit and recurring deposit are the time deposits.

(iv) M_3 incorporates fixed deposit. Other components are Currency held by the public (C), Demand Deposits with commercial bank (DD) and Other Deposits with the RBI (OD).